Human Geography

Jon C. Malinowski
United States Military Academy

David H. Kaplan
Kent State University

Mc Graw Hill

Connect
Learn
Succeed™

HUMAN GEOGRAPHY

2 3 4 5 6 7 8 9 0 RJE / RJE 1 0 9 8 7 6 5 4 3

ISBN 978–0–07–312294–6
MHID 0–07–312294–7

Vice President, Editor-in-Chief: *Marty Lange*
Vice President, EDP: *Kimberly Meriwether David*
Senior Director of Development: *Kristine Tibbetts*
Publisher: *Ryan Blankenship*
Sponsoring Editor: *Todd L. Turner*
Senior Developmental Editor: *Joan M. Weber*
Executive Marketing Manager: *Lisa Nicks*
Senior Project Manager: *Sandy Wille*
Buyer: *Susan K. Culbertson*
Lead Media Project Manager: *Judi David*
Designer: *Tara McDermott*
Cover Image: © *Buena Vista Images/Getty Images*
Senior Photo Research Coordinator: *Lori Hancock*
Photo Research: *Danny Meldung/Photo Affairs, Inc.*
Compositor: *Lachina Publishing Services*
Typeface: *10/12 Times LT Std*
Printer: *R. R. Donnelley*

Library of Congress Cataloging-in-Publication Data

Malinowski, Jon C.
  Human geography / Jon Malinowski, David Kaplan.—1st ed.
     p. cm.
  Includes index.
  ISBN 978–0–07–312294–6 — ISBN 0–07–312294–7 (alk. paper) 1. Human geography—
Textbooks. I. Kaplan, David H., 1960- II. Title.
  GF43.M27 2013
  304.2—dc23
                                                          2011026361

The opinions expressed by the authors are theirs and do not reflect the official position of the United States Military Academy, Kent State University, the Department of the Army, or the Department of Defense.

www.mhhe.com

Jon C. Malinowski

Jon C. Malinowski received his B.S. in foreign service from the Edmund A. Walsh School of Foreign Service at Georgetown University and earned his M.A. and Ph.D. in geography from the University of North Carolina at Chapel Hill. He has been a member of the geography faculty at the United States Military Academy at West Point since 1995. In addition to scholarly articles, he is the co-author of several books, including geography texts and trade books on summer camp and West Point's changing landscape. His research interests have focused on spatial cognition, children's geographies, and cultural geography and he has taught courses on Asia, North America, the Middle East and Africa, world regional geography, human geography, behavioral geography, economic geography, and the historical geography of the Hudson Valley. In addition to teaching and research, Dr. Malinowski has held administrative positions in the Environmental Perception and Behavioral Geography Specialty Group of the Association of American Geographers and in the Geography Program at the Academy. He also serves as a member of the Board of Directors for YMCA Camp Belknap in Tuftonboro, New Hampshire.

David H. Kaplan

David H. Kaplan is a professor of geography at Kent State University. He received his Ph.D. from the University of Wisconsin at Madison and his B.A. from The Johns Hopkins University. Dr. Kaplan has published over 40 peer-reviewed articles and chapters, and he has seven books published: *Segregation in Cities, Nested Identities, Boundaries and Place, Urban Geography, Landscapes of the Ethnic Economy, Perthes World Atlas*, and the four-volume *Nations and Nationalism: A Global Historical Overview*. His research interests include nationalism, borderlands, ethnic and racial segregation, urban and regional development, housing and finance, and transportation. In his free time, he enjoys spending time with his family, cooking, bicycling, skiing, and gaining a deep appreciation of different places.

DEDICATION

We would like to dedicate this book to those teachers who first inspired us to study the great field of geography.

Jon C. Malinowski and David H. Kaplan

BRIEF CONTENTS

CONTENTS

Chapter 9
Race, Ethnicity, and Gender   182

Chapter 10
A World of Nations and States   202

Chapter 11
Geography of Governance and Representation   226

Chapter 12
Environment and Conservation   254

Chapter 13
Urbanization and Urban Networks 278

Chapter 14
The Changing Structure of the City 300

Chapter 15
The Geography of Economic Activity and Agriculture 322

Chapter 16
Geographies of Production and Consumption 344

Chapter 17
Distribution and Transportation   368

Chapter 18
Development and Geography   390

It's fairly likely that, when you think of geography, your mind pictures maps or some of the global issues facing us in the modern age, such as global warming, cultural conflict, or immigration. But before we start tackling large-scale issues, take a minute to think about your hometown and answer the following questions:

- Why did people settle in your town in the first place?
- Is there a section of your town where richer or poorer people live?
- Are factories and other businesses evenly distributed or concentrated in particular parts of town?
- What sports teams do most people in your town support? Why?
- Is the ethnic or racial makeup of the town diverse, or all the same?
- Is your town famous for anything? Why?
- Is your town politically conservative or liberal? Why?

The answers to these questions should begin to show you that the world's surface is not uniform. As we all know, people, ideas, and things are not evenly distributed, and there are reasons that this is the case. Take the example of Springfield, Vermont, the hometown of one of this textbook's authors. People settled there for a variety of reasons, but the town grew because of a river that runs through the area and that has good waterfalls, which were able to turn water wheels for small factories. In time, the town became a manufacturing center of machine tools and was tied to a global economic system. Today, manufacturing has largely shifted to other locations in the United States and overseas, so the town is no longer as prosperous as it once was. Traditionally, the poorer citizens lived closer to the river, where the factories were located, and the wealthier citizens occupied larger plots of land on the hills that ring the center of town.

This one small town has a story, and that story is tied strongly to geography. Geographers believe that phenomena on the earth's surface are not random, but rather, the result of a complex series of processes going on at the local, regional, national, and international scales. This book will introduce you to how geographers attempt to make sense of the diverse reality of human populations on the earth's surface. In this preface, we introduce you to the discipline of geography, as well as the unique modular format for this textbook.

What Is Geography?

So, what exactly is *geography*, and more specifically, what is *human geography*? For many of you, geography means memorizing state capitals and rivers, as you did in elementary school. While geographers feel that this sort of information is important, it is not what you will be reading about in this book. Rather, we want to introduce you to what professional geographers focus on as they research and analyze the world.

Let's start with the word *geography* itself. Can you guess what the word means? The word root *geo-* means "earth," but what about the second part of the word? The *graph* part of the word means "writing," so the word *geography* literally means "writing about the earth" in ancient Greek. As you will see in Chapter 2, geography started out with people writing about or describing their world. If you take a trip, often you write or e-mail to friends about what you saw. But the next step after describing something is to ask, "Why?" The core of geography is identifying what exists on the world's surface and attempting to explain why it is there. This may seem simplistic, but when you start trying to explain war, famine, or global migration, the answers to the questions of what, where, and why get complicated.

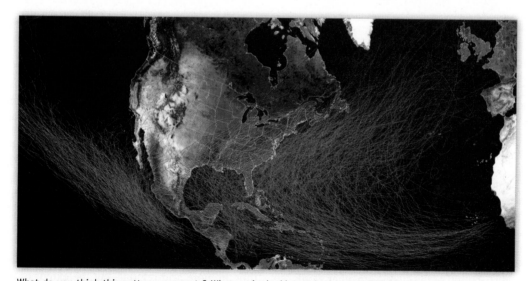

What do you think this pattern represents? What you're looking at is the spatial distribution of hurricanes in the United States from 1851 to 2008 on the East Coast and 1949 to 2008 on the West Coast. Is there a pattern? Clearly there is. So, geographers see a pattern and then want to know why. In the East, for example, storms form over the warm waters in the equatorial regions off of Africa, and then the prevailing winds carry them westward, where they strike the Caribbean and the southeastern United States. There is a pattern and a process.

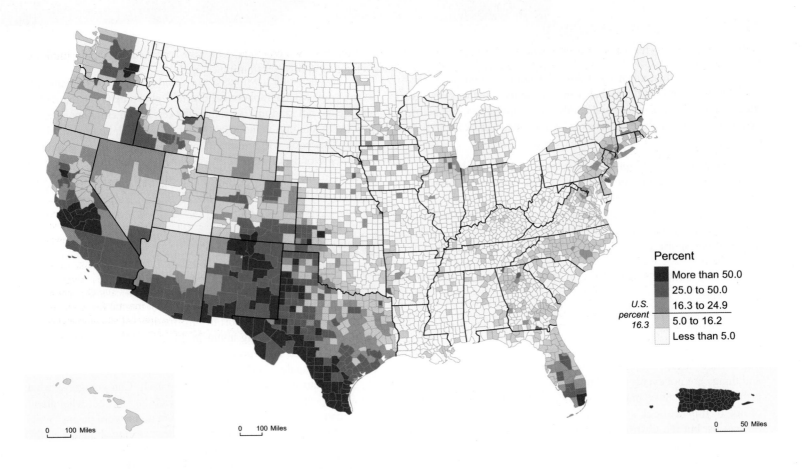

Here's another example: the population of many parts of the United States is becoming increasingly Latino or Hispanic due to immigration and population increases. This map shows Hispanics and Latinos as a percentage of the entire population as recorded in the 2010 Census. What might explain the pattern? In many areas, as the population becomes more Hispanic, one starts to see more signs in Spanish and more businesses that cater to Hispanics. The same situation often occurs when a new cultural or ethnic group enters an area. Why does this happen? The new population is interacting with the environment and changing it gradually. How many roads or stores in your community have a name that reflects the ethnic heritage of the area?

So, more formally, geography can be defined as the academic discipline that studies the pattern of phenomena on the earth's surface, the processes that create those patterns, and the interaction between humans and the environment. Basically, geographers are interested in where things are and why they are there. This includes physical things, such as mountains, rivers, or churches, but it can also include human populations, such as cultural or ethnic groups, or even ideas, such as democracy or freedom of speech. The emphasis on where things are is often referred to as the *spatial perspective*. The word *spatial* means "relating to space" and is often used instead of the word *geographic*. For example, if you are studying the spatial distribution of McDonald's restaurants, you're studying the geographic distribution of the stores—in other words, where they are located. Let's look at two examples of how geographers look at the world.

Geographers study and analyze patterns on the surface of the earth. Geographers also emphasize the relationship between humans and the environment. Think about areas where there is persistent flooding. How do humans respond to flooding? Some people just move away. Others modify their homes to put them on stilts. Still others dam up the river or create levees to protect an area. There is no single human response to flooding. Geographers study these interactions between people and their environment.

In addition, geographers examine how human activity shapes the environment. In the late summer of 2011, wildfires in Texas raged out of control, consuming an area the size of Connecticut and burning over 1000 homes. Fires like this occur all of the time in more arid regions, but the extent of these particular fires may be a worrisome indicator of increased global climate change caused in part by human activity.

Thinking Geographically

Before we dive into the basic concepts and history of human geography in the first two chapters, let's take some time to begin thinking geographically. Take a few minutes to really look at the map, which shows the population distribution of the United States.

Why does a line of population go right down the middle of California (point A)? What is there? It's not Los Angeles or San Francisco. The answer is agriculture. This is the productive Central Valley, which produces 8 percent of all U.S. agricultural output on just 1 percent of the nation's farmland. So, just as our ancestors did thousands of years ago, humans still settle in areas that are fertile. Of course, what is different is that today the farmer's output is packed within minutes of picking, labeled by machines, and immediately shipped out to the four corners of the globe. In the modern era, the local is tied to the global like no other time in our history.

Note the line of population at point B. This line extends from Indianapolis to St. Louis and then on to Oklahoma City. What might explain a line of population that is straight? In this case, it's transportation routes. Historically, the cities of St. Louis and Indianapolis were connected by rail. Today, Interstates 70 and 44 follow the same route. I-44 follows much of the path of Route 66, made famous in songs and movies. In this case, the human settlement pattern is not caused by a physical feature on the earth's surface but rather human-built features.

Why are cities such as Chicago and Detroit located where they are (points C and D)? What advantages do they have? One factor is that they both offer access to water, specifically the Great Lakes water system that connects the Midwest with the eastern seaboard by way of the St. Lawrence Seaway, and via canals and railroads before that. Chicago became a railroad hub, allowing products from the Great Plains to be processed and then shipped to other locations. Can you identify other major cities that are at critical transportation junctions? This shows us that sometimes cities grow because of economic growth or transportation needs.

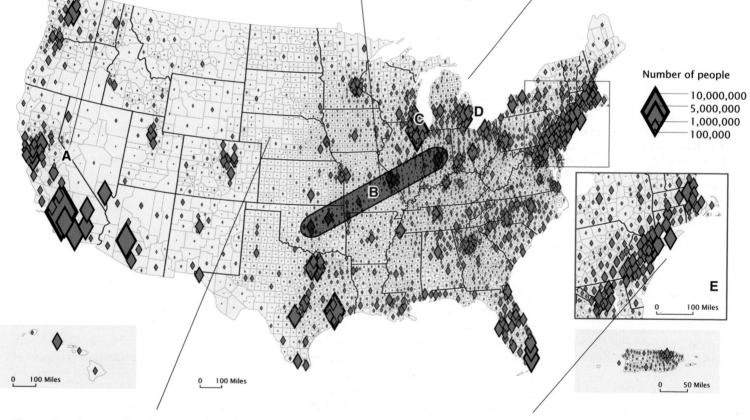

Number of people

10,000,000
5,000,000
1,000,000
100,000

0 100 Miles

0 100 Miles

0 100 Miles

0 50 Miles

Why are there fewer people in the western half of the United States? One major factor is physical geography. The region is dry and remote and cannot as easily support large human populations. Human patterns are often influenced by physical patterns. Can you find other areas where the human pattern seems to follow a physical feature, such as a mountain range or a river?

Why is the population so strongly clustered along the coast near point E? This is the Boston to Washington, DC, corridor. The answer, of course, relates to immigration patterns. Early settlers from Europe tended to arrive in northeastern ports, and therefore these entry cities grew. They also became industrial centers that created products for the home market and for export, and thus they attracted more immigration because of economic opportunities. Can you think of other areas of the United States that have grown because they have been arrival destinations for immigrants?

The Value of This Book

We believe that students and faculty will find this text more appealing than their current text. There are several areas in which the content of this text diverges from current texts:

1. We include a chapter on the history of geographic thought, often omitted from texts, which includes modern social theoretical perspectives. This chapter can be used at the beginning or at the end of the course, as the instructor sees fit.
2. We include a chapter on health and disease.
3. We provide thorough discussions of world religions, which we feel is crucial in a post–9/11 world.
4. We include innovative examples from today's culture, including new music and NASCAR racing, which most students will find more relevant than the examples often used by text authors.
5. We focus on political representation and administration in a single political geography chapter.
6. We package the discussion of secondary and service sectors into the geography of production and consumption.
7. We include a chapter on transportation and communications.
8. We focus on some of the major issues in the world today, including the drug trade and vast disparities in development between countries in the world.

Our Book	Other Books
Short chapters divided into 8 to 10 2- to 4-page self-contained modules	Long chapters with a hierarchical outline structure
Maps, photos, and graphics that are central to each module	Text-centric chapters, with graphics as an afterthought
Easily customizable to instructor's class organization	Hard to customize—instructors expected to follow the book
Accessible, contemporary writing	Difficult to follow, with many outdated references
Features that allow each student to consider and engage the material	A standard list of questions at chapter end

Key Features of This Text

Modular Approach   This book uses the modular approach, which allows both instructor and student a great deal of flexibility. Each chapter is divided into 8 to 10 2- to 4-page modules. Each module includes photos and graphics, which, when integrated with figures provided by the instructor, will create self-contained "modules." For the most part, two or three modules can be covered in a relatively short class. More modules might be covered in a longer class. It is up to the instructor to decide. This layout makes the book unique in the field and provides a big advantage to students and instructors.

For the student, the book is easier to manage, more fun to read, and more logical than a running narrative. Readers will have a clear understanding of where discussions of key concepts start and stop. Graphics on each 2-page spread support the text on those pages, so students don't have to flip back and forth. Captions require students to think about the content of both the graphics and the text material.

For the instructor, this layout provides fantastic flexibility. Rather than combing through the text to find relevant passages, it is now possible to mix and match modules to construct a daily lecture. For a 50-minute lecture, 2 or 3 modules can be selected from the same or different chapters. Instructors who teach three times a week might choose 2 modules, while those teaching twice a week could assign 3 modules.

If you don't like the way we organized a chapter, you can easily create your own organization based on modules from the same or different chapters. For example, if you prefer to teach Judaism before Hinduism, the modular system allows you to more easily assign the students the correct reading. Add a module on nationalism from a different chapter to discuss how religious differences have political consequences. You can pair some of the migration modules with development modules, population modules with environmental modules, and so on. In each case, the graphics in each module deliver an excellent beginning to a compelling lecture, as well as a way to hold student interest in our geographic world.

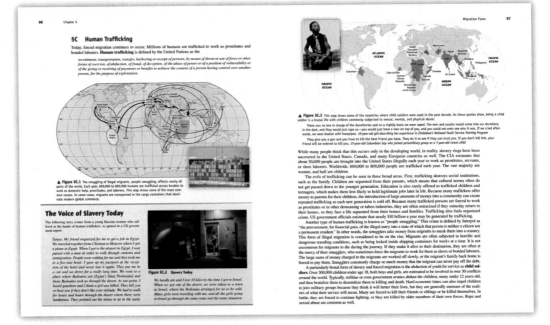

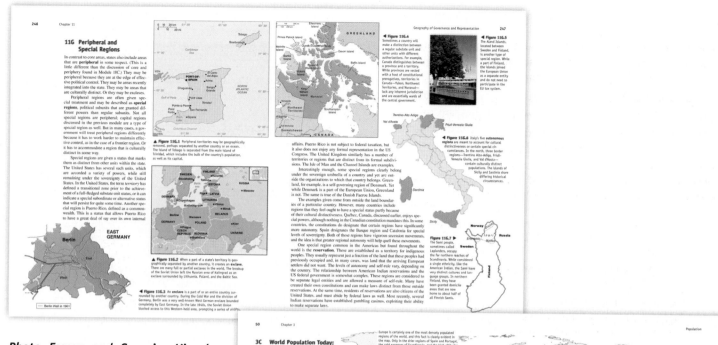

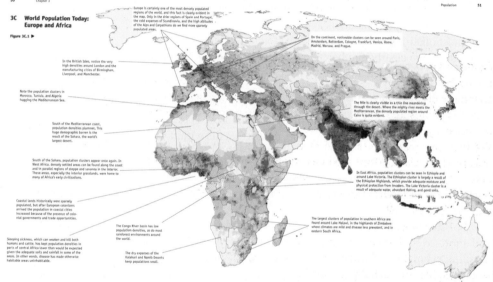

Photo Essays and Superior Visuals

A study on textbook usage found that students react most strongly to the graphic content of their texts (Inside Higher Ed, 2007). They are more likely to use the textbook if the graphics are strong.

Because geography texts cover the same basic concepts, all theories are generally presented in the same way. Instructors get familiar with a particular presentation, and texts may be afraid to deviate from those norms. In this book, every effort is made to blend the text with the graphics to clarify and illustrate the concepts. At the same time, this book retains intellectual rigor in presenting the latest material in human geography. Graphics and text work together to provide students with the latest information, but presented in the most understandable way.

Accessible Writing

No textbook works if students do not read it. Too often, complex information can be passed along to students in a style that does not sound as if it was lifted from a grammar text. This is not to say that the writing style needs to be "dumbed down" for today's students or condescending, but a voice that approximates trade books and intelligent magazines will appeal to students with several pages to read each week.

All attempts are made to use contemporary examples that either relate to students' experiences or introduce them to a vital example from a wider world. We make the writing in this book more accessible to students while maintaining a proper level of scientific rigor.

Student Engagement We have developed other features to encourage readers to pause and reflect on what they are reading. First, captions are written to think about the content of the graphics they introduce. Second, at the end of each chapter, students will find questions and exercises that go beyond the simple one-line questions often placed there by authors. Each chapter includes key terms, short questions, longer essay-style questions, and possible topics for further study. What is more, we provide a summary activity that ordinarily revolves around a graphically portrayed model or concept.

How to Use This Book

We believe that this book should be fairly intuitive. As with all textbooks, we include chapters oriented around a particular theme. Our 18 chapters package different chunks of information and include a variety of pedagogical materials at the end. Where this book differs from most other texts is in the structure of self-contained modules. All modules are clearly numbered and lettered, and most span only 2 facing pages in the text. A few cover 4 pages. This makes the information easier to access and to refer to.

The important thing to remember about the modules is that they can be used in any manner the instructor chooses. There is no need to reference the preceding module, unless that fits within your

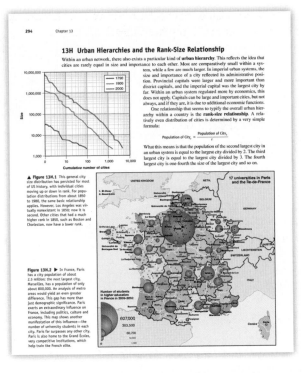

curricular plan. It may be just as practical in a single class period to include 3 modules from 3 different chapters. Our numbering system makes this easy. It also makes it much simpler when designing a syllabus. There's no need to figure out the specific pages a student must read. Instead, merely indicate the modules. The number of modules and their arrangement are completely up to you.

Acknowledgments

On some days, bringing a new textbook to life seems almost like a Herculean task. Over the past few years, we have been tremendously fortunate to have the support of our friends, family, colleagues, and students as we developed and wrote our book. Without their kind words, willingness to listen, and helpful suggestions, this first edition would not have been possible.

Jon Malinowski would like to thank Drs. Gesler, Birdsall, and Florin for their mentorship at a crucial time in his development as a geographer. For their friendship, Jon would like to thank Dr. Frank Galgano, Dr. Christopher Thurber, Mike Auricchio, and his colleagues and cadets at West Point. And above all, Jon thanks his parents and family for their unwavering love and support.

Dr. Martyn Bowden and Dr. Saul Cohen were the first geographers to introduce Dave Kaplan to their field. Since those early years, Dave profited from reading, listening, discussing, and collaborating with geographers from throughout the world. Dave has also benefited from the help of his students, and in this instance, he would like to thank Emily Fekete, Nick Wise, Megan Petroski, and Gina Butrico for their invaluable support in producing this book. Dave would also add a special thanks to Veronica Jurgena, who provided advice, encouragement, and technical assistance at every stage of the process.

The authors wish to thank the following for reviewing drafts of the book and for providing meaningful feedback:

Nurudeen Alao
University of California–Irvine

Christiana Asante
Grambling State University

Andrew Baker
IUPUI

Chris W. Baynard
University of North Florida

Mark Bonta
Delta State University

Scott Brady
California State University–Chico

Wayne Brew
Montgomery County Community College

Craig S. Campbell
Youngstown State University

Scott Carlin
Long Island University—C.W. Post Campus

J. Chris Carter
Long Beach City College

William K. Crowley
Sonoma State University

William Dakan
University of Louisville

Fiona M. Davidson
University of Arkansas

Phyllis P. Duryee
Franklin University

Owen Dwyer
Indiana University–Indianapolis

Marcia R. England
Miami University of Ohio

Kyle T. Evered
Michigan State University

David Albert Farmer
Wilmington University

Mark Guizlo
Lakeland Community College

Joshua Hagen
Marshall University

Daniel Hammel
University of Toledo

Marc A. Healy
Elgin Community College

John Heppen
University of Wisconsin–River Falls

Scott Hunt
Columbus State Community College

Oren Katz
California State University–Los Angeles

Lee Liu
University of Central Missouri

Taylor E. Mack
Louisiana Tech University

Alan P. Marcus
Towson University

Darla K. Munroe
The Ohio State University

Douglas C. Munski
University of North Dakota

Carol Nickolai
Community College of Philadelphia

Lashale Pugh
Youngstown State University

Victoria S. Randlett
University of Nevada–Reno

Murray D. Rice
University of North Texas

Anu Sabhlok
University of Louisville

James C. Saku
Frostburg State University

Steven Schnell
Kutztown University of Pennsylvania

Roger Mark Selya
University of Cincinnati

Sherman E. Silverman
Prince George's Community College

Christopher D. Storie
Winthrop University

Ray Sumner
Long Beach City College

Benjamin F. Timms
Indiana University–Bloomington

W. Michael Wheeler
Southwestern Oklahoma State University

David Wilson
University of Illinois–Urbana/Champaign

J. Gaines Wilson
University of Texas at Brownsville

Dawn Wrobel
Moraine Valley Community College

Keith Yearman
College of DuPage

Finally, tremendous thanks to the team at McGraw-Hill, listed in full on the copyright page. In addition, we would like to acknowledge the years of enthusiastic encouragement from Rose Arlia and Daniel Lange—McGraw-Hill's book representatives who helped spur us into doing this project. We wish to single out and thank Marge Kemp for believing in this book in its infancy and Joan Weber for her patience and hard work. Special thanks as well to Todd Turner for his skilled oversight of the project and to Lisa Nicks for her marketing efforts.

Jon C. Malinowski
David H. Kaplan

Supplements

McGraw-Hill offers various tools and technology products to support *Human Geography*. Students can order supplemental study materials by contacting their local bookstore or by calling 800-262-4729. Instructors can obtain teaching aids by calling the Customer Service Department at 800-338-3987, visiting the McGraw-Hill website at www.mhhe.com, or contacting their McGraw-Hill sales representative.

Digital Supplements

McGraw-Hill Connect Geography (www.mcgrawhillconnect.com) is a web-based assignment and assessment platform that gives students the means to better connect with their coursework, with their instructors, and with the important concepts that they will need to know for success now and in the future.

With Connect Geography, instructors can deliver assignments, quizzes, and tests online. Questions from the text are presented in an auto-gradable format and tied to the text's learning objectives. Instructors can edit existing questions and author entirely new problems. They can also track individual student performance—by question, by assignment, or in relation to the class overall—with detailed grade reports. Integrate grade reports easily with Learning Management Systems (LMS), such as WebCT and Blackboard, and much more.

By choosing Connect Geography, instructors are providing their students with a powerful tool for improving academic performance and truly mastering course material. Connect Geography allows students to practice important skills at their own pace and on their own schedule. Importantly, students' assessment results and instructors' feedback are all saved online, so students can continually review their progress and plot their course to success.

Like Connect Geography, **McGraw-Hill ConnectPlus Geography** provides students with online assignments and assessments, plus 24/7 online access to an eBook—an online edition of the text—to aid them in successfully completing their work, wherever and whenever they choose.

McGraw-Hill Higher Education and Blackboard have teamed up!
What does this mean for you?

1. **Your life, simplified**. Now you and your students can access McGraw-Hill's Connect and Create™ right from within your Blackboard course—all with a single sign-on. Say good-bye to the days of logging in to multiple applications.
2. **Deep integration of content and tools**. Not only do you get single sign-on with Connect and Create, you also get deep integration of McGraw-Hill content and content engines right in Blackboard. Whether you're choosing a book for your course or building Connect assignments, all the tools you need are right where you want them—inside Blackboard.
3. **Seamless gradebooks**. Are you tired of keeping multiple gradebooks and manually synchronizing grades into Blackboard? We thought so. When a student completes an integrated Connect assignment, the grade for that assignment automatically (and instantly) feeds your Blackboard grade center.
4. **A solution for everyone**. Whether your institution is already using Blackboard or you just want to try Blackboard on your own, we have a solution for you. McGraw-Hill and Blackboard can now offer you easy access to industry-leading technology and content, whether your campus hosts it or we do. Be sure to ask your local McGraw-Hill representative for details.

McGraw-Hill Tegrity is a service that makes class time available all the time by automatically capturing every lecture in a searchable format for students to review when they study and complete assignments. With a simple one-click start-and-stop process, you capture all computer screens and corresponding audio. Students replay any part of any class with easy-to-use browser-based viewing on a PC or Mac. Educators know that the more students can see, hear, and experience class resources, the better they learn.

With Tegrity, students quickly recall key moments by using Tegrity's unique search feature. This search helps students efficiently find what they need, when they need it across an entire semester of class recordings. Help turn all your students' study time into learning moments immediately supported by your lecture.

To learn more about Tegrity, watch a two-minute Flash demo at http://tegritycampus.mhhe.com.

Customizable Textbooks

McGraw Hill create

Create what you've only imagined. Introducing **McGraw-Hill Create**—a new, self-service website that allows you to create custom course materials—print and eBooks—by drawing upon McGraw-Hill's comprehensive, cross-disciplinary content. Add your own content quickly and easily. Tap into other rights-secured third-party sources as well. Then, arrange the content in a way that makes the most sense for your course. Even personalize your book with your course name and information. Choose the best format for your course: color print, black and white print, or eBook. The eBook is now viewable on an iPad! And when you are finished customizing, you will receive a free PDF review copy in just minutes! Visit McGraw-Hill Create—www.mcgrawhillcreate.com—today and begin building your perfect book.

Presentation Center

www.mhhe.com/malinowski1e

Within the Instructor's **Presentation Center**, instructors have access to PowerPoint lecture outlines, which appear as ready-made presentations that combine art and lecture notes for each chapter of the text. For instructors who prefer to create their lectures from scratch, all illustrations, photos, and tables are pre-inserted by chapter into blank PowerPoint slides.

An online digital library within Connect contains photos, artwork, animations, and other media types that can be used to create customized lectures, visually enhanced tests and quizzes, compelling course websites, or attractive printed support materials. All assets are copyrighted by McGraw-Hill Higher Education but can be used by instructors for classroom purposes. The visual resources in this collection include

- **Art.** Full-color digital files of all illustrations in the book can be readily incorporated into lecture presentations, exams, or custom-made classroom materials. In addition, all files are pre-inserted into PowerPoint slides for ease of lecture preparation.
- **Photos**. The photo collection contains digital files of photographs from the text, which can be reproduced for multiple classroom uses.
- **Tables.** Every table that appears in the text has been saved in electronic form for use in classroom presentations and/or quizzes.

Computerized Test Bank Online

A comprehensive bank of test questions is provided within a computerized test bank powered by McGraw-Hill's flexible electronic testing program EZ Test Online (www.eztestonline.com). EZ Test Online allows you to create paper and online tests or quizzes in this easy-to-use program!

Imagine being able to create and access your test or quiz anywhere, at any time, without installing the testing software. Now, with EZ Test Online, instructors can select questions from multiple McGraw-Hill test banks or author their own, and then either print the test for paper distribution or give it online.

Test Creation

- Author/edit questions online using the 14 different question type templates.
- Create printed tests or deliver online to get instant scoring and feedback.
- Create question pools to offer multiple versions online—great for practice.
- Export your tests for use in WebCT, Blackboard, PageOut, and Apple's iQuiz.
- Tests are compatible with EZ Test Desktop tests you've already created.
- Sharing tests with colleagues, adjuncts, and TAs is easy.

Online Test Management

- Set availability dates and time limits for your quiz or test.
- Control how your test will be presented.
- Assign points by question or question type with a drop-down menu.
- Provide immediate feedback to students or delay until all finish the test.
- Create practice tests online to enable student mastery.
- Upload your roster to enable student self-registration.

Online Scoring and Reporting

- Use automated scoring for most of EZ Test's numerous question types.
- It allows manual scoring for essay and other open response questions.
- Manual re-scoring and feedback are also available.
- EZ Test's grade book is designed to easily export to your grade book.
- View basic statistical reports.

Support and Help

- A user's guide and built-in page-specific help is included.
- Flash tutorials help you get started on the support site.
- A support website is included: www.mhhe.com/eztest.
- A product specialist is available at 1-800-331-5094.
- Online training is available at http://auth.mhhe.com/mpss/workshops/.

Related Titles of Interest

McGraw-Hill offers a multitude of reference materials providing valuable geography-related supplements at a discounted price when packaged with your text. Students of geography and other disciplines, as well as the general reader, will find these unique materials invaluable to their understanding of geography. Ask your McGraw-Hill sales representative about the following.

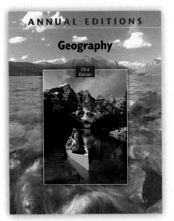

Annual Editions

The Annual Editions series is designed to provide students with convenient, inexpensive access to current, carefully selected articles from the public press. They are updated on a regular basis through continuous monitoring of over 300 periodicals. Each volume presents articles written for a general audience by experts and authorities in their fields. Newly introduced features in Annual Editions include unit-specific Learning Outcomes and Critical Thinking questions following each article. Other organizational features include an annotated listing of selected World Wide Web sites; an annotated table of contents; a topic guide; a general introduction; brief overviews for each section; and an online Instructor's Resource Guide with testing materials. Using Annual Editions in the Classroom is offered as a practical guide for instructors. www.mhhe.com/annual editions.

Annual Editions: Developing World 12/13, by Griffiths (ISBN 978-0-07-805100-5; MHID 0-07-805100-2)

Annual Editions: Geography, 23/e, by Pitzl (ISBN 978-0-07-351551-9; MHID 0-07-351551-5)

Annual Editions: Global Issues 11/12, by Jackson (ISBN 978-0-07-805084-8; MHID 0-07-805084-7)

Annual Editions: World Politics 11/12, by Purkitt (ISBN 978-0-07-805093-0; MHID 0-07-805093-6)

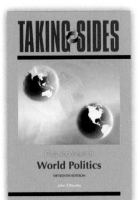

Taking Sides

Taking Sides volumes present current issues in a debate-style format designed to stimulate student interest and develop critical thinking skills. Each issue is thoughtfully framed with an issue summary, an issue introduction, and a postscript or challenge questions. New features for this series include Learning Outcomes and Critical Thinking and Reflection questions for each issue. The pro and con essays—selected for their liveliness and substance—represent the arguments of leading scholars and commentators in their fields. Taking Sides readers also offer annotated listings of selected World Wide Web sites. An online Instructor's Resource Guide with testing materials is available for each volume. Using Taking Sides in the Classroom is an excellent resource that offers practical suggestions for fostering critical thinking in the classroom when using the Taking Sides readers. www.mhhe.com/takingsides

Taking Sides: Clashing Views on African Issues, 4/e, by Moseley (ISBN 978-0-07-805008-4; MHID 0-07-805008-1)

Taking Sides: Clashing Views in Energy and Society, by Easton (ISBN 978-0-07-812755-7; MHID 0-07-812755-6)

Taking Sides: Clashing Views on Global Issues, 7/e, by Harf/Lombardi (ISBN 978-0-07-805024-4; MHID 0-07-805024-3)

Taking Sides: Clashing Views on Latin American Issues, by DeGrave et al. (ISBN 978-0-07-351504-5; MHID 0-07-351504-3)

Taking Sides: Clashing Views in World Politics, 15/e, by Rourke (ISBN 978-0-07-805010-7; MHID 0-07-805010-3)

Global Studies

Global Studies is a unique series designed to provide comprehensive background information and selected world press articles on the regions and countries of the world. Designed to facilitate students' learning and understanding of the region, Critical Thinking questions follow each world press article. Global Studies volumes also include an annotated listing of World Wide Web sites. An online Instructor's Resource Guide with an extensive question bank for use in discussion and testing supports each volume. www.mhhe.com/globalstudies

Global Studies: Africa, 13/e, by Krabacher et al. (ISBN 978-0-07-352776-5; MHID 0-07-352776-9)

Global Studies: China, 14/e, by Zhu (ISBN 978-0-07-802619-5; MHID 0-07-802619-9)

Global Studies: Europe, 10/e, by Frankland (ISBN 978-0-07-337976-0; MHID 0-07-337976-X)

Global Studies: India and South Asia, 10/e, by Dhussa (ISBN 978-0-07-802617-1; MHID 0-07-802617-2)

Global Studies: Japan and the Pacific Rim, 10/e, by Collinwood (ISBN 978-0-07-337985-2; MHID 0-07-337985-9)

Global Studies: Latin America and the Caribbean, 14/e, by Goodwin (ISBN 978-0-07-352777-2; MHID 0-07-352777-7)

Global Studies: The Middle East, 13/e, by Layachi (ISBN 978-0-07-352775-8; MHID 0-07-352775-0)

Global Studies: Russia and the Near Abroad, 12/e, by Ioffe (ISBN 978-0-07-340147-8; MHID 0-07-340147-1)

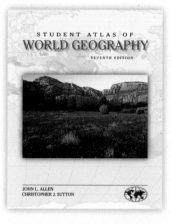

Student Atlas

The Student Atlas series combines full-color maps and data sets to introduce students to the importance of the connections between geography and other areas of study, such as world politics, environmental issues, and economic development. These thematic atlases will give students a clear picture of the recent agricultural, industrial, demographic, environmental, economic, and political changes in every world region. Each Student Atlas is supported by an online Instructor's Resource Guide with testing materials. www.mhhe.com/studentatlas

Student Atlas of World Geography, 7/e, by Allen/Sutton (ISBN 978-0-07-352762-8; MHID 0-07-352762-9)

Student Atlas of World Politics, 9/e, by Allen/Sutton (ISBN 978-0-07-340148-5: MHID 0-07-340148-X)

Sights & Sounds CD-ROM by David Zurick, Eastern Kentucky University

(ISBN 978-0-07-312210-6; MHID 0-07-312210-6)
This CD-ROM offers a unique opportunity in "seeing and hearing" the music and cultural perspectives of 10 regions:

- North America: Appalachia
- Central America: Oaxaca, Mexico
- South America: Ecuador
- Europe: British Isles
- Africa South of the Sahara: Tanzania
- South Asia: Nepal
- Middle East
- Insular Southeast Asia: Bali, Indonesia
- East Asia: China
- South Pacific: Samoa

Klett-Perthes World Atlas

(ISBN 978-0-07-329073-7; MHID 0-07-329073-4)
This high-quality world atlas by well-known mapmaker Klett-Perthes features over 300 pages of detailed climate, physical, political, population, regional, and thematic maps, as well as statistical information for all countries. Also included is a glossary of important terms, an extensive index, and instructions on how to read a map—a must for all geography students! Ask your McGraw-Hill sales representative for further details on how to package this outstanding atlas with *Human Geography*. Explore the many products and resources available from Klett-Perthes by visiting their website at www.klettmaps.com.

Instructors: Ask your sales representative about packaging options—special discounts may be available with some of the titles listed above!

Major Geographic Concepts

In this chapter, we introduce you to the geographer's vocabulary: the terms and concepts human geographers use in their studies. Many of these terms and concepts are the same as those used by cognate social sciences and history. By *cognate*, we mean disciplines that are in some way affiliated with a branch of human geography; for example, political science is a cognate of political geography. We introduce, define, and describe the more specialized geographical terms and concepts over the course of the book, paying special attention to their geographical content. At the same time, there are some specific geographic concepts that make geography the field that it is. These concepts are shared by human and physical geography and are an important reason that physical geography, which examines natural phenomena, and human geography, which deals with human phenomena, are in the same discipline.

The term phenomenon may seem a bit odd when you first hear it. Phenomenon pertains to nearly any type of object, animate or inanimate, that can be sensed. It also refers to something that can be perceived or mentally constructed, such as an attitude or a quality, even though it cannot be immediately sensed. All geographic phenomena are rooted in a spatial context, and geographers are interested in where various phenomena are located, where they are distributed spatially, and how they vary over an area.

This chapter covers the concepts that you will come across in many different areas of human geography, topics that range from migration to trade to studies of elections. These concepts are essential because they are what make geography unique.

1A   Pattern and Process

Major concepts in geography can be distinguished by pattern and process. If you look at a map of the world or a map of a city, you are seeing a spatial **pattern** of different phenomena at any one point in time. Here we describe two familiar patterns that show the distribution of human geographic phenomena and how they can change over time. The term **phenomenon** (the singular of *phenomena*) includes all sorts of attributes that can be considered geographically. These can be physically present (such as a body of water), an attribute of human society (such as regions), or even an attitude that exists in the mind.

Because geography covers such a wide range of phenomena, concepts pertaining to a particular set of phenomena, such as electoral activity, are also shared with the discipline that studies political activity—in this case, political science. Political science is considered a **cognate** discipline to geography because the disciplines share the study of a particular set of phenomena.

Figure 1A.1 ▶ Every couple of years, a major national election occurs in the United States. (a) This map shows the electoral college results during two presidential years. The pattern shown in the top map shows the distribution of electoral votes by state. The colors correspond to the political party of the winner: blue for the Democratic Party, red for the Republican Party. These two elections did not have significant third-party candidates and, although decisive, were not blowouts.

The 2008 election resulted in the victory of Barack Obama against John McCain. This electoral pattern provides a number of insights. It shows the strong position of the Democratic Party in the Northeast and along the coasts. It shows the predominance of the Republican Party in the Southeast, in the Great Plains, and in the interior West. It shows the midwestern states, Florida, and parts of the Southwest as more of a battleground.

The electoral map changes every two years, and over the long term, major shifts can be seen. (b) This map shows the same phenomenon over a century before the 2008 map. William McKinley was elected president that year against William Jennings Bryan. What is interesting is how so many of the areas of strength have flipped. The Southeast and much of the Southwest are solidly in Democratic hands. The Northeast and West Coast states are predominantly Republican. So why did the patterns change? What led to the changing strength of political parties in different parts of the United States? How has this change affected the nature of the political parties?

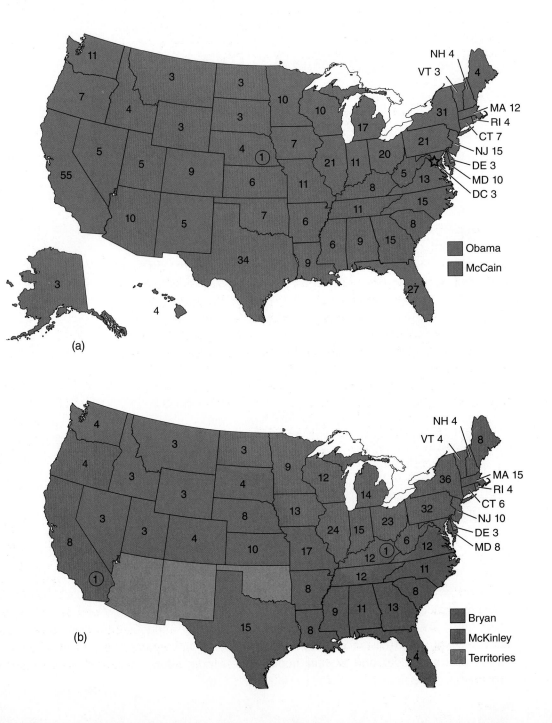

Figure 1A.2 ▶ A second, perhaps less obvious example is a common road map. A road map displays a number of different elements that exist at a particular point in time, such as cities, towns, and unincorporated land. It shows some natural features: rivers, lakes and ponds, perhaps the coastline. Sometimes it shows elevation levels, but probably only extremes. Of course, the prime purpose of any roadmap is to get people where they need to go, so it emphasizes the transportation networks, particularly roads and highways.

(a) This recent Ohio road map designates highways of different sizes, exits and intersections, and perhaps a few other things (such as rest stops) that might interest people who are traveling on the road. Road maps that cover smaller areas also include airports, railroad tracks, railroad stations, and maybe some bicycle lanes. It likely displays various points of interest, major shopping areas, schools, and parks. In fact, the number of items on a roadmap is truly mind-boggling. But consider this roadmap as a pattern, representing a slice of time.

(b) More than 50 years ago, this roadmap was completely different. The major cities and towns are there. Many of the same roads are found in the state. But the biggest change is that there are no major interstate highways—most people traveled on what we would consider now to be small, secondary roads. Less apparent on this map, but a fact of transportation at that time, is the much more important role for the passenger rail system. Railroad lines take people long distances. Missing from this map are many of the airports that are such an important part of long-distance travel today. What factors led to the changing transportation networks between the two maps? How would this have affected other aspects of Ohio's geography?

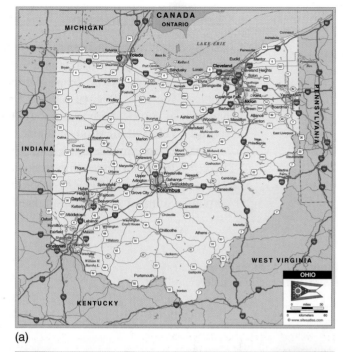

(a)

(b)

Maps are a wonderful way to demonstrate the importance of pattern. Taking two maps that show the same phenomenon but at different points in time begs the question of why the patterns changed and what were the consequences of this change. **Process**, then, is the action that brings about a particular pattern. Process represents the evolution and development of something over time. Geographers like to study process, because it helps explain why things are the way they are, and it reveals some of the mechanisms that help create the patterns we see today.

When geographers think about process, they are interested in a few basic things. They want to know

- when a process began and when it ended,
- the logical ordering of a sequence of processes,
- the relationship between different processes that might have affected the spatial location or distribution of a phenomenon, and
- why the sequence of processes occurred when it did.

Processes in human geography do not always have to result in a particular pattern—in other words, processes are not **deterministic**. Rather, processes are more **probabilistic**, meaning that they tend to result in a pattern, but they may result in other patterns as well. Processes are often **multivariate**—they may involve several different factors, and it can be hard to untangle the relative significance of each. They are also **multiscalar** in that they take place at different spatial scales (see Module 1D). While we need to first examine a phenomenon such as urbanization at a single spatial scale, it soon becomes clear that processes at other scales are heavily involved. For example, decisions about the introduction of a new highway or a new national park are often made at much higher scales; making decisions about where to build new housing and evaluating the demand for such housing may occur at lower scales, each dependent on a separate set of processes.

1B   Absolute and Relative Location

The key geographic attribute of any place is its location on earth. If we didn't consider locations, we would not be doing geography, so geographers always want to know *where* something is. There are two basic ways in which location can be determined. First, **absolute location** dictates where each place exists on a reference system. The most basic of these is the **geographical coordinate system**, which gives each place a unique value based on its latitude and longitude.

The **relative location** of a place has to do with its location compared to other places—its location in context. Places are discussed with regard to particular attributes. For example, the location of factories could be considered in relationship to nearby natural resources, transportation networks, labor supply, and other characteristics that can show where factories are located and which are successful. Relative location helps explain a number of geographic facts.

Figure 1B.1 ▶ Places are indicated by **latitude** and **longitude**.

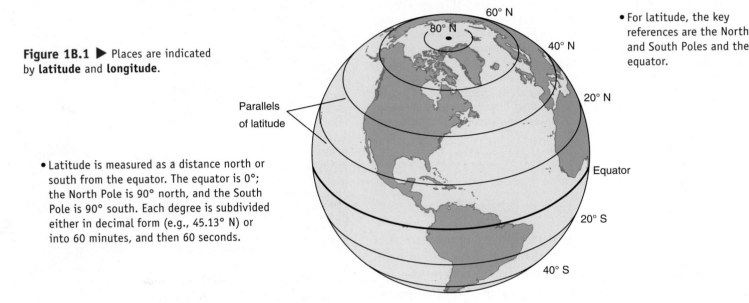

• For latitude, the key references are the North and South Poles and the equator.

• Latitude is measured as a distance north or south from the equator. The equator is 0°; the North Pole is 90° north, and the South Pole is 90° south. Each degree is subdivided either in decimal form (e.g., 45.13° N) or into 60 minutes, and then 60 seconds.

• Longitude runs east of this line or west of the prime meridian between 0° and 180°. The Americas are west longitude; most of Europe, Africa, and Asia are east longitude. Like latitude, degrees of longitude are subdivided decimally or into minutes and seconds.

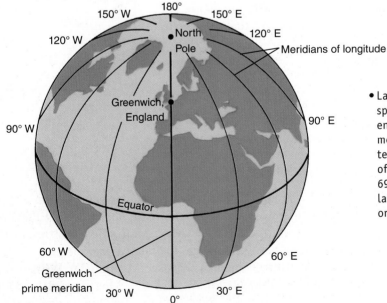

• Latitude and longitude correspond to distances, but in different ways. Each degree of latitude measures about 69 miles no matter where it is located. A degree of longitude is equal to about 69 miles at the equator (same as latitude), about 53 miles at 40° N or S, and 0 miles at the poles.

• For longitude, the key reference is an arbitrary line called the **prime meridian**. This line crosses through Greenwich (London), England, and connects both poles. The prime meridian is 0° and the other side of the prime meridian is 180°—generally the location of the **international date line**.

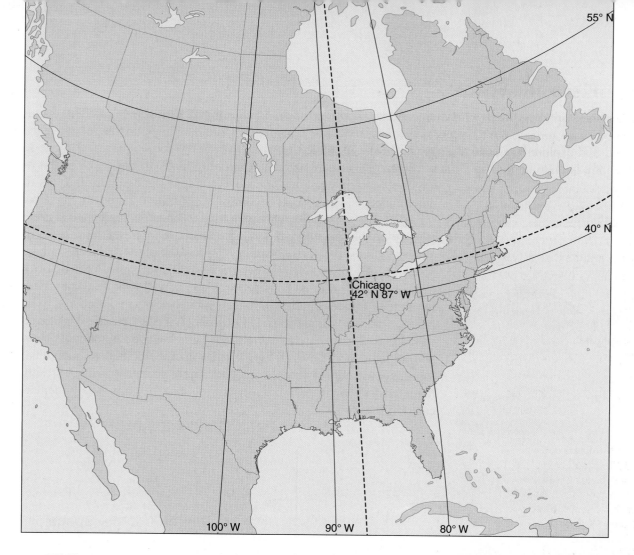

While geographers occasionally discuss absolute location, particularly if working with global positioning systems or as part of a project in mapping, human geographers are much more comfortable with relative location. At the heart of geography is the issue of how some geographical phenomena relate spatially to other geographical phenomena and what this means. Relative location is suggested in many geographical descriptions like the following:

- land-locked country: a country that does not have direct access to the sea
- edge city: a district on the outskirts of a major city that, unlike a traditional suburb, includes many aspects of a central business district
- agricultural hinterland: a farming area surrounding a town or city that provides it with food
- cancer alley: a corridor alleged to have an above-average rate of cancer incidence tied to its proximity to petrochemical plants

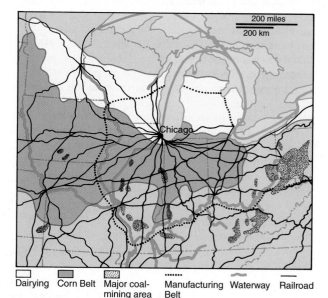

Figure 1B.3 ▶ During the nineteenth century, Chicago rose to become the second most important city in the United States, surpassing all but New York. Not even the Great Chicago Fire of 1857 could derail its ascent. Relative location explains a great deal about Chicago's success. It was based in a natural harbor at the bottom of Lake Michigan, part of the Great Lakes system. Chicago rapidly became the central place for the enormous grain and livestock lands that made up the new American Midwest. Not surprisingly, food processing was among Chicago's first industries. Chicago also benefited from the location of the railroad system. This provided the city with a natural switch point between water traffic (by Great Lake freight ships) and land traffic (over the railroads). Because of these earlier advantages, Chicago continues to maintain its dominance today. However, it has supplemented early transportation linkages with the development of one of the world's busiest airports, O'Hare International, which brings in over 50 million passengers a year.

1C   Place and Space

Geographers are concerned with where, and *where* is often defined in terms of a specific **place**. This seemingly ordinary term is one of geography's key concepts. Geography looks at things as they exist on the ground and explores the spatial perspective, and its basic unit is one or more specific places. A place in geography is quite similar to a date in history. It is a fundamental building block in the development of larger spaces, interactions and flows, regions, landscapes, and lots of other concepts. Place exists in almost everything that geographers do.

Place has very different connotations, depending on how it is used. A place can be something that is quite objective, representing a series of attributes found at a fixed location. This kind of place is usually named.

A second key concept in geography is that of **space**. It is difficult to refer to space without considering place as well. One way is to think in terms of dimensionality. In other words, places are considered to be points, with zero dimensions. On the other hand, spaces are considered to be areas. Spaces have two dimensions and include a number of places within them. While overall "space" may itself be boundless, individual "spaces" have edges of some sort. They might not necessarily be strictly bounded—although very often they are—but they are usually demarcated in some way.

(a)

(b)

▲ **Figure 1C.1** Venice, Italy, is a place that is usually quite specific. (a) This picture of Venice shows a few things you would not expect to see elsewhere, such as gondoliers and the Rialto Bridge. (b) A place can also indicate a generic geographical type, as shown in this picture of Cetara on Italy's Amalfi coast. This is perhaps more generic, showing an ancient seaport community along the Mediterranean. We might speak of a coastal community or an ethnic neighborhood as a place. Another understanding of place can be considered subjectively. Here, place is more than simply a set of attributes but something that connotes a whole set of meanings, particularly to the people who know that place well. This is often described as **sense of place**. For example, a historic seaport, such as depicted here, might conjure feelings of fascinating old buildings and a sense of history, but also the ease and relaxation that we often associate with being on the water.

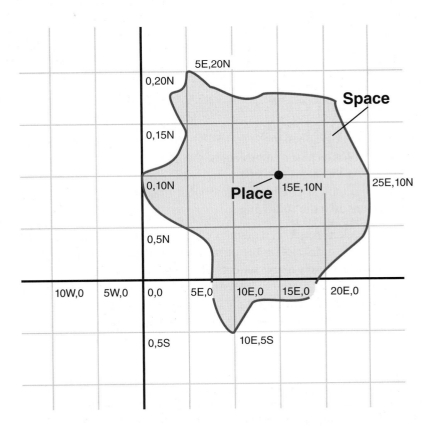

▲ **Figure 1C.2** Like place, space can be considered in a number of ways. It can be viewed as something quite objective. In this way, it serves as a kind of void, within which are a series of places, each with specific locations. Space operates as an arena within which activities take place. This is sometimes described as absolute space, or **Euclidean space**. The absolute locations discussed in the previous module and absolute distance (presented in Module 1F) exist in Euclidean space.

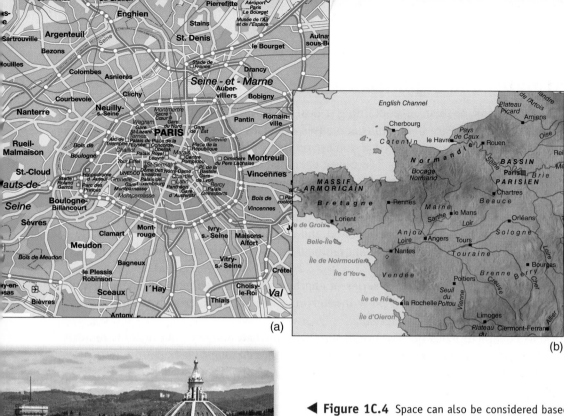

(a)

(b)

◀ **Figure 1C.3** Space can also be considered in more relative terms, often in regard to a particular place or set of places. The use of terminology such as *site* or *situation* considers space in this way. (a) A **site**, for example, constitutes the immediate environment of a place, whereas (b) **situation** is concerned primarily with the way in which a particular place relates to the space that surrounds it. This refers back to the discussion of relative location in the previous module. In the map in (a), Paris is shown in regard to its immediate site: the Seine River, the city itself, the suburbs, the parks, and various transportation arteries. The map in (b) places Paris within a broader context, or situation: its location in relation to other parts of France, to the great northern European plain, and the various river systems.

◀ **Figure 1C.4** Space can also be considered based on how it is perceived. Humanist geographers may discuss spaces that are relatively sacred and counterpoise these with spaces that are decidedly secular. In a church, the especially sacred spaces include the high altar and other altar spaces. Confessionals confer a space of privileged communication between the parishioner and the priest. Movement across an area is more than simply a trip from one point to another—it is charged with a particular set of symbols and emotions. Space may also be viewed as something understood and experienced in a slightly different way. The construction of mental maps (see Module 2F) that are the product of an individual viewpoint is an example of this.

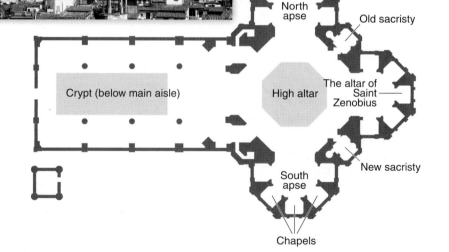

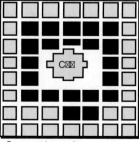

Sector growth toward suburbia

Compact inner city

Figure 1C.5 ▶ It is important to keep in mind that space can be produced for a particular end. Specific spaces can be created to constrain the options of people. Consider the creation of the ghetto, a space of extremely high spatial segregation and concentration of a racial or ethnic group. The ghetto is not a "natural" occurrence. Rather, it is something produced as an area that encloses a group of people that have been branded as somehow distinct and is isolated from the rest of society. In so doing, it effectively limits the options of those who live within the ghetto, as well as the options of those living outside the ghetto. These diagrams show two common patterns for the African American ghetto that emerged in the twentieth century. The lower diagram displays the ghetto as a ring around the central business district, while the upper shows the ghetto as a sector of the city that grew out toward the suburbs.

1D   Place Attributes and Significance

One way to view places is to think of them as containing a host of attributes. In the **geographical grid** shown here, characteristics or attributes are in columns and cases or places are in rows.

This grid is similar to a number of spreadsheets that you are probably already familiar with but, because this is geographical, places are represented in rows. Moreover, each place has a specific **geographical location**. The types of places we study depend very much on the **scale of analysis**, which tells what is being studied. For example, the entire world might be the scale of analysis, and the places studied might be countries. Alternatively, the scale of analysis might be a city and the places considered might be neighborhoods, streets, or bus stops. The types of places that are cataloged and considered have to do with the scale of analysis and the topic of interest. The reason this is a geographical grid is because each place has a location as well, so it can be positioned on a map.

Each place will be marked by a comprehensive series of characteristics or attributes that help describe it. Although the scale of analysis and topic of interest will determine which characteristics we focus on, all places are marked by an array of different characteristics.

What can some of these characteristics be? We might start with a whole range of physical characteristics. Even though this is human geography, the physical aspects of different places can be vitally important, since geographers pay attention to both the human and the physical aspects of things.

Among the physical characteristics are a particular elevation, a climate, soil, rock formations, topography, vegetation, crops, land use, and other aspects. Places can also be marked by a variety of human characteristics, including population, cultural groups, businesses, socioeconomic status, education levels, political systems, and institutions; in fact, the list can go on and on.

Often, it is difficult to define a place by a fixed characteristic. How can we talk about the religion of a place that includes people practicing lots of different religions? Sometimes, we can apply a characteristic to an entire place. If we are looking at countries, each country is marked by a particular political system that applies to the entire country. This may be considered a **pure characteristic**. But the characteristics of the population within the country can be trickier to determine. How does one determine the culture of a country, for example? We may mark a country as Catholic, but we are really saying that Catholicism is the dominant religion in the country. There may be other, very significant religions that are being practiced, and

▼ **Figure 1D.1**

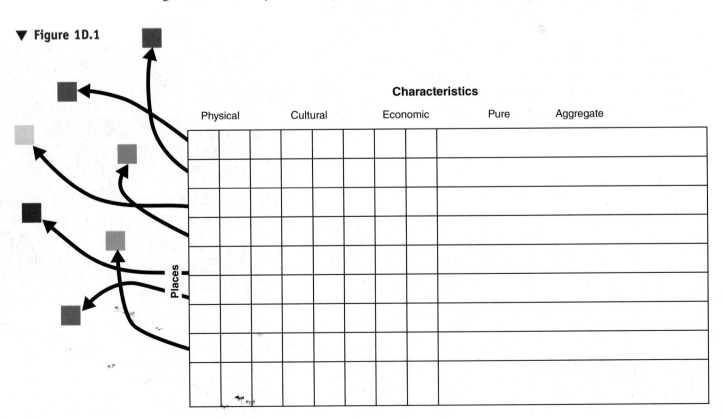

a geographer may wish to understand these as well. We may say that this city is marked by a particular socioeconomic status. For example, some cities are clearly wealthier than others. But "wealthy" cities usually contain a number of poor people and "poor" cities include people who are fairly affluent. When looking at characteristics, we are very often looking at **aggregate characteristics**, the dominant characteristics that are found within a place.

A few key ideas are important in considering the location and attributes of places:

1. While places contain myriad characteristics, some characteristics are more significant than others. The **relative significance** depends on the scale of analysis and the topic of interest. A study of religion, for example, may not be very concerned with characteristics related to the topography of a place, unless natural features are seen as a key factor. Relative significance can also apply to the fact that a given attribute may be significant, but in different ways in different contexts. In the United States, a map of religions can help us understand patterns of faith, ethnicity, and even political attitudes. But religious differences in the United States have a significance that is separate from religious differences in a place such as Bosnia-Herzegovina.

2. Much of the significance of an attribute is established by **scale**. Geographers are very interested in scale, whether it is global scale, local scale, or something in between. Scale determines the frame of reference and shows which characteristics are especially important. Scale also comes up because geographers like to think about the interactions of different places at different scales. How does politics at the urban scale interact with politics at the national scale, and how does this interact with politics at the global scale?

3. The third key aspect of places is that they have a location in space. As discussed earlier, geographers have two ways of identifying location—absolute and relative. When the attributes of places are considered, and especially when places are compared to each other, both types of location can be important. Absolute locations can provide a measure of distance. The relative location can help us compare place attributes.

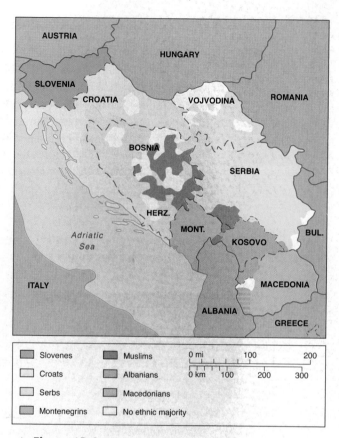

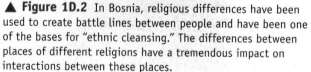

▲ **Figure 1D.2** In Bosnia, religious differences have been used to create battle lines between people and have been one of the bases for "ethnic cleansing." The differences between places of different religions have a tremendous impact on interactions between these places.

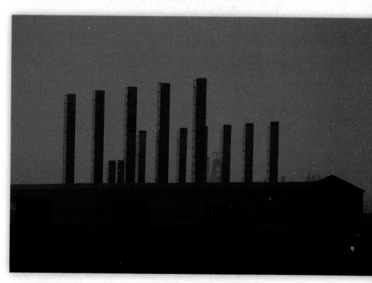

▲ **Figure 1D.4** The location of nearby natural resources, transportation networks, and labor supply can help determine the best place to locate a factory. Steel factories, such as this mill in Ohio, were traditionally located near sources of coal and iron, and if these resources were not close at hand, there had to be essential transportation networks to bring in raw materials. Factories also depended on a steady water source.

◀ **Figure 1D.3**
Globalization, which is often defined as the broader integration of more places around the world, has a lot to do with the interaction of economics at various scales. These people are protesting the role of globalization—specifically, overseas production of goods and international trading practices—in undercutting wages and in harming the environment.

1E   Mapping Spatial Distributions

In Module 1A, we described how geographers look for patterns. In considering how phenomena are arranged in space, geographers speak of **distribution**. This is often a more precise way of describing a pattern. Distributions are rarely even. Often, something will be concentrated in a few areas and sparse in several others. The distribution of any phenomenon creates a pattern that can be analyzed in its own right, but it can be particularly helpful when compared to the distribution of other phenomena. Modern geographic information systems, discussed in Module 2H, have allowed for even more complex analyses of spatially distributed data.

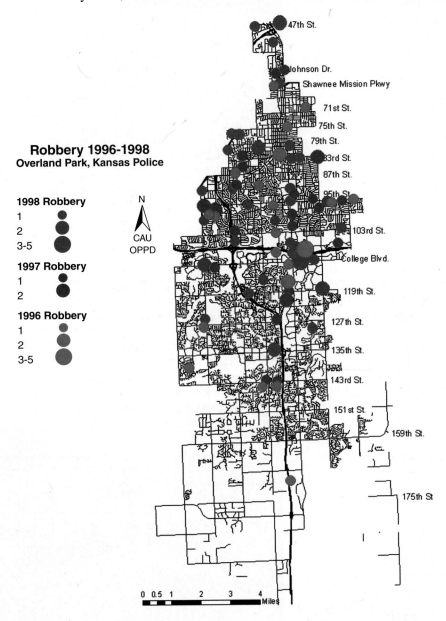

Figure 1E.1 This is a crime map of a city, which shows each incident of robbery as a particular point on the map. A simple dot map would just show each incidence as a dot. This map uses different sized circles to reflect more incidences of robbery at each location. The colors depict at what year the robberies took place, which allows us to see whether the pattern of criminal activity has changed over time. How would you describe the distribution of robberies: dispersed, clustered, or random? Would other criminal activity follow these same patterns? What would the distribution of homicides look like?

Most things in geography can be mapped, and the mapping allows us to look at the distribution in some detail. **Thematic maps** are maps that show the distribution, flow, or connection of one or more characteristics. We use thematic maps to show how different attributes are distributed, and many of the maps in this textbook are thematic maps. The type of map that is used to show a particular distribution can be key to understanding how this distribution occurs. In one type of map, every incident is displayed as a point. This type of map can be described as a **point pattern**, or point distribution, map. If there are a lot of incidences of a particular phenomenon, then it becomes necessary to have each point stand for a number of items—say, 20 per point. Maps of population density are point maps with each point representing thousands or even tens of thousands of people.

Point pattern maps make it easier to show whether a distribution is **dispersed** or **clustered**. The distribution may show itself to be either highly clustered, with distinct pockets, or more dispersed, where there does not seem to be any type of agglomeration and incidences are well separated from one another. Particular kinds of businesses may be clustered, if these businesses see a benefit in agglomeration. Or they may be dispersed, if each business seeks to capture its own market. We might see whether crime is clustered in particular parts of a city or dispersed in all parts of the city. Sometimes geographers use the term **random distribution** for a phenomenon that is neither clustered nor dispersed.

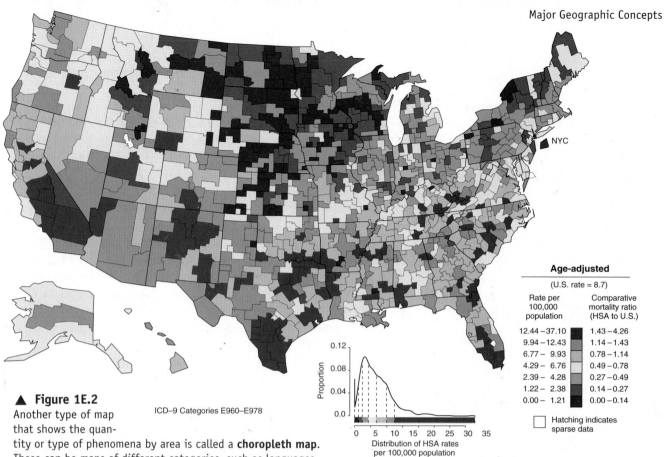

▲ Figure 1E.2

ICD–9 Categories E960–E978

Age-adjusted

(U.S. rate = 8.7)

Rate per 100,000 population	Comparative mortality ratio (HSA to U.S.)
12.44 – 37.10	1.43 – 4.26
9.94 – 12.43	1.14 – 1.43
6.77 – 9.93	0.78 – 1.14
4.29 – 6.76	0.49 – 0.78
2.39 – 4.28	0.27 – 0.49
1.22 – 2.38	0.14 – 0.27
0.00 – 1.21	0.00 – 0.14

☐ Hatching indicates sparse data

Another type of map that shows the quantity or type of phenomena by area is called a **choropleth map**. These can be maps of different categories, such as languages, religions, or vegetation. Or they can be maps of different amounts or quantities, such as per capita income. The shading or color of each areal unit depicts the quantity or category of data. Any choropleth map begins with a base map, which is then divided into subunits. After this, we need to figure out what kind of data needs to be mapped. The **density** of a distribution is best explored in a choropleth map. The density shows the number of some phenomenon divided by some sort of control group. For instance, we could take the same map of the city that we used in Figure 1E.1 and divide it into census tracts or wards and then show how many robberies were committed in each ward. We might even choose to standardize this by dividing the number of robberies by the population of the ward.

In this example, we use another crime—homicides—and another scale—counties in the United States. The actual proportion of homicides is then divided into what are called **class intervals**—each class interval is assigned a shade (often colors are used as well). This map allows us to indicate those counties that have a major problem with homicide compared to those where homicide is not as great an issue. This can be a useful gauge of what is taking place in the country.

Figure 1E.3 ▶ The final type of map used to display distributions is an **isoline map**, which consists of lines that connect points of equal value. Isoline maps do a good job of showing the peaks and valleys of a particular distribution. Isoline maps can be helpful in handling **continuous data**, data that occur everywhere but where we have only a few observations. While this type of map is more popular in physical geography (a topographic contour map is a well-known isoline map), it can be an interesting way to observe human geographic patterns.

In the case of crime data, an isoline map helps draw a contrast between areas with high levels of robberies and areas with lower levels. The "crime surface" of a city can be readily measured. In this case, the left map shows the relative density of robberies in New York City, with darker areas indicating a higher rate of crime.

In the case of these sorts of isoline maps, the phenomenon may exhibit a particular type of pattern. It may follow a particular line or shape, or it may coincide with another type of distribution. The relationship between the spatial distributions of two or more phenomena is described as **covariation**—which means that they tend to vary in the same way. Covariation can be a very important tool in understanding why phenomena are arranged the way they are. Here the map showing rob-

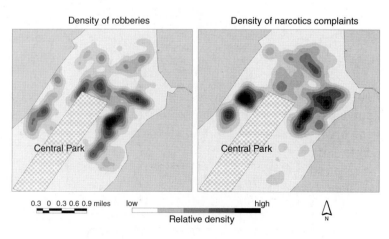

Density of robberies

Density of narcotics complaints

Central Park

Central Park

0.3 0 0.3 0.6 0.9 miles   low ———————— high
Relative density

N

beries in New York is compared to a map showing the pattern of narcotic complaints. This covariation may offer some explanation for robbery "hot spots" and provide some clues of how to reduce the number of robberies.

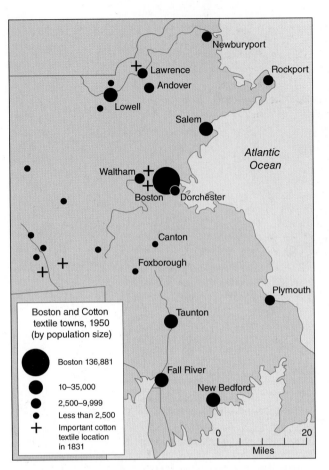

▲ **Figure 1F.1** This map of textile towns in nineteenth-century Massachusetts shows places that share a place similarity in terms of industry. Why were all these towns involved so heavily in textiles? Was there any common factor that led to this pattern?

1F Spatial Interactions and Distance

Many questions in geography begin with observing interesting patterns. And many of these patterns emerge because of the relationships that exist between places. Other social sciences also consider places, but they are less likely to consider the relationship between places and how this is affected by *where* these places happen to be.

One key aspect of geographic thinking is that places often bunch together on a number of common characteristics or traits. Places can be very similar, and this is particularly true of places that are close to each other. **Place similarity** can apply to either a single attribute or multiple attributes. Places may be bunched together based on their cultural features, they may be politically consolidated, or they may share economic similarities. Once a similarity is detected, the geographer might then ask why.

A second aspect of geography is that places interact even if they do not share characteristics. Often, the differences between places spur the greatest interaction. **Place interaction** can take any number of forms. Movement of people is a common interaction between places. Other interactions are the flow of goods and services, the movement of ideas, the movement of communications through space, and a variety of other interactions that tie places to each other.

Spatial interaction is a term used to describe the movement and interconnections between different places. These interactions create a network, which geographers attempt to understand. Geographers often describe this network as **spatial connectivity**.

Interaction is influenced by **accessibility**, which indicates how easy it is to move between different places. Accessibility depends on where the places are, what type of interaction is being addressed, the distance between places, the barriers between places, and what sorts of things might help facilitate movement between places. Commuting patterns that involve daily flows of people from home to work are quite different from our connections through cyberspace.

A **flow map** is often the best way to depict the interactions between places. Depending on the type of attribute being measured, a flow map can show (1) the places between which interaction occurs, (2) the volume of that interaction, and (3) the direction of that interaction.

Spatial interactions are heavily dependent on **distance**, a key concept in geography. Clearly, distance matters: guest worker flows are more likely to occur between nearby countries. The same would be true if we looked at other types of interaction: shopping between homes and stores, commuting between homes and work, or trading between countries.

◄ **Figure 1F.2** This recent map shows the interaction between Taliban strongholds in Pakistan, a major source of terrorism in Pakistan and neighboring Afghanistan. We know that terrorists do not work in isolation but, instead, are connected to other terrorists within a large network. Understanding the levels of interaction between terrorists may help us understand where terrorist organizations get their funding, where they find safe havens, and perhaps where they are in the best position to strike. Not understanding this network appropriately may result in false conclusions about terrorist relationships that do not exist.

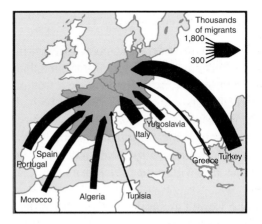

◀ **Figure 1F.3** Any sort of human migration is highly directional: people depart from one place and arrive at another. A good migration map uses the width of the line to show the volume of migration from place A to place B, another line to show the volume of migration from place B to place A. This map shows the flow of guest workers or labor migrants from source countries to destination countries. Where are some of the biggest flows? What do the major source countries have in common?

Figure 1F.4 ▶ These two maps are only 27 years apart, but they show a massive difference in terms of travel time. (a) In 1830, it took one week to travel from New York to Ohio and three weeks to go to Illinois. Other distances took equally long. (b) By 1857, this had all changed. New York to Ohio took only a day, and it took only two days to get to Chicago. What happened to shrink these times?

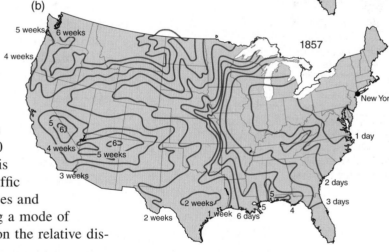

There are a number of ways to measure distance. **Absolute distance**, or **Euclidean distance**, measures the straight line mileage between two places. This straight line distance is less useful than some other ways to measure distance. In traveling, people need to follow existing transportation routes, leading to distance measures that vary a bit—we might call this **travel distance**.

Another way of measuring distance considers the actual time it takes to get from one place to another, accounting for the different levels of accessibility. This measures distance in terms of time, or **travel time**. As any traveler can tell you, this type of distance varies tremendously. One reason is time of day. The distance between your home and where you go to school can be traversed in about 10 minutes with no traffic (say, at 2:00 a.m.). Or it can take 20 minutes at 8:30 a.m., when traffic is heavy. Factors such as the type of roads, construction, traffic volume, the number of lights, and the number of businesses and residences on the roadways determine travel time. Taking a mode of transportation other than a car has an enormous impact on the relative distance as well.

Distance decay refers to the idea that, all else being equal, as the distance between two places increases the volume of interaction between these places decreases. This measure also depends on the level of accessibility based on transportation technology and infrastructure. As transportation technology and infrastructure improve, the amount of time it takes to get from one place to another—termed the **friction of distance**—decreases.

While distance is often measured by either physical distance or time, it can also have a different connotation as something that is perceived, what we call **cognitive distance**. For example, for many people the trip back from a place often seems to be shorter than the trip there. This may have to do with familiarity—once a pathway is known and becomes routine, the perceived distance is less. Likewise, strong emotions can make the distance between places seem much greater than they are. For instance, a walk in a bad neighborhood feels a lot longer than a walk in a comfortable, familiar place. The cognitive distances that people experience influence how they interact.

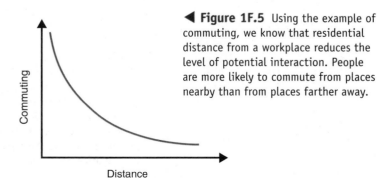

◀ **Figure 1F.5** Using the example of commuting, we know that residential distance from a workplace reduces the level of potential interaction. People are more likely to commute from places nearby than from places farther away.

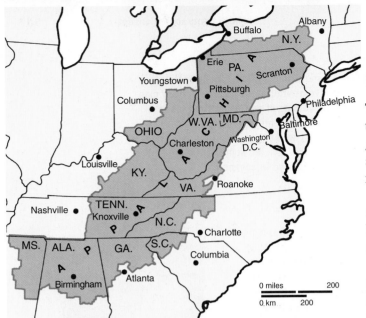

▲ **Figure 1G.1** The establishment of criteria is also important when we consider a region. Any defined region depends on certain criteria or conditions that have to be specified. Sometimes regions are created for a specific political or economic reason. This map depicts the boundaries of the Appalachian region, at least according to some criteria specified by the US government. You can see that this region includes parts of 12 states and all of West Virginia. Many cities are also found within this official Appalachia, including some you may not expect, such as Pittsburgh. Another set of criteria would result in a region with different boundaries.

1G   Regions

The concepts of place similarity and place interaction come together in the idea of a **region**. *Region* is a term that people use all the time, but geographers use it in a much more specific way. Regions are a way of subdividing space into categorizable geographic units. To start with, a region is composed of two or more places and has spatial dimensionality.

Regions are units that geographers use to organize space. They are composed of separate places. Regions also have some type of **boundary** that distinguishes the area within the region from the area outside the region.

A geographic region can be viewed as similar to a **period** in history. Periods are a way to slice up time and are essential to historical understanding. For example, the period known as the Civil War can be open to a variety of interpretations. Depending on whom you are talking to, the Civil War constitutes only that period between the beginning of conflict and the surrender of General Lee at Appomattox: between 1861 and 1865.

But there are other ways to consider the Civil War period. We might begin with the sectionalism that began to divide the North and the South as early as the 1820s with the Missouri Compromise. Or we can look at the beginnings of political hostilities, evident by the 1840s, with a number of Supreme Court decisions and congressional acts.

On the other side, we might consider the end of the Civil War as not truly taking place until after the Reconstruction era, which ended in the 1870s, and the bitterness that lasted well into the twentieth century. The point is not to come up with a uniform definition of the period known as the Civil War but to realize that the Civil War as a period depends on **criteria**.

Formal regions are composed of places that have one or more characteristics in common. The characteristics can be almost anything listed in the geographical grid (see Module 1D). But the formation of such regions depends, as do so many items in geography, on scale and on the units used to compose the region.

Consider a map of religious regions, where the regions are composed of countries. In this case, the dominant religion of each country is used to construct a world map of religious regions. But this can be misleading, since we know that many countries do not follow a single religion but, instead, are divided among a number of religious faiths (see Chapter 8). Sometimes, the dominant religion varies within areas of each country. In this case, we might come up with a more sophisticated and concise picture of religious geography by using country subdivisions.

Figure 1G.2 ▶ A political region such as the British Commonwealth is defined on the basis of particular criteria pertaining to membership in this commonwealth, which is made up of countries that were at one point British colonies. Notice in these cases that the places used to delimit the region are countries.

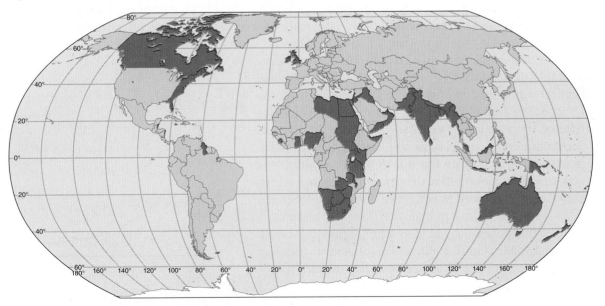

Figure 1G.3 ▶ Organizations such as the World Bank categorize the world on the basis of per capita income. Here countries are grouped on the basis of per capita income, labeled here as GNI per Capita, with the shades corresponding to very low income, low income, lower-middle income, upper-middle income, and high income. This is a form of regionalization. Many organizations, such as the World Bank, do not distinguish between high- and low-income areas *within* a country but treat each country as a single unit and use an aggregate measure, like an average, to determine level of income.

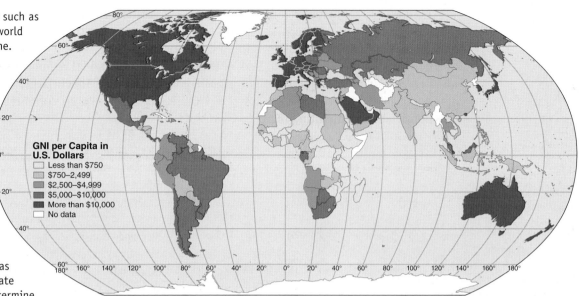

GNI per Capita in U.S. Dollars
- Less than $750
- $750–2,499
- $2,500–4,999
- $5,000–10,000
- More than $10,000
- No data

Religious regions of Switzerland as of 2000

Catholic
- Absolute majority over 50%
- Plurality between 40% and 50%

Protestant
- Absolute majority over 50%
- Plurality between 40% and 50%

No religion dominant
- No religion exceeds 40% of the population

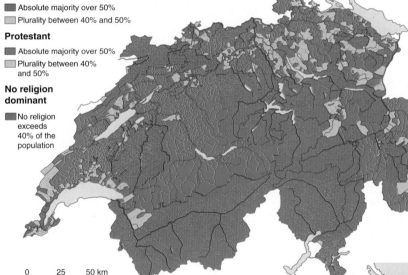

0   25   50 km

◀ Figure 1G.4 A country such as Switzerland, with its diverse linguistic and religious traditions, can be differentiated between Protestant and Catholic areas, yet these divisions are fairly fine-grained and not always clear-cut. Some places show an absolute majority (over half) of Catholics or an absolute majority of Protestants. Other places show a relative majority (between 40% and 50%) of these groups, whereas in some regions there is no clearly dominant religion. When looking at a map like this, another important thing to consider is how criteria themselves are defined. How do we define something like a religious region? Does it have to do with official policies, or the number of people who say they practice that religion, or attendance at each religious institution over the course of a week?

Figure 1G.5 ▶ Think of a map of music regions. Is there a bluegrass region, a grunge rock region, and a hip-hop region? Depending on the criteria, these types of regions might be delineated. But what are we using to operationalize the criteria? Is a bluegrass region made up of places where bluegrass musicians come from, where a certain percentage of radio airplay is bluegrass, or something else? In this map, the influence of country music is operationalized by the distribution of country music stations. The region that is established may also be internally divided between areas of high intensity and areas where there is less intensity.

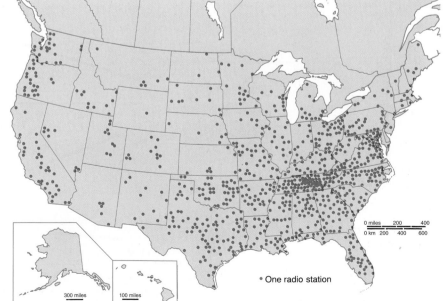

• One radio station

Another type of region is constructed out of places that interact. These **functional regions** do not rely on places that have similar characteristics but, rather, on places that have some type of relationship. The connections can be exceptional or routine, small- or large-scale.

There are a variety of ways to look at these regions. Functional regions can be constructed at the individual level. Functional regions might also be constructed at a much larger scale. A region composed of commuting patterns from town to town or from residential areas to commercial, industrial and business areas constructs a commuting region.

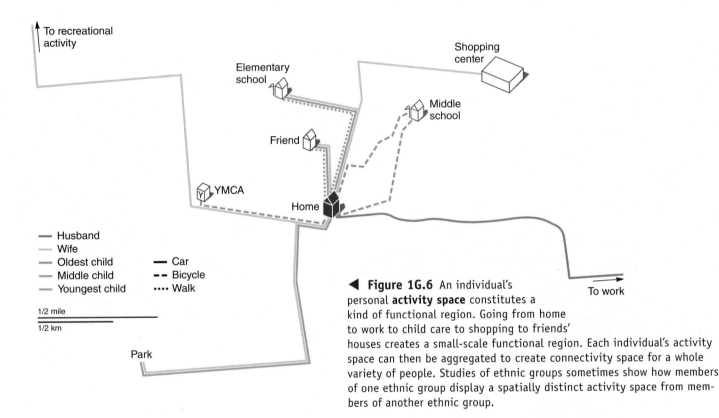

◄ **Figure 1G.6** An individual's personal **activity space** constitutes a kind of functional region. Going from home to work to child care to shopping to friends' houses creates a small-scale functional region. Each individual's activity space can then be aggregated to create connectivity space for a whole variety of people. Studies of ethnic groups sometimes show how members of one ethnic group display a spatially distinct activity space from members of another ethnic group.

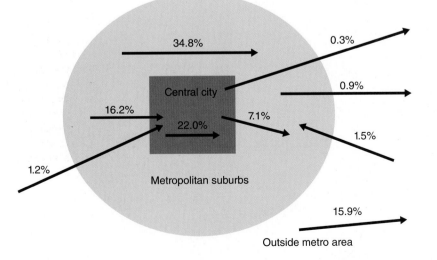

◄ **Figure 1G.7** Functional regions can be constructed at a larger scale, such as a commuting region that encompasses many towns. Defining a commuting region is actually quite significant for policy. The US Census Bureau uses such regions as a way of defining metropolitan areas. Those places having a commuting relationship are included in the same metropolitan area. Where no clear relationship exists, a place is considered to be outside the metropolitan area. The Census also uses a threshold standard: at least 25% of all workers in outlying counties must commute to a metropolitan area's central county, or at least 25% of jobs in an outlying county must be taken by workers who live in a metropolitan area's central county or counties.

Functional regions can change as the level of interactions changes. Over time, interactions can shift from one set of places to another set of places. They can expand or they can shrink. As with formal regions, the important thing is to consider the criteria being used to define these regions. It is also useful to think about what exactly the functional region will be used for. A marketing geographer may be interested in the potential market and in the interactions of customers with a variety of shopping spaces. A transportation geographer might be looking at the interactions of people from one place to another, using the roadways and other transportation arteries.

A third type of region might be described as a **vernacular region**. These are regions that people construct in their mind and may be very difficult to dissect. Although criteria define a formal or functional region, this does not apply in the case of a vernacular region.

Figure 1G.8 ▶ Within the United States, "the South" designates a distinct region. People speak of the South, everyone has a general idea about where it is located, and several universities even have institutes of "Southern Studies" to help analyze this region. But it is very difficult to define the South. If it were a question of latitude, Hawaii would be part of that region, but it is not. We could use the example of those states that constitute the Confederacy or states south of the Mason-Dixon line. While useful, the South does not necessarily follow these designators. The South can be a question of history, climate, ethnicity, or style. It might be defined in terms of states and state boundaries. But often areas such as southern Indiana and southern Illinois are considered to be a part of the South, whereas most of Maryland is not. And then there is Florida, where the northern part of the state is far more "southern" than southern Florida. These factors indicate that the South has more to do with a state of mind than anything else. In this map, the shadings reflect the degree to which certain states have been considered as part of the South, with the darkest red indicating a consensus opinion.

◀ **Figure 1G.9** To define vernacular regions, sometimes geographers resort to tracing self-designation: Where do people feel they belong in a particular region? Geographer Wilbur Zelinsky defined the South by counting all of the entries in telephone books that used the term *Dixie*. As with many vernacular regions, often the best way to find them is to determine exactly how people identify themselves and their places.

(a)

(b)

(c)

1H   Idea of Landscape

Landscape is a very old term that has changed its meaning over the years. Originally, the term referred primarily to estates or manors. Later, it began to acquire a strong aesthetic expression as it applied to landscape paintings. From its German root, *landscape* has also signified a bounded area of human occupation. Yet in most of our more modern usages, landscape has represented something more ambiguous. Unlike a region, which is defined by distinct criteria, a landscape is more likely to be defined as a mélange—a mixture of sometimes incongruous elements.

Some earlier cultural geographers—notably, Carl Sauer (see Module 2E), looked at a landscape as an assemblage of different elements that came together in one area. Landscapes could provide a visual cultural history, since people altered the landscape as they went about their daily work. More recently, there has been an interest in how landscapes comprise physical, human, and symbolic elements. Landscapes also reflect identity, and geographers examine how landscapes represent particular identities and how these representations may change.

Landscapes exist at a variety of spatial scales. They can encompass a very large area of land. They can represent a particular type of land. They can also represent something at a much smaller scale, even the interiors of buildings. Landscapes are perceived in many different ways. There is a purely visible way of examining a landscape; these are the elements of a landscape that are clear and tangible. There is also a visual way of examining landscape in which the visible elements in the landscape are distinguished by relative significance. Depending on what we are seeking to get out of the landscape, certain features acquire a high significance. For a person parking a car, the visual landscape is dominated by parking spaces. When we look at a particular landscape, we cannot help but think about other things that landscape brings up. This is what might be described as the vicarious nature of landscape, having to do with the way in which the landscape we see plays into our thoughts and emotions. The landscape in this case becomes quite evocative; it brings in emotions and memories from the past and ties these into other landscapes that you are familiar with.

◀ **Figure 1H.1** Landscapes can be ordinary or special. The **ordinary landscape** (sometimes called a vernacular landscape) is a landscape that people encounter in their daily experiences. Understanding these ordinary landscapes can be very important, because they help us understand the culture and the ways of life of the people who live in it, as well as how a place is affected by people. As J. B. Jackson put it, "The beauty that we see in the vernacular landscape is the image of our common humanity: hard work, stubborn hope, and mutual forbearance striving to be loved" (Groth and Bressi 1997, 18). These three images represent the ordinary landscapes of (a) nature, (b) prayer, and (c) shopping. What country do these landscapes come from? How would the American landscape be different?

(b)

Figure 1H.2 These landscape images are iconic in different ways. (a) The Statue of Liberty in New York Harbor helps people identify one aspect of American identity: the US role as a country of immigrants. (b) Our notion of the American West is filled with iconic landscape images, including a dusty Main Street lined with saloons, a general store, a boarding house, and a sheriff's office. (c) Our vision of the South Pacific is often characterized by this landscape of palm trees swaying on a lagoon.

(a)

(c)

There is also a class of distinctive landscape types that bring to mind images and symbols essential to identity. These can be described as **iconic landscapes**. An iconic landscape can be unique to a particular place. Other iconic landscapes may not be unique to particular places but can evoke a whole class of places. Sometimes particular symbols end up representing an entire culture or group of cultures, adding to our sense of a much larger area. In this way, of course, these symbols can also be misleading and readily used for all sorts of ends: projecting power, fostering certain ideas, subtly evoking a particular sensibility.

While many landscapes come from the outside, **interior landscapes** are those found inside a building, a house, or another structure. While invisible to outside eyes, these landscapes can be a vital part of people's identity.

(a)   (b)

▲ **Figure 1H.3** Interior landscapes can be constructed (a) formally, as an architect might design a grand lobby, or (b) informally, as families scatter elements of their identity around a house.

Key Terms

absolute distance (1F)	isoline map (1E)
absolute location (1B)	landscape (1H)
accessibility (1F)	latitude (1B)
activity space (1G)	longitude (1B)
aggregate characteristics (1D)	multiscalar (1A)
boundary (1G)	multivariate (1A)
choropleth map (1E)	ordinary landscape (1H)
class intervals (1E)	pattern (1A)
clustered (1E)	period (1G)
cognate (1A)	phenomenon (1A)
cognitive distance (1F)	place (1C)
continuous data (1E)	place interaction (1F)
covariation (1E)	place similarity (1F)
criteria (1G)	point pattern (1E)
density (1E)	prime meridian (1B)
deterministic (1A)	probabilistic (1A)
dispersed (1E)	process (1A)
distance (1F)	pure characteristic (1D)
distance decay (1F)	random distribution (1E)
distribution (1E)	region (1G)
Euclidean distance (1F)	relative location (1B)
Euclidean space (1C)	relative significance (1D)
flow map (1F)	scale (1D)
formal regions (1G)	scale of analysis (1D)
friction of distance (1F)	sense of place (1C)
functional regions (1G)	site (1C)
geographical coordinate system (1B)	situation (1C)
geographical grid (1D)	space (1C)
geographical location (1D)	spatial connectivity (1F)
globalization (1D)	spatial interaction (1F)
iconic landscapes (1H)	thematic maps (1E)
interior landscapes (1H)	travel distance (1F)
international date line (1B)	travel time (1F)
	vernacular region (1G)

Basic Review Questions

1. What is the distinction between pattern and process?
2. What is the difference between probabilistic and deterministic processes?
3. How does a multivariate explanation consider a process?
4. How is absolute location related to latitude and longitude?
5. How many degrees total are there in longitude, and how is this measured between the prime meridian and the international date line?
6. How many degrees are there in latitude, and how is this measured between the equator and the poles?
7. How does relative location differ from absolute location?
8. What is a way to define a place: specifically, generically, and subjectively?
9. What are ways to consider space, and how is this related to place?
10. What types of place attributes are found on a geographical grid?
11. What might determine the relative significance of characteristics?
12. How is scale important when considering a place?
13. What are the differences between point maps, choropleth maps, and isoline maps?
14. What is the difference between a dispersed and a clustered distribution?
15. How would a map demonstrate the covariation of two phenomena?
16. How does a flow map help demonstrate spatial interactions?
17. How does accessibility relate to connectivity?
18. How does distance decay show the friction of distance?
19. What is the relationship of criteria to a region?
20. Define the difference between formal, functional, and vernacular regions.
21. Landscapes can be ordinary or iconic. What is the distinction between these types?

Advanced Review Questions (Essay Questions)

1. How does the pattern of the map of US elections in 2006 differ from the pattern of US elections in 1946? What would be some of the processes leading to this change, and how would these processes be considered multivariate?
2. How might you measure the absolute location of any US city? How would this city be considered in regard to its relative location, and what would be three aspects of its relative location?
3. Explain how a place can be perceived specifically, generically, and subjectively (give an example). How would the subjective perception provide a sense of place? How is space distinct from place, and how might spaces be created?
4. Describe the characteristics of five places. What might determine the most significant characteristics of each place? How might this be affected by the scale of analysis at which the place is being examined?
5. What is the difference between point pattern maps and thematic maps in regard to the unit of analysis? What would be the best map to measure median income, and why? What map might be best used to depict population density, and why?
6. What are three basic ways to consider distance? Which of these might help determine the best means of getting around by train or airplane, and why? How has the friction of distance declined over time?
7. Name an example of a formal region, a functional region, and a vernacular region (not examples from the text). Defend your choices. How is a region in geography similar to a period in history?
8. What makes the Statue of Liberty an iconic landscape? How might some of the same ideas represented by the Statue of Liberty also be depicted in some other ordinary landscapes? Name an ordinary landscape from your home town and discuss what it represents.

Further Study Topics

- The way a place is perceived varies, depending on who is doing the perceiving. Think of a place you know, and consider how someone who is a visitor might have a different perception than someone who is a resident. In what ways do the attributes that make up your college campus seem different now than when you first arrived?

- Some critics charge that globalization is erasing many of the unique characteristics of places. Do you agree or disagree with this assessment, or does it depend on what is being examined? In some instances, might globalization heighten the differences between places?

- Maps can be a helpful way of understanding how phenomena are distributed. If you had access to a set of maps and were interested in buying a house in a city, what sorts of maps might you use to help you pick the ideal neighborhood?

- Consider a landscape you know. It can be part of an urban neighborhood, an area in a suburb, part of a small village, or a spot of countryside. What elements make up the landscape? Which of these are clear and tangible? Which seem more significant than others? How do some of these elements evoke certain emotions? Finally, what sorts of themes does the landscape represent?

Summary Activities

Find an atlas that includes an index of places in the back. Using this atlas, identify 10 places: cities in the same country, states or provinces of a country, or even different countries. Using this geographical grid, determine the location (absolute and relative) and other attributes that might be important in studying these places. Depending on the places you select, these include resources, income, population, language, and religion, and any other attributes that you think might be of interest.

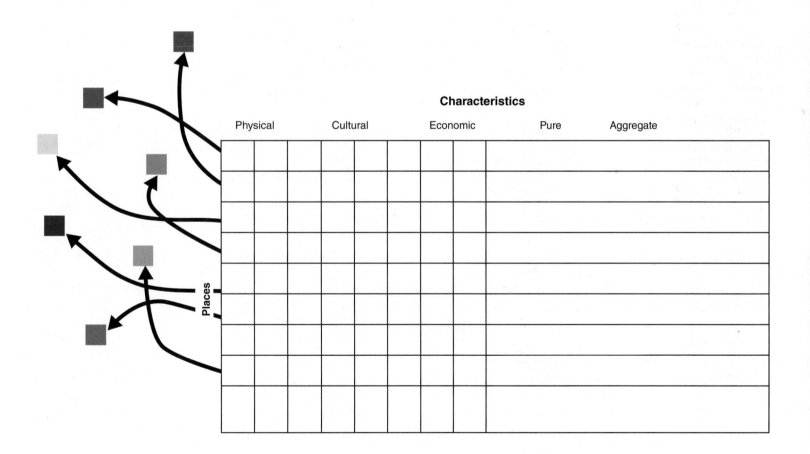

CHAPTER 2

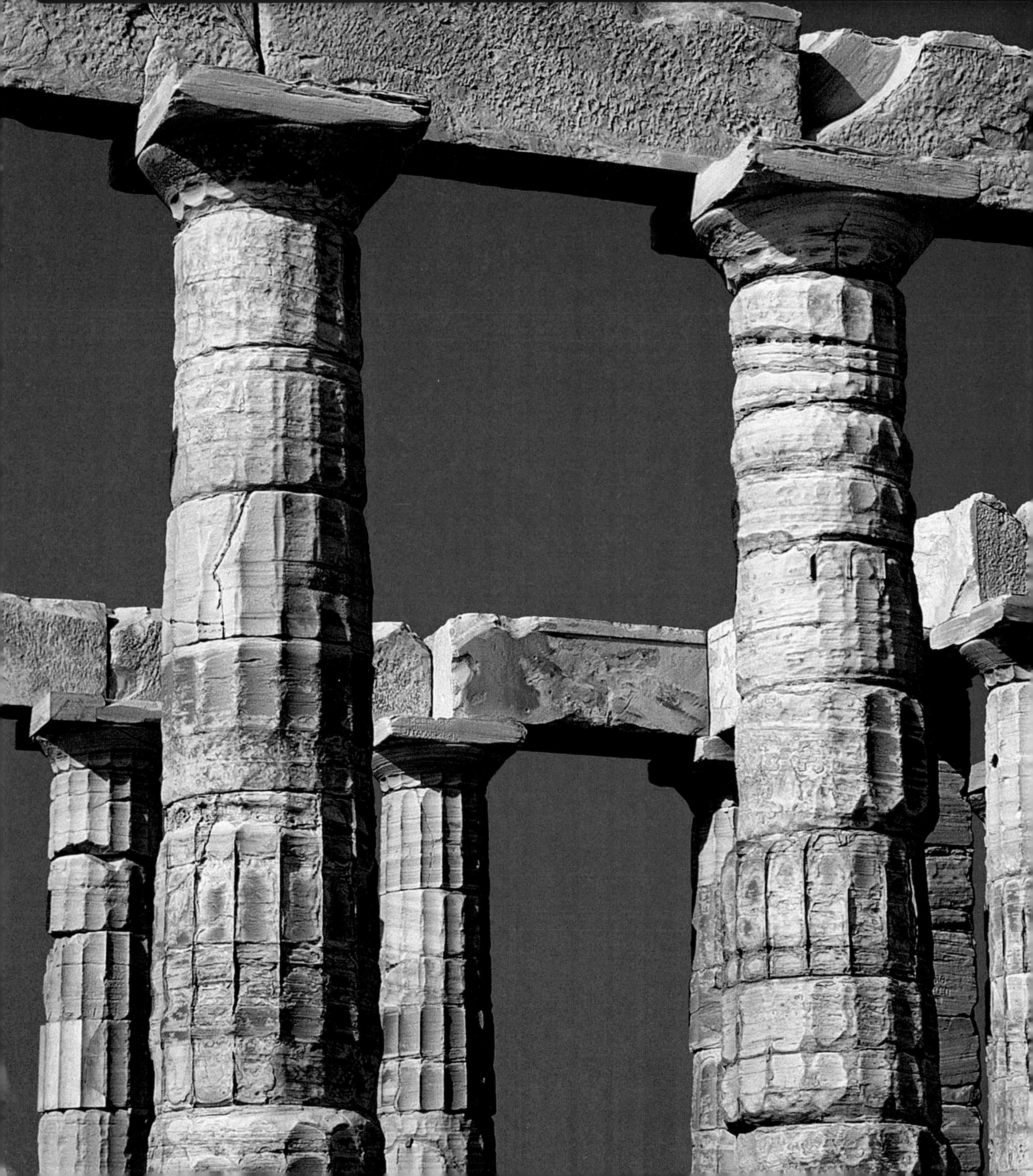

Geography through the Ages

In this chapter, we introduce you to over 2,500 years of geography history. Why? Because whenever you study a physical or social science for the first time, you really need to understand how thinking about a particular subject developed. Picture yourself as a Greek 2,000 years ago. You know that there is world beyond Greece, but you don't have any accurate maps, and the only descriptions you have are the stories that traders and sailors bring back. Often, the stories they tell are quite crazy as well. Do you believe them when they tell you about animals that stand 18 feet high, with long necks to eat leaves from the tops of trees? Do you believe them when they tell stories of great cities in far-off lands? And if you do believe them, how do you go about classifying and collecting this information?

In the first module of Chapter 1, we discussed human geography as interested in pattern and process. There are patterns on the earth's surface (e.g., people live in some places but not others), and geographers want to know how these patterns were created (i.e., the process). In the most crude form of summary, the history of geography is about humans discovering and learning the patterns of the earth's surface and then trying to explain them. Thousands of years ago, the emphasis was probably more focused on the patterns because humans knew little about the lands beyond their homes. But as more and more of the world became known, emphasis shifted to more complex explanations of what was being observed. As you read through this chapter, think closely about pattern and process, observation and explanation, and how the way we view the world changed over time.

2A   Ancient Geography

To early humans, the world was largely *terra incognita*—in other words, unknown land. Certainly, humans knew about their own homelands, and a bit about the other peoples they came in contact with along trade routes or other ways, but for the most part the difficulty of travel meant that much of the world was a mystery.

So it is not surprising that early geography focused on two basic elements of knowledge, **description** and **measurement**. *Description* simply means the recording of knowledge about the peoples and environments of the earth. *Measurement* refers to human understanding about the shape and size of the world. We take it for granted that there are seven continents, that people have different skin color in some parts of the globe, and that it gets colder as you travel toward the poles, but all of these truths had to be discovered and accepted by humanity.

Humans began making maps to record descriptions and measurements of the known world thousands of years ago. In 2009, scientists announced that they had found what is believed to be a 14,000-year-old map on the wall of a cave in Spain. An 11,000-year-old Babylonian map is believed to be the oldest world map, and Chinese maps survive from 6,000 years ago. Ancient peoples clearly had an interest in mapping and understanding their world.

To the ancient Greeks, **Homer** was often considered the father of geography because his literary works, such as *The Iliad* and *The Odyssey*, have many descriptions of places around the Mediterranean. The Greek philosopher **Hecataeus** took a more factual approach to description of the earth by compiling his own experiences with stories and descriptions of far-off locations from sailors who passed through the Greek port of Miletus. His book, the *Ges Periodos*, is a coastal survey of much of the Mediterranean and surrounding areas and focuses on the nature of towns, rivers, animal life, and ethnic groups. **Herodotus**, also a Greek philosopher and often described as the first historian, also included detailed geographic descriptions in his writings. Copies of his *Histories* endured the centuries and can be read today.

▲ **Figure 2A.1** To the ancient Greeks, myths were often as real as reality. Homer's works, such as *The Odyssey*, were considered geographic because they described the Mediterranean region, but the descriptions of monsters— such as the Scylla, shown here—did not always help paint an accurate picture of the world.

Figure 2A.2 ▶ Because of the perfect form of a sphere, the Greeks soon conceptualized ways of dividing up the world into zones known as *climata*. Because the Mediterranean has a temperate climate and the Greeks knew that it got colder when traveling north and warmer when traveling south, they envisioned the northern zones of the world as too cold for habitation and the equatorial parts of the world as too hot for humans. In other words, they felt that, if someone traveled south, the land would get warmer and warmer until it would be too hot to even pass through. This meant that, for all practical purposes, the southern half of the earth was considered unreachable.

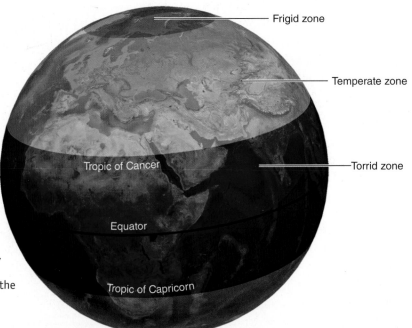

While some ancient Greeks described the world, others were busy trying to understand its shape and measure it accurately. Despite popular belief, most intellectuals in the ancient world did not believe that the world was flat. In fact, ancient peoples had numerous ideas about the shape of the earth. Homer envisioned a flat disk surrounded by a river. The ancient Peruvians pictured the world as a box, while the Aztecs conceptualized it as a square with four other squares attached to it, one on each side. But by the fifth century BC, as evidenced in the works of Plato, the Greeks had begun to accept the concept of the earth as a globe. Originally, this was based on mathematical aesthetics. In other words, the Greeks saw a sphere as a perfect mathematical form. But in time, they realized that a sphere could also explain occurrences such as eclipses and the phases of the moon.

As history progressed, ancient scholars began to divide up the world using north–south lines and east–west lines similar to the lines of latitude and longitude we still use today. This type of system allows each place on the surface of the earth to have unique coordinates. Once each place has coordinates, it becomes much easier to make accurate maps. One famous map of the world was that of **Ptolemy**, who wrote a complex geography of the world in the second century AD. Versions of his maps were used for 1,500 years, despite serious errors. Most notably, Ptolemy felt that Asia extended farther to the west from Europe than it actually does in terms of longitude. This error would change human history in the fifteenth century.

Early scholars also developed estimates of the earth's size. Eratosthenes's efforts are perhaps most widely known. Using geometry, and with a little bit of luck, **Eratosthenes** calculated that the planet's circumference was 28,700 miles, only 15% off the actual circumference of 24,902 miles at the equator. But other estimates existed as well. Both the scholar Posidonius and the geographer Strabo used estimates closer to a circumference of 18,000 miles. Can you think of how this error might affect navigation?

▲ **Figure 2A.3** As you can see, Ptolemaic maps were fairly accurate in their depiction of the world's shape, but they erroneously showed Asia extending much farther to the east than it actually does. This error may have led Columbus to believe that he could sail west to reach Asia.

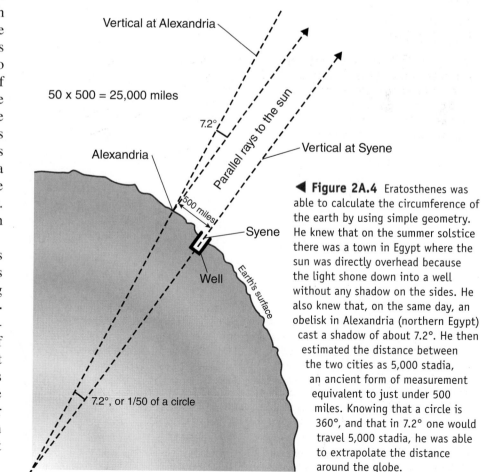

◀ **Figure 2A.4** Eratosthenes was able to calculate the circumference of the earth by using simple geometry. He knew that on the summer solstice there was a town in Egypt where the sun was directly overhead because the light shone down into a well without any shadow on the sides. He also knew that, on the same day, an obelisk in Alexandria (northern Egypt) cast a shadow of about 7.2°. He then estimated the distance between the two cities as 5,000 stadia, an ancient form of measurement equivalent to just under 500 miles. Knowing that a circle is 360°, and that in 7.2° one would travel 5,000 stadia, he was able to extrapolate the distance around the globe.

2B   The Middle Ages

After the fall of the Roman Empire, Europe was dominated by the power of the Catholic Church. The leadership of the Church was less interested in an accurate geographic description of the world and more interested in explaining the world in terms of Christian scriptures. For this reason, the status of geography in Europe is generally considered to have declined for the thousand years following the fall of the Roman Empire in the fifth century. But beyond Europe, as we will see, geography flourished in non-European cultures.

One aspect of geography that declined dramatically in Europe during the Middle Ages was the quality and accuracy of maps. The Church had little need for the maps of Ptolemy and others from the ancient world. For centuries, the most common map of the world was something we now call a **T-O map**.

In monasteries, where some scholarship was allowed, monks had access to some ancient texts containing geographic knowledge and themes. But for much of the medieval period, only works in Latin or those translated into Latin were read, and thus the works of the ancient Greeks were lost unless they had been translated into Latin. Naturally, Europeans needed basic geographic knowledge to move around the known world, but there was little attempt to explain or measure the world in the way that had been pursued by the ancients.

But the Muslim world was a bright spot in geographic knowledge during the Dark Ages in Europe. Islamic tradition dictated that all good Muslims should be able to read the Koran, the Muslim holy book. Therefore, literacy rates were high in Muslim areas, and Muslim travelers and scholars wrote detailed accounts of the places they came in contact with during trade, conquest, or conversion. European Christendom did not embrace reading and writing as much, and typically only priests, church officials, and the wealthy had any chance to learn to read or write.

The early rulers of Baghdad, founded in the eighth century, encouraged scholars to translate the works of the Greeks and Romans into Arabic, and thus the geographic knowledge of those civilizations were not lost, as they were in medieval Europe. As the centuries passed, Muslim geographies were generally much more detailed than anything being written in Europe. Because the center of Islam was farther to the east than Christianity, Muslim writers had more detailed knowledge of Asian locations. Furthermore, some Muslim scholars even tried to explain the world, writing about how mountains erode, for example. Some of these ideas would not resurface in modern geography until hundreds of years later.

Two of the most notable Muslim geographers, **al-Idrisi** and **ibn-Battuta**, deserve special note. Al-Idrisi (1100–1165) was educated in Spain and came into the favor of Roger II, the king of Sicily. The primary accomplishment of al-Idrisi was to more accurately combine ancient geographic knowledge with the firsthand knowledge of Muslim traders who

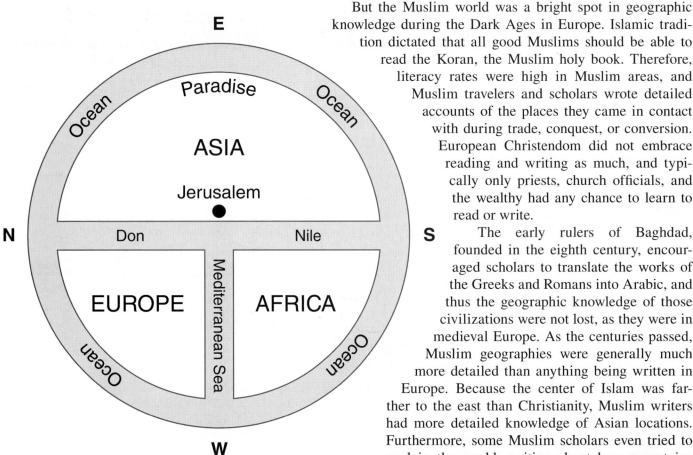

▲ **Figure 2B.1** A T-O map depicts a round world with three continents separated and surrounded by water. The three continents, Europe, Africa, and Asia, were believed to have been settled by Noah's sons Japeth, Ham, and Shem, respectively. Jerusalem was placed at the middle of the map based on biblical passages, and the Garden of Eden was in the East at the top of the map. The tradition of placing East (the Orient) at the top of the map is the origin of our phrase "to orient" something. In short, the T-O map reflected a Christian spiritual view of the world based on the Bible.

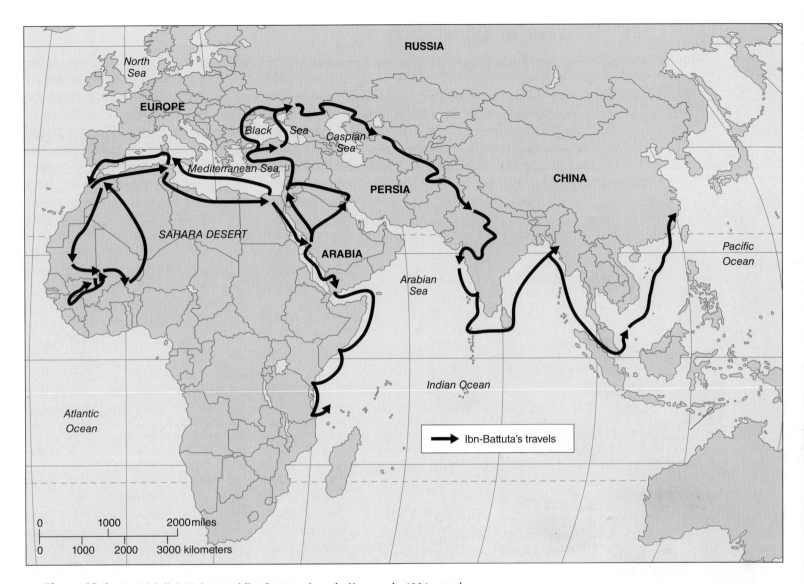

▲ **Figure 2B.2** Abu Abdullah Muhammad ibn-Battuta, born in Morocco in 1304, remains one of the most amazing travelers and geographers ever. During his lifetime, he traveled over 75,000 miles across Northern and West Africa, southern and eastern Europe, the Middle East, South Asia, China, and Southeast Asia. Given the slow travel speeds at that time, his journeys are beyond remarkable. After 30 years of travel, ibn-Battuta dictated an account of his travels, containing detailed descriptions of the places he visited.

had traveled the world. This resulted in the completion of both more accurate maps of the world and a written geography of the known world.

Outside of Europe and the Muslim world, geographic knowledge was being expanded by other peoples as well. The Chinese were keeping geographic records of natural resources as early as the fifth century BC, and we have centuries of Chinese geographic writings about the human and physical geography of places both far and near. The Chinese also attempted to understand geographic processes, such as the effects of water on the natural landscape. Chinese explorers are also believed to have reached areas as far away as Europe and Africa. The Scandinavians were also expert explorers and settled locations in Iceland and Greenland before AD 1000. On the other side of the planet, locations in the South Pacific, such as the famed Easter Island, had already been settled by Polynesian travelers in boats before the fifth century AD.

2C   The Age of Exploration

After the fourteenth and fifteenth centuries, exploration by Muslim and Chinese peoples declined, but Europe emerged from its period of relative geographic isolation and began a period of global conquest and discovery that would change the world forever. The purpose of this section is not to rehash the basic history of famous explorers but, rather, to examine how the era changed and expanded geographic knowledge.

A natural starting point is **Prince Henry the Navigator**, who actually did very little navigating. Despite the misleading name, Prince Henry is one of the most important people in the history of geographic discovery. In 1418, according to some historians, the young royal began employing cartographers, geographers, astronomers, and other experts near his home close to the Portuguese city of Lagos. Using the knowledge gained from these scholars, he financed a series of money-making expeditions to Africa. In doing so, the Portuguese gained better knowledge of the coast of Africa and dispelled the myth that the tropics were uninhabitable. Furthermore, the Portuguese developed a new ship, the *caravel*, that allowed longer expeditions down the African coast and eventually into the Atlantic. Henry's experts also improved navigation aids, such as compasses and astrolabes. By the end of the fifteenth century, Portuguese explorer Vasco da Gama was able to sail around the southern end of Africa. Unfortunately, by the middle of the fifteenth century, the Portuguese travels along the coast of Africa accelerated the European slave trade as investors found they could make more money trading in flesh than in gold or other commodities.

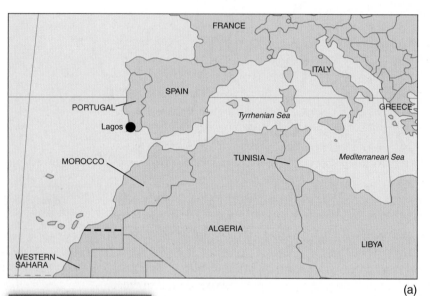

(a)

(b)

▲ **Figure 2C.1**
(a) From ports such as Lagos in southern Portugal, (b) Prince Henry and other Portuguese patrons were able to finance missions of exploration along the coast of Africa that eventually allowed Portugal to reach Asia.

Despite improvements in technology and knowledge, explorers still faced numerous problems that made navigation over long distances difficult. First, it was difficult for ship captains to know where they were located 500 years before the global positioning system (GPS) was invented. Latitude, location north or south of the equator, was relatively easy to calculate by measuring the angle of the sun or certain stars above the horizon. Devices such as the astrolabe, and later the sextant or octant, were common and accurate. But longitude, location east or west of a known point, is not as easily measured. Because the earth rotates at a fixed rate (15° per hour), if you have a clock that shows your local time and the time at a known longitude (such as longitude 0°), you can use the difference in those times to determine your location. If the sun rises at 6:00 a.m. in London, it will rise at 7:00 a.m. London time 15° to the west. This is why today we use time zones

Figure 2C.2 ▶ Despite the gains in geographic understanding made during the fifteenth century, there were still numerous errors and shortcomings, which had a profound effect on explorers of the period. A notable example is **Christopher Columbus**, the Italian-born explorer who worked for the king and queen of Spain. Despite what he is remembered for, Columbus was not seeking the "New World" when he set out in the 1490s. Rather, he was searching for a quicker route to Asia to ensure that the Spanish would control the lucrative spice trade with Asia. As discussed in section 2A, Eratosthenes's estimate of the circumference of the earth was not the only one considered accurate, and Columbus believed that the earth's circumference was closer to 18,000 miles than the true 24,902 miles (at the equator). Because of this, and because Ptolemaic maps still in use showed Asia extending farther to the east than it actually does, Columbus believed that Asia could be reached by sailing just a few thousand miles to the west. On the map, you can see the approximate location of where Columbus believed Japan was situated, as well as the estimated boundary of China.

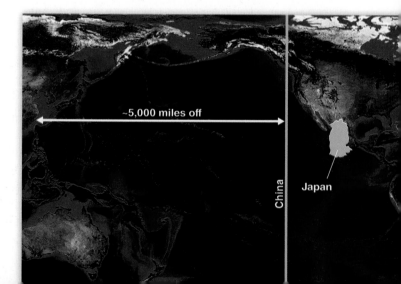

(a)

(b)

◀ **Figure 2C.3** (a) This clock, designed by John Harrison, was one of the first to accurately keep time at sea, allowing mariners to determine accurate longitude. Because the British government offered a huge reward to the inventor of an accurate timepiece, lots of quacks tried to invent clocks, and thus the mentally ill in eighteenth-century paintings were often depicted as working on clocks or longitude. (b) In this illustration from 1763, an insane asylum patient can be seen scrawling longitude calculations on the back wall.

and a common prime meridian (0°) to adjust our clocks, so that everyone gets up at roughly the same time and knows the time at any other location on the planet. (See Module 1B for a discussion of geographic coordinates.)

But clocks during the Renaissance period were generally based on a pendulum swinging back and forth to move the gears. On a ship rocking from the waves, a pendulum-based clock was largely useless because the waves would throw it off, making it impossible to keep track of what time it was at a known longitude. Thus, sailors went for centuries with poor estimates of longitude, often missing islands outright or crashing into coastlines at night. Maps, too, were inaccurate because longitudinal locations could only be estimated. After a horrible shipwreck in 1714, the British Parliament offered an award of £20,000 to anyone who could produce a clock that would be accurate to just two minutes or less when crossing from Europe to the Caribbean and back. This amount of money was a fortune in the day (about $8 million to $10 million by today's standard), and all sorts of inventors and quacks tried to win the prize. Numerous gains were made by various people during the eighteenth century, but it wasn't until 1775 that the ultimate prize was awarded to a clockmaker named **John Harrison**. With an accurate method of determining longitude and latitude, maps and navigation improved tremendously and a more complete view of the world came into focus.

Another problem with long-distance navigation during the Age of Exploration was the problem of **scurvy**, a nutritional disease that causes weakness, mushy gums and tooth loss, spots on the skin, diarrhea, the opening of scars, and the breakdown of bones previously broken and healed. Sailors traveling near coastlines, as they had for most of human history, did not face the problems of scurvy because they took in fresh food regularly. But as Europeans began crossing oceans, fresh fruits and vegetables could not be preserved, and vitamin C deficiencies began to lead to scurvy. In the 1600s, ship captains first learned that eating lemons or other fresh produce can quickly reverse the effects of scurvy, but it wasn't until the eighteenth century and the voyages of Captain Cook that fresh fruits and vegetables were supplied regularly to sailors.

Technological advancements in navigation, along with faster ships, allowed the European powers to expand their control over vast areas of Africa, Asia, and the Americas after the fifteenth century. Never before could cultural ideas and economic products move as quickly, and the consequences were dramatic. European culture traits spread nearly everywhere, including Christianity. Most notable was what is called the **Columbian Exchange**, which refers to the interaction between the Eastern and Western Hemispheres after the arrival of Europeans in the Americas. Europeans brought diseases, such as smallpox, malaria, and measles, that wiped out an estimated 50% to 90% of the indigenous population of the "New World." Crops and livestock were also exchanged. Potatoes, tomatoes, and corn were taken back to Europe from their area of origin, forever changing the European diet, while apples, citrus fruits, and bananas were brought to the Americas. Animals were also exchanged. Horses, for example, were introduced to the Americas from the Old World.

▼ **Figure 2C.4** To determine longitude, a sailor must measure the ship's speed and how long the ship has traveled at that speed. Speed could be measured by throwing a chip log (a) off the back of a ship (b). This was a piece of wood attached to a rope that had knots tied in it every 47 feet 3 inches. While one sailor watched a 30-second hourglass, another counted how many knots passed through his hand as the ship moved away from the chip log. This is the origin of the nautical speed measurement known as the **knot**.

(a)

(b)

2D   The Birth of Modern Geography

History books often discuss the legacy of the Age of Exploration in terms of what was discovered and the impact of the European presence on the world. But the increased interaction among the peoples of the world began to stimulate an increased interest in how the world worked. As was discussed in Chapter 1, geographers often focus on pattern and process, so it makes sense that as the world's patterns became clearer, more scientists attempted to explain what was being observed. In the seventeenth and eighteenth centuries, scholars began to classify plants and animals, explore the linkages between humans and the environment, and hypothesize about the origins of continents. Two geographers who bridged the gap between the work of the past and modern geography were the Germans **Alexander von Humboldt** and **Carl Ritter**.

Geographers in the second half of the nineteenth century and early twentieth century focused on many different aspects of the discipline, but three areas dominated: scientific exploration, environmental determinism, and regional geography. We deal with the first two here; regional geography is addressed in the next

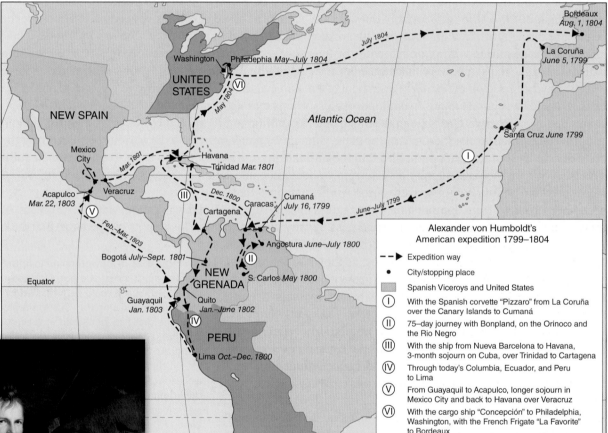

(b)

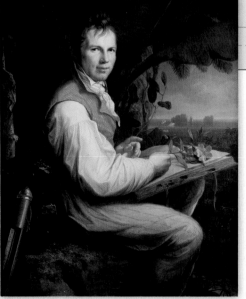

(a)

▲ **Figure 2D.1** (a) Alexander von Humboldt (1769–1859) was a wealthy, well-educated Prussian who had already traveled extensively in Europe before embarking on a five-year expedition to the Americas between 1799 and 1804. (b) Von Humboldt traveled to what is now Mexico and throughout northern South America. He also made stops in the young United States and was a friend of Thomas Jefferson. During his journeys, he collected thousands of plant and rock specimens, climbed volcanoes and mountains, and observed how the colonial governments had changed the landscape through deforestation and other means. Upon returning to Europe, he lived in Paris and began writing a 30-volume account of his American expedition. Designed for both a scientific and a nonscientific audience, the work was read and admired by the scientists of the day. Von Humboldt stressed careful observation of nature in the support of science and thus helped pave the way for societal appreciation of scientific inquiry.

Figure 2D.2 ▶   Carl Ritter (1779–1859) was the first-ever professor of geography at the University of Berlin, a post he held for nearly 40 years. Unlike past geographers, who had focused on describing the earth, Ritter advocated searching for the interconnections among things. He expected his students to carefully observe the earth and its phenomena before drawing conclusions, rather than using existing opinions or theories to guide their thinking. Although Ritter's ideas were not without criticism, he is remembered for pushing geography toward scientific observation and for advocating that geographers study the earth as the home for humanity. By the last three decades of the nineteenth century, geography was routinely being taught as an academic subject in German universities and by professional geographers.

module. The interest in **scientific exploration** was driven in part by the rise of geographic societies, such as the Royal Geographic Society, founded in 1830, and the American Geographic Society, founded in New York in 1851. These and similar societies were made up of scholars, public leaders, adventurers, and businesspeople dedicated to expanding geographic knowledge. In the spirit of von Humboldt and others, these geographic societies sponsored scientific expeditions that helped further knowledge about earth processes. The findings of these expeditions were often published in society journals. Probably the best surviving example of this is the National Geographic Society, which still supports scientific missions and shares findings with the public.

While some geographers focused on gathering more information about the world in a systematic way, others tried to come up with broad, general theories to explain the world. One such theory that dominated geography in the last decades of the nineteenth and first decades of the twentieth centuries was the now disgraced idea of **environmental determinism**. The basic premise of this theory is that human culture is caused by the environment a society lives in. Geographers such as Frederich Ratzel in Germany and Ellsworth Huntington and Ellen Churchill Semple in the United States were key proponents of environmental deterministic ideas. Huntington, for example, studied climate and made broad, and by today's standards, oversimplified connections between a place's climate and the culture to be found there. For example, to environmental determinists, people who lived in the tropics were lazy and prone to moral lapses, while people in mountain climates were hardy and hardworking. These ideas often were linked to race, because the hot parts of the world have darker-skinned peoples, and therefore certain races were broadly and wrongly stereotyped, while whites living in middle latitudes were seen as having the "best" cultures.

The ideas of the environmental determinists were challenged by some scholars, including the French geographer Vidal de la Blache, the theorist credited with the ideal of **possibilism**. The possibilists believed that the environment does not determine a society's culture. Rather, they believed that humans develop their own culture, but within constraints set by the environment. Thus, people in cold regions probably will not run around naked, but the clothes, building types, and food systems they develop to deal with the cold are their choice over time. Although environmental determinism remained a common idea well into the twentieth century, and still appears in some writings today, it had been largely discredited by scholarly geographers by the 1940s as racist and supportive of European and American imperialism.

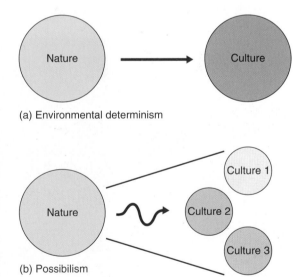

▲ **Figure 2D.3**   (a) Environmental determinism is the belief that natural conditions (terrain, climate, etc.), whether good or bad, essentially determine how a culture will form. (b) Followers of possibilism reject a strict, deterministic link between nature and culture, arguing instead that nature places some constraints on culture, but ultimately humans are free to choose how they adapt to their environmental conditions. Thus, different cultures can emerge in areas with the same natural conditions.

2E   The Twentieth Century

The twentieth century brought great changes to the discipline of geography and to ways of thinking about and understanding human patterns on the landscape. Within the discipline, geographers argued among themselves about whether geography should study unique aspects of the earth's surface or look for universal laws that apply everywhere on the globe. They also debated whether the oddities of the human mind should factor into understanding human activities, and they argued whether we could really know anything for certain at all.

As mentioned in the last module, American geography's interest in environmental determinism was waning by the 1920s, and geographers were conceptualizing the role of culture and geography in new ways. An important theorist who changed the way geographers look at the cultural landscape was Carl Sauer, a geographer at the University of California, Berkeley, from the 1920s to the 1950s. Sauer did not believe in environmental determinism, instead emphasizing the impact of human cultures and physical processes on a landscape over time. (See Module 1H for a discussion of landscapes and geography.)

By the 1930s, there had been an increased interest in regional geography. As explained earlier in the text, a region is an area that has common characteristics, such as a common language or physical landforms, or that is connected by a common network, such as a railroad network. For many geographers, there was a strong attempt to divide the world into areas of common characteristics to make it easier to classify and understand the infinite diversity of the planet. In short, geographers were interested in being able to sci-entifically differentiate among the places of the earth by grouping similar places together. During the first half of the twentieth century, many geographers researched and wrote detailed **regional geographies** of the world and parts of the world that discussed all aspects of a region, including language, religion, agriculture, industry, and political patterns.

But as geography focused primarily on understanding and identifying regions, a different set of skills was needed to complete the task. This was the realm of **topical**, or specialized, **geography**. In order to under-stand the Great Plains of the United States, for example, one needed to understand agricultural patterns and farming systems, so most geographers during the period adopted a topical specialty and focused on some-thing more specific than a whole region. Some geographers, for example, studied cities (urban geographers), while others looked at manufacturing patterns (economic geographers); still others researched voting patterns

▲ **Figure 2E.1** One of the benefits of a regional approach to human geography is that it allows you to see that New England is a part of the United States that has many common characteristics among its six states, but the regional approach also enables you to look at smaller parts of New England, such as a town, and to investigate how that smaller area is similar to and different from the larger region. This Vermont town shares characteristics with other parts of New England but also has unique features that set it apart within the region.

Human geography						Physical geography			Geographic techniques			
Cultural geography	Political geography	Historical geography	Economic geography	Urban geography	Population geography	Climatology	Geomorphology	Biogeography	Cartography	Geographic information science	Geostatistics	Qualitative methods

▲ **Figure 2E.2** Geography is a broad and complex discipline that includes subdisciplines in human geography, physical geography, and geographic techniques. Which subdisciplines do you think overlap each other? Can you speculate on which academic fields outside of geography each subdiscipline is connected with?

(political geography). Together, their specialized findings better helped the discipline of geography to understand the similarities and differences among regions.

Not all geographers, however, felt that the regional approach was the best for geography. Many adopted the approach of **systematic geography**, which focuses on specializing in a particular type of geography, such as economic geography, political geography, or urban geography, and then applying theories to places and regions. So a person might be an expert on voting patterns in general and then can look at elections in many different places, rather than focusing all of his or her attention on one region.

In addition, critics of the regional approach argued that, by focusing on particular parts of the planet, often in great detail, geographers were ignoring the opportunity to look for universal laws or truths. In other words, they felt that geographers should be looking for scientific explanations that might apply to everywhere on the earth. In the 1950s, geographers such as Fred Schaefer argued that geographers should adopt more positivistic research methods, as do other sciences. **Positivism** argues that all knowledge can be pursued by the scientific method, and thus a strong emphasis is placed on observation and measurement. If something cannot be verified through the scientific method, it is not considered valid. Because computers were also becoming available to scientists at the time, many positivistic geographers began relying on statistical methods to "prove" theories. This period is often referred to as the era of "geography as spatial science" or the **quantitative revolution** in geography, an attempt to find universal laws that explain geographic patterns and processes.

$$Interaction_{ij} = \frac{k(Population_i \times Population_j)}{(Distance_{ij})^2}$$

(a)

Another important development in mid-twentieth-century geography was natural hazards research. A pioneer in this field was Gilbert White, who made his mark researching the causes of flooding. White realized that flood damage and losses are the result of not only physical processes but also human activities, perceptions, and decisions. In 1945, he wrote, "Floods are 'acts of God,' but flood losses are largely acts of man." Modern geographers continue the work of White and others on natural hazards because of the emphasis on human-environment interaction.

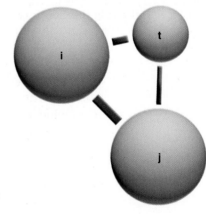

(b)

Figure 2E.3 ▶ The gravity model is an example of the "spatial science" and positivistic trends of the post–World War II period in geography. (a) Based on studies of retail trade patterns published by Reilly in 1931, geographers in the 1950s and 1960s attempted to predict migration and other human movements between two cities (City i and City j) as a function of the population of the two cities and the distance between the cities. Two large cities close together will interact more than two small cities close together. Likewise, cities that are farther apart will have less interaction than cities that are closer together. What variables that might explain the interaction between cities are left out? In part (b), the model would predict that there would be the highest interaction between Cities i and j, less between i and t because t is smaller in population, and the least between j and t because of the longer distance between them. But what variables are not included in the model that might affect migration?

2F   Behavioral and Humanistic Geography

By the middle of the 1960s, some geographers had begun to criticize what they felt was an overreliance on mathematical models. Specifically, they felt that the models being used often did not give any or adequate attention to human motivations or the complexity of decision making. For example, if we look again at the gravity model, it is one way of predicting the interaction between two cities, but does it take into account human decisions? In fact, there is no human variable in the model, just city size and distance. But do human decisions factor into migration decisions, such as moving from one city to another? Of course they do. People move because they like an area, or because their family is there, or because they saw a picture and thought it looked nice. This desire to add more human decision making into spatial models led to the birth of what is known as **behavioral geography**, a focus on the psychological processes that underlie geographic decisions. People may choose to live in a particular neighborhood because of something concrete, such as price, but they may also cite reasons such as safety or aesthetics or just that they "like" the area. These types of feelings are not always easy to drop into a mathematical model; thus, they require new methods and forms of research. Behavioral geographers argued that they were putting humans back into the study of human geography.

One way that behavioral geographers attempted to understand geographic decisions made by humans was through the concept of the **mental map**. Mental maps are the representations of the real world, which we have in our heads. If you ask an upper class student to describe your campus and a new student to do the same, you'll probably find that they have different mental maps of the area. The experienced student may have a more detailed map about where things are but might also have a better idea about the qualities of certain places. That person might

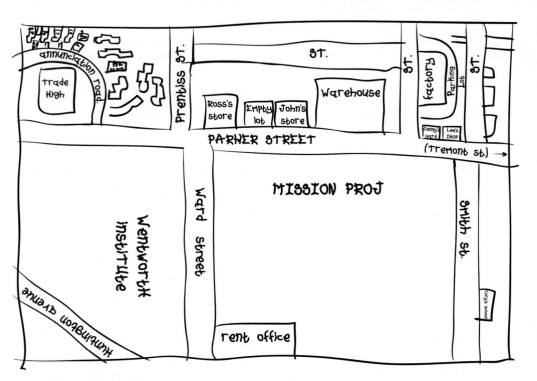

▲ **Figure 2F.1** This map sketched by a young child is from a study conducted in Boston in the 1960s. The boy lived in the area near the top of the drawing that shows the most detail. The area labeled "Mission Proj" was a housing development where the majority of the population was a different ethnicity than the boy, and he reported that he was afraid to go there. Notice how the boy's mental map of that area is much less developed and is more distorted. What physical or social barriers might make certain parts of a city a mystery to children or to people from a different part of town?

know some shortcuts or might know that a particular path is muddy after a storm and therefore not ideal for a bike ride. In other words, that person's mental map of the campus might be expected to affect his or her geographic decisions. Furthermore, think about how the mental map of a town might be different for a blind person than a sighted person.

Our mental maps can include more than just concrete information about where things are located. To use the same example of new versus experienced students, upper class students may know that some areas of campus are safer after dark than others. Or they may just perceive that an area is more or less safe, even if they have no crime statistics or proof. The reality is that our mental maps of the world include many elements based on poor or incomplete information. To capture the complexities of mental maps, behavioral geographers developed ways of surveying people that better uncovered their beliefs, attitudes, concerns, and preferences about the environment. This information was then used to create new models of geographic decision making.

But not all geographers felt that the behavioral approach was adequate. Critics argued that behavioral geographers were too reliant on the positivist approach (i.e., the scientific method) and that human behavior couldn't be plugged into an equation so easily. They argued that mathematical spatial models describe how the world works under idealized conditions instead of how it works in real life. This criticism led to the rise of various forms of **humanistic geography**. In general, humanistic geographers put less emphasis on explaining the world and more emphasis on the meaning that humans place on the environment and surroundings. For example, a humanistic geographer might argue that environmental destruction in a community indicates not only that there is a pattern of urbanization or industrial growth, but also that the culture of the society may not value the environment. In other words, investigating what humans value in the world around us helps us better understand the world.

One of the most important geographers of the humanistic tradition is Yi-Fu Tuan. Tuan wrote extensively in the 1970s about the importance of meaning and the connections humans have with places. He explored concepts of **topophilia**, love of place, and **topophobia**, fear of place, and emphasized aesthetics, contact with the physical environment, and the importance of cultural ideas, such as patriotism. We may feel attached to a place because of how it looks or because it's physically comfortable. But more abstract concepts can also affect attitudes toward place. For example, Americans visiting the site of the World Trade Center attacks might feel sadness and anger because of the loss of human life, but also because it was an attack on America and our sense of patriotism. Or a religious person might feel a deep connection with a particular church, shrine, or temple, not only because of the design or location of the building but also because of his or her own spiritual beliefs.

▲ **Figure 2F.2** Humanistic geographers often focus on why humans form emotional bonds with certain types of landscapes. Looking at this photo of Siena, Italy, would you rather spend time in the town exploring the streets and alleyways or in the countryside among the fields and trees? Why do you think you connect more with one than the other?

▲ **Figure 2F.3** Think about your favorite place as a child. What did you like about that place? What were some of the special qualities of your favorite place that might not be obvious to a stranger?

2G   Structuralist Geographies

During the 1960s and 1970s, as some geographers were exploring behavioral geography and humanistic geography, others were drawing from more radical ideas to try to explain the world. Poverty, the war in Vietnam, and the civil rights movement energized some geographers to challenge accepted notions of the world order, such as capitalism. But to understand these ideas, we have to start by understanding what is meant by *structuralism*.

Behavioral geographers and humanistic geographers generally focus on the actions, thoughts, or attitudes of humans. There is a general assumption in their work that human decisions or a person's attitudes guide his or her actions in the world. **Structuralism** argues that humans actually have very little control in the world. Instead, structuralists believe that the world is actually the product of unobservable social structures that create what we observe on a daily basis. For example, a structuralist might say that a college student is not at a particular college because of personal choice but because of an unseen economic and social system that expects young men and women to go to college and then divvies out students to particular schools based on grades, sports ability, or economics. Naturally, a college student has some choices, but a structuralist would argue that the structure of society is more important. Social theory debates in geography (and other social sciences) often raise the question of how much weight is given to **structure** (larger economic or social systems) as opposed to **agency** (human decision making).

How does a theory like Marxism apply to geography? In practice, Marxist geographers focus on issues of inequality that they felt were caused by the capitalist system, such as poverty. Think about world hunger, for example. Is hunger caused by a lack of food in the world, or is the world's food poorly distributed? A Marxist geographer might argue that the capitalist system causes hoarding or wasting of food by rich countries at the expense of poor countries. Or they might argue that capitalism encourages people to grow crops for sale, such as inedible tobacco, instead of crops that can be eaten by the local population.

But some geographers interested in social theory and its application to geographic research felt that Marxist and other structuralist geographers went too far in looking only at structures. They felt that the role of the human (agency) was underestimated and that an overreliance on structure was deterministic. In other words, it predicted the same societal outcomes, no matter what a person or society might do. Some of these critics turned to the social theory of structuration as a possible compromise. **Structuration** in its most basic form proposes that society, and therefore the human landscape, is like a set of rules on which humans can choose to act or not act. For the most part, humans choose to reproduce the status quo, but at times we can also change it. For example, slavery lasted for hundreds of years and over scores of generations, but in time, most human societies chose to end it as a common social practice. How is this geographic? Many structurationists have focused on what are known as **locales**. They have argued that the intersection between societal structures (such as capitalism) and agency (human decisions) takes place in regions or even smaller places. Thus, if a geographer studied, for example, the economy of a particular region, he or she could better understand how the capitalist system had been implemented by humans. This led many researchers to return to studying regions and places, which had not been as common in an era of positivist spatial science or in the search for global structures.

Figure 2G.1 ▶ According to anthropologist Claude Lévi-Strauss, the world we live in is like a machine that makes jigsaw puzzles. The machine is programmed or designed to make a variety of specific cuts in the cardboard. The way the machine cuts is random, so it can produce a variety of similar but different puzzles. Each puzzle is analogous to part of the world around us. This is known as the **superstructure**. But by looking at the world around us, at a single puzzle, we cannot understand the machine itself. So the details of how the machine is designed or how it is programmed remain a mystery. Structuralists try to theorize about the machine, which they cannot experience directly, and then observe the earth to see if the theory (the **infrastructure**) explains the superstructure.

SUPERSTRUCTURE
The world around us
The cultural landscape

INFRASTRUCTURE
The unseen "machine" that creates the superstr
Cultural, economic, and political systems

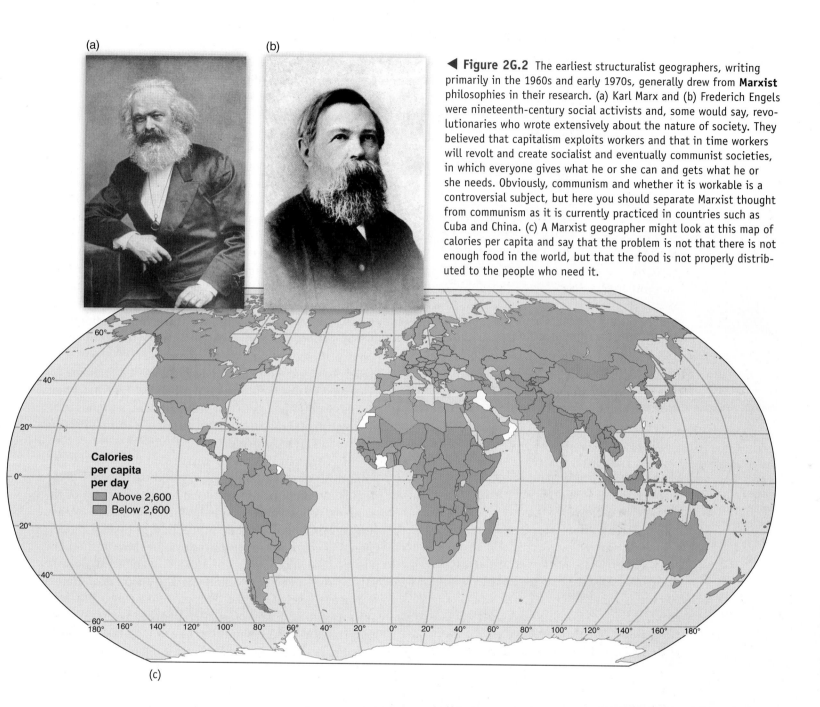

(a)

(b)

◀ **Figure 2G.2** The earliest structuralist geographers, writing primarily in the 1960s and early 1970s, generally drew from **Marxist** philosophies in their research. (a) Karl Marx and (b) Frederich Engels were nineteenth-century social activists and, some would say, revolutionaries who wrote extensively about the nature of society. They believed that capitalism exploits workers and that in time workers will revolt and create socialist and eventually communist societies, in which everyone gives what he or she can and gets what he or she needs. Obviously, communism and whether it is workable is a controversial subject, but here you should separate Marxist thought from communism as it is currently practiced in countries such as Cuba and China. (c) A Marxist geographer might look at this map of calories per capita and say that the problem is not that there is not enough food in the world, but that the food is not properly distributed to the people who need it.

Calories
per capita
per day
■ Above 2,600
■ Below 2,600

(c)

Humans are free agents who can act independently in the world and make their own decisions.

Cultural, social, and/or economic structures limit or eliminate human independence.

Figure 2G.3 ▶ The social theories discussed in this chapter vary in terms of their emphasis on human agency versus hidden societal structures. This graphic shows roughly how the major social theories embraced by geographers weigh the importance of structure or human agency.

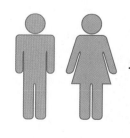

Human agency

Structure

2H   Recent Decades

To summarize human geography in the twentieth century, the discipline went from exploration and a focus on environmental determinism to a concentration on regions to a quantitative revolution, and then decades of reaction to it. But change is constant, and geography continued to evolve in the last decades of the twentieth century and into the twenty-first century. Two trends emerged during this period. One was a continuation of the social theory that had begun with humanistic and radical geographies, but the other was a surprising return to a positivistic tradition sparked by new technological advancements.

Theoretical positions in geography that thrived at the end of the twentieth century included postmodernism, poststructuralism, and feminism. **Postmodernism** is a complicated set of ideas. To understand postmodernism, you first have to understand modernism. **Modernism** refers to twentieth-century trends in art, architecture, and literature that represented a break from traditions of the past. But over time, modernist aesthetics began to appear everywhere. The movement that broke from tradition had become traditional. Some scholars reacted to this by developing postmodern (i.e., "after the modern") ideas. Postmodernists generally saw modernism as very rational, as evidenced in practical architectural styles. But they noted that the world often does not seem rational, and thus postmodernism often focuses on the differences from the norm that are found in the world.

In geography, postmodernists often focus on the singular aspects of particular places and on regional diversity. The search for universal truths characteristic of the quantitative revolution is often a target for postmodernist geographers, because they argue that, if spatial models cannot account for every difference in the world among places, then those types of models cannot possibly be valid. Thus, different techniques and theoretical frameworks are needed. In the end, postmodernism has been most useful as a way of challenging the assumptions of long-standing theories in order to examine the complexities of regional differences and the uniqueness of places.

▲ **Figure 2H.1** The building on the left, the Seagram Building in New York City, is a classic example of modernist architecture, with its rational design and simple lines. Just a few blocks away, however, the Sony Building is considered postmodern. It is less formal and has unexpected angles and elements not found on modernist buildings, such as the unique roof line. Postmodern social theory also challenges the conventional thinking of the past and often questions whether we can really know anything.

◀ **Figure 2H.2** The first electronic computer, ENIAC, was completed in 1946. It weighed 27 tons and took up 680 square feet. Throughout the 1950s, 1960s, and 1970s, computers got much smaller and more powerful, but they were still rare, slow, and complicated to use, and they were generally poor at producing any kind of graphics. Even 20 years ago, complex commands to perform statistics on a database had to be input into a workstation and then sent electronically to a remote supercomputer. Researchers had to walk to the basement of another building later in the day to pick up the printed output. If a mistake was made, it was only detected when the printout was picked up, and the process had to be repeated. This made research quite slow. Now many of the same statistical techniques can be completed on nearly any personal computer with freeware from the Internet.

Poststructuralism has its origins in critiques of structuralism that emerged in the 1960s among a group of French thinkers, including Michel Foucault. Remember from the last module that structuralists look for unseen structures that drive social systems. Poststructuralism questions the search for deep structures and focuses instead on individuals, local differences, and historical factors that affect the social world. Many geographers embraced poststructuralist approaches in the 1980s, and Foucault's work has probably been the most important to geographers who embrace social theory. One way poststructuralism influenced geography was to emphasize that a landscape can have different meanings to different people. This drove many geographers to look at how marginalized groups view and use landscapes. For example, a majority population may see the revitalization of an economically depressed area as a positive transformation of a decayed landscape, but some residents of that area may see it as a destruction of their homes and social network.

Another recent trend in work by human geographers has been the exploration of feminist theory. **Feminism** is a catch-all term in the social sciences that includes scores of theories and philosophies that, in general, focus on the status and rights of women. Within geography, one focus of feminist perspectives has been to emphasize the important contributions of female geographers and to promote women in the discipline. Another focus has been on the struggles of women in other theoretical debates in geography. And finally, feminist geographers have contributed to the study of social inequality in particular places and regions. For example, in Saudi Arabia, women do not have the right to move freely around their country because of cultural traditions and a strict interpretation of Islam. The result is that Saudi men and women have very different geographies.

While some geographers were continuing to focus their attention on social theories, others were returning to more positivistic approaches as computer

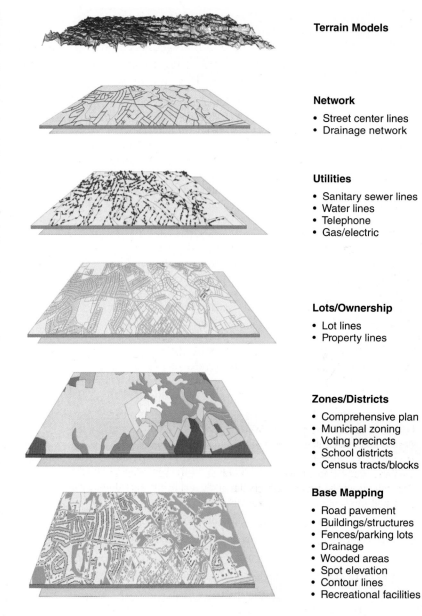

Terrain Models

Network
- Street center lines
- Drainage network

Utilities
- Sanitary sewer lines
- Water lines
- Telephone
- Gas/electric

Lots/Ownership
- Lot lines
- Property lines

Zones/Districts
- Comprehensive plan
- Municipal zoning
- Voting precincts
- School districts
- Census tracts/blocks

Base Mapping
- Road pavement
- Buildings/structures
- Fences/parking lots
- Drainage
- Wooded areas
- Spot elevation
- Contour lines
- Recreational facilities

▲ **Figure 2H.3** Modern GIS applications allow geographers to layer different types of spatial information to better analyze human and physical patterns on the earth's surface.

technologies became more readily available. The biggest impact that improvements in computing had on geography was probably in the development of **geographic information systems**, commonly abbreviated as GIS. A GIS generally is a computer system that can capture, store, analyze, and output geographic data. A GIS most commonly involves the layering of geographic data, so the data can be measured and analyzed in various combinations. For example, the location of cancer cases could be overlaid on a map of pollution sites to see if there might be a connection. Google Earth is a great example of a practical application of GIS technology. You can see a base map, or a map of roads, or even the locations of every waffle house in the country. Each layer is its own entity, but they can be combined to produce unique maps. Complex spatial statistics are also much more easily calculated within a GIS, allowing geographers to search for patterns hidden from researchers in the past. The ease of use and wide availability of GIS technologies have led to a massive increase in the availability of geographic information in digital form, much of it free and widely available.

Key Terms

agency (2G)
Alexander von Humboldt (2D)
al-Idrisi (2B)
behavioral geography (2F)
Carl Ritter (2D)
Christopher Columbus (2C)
Columbian Exchange (2C)
description (2A)
environmental determinism (2D)
Eratosthenes (2A)
feminism (2H)
geographic information systems (2H)
Hecataeus (2A)
Herodotus (2A)
Homer (2A)
humanistic geography (2F)
ibn-Battuta (2B)
infrastructure (2G)
John Harrison (2C)
knot (2C)
locales (2G)
Marxist (2G)

measurement (2A)
mental map (2F)
modernism (2H)
positivism (2E)
possibilism (2D)
postmodernism (2H)
poststructuralism (2H)
Prince Henry the Navigator (2C)
Ptolemy (2A)
quantitative revolution (2E)
regional geography (2E)
scientific exploration (2D)
scurvy (2C)
structuralism (2G)
structuration (2G)
structure (2G)
superstructure (2G)
systematic geography (2E)
T-O map (2B)
topical geography (2E)
topophilia (2F)
topophobia (2F)

Basic Review Questions

1. Why was early geography focused on description and measurement?
2. What contributions to geography were made by Herodotus and Hecataeus?
3. What was wrong with Ptolemy's map of the world?
4. What contributions to geography were made by Eratosthenes?
5. What are the main features of a T-O map?
6. Why were literacy rates higher in Muslim areas during the Middle Ages?
7. What were the accomplishments of al-Idrisi and ibn-Battuta?
8. How did Prince Henry the Navigator further geographic knowledge?
9. Which was easier to calculate for ancient mariners, latitude or longitude? Why?
10. What were the accomplishments of Carl Ritter and Alexander von Humboldt?
11. Define environmental determinism and explain the criticism of it.
12. What is positivism?
13. What is the quantitative revolution?
14. What do humanistic geographers emphasize?
15. Explain what a mental map is.
16. What is topophilia?
17. What are the key components of structuralism?
18. What is post-structuralism and how does it differ from structuralism?
19. What is meant by a feminist approach to geography?
20. What is a GIS?

Advanced Review Questions (Essay Questions)

1. Why were measurement and description so important for geographers in the ancient world? Are measurement and description still important today? Why or why not?
2. Why did geography stagnate in Europe during the Middle Ages, and how did scholars in other parts of the world help fill the intellectual void?
3. Why was longitude so difficult for seafarers to measure before the eighteenth century? How did its measurement advance geographic study?
4. Why did many scholars consider environmental determinism to be racist? How does possibilism differ from environmental determinism? Do deterministic ideas continue in modern society?
5. What are the pros and cons of a positivist approach advocated by proponents of the quantitative revolution? What aspects of human geography cannot be explained with statistics?
6. How might mental maps change over time? Why is this important to geographers?
7. Explain the role of structure and agency in structuralist geographies. Why is Marxism considered a structuralist theory?
8. How does postmodernism differ from modernism? What is the focus of postmodern geographic studies?

Further Study Topics

- Some scholars refer to the Age of Exploration as the Age of Encounters to better emphasize the two-way nature of the interaction between Europeans and non-Europeans as empires spread across the world, seeking financial gain. From a geographic viewpoint, what types of phenomena were transferred around the world by the European colonial process?

- Jared Diamond's bestselling book *Guns, Germs, and Steel* brought geographic topics to a modern audience, many of whom thought that geography meant memorizing state capitals in fifth grade. But Diamond's book has also been criticized as putting forth arguments that can be seen as environmentally deterministic. Read Diamond's book and see what you think. Is criticism of Diamond on charges of environmental determinism valid?

- Many traditions of modern geography focus on the meaning that people attach to certain environments. Take a critical look at your hometown or campus community and think about how different groups in the community value or do not value certain locations, neighborhoods, or districts in the area. What causes certain places to be valued by some, but not all?

- How is GIS being used by your state or province? Does the state or province have publically available data and GIS products? If so, what types of data are available?

Summary Activities

1. Put the following figures in the history of geography in chronological order and write a summary of their importance.

   a. Homer
   b. Yi-fu Tuan
   c. Prince Henry the Navigator
   d. Carl Ritter
   e. Alexander von Humboldt
   f. Hecataeus
   g. Ptolemy
   h. Carl Sauer
   i. al-Idrisi
   j. ibn-Battuta

   _____ _____
   _____ _____
   _____ _____
   _____ _____
   _____ _____
   _____ _____
   _____ _____
   _____ _____
   _____ _____
   _____ _____

2. In the space provided, draw and label a T-O map.

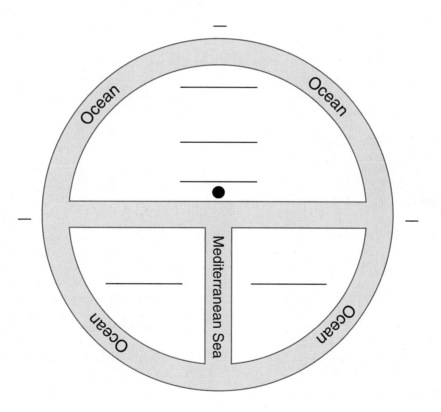

Population

In 2010, the world's population grew by over 228,000 people per day. That's over two times the population of the state of California in a single year. Of the 83 million new people added, more than 97% were born into the less developed areas of the world. As they age, where will these people find housing? Is there enough land or jobs for them? What about sewer lines, public transportation, or classrooms? To think that so many people can be added to the planet each year without some consequences or adjustments would be foolish. Population matters, and as geographers, especially human geographers, we must have a working knowledge of population patterns and the dynamics of population change around the world. By studying the distribution of people, we can better understand the cultural and economic patterns discussed later in this text.

In this chapter, we introduce you to the basic concepts that geographers use to measure and track population growth. We will look closely at where people live on the planet today. Then we will focus on how, as social scientists, we measure fertility and mortality, as well as population change.

Billions of people

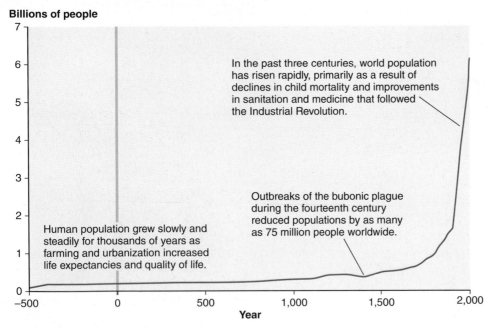

In the past three centuries, world population has risen rapidly, primarily as a result of declines in child mortality and improvements in sanitation and medicine that followed the Industrial Revolution.

Human population grew slowly and steadily for thousands of years as farming and urbanization increased life expectancies and quality of life.

Outbreaks of the bubonic plague during the fourteenth century reduced populations by as many as 75 million people worldwide.

▲ **Figure 3A.1** World population growth, 2,500 years ago to the present.

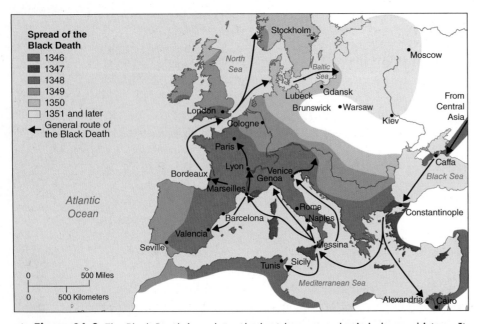

Spread of the Black Death
- 1346
- 1347
- 1348
- 1349
- 1350
- 1351 and later
- ← General route of the Black Death

▲ **Figure 3A.2** The Black Death is perhaps the best-known pandemic in human history. It was likely caused by the bubonic plague, although in recent years scientists have questioned this to some degree. The disease, caused by the bacterium *Yersinia pestis*, is believed to have been widespread in certain types of rats and was then transmitted to humans through fleas that fed on both animals. Once it infected humans, transmission was also possible through the air. The plague probably began in Central Asia and spread east and west during the 1340s along the Silk Road, a series of ancient trading routes that crisscrossed the continent. Infected people, as well as rats and fleas carried in cargo, moved out across the world. In the end, the disease killed an estimated 75 to 200 million people in Eurasia and Africa. In Europe alone, close to 50% of the population died in just a four-year period from 1347 to 1351. The Italian writer Boccaccio, a witness to the plague, wrote, "How many valiant men, lovely ladies and handsome youths whom even Galen, Hippocrates and Aesculapius would have judged to be in perfect health, dined with their family, companions and friends in the morning and then in the evening with their ancestors in the other world?"

3A   Population Growth in the Past

Population growth has not always been as rapid as it is today. Two thousand years ago, global population totaled about 300 million people and roughly 300,000 people were being added per year. Compare that to over 80 million a year today. Population grew so slowly that not until the early 1800s did the world's population reach a billion people. Less than 200 years later, the planet's total is now over 7 billion. It took nearly all of human history to reach a billion people and in just over two centuries the world population has increased by 6 billion. This incredible increase raises an obvious question, "Why?"

To answer this question, we need to explore two major "revolutions" in human history that caused significant population growth. The first occurred approximately 12,000 years ago when humans, in large numbers, began to give up hunting and gathering to settle down in one location as farmers (see Modules 16A and 16D). Wild strands of wheat and other grain crops were now planted in particular locations, allowing humans to settle in one place for an entire year. Before this, people had to move periodically to find food or game animals. The domestication of agriculture and livestock has often been called the **Neolithic Revolution** (*Neolithic* means "New Stone Age") because for a long time archeologists believed that it happened quite quickly, as if humans suddenly figured out that seeds could be planted and crops grown. Today, many scholars feel that the transition from hunting/gathering to farming occurred gradually over thousands of years. The first locations of domesticated plants were probably in the "Fertile Crescent" of the Middle East, in what is now primarily Iraq and Syria, and in Iran for the domestication of livestock, but archeological evidence shows that similar changes took place all around the world within a few thousand years of each other. But whether it happened gradually or quickly is not really the main point—

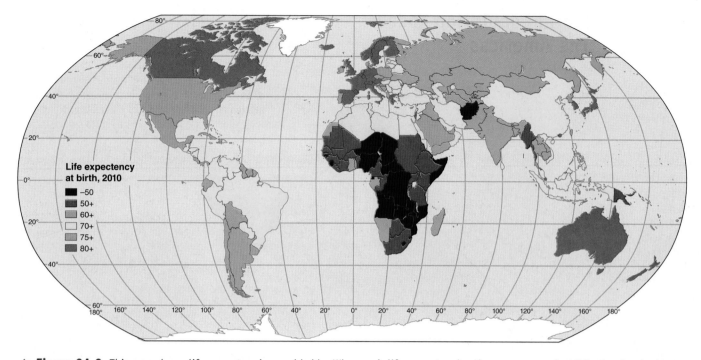

▲ **Figure 3A.3** This map shows life expectancies worldwide. Why aren't life expectancies the same everywhere? In the developing world, life expectancies have increased by over 20 years in recent decades but, on the whole, people in poorer areas of the world live about 12 years less than those in wealthier, developed countries. But while the global trend has been upward, Russia and some of the other countries of the old Soviet Bloc have actually seen a decline in life expectancies in recent decades. This is likely due to a decline in health care after the fall of the Soviet Union, smoking and alcohol abuse, and inadequate availability of medicine. But this is an exception globally. AIDS has also devastated some areas of the world, most tragically in sub-Saharan Africa (see Module 4D).

what is important is the impact of this innovation. Specifically, a stable food supply meant that human populations began to increase.

From about 10,000 BCE until 1750 or so, the world's population grew slowly but steadily, although plagues occasionally caused significant reductions in human numbers. The most well known is the Black Death, which devastated Europe, Southwest Asia, and much of the rest of Eurasia in the 1300s. By some accounts, more than a third of Europe's population was killed and it took centuries for population numbers to rebound.

By the mid-eighteenth century, northern Europe had begun entering the phase commonly known as the **Industrial Revolution** (see Module 16A for a full discussion). Innovations in textile machinery made factories possible, and farming innovations allowed or forced many farmers and rural workers to give up the agricultural life for more predictable factory work. Along with the revolution came innovations in science and public health. Sophisticated water and sewer systems, improved medical techniques, and better prevention of famines caused a significant drop in death rates in industrialized areas. It is this decline in mortality, not an increase in fertility, that caused a global rise in population in the nineteenth and twentieth centuries. In fact, fertility rates dropped over the past century, but deaths dropped more than births, so the population grew. Geographically, twentieth-century population growth was greatest in the developing world, even though many areas have yet to industrialize. This is because public health improvements, such as clean drinking water and immunization, have spread around the world. In 1900, a quarter of all humans lived in Europe. Today, only about 11% of the world's population is European.

Another twentieth-century change that caused populations to increase was a significant increase in **life expectancies**. An American or European born in 1900 could expect to live for only 45 to 50 years. This had increased 20 years by 1950 and today the average American or European lives over 75 years. Much of these gains were made through reductions in infant mortality.

3B   World Population Today: The Americas

▼ **Figure 3B.1**

Within the United States, notice the relative difference in population densities in the western and eastern halves of the country. The western areas receive much less rainfall than the east, making agriculture much more difficult. Because of this, this area was never settled in large numbers. The eastern half of the United States, however, is well-watered and has mild temperatures.

Notice the lack of population in most of Canada. The harsh, cold climate and remote environment of these areas offer little incentive for human settlement. In fact, most of Canada's population is located in a narrow band along its southern border with the United States.

In Middle America, a dense cluster of people can be seen in around Mexico City, by far the largest city in Mexico and one of the largest on the planet. Further south, notice the cluster on the west coast of Central America. The climate here, especially in elevated areas just inland from the coast, is much milder than the hot, tropical lowlands along the eastern coast. Finally, notice the dense populations on many of the largest islands of the Caribbean. Cuba, Jamaica, and Hispaniola, which includes the countries of Haiti and the Dominican Republic, all have high population densities.

The U.S. West Coast has several significant population clusters. Major cities such as San Diego, Los Angeles, and San Francisco are clearly visible. Also apparent is a dense cluster of people in California's Central Valley, one of the world's major agricultural hearths.

Note the large empty spaces that correspond with the Amazonian rainforest. Tropical rainforests are not unpopulated. They have always supported small populations, but the key word is small. Farming is difficult in these environments because the abundant rainfall leaches the nutrients out of the soil. So, traditionally, groups that lived in the rainforest survived by hunting and gathering, which can be quite successful as long as populations remain small. Today, a few larger clusters can be seen in the Amazon. One is the city of Manaus in the middle of the Amazon. It grew rapidly in the last half of the nineteenth century as rubber exports exploded after the development of vulcanization by Charles Goodyear in 1839.

Population clusters are right on the ocean, packed into cities such as Rio de Janeiro, São Paolo, Salvador, and Recife. Compare this to populations on the western coast.

South America has two additional areas of sparse population. The first is the Atacama Desert, the world's driest desert. The second is the extreme southern part of the continent, which includes the Patagonia. Cold temperatures and rugged terrain make this area unsuitable for large human populations.

Note that western population clusters are actually inland, located for the most part high in the Andes Mountains. This is one of the only places in the world that has high population densities at such high altitudes. Coastal areas here tend to be dry because of cold ocean currents offshore and a rainshadow caused by the Andes, but at higher elevations, more rainfall makes agriculture possible. Historically, this was the territory controlled by the mighty Inca Empire.

▼ **Figure 3B.2 Arithmetic and Physiologic Density**   As you think about population densities, keep in mind that not all places on the planet are equally as habitable for humans. So when geographers consider the population density of an area, we think of it in two ways. The most basic way is what is called **arithmetic density**, which is the population of a region or country divided by its total area. This is a quick and easy way to calculate densities. The world today has about 45 to 50 people per square kilometer of land, but some countries have considerably higher or lower densities. The former Portuguese colony of Macau, now part of China, has a density of over 18,500 people per square kilometer, and the tiny coun-

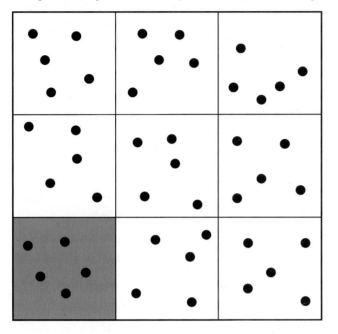

try of Monaco in Europe has nearly 17,000 people per square kilometer. At the other extreme, Australia has less than three people per square kilometer. In this diagram, each square is 1 square kilometer, so the arithmetic density would be five people per square kilometer. But many countries have a lot of land that humans cannot inhabit because it is too dry, too mountainous, too cold, or too wet. So demographers and population geographers also talk about **physiologic density**, which is the number of people per unit of arable (i.e., farmable) land. These numbers are obviously much higher than arithmetic densities for many countries. In the diagram, only the green square is farmland, so the physiologic density is 45 people per square kilometer because the 1 square kilometer of arable land supports the whole country. India has an arithmetic density of about 360 people per square kilometer, but its physiologic density is over 4,000 per square kilometer. Thus, if India had no access to outside food sources, it would have to support over 4,000 people on each square kilometer of farmland. As cities grow around the world, the amount of arable land declines and physiologic densities go up. What are the possible consequences of this?

◄ **Figure 3B.3** This photo looking west from the Strip in Las Vegas shows two ways that humans have changed population densities in some areas over the past century. First of all, improvements in the technology to capture, move, and store water have allowed desert areas that previously supported sparse populations to become large cities. Second, steel construction has led to taller buildings, allowing large numbers of people to live in close proximity.

3C   World Population Today: Europe and Africa

Figure 3C.1 ▶

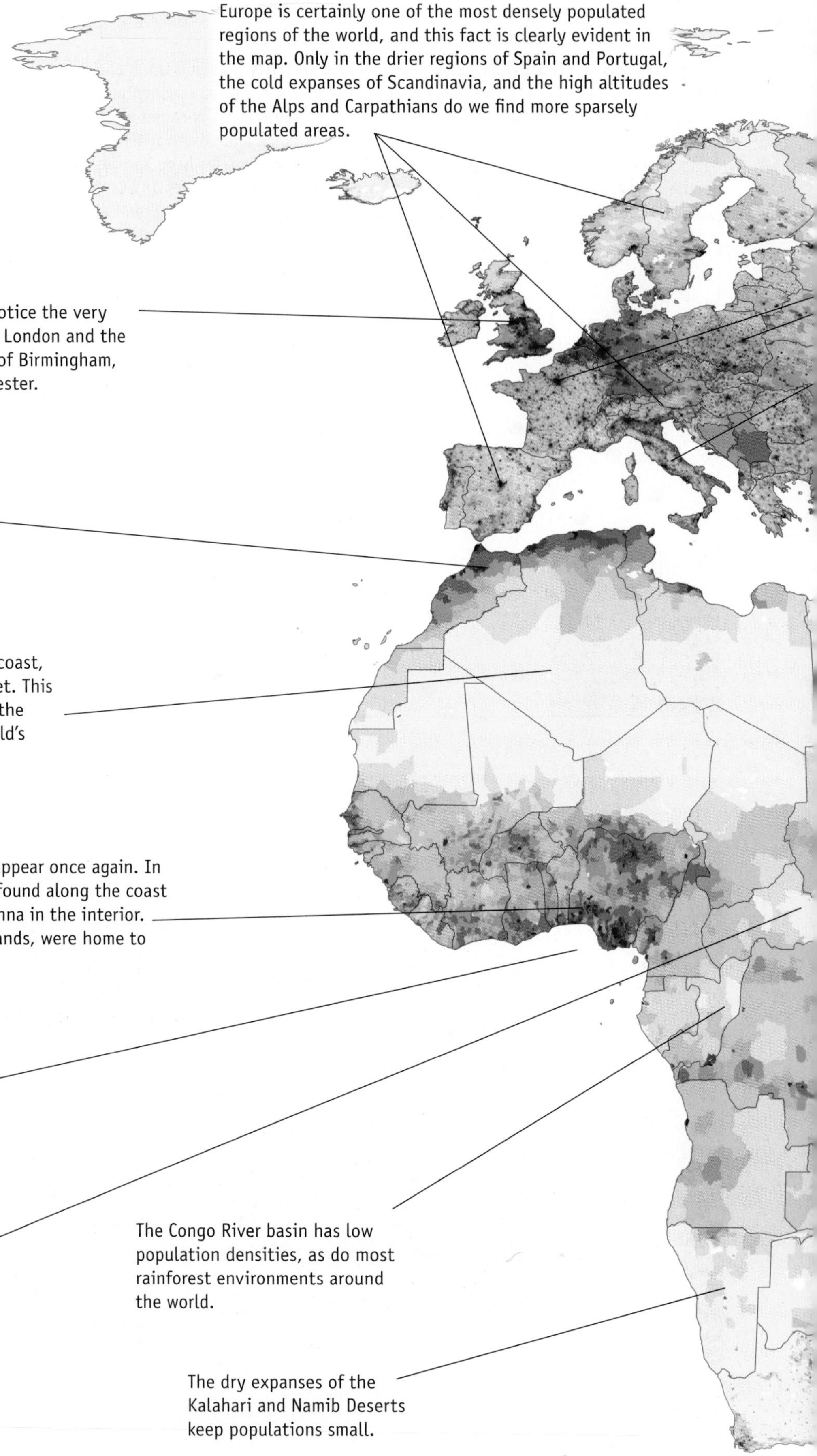

Europe is certainly one of the most densely populated regions of the world, and this fact is clearly evident in the map. Only in the drier regions of Spain and Portugal, the cold expanses of Scandinavia, and the high altitudes of the Alps and Carpathians do we find more sparsely populated areas.

In the British Isles, notice the very high densities around London and the manufacturing cities of Birmingham, Liverpool, and Manchester.

Note the population clusters in Morocco, Tunisia, and Algeria hugging the Mediterranean Sea.

South of the Mediterranean coast, population densities plummet. This huge demographic barren is the result of the Sahara, the world's largest desert.

South of the Sahara, population clusters appear once again. In West Africa, densely settled areas can be found along the coast and in parallel regions of steppe and savanna in the interior. These areas, especially the interior grasslands, were home to many of Africa's early civilizations.

Coastal lands historically were sparsely populated, but after European colonizers arrived the population in coastal cities increased because of the presence of colonial governments and trade opportunities.

Sleeping sickness, which can weaken and kill both humans and cattle, has kept population densities in parts of central Africa lower than would be expected given the adequate soils and rainfall in some of the areas. In other words, disease has made otherwise habitable areas uninhabitable.

The Congo River basin has low population densities, as do most rainforest environments around the world.

The dry expanses of the Kalahari and Namib Deserts keep populations small.

On the continent, noticeable clusters can be seen around Paris, Amsterdam, Rotterdam, Cologne, Frankfurt, Venice, Rome, Madrid, Warsaw, and Prague.

The Nile is clearly visible as a thin line meandering through the desert. Where the mighty river meets the Mediterranean, the densely populated region around Cairo is quite evident.

In East Africa, population clusters can be seen in Ethiopia and around Lake Victoria. The Ethiopian cluster is largely a result of the Ethiopian Highlands, which provide adequate moisture and physical protection from invaders. The Lake Victoria cluster is a result of adequate water, abundant fishing, and good soils.

The largest clusters of population in southern Africa are found around Lake Malawi, in the highlands of Zimbabwe where climates are mild and disease less prevalent, and in eastern South Africa.

3D   World Population Today: Asia and Oceania

Figure 3D.1 ▶

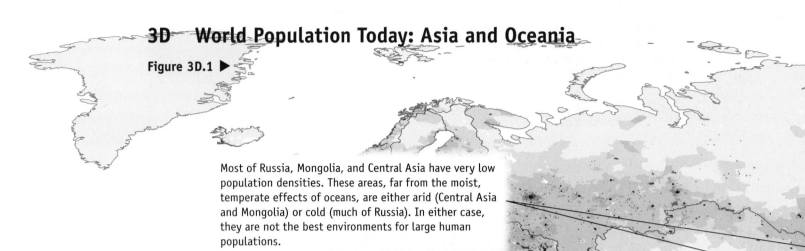

Most of Russia, Mongolia, and Central Asia have very low population densities. These areas, far from the moist, temperate effects of oceans, are either arid (Central Asia and Mongolia) or cold (much of Russia). In either case, they are not the best environments for large human populations.

Southwest Asia, what is often called the Middle East, has moderate population clusters, but here too the environment is not suited for high population densities.

India alone has 1.2 billion people and will likely surpass China as the world's most populous country in the next half century. Literally hundreds of millions of Indians live in the fertile Ganges Plain.

The Ganges River meets the Brahmaputra River to create a large, fertile delta that is primarily the territory of Bangladesh. Although devastating floods and typhoons periodically strike the region, traditional farmers have long found the fertile area to be life-sustaining. Bangladesh alone has a population of over 141 million people, half the population of the United States.

The Tibetan Plateau, an expanse of high, dry wasteland separated from the wetter areas to the south by the Himalayas, is largely empty of population.

Japan and South Korea are important population clusters in East Asia.

The fertile lowlands of eastern China, fed by the Yellow and Yangtze Rivers and temperate monsoons, have supported significant populations for thousands of years.

Important population clusters in Southeast Asia include the northern Philippine island of Luzon, the Indonesia island of Java, and coastal Malaysia along the Strait of Malacca south to the city-state of Singapore.

Indonesia is the world's fourth most populous country behind China, India, and the United States. In 2010, it had nearly 236 million people.

Oceania is sparsely populated, but the islands of Melanesia are home to the most people.

Australia is sparsely populated. The main population cluster is in the southeast, where mild climates are prevalent. Much of the continent's interior is arid and only small populations live there.

3E   The Basic Demographic Equation and Fertility

The population of an area, such as a country, state, or city, can be expressed by the following equation, often called the **basic demographic equation**:

Future population = current population + births − deaths + immigrants − emigrants

This equation makes sense. People are born and people die. Some people leave, while others arrive. The rest of this chapter essentially looks at the components of the basic demographic equation. First, we explore births by learning about fertility rates and birth patterns around the world. The great differences in birth rates from country to country are an important factor in the global demographic situation. Next, we delve into mortality rates and patterns to explain the impact of deaths on population change and distribution. Then, we focus on the future of the world's population.

Fertility

Between two and three children are born each second, which means that about 10 to 15 babies were born just in the time since you started reading this sentence. Even though birthrates have declined in the past few decades, the size of the world's population means that even low birthrates can translate into large increases in total population.

Fertility refers to how many children are born in a given time period. The most common, and basic, measure of fertility is known as the **crude birth rate (CBR)**. The CBR is simply the number of children born per 1,000 people in a population. Thus, if the CBR for a country is 25, that means that, for every 1,000 people in the country, 25 babies were born during a one-year period.

Another commonly used measure of births is the **total fertility rate (TFR)**, which measures how many children, on average, a woman can expect to have in her lifetime, given the current fertility rates. World-wide, the TFR averages 2.5, but the numbers vary widely by region.

Considering that the TFR is the average number of children per woman, what does the rate have to be for the population to stay the same? If you said 2.0, you made a good, but incorrect, guess. A TFR of 2.0 would seem to make sense because, if two parents have two children, the population will stay the same. But

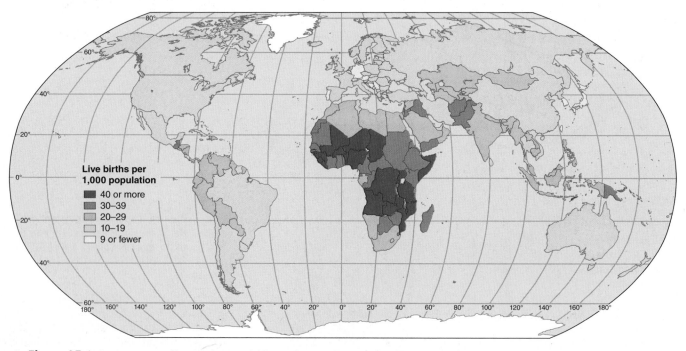

▲ **Figure 3E.1** In 2010, according to the Population Reference Bureau, the highest CBR in the world was 48 in the African country of Niger. The lowest rate was found in Monaco, where just 7 babies are born per 1,000 people. Much of Eastern Europe also has low rates (8–10 per 1,000), as do some of the more developed countries in Asia, such as Taiwan, Japan, and Singapore. Thus, globally, the crude birth rate ranges from about 7 to 52. What might explain the differences among regions of the world?

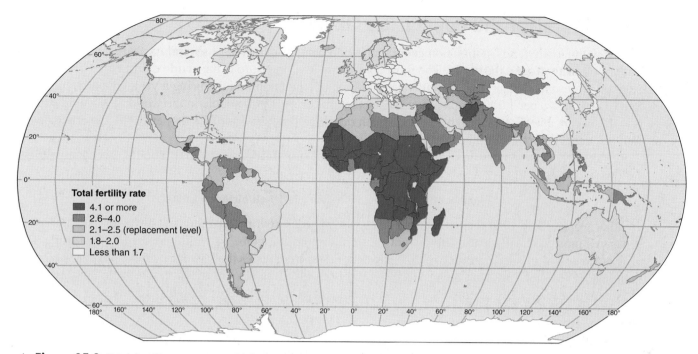

▲ **Figure 3E.2** Total fertility rates vary widely around the world. In sub-Saharan Africa, for example, the TFR was 5.2 in 2011. Europe, however, had a TFR of only 1.6. By country, the highest rates can be found in West Africa, where several countries have TFRs of over 5.5. Total fertility rates used to be high in the developed world as well. In 1850, the TFR in the United States was over 5.0, and 50 years ago it was still over 3.5. Today, the United States has a TFR of just 2.0.

some children do not live to adulthood, and some women choose not to have children or cannot conceive a child. Thus, the TFR has to be about 2.1–2.3 for a population to stay about the same size. This is known as the **replacement level of fertility**, or **zero population growth**. In developed countries, where few babies die before adulthood, the replacement level is closer to 2.1. In the developing world, where health care is poor and disease more prevalent, the replacement level is closer to 2.2 or 2.3. The world TFR is currently about 2.7, meaning that global population is rising because the TFR is above the replacement level.

So why are fertility rates higher in some places and lower in others? The answer is complicated and involves a variety of biological, social, and cultural issues. In general, however, fertility is influenced by factors such as the following:

- Health: poor health can reduce fertility.
- Economics: children cost money, so fertility declines in times of economic trouble.
- Education: the availability of education for women tends to reduce fertility.
- Culture: some societies place high value on large families; societies also have different attitudes toward contraception and abortion.

Figure 3E.3 ▶ Fertility rates vary widely among countries. In Afghanistan, the total fertility rate is 6.3, meaning that the average Afghan woman will have between six and seven children in her lifetime. Even with high infant mortality rates, about 44% of the country's population is under 15 years old.

3F   Mortality and Population Change

Just as with fertility rates, population geographers and demographers have several measures to examine the pattern of death around the world. The most commonly used measure is the **crude death rate (CDR)**. This statistic represents the number of deaths per 1,000 people in a population during a year. Globally, the average CDR is just 8 per 1,000 people. That means that, for every 1,000 people in the world, you would expect 8 to die during a year. And unlike the crude birth rate, which ranges from 7 to 48 per 1,000, the crude death rate has a much narrower range.

Another common measure of mortality is the **infant mortality rate (IMR)**. The IMR is calculated as follows:

(Number of infants who die before age 1 / all births) x 1,000

In other words, the IMR is the number of babies who die each year before their first birthday. Like the other measures presented earlier, the IMR is not uniform around the globe or within countries. Worldwide, the IMR averages 44 infant deaths per 1,000 births, but in some countries the rate can be much higher. Afghanistan has an IMR of 131. That means 13.1% (131/1,000) of all babies are dying before their first birthday! Compare that to an IMR of only 2.2 in Iceland. This incredible and depressing differential says a lot about the variable quality of healthcare around the world.

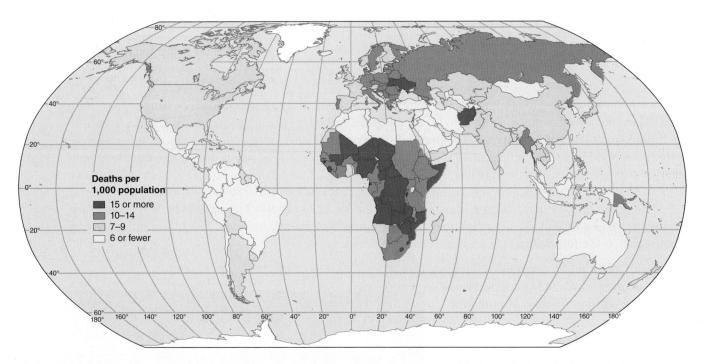

▲ **Figure 3F.1** The highest CDRs in the world are in the range of 17–20. The country with the highest crude death rate is currently the Democratic Republic of the Congo (17), a country plagued with civil war and strife. The lowest CDRs are below 5, and in 2011 Qatar had a death rate of just 1 person per 1,000. Therefore, the range of the crude death rate is about 1–20, much lower than the crude birth rate. This discrepancy explains why the world's population is growing. Quite simply, more people are being born than are dying.

Natural Population Change

Now that both the crude birth rate and crude death rate have been introduced, you can calculate the **rate of natural increase (RNI)** for a country. The RNI is calculated as follows:

RNI = crude birth rate − crude death rate

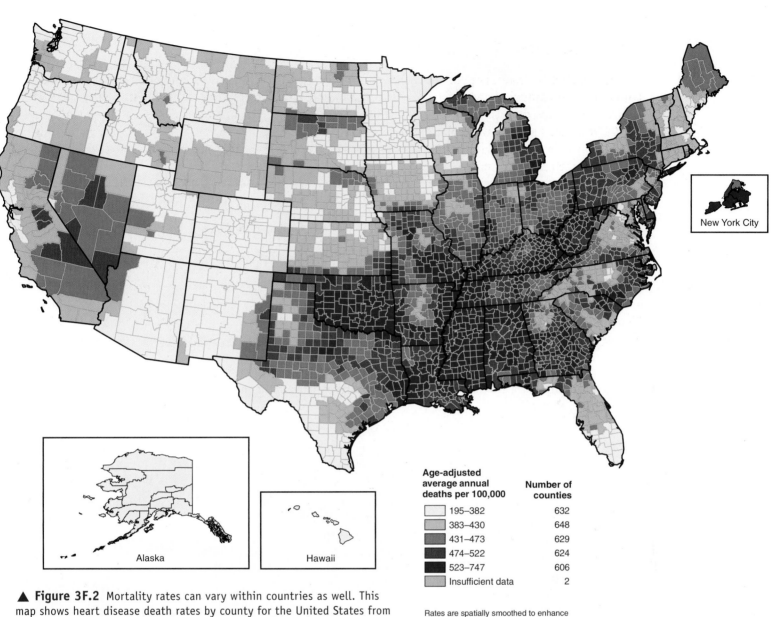

Age-adjusted average annual deaths per 100,000

	Age-adjusted average annual deaths per 100,000	Number of counties
	195–382	632
	383–430	648
	431–473	629
	474–522	624
	523–747	606
	Insufficient data	2

New York City

Alaska   Hawaii

▲ **Figure 3F.2** Mortality rates can vary within countries as well. This map shows heart disease death rates by county for the United States from 2003 to 2006. Instead of deaths per 1,000 people, the map uses deaths per 100,000 people. There is clearly a regional pattern to the death rate. Much of the South and Appalachia has higher mortality due to this disease. What factors might explain these differences? How might you find these factors if you were a medical geographer or public health official?

Rates are spatially smoothed to enhance the stability of rates in counties with small populations.

ICD-10 codes for heart disease: I00-I09, I11, I13, I20-I51

Data Source: National Vital Statistics System and the U.S. Census Bureau

Basically, the RNI is the difference between births and deaths. Quite often, RNI is expressed as a percentage. Because both the CBR and CDR are calculated per 1,000 people (and a percentage is 100 people), the RNI as a percentage is

RNI (%) = crude birth rate − crude death rate / 10

So, if a country's CBR is 30 and its CDR is 10, the rate of natural increase is 30 − 10, or 20 per 1,000 people. As a percentage, this is 2.0% (20/10). If a country's CBR is 25 and its CDR is 7, what is the RNI as a percentage? That's right, 1.8%, calculated as (25 − 7)/10. Try one more: What is the RNI as a percentage if the CBR is 24 and the CDR is 16? The answer is 0.8%.

Be aware, however, that the rate of natural increase is not the same as the rate of population change. A country can have a lot of migrants coming or going, which would change the size of the population. The rate of natural increase looks at just the effect of births and deaths. When migration is factored in, we have what is known as the **rate of population growth**, usually expressed as a percentage.

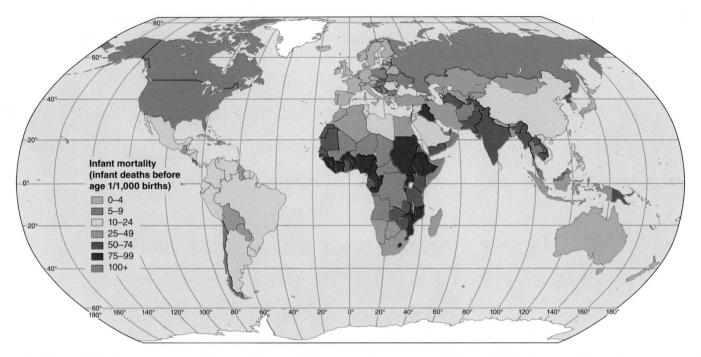

▲ **Figure 3F.3** What patterns are evident in this map of infant mortality rates around the world? What factors might explain the pattern?

Figure 3F.4 ▶ Worldwide, several countries have rates of natural increase that exceed 3.0% per year. On the other end of the spectrum, much of Eastern Europe has negative rates of natural increase. For example, Bulgaria, Belarus, and even Germany have negative rates of natural increase. While we rarely think of declining populations as being a problem, when a population gets smaller it can be more difficult to properly staff jobs in the economy, and tax revenues decline. There is also a social burden of financially supporting a large senior population. Who will care for these seniors enjoying a summer's day in Krakow, Poland?

Whether you use the rate of natural increase or the rate of population growth will depend on whether or not you want to consider the impact of migration (rate of population growth) or just births and deaths (rate of natural increase). On a global scale, migration is not a factor because other than astronauts, there is no emigration or immigration. For countries, regions, or smaller areas, migration might be an important consideration when calculating a doubling time.

Rates of natural increase have declined significantly in the last half century. In the 1950s and 1960s, the RNI was often over 2.0% a year and rarely fell below 1.8% a year. The primary reason for the high rates was a global reduction in mortality brought about by better public health measures and modern medicine. But starting in the 1970s, better access to contraceptives and later marriages led to a steady decline in the rate of natural increase. In 2011, the RNI was 1.2% a year. While this number is considerably lower than what it was a half-century ago, it still means that 70 million people are being added to the world each year. In the 1980s and 1990s, more than 80 million people were being added to the planet annually.

Over the next 50 years, the rate of natural increase is expected to continue to decline. The U.S. Census Bureau predicts that the RNI might be as low as 0.5% by mid-century. This will mean that the number of people added to the global population each year will drop to 50 million annually. While much lower than today's figures, it still equates to a billion more people on earth every 20 years or so.

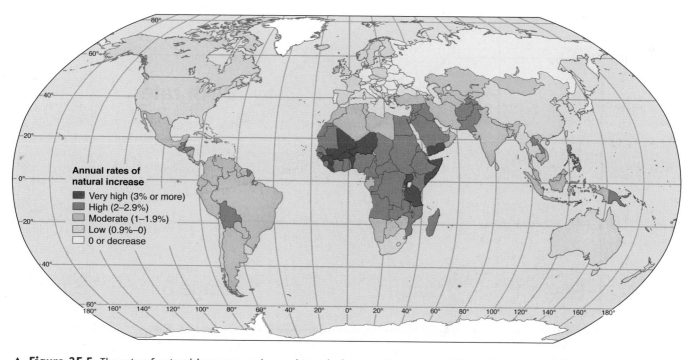

▲ **Figure 3F.5** The rate of natural increase can be used to calculate another demographic measure, the **doubling time**, which not too surprisingly represents the amount of time it will take for a population to double if the rate of natural increase continues at the same rate. Doubling time is calculated as follows:

70 years / rate of natural increase (%)

So, if a country's rate of natural increase is 3.5%, the doubling time is (70/3.5), or 20 years. At the world's current growth rate of 1.2%, the planet's population will double in slightly more than 58 years. Naturally, this assumes that the growth rate will not change between now and then, which is unlikely, but this measure gives you a rough idea of where a country or region might be headed demographically.

3G   The Demographic Transition Model

We've looked at a few theories of population growth, but how exactly do populations grow? Do birth rates increase or do death rates decline? If so, why? One classic, and debated, model of how populations change is known as the **demographic transition model (DTM)**. This model is based on changes that occurred in Europe during the eighteenth, nineteenth, and early twentieth centuries as a result of the Industrial Revolution. The basic point of the model is that, as a country modernizes, its fertility and mortality rates decline. These changes can be discussed in terms of four stages or time periods.

▼ **Figure 3G.1**

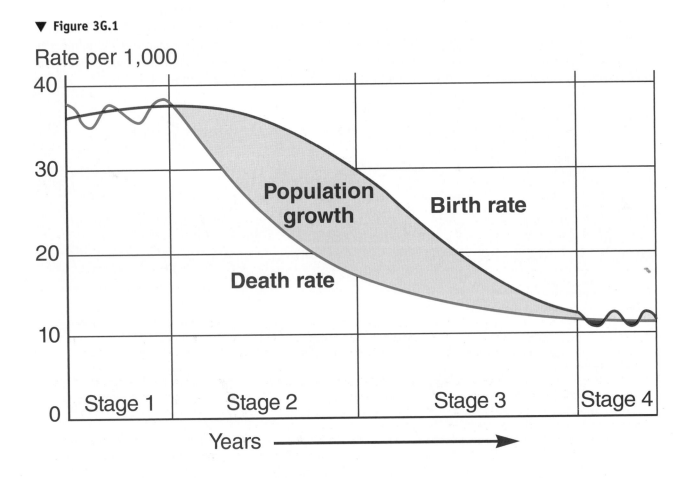

The demographic transition model is a nice way to conceptualize what happens as a country modernizes, but does it explain what is happening in the world today? The great, definitive, academic answer is a resounding "maybe not." Most scholars seem to agree that the DTM explains what happened in many of the industrialized countries of the world, including much of Europe and the United States. But in the past two decades, its ability to predict change in the developing world has been questioned. For population in the developing world to change as predicted by the DTM, it must be assumed that the conditions that prevailed when Europe and the United States were industrializing are the same conditions that now prevail in the developing world. But if conditions are not the same, the model breaks down and the future of population growth in these countries becomes questionable.

Stage 1

Stage 1, the initial period, represents a country or region that has not yet begun significant modernization. In other words, it is a preindustrial, probably agrarian society. During this stage, both birth rates and death rates tend to be high. A lot of children are born, but the high birth rate is offset by a lot of deaths. War, famine, disease, and generally poor healthcare keep death rates high. Thus, although birth rates are high, the population tends to stay at about the same size because births and deaths cancel each other out.

In the world today, there are no large areas or regions where a Stage 1 scenario prevails. But a few countries, and smaller areas within countries, still show both high birth rates and high death rates. Zambia, for example, had a CBR of 46 and a CDR of 15 in 2011. Even here, however, births are quite a bit higher than death rates, a pattern more indicative of Stage 2.

Stage 2

In Stage 2, death rates decline dramatically while birth rates stay about the same. In Europe, this decline was due to two factors: increased harvests brought about by better agricultural techniques reduced death and illness related to malnutrition or famine, and sanitary conditions began to improve in urban areas, reducing disease-related deaths. The net result of these two factors was a rapid reduction in mortality. Birth rates, however, remain high during this period. In Europe, birth rates actually increased a bit during this stage because young people could get factory jobs instead of working as apprentices for years; thus, they were marrying and starting families at a younger age. But overall, fertility rates during Stage 2 stay at a constant, high level.

The net result of high birth rates and declining death rates is rapid population growth because fertility and mortality are not canceling each other out, as they did in Stage 1. So, rapid population growth and modernization, according to the model, are linked. Note that total population grows during this stage.

Many countries of the world seem to be in Stage 2. Sub-Saharan Africa, for example, has crude birth rates, on average, of 38, while the crude death rate is just 13. Some Asian countries also show similar birth and death rates. Laos, in 2011, had a crude birth rate of 31 and a crude death rate of 8.

Stage 3

In Stage 3, birth rates decline significantly. In Europe, this began to happen in the middle to late 1800s. The reasons for the decline in fertility are debated by scholars, but several good possibilities have been discussed, such as children becoming less important as earners or labor for families and people choosing to spend money on things other than children as an economy grows.

Death rates continue to decline during Stage 3 of the model, which means that birth rates are still higher than death rates during this period. The result, as in Stage 2, is population growth. But, as fertility rates get closer to mortality rates, overall population growth slows and eventually begins to level off, although it can take a generation or two before this happens because babies already born will grow up and have their own children.

Many countries show birth rates and death rates characteristic of Stage 3. Turkey, for example, had a CBR of 18 and a CDR of just 6 in 2011. Argentina's CBR was 19 and its CDR just 8 during the same year. The death rates in these countries are close to being as low as in any country on the planet, but their birth rates are still higher than those of the most industrialized countries.

Stage 4

The last stage of the DTM represents what is essentially a modern, industrialized country. Both birth rates and death rates have leveled off, with birth rates almost always remaining higher than death rates. This means that the population will continue to grow at a steady pace—but not rapidly, as it did in Stages 2 and 3.

Stage 4 countries include the United States, much of Europe, and a few countries in Asia. Japan, for example had a crude birth rate of just 8 and a death rate of 9 in 2011. Japan's population is thus close to being level. In the United States, the 2011 CBR was 13 and the CDR was 8. Some theorists have hypothesized that there is a Stage 5 of the demographic transition in which birth rates are consistently lower than death rates. Because of this, a country's population would be expected to decline over time. Some countries in Europe exhibit the conditions of Stage 5.

3H   Population Profiles

One common tool that demographers and geographers use to better understand a population's structure is the **population profile** (or pyramid). A population profile shows the number or percentage of a population that is a particular age (or age range). Males and females are divided, so that their numbers can be compared for any given age range. For example, when looking at the population profiles, note that there are more older women than older men. Women generally live longer than men and this is graphically represented in the profiles shown here.

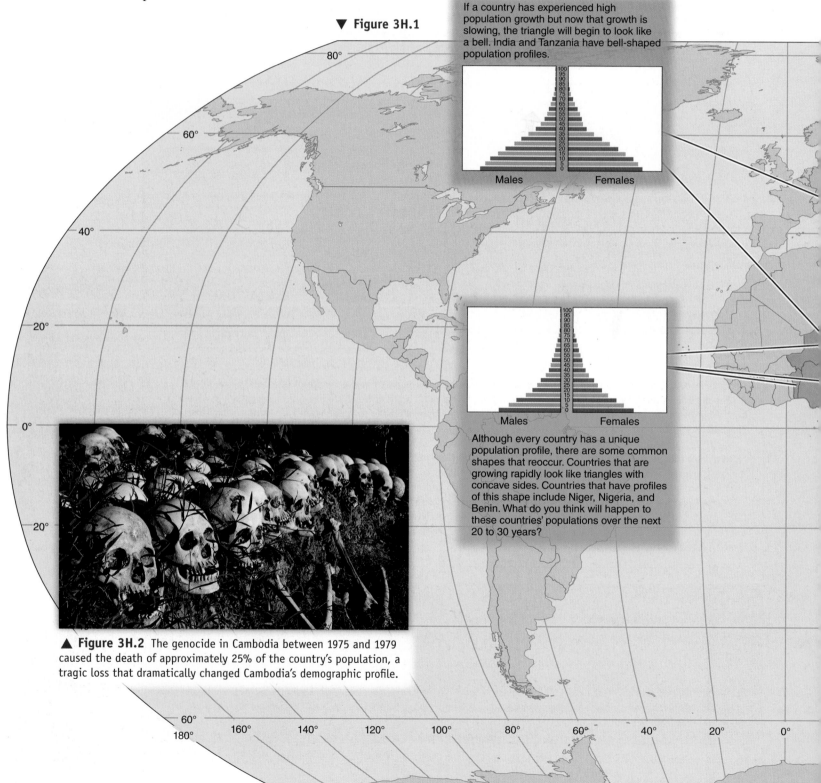

▼ **Figure 3H.1**

If a country has experienced high population growth but now that growth is slowing, the triangle will begin to look like a bell. India and Tanzania have bell-shaped population profiles.

Although every country has a unique population profile, there are some common shapes that reoccur. Countries that are growing rapidly look like triangles with concave sides. Countries that have profiles of this shape include Niger, Nigeria, and Benin. What do you think will happen to these countries' populations over the next 20 to 30 years?

▲ **Figure 3H.2** The genocide in Cambodia between 1975 and 1979 caused the death of approximately 25% of the country's population, a tragic loss that dramatically changed Cambodia's demographic profile.

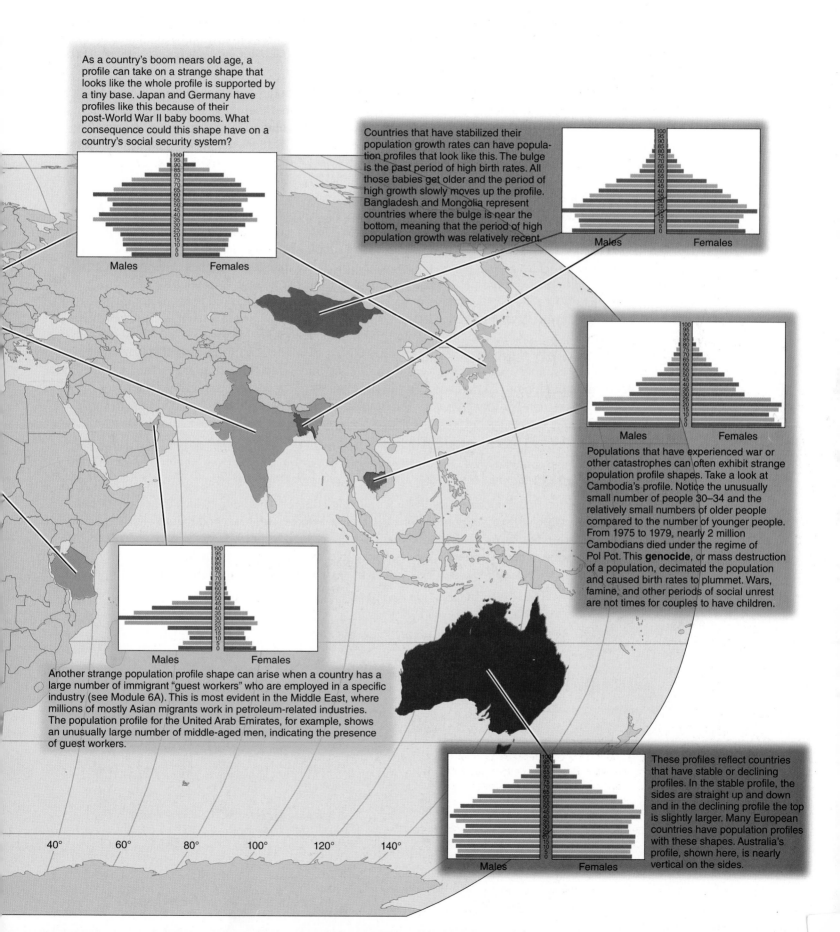

As a country's boom nears old age, a profile can take on a strange shape that looks like the whole profile is supported by a tiny base. Japan and Germany have profiles like this because of their post-World War II baby booms. What consequence could this shape have on a country's social security system?

Males   Females

Countries that have stabilized their population growth rates can have population profiles that look like this. The bulge is the past period of high birth rates. All those babies get older and the period of high growth slowly moves up the profile. Bangladesh and Mongolia represent countries where the bulge is near the bottom, meaning that the period of high population growth was relatively recent.

Males   Females

Males   Females

Populations that have experienced war or other catastrophes can often exhibit strange population profile shapes. Take a look at Cambodia's profile. Notice the unusually small number of people 30–34 and the relatively small numbers of older people compared to the number of younger people. From 1975 to 1979, nearly 2 million Cambodians died under the regime of Pol Pot. This **genocide**, or mass destruction of a population, decimated the population and caused birth rates to plummet. Wars, famine, and other periods of social unrest are not times for couples to have children.

Males   Females

Another strange population profile shape can arise when a country has a large number of immigrant "guest workers" who are employed in a specific industry (see Module 6A). This is most evident in the Middle East, where millions of mostly Asian migrants work in petroleum-related industries. The population profile for the United Arab Emirates, for example, shows an unusually large number of middle-aged men, indicating the presence of guest workers.

40°   60°   80°   100°   120°   140°

These profiles reflect countries that have stable or declining profiles. In the stable profile, the sides are straight up and down and in the declining profile the top is slightly larger. Many European countries have population profiles with these shapes. Australia's profile, shown here, is nearly vertical on the sides.

Males   Females

3I   Population Change in the Future

So far, we've looked at population in the past and the present. But what about population prospects in the future? Where is global population headed? To look to the future, it helps us to first understand how geographers and other scholars think about population growth. Is a rising population a good thing or a bad thing? Can the world sustain a few billion more people, or will chaos arise?

For much of human history, people did not really think much about population because it was rarely a problem. There was generally plenty of space for everyone. Remember that the planet's population did not reach a billion until less than 200 years ago. But as the Industrial Revolution brought population growth and social change to England in the 1700s, theorists there began to think about the possible impacts of rising populations. In 1798, **Thomas Malthus** published a short work, *An Essay on the Principle of Population*, arguing that population growth in the future would be guided by two postulates and one assumption. His postulates were that food is necessary for survival and that sex between men and women would continue to occur. Few would doubt these postulates. Then Malthus said that population, if not restrained by disease, vice, war, or similar checks, would grow at a geometric rate. That is, population would grow from 1 to 2, 2 to 4, and then to 8, 16, 32, 64, and so on. But, he argued, food supplies would grow only arithmetically, or 1, 2, 3, 4, 5, 6, 7, and so on. Thus, human populations would grow faster than food supplies. Malthus recognized that restraint could lower fertility rates, but he felt this was unlikely, and thus war, famine, and other horrible consequences were likely in the future. Today, we recognize that Malthus did not consider the role that technology would play in developing better fertilizers, types of seeds, and farming techniques; nevertheless, Malthus's ideas were an important addition to our thinking about population issues.

For a long time, very few people really considered Malthus to be correct. Europe was able to deal with its rising population by sending a lot of immigrants to the United States and other destinations, and technology allowed more and more food to be produced. But in the mid-twentieth century, scholars began returning to Malthus's ideas. Today, **neo-Malthusians** carry on Malthus's general notion that population growth can lead to global chaos. Notable was the publication in 1968 of *The Population Bomb* by Paul Ehrlich. Ehrlich wrote:

> *The battle to feed all of humanity is over. In the 1970s and 1980s hundreds of millions of people will starve to death in spite of any crash programs embarked upon now. At this late date nothing can prevent a substantial increase in the world death rate.*

While Ehrlich's prediction did not come true, and worldwide famines have been reduced in recent decades, neo-Malthusian ideas are still very common. One difference between Malthus and the neo-Malthusians is that recent theorists often talk about environmental, as well as social, chaos. For example, overpopulation can lead to deforestation as people cut trees for farmland. In turn, some scientists believe that the loss of forests contributes to global warming. Thus, a link can be made between rising populations and environmental problems (see Module 13I).

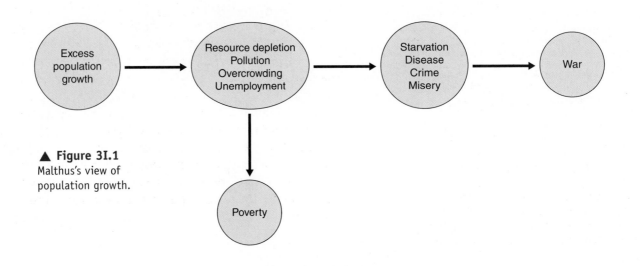

▲ **Figure 3I.1**
Malthus's view of
population growth.

▲ **Figure 3I.2** The Green Revolution resulted in higher yields for some crops more than others. (a) Rice, (b) wheat, and (c) maize (corn) were the three grain crops that science focused on, leaving areas of the world using other crops as their staples lagging behind. For example, yams, a staple for millions in West Africa, saw few gains during the first decades of the Green Revolution.

But not all modern demographic theorists agree with the pessimistic view of the neo-Malthusians. A famous dissenting view was put forth in 1965 by a Danish economist named **Ester Boserup**. Boserup argued that population growth actually stimulates societies to innovate and produce more food. In other words, people and technology will adapt to meet the challenges of a rising population. If populations rise, harder work and new farming techniques will raise food yields. Development of these techniques did actually result in a "Green Revolution" that helped increase agricultural yields considerably in the last decades of the twentieth century (see Module 15H for an extended discussion of the Green Revolution).

Boserup and other technology-focused scholars are not without their critics. The Green Revolution increased yields, but at greater cost to the farmers. Fertilizers, pesticides, and better seeds are more expensive than traditional methods. Some of the new farming techniques require more water and fertilizer and thus can have negative effects on the environment. But despite the problems of the Green Revolution (see Module 15H), for our purposes it is simply important to acknowledge the viewpoint of Boserup and others that technology will provide for growing populations. This view contradicts the more pessimistic view of the neo-Malthusians.

Another theoretical view on the future of population growth is held by some Marxists, such as communists and socialists. This view tends to downplay population growth itself and, instead, focuses on the poor distribution of food around the world as the source of population-related problems, such as famine. In other words, the rich countries of the world do not share enough food with poorer countries.

Today, theorists in the debate about the world's population are often grouped into two camps, labeled by one expert as the **implosionists** and the **explosionists**. Implosionists point at declines in fertility in most countries and argue that the world has turned the corner on population growth. They see a future in which the problem is not high population but, rather, lower populations. Industrialized countries require people to fill jobs, and without enough people, labor shortages can severely cripple a country's economy. Japan and parts of Eastern Europe are already facing problems related to a declining labor force. Explosionists tend to be more Malthusian in their view and warn that, although fertility rates have declined, the world will continue to see rapid population growth for decades to come.

3J　Population Planning

The demographic transition model describes a natural sequence of population change linked to modernization. In the modern world, however, governments have demonstrated the ability to rapidly increase or decrease population through government programs. Most of the time, governments have attempted to reduce populations, but sometimes the emphasis is on increasing fertility.

Historically, **population planning** has been quite controversial. Many religions see birth control as immoral, so proposals or attempts to reduce population sizes through the use of contraceptives has often been opposed. A famous example is the 1873 "Comstock Law" in the United States that made it illegal to distribute any information about contraception through the mail. Related laws stayed on the books until the 1960s in some states.

After World War II, organizations such as the United Nations Population Commission and the International Planned Parenthood Federation (IPFF) began to advocate for more family planning globally. International advocacy increased in the 1960s and 1970s as fear of a population-induced global crisis increased.

International groups involved in population planning generally focus on several areas:

- Changing cultural attitudes that keep population rates high (or low)
- Training population planning staff around the world
- Providing contraceptives to poor countries
- Helping countries improve their demographic statistics through better censuses and recordkeeping
- Working to improve education for women
- Providing technical assistance to personnel in developing countries

▼ **Figure 3J.1** The connection between education and birth rates is clear. Girls with even some education, such as the Senegalese girls pictured, are less likely to have begun having children as teenagers. In Egypt, a woman with a high school education has one fewer child than an uneducated woman does. In Peru, the difference is over three fewer children for a woman with a secondary education. Educated women have more options in the workforce and thus tend to get married later. Delaying marriage is an effective way to reduce fertility rates around the globe. For example, in Turkey, one-fifth of women ages 15–19 who had no schooling were already married in a 1998 study. Among women with some secondary schooling, only 1 in 50 was married.

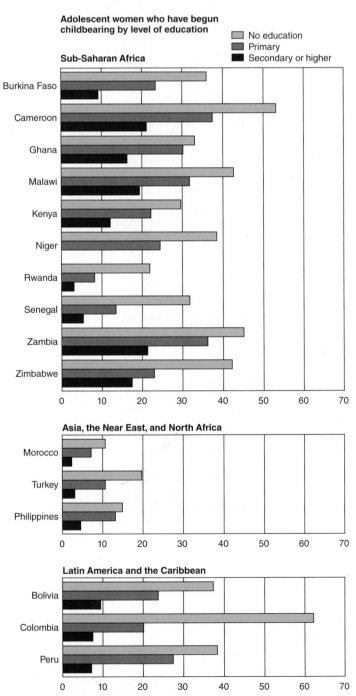

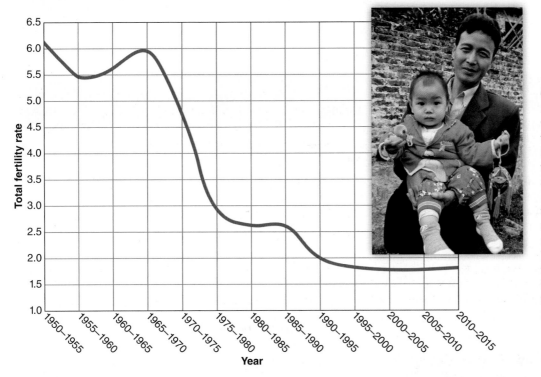

◀ **Figure 3J.2** The impact of China's One-Child Policy has been dramatic. In 1950, the total fertility rate in China was 6.2. As the graphic shows, high fertility began to drop in the early 1970s because of government policies and then fell dramatically in the late 1970s and late 1980s as part of the One-Child Policy. Now, it is just 1.5. This means that China's population, if the numbers are to be believed, will level off and decline if the present rates persist. There is a marked geographic pattern to the success of the One-Child Policy. China's cities and urban zones have seen the most dramatic declines, while the rural areas have lagged behind.

While contraceptive use remains controversial for many groups, about 61% of women aged 15–49 worldwide use some modern method of contraception, but there is a marked geographic difference from region to region. While 74% of women in North America use some sort of modern contraceptive, the number is just 29% of women in Africa and 55% of women in Asia, if China is excluded.

But modern population planning programs focus on much more than just reducing fertility through the use of contraceptives. This was made quite clear at the 1994 International Conference on Population and Development (ICPD) held in Cairo, Egypt. The Programme of Action that came out of this meeting urged countries to make social development a central part of their population policies. Specifically, the social status of women was emphasized. It has become clear that higher levels of education and greater civil rights for women tend to lead to a reduction in fertility.

Often, countries take dramatic steps to try to increase or decrease population growth. China's attempt to control its population is the most well known. In 1979, China instituted what is commonly referred to as the **One-Child Policy**, although a more accurate description would be the One-Birth Policy. Under this plan, most couples in China are allowed to have only one birth. This birth is carefully monitored to ensure a healthy delivery. In urban areas, couples are often rewarded for adhering to the policy with larger salaries or more spacious housing. Couples who illegally have a second child can be fined severely, and reports indicate that forced abortions and other punishments have occurred. Extra children born without permission do not legally exist and therefore cannot attend school unless the school officials are bribed, and many have difficulty later in life getting any kind of government license, such as permission to marry or to travel.

▲ **Figure 3J.3** Look at this population profile of China. Notice that there are several million more young boys than girls. This is not biologically normal, so what accounts for the "missing" girls? Historically, Chinese couples have favored sons. The main reasons for this is that boys often take care of their parents in old age, while girls leave their families to live with their husband's parents and family. Thus, to have no sons means little or no security in old age. When China implemented the One-Child Policy, couples began hiding female births, harassing government officials, or selectively aborting female fetuses to ensure that they would be able to try for a son. While the Chinese government's efforts did help a bit, there is still an alarming number of missing Chinese women. A population usually has about 108 boys for every 100 girls, but China now has nearly 120 boys for every 100 girls. This translates to about 40 to 60 million women that statistically should exist but do not. Some experts fear that, as young men in China age and cannot find wives, social unrest may rise. The problem is not exclusive to China. In India, the development of cheap and affordable ultrasound has led to more selective abortions by parents who choose to keep only boy babies.

Key Terms

arithmetic density (3B)
basic demographic equation (3E)
crude birth rate (CBR) (3E)
crude death rate (CDR) (3F)
demographic transition model (DTM) (3G)
doubling time (3F)
Ester Boserup (3I)
explosionists (3I)
fertility (3E)
genocide (3H)
implosionists (3I)
Industrial Revolution (3A)
infant mortality rate (IMR) (3F)

life expectancies (3A)
Neolithic Revolution (3A)
neo-Malthusians (3I)
One-Child Policy (3J)
physiologic density (3B)
population planning (3J)
population profile (3H)
rate of natural increase (RNI) (3F)
rate of population growth (3F)
replacement level of fertility (3E)
Thomas Malthus (3I)
total fertility rate (TFR) (3E)
zero population growth (3E)

Basic Review Questions

1. What is the world's population today?
2. Approximately how many people are being added to the world's population each year?
3. What was the Neolithic Revolution?
4. What was the Industrial Revolution?
5. How did the Black Death spread in the fourteenth century?
6. Why do death rates usually drop as a country becomes more industrialized?
7. Where are the population clusters in Middle America?
8. Why are population densities low in the Amazon?
9. Where are the population clusters in Europe?
10. Where are the population clusters in Africa?
11. Why is there a population cluster in the Ethiopian Highlands?
12. What is the difference between arithmetic and physiologic density?
13. Where are the population clusters in Asia?
14. What factors make Bangladesh a population cluster?
15. What is the crude birth rate, and what are its highs and lows in the world?
16. What is the total fertility rate?
17. What is the replacement level of fertility?
18. What is the crude death rate, and what is its global range?
19. What is the global range of the infant mortality rate?
20. How is the rate of natural increase calculated?
21. How do you calculate doubling time?
22. What is the demographic transition model?
23. In what stage of the DTM is the United States?
24. What is a neo-Malthusian?
25. What did Ester Boserup argue?
26. What is China's One-Child Policy?
27. When was the "baby boom" in the United States?
28. What do population profiles show, and how do they help us understand a country's past and possible future?

Advanced Review Questions (Essay Questions)

1. Why did the Neolithic Revolution lead to larger human populations and the rise of cities? What services does a city need if it has a surplus of agricultural goods?
2. How did the Industrial Revolution lead to higher populations?
3. Why is the crude birth rate "crude"? If it is "crude," why do we use it? Which demographic statistics do you think are the most reliable, and which are probably more inaccurate?
4. Do physiologic densities change over time? Why? How might urbanization affect physiologic density? Do cities grow at the expense of farmland?
5. How is the environment related to population density in Africa? What types of environments support larger or smaller populations? If the population of an area goes up, what might be some of the environmental effects?
6. Why isn't the replacement level of fertility 2.0? Why is the replacement level higher in developing countries? What might a government do to encourage a higher or lower total fertility rate?
7. Why are fertility rates higher in some places in the world than in others? How do environmental, historical, and political factors affect fertility rates?
8. Describe each stage of the demographic transition model and explain what happens to birth and death rates as a country develops. What factors might slow or speed up the process?
9. Compare and contrast implosionist and explosionist viewpoints on world population growth. What facts can be used to support or refute each?
10. What do population planning groups focus on to reduce fertility rates? Why are population planning programs controversial?
11. Why is the status of women important in lowering birth rates?

Further Study Topics

- What geographic and technological changes in the world today make global plagues more or less likely to occur? What barriers are there to the spread of pandemics? Which are more dangerous to the planet, diseases that kill quickly or diseases that kill slowly?

- Does a Malthusian or neo-Malthusian argument about world population growth have any justification in a world where technology can produce more and more food through genetic modifications? How did the Green Revolution change food production, and what is the importance of genetically modified foods today?

- The chapter discusses the Cambodian genocide. What other genocides occurred in the twentieth century, and what were their demographic impacts? Are there long-term demographic consequences to genocide?

- What countries in the world are actively encouraging higher population growth, and what countries are trying to curb growth? Why would a country want to encourage people to have children if population growth taxed global resources?

- Organizations that work to improve the sanitation and general health of the developing world are generally seen to be positive actors on the global stage. But some worry that these well-minded groups are lowering death rates without affecting a corresponding reduction in birth rates. Is there a danger that countries could get stuck in Stage 2 of the demographic transition model? If they did, what could be some of the consequences?

- Why did Ehrlich's prediction of a substantial increase in death rates in the 1970s and 1980s not come true?

- Nearly 20 years after the 1994 International Conference on Population and Development, what progress has been made in improving the status of women worldwide? In areas where progress has not been significant, what are the barriers to advancement?

- What countries have a problem of "missing women" today? Should the international community take an active role when a country has a biologically unnatural birth rate?

Summary Activities

Look at each population profile at the right and describe what might be happening demographically in each country.

Using a table of world population statistics, such as those available at prb.org, list three countries that are in Stage 2, Stage 3, and Stage 4 of the demographic transition model.

Stage 2 Countries

1.

2.

3.

Stage 3 Countries

1.

2.

3.

Stage 4 Countries

1.

2.

3.

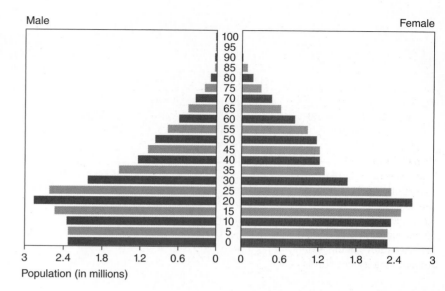

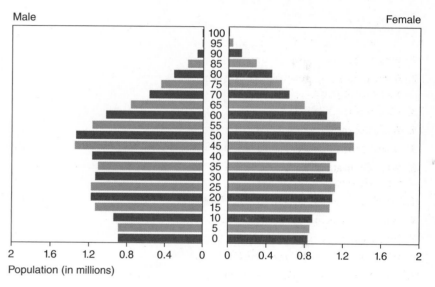

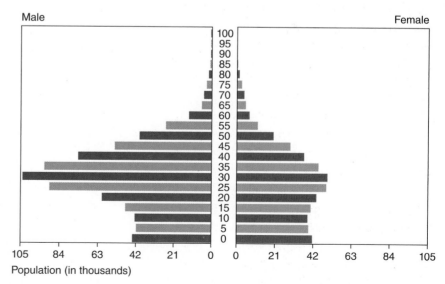

CHAPTER 4

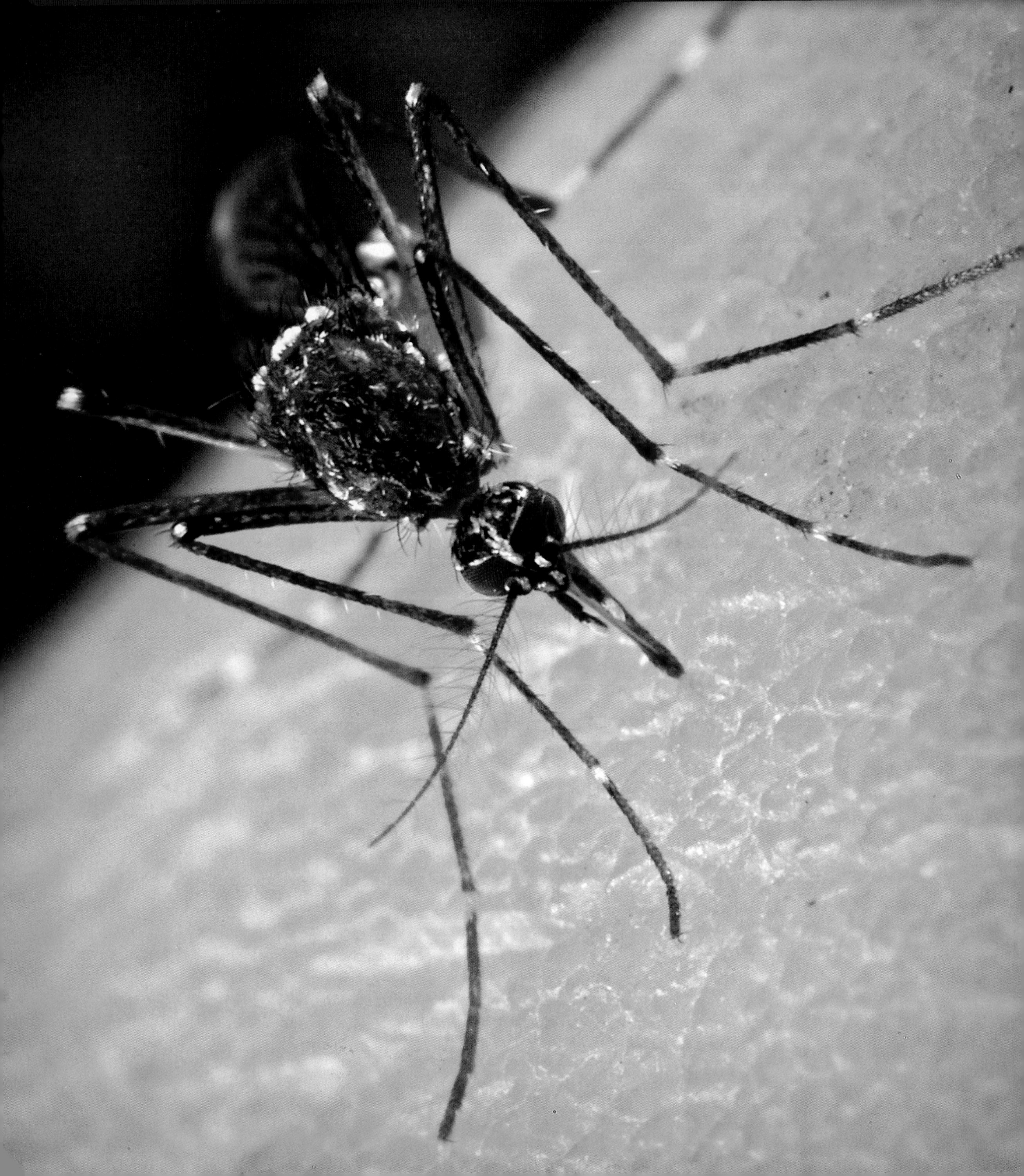

Geography of Health and Disease

CHAPTER MODULES

In Chapter 3, we explored the geography of births and deaths, but the story of the human population is obviously much more than being born and eventually passing away. Humans thrive and they get sick, and the health of a country's or a region's people affects that region's economy, education system, and ability to grow and adapt.

Medical geography, or health geography, is the application of geographic ideas, information, and theories to the study of disease, health, and health care. In an era of rapid transportation, when a person in Hong Kong can board a plane and land in New York the same day, the study of how diseases diffuse is critical to global health initiatives, and

geographers can play an important role. Twenty-first century scares over severe acute respiratory syndrome (SARS) and avian flu are reminders of how small the world has become.

Health care, too, is a geographic phenomenon. Doctors, nurses, and hospitals are often not evenly distributed on the landscape. And even when they are, not everyone has equal access to health facilities. Do poor people in the United States have equal access to the health care facilities in their community as their rich neighbors? In many cases the answer is no. In this chapter, we explore the geography of health by looking at both disease and disease diffusion, as well as access to health care.

4A   Health and Geography

Why should geographers be interested in health and disease? Isn't that for medical professionals? Certainly, disciplines such as epidemiology, the study of the causes and spread of disease, play a critical role in understanding health around the world. But geographers, with their feet firmly grounded in the study of both the physical environment and patterns of human activity, have contributed to academic research on health in many ways.

Human-Environment Relationships

Human health is fundamentally affected by the environment (see Chapter 12). Wet, swampy areas are traditionally the breeding ground for insects, such as mosquitoes, that spread diseases such as malaria or yellow fever. People's diets are different in cold areas versus warm areas of the world, and between wet and dry regions. Parts of the world prone to catastrophes can have a rapid, profound change in the quality of its inhabitants. Pollution can also affect disease (see Module 12E). In recent U.S. history, there are numerous well-documented cases of pollution-related epidemics. Geographers are also well suited to understanding the linkages between environmental change and the potential impacts on human health (see Module 12I).

Culture

Culture and its impacts are addressed more completely in Chapter 6, but health and disease are affected by a region's culture, and geographers have long studied cultural patterns. Can you think of ways in which a society's culture might affect health or disease? In the United States, for example, there is a great cultural debate about abortion. Disagreements between liberals and conservatives over abortion have led to varying state health policies about whether public money can be spent on certain medical procedures. You can see how this is not just a cultural, but also a geographic, issue. Attitudes toward abortion are not the same in all places of the United States, and thus health policies have a geographic pattern.

Around the world, some cultures still allow a man to have many wives. This practice, called **polygyny**, has had an effect on HIV/AIDS rates in some countries. An infected man can very rapidly spread the AIDS virus to many women, and thus potentially many children. In countries that do not culturally sanction polygyny, this can still happen, but it is less likely because sexual relations with many women might be more socially unacceptable. Another example is the initial lack of public money to fight AIDS in the United States in the 1980s, in part because of the connection between AIDS and the gay community at that time. Societal attitudes against homosexuality led to resistance on the part of some to research the disease.

▼ **Figure 4A.1 Pollution-Related Environmental Disease: Love Canal** In the 1940s, a chemical company began dumping toxic waste in an abandoned waterway known as the Love Canal in Niagara Falls, New York. By the 1950s, the company had sold the property to the city government, which, at the advice of the company, built a school on the waste site and allowed houses to be built in the area. By the 1970s, residents had become concerned over the high rate of birth defects and diseases such as asthma and epilepsy. In time, they learned the truth—their neighborhood rested on top of 21,000 tons of chemical waste. In the late 1970s, President Jimmy Carter declared an emergency and relocated the residents. Lawsuits and investigations followed, and today the area is abandoned. Geographers have the statistical tools to investigate whether an outbreak of diseases or health conditions in a particular area is the result of a random occurrence or is abnormally clustered.

Movement

Diseases move, and geographers study diffusion (Module 6D), thus making geography an obvious academic discipline for the study of infectious disease. Compare the dynamics of a disease like HIV/AIDS to one like Ebola. HIV can stay in a person's body without visible signs for years. Thus, an individual affected by HIV is able to travel long distances, even around the world, without being detected as a disease carrier. Conversely, Ebola virus kills humans in less than two weeks. Thus, it is less likely that an infected person will be able to travel to as many places before dying or showing symptoms. But of course, some diseases are more easily transmitted, meaning that they can spread more rapidly. A human geographer has the training to identify and interpret these complex dynamics of movement.

▼ **Figure 4A.2 Global Climate Change and Human Health** Groups such as the World Health Organization warn that, if the planet's climate changes dramatically in the coming decades, there could a profound impact on human health. Possible effects include:

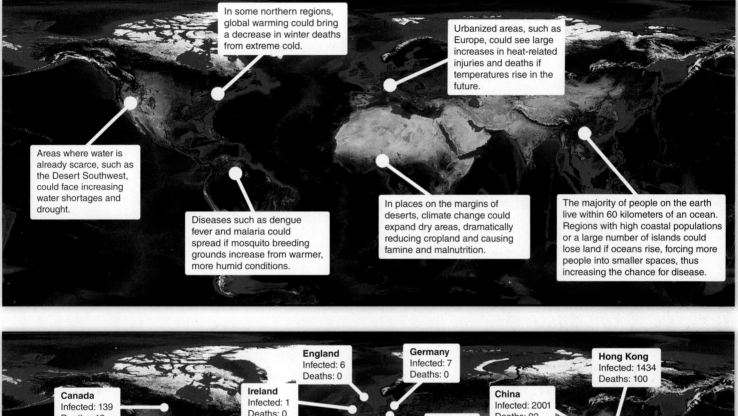

In some northern regions, global warming could bring a decrease in winter deaths from extreme cold.

Urbanized areas, such as Europe, could see large increases in heat-related injuries and deaths if temperatures rise in the future.

Areas where water is already scarce, such as the Desert Southwest, could face increasing water shortages and drought.

Diseases such as dengue fever and malaria could spread if mosquito breeding grounds increase from warmer, more humid conditions.

In places on the margins of deserts, climate change could expand dry areas, dramatically reducing cropland and causing famine and malnutrition.

The majority of people on the earth live within 60 kilometers of an ocean. Regions with high coastal populations or a large number of islands could lose land if oceans rise, forcing more people into smaller spaces, thus increasing the chance for disease.

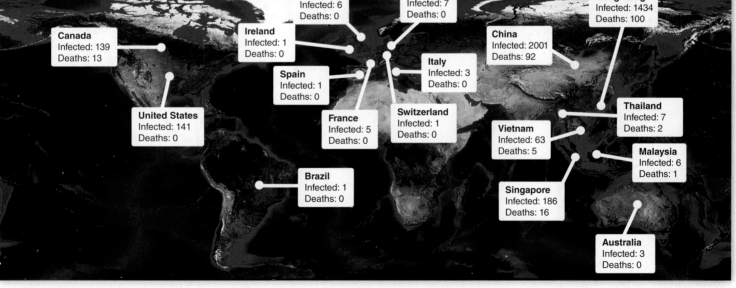

Canada
Infected: 139
Deaths: 13

England
Infected: 6
Deaths: 0

Germany
Infected: 7
Deaths: 0

Hong Kong
Infected: 1434
Deaths: 100

Ireland
Infected: 1
Deaths: 0

China
Infected: 2001
Deaths: 92

Spain
Infected: 1
Deaths: 0

Italy
Infected: 3
Deaths: 0

United States
Infected: 141
Deaths: 0

France
Infected: 5
Deaths: 0

Switzerland
Infected: 1
Deaths: 0

Thailand
Infected: 7
Deaths: 2

Vietnam
Infected: 63
Deaths: 5

Malaysia
Infected: 6
Deaths: 1

Brazil
Infected: 1
Deaths: 0

Singapore
Infected: 186
Deaths: 16

Australia
Infected: 3
Deaths: 0

▲ **Figure 4A.3 SARS** The global outbreak of severe acute respiratory syndrome, or SARS, between November 2002 and July 2003 illustrated the dangers of communicable diseases in an age of air travel. From its source areas in China, cases spread to North American cities, such as Vancouver and Toronto, by airline passengers, resulting in a public health crisis in both Canada and the United States. Officials at that time advised against all but essential travel to Toronto, one of the areas of greatest concern. Diffusion in the modern age is much more rapid than during the days of travel by sea or land alone. What do the primary areas of SARS infection have in common? How are they all connected? Why do you think large areas of Africa were not affected?

4B   Human Ecology of Disease

The term **ecology** refers to the relationship between organisms (plants or animals) and their environment. Therefore, the term **human ecology** refers to the interconnections between human populations and the physical world. So when we look at what impacts human health or disease, it makes sense as geographers to take an ecological perspective. If humans, for example, farm an area until the soil nutrients are depleted, there may be consequences of nutritional deficiencies for the community. Humans affect their environment, and the environment affects humans. Because geographers study the surface of the earth, a human ecology approach to disease makes good sense for medical geographers.

▲ **Figure 4B.1** We commonly think of pollution and poor sanitation as leading to poor health, but this is not always the case. Sometimes, seemingly positive changes to human environments can cause adverse effects. In the late nineteenth century and the first half of the twentieth century, there was an increase in the number of children afflicted with polio, a crippling disease that can lead to paralysis and deformity when it doesn't kill. The reason? Better sanitation and smaller families. Polio is caused by a viral infection and was traditionally spread through contact with water or food contaminated by fecal matter. But better sanitation and smaller families led to less contact with the virus during infancy; thus, children did not build up natural immunities. There were large outbreaks of polio in North America until the 1950s in the United States, when the first polio vaccine, developed by Jonas Salk, was introduced. In 1952 alone, 58,000 polio cases were reported, leading to over 3,000 deaths and over 21,000 people paralyzed. Infected children often had to wear leg braces and undergo painful therapy. Some polio patients even required "iron lungs" to assist them with breathing. But a strong public health campaign for vaccination reduced cases dramatically in the United States and most of the rest of the world. The disease persists in places such as India and parts of Africa. If your parents or grandparents were alive in the 1950s, ask them about polio.

If you think about the environments that humans live and work in, they can be classified by scale (see Module 1D). Microscale environments include your house or dorm room, your car, and the classrooms you go to. Mesoscale environments (*meso* means "medium") include your town or region. Macroscale environments include large areas, such as a country. At each scale, there are factors that can positively or negatively affect human health.

Health can be affected by a variety of factors that geographers refer to as *insults* or *stimuli*. These can be grouped as chemical, physical, infectious, or psychosocial. **Chemical insults** include things such as drugs and exposure to carbon monoxide or other noxious gases. **Physical insults** include traumas from events such as accidents, radiation poisoning, or electrical shock. The effects of viruses, bacteria, or protozoa are **infectious stimuli**. Finally, **psychosocial insults** include the positive or negative effects of crowding, anxiety, love, and sense of belonging.

Each of these insults can manifest itself at different scales and are thus inherently geographic. A chemical insult, such as air pollution, can cover a wide area or be localized because of a chemical plant in your town. Many of these negative stimuli can move over large distances. Chemicals can be carried by the air or can get into water systems. Infectious diseases can diffuse by person-to-person contact or can be transported long distances in a short period of time if an infected person hops onto an overseas flight.

One easy way of thinking about the human ecology of disease is through the triangle of human ecology. In this model, the state of human health in an area is at the nexus of three major factors: population, habitat, and behavior.

Population does not simply refer to numbers of people; the term refers to a group or society's age, gender, and genetic characteristics. A population that is, on average, older may have different types of health issues than a younger population. Cancer and heart disease tend to affect older populations. Genetics obviously affects individual health, but it can also affect a larger population, although the connections are more complex. For example, studies have shown that the Chinese metabolize alcohol at a slower rate than most European populations. There is also evidence that men of African descent are more likely to have a genetic mutation that makes them process testosterone more efficiently than most Caucasians. This leads to stronger bones in these men, but also an increased likelihood of prostate cancer.

Habitat refers to both natural characteristics and cultural and human-made aspects of an environment. For example, urban environments tend to show higher rates of asthma than rural locations. A person's home can also affect health. Some people have homes without a proper floor or roof, thus increasing the chance of getting colds or similar problems. Rich communities may have more homes with air conditioners, which would reduce illnesses during heat waves. A century ago, poorly ventilated homes burning coal for heat or cooking contributed to respiratory diseases, such as tuberculosis. Lung cancer from radon exposure can be caused simply by living in an area with certain subterranean characteristics, such as a lot of granite or shale.

Behavior refers to the effect of things such as cultural beliefs and social organization. Some cultures put less importance on modern medical care than others, or they have traditional beliefs that are not in line with modern medical practices or are just erroneous. For example, some cultures believe that a man can be cured of a sexually transmitted disease by having sex with a virgin woman. This is, of course, dangerously false. Another example is the emphasis that a society places on health education in schools. Diet is also an important part of behavior. Bad American eating habits have led to record levels of obesity, heart disease, and diabetes.

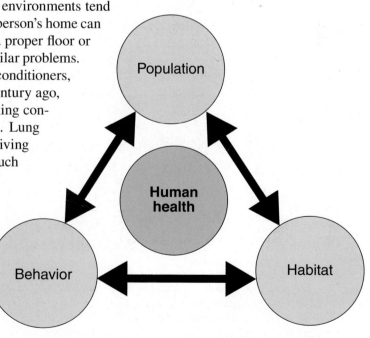

▲ **Figure 4B.2 Triangle of Human Ecology** The Triangle of Human Ecology reminds us that health can be affected by a variety of factors that are interrelated. Can you describe some of the relationships between each of the three major factors?

▼ **Figure 4C.1** In 1854, a cholera outbreak ravaged the Soho neighborhood in London's West End. Physician John Snow did not believe, as most medical officials did in his day, that diseases such as cholera were caused by bad air. By talking to Soho residents and mapping the locations of cholera cases, shown as dots on this map, he was able to hypothesize that a contaminated well in the neighborhood was the source of the outbreak. Later, he was able to use statistical methods to better make his case.

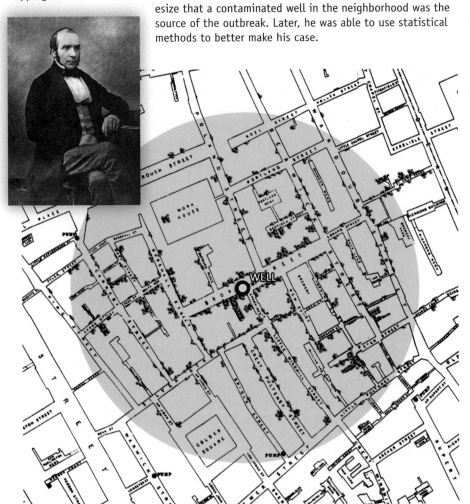

4C   Disease Basics

The study of disease patterns and transmission is a key component of medical geography. John Snow's work in London on cholera highlights how modern researchers became increasingly aware that understanding patterns of disease can help fight disease and disease transmission.

Some diseases are always present in a population of animals or humans. In the United States, chicken pox is an example, with cases happening from time to time. There are more cases in the winter and spring, when more people are indoors, but in general the disease is always present. A disease such as this, which is always present, is known as **endemic**. In the U.S. population, arthritis and heart disease are examples of endemic diseases.

When a disease occurs in large numbers in a population that does not normally experience the disease, or when the number of new cases of a disease is more than would normally be expected, it is said to be **epidemic**. Today, the flu and AIDS are well-known epidemic diseases. When an epidemic covers a large area, or even the whole world, it is said to be a **pandemic**. HIV/AIDS would certainly be considered a pandemic.

A useful way of understanding the dynamics of disease is to think in terms of an agent, a vector, and a host. An **agent** is the organism that causes a disease, such as bacteria, viruses, protozoa, or tiny

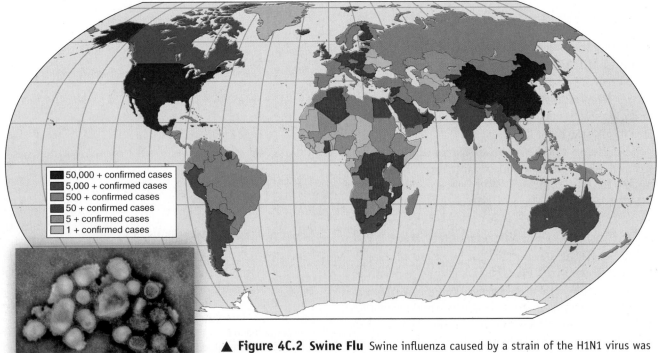

- 50,000 + confirmed cases
- 5,000 + confirmed cases
- 500 + confirmed cases
- 50 + confirmed cases
- 5 + confirmed cases
- 1 + confirmed cases

▲ **Figure 4C.2 Swine Flu** Swine influenza caused by a strain of the H1N1 virus was a major concern to health organizations in 2009 and likely accounted for over 15,000 deaths. This map of cases shows that the disease was truly a pandemic, as are many strains of influenza.

Figure 4C.3 ◢ **Intermediate Hosts** Schistosomiasis is an endemic disease affecting about 200 million people worldwide, especially in Africa and South America. In humans, the disease causes a massive immune response, resulting in internal scarring, anemia, learning disabilities, and damage to internal organs. The agent, a fluke (worm), lives in fresh water in one stage of its life. The free-swimming larvae are able to penetrate the bodies of snails that also live in the water. Inside the snail, larvae transform and mature into a young adult stage before being ejected back into the water. At this stage, the worm is able to infect mammals. Humans bathing, working, or swimming in the water can be infected. Inside the human body, the primary host, the worm matures and within six to eight weeks can produce hundreds or even thousands of eggs per day, depending on the species of fluke. In time, some of the eggs are excreted in human feces. In areas with poor sanitation, this puts the eggs back into the water, where they hatch and the cycle continues. This disease is a prime example of how an intermediate host is vital to a disease's life cycle and ability to infect humans. The map shows areas of the world where schistosomiasis is a risk to humans.

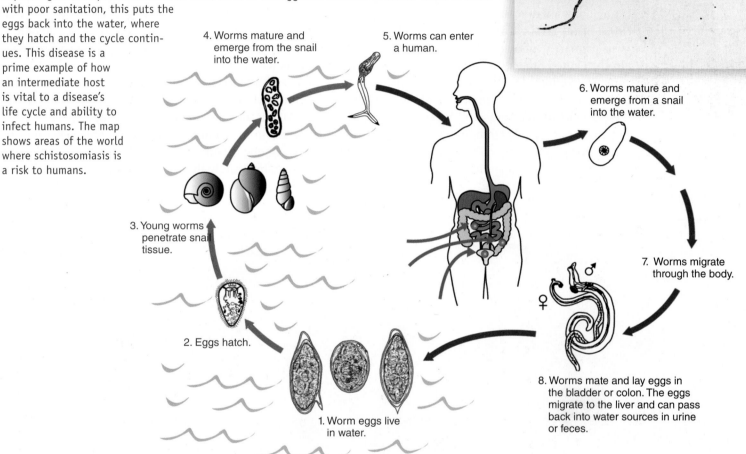

4. Worms mature and emerge from the snail into the water.

5. Worms can enter a human.

6. Worms mature and emerge from a snail into the water.

3. Young worms penetrate snail tissue.

7. Worms migrate through the body.

2. Eggs hatch.

8. Worms mate and lay eggs in the bladder or colon. The eggs migrate to the liver and can pass back into water sources in urine or feces.

1. Worm eggs live in water.

worms called flukes. A **host** is the life form, animal or human, that has the disease caused by the agent, and the **vector** is the means by which the agent is transmitted to the host. Common vectors include mosquitoes, flies, ticks, bats, and rodents. Many vectors are blood-feeders and transmit the agent by feeding on infected blood in one host and then transmitting it to another host through another bite. An agent can also multiply or even mutate inside a vector. There can also be intermediate or secondary hosts. In other words, an agent can live in one organism for a while before being transmitted into a different host. Sleeping sickness in Africa is one example. The agent, a protozoa, lives in tsetse flies until the fly bites an animal or a human. Finally, some diseases are spread from one human directly to another human through physical contact or close proximity. In these cases, there is essentially no vector.

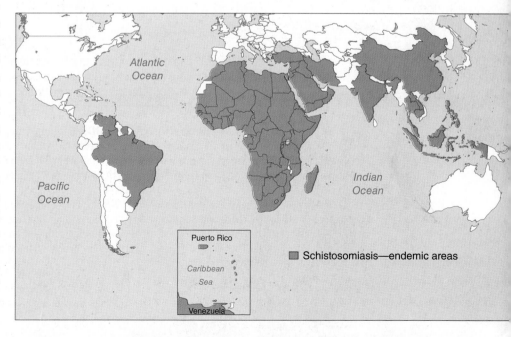

Atlantic Ocean

Pacific Ocean

Indian Ocean

Puerto Rico

Caribbean Sea

Venezuela

■ Schistosomiasis—endemic areas

4D HIV/AIDS

Across the globe, **HIV/AIDS** killed as many as 1.8 million people in 2009 alone, and over 25 million people have lost their lives to the pandemic disease since 1981. Understanding the geography of this horrible disease, which infects an estimated 33 million people worldwide, will help you better understand the challenges of controlling and someday eradicating this killer.

As geographers, we know that looking only at data at the country level can mask important dynamics at a subnational scale. This has certainly been true of HIV/AIDS. For example, in the 1980s as many as 90% of all HIV cases in the United States were among homosexuals, while in Africa the early epidemic was primarily among heterosexuals. Thus, the diseases took on a much different geography in each region. In the United States, early cases were concentrated in areas with higher gay populations, such as New York and San Francisco. The pattern was different in Africa, with the disease following, in some cases, truck routes used by straight men who often frequented prostitutes while away from home. Truck drivers are not responsible for the spread of AIDS in developing countries, but they are one piece of the process.

The rate of HIV infection has also been more common in urban areas than rural areas. The pool of infected people in a rural location is simply much smaller. Among urban areas in Africa, for example, those that are major commercial centers or located at border crossings show the highest infection rates. This is

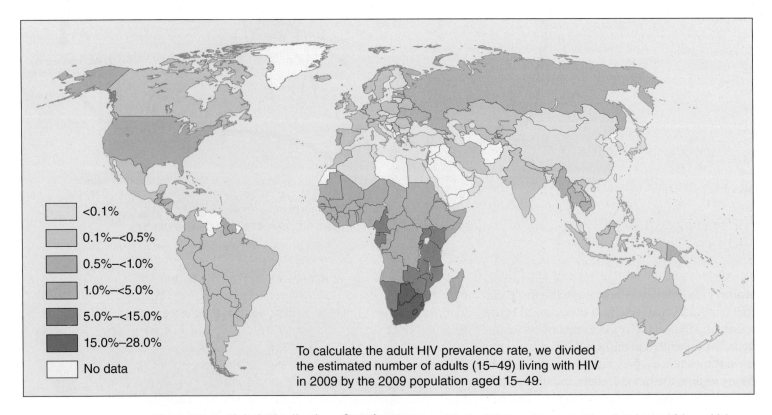

Legend:
- <0.1%
- 0.1%–<0.5%
- 0.5%–<1.0%
- 1.0%–<5.0%
- 5.0%–<15.0%
- 15.0%–28.0%
- No data

To calculate the adult HIV prevalence rate, we divided the estimated number of adults (15–49) living with HIV in 2009 by the 2009 population aged 15–49.

▲ **Figure 4D.1 Global Distribution of HIV/AIDS** Geographically, HIV is most common in sub-Saharan Africa, which accounts for two-thirds of all cases worldwide, or nearly 23 million cases. Next, the disease is most commonly found in South, East, and Southeast Asia, where 4.9 million people are infected. Latin America has 1.4 million cases, about the same number as Eastern Europe and Central Asia. North America and Western Europe combined have 2.3 million people living with the disease.

The map shows the global distribution of HIV/AIDS, but it hides some important spatial details. For example, although AIDS is most prevalent in Africa and Southeast Asia, it is spreading the fastest in Eastern Europe and the former Soviet Union. This is because health care systems in these areas have tended to break down in the post–Communist era, while the use of injected drugs has increased. The number of cases in the region nearly doubled between 2001 and 2009.

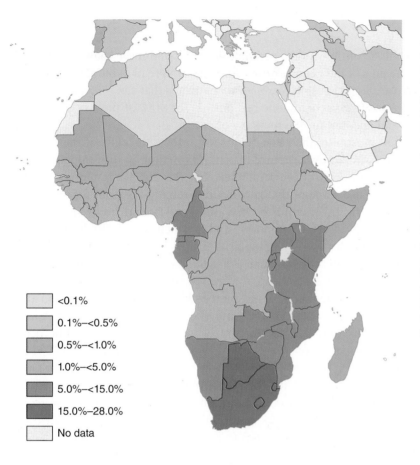

<0.1%

0.1%–<0.5%

0.5%–<1.0%

1.0%–<5.0%

5.0%–<15.0%

15.0%–28.0%

No data

◀ **Figure 4D.2 AIDS in Sub-Saharan Africa, by Country** HIV/AIDS is the number-one killer in Africa, and the sub-Saharan region has two-thirds of all HIV-infected persons in the world. Geographically, the disease is most severe in central and southern Africa, where some countries now have nearly a quarter of their population infected. Lesotho and Botswana each have infection rates exceeding 20%, and as of 2009 Swaziland had an HIV prevalence rate of 26%. One-third of all HIV-infected infants die in their first year if not treated, and life expectancies have taken a downturn. The average life expectancy in Lesotho, for example, has dropped 15 years since the mid-1990s, according to the World Bank. High death rates among young adults have reduced economic productivity because young workers are sick or dying. AIDS has also led to increased prevalence of pneumonia and tuberculosis in areas with high infection rates, as well as millions of orphaned children.

likely because these areas have higher rates of migrants going in and out. Over time, migrants who return to rural towns can spread the disease there as well, but there remains a rural-urban divide. It is, however, easier to combat HIV/AIDS in cities because access to medical care, drugs, and education programs is more readily available.

Because HIV is primarily contracted through sexual contact, prevention measures are commonly directed to sex education programs. Abstinence, delayed sexual activity, monogamy, condom use, counseling, and testing are all emphasized. But because many countries have few resources for health care, HIV/AIDS presents a formidable challenge. There have been successes, however. The development of retroviral drugs has greatly benefited HIV patients in areas where the drugs are affordable and readily obtained. There have also been decreases in transmission of the disease from infected mothers to their infants. Free syringes and drug treatment programs have reduced HIV rates in some areas where the sharing of needles during drug use is a contributing factor. In some areas, public health officials have instituted complex counseling programs to work with couples and families to improve understanding about the disease, safe sex practices, and access to affordable testing. This includes mobile testing facilities that can take health workers to remote areas that might otherwise be ignored.

There are also geographic issues related to the spread and prevention of HIV that are less obvious, but still geographic. One is the vast economic disparity between the developed and developing worlds. Continents such as Africa have much less money to spend on health care and education, which in turn can lead to higher infection rates (through lack of awareness) and poor prevention programs. In many countries, too, the status of women is poor. This can lead to women not getting the health care or education they need to reduce the likelihood of contracting or spreading HIV.

4E   Common Diseases

Malaria is a global problem, with about 40% of the world's population at risk and more than half a billion cases each year. Malaria is caused by parasites of the genus *Plasmodium* and is spread to humans by the bite of infected Anopheles mosquitoes. There are four types of *Plasmodium* parasites that can infect human populations, but the most deadly is *Plasmodium falciparum*, alone responsible for 90% of the world's malaria deaths. Children are particularly at risk and account for the majority of cases.

When a person is bitten by an infected mosquito, the parasite quickly infects the cells of the liver and reproduces. After a couple weeks, some cells in the liver rupture from the infection, in turn infecting some red blood cells. In time, more and more blood cells become infected, but the disease remains relatively hidden from the body's immune system. Because some of the parasites can remain dormant for up to three years, an infected person may have reoccurring bouts with the disease years later if he or she does not receive treatment. Malaria symptoms include fever, chills, vomiting, and headaches, and the disease can be fatal if untreated. Treatment generally includes the use of antimalarial drugs. Historically, the drug chloroquine was most commonly used, but in recent decades, *Plasmodium falciparum* has grown resistant to chloroquine, requiring the use of other drugs. There is no cheap or effective vaccine.

At the local scale, malaria is associated with water because mosquitoes lay eggs in water. Thus, in areas with high rainfall or near-stagnant or slow-moving water, malaria may be endemic, while in other areas it may be only seasonal. Historically, wet areas were drained to control malaria, but today public health officials focus on controlling mosquito populations through the use of indoor residual spraying (IRS) and the use of long-lasting insecticidal nets (LLINs). IRS involves spraying interior walls of buildings with insecticides. If a mosquito bites one person in a household and then lands on a wall treated with insecticide, it will die before it can infect someone else. The nets operate in a similar way and cost only a few dollars per net. When combined with efforts to drain areas of stagnant water, malaria often can be controlled, but at a high cost. In Africa, the World Health Organization estimates that malaria alone accounts for 40% of public health expenditures, up to half of all admissions to hospitals or clinics, and up to 60% of outpatient visits. In addition, infected children often cannot attend school and thus reduce their ability to hold a good job later in life.

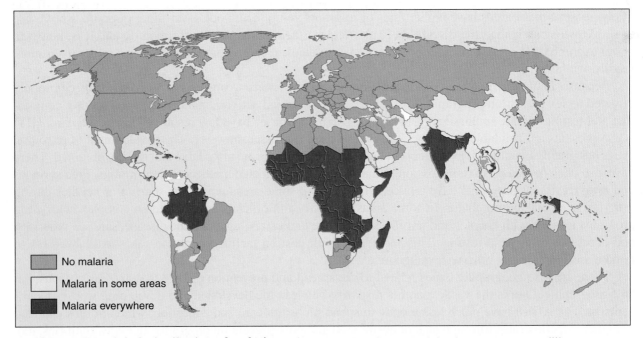

▲ **Figure 4E.1 Global Distribution of Malaria** The vast majority of cases and deaths, as many as a million a year, are in sub-Saharan Africa, where the disease is endemic. In Africa, malaria causes an average decline of 1.3% in a country's annual economic growth, which over the years has led to a poverty gap between countries where malaria is and is not common. In poor families, malaria reduces the ability of productive workers to earn a living, and any savings a family has to go to health care and treatment. The disease is also endemic in Latin America and across South and Southeast Asia in areas below 1,500 meters.

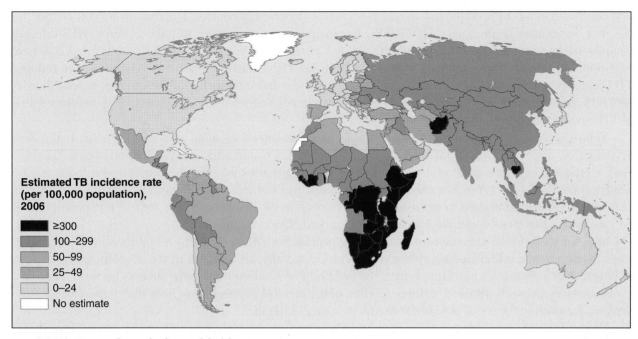

▲ **Figure 4E.2 Tuberculosis Worldwide** Tuberculosis is a disease that affects nearly the entire world. Can you see any patterns that might explain why some areas are more or less affected?

Tuberculosis, or **TB**, is one of the world's great killers. Each year, 9 million people get a new case of the lung disease, and nearly 1.5 million die from it. A full third of the world's population, over 2 billion people, have been exposed to the TB bacteria. TB is most commonly a pulmonary disease. In other words, it affects the lungs, with symptoms including chest pain, coughing or coughing up of blood, fever, fatigue, and weight loss. In a quarter of all cases, it moves from the lungs to affect other parts of the body.

Tuberculosis is difficult to control and eradicate because it is easily spread from an infected person to a noninfected person through coughing, speaking, or sneezing. A single sneeze can release up to 40,000 droplets of infected spit, and even a single droplet can infect someone else. Because of the ease of transmission, public health measures usually focus on isolating infected patients until they're no longer contagious.

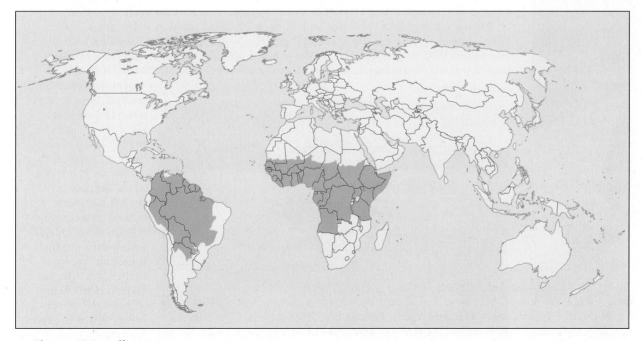

▲ **Figure 4E.3 Yellow Fever** Why is yellow fever a disease of the tropical regions? What problems might be associated with reducing the impact of the disease in these areas?

Tuberculosis has been on the rise in recent years after a period of control. The reasons for this are numerous, but one reason is the rise of HIV/AIDS. Because of their weakened immune systems, HIV-infected persons are quite susceptible to TB, and it is a major killer of AIDS patients. In Africa, where AIDS is so common, TB is a deadly bedfellow. A second reason for TB's return is that many countries have reduced TB control programs and public health money for treatment and monitoring of the disease. Again, the rise of AIDS in many areas has tapped public health money in poor countries. Finally, new, drug-resistant forms of TB have made control much more difficult.

Yellow fever is a mosquito-transmitted viral disease that causes an acute hemorrhagic fever. In the most severe cases, about 15% of all infections, coma or death can occur after internal hemorrhaging. The disease is endemic in Africa and Latin America, infecting approximately 200,000 people and causing 30,000 deaths annually. In the 1960s, the disease was almost wiped out, but many countries stopped immunizing children, allowing the disease to survive. In order to contain the disease, 60% to 80% of a population must be vaccinated, but many countries have not even reached 30% immunization.

Most of us think of **diarrhea** as a temporary problem or as the result of a bad meal. However, diarrheal disease is one of the leading killers worldwide, especially for children in the developing world. It is, of course, not a disease in itself but, rather, the symptom of a variety of agents, such as bacteria, parasites, viruses, and rotaviruses. About 2 million children under age five die each year from diarrhea-induced dehydration, accounting for about 18% of all deaths in young children.

To eliminate the problem would require massive improvements in sanitation and access to clean drinking water throughout the developing world. Nearly 1.1 billion people worldwide do not have access to clean drinking water, and nearly 2.5 billion have no adequate sanitation, so exposure to contaminated water is a

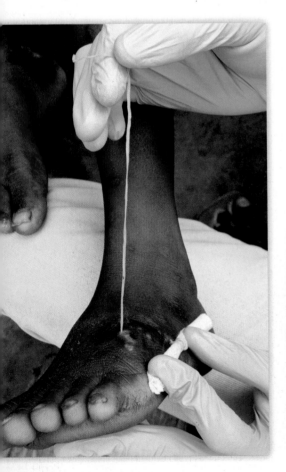

▼ **Figure 4E.4 Success Story: Guinea Worm** Guinea worm disease, also known as dracunculiasis, is a roundworm that is contracted when humans drink stagnant water containing water fleas carrying the worm's larvae. Once in the stomach, the water fleas are destroyed by stomach acid, allowing the larvae to mate inside the abdomen. Over time, the male dies and the female worm grows to 1 meter long and eventually begins to emerge from the body through a painful blister, usually on the legs. Humans often try to relieve the pain by cooling it in water. When this happens, the female worm releases tens of thousands of larvae back into the water. To remove the worm, it must be slowly pulled, inches at a time, a process that can take weeks or months.

The near eradication of the Guinea worm is one of the great successes of the global public health community. Just a couple of decades ago, there were approximately 3.5 million cases in 20 countries in Africa and Asia. In 2010, fewer than 1,800 cases were reported. Some estimates suggest that the disease may be wiped out in just a few years, which would make it the first disease eradicated since

smallpox three decades ago. The success has largely come due to health education and behavior change, such as filtering all drinking water. The child to the left is drinking through an inexpensive filtering straw. Today, Guinea worm disease is endemic only in south Sudan, Mali, and Ethiopia. South Sudan accounts for approximately 95% of all cases reported (in 2010).

problem that will be around for years to come. Because of this, public health officials have focused not on eliminating the cause of the problem but, rather, on reducing the effects of dehydration for the victims. In the late 1960s, researchers in India and Bangladesh developed what is commonly known as oral rehydration therapy (ORT), which involves giving patients suffering from acute diarrhea a solution of salt and sugar. This solution is able to be absorbed by the body when regular water is not. It also restores electrolytes. In modern hospitals, patients are treated by the use of intravenous solutions, but this requires a needle and proper medical training, which is much less common in poorer areas of the world. The ORT solutions are easily mixed and prepared and require almost no training. Between 1980 and 2000, the use of ORT reduced annual deaths of children under five by diarrhea from nearly 5 million a year to just under 2 million a year. While the exact formula of the solution has been changed over the years, the basic concept remains.

Like acute diarrhea, most Americans and Europeans do not think of **influenza** as a major killer, but historically, and for many worldwide, it is just that. The 1918 flu pandemic spread to nearly every corner of the globe between 1918 and 1920 and, in the end, killed as many as 100 million people, up to 5% of the world's entire population at the time.

Today, the flu continues to be a serious health concern. Caused by a virus, the flu causes fever, aches and pains, headaches, and sore throats. But the flu often leads to pneumonia, and pneumonia is a killer of children, the sick, and the elderly. Because influenza outbreaks are worse during the winter, there is a geographic and temporal difference between outbreaks in the Northern and Southern Hemispheres because winter occurs at different times. In addition, various strains of the influenza virus can cause epidemics, so medical experts have to track numerous strains at different times of year in each hemisphere. Vaccines can be effective, but this requires quick identification of new strains and mutations of existing strains across the globe. Recent research has shown that China is the point of origin for most new types of flu. The reasons for this are complicated, but some scientists believe that, because animals and humans often live in close proximity in Chinese villages, it is easier for new types of flu to spread from animals, such as pigs, to humans. With China increasingly connected to the rest of the world through trade and tourism, there is an increased need for careful monitoring of flu outbreaks in China.

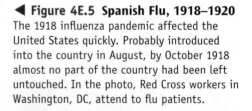

◀ **Figure 4E.5 Spanish Flu, 1918–1920**
The 1918 influenza pandemic affected the United States quickly. Probably introduced into the country in August, by October 1918 almost no part of the country had been left untouched. In the photo, Red Cross workers in Washington, DC, attend to flu patients.

Approximate dates of onset

- Before Sept. 14
- Between Sept. 14 and Sept. 21
- Between Sept. 21 and Sept. 28
- Between Sept. 28 and Oct. 5

4F   Snapshot of Global Health

▼ **Figure 4F.1 Map of Physicians per 10,000 People** This map shows physicians per 10,000 people in a country. What do you think explains this pattern? What are the long-term problems that might arise from not having enough health workers in a country?

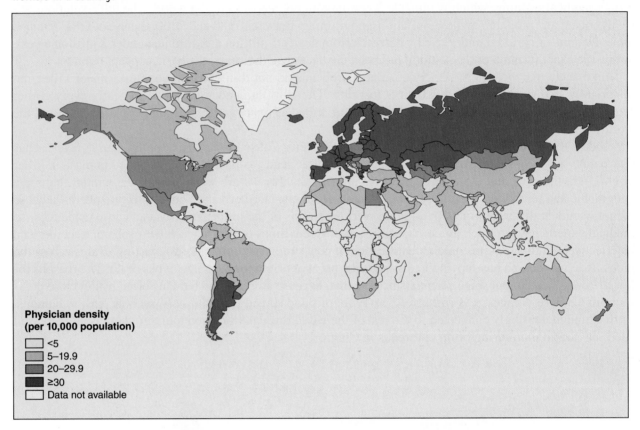

▼ **Figure 4F.2 Access to Safe Drinking Water** This map shows access to safe drinking water around the world. What problems might arise or are made worse by not having access to safe drinking water?

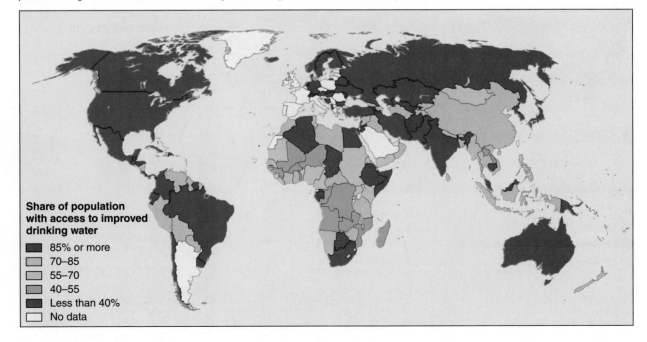

▼ **Figure 4F.3 Percentage of the Population with Access to Proper Sanitation** This map shows that, in some areas of the world, less than 50% of the population has access to proper sanitation. What groups in a population are most at risk when sanitation is poor?

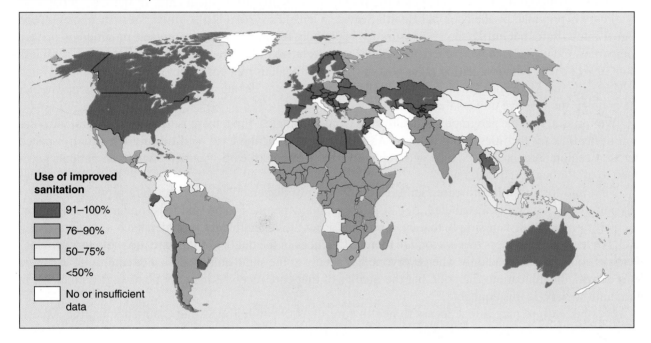

Use of improved sanitation
- 91–100%
- 76–90%
- 50–75%
- <50%
- No or insufficient data

▼ **Figure 4F.4 Percentage of the Population Undernourished** Much of the world's population fails to get enough calories, or the proper combination of nutrition. What key factors explain the undernourished areas of the world? Does the world produce enough food? If so, is it adequately distributed?

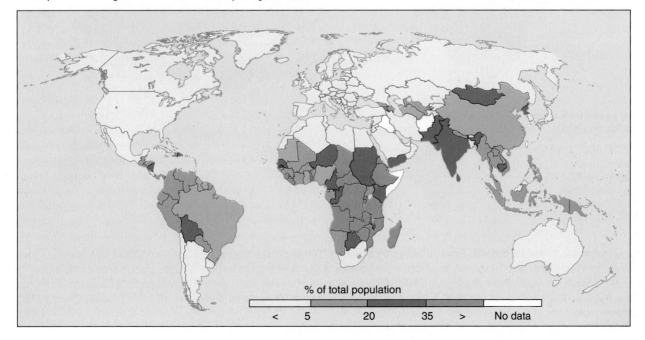

% of total population

<   5   20   35   >   No data

4G Geography of Health Care

Many medical geographers spend their careers studying access to health care. Timely and regular health care is a key component of human wellness, and even in the United States it is well established that poverty reduces access to good health care.

The delivery of health care resources varies widely by country. In some countries, such as the United Kingdom, a national organization handles the provision of nearly all medical care. In the UK, about 97% of all care is provided by the National Health Service. Canada's system is also universal—that is, everyone is guaranteed care, but unlike the UK, insurance is publicly funded, with the care itself provided by private companies. Conversely, in the United States a large percentage of health care is privately funded, with less than 30% of the population getting all or part of their health needs met only from government sources such as Medicare and Medicaid. This is, of course, the source of a huge debate in the United States about whether the country should have universal care for all citizens.

We can examine the geography of health care from two angles. First, there is the actual geographic location of health care facilities and providers. As you can guess, health care facilities are not equally spaced across a region. Second, there is the geography of access to health care—namely, where do patients go or need to go for health care, and why?

First and foremost, health care facilities are not evenly dispersed. And health care providers, such as physicians, are not evenly distributed. Because of this, many people can be said to be underserved. But how is equality measured? Is it simply that everyone has access to a health care provider, such as a doctor? But even if everyone has access to a doctor, are there differences in the quality of the care those doctors provide? Perhaps equity is achieved only when everyone has access to the same quality of health care. A government may provide health care to the poor, but the quality of that care received may not be as high as the rich in the same society. Is this equitable?

Second, culture may affect access to health care. A 2008 study found that Spanish-speaking Americans have a harder time accessing the health system and are more likely to use preventative medicine.

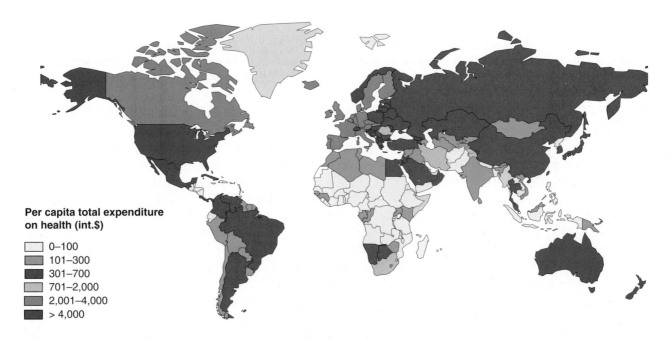

▲ **Figure 4G.1 Public Health Expenditures by Country** In the United States, an average of $7,285 was spent per person in 2007 on health care, according to a 2010 report by the World Health Organization. On the opposite end of the scale, the Democratic Republic of the Congo spent only $17 per person in the same year. Obviously, the quality of a country's health care and its citizen access will vary widely based on these numbers. What might be done to rectify this problem? Should this be a responsibility of the international community?

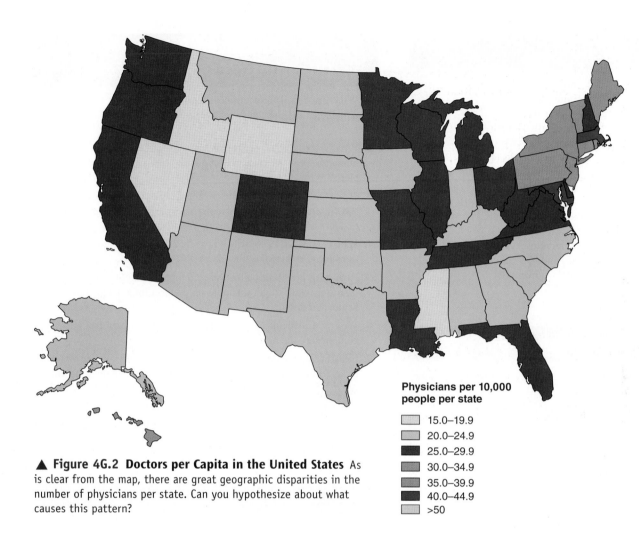

**Physicians per 10,000
people per state**

☐ 15.0–19.9
☐ 20.0–24.9
■ 25.0–29.9
▨ 30.0–34.9
▨ 35.0–39.9
■ 40.0–44.9
☐ >50

▲ **Figure 4G.2 Doctors per Capita in the United States** As
is clear from the map, there are great geographic disparities in the
number of physicians per state. Can you hypothesize about what
causes this pattern?

The problem was particularly bad in areas where the Hispanic population is rapidly increasing. Critics
countered that Spanish-speaking households were actually more likely to be poor and less acculturated
into U.S. society, but the fact remains that some populations in North America have poorer access to
existing health care resources.

In fact, access to health care is limited by functional, geographical, social, and financial factors. **Functional factors** are simply the presence or absence of health care resources. If there are no hospitals in an
area, access to hospital resources by people in that area will be lower. In general, the more common the
health resources, the more likely it is that the services will be available for a population.

Geographical factors include the proximity of the resources to the population. In rural areas, the nearest hospital may be hundreds of miles away. In poor countries, it may be days on dirt roads to a full-service
facility. Even in American cities, travel time (see Module 2F) can make a close hospital "far away." If a
poor citizen has to take four different buses to reach a hospital, the travel time may be the same as someone
driving 60 miles in a rural area.

Access to health care may be affected by **social factors**, such as racism or sexism. Historically, blacks
were excluded from many hospitals in the United States. In India, caste discrimination, although illegal,
still restricts members of lower castes from receiving some of the health care they need. And as described
earlier, cultural differences, such as language, can be a barrier to obtaining services.

Finally, **financial factors** limit access to health services for people who cannot afford to use them. For
example, poor health insurance coverage can affect initial diagnoses of illnesses, the treatment of long-term
conditions, and the management of diseases. Because poor communities tend to have poorer insurance coverage, there can be geographic differences in the quality of health care within a particular city or region.
Thus, even if a city has good hospitals, the quality of insurance may affect the overall care.

Key Terms

agent (4C)
behavior (4B)
chemical insults (4B)
diarrhea (4E)
ecology (4B)
endemic (4C)
epidemic (4C)
financial factors (4G)
functional factors (4G)
geographical factors (4G)
guinea worm disease (4E)
habitat (4B)
HIV/AIDS (4D)
host (4C)
human ecology (4B)

infectious stimuli (4B)
influenza (4E)
malaria (4E)
medical geography
pandemic (4C)
physical insults (4B)
polygyny (4A)
population (4B)
psychosocial insults (4B)
schistosomiasis (4C)
social factors (4G)
tuberculosis (TB) (4E)
vector (4C)
yellow fever (4E)

Basic Review Questions

1. What is medical geography, and how does it differ from other branches of geography?
2. How is human health affected by the environment?
3. What is human ecology?
4. What was the importance of John Snow's study of cholera in London?
5. What was Love Canal?
6. What is meant by *polygyny*?
7. What is SARS?
8. Explain the difference between endemic, epidemic, and pandemic diseases.
9. Define *agent*, *host*, and *vector*.
10. What are some common vectors?
11. Explain the life cycle of schistosomiasis.
12. What is malaria, and how is it spread?
13. What is tuberculosis, and how many people does it kill each year?
14. What is yellow fever, and how is it spread?
15. How many people were killed by the flu epidemic of 1918–1920?

Advanced Review Questions (Essay Questions)

1. What are the different types of insults or stimuli that can affect human health? Have any become more or less relevant in the modern era?
2. What is the triangle of human ecology, and how does it help explain human health? What aspects of the model are most useful for geographers? Why?
3. Using the agent-host-vector concept, explain the life cycle of HIV/AIDS, schistosomiasis, and malaria. How do health organizations try to address each part of the disease's life cycle?
4. Why is HIV/AIDS so difficult to stop? How do prevention organizations try to reduce the spread of HIV?
5. How have health organizations attempted to fight malaria? Why is it so important to get a handle on malaria infections from a public health standpoint?
6. Why is it difficult to control tuberculosis, and how has HIV/AIDS complicated the fight?
7. Explain why acute diarrhea is such a significant killer in the world today. How does economic development exacerbate the problem?
8. What are some functional, geographical, social, and financial factors that affect access to and provision of health care?
9. Describe the global geography of health. Where are the least healthy regions of the world?

Further Study Topics

• When malaria was being eradicated in the United States, why were white areas often targeted before minority areas? How might racism or other forms of discrimination affect provision of health care services in the present day?

• Investigate and discuss other significant diseases that affect the developing world. Possible diseases are river blindness, sleeping sickness, and guinea worm disease.

• Why has HIV/AIDS persisted in Africa while its prevalence has declined in some other parts of the globe?

• Using your school's archives, research societal responses to polio before the introduction of Salk's vaccine. What steps did parents take to reduce their children's exposure to the disease? Are there parallels between society's reaction to polio and any diseases common today?

• Research the geography of mortality by certain causes (heart disease, smoking, suicide, etc.) in the United States. What patterns can you find, and what might explain the patterns?

• What are the leading causes of death on each of the continents? What accounts for the differences?

Summary Activities

1. For each disease listed, indicate the agent, host, and vector:

   Malaria

   Yellow fever

   HIV

   Schistosomiasis

   Influenza

2. The following map from the Centers for Disease Control and Prevention shows death by lung disease for men in the United States. Below the map speculates on what might cause the pattern.

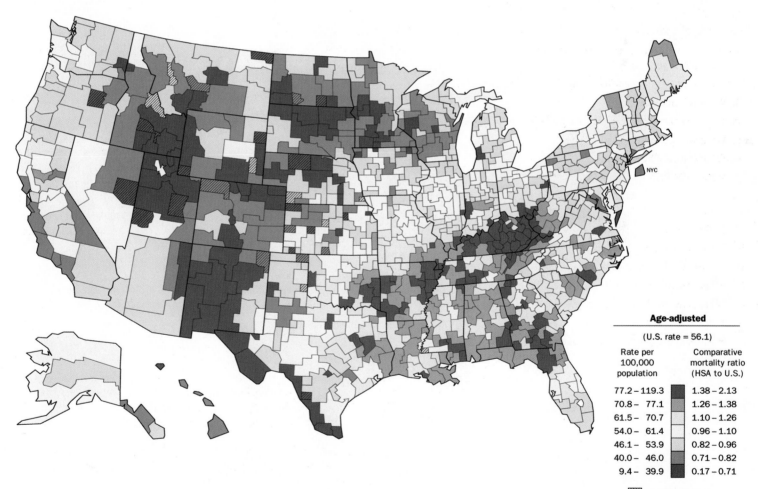

Age-adjusted

(U.S. rate = 56.1)

Rate per 100,000 population	Comparative mortality ratio (HSA to U.S.)
77.2 – 119.3	1.38 – 2.13
70.8 – 77.1	1.26 – 1.38
61.5 – 70.7	1.10 – 1.26
54.0 – 61.4	0.96 – 1.10
46.1 – 53.9	0.82 – 0.96
40.0 – 46.0	0.71 – 0.82
9.4 – 39.9	0.17 – 0.71

Hatching indicates sparse data

CHAPTER 5

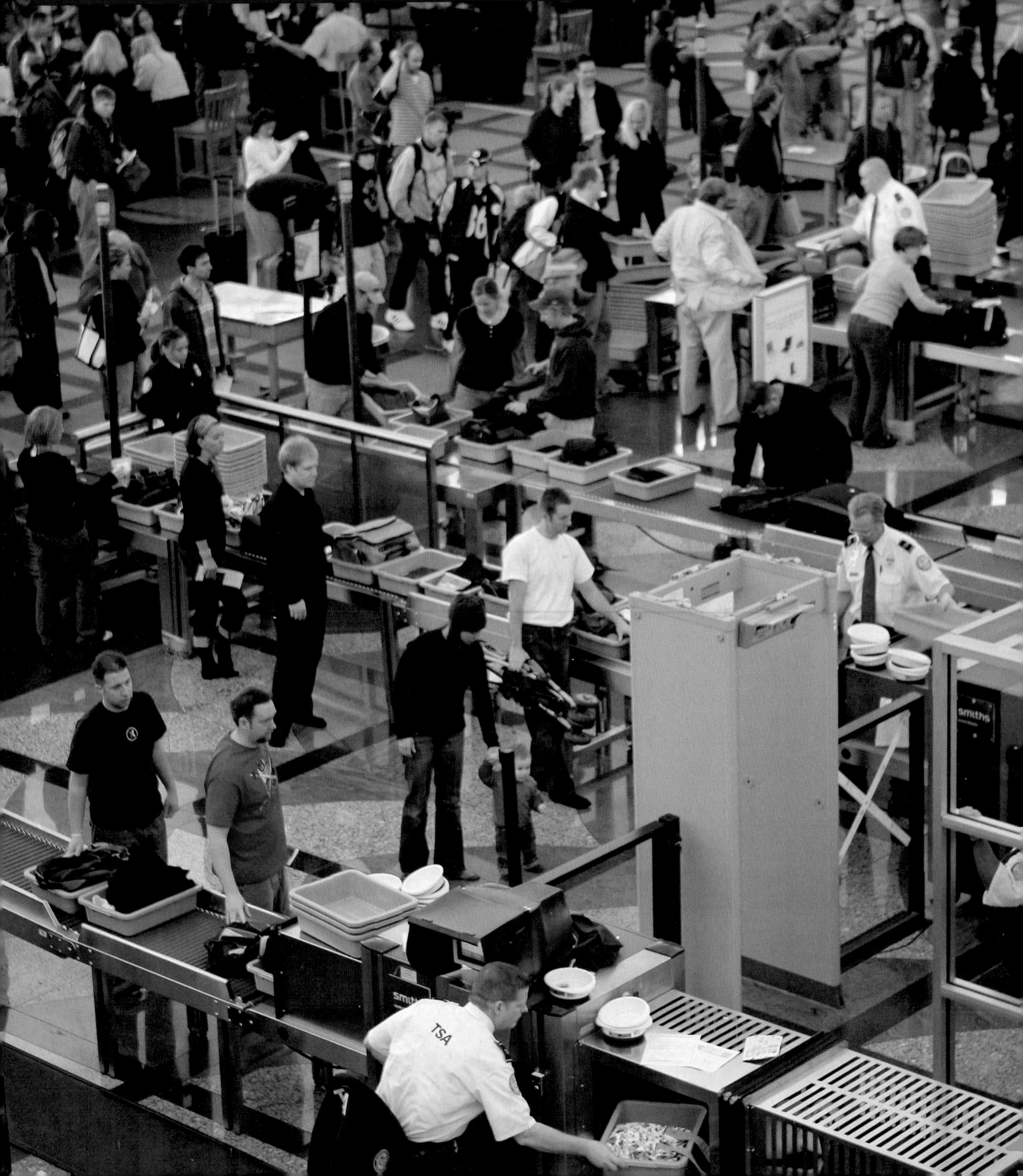

Migration Flows

CHAPTER MODULES

So far, we have covered only part of the demographic equation: births and deaths. But as discussed in an earlier chapter, population is also affected by immigration and emigration. In other words, as people move either in or out of an area, that area's population changes. More importantly, migration can change the composition of an area because migrants are not evenly divided among all ages and ethnicities.

Today, about 175 million people live outside their country of birth, and each year 5 million to 10 million people migrate from one country to another. Most move from countries in the developing world to other developing countries. Much of this movement is to take advantage of economic opportunities, but some migrants are fleeing persecution or violence. A small number of migrants move from one industrialized country to another, or from the developing world to the developed, but this accounts for just a fraction of all international migration. Some of the most active migration streams from the developing to the developed world are from Latin America and Asia to the United States and Canada and from the Middle East and North Africa to Europe.

In the developed world, migration *between* countries has been less important than migration *within* countries. Specifically, rural-to-urban migration (see Module 5B) has been the story of migration in countries such as the United States over the past century. Certainly, the United States welcomed millions of migrants during the late nineteenth and early twentieth centuries, but the movement of farmers and their families to the cities has been significant. Fifty years ago, about half of all Americans lived in urban areas. Today, that number is over 78%. In the next 50 years, tens, if not hundreds, of millions of rural residents in the developing world will also move to cities, placing a great burden on governments to provide housing, education, health care, and sanitation for these increasing city populations. Today, only about 44% of people in developing countries live in cities.

5A   Migration versus Movement

Migration is a permanent relocation of one's place of residence and generally considered to be a long-distance move. If a person moves from one apartment to another, he or she is usually not said to have "migrated." Thus, the classic view of migration is a migrant leaving one country or region and moving permanently to another, or **international migration**. However, **internal migration** occurs within a country, and some other types of population movements are important to consider.

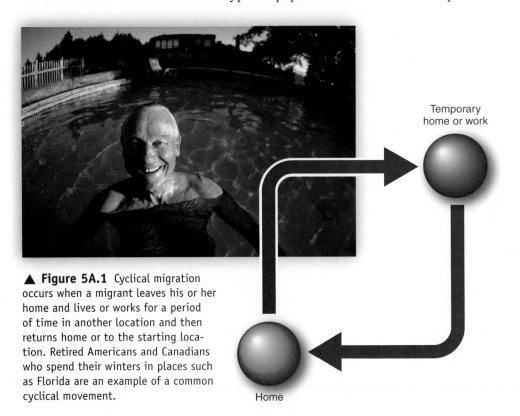

▲ **Figure 5A.1** Cyclical migration occurs when a migrant leaves his or her home and lives or works for a period of time in another location and then returns home or to the starting location. Retired Americans and Canadians who spend their winters in places such as Florida are an example of a common cyclical movement.

Temporary home or work

Home

Cyclical movements occur when people move back and forth between two places or among a few locations. On a small scale, each day hundreds of millions of people commute back and forth to work, requiring transportation and other services that tax the budgets of cities everywhere. Cyclical movements can also be seasonal. In the United States, for example, millions of Americans, mostly retirees, move to warm southern locations for the winter months. When spring arrives, they head back north. This movement has significant economic consequences for both the hometowns and the warmer destinations. Cyclical movements are also common for pastoral nomads, farmers who move with their animals during the course of a year. As water and vegetation availability changes, the nomads pack up and move to another location, but they often go back to the same locations at the same time each year, creating a cyclical pattern. Seasonal agricultural workers are also cyclical migrants, following planting and harvesting seasons each year. In the United States, for example, migrant farm workers often start in southern areas and move north as the weather warms, returning again to warmer areas in the winter.

Another type of population movement is termed **periodic movement**, population moves, often over long distances that occur from time to time but are not permanent. It is similar to cyclical movements but the length of time spent away from home is longer. Going away to college or to join the military are examples. Another common example of this involves **guest workers** who are allowed to enter a country for a specified period of time to work in certain industries, but after the end of their work period they return home. The number of guest workers around the world is staggering. In the Gulf States of the Middle East, over 11 million people are from other countries, mostly South and Southeast Asian countries, such as India, Bangladesh, and the Philippines. These workers often have to endure horrible living conditions, abuse at the hands of employers, and great cultural differences. The benefit is good pay, at least by standards in their home countries. Guest workers send home much of the money they make. These payments are known as **remittances**.

But guest workers can induce real social challenges in countries where they work. Many times, the home country needs workers but is poorly prepared for the cultural effects of having a large number of immigrants from a different culture. In Europe, Germany, Austria, and Belgium there have been attacks on immigrant groups, such as Turks, who have gone there to work and in many cases have taken along family members. Fear that Muslim immigrant groups are taking extremist family members with them has fueled many right-wing political groups opposed to immigration. In the Flanders region of Belgium, the anti-immigration Vlaams Belang party has increased its support from just 10% of the population to nearly 30% since the late 1990s. Some of this support comes from the Jewish population who have experienced rising anti-Semitism in some areas as the Muslim population has increased.

◀ **Figure 5A.2a** Many Americans equate migration with Ellis Island and the large influx of Europeans a century ago, but migration is much more complicated than just intercontinental mass migrations. This photo shows immigrant children arriving in New York in 1908.

▲ **Figure 5A.2b** As discussed on the opposite page, some migrants are only practicing cyclical movements, as is this migrant farmworker who might move to a different area with the seasons. Migration is not always long-distance and permanent.

▲ **Figure 5A.2c** As geographers, we're interested not only in the geography of migration but also in its effect on the origin and destination points. In the United States, migration has dramatically changed the culture of destination communities. For example, Dearborn, Michigan, is now over one-third Arab.

◀ **Figure 5A.2d** Migration is often involuntary. Some refugees, such as these refugees from Sudan, are either forced or impelled to migrate because of war or threats of violence. Refugees are discussed in Module 5D.

5B   Types of Migration

There are many types of migration. Perhaps the most basic form is **primitive migration**. This type of human movement occurs when human populations run out of food; it is especially common among groups that remain hunters and gatherers. Environmental change, natural disasters (such as drought), or plagues (such as attacks of locusts) can lead humans to move in search of food.

Before the modern era, most migration was **mass migration** (also known as group migration). As the name implies, mass migration involves a large group of people moving together. This can be a community, an entire tribe or ethnic group, or even an army that resettles in an area it has invaded. Colonization, such as British settlement in North America, can also be considered mass migration.

Free migration is defined as a decision to relocate permanently to another location without the coercion, support, or compulsion of any government or group in power. In other words, people decide to migrate without being forced or coerced to do so. In the history of the United States, free migrants totaled nearly 40 million or more as individuals moved alone or with their families from their homeland to seek new opportunities. Most of this migration has been from Europe, but in recent decades, the sources of migration have shifted to Latin America and Asia.

Today, free migration has largely been replaced by **restricted migration**. Because most countries now have complex rules that limit the number of people who can cross their borders to seek residency, migration is no longer "free" for most migrants. In the United States, the Emergency Quota Act of 1921 was the

▲ **Figure 5B.1** An immigrant to the United States takes a loyalty oath at a naturalization ceremony. Is migration to the United States in recent decades free or restricted?

▼ **Figure 5B.2** (1) Between the sixteenth and nineteenth centuries, between 9 and 12 million Africans arrived in the Americas as slaves. Because many died during the passage, the actual number enslaved is much higher.

(2) In the 1830s, nearly 50,000 Native Americans were forcibly moved from their homes in the southern United States and forced to resettle in present-day Oklahoma. Thousands died on route in what has been called a "Trail of Tears."

(3) The 1923 Treaty of Lausanne, signed by the governments of Turkey and Greece, led to the forced movement of 2 million people. Muslim Greeks were made to migrate to Turkey, and Greeks in Turkey were forced to migrate to Greece.

(4) When the Nazis came to power in Germany in 1933, the persecution of Jews increased dramatically. By 1939, nearly a half million Jews had been forced to flee from Germany and Austria.

(5) The 1947 Partition of British India into the countries of Pakistan and India caused the movement of millions of Hindus from Pakistan to India and Muslims from India to Pakistan. Sikhs, Jains, and other religions were also affected. In total, over 12 million people were displaced and 500,000 or more likely perished in the mass migrations that followed.

(6) The 1948 Palestine war between the newly created Israel and its Arab neighbors caused the migration of over 600,000 Palestinian Arabs who lived in what became Israel and about 10,000 Jews in Palestine.

(7) After the communist Khmer Rouge came to power in Cambodia in 1975, its leader, Pol Pot, ordered the evacuation of all cities, causing about 3 million Cambodians to move. By the end of the Khmer Rouge rule in 1979, 2 million of Cambodia's 8 million people had died.

(8) The construction of the Three Gorges Dam in China during the 1990s and 2000s led to the relocation of over a million people.

(9) Between the late 1700s and late 1800s, over 161,000 convicts were forced to relocate to Australia, largely to reduce the strain on the British penal system.

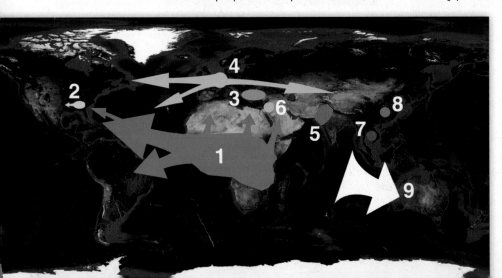

first major legislation to limit migration. The act restricted migrants from any country to 3% of the population from that country living in the United States in 1910. Although these numbers have been changed over the years, the act remains important because it forever changed the way immigration is handled in the United States.

Two other types of migration are **impelled** and **forced migration**. In both cases, migrants are pressured by a government or another institution in power to move. Impelled migrants may have some choice in the decision, but they feel pressured to do so. The classic example of this is the migration of Jews from Germany under the Nazi regime of the mid-1930s. During this period, anti-Semitic laws were passed that made it more difficult for German Jews to live and work in the country. This impelled many to leave the country. By the late 1930s and early 1940s, German Jews had been forced to leave their homes as the Nazis began moving Jews to ghettos and extermination camps. This is considered forced migration.

Human history has many examples of large-scale forced migration. The slave trade in the sixteenth through nineteenth centuries brought millions of Africans to plantations in the United States to work as laborers. Examples of forced internal migration in the United States include the Trail of Tears, the forced movement of Native Americans from Georgia to Oklahoma in 1838–1839, and the relocation of Japanese Americans to internment camps during the 1940s.

In world history, there are many examples of forced migration in addition to Nazi resettlement. Of course, the African slave trade is the most widely known. This migration dramatically affected the history of nearly every country in the Americas. In addition to the movement of as many as 20 million Africans to North and South America, for centuries there was a slave trade between East Africa and the Arabian Peninsula that may have included as many as 18 million Africans between the seventh and nineteenth centuries. In Module 5C, you will read about human trafficking, a modern example of forced migration and human slavery that remains common in all parts of the world. Forced internal migration continues to occur around the world as well.

It's also important to remember that migration can take place within a country as well as between countries. The most important type of internal migration affecting the world today is **rural-to-urban migration**. In general, countries with low levels of industrialization have urban populations that account for about 24% to 40% of their total population. But industrialized countries often have urbanized populations of over 75%. So, as a country's economy industrializes, people tend to move to urban areas (see Module 13D for a discussion of industrialization's role in rural-to-urban

▲ **Figure 5B.3** The construction of the massive Three Gorges Dam in Central China has been a priority of the Chinese government for the past three decades. During the 1990s and 2000s, an estimated 1.24 million people were forced to leave their homes because construction of the dam would lead to the flooding of their homes. The Chinese government is also encouraging millions more to leave areas along the Yangtze River before the year 2020. The forced moves have been quite controversial and the Chinese government has been accused of not providing proper relocation support for displaced residents. The top image shows the reservoir that has grown upstream from the Dam, which can be seen near the bottom right of the photo.

migration). These internal migrations can have significant impacts on a country because each new urban resident needs food, shelter, social services, and employment. Meanwhile, because people are leaving rural areas, there are fewer farmers to supply resources to urban areas. China, for example, is expected to see hundreds of millions of its citizens move to cities in the coming decades.

◀ **Figure 5B.4 Measuring Migration** There are a few basic measures of migration that you should know. The most basic is **gross migration**, which is simply the total number of people who leave and enter a country. **Net migration** is the difference between the number of people who leave and the number of people who arrive in a country. If more people leave than arrive, net migration is negative. **Out-migration** is the total number of people who leave a country, and **in-migration** is the total number of people who arrive.

5C   Human Trafficking

Today, forced migration continues to occur. Millions of humans are trafficked to work as prostitutes and bonded laborers. **Human trafficking** is defined by the United Nations as the

recruitment, transportation, transfer, harboring or receipt of persons, by means of threat or use of force or other forms of coercion, of abduction, of fraud, of deception, of the abuse of power or of a position of vulnerability or of the giving or receiving of payments or benefits to achieve the consent of a person having control over another person, for the purpose of exploitation.

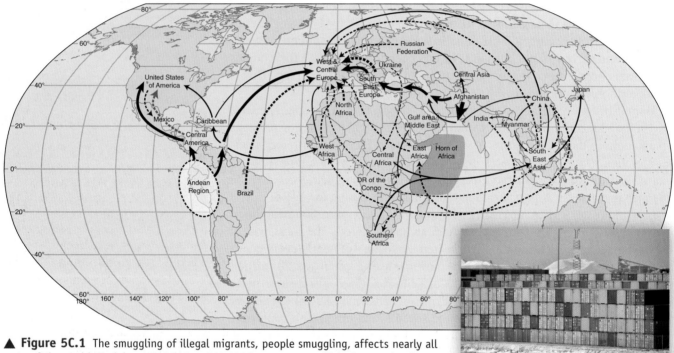

▲ **Figure 5C.1** The smuggling of illegal migrants, people smuggling, affects nearly all parts of the world. Each year, 600,000 to 800,000 humans are trafficked across borders to work as domestic help, prostitutes, and laborers. This map shows some of the most common routes. In some cases, migrants are transported in the cargo containers that dominate modern global commerce.

The Voice of Slavery Today

The following story comes from a young Russian woman who suffered at the hands of human traffickers, as quoted in a US government report:

Tanya: My friend organized for me to get a job in Egypt. We traveled together from Chisinau to Moscow where I got a plane to Egypt. When I got to the airport in Egypt, I was paired with a man in order to walk through customs and immigration. People were waiting for me and they took me to a five-star hotel. I gave up my passport at the reception of the hotel and never saw it again. They put me in a car and we drove for a really long time. We went to a place where Bedouins are [Egypt's Sinai Peninsula] and those Bedouins took us through the desert. At one point, I heard gunshots and I think a girl was killed. They kill you or beat you if they don't like your attitude. We had to walk for hours and hours through the desert where there were landmines. They pointed out the mines to us in the sand.

Figure 5C.2   Slavery Today

We hardly ate and I lost 10 kilos by the time I got to Israel. When we got out of the desert, we were taken to a town in Israel, where the Bedouins arranged for us to be sold. Many girls were traveling with me, and all the girls going to Israel go through the same route and the same situation.

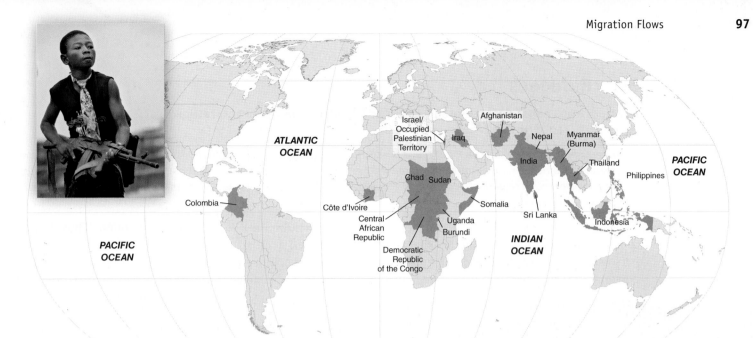

▲ **Figure 5C.3** This map shows some of the countries where child soldiers were used in the past decade. As these quotes show, being a child soldier is a brutal life with children commonly subjected to sexual, mental, and physical abuse:

> There was no one in charge of the dormitories and on a nightly basis we were raped. The men and youths would come into our dormitory in the dark, and they would just rape us—you would just have a man on top of you, and you could not even see who it was. If we cried after-wards, we were beaten with hosepipes. *19-year-old girl describing her experience in Zimbabwe's National Youth Service Training Program*

> They give you a gun and you have to kill the best friend you have. They do it to see if they can trust you. If you don't kill him, your friend will be ordered to kill you. *17-year-old Colombian boy who joined paramilitary group as a 7-year-old street child*

While many people think that this occurs only in the developing world, in reality, slavery rings have been uncovered in the United States, Canada, and many European countries as well. The CIA estimates that about 50,000 people are brought into the United States illegally each year to work as prostitutes, servants, or slave laborers. Worldwide, 600,000 to 800,000 people are trafficked each year. The vast majority are women, and half are children.

The evils of trafficking can be seen in three broad areas. First, trafficking destroys social institutions, such as the family. Children are separated from their parents, which means that cultural norms often do not get passed down to the younger generation. Education is also rarely offered to trafficked children and teenagers, which makes them less likely to hold legitimate jobs later in life. Because many traffickers offer money to parents for their children, the introduction of large amounts of money into a community can create repeated trafficking as each new generation is sold off. Because many trafficked persons are forced to work as prostitutes or in other demeaning or taboo industries, they are often ostracized if they someday return to their homes, so they face a life separated from their homes and families. Trafficking also fuels organized crime. US government officials estimate that nearly $10 billion a year may be generated by trafficking.

Another type of human trafficking is known as "people smuggling." This crime is defined by Interpol as "the procurement, for financial gain, of the illegal entry into a state of which that person is neither a citizen nor a permanent resident." In other words, the smugglers take money from migrants to sneak them into a country. This form of illegal migration is considered to be on the rise. Migrants are often subjected to horrific and dangerous traveling conditions, such as being locked inside shipping containers for weeks at a time. It is not uncommon for migrants to die during the journey. If they make it alive to their destination, they are often at the mercy of their smugglers, who sometimes force the migrants to work for them as slaves or bonded laborers. The large sums of money charged to the migrants are worked off slowly, or the migrant's family back home is forced to pay them. Smugglers commonly charge so much money that the migrant can never pay off the debt.

A particularly brutal form of slavery and forced migration is the abduction of youth for service as **child soldiers**. Over 300,000 children under age 18, both boys and girls, are estimated to be involved in over 30 conflicts around the world. Typically, militias or even government armies abduct the children, many under 12 years old, and then brutalize them to desensitize them to killing and death. Hard economic times can also impel children to join military groups because they think it will better their lives, but they are generally unaware of the realities of what their service will mean. Many are forced to kill their friends or siblings or be killed themselves. In battle, they are forced to continue fighting, or they are killed by older members of their own forces. Rape and sexual abuse are common as well.

5D   Refugees

Refugees are a particular type of migrant. The US government defines a **refugee** as

any person who is outside any country of such person's nationality or, in the case of a person having no nationality, is outside any country in which such person last habitually resided, and who is unable or unwilling to return to, and is unable or unwilling to avail himself or herself of the protection of that country because of persecution or a well-founded fear of persecution on account of race, religion, nationality, membership in a particular social group, or political opinion.

This definition is essentially the same as the one introduced in the 1951 Geneva Convention. Thus, forced or impelled migration can lead to someone being considered a refugee under international law. Generally, a person is considered a refugee when the government of the country to which he or she travels declares the person to be one. Until that time, that person is considered to be an **asylum seeker**.

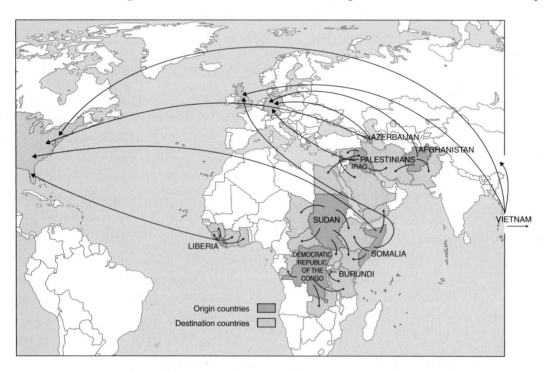

▲ **Figure 5D.1 Major Refugee Movements of the Past Few Years** Notice that refugees are moving in all parts of the world. Africa has seen numerous refugee movements involving hundreds of thousands of people in each case. Sudan, Burundi, Somalia, and the Democratic Republic of the Congo each have over 400,000 refugees living in other countries. These numbers certainly reflect the political and economic chaos in these regions. In all, there are nearly 3.5 million refugees just from African countries, but few areas of the world are immune from this challenging problem.

Worldwide, the number of refugees is staggering. About 12 million people are either refugees or asylum seekers. In addition, twice as many people, about 24 million persons in total, are displaced from their homes in their own country. These migrants are classified as **internally displaced persons**.

Millions of refugees end up in what is known as **refugee warehousing**, the long-term housing of refugees in a specific location without allowing them to assimilate into the receiving country. Refugees often are housed in temporary "camps" when they enter a new country, but quite often these camps are made permanent settlements, which may be isolated from the rest of the country. Thus, the refugees are stuck living in these camps, unwanted by the receiving country and unable to return home. Nearly 8 million refugees worldwide, 67% of the world's total, have been warehoused for more than 10 years.

Managing a refugee camp presents numerous challenges. Camps can range in size from a few thousand people to hundreds of thousands. The 1994 genocide in Rwanda resulted in a refugee camp at Goma in the Democratic Republic of the Congo (then Zaire) to grow to over 1 million people. Naturally, a camp of this size presents challenges for shelter, food, water, and sanitation. Food must be supplied by aid organizations or the host country at a goal of about 2,100 calories per person each day. A considerable problem in many camps is finding fuel, such as wood, for cooking meals. Aid groups generally provide basic foods, such as grains, that must be cooked. Clean water is necessary as well for both drinking and food preparation. Much of the water available in areas with refugees is contaminated with microorganisms, so treatment is necessary to avoid outbreaks of waterborne diseases, such as cholera (see Module 4C). Cholera can kill refugees within hours or days and can spread quickly in crowded areas, such as a refugee camp. Remember that cholera was a real concern for parts of Asia hit by the tsunami in December 2004. Sewage can also lead to the spread of disease, but building latrines for thousands or tens of thousands of refugees is very difficult. This adds to the poor quality of life within many camps. Medical care is usually available in refugee camps because of the work of international agencies, such as Médecins Sans Frontières (Doctors without Borders), but health care is usually quite basic. Many refugees are from areas at war or under other crises and may have had to walk for many miles each day to reach the camps, so their level of health may be quite low to begin with.

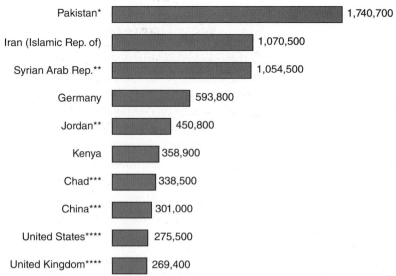

Pakistan*	1,740,700
Iran (Islamic Rep. of)	1,070,500
Syrian Arab Rep.**	1,054,500
Germany	593,800
Jordan**	450,800
Kenya	358,900
Chad***	338,500
China***	301,000
United States****	275,500
United Kingdom****	269,400

Figure 5D.2 ▶ This graph shows the countries that host the most refugees. The Palestinians are the group of refugees who have been warehoused the longest. Some Palestinian refugee camps, such as some in Jordan, are over 40 years old. There are also Eritreans in Sudan and Filipinos in Malaysia who have been in refugee status for over three decades. Numerous problems arise when refugees are forced to stay in "temporary" settlements for long periods of time. Many host countries have security fears and try to keep settlements physically separated from the rest of the country. Because of this, settlements are economically isolated and must rely on international aid and the generosity of the host country for food, clothing, and other necessities. Over time, the amount of economic support may dwindle, causing unrest in the warehousing areas. In the era of global terrorism, many countries try to isolate refugees because they fear that unwanted persons might be entering their country, but the isolation created can actually breed civil discontent and rebellion if the refugee areas are not properly cared for.

* Includes Afghans in a refugee-like situation.

** Government estimate.

*** The 300,000 Vietnamese refugees are well integrated and in practice receive protection from the government of China.

**** UNHCR estimate based on 10 years of individual recognition of asylum seekers. Figures exclude resettled refugees.

▲ **Figure 5D.3**
Repatriation is the process of moving refugees back into their home country or region. On the surface, this seems to be a positive event, but the process can be difficult. For example, the recent crisis between government forces and rebel groups

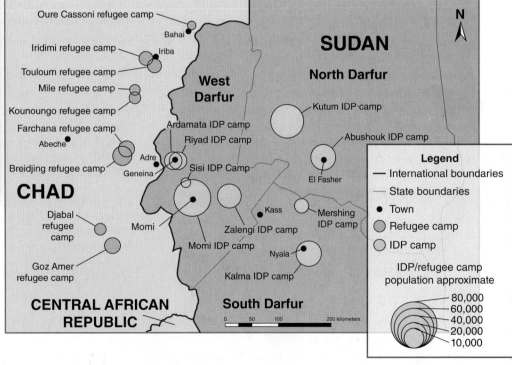

in the Darfur region of Sudan created an estimated 2 million refugees in Sudan or in neighboring countries, such as Chad and Kenya. But in January 2005, a cease-fire was agreed upon and, although violence continued, some groups began talking about the possibility of moving refugees back into their home regions in Sudan. But officials and aid groups faced many challenges. First, many areas had been destroyed by fighting, so roads, buildings, and other key aspects of the infrastructure needed to be repaired at significant cost. Next, a security apparatus needed to be installed to make returning migrants feel safe enough to return. Legal issues also needed to be addressed. For example, when refugees leave in large numbers, their homes and property are often occupied by other people or groups. When the refugees return, they naturally want their land and belongings back, so a legal system must be in place to handle complaints and claims.

5E   Why Do People Migrate?

So why do people migrate? Geographers and other social scientists have pondered this question for more than a century. The decision to move, sometimes far from homeland and family, is one of the most important choices that a person ever makes. Think of how afraid and uncertain a young European peasant farmer must have been in 1900 to leave his farm and the only place he has ever known to take his entire family to America. Today, the same feelings may be experienced by a teenage Filipino girl who decides to leave home to work as a house servant in Saudi Arabia or Kuwait.

The theories put forward are quite varied. The earliest modern theory of migration dates back to the 1880s and a British geographer named Ernst Georg Ravenstein. Ravenstein studied migration within Great Britain and came up with a few generalizations about population movements. In a paper published in 1885, Ravenstein outlined a series of "laws" that he felt governed migration. **Ravenstein's laws** of migration are as follows:

1. Most migrants travel only a short distance and toward major cities or industrial areas, what Ravenstein called **centers of absorption**. The longer the distance to be traveled, the fewer the migrants that can be expected. In other words, more people migrate a short distance than a long distance.
2. As migrants move toward these centers of absorption, they leave gaps, which are filled by migrants from farther away. This creates a flow of migrants from remote areas to less remote areas and finally to the cities.
3. Flows of migration also create counterflows that take people away from the cities, but in less numbers.
4. Long-distance migrants are more likely to be heading to a major city.
5. Urban residents are less likely to migrate than are people who live in the country.
6. Women migrate more than men, but they tend to migrate shorter distances. Ravenstein believed that long-distance migrants were more apt to be men.

Ravenstein's observation that more people move short distances compared to long distances is a good example of the idea of distance decay (see Module 1F). **Distance decay** simply means that we expect more interaction among places that are closer rather than farther away, a concept known as **Zipf's law**. In other words, more people will migrate to closer places than far-away places. In terms of migration, this generally makes sense because migrants have more information about nearer places and are more likely to be able to

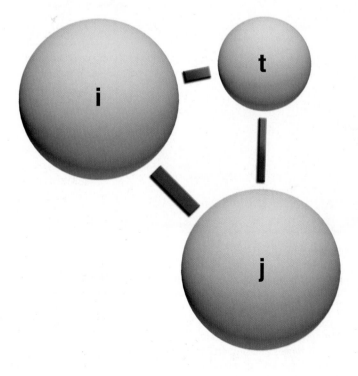

◀ **Figure 5E.1** A more recent geographic concept known as the **gravity model**, which we introduced in Module 2E, is largely based on the idea of distance decay. The gravity model describes the interaction between two cities, such as migration, as a function of the population of the two cities and the distance between them. Just as in physics, where the force of gravity is greater between objects with larger masses, two large cities will have more interaction between them than one large city and one small city. In this example, we would expect there to be more migration between cities *i* and *j* than between *i* and *t* or *i* and *j*. Is this model too simplistic?

get to nearer places. Because of this, if migrants wish to travel to somewhere far away, they will often move to a closer town, then to a town farther away, and so on until they reach their final destination. This kind of movement pattern is referred to as **step migration**.

Whether or not Ravenstein's ideas are just theories or actually "laws" has been debated for over a hundred years. A good example of a migration stream that defies Ravenstein's laws, and one that Ravenstein himself recognized, was the movement of American immigrants to the rural frontier far from major cities. This is counter to Ravenstein's initial theory that most long-distance migrants head to major cities. But in general, Ravenstein's ideas have held up well. Also, the speed at which people can move around the world may change the assumption that migrants move to nearby areas more than far-away destinations. Everywhere in the world is now only a day's travel by air.

One of the most important migration theorists was Everett Lee. In 1966, Lee put forward what is commonly referred to as the **push-pull model** of migration. Lee felt that there were factors that pushed people away from their homelands and pulled people to new areas. Take a moment to think about what reasons you feel would push a person from his or her home. Certainly, poverty, unemployment, war, violence, and social inequality are among the most important push factors. Pull factors might include job opportunities, religious freedom, and overall quality of life.

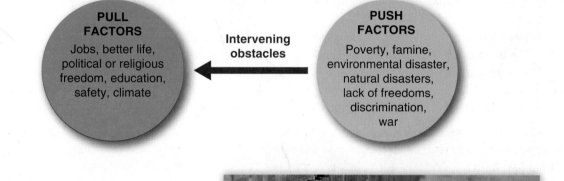

PULL FACTORS
Jobs, better life, political or religious freedom, education, safety, climate

Intervening obstacles

PUSH FACTORS
Poverty, famine, environmental disaster, natural disasters, lack of freedoms, discrimination, war

Figure 5E.2 ▶ Everett Lee acknowledges that, in addition to push and pull factors, other considerations are important. First is what are called **intervening obstacles**. These are variables that a migrant must consider when weighing the pluses and minuses of a potential move. Most significant are the cost of the move, the difficulties of crossing borders and obtaining visas, and the psychological difficulties of breaking ties with friends and family. For example, a migrant may want to leave his or her home country, but if the person thinks he or she will have little chance to obtain an entrance visa, the person may choose not to try the move. In the photo, a member of the US military works on a security fence along the border with Mexico. How do you think the debate over immigration in the United States might change the decision-making process of migrants intending to cross into the United States from Mexico?

Child

Birth

Birth of siblings

Starting school

Starting high
  school

Finishing high
  school

Young Adults

Starting college

Ending college

Getting a new job

Marriage

Job promotion

▲ **Figure 5E.3** Another factor in the decision to migrate is a person's **life cycle**. People are more likely to move at critical times in their lives. For example, a couple may choose to move right before the birth of a child, or just after it. They may then choose to move just before or after the child is old enough to enter school in order to take advantage of a better school. Or they may delay a move to let a child finish high school. College is a time when many people around the world migrate away from their homes for the first time, while their parents consider leaving a large but now empty house for a smaller one. Graduation from college often brings another move, as does employment. Toward the end of our lives, many people move closer to family or to a retirement community.

The theorist Samuel Stouffer added to migration theory by introducing the concept of **intervening opportunities**. He said that the amount of migration movement between two places, A and B, is affected by the number of other possible migration destinations that a migrant leaving location A can choose from before reaching B. If other locations with positive characteristics are available, the migrant may choose to stop and settle there. So an immigrant who reached the United States in 1900 might have made the decision to go on to Chicago, but if he or she were offered work in New York, the person might have chosen to stay there.

Economics is obviously a key component of many migrants' decision to move, and economists and economic geographers have used that fact to think about migration. One microeconomic model of migration is the **factor mobility model**. This model argues that differences in wage rates cause people to migrate from low-wage areas to high-wage areas. In reality, this does not always happen. For example, a new migrant who does not find a job after moving to a new area might choose to return home, even though wages are lower there. Second, people sometimes choose to stay in one place for personal reasons, even if a higher wage can be earned elsewhere. Another economic model is the **human capital model**, which argues that people move not just for macroeconomic reasons but also for individual reasons. Specifically, people who have the most to gain and the least to lose are those most likely to migrate. For example, many young people have no real job to leave, and because they can earn money for decades, they are more likely to migrate. Furthermore, the educated are more likely to migrate because they are better able to get a job when they get to their destination, and thus the risks are lower.

To many theorists, psychology is quite important to the decision to migrate. Few migrants know exactly what is going to happen when they get to their destination. What is important is what they think is going to happen. If they predict that they will find a good job, that belief alone might be enough to stimulate a move. Behavioral geographers have repeatedly shown that perceptions about the world are often just as or even more important than reality in governing human geographic behavior.

Older Adults

Retirement

Death of a spouse

Failing health

5F Consequences of Migration

The movement of large numbers of people in or out of an area can lead to significant challenges for the receiving or the sending area. So many people entered New York City in the 1830s and 1840s, for example, that housing demands could not keep up. Landlords in the Five Points section of the city, depicted in the movie *Gangs of New York*, took to cramming people into small tenement apartments. A single building 25 feet wide and 70 feet deep might house over two dozen families, each occupying a space of about 180 square feet. Today, housing continues to be a challenge in areas taking in large numbers of immigrants, but the effects of immigration are more widespread than just lodging. In general, the consequences of migration can be characterized as demographic, economic, or social.

Demographic consequences occur when migrants change the basic structure of a population. In Module 3H, we looked at population pyramids for Persian Gulf oil states that import large numbers of young men to work as laborers. This type of migration has skewed the demographic profile of countries such as Kuwait, Saudi Arabia, and the United Arab Emirates. Many southern US states, such as Florida and Arizona, have higher-than-expected numbers of older people because retirees have resettled there.

Naturally, the ethnic composition of a population can also be affected by immigration. The US population is increasingly Hispanic and Asian because of Latin American and Asian immigration. Populations of both groups are expected to triple by 2050. One consequence of this is that the white, non-Hispanic population will decrease from nearly 70% of the population today to approximately

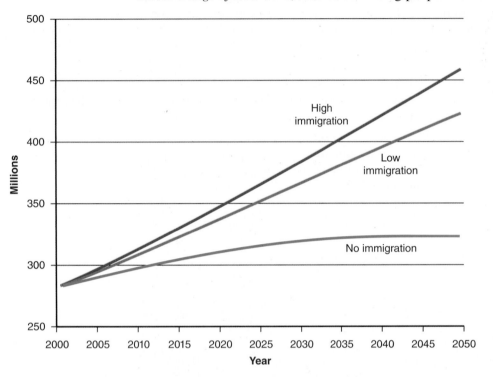

▲ **Figure 5F.1** The US Census Bureau estimates that, if all immigration into and out of the United States had stopped in 1992, the country's population would have been 8 million people less in 2000 than recorded. By 2050, the US population may be over 100 million persons larger than if immigration had stopped in 2000. This chart shows what the US population growth might look like with no net migration, low rates of net migration, and high rates of net migration. Immigrants, once they settle, often start families, so it is not just the number of people arriving that matters, but also the long-term addition to the population by the children of immigrants. Because immigrants tend to be younger, the proportion of the elderly in a receiving area can actually decrease when immigrants arrive in large numbers.

Figure 5F.2 ▶ Immigration can also have a positive effect on an economy when the migrants bring skills that the host country needs. For example, in the United States many rural areas, small towns, and poor urban neighborhoods rely on foreign-trained doctors and nurses who are willing to work for salaries that are below US averages for medical professionals but higher than in their home countries. Special visa exceptions, although cut during the 1990s and after the 9/11 attacks, allow some of these professionals to stay in the country longer than most temporary migrants.

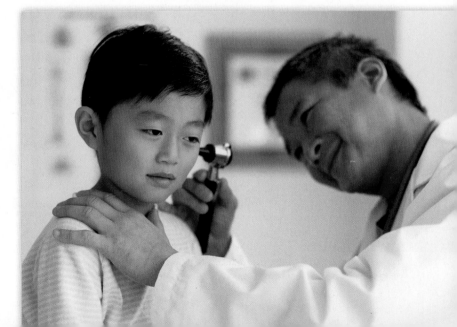

◄ **Figure 5F.3** The Irish, such as this immigrant boy in 1916, are a good example of a group much maligned when they first arrived in the United States in the nineteenth century. Since many New Yorkers were English, they carried preexisting prejudices about the Irish. Many residents were also anti-Catholic and distrusted Irish immigrants. So strong was the mistrust that many shopkeepers placed "No Irish" signs in their store windows. New Irish immigrants were offered jobs considered to be too dangerous for slaves. The loss of a slave was a cost too great to bear, but the loss of an Irish immigrant was not so disconcerting. In Boston, a key destination for Irish immigrants, a political party named the Know Nothings rose to power in the 1840s on a strong anti-Irish agenda. The party quickly held numerous local and state positions, including several governorships. These political leaders instituted anti-Irish laws, such as forcing students to read from the Protestant King James Bible in school. Poor Irish immigrants were also targeted for deportation back to Ireland for being a drain on the local economy. In San Francisco, two Irish immigrants were lynched. In time, Irish Americans rose up the social ladder and discrimination waned.

50%. At the same time, the Hispanic population will rise from under 13% of the population in 2000 to over 24% by midcentury, and the Asian population will double, from 4% to 8%.

Immigration also has **economic consequences**, and these can be either positive or negative. During the Industrial Revolution in Europe, population levels rose sharply. The need to house, feed, educate, and employ this population increase strained many European societies. Luckily for Europe, the United States and Canada began welcoming immigrants in large numbers to work in the growing industrial and agricultural sectors of the North American economy. Thus, migration served as a safety valve for Europe.

Immigration also creates debates over the economic pros and cons of undocumented workers. Studies of the economic effects of illegal immigration in Arizona, some by anti-immigration groups, have argued that illegal migrants cost Arizona over $2 billion each year in health care, education, lost taxes, and public services. Immigration advocacy groups counter that the taxes paid by illegal migrants and the benefits to companies from cheap labor offset the costs to local and state governments. Even if we separate the issues of legal and illegal migration, a large influx of people into an area will require more housing, more school rooms, and more health care facilities. In 2010, the debate over undocumented workers in Arizona erupted into a national debate when Arizona policymakers sought to step up efforts to identify illegal migrants in the state.

Finally, migration can have important **social consequences** for a society. In most cases, migration brings one group of people into contact with other groups of people. This can lead to better cultural understanding among the groups but also conflict and discord. The history of New York City is full of conflicts. As each new group of people arrived in the city (Irish, Italian, black, Chinese, Jewish, Puerto Rican, etc.), prejudice, resentment, and misunderstanding reared their ugly heads. Eventually, each of these groups, and countless others, became part of the fabric of the city, but at first there was conflict. This is true of large cities in Europe as well.

Figure 5F.4 ▶ Immigration can also create new connections between cultures that may have never interacted at a significant level—for example, the phenomenon of Cuban-Chinese restaurants. Chinese immigrants first arrived in Cuba in the middle of the nineteenth century to work on sugar plantations. In 1882, a law in the United States called the Chinese Exclusion Act banned Chinese laborers from entering the country. New immigrants sought other destinations, including Cuba and other Latin American countries. In addition, rising anti-Chinese sentiment within the United States impelled many Chinese Americans to leave for Cuba and other locations. By the mid-1800s, Havana had nearly 40,000 Chinese. But the communist revolution that brought Fidel Castro to power in 1959 forced many Chinese Cubans to flee. New York, with its large Chinatown, was a popular destination. However, many of these new immigrants no longer considered themselves Chinese. Many families had been in Cuba for a century and had adopted the Latin and Caribbean cultural traits of Cuban society. One result of this cultural merger was the evolution of food that reflected both Chinese and Caribbean diets. Today, several Cuban-Chinese restaurants remain in New York City and other American cities.

5G   Migration History of the United States

Obviously, the United States is a nation of immigrants. Nearly the entire US population has origins in some other part of the world. From a geographer's standpoint, we want to understand migration in three ways. First, we want to know when people migrated. Migration to the United States can be broadly grouped into four phases: the colonial period, the first wave of European immigrants, the second wave of European immigrants, and the era of restricted immigration. Second, we want to know where people came from during particular time periods. Third, we want to know where people settled during each time period.

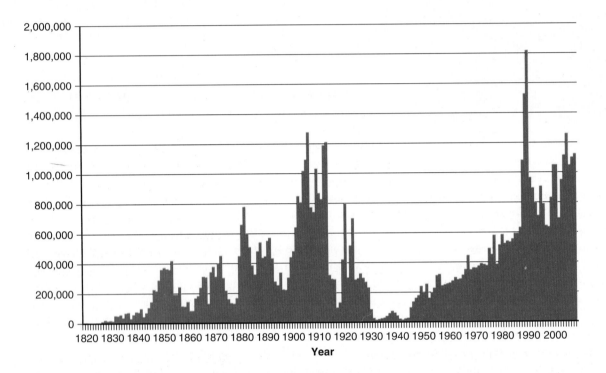

▲ **Figure 5G.1** This graph shows the amount of immigration to the United States from the early nineteenth century to today. Just by looking at the chart, try to explain why migration may have gone up or down at certain time periods. What happened to cause the peaks and valleys?

The **colonial period** of US immigration includes the period from about 1600 until the American Revolution. In general, migrants to the United States can be grouped into two categories: white northern and western Europeans and black Africans. Black Africans were brought against their will to the Americas as part of the forced migration of the Atlantic slave trade. About 360,000 Africans immigrated to the United States before 1790, and most settled in the American South because of the use of slaves for agriculture. European migrants before 1790 were largely from the British Isles (England, Ireland, Scotland, and Wales) and settled mostly in New England and the Southeast. Migrants to the Hudson Valley of New York and the Middle Atlantic states were a bit more diverse and included a large number of Germans (over 100,000 before

◀ **Figure 5G.2** These children are preparing for a Scandinavian festival on Washington Island, Wisconsin, in 1957. Over 50 years later, there is still a Scandinavian-themed festival held yearly. When large numbers of migrants from the same region settle in a particular area, they often bring aspects of their culture that persist for decades or even centuries.

◀ **Figure 5G.3** Ellis Island, pictured, was the arrival point for millions of immigrants in the late 19th and early 20th centuries. In 1921, the US government passed the first of several sets of laws to put restrictions on migration. The effect of these laws was that the number of immigrants during the 1920s, 1930s, and 1940s was significantly lower than in previous decades. The global depression of the 1930s and World War II also greatly disrupted migration patterns. After the war, migration slowly increased as the government gradually relaxed immigration rules, but more importantly, the source location for most migrants changed. Today, most migrants to the United States do not come from Europe but, rather, have homelands in Asia or Latin America. Because of this, recent immigrants have been more likely to settle in the American South, Southwest, and Pacific Northwest. In recent decades, the United States has also struggled with the issue of undocumented (illegal) immigrants. The number of illegal immigrants living in the United States is estimated at over 12 million.

1790) and Dutch (especially in the Hudson Valley). In the South and Southwest, many Spanish settlements were also established during this time period.

The **first wave of European immigration** occurred between 1800 and 1880. Like the colonial period, nearly all the migrants during this period were from western and northern Europe. England remained the largest supplier of migrants, but Germans, French, Scots, and Irish were also important components of the immigration stream. When reading about immigration during this period, you might also hear the term Scots-Irish (or Scotch-Irish). This refers to Scots who migrated to Northern Ireland from the seventeenth century onward, then later to North America. Unlike most Irish settlers, most Scots-Irish were Protestant. Overall, nearly all of the new European settlers during this time period settled on the East Coast. Why? At that time, it was the only territory the United States controlled. Toward the end of this period, especially after 1840, railroads increasingly allowed people to move away from the coast, so the first "frontiers" of the United States—such as the Appalachians, western Pennsylvania, western New York, and the eastern parts of the Midwest—were settled largely by western and northern Europeans.

The **second wave of European immigration** is the period from 1880 until 1921, when the first serious immigration restrictions were passed into law. During this phase, immigration reached hundreds of thousands of people per year. The primary change during this period of migration was the origin of the migrants. Although most continued to come from Europe, there was shift from western and northern European to eastern and southern European countries of origin. Increasingly, Italians, Poles, Scandinavians, Hungarians, Russians, and Greeks replaced English, Irish, and French migrants. Although many of these migrants settled in eastern US cities, such as Boston, New York, and Philadelphia, because the frontier had moved westward, many migrants during this period settled in the Midwest and Great Plains. Some parts of these regions still have very high concentrations of a particular European ethnic group.

Figure 5G.4 ▶ In recent decades, immigrants to the United States have increasingly come from Asia and Latin America, rather than Europe. Where have these immigrants settled in the country?

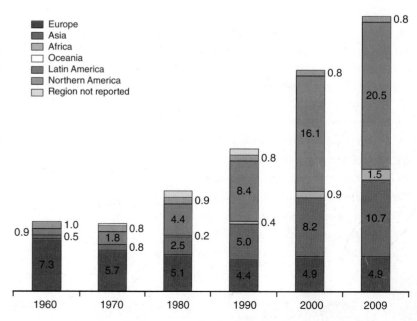

Key Terms

asylum seeker (5D)
centers of absorption (5E)
child soldiers (5C)
colonial period (5F)
cyclical movements (5A)
demographic consequences (5F)
distance decay (5E)
economic consequences (5F)
factor mobility model (5E)
first wave of European
    immigration (5F)
forced migration (5B)
free migration (5B)
gravity model (5E)
gross migration (5B)
guest workers (5A)
human capital model (5E)
human trafficking (5C)
impelled migration (5B)
in-migration (5B)
internally displaced persons (5D)
internal migration (5A)
international migration (5A)

intervening obstacles (5E)
intervening opportunities (5E)
life cycle (5E)
mass migration (5B)
migration (5A)
net migration (5B)
out-migration (5B)
periodic movement (5A)
primitive migration (5B)
push-pull model (5E)
Ravenstein's laws (5E)
refugee (5D)
refugee warehousing (5D)
remittances (5A)
repatriation (5D)
restricted migration (5B)
rural-to-urban migration (5B)
second wave of European
    immigration (5G)
social consequences (5F)
step migration (5E)
Zipf's law (5E)

Advanced Review Questions

1. Are there still examples of primitive migration in the world today? If so, where? Will it continue?

2. What are the consequences of rural-to-urban migration for a country? Think about what must be accomplished to accommodate rising urban populations.

3. Why is repatriation difficult? What other options do countries and international organizations have?

4. Are Ravenstein's laws valid today? What parts are no longer valid? Why?

5. Is the push-pull model valid or too simplistic? What are the primary push and pull factors for today's migrants? Have these changed from a century ago?

6. Does distance decay still apply in a modern world, with the Internet and advanced technology?

7. Compare and contrast the factor mobility model and the human capital model.

8. Trace and explain the history of migration in the United States from the colonial period onward. What were the push-pull factors at each time of high migration in US history? What were some of the barriers to migration throughout US history? Finally, where did immigrants settle during each major period of US immigration?

Basic Review Questions

1. What percentage of people in the developing world live in cities?
2. Define *migration*.
3. What is meant by *cyclical movements*?
4. What is periodic movement?
5. What are remittances, and what is their importance to guest workers?
6. What are the different types of migration?
7. What are some historical examples of forced or impelled migration?
8. How is China's Three Gorges Dam related to migration?
9. What is the difference between net and gross migration?
10. What is human trafficking?
11. What is the difference between a migrant and an internally displaced person?
12. Explain refugee warehousing.
13. What is repatriation?
14. Explain Ravenstein's laws.
15. What is meant by *distance decay* and *Zipf's law*?
16. Explain step migration.
17. What are intervening opportunities?
18. What are some of the demographic consequences of migration?
19. What are some economic consequences of migration?
20. What are the social consequences of migration?
21. What was the second wave of European immigration?

Further Study Topics

- Apply the concepts of social, demographic, and economic consequences to the debate over Mexican and Latin American migration to the United States. Do theories of migration adequately address illegal migration, or are they designed to explain only legal migration?

- In some cases, refugees have been living outside of their country or region of origin for decades. Does the international community have any responsibility for solving lingering refugee problems?

- How does technology affect migration in the world today? Speculate on some of the effects of economic, transportation, and communication technologies on the decision of migrants to move.

- Where does the use of child soldiers persist in the world? Why don't more governments try to stop it?

- Human trafficking for sex remains a billion-dollar, global industry. Research the current patterns of the global sex trade and discuss the geographic and other factors that allow it to persist. Where are the most troublesome locations for sex trafficking? Does the problem affect the United States?

- Are US immigration laws, either historically or presently, motivated by racism or ethnic bias? Why or why not?

Summary Activities

On the graphic below, indicate the following:

In Box 1, sketch the number of migrants that came to the United States each decade.

In Box 2, briefly indicate where migrants came during each time period.

In Box 3, indicate where migrants settled during each time period.

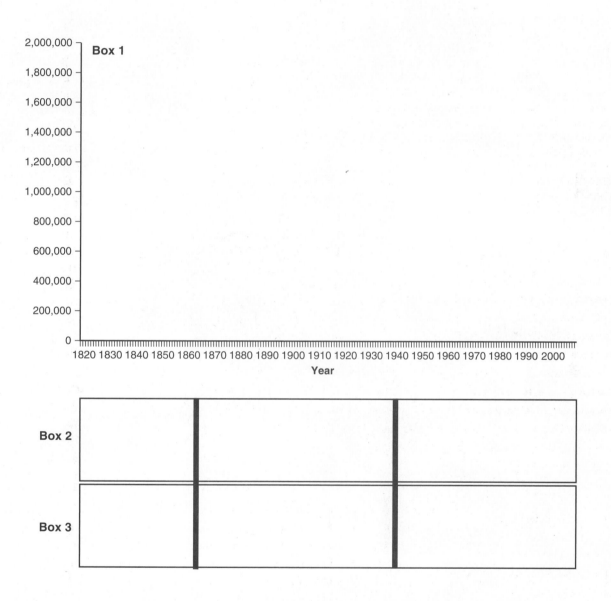

CHAPTER 6

Culture and Cultural Landscapes

CHAPTER MODULES

If we asked you "What are you?" how would you answer? What defines you? How do you see yourself? If you had to describe yourself and your place in the world, what would you say? Humans derive their identity from many different sources, so naturally the answers to this question would be extremely diverse. Some people define themselves based on where they live ("I'm a Texan"), while others might refer to religion ("I'm a Muslim"). Still others might use race or ethnicity as an identifier ("I'm Asian") or a historical marker in their lives ("I'm a Holocaust survivor"). Someone might use nationality ("I'm British"), political beliefs ("I'm a Republican"), or an occupation ("I'm a firefighter").

Who we are as humans is complicated, but a great deal of identity in the world is derived from our cultural and ethnic backgrounds. Culture and ethnicity are difficult concepts to understand, but they are the focus of a great deal of attention by geographers. Culture and ethnicity are both etched on the global landscape for us to see and study, and they are often the source of conflict and pivotal points in history. In this chapter, we look at culture and cultural geography in general. In the next two chapters, we investigate religion and language, two important components of culture, and then in Chapter 9 we focus on ethnicity and the geography of ethnic groups.

6A   Culture and Cultural Geography

Cultural geography is the study of both the distribution and diffusion of culture traits and how the culture modifies the landscape around us. It is an important subfield within the discipline of geography and has contributed a great deal to the larger field over the past century. But what exactly is culture and what is a culture trait?

Culture can be defined as shared patterns of learned behavior, attitudes, and knowledge. This is just one of countless definitions, but it works for our purposes. We can break down the definition a bit further.

What is meant by "shared patterns"? This means that things that are part of our culture are believed or practiced by a lot of people, so toothpaste is part of our culture because a lot of people use it. But if you brush your teeth with mustard, it should not be considered part of our culture because it is not a behavior shared by a lot of people. The word *patterns* also implies that we will find an element of a culture repeated over and over again in different places.

The word *learned* is important because it excludes race as a part of culture. Culture is not inherited. It is taught to children as they grow up. For example, if a racially Asian baby is raised in the United States by white Polish immigrant parents, will the baby grow up speaking Japanese and eating miso soup for breakfast? Not unless that is what the parents teach their child. Both language and food choices are taught or learned as we grow up. Many times race and culture seem to be related because skin color is often a common feature across a cultural group, but it is not a requirement.

▲ **Figure 6A.1 Culture in the Landscape** Look at this photo and try to identify all of the things that are traits of American culture that might not be found around the world. How many can you see? Don't just think about what people are wearing or doing, although that's important. Also think about what the photo says about what Americans value. Can those things be seen in the photo?

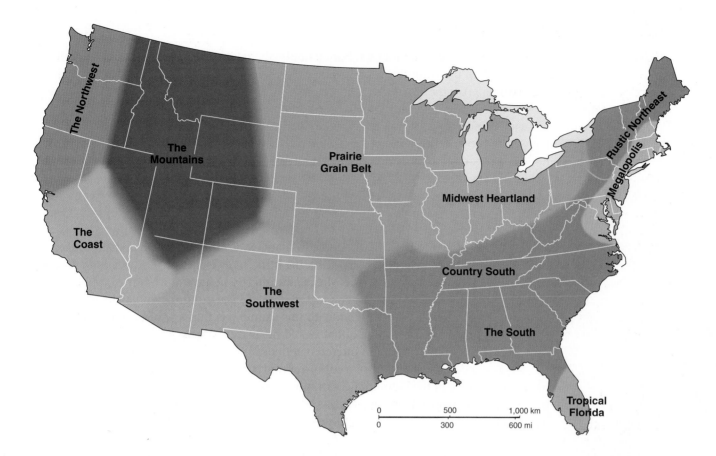

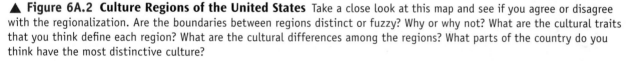

▲ **Figure 6A.2 Culture Regions of the United States** Take a close look at this map and see if you agree or disagree with the regionalization. Are the boundaries between regions distinct or fuzzy? Why or why not? What are the cultural traits that you think define each region? What are the cultural differences among the regions? What parts of the country do you think have the most distinctive culture?

Scholars refer to a single component of a culture as a **culture trait**. The wearing of a baseball cap by an American teenager is a trait of American culture that is less common in some other places in the world. So, too, is eating cereal for breakfast or using certain slang terms. These are all culture traits of American and many other cultures. This raises an important point. Culture traits do not have to be unique to one culture. In France, for example, people do not work on Sunday, sharing a culture trait with the United States and Canada related to religious beliefs. But most people in France speak French, while only a portion of North Americans do the same. So we share some traits, while others are unique.

If an area shares a large number of culture traits, geographers refer to it as a **culture region**. North Africa could be defined as a culture region because of similarities in language (Arabic and Berber variants) and religion (Islam). In the United States, a region such as New England could be defined as the area in which many people root for the Red Sox, pronounce *chowder* "chowda," and use the word *wicked* as an adjective for something extreme, as in "It's wicked cold out there!"

Culture regions can be grouped into even larger areas called **culture realms** that are based on a few broad cultural similarities. For example, Northern Europe, Western Europe, the Mediterranean region, and Eastern Europe could be combined to form a European culture realm because there are general similarities in religion, daily life, and to some extent language. Can you think of culture traits that might be found in different European countries and not in Asia, sub-Saharan Africa, or even the United States? The history of the United States is closely tied to Europe's, but do we have cultural differences?

6B   Culture Complexes

Individual culture traits themselves are often related. For example, the common practice of giving employees Sundays off is a culture trait of the United States. Another fact about the United States is that the majority of Americans are Christians. Are these culture traits related? Yes, Sunday is the Sabbath to Christians. In many states, alcohol sales are prohibited on Sunday or Sunday morning. These regulations, commonly known as "blue laws," are related to Christianity and resting on Sunday. The leaders of many early colonial settlements considered the consumption of alcohol on the Sabbath to be improper and banned liquor sales outright. Thus, commerce, religion, and leisure time are all related culturally.

▲ **Figure 6B.1** How many movies or television shows can you name that feature cars?

When several culture traits are related, they can be referred to as a **culture complex**. Think of a culture complex as a bundle of culture traits that have something in common. The Masai culture of East Africa is often used as an example of a culture complex. Cattle are important to the Masai people in many ways. Cattle are the primary basis of their diet because the Masai eat and drink the milk, blood, and meat. Cattle are also the source of wealth and prestige in the Masai culture. If you have more cattle, you're more important. So diet and society are connected in the Masai culture complex because they have cattle in common. The problem with this example is that few of us have ever spent any time with the Masai, although that would be an amazing experience. This makes it difficult to really understand the interconnections among their culture traits.

A more accessible example of a culture complex in U.S. and Canadian culture relates to the importance of the automobile. For most Americans, cars are a source of status and prestige. Many people drive nice cars as a symbol of their place in society. Cars are also a key component of our popular culture. Movies are made about cars, such as *American Graffiti*, *Days of Thunder*, *The Fast and the Furious*, *Gone in 60 Seconds*, *Transformers*, and *Smokey and the Bandit*. Songs are sung about cars and driving, including "Route 66," "I Can't Drive 55," "Low Rider," and "Little Deuce Coupe." Just think about how many rock, country, and rap songs feature cars or trucks.

Automobiles are also part of our social fabric. The United States provides very little public transportation to its citizens because so many people have automobiles. The classic American vacation is to put the family in the car and drive somewhere, a scenario portrayed in movies going back a half century. College students relish the "road trip." Americans spend billions of dollars a year on things to hang in their cars to make them smell better or to put on the outside to make them look better. Teenagers often work their first jobs to save up for a car so they can have more freedom from their parents. Just think of how many movies and television shows use the image of a teenage couple making out in a car on a hill overlooking a city or town. It's part of our collective culture. All of these culture traits are interrelated by a connection to the common car.

Is there a geography to auto-related culture in the United States? Absolutely; the following are a few examples.

- Traditionally, the automobile industry was located in the northern and northeastern parts of the United States, in places such as Detroit, Michigan. Now, the industry has diffused to the South and to overseas locations. Thus, there is an economic geography to the automobile.
- People drive different types of cars in different states. Trucks are more popular in some areas than in others. One way of looking at popularity is to examine car theft statistics. A 2010 survey by the National Insurance Crime Bureau found that the Honda Civic was the most popular target of thieves in New York, while in Texas it was a Chevy pickup. In Ohio, it was the Dodge Caravan. There is clearly a geography of automobile preference.
- Almost all NASCAR Grand National drivers in the late 1960s were almost entirely from Virginia and the Carolinas. After 1970, due in part to greater national television coverage of the sport, drivers began to be drawn from the Midwest and Northeast. Now, NASCAR drivers come from nearly everywhere in the country, but there is still a concentration of racetracks in the southeastern states. Tracks outside this area are generally located relatively close to major metropolitan areas to ensure a large audience at races. Clearly, there is a geography of auto sports.

Figure 6B.2 What do these photos say about the role of cars in American culture?

6C   The Components of Culture

After exploring the idea of a culture complex of interrelated culture traits, it is clear that culture is a very complicated and multifaceted concept. Many Americans would consider hot dogs to be a part of American culture, but so are the ideas of democracy and freedom. So both hot dogs and democracy are elements of American culture, but clearly they are not similar things. Because culture covers the spectrum from basic physical objects to abstract ideas, geographers and other social scientists divide culture, and culture traits, into three subsystems: the technological subsystem, the sociological subsystem, and the ideological subsystem.

The **technological subsystem** is the material objects that a culture produces, as well as the procedures for using those objects. An individual culture trait that falls within the technological subsystem is known as an **artifact**. Usually when we use this term, we think of an archeologist digging up a shard of pottery or an arrowhead, but in this case the term is used in a much broader sense. Anything that a culture produces is an artifact. A pair of jeans, baseball cards, an iPad, and a bag of potato chips are all artifacts of American culture. Also included in the technological subsystem are the procedures or techniques for using these artifacts. For example, some Native American cultures made canoes. The techniques for making and using a canoe would be part of the technological subsystem, along with the canoe itself. How do you update a Facebook page? You probably know, but these procedures are modern techniques that someone living isolated from the modern world does not comprehend.

Of course, many modern artifacts are available to people all around the world. Given the nature of the global economy, technologies are widely distributed, so at least in this subsystem of culture there is a lot of **cultural convergence**, meaning that two or more cultures share culture traits to such an extent that many aspects of their cultures are very similar. Many Japanese regularly eat hamburgers and drink Coca-Cola, while many Americans regularly eat sushi and read manga (Japanese comic books).

The second subsystem of a culture is the **sociological subsystem**. This component guides how people in a culture are expected to interact with each other and how their social institutions are structured. If two people meet for the first time, are they expected to kiss, shake hands, bow, ignore each other, or fight? The acceptable response is guided by the culture. Similarly, how far apart should two people stand when talking to each other? In some cultures, this distance might only be a few inches, while in other areas of the world it may be several feet apart. Culture traits in the sociological subsystem are known as **sociofacts**. So the socially accepted Western norm of shaking hands when meeting someone is a sociofact.

Social institutions are also part of a culture's sociological subsystem. In some parts of the world, a family commonly includes parents, children, grandparents, and other close relatives. In the United States, nuclear families of just two parents and their children are more common. Single-parent families are accepted and commonplace in American culture, but this is not true of some other cultures. Government institutions are also governed by the sociological subsystem. In the United States, the leader of the country is elected. In other cultures, hereditary monarchs are accepted. The structure of legal and educational organizations also reflects our culture. For example, most American children have summers off from school. In the nineteenth century, the school year was structured to allow farm children the time to help care for crops when they were most needed. The structure of the education system was altered to meet the needs of the economic system. Today, although few Americans are full-time farmers, the structure remains.

◀ **Figure 6C.1 Artifacts 1**   Can you identify each of these objects? What would a person who lived 100 years ago think they are? How do these artifacts of our time represent our culture?

▲ **Figure 6C.2 Artifacts 2** Can you identify each of these common household objects from the nineteenth century? If not, what does that say about how our culture has changed? The objects are (a) an ice cream maker, (b) a clothes wringer, (c) a carpet beater, (d) a man's shirt collar (men used to replace the collar of a shirt), (e) a refrigerator (the ice goes in the top section), and (f) a holder to take canning jars out of hot water.

The third component of culture is the **ideological subsystem**, which is the ideas, beliefs, values, and knowledge of a culture. Individual culture traits in this subsystem are called **mentifacts**. Ideas such as democracy, freedom, and justice are values that some cultures hold important, while others do not. Americans see individual rights and freedoms as very important, and in general, individualism is encouraged and praised. But in some Asian cultures in which Confucianism is deeply ingrained, individualism is not as highly valued. Instead, loyalty to a group or an authority figure is more important. What was accepted as "freedom" in Nazi Germany was certainly not what was considered freedom in the United States during the same period. Finally, over time, values and beliefs can change dramatically.

As mentioned previously, all three subsystems of culture can be related. Religion, for example, often encompasses culture traits in each of the three subsystems. Certainly, the ideas and values that a religion teaches are mentifacts. But religions also affect social organizations, such as marriage or the treatment of elders. These norms of interaction are sociofacts. Finally, religious organizations produce all sorts of artifacts. Churches, temples, and mosques (and everything that fills them) are cultural artifacts. As we discuss certain religions in more detail in Chapter 7, think about how the ideological, sociological, and technological subsystems are affected.

Figure 6C.3 ▶ Mentifacts
What ideas in American culture are invoked in this photo of a man voting?

6D   Cultural Diffusion

The movement of culture traits from one place to another is called **cultural diffusion**. **Diffusion**, or **innovation diffusion**, is an important concept to geographers, and it generally consists of the movement of people, ideas, or things from a point of origin to another location over time. *Diffusion*, of course, refers to non-cultural phenomena as well as culture traits. Diseases, for example, diffuse across space and time (see Modules 4A and 4C). If one person in a dorm gets a bad cold, other people in the same building who come in contact with the infected resident may get sick. They, in turn, go to class and may spread it to other students. If these students live in a different dorm building, the disease may diffuse over the entire campus. But ideas and innovations can also diffuse. Rumors are a good example, spreading quickly from person to person. Geographers are interested in identifying the pathways of diffusion and understanding what **barriers to diffusion** exist to slow or stop movement.

Geographers have many terms and theories to describe and explain the concept of diffusion. Most phenomena begin somewhere, and sometimes we can identify the origin. The place where something begins is termed the **hearth**. Most phenomena have at least one hearth; some, such as agriculture, have multiple hearths. The hearth of a phenomenon can be well known. In the case of religion, the hearth is usually associated with a historical figure and, so, is known. In fact, it almost always carries a great deal of symbolic weight.

▲ **Figure 6D.1** We know that the hearth of Islam is Mecca. This place became enshrined in the Islamic religion and long ago emerged as a place of pilgrimage for the hundreds of millions of Muslims around the world.

Figure 6D.2 ▶ Hagerstrand divides his population into people who do not know of an innovation, people who do know the innovation but choose not to adopt it, and people who adopt the innovation. Over time, the percentages of adopters and of people who know of the innovation increase at the expense of those who do not know of it. If it is a successful innovation, many people who know of it will eventually adopt it. If there are some major barriers to adoption, the number of non-adopters will remain high, even as they gain knowledge of the innovation. Hagerstrand also includes a population of people who are simply too geographically isolated to have any knowledge of the innovation.

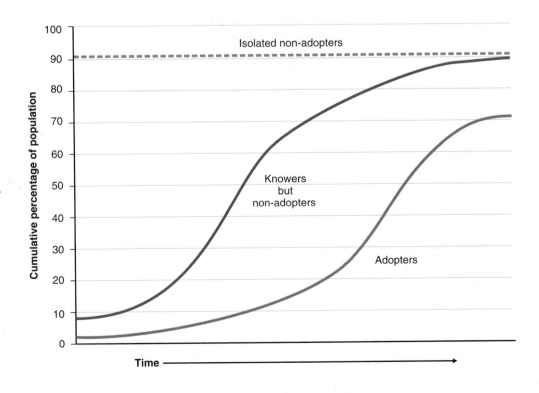

In the 1950s, Swedish geographer Torsten Hagerstrand developed a model of diffusion. While this process has been turned into a mathematical model, complete with equations, for our purposes let's consider this as a stage, or sequential, model that shows how diffusion progresses.

Diffusion results from the transfer of an idea or a thing from one place to another. The transfer can occur through communication, observation, marketing, or a physical means. The agent of diffusion is termed a vector, and the type of vector can help explain exactly how various items diffuse and where they are most likely to be experienced or adopted. In the case of diseases, the vector can be sexual contact (in the case of AIDS), mosquitoes (in the case of malaria), and drinking water (in the case of cholera) (see Modules 4D and 4E).

History is littered with countless "great ideas" that never caught on. So how does an innovation successfully broadcast to a larger group?

In his book *The Tipping Point*, Malcolm Gladwell came up with some interesting insights into how ideas or practices may diffuse by focusing on particular vectors. In his view, the diffusion occurs via a few basic principles. The first principle Gladwell terms "the law of the few." This means that ideas and items alike are diffused through the efforts of a select group of people. Some of these people may be particularly well connected to lots of other people. Some may be particularly well informed and good at explaining things to others. And some may be remarkably good at selling an idea. Each of these people helps move an idea to a larger population.

Gladwell calls the second principle the "stickiness factor." This refers to how well an idea resonates once it is introduced. People need to see a good reason for the idea or item and how to fit it into their lives. For many people, something as difficult as learning a new language or adopting a new technology becomes "sticky" only when there is a real need to learn.

The third principle introduced by Gladwell has to do with the "power of context." Diffusion relies on prevailing conditions: the place and time have to be right to accept the new thing; otherwise, it just falls flat.

The diffusion of an innovation depends on acceptance. Conversely, acceptance depends a great deal on what is being diffused. New technologies may be readily accepted as long as the price is right and the product is good. When videocassette recorders were introduced in the 1980s, it did not take long for electronics stores to sell them at a very rapid clip. These were clearly something that people found quite useful to their lives. Soon, specialty video stores opened up as a way to provide movies to rent. The introduction of DVD technology in the 1990s was also rapidly accepted.

But what if something represents a difficult change, often true of more profound cultural innovations? Consider what it would mean to change a language, religion, or way of making a living. Even when all of the circumstances are favorable to the diffusion, these attributes can take a very long time to be accepted.

▲ **Figure 6D.3** Paul Revere's message mobilizing residents from Boston to Concord worked because of who Revere was—a well-connected and respected man whom people listened to.

▲ **Figure 6D.4** *Sesame Street* has become the most successful children's program of all time because it divided its programming into several small chunks, retaining the attention of children used to the rapid-fire delivery of commercial television.

◀ **Figure 6D.5** Can crime be reduced by focusing on the little things? An influential theory suggests that criminal activity thrives in a context where small insults—graffiti, panhandling, petty vandalism—are allowed to occur. Clean up the context and people are less likely to commit major crimes. How might the physical appearance of a neighborhood encourage or discourage certain behaviors?

Geographers have categorized some of the spatial patterns involved in the diffusion of phenomena from one place to another. Three patterns have been commonly identified.

The first pattern is **relocation diffusion**, the diffusion of a particular phenomenon that results from the migration of people who practice that phenomenon. In other words, people move and take their cultural baggage, economic know-how, and technology with them. They also take diseases.

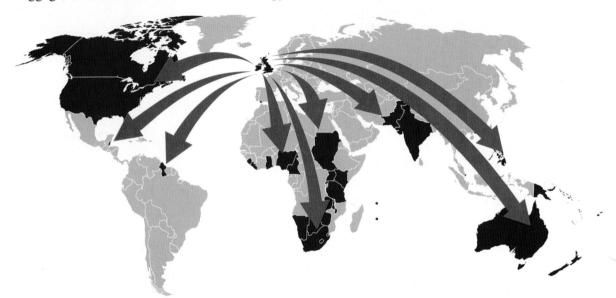

▲ **Figure 6D.6** From 1600 to 1900, the English language spread from England to much of the rest of the world. This map shows countries in which English is an official language. Much of the spread had to do with the movement of English men and women to these areas, taking their language with them. This did not have to be the case; in many instances of migration, people adopt the language of the place they move to, and the usage of their original language withers away after a couple of generations. This did not happen with English. Because migration is such a common occurrence, many types of phenomena have been spread via relocation diffusion.

▲ **Figure 6D.7** Walmart is an economic and cultural phenomenon that shows clear lines of dispersal from a hearth area in Arkansas to much of the rest of the Southeast, to its eventual saturation of most of the United States. Walmart's diffusion depended on a number of different things, most notably a marketing strategy. At the same time, it depended on locating stores in what it viewed as more hospitable terrain. Urban areas were mostly shunned in favor of small towns, although this has changed in recent years.

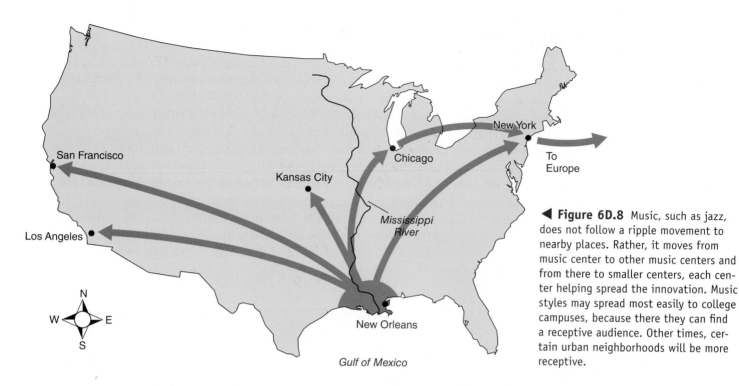

◀ **Figure 6D.8** Music, such as jazz, does not follow a ripple movement to nearby places. Rather, it moves from music center to other music centers and from there to smaller centers, each center helping spread the innovation. Music styles may spread most easily to college campuses, because there they can find a receptive audience. Other times, certain urban neighborhoods will be more receptive.

The second pattern is **contagious diffusion**. In this case, the phenomenon spreads to nearby places. Diffusion often depends on contact, close communication, and even observation. As a result, it makes sense that phenomena ripple out from the hearth. Some types of phenomenon that undergo this type of contagious diffusion are farming techniques, diseases, and sometimes different cuisines.

Diffusion patterns are not often continuous; phenomena can skip across space. **Hierarchical diffusion** is a pattern whereby things move from one place to other places that have some similarities or are otherwise going to be more receptive. These places are often large cities, college campuses, or places that share a cultural affinity with each other and the phenomenon being diffused. In fact, there can be all different types of hierarchies established when transmitting different phenomena from one place to another. The actual process of diffusion depends on what is being diffused. Fashions, contraceptives, and slang are examples of this kind of diffusion.

One could also consider a kind of **reverse hierarchical diffusion**, in which a particular innovation begins in places that are distinctly not centers and then over time begins to make its way up conventional hierarchies. Sometimes these are referred to as "groundswells" because they emerge from the smallest places. Some political movements, religious revivals, even sports have diffused in this way. This could be viewed as a type of hierarchical diffusion, but the process appears as a bottom-up movement rather than as a typical movement down the hierarchy.

Figure 6D.9 ▶ The populist movement of the 1890s was a reaction against the alleged stranglehold of northeastern banks and industrial interests on the agricultural heartland. Populism arose as a true grassroots movement, coming out of small towns and rural areas in the Great Plains. William Jennings Bryan later became the standard bearer for this movement, nominated by the Democratic Party to run for president three times.

6E   Culture Hearths

If culture traits diffuse out from a point of origin, where did significant aspects of human culture begin? For a great many aspects of human culture, the answer to this question is vague. We often know roughly where a particular innovation began, but not exactly where. Roughly 8,000–10,000 years ago, the domestication of agriculture and livestock led to civilization, the settling down of people in permanent settlements. This dramatic change from a wandering, nomadic way of life led to surpluses in agriculture (see Module 15D), allowing some members of society to devote their time to science, religion, trade, government, and engineering. Many of the innovations that they created are still parts of our culture today. Ideas such as mathematics, writing, legal systems, and religious ideas emerged out of these newly "civilized" urban areas. While individual innovations may have begun nearly anywhere on the planet, geographers and other scholars recognize a handful of places that had an unusually large impact on the planet by virtue of being the foundry that produced a large number of influential new ideas and technologies. These locations are referred to as **culture hearths**, areas from which important culture traits, including ideas, technology, and social structures, originated.

Mesopotamia

Many historians believe that civilization originated in Mesopotamia, an area now largely in Iraq. The word *Mesopotamia* means "between rivers," referring to the Tigris and Euphrates Rivers. This fertile area was ideal for early human populations to settle and farm. Early Mesopotamian civilizations included groups such as the Sumerians, the Babylonians, and the Assyrians. Their important contributions include the creation of writing, innovations in mathematics and astronomy that are still used today, and architectural developments that allowed them to build large ziggurats, pyramid-shaped temples. Perhaps the most widely mentioned contribution of Mesopotamia, however, is the development of complex legal systems, such as the Code of Hammurabi, developed starting about 3800 years before the present (1790–1750 BC). A series of 282 laws cover business agreements, marriage and divorce, property crime, and violent crime, such as "If any one gives another silver, gold, or anything else to keep, he shall show everything to some witness, draw up a contract, and then hand it over for safe keeping. If he turns it over for safe keeping without witness or contract, and if he to whom it was given deny it, then he has no legitimate claim."

The Americas

There were two important culture hearths in the Americas. Numerous cultural groups were located in the Andes Mountains of South America, culminating in the most well known, the Inca Empire. The Inca Empire arose in the fifteenth century and lasted until the arrival of the Spanish just a century later. The Incas unified the peoples of the Andes and are known for building thousands of miles of roads high in the mountains that still exist today. The Incas kept control by forcing a proportion of conquered peoples to resettle to other areas. Strong taxes were also levied to support the central government. They also established two capitals, one at Quito in the northern Andes and another at Cusco in the southern Andes, for better control over their long, thin empire. One legacy of the Incas is the persistence of Quechua, the empire's official language, which still is used today in the Andes. Meso-American civilizations, such as the Mayans, built elaborate pyramids that still survive today. The Aztec culture, centered on what is now Mexico City, had extremely complex religious systems, a detailed calendar, and an effective bureaucracy.

West Africa

For much of modern history in the United States and Europe, little was known or taught about the early cultures of sub-Saharan Africa, such as the important West Africa hearth. The reasons for this are complicated, but they include a lack of known written information and racism. Oral histories were common in this area, so many of the descriptions of these areas come from Islamic traders and others passing through. Some Western scholars simply refused to believe that ancient African peoples were capable of having established large political units. But we know today that ancient West African civilizations, such as Mali, Ghana, and Songhai, were impressive by any world standard. The Mali Empire, for example, flourished from the twelfth to sixteenth centuries AD in the broad grasslands south of the Sahara and along mighty rivers, such as the Niger. Trade in gold, salt, and other commodities at cities such as Timbuktu made the empire very wealthy and allowed art, religion, and other components of society to flourish.

Greco-Roman

The Greco-Roman culture hearth evolved a bit later than the others discussed here. Ancient Greece has its precursors in the Minoan civilization, which existed on the island of Crete between 2500 and 1500 BC, and the later Mycenaean civilization, which arose about 1400 BC. Classical Greece flourished after 800 BC and lasted for about 500 years. Although the Greeks had a well-organized political system, they are most remembered for their contributions to art, philosophy, and science. Significant legacies include the great philosophical works of Plato and Aristotle, some of the oldest surviving theatrical works, and contributions to science, such as the idea that the earth and the other planets revolve around the sun. Ancient Rome is traditionally said to have been founded in 753 BC, but the most important achievements of the civilization occur after the founding of the Roman Republic in 509 BC and the establishment of the Roman Empire in 27 BC. The empire began to collapse in the fifth century AD. While the Greeks are remembered for their scientific, artistic, and philosophical ideas, the Romans are recognized primarily for their achievements in government structures, military organization, engineering, and bureaucracy. Rome was able to extend far beyond its borders and control large areas of the world successfully and efficiently. A surviving geographic reality of the importance of Rome is the fact that large areas of Europe still speak languages derived from Latin.

Indus Valley

The early civilization of the Indus River valley was centered on cities such as Harappa and Mohenjo-Daro. Flourishing about 2500–1800 BC, the cities of the so-called Harappan civilization were arranged in a grid pattern and serviced by an early but working drainage system. Large communal baths, possibly for ritual purification, have also been uncovered. Excavations at Harappa also reveal organized facilities for storing and processing grain, which indicates the importance of agriculture to these early cities.

North China

The North-Central Chinese culture hearth was centered near where the Wei and Yellow Rivers converge. This area saw the domestication of millet and rice more than 7,000 years ago. Later, soybeans were also cultivated, as were tea and a variety of fruits and vegetables. Politically, the area included a variety of small, regional groups, but by about 5,000 years ago these groups had begun to interact more. By about 1,800–1,600 BC, many areas had been consolidated under what is called the Shang dynasty. The Shang period is remembered for elaborate bronze art, the first Chinese writing system, and a well-organized political system, which was based on kinship ties.

Figure 6E.1 Major Culture Hearths

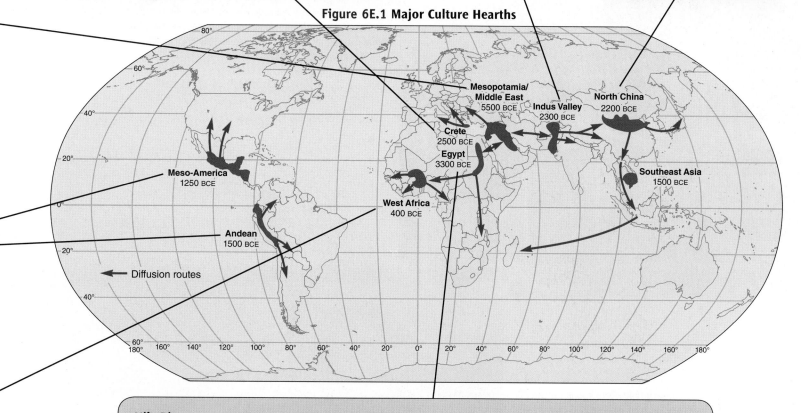

Nile River

For modern geographers, the achievements of the Nile River culture hearth are easier to envision because they left for us the glorious pyramids that have been a tourist destination for thousands of years. In fact, 2,000 years ago ancient travelers from around the Mediterranean would travel to Egypt to see them. But naturally, we know that the legacies of ancient Egypt go beyond giant burial structures. The Egyptians had complex theological, political, and social systems. The first dynasties arose just after 3000 BC and continued until the Macedonians conquered the region in the fourth century BC. Like other early culture hearths, the Egyptians cultivated a variety of grains and had a complex trade system. This allowed Egyptian science, math, and technology to influence other civilizations around the Mediterranean and to the south along the Nile.

6F   Cultural Landscapes

To many geographers, the central focus of cultural geography is the **cultural landscape**. As introduced in Module 1H, *landscape* refers to the appearance of a location, the items in a location that give it a particular appearance, or the general area itself. For example, *a natural landscape* might refer to the vegetation, rocks, and water bodies in that area. *The cultural landscape*, therefore, refers to the cultural impacts on an area, including buildings, agricultural patterns, roads, signs, and nearly everything else that humans have created.

North American geography's emphasis on the cultural landscape dates to the 1920s and a geographer named Carl Sauer. Before Sauer, the most common view of culture emphasized the effect that the natural environment has on culture, rather than the effect that culture has on the physical landscape. This view was epitomized by the notion of environmental determinism, which was addressed in Module 2D. Sauer was one of several geographers who challenged the view that nature determines culture. While he acknowledged that the physical environment can influence human actions, he emphasized that cultural groups modify their environments extensively.

If humans enter a wilderness area to settle, they will build towns that have buildings in the style that is popular in their culture. They might lay out the community in the same way as was done in their homeland. They may put up signs written in their own language. They may start farming using methods they learned

Figure 6F.1 Cultural Landscapes

◀ Ordinary, day-to-day landscapes are important to geographers because it is in these environments that our culture forms. Thus, we would expect culture, and change in culture, to be expressed here. What culture traits can you see in this photo? Which represent old ideas and which represent new?

▶ While our first tendency may be to focus on the mountains or trees, the imprint of culture is strong in rural areas. For example, in this photo from northern Italy, the cultural landscape includes not only the building and roads, including a Christian church, but also the land-use pattern. The large, grassy areas are the result of cultural preferences for grass around homes and agricultural traditions, such as grazing.

back at home. In each case, the structure or appearance of the landscape is modified. If two nearly identical areas of wilderness are settled by two distinct cultural groups, the resulting cultural landscapes will be different. As each group develops and adapts to the new area, its culture may change, and this change, according to Sauer, will be reflected in the environment.

Similarly, if an area is settled by a particular culture, but later another cultural group moves in, the landscape will be modified again. Over time, each new group tends to leave some evidence of itself in the cultural landscape. This was Sauer's main goal for cultural geography—using the cultural landscape to uncover evidence of past cultures. He, and countless geographers after him, focused on "reading" the visual clues in a landscape to identify and better understand past cultural influences in a particular area. For example, if you were in a largely Asian community but noticed that most of the street names were French, that would be a clue to a past reality about that area.

The emphasis so far is clearly on material culture, but later cultural geographers also note that cultural landscapes can reflect the presence of nonmaterial culture, including ideology or power. For example, many communities in the American South have great geographic disparities between where whites live and where blacks live. This spatial difference reflects the ideological culture trait, the mentifact, held by the majority of whites in the past that the two groups should not live near each other. The physical layout of the city was thus arranged to support this idea. Often, the two groups were literally separated by train tracks to add more of a barrier. A more recent example might be a community's acceptance or rejection of gay lifestyles. Some communities openly welcome the flying of the rainbow flag, a symbol of the gay community, but in other areas this might cause a backlash. Therefore, the liberal or conservative nature of the community might thus be visible.

That nonmaterial culture can be identified in the landscape reflects the work of late twentieth-century cultural and social geographers on the subject of the **social construction of space**. Namely, this is the idea that society shapes the spatial nature of our world. How is the cultural landscape of your community reflective of the values of your community?

▶ Researchers tend to focus on either locals' difference as a reflection of cultural or ethnic diversity or on similarities among places caused by some larger cultural or national ideal. Thus, local areas can be distinct, but also may be changing to reflect national trends. In other words, even though this Japanese neighborhood has a McDonald's restaurant, part of a global chain, it has not lost its local, Japanese character.

◀ Some landscapes show signs of recent change. In this scene, we can see the impact of recent Hispanic immigration into a community. The signs have both English and Spanish words, and the flags show a diverse clientele drawn from several different countries.

6G   Folk Culture and American Foodways

You will often hear the terms *folk culture* and *popular culture*, but what are the differences between the two? **Folk culture** generally refers to culture traits that are traditional, no longer widely practiced by a large amount of people, and generally isolated in small, often rural, areas. **Popular culture**, on the other hand, refers to aspects of a culture that are widespread, fast-changing, and transmitted by the mass media. Think about something like quilt-making. Although nearly every household had someone who could sew a quilt 200 years ago, today it is a folk tradition only. On the other hand, kids carrying lunchboxes featuring characters from the latest movie to elementary school is a popular culture fad. It is widespread and perpetuated by the popular media, but it is unlikely ever to be considered a "tradition."

One of the most common types of folk culture that affects daily life are **foodways**, which means how we prepare and consume food. While much of what we eat is motivated by popular culture (think of the latest kids' cereal with a cartoon character on the box), there are still folk traditions that affect food choices in some parts of the country. Before you read ahead, can you think of types of food that you eat in your part of the country that are not eaten as much in other regions? Why?

◄ **Figure 6G.1 New England Food** Traditional New England foods are a product of the region's geography. Seafood dishes, such as lobster and clam chowder, are common because much of the region's population lived close to the ocean. From native peoples the early settlers of New England were introduced to the "three sisters": corn, beans, and squash. Any traditional New England feast is bound to have something from at least one of these three categories, although corn was used less as a grain than it was in the South because wheat was available to richer residents through imports. Items like baked beans use ingredients such as molasses, which was not produced in New England at all but was readily available from European trading ships moving up the coast from the Caribbean before sailing back to Europe. With honey and maple syrup also available, New England foods are often sweet. Hot spices are rare in northeastern cooking because the climate is not conducive to growing peppers and hotter spices.

◀ **Figure 6G.2 Southern Food** Southern food is well known for having a distinct character. The reasons that Southern cuisine is different are due to geography and history. First, African slaves and immigrants made a huge impact on cooking. In many households, African slaves were responsible for nearly all food preparation and they changed the traditional recipes of their English owners to reflect their own traditions. The use of okra to produce thick soups and gumbos is a direct result of African cooking traditions. So is frying food, such as fried chicken and fritters. Both draw on West African techniques. Speaking of chicken, although foods like fried chicken are considered southern staples, it has become more common only in the last century. In the eighteenth and nineteenth centuries, chickens were most commonly used for eggs rather than meat. Pork was much more common as a meat in the South and continues as a typical southern food in dishes such as barbeque. Corn is also traditionally Southern. Foods like grits and hushpuppies are quintessentially Southern and can rarely be found outside the region. Try ordering a bowl of grits in Maine and you may have a hard time. Rice is also common in traditional Southern cooking but not Northern cooking. While we sometimes think of rice as Asian, rice growing was common in parts of Africa where slaves originated. Rice was introduced to the United States before 1700 and flourished in places such as South Carolina because slave laborers had prior knowledge of rice cultivation techniques. Many Southern soups utilize rice, and red beans and rice is a common Southern dish.

Figure 6G.3 ▶ Southwestern Food Southwestern foods represent the combined geographic influences of Mexicans, Spanish settlers, Native Americans, and eastern cowboys and migrants. The most notable difference between Southwestern cooking and the cuisine of the rest of the United States is the use of the chili pepper to make the food spicy. Beans and corn are widely used in Mexican and Native American cooking and continue to be popular in the region. The Spanish are responsible for introducing more meat into the diet, particularly pork and beef.

◀ **Figure 6G.4 Midwestern Food** Geographically, the Midwest was primarily settled by central, eastern, and northern Europeans. Foods in this region tend to make use of agricultural produce grown locally and are often simple and hearty casseroles and fruit pies. Because dairy products are abundant in the region, cheese and cream are often used in dishes such as casseroles. Grains are also common in the breadbasket of America, which allowed immigrants to continue to eat items such as Polish *pierogis* and various types of pancakes and allowed German immigrants to help make the region the beer capital of the country.

6H Popular Culture: House Types

Cultural geographers are traditionally quite interested in architecture because what we build often stays on the landscape for a long time. Thus, old buildings offer a way of examining cultural ideas of the past. For example, old school and government buildings often are named after people who were well known in their time but are generally unknown today, or the buildings may have carvings or artwork that represents what people in the past felt were important events or people.

House styles are an excellent way to examine popular trends of the past. People generally build new homes in the style that is popular at the time. Few people, for example, build castles today. If you drive through an area with new homes, they generally all look the same or at least have a small number of styles. People rarely build one-of-a-kind homes. Notice, too, that the colors of homes are usually quite limited. You rarely see a fluorescent orange home. Because people are relatively conservative about their home styles, most homes built in a certain decade are generally of the same small number of styles. And because homes usually stay around for decades or longer, we can often look at a home and tell roughly when it was built.

▲ **Figure 6H.1 Early American Homes** The typical home of the well-off colonial American was what we now call a *Georgian* style home. Notice in the photos that the homes are generally rectangular and the home's gables are on the side of the house. In other words, the roofline runs from the side of the home to the other side. On very old homes, the roof rarely overhangs the walls, as seen in this 1790 colonial in Connecticut (a). On homes built toward the end of the eighteenth century and into the early nineteenth century, this basic style was often supplemented with small flourishes, such as a semicircular fanlight over the front door, as seen in the second photo (b) showing the 1820 Davenport House in Savannah, Georgia.

◀ **Figure 6H.2 Early Nineteenth-Century Homes** In the early nineteenth century, Americans were in love with ancient Greek and Roman civilizations because we felt that our new republic was similar to these great ancient societies. Many towns that were founded during this time have classical names, such as Utica, Ithaca, Rome, and Athens, and children were sometimes given classical names, such as future president Ulysses S. Grant, born in 1822 (Ulysses was actually his middle name). Can we see this interest in ancient civilizations in our homes? Yes. Notice that Greek Revival homes from this era often have columns and other touches that make them look like ancient temples. (a) The first image is a home in Madison, Indiana, built in the late 1830s. For the first time in history, a large number of homes were built with front-facing gables. In other words, the roofline runs from front-to-back rather than side-to-side. Even smaller houses (b), such as this 1840s brick house in Madison, were front gabled. These features make the homes look more like ancient structures, such as the Parthenon.

Figure 6H.3 ▶ Mid-Nineteenth-Century Homes The (a) *Gothic Revival* and the (b) *Italianate* house styles were, for the most part, built between the 1840s and 1870s. Thus, if you see an area with a large number of these houses, it tells you that the area was flourishing at that time because a lot of people were building new homes. This was the era of railroad expansion, and many towns witnessed economic booms.

▲ Figure 6H.5 Victorian Homes *Victorian* homes were built from about the 1870s to 1900. Many of these homes have crazy rooflines, odd-shaped windows, porches, and ornamental designs on the outside walls. If you think about a bed & breakfast or a horror-movie house, chances are you're thinking about a Victorian home. These types of homes are rarely built today. The examples here are in the Queen Anne style of Victorian architecture and were built in 1893 and 1881.

▲ Figure 6H.4 Second Empire Homes The *Second Empire* style was only built between 1855 and about 1875, with most built in the 10 years after the Civil War. They were based on trendy styles in Europe at the time and feature the unique mansard roof. Because these were rarely built after the mid-1870s, they are a great indicator of an area that was booming just after the Civil War. Both of these examples were built in the early 1870s.

$2,065⁰⁰ Completely BUILDS AND FINISHES This $3,000.00 Ten-Room Residence

As Proven by Our FREE Plans, Specifications and Complete Itemized Bill of Materials. THESE PLANS ARE FREE OF CHARGE TO YOU ON CONDITIONS EXPLAINED ON PAGE 2.

▲ Figure 6H.6 Early Twentieth-Century Homes Common house types in the early twentieth century included *Prairie*-style homes, *Tudor* designs, and (a) smaller bungalow-style homes. Catalog homes, which could be purchased from Sears, Roebuck & Co. and other companies, were also common before World War II. (b) The Sears house, sold around 1910 for $2,065, would be delivered to the building site and the homeowner would hire local carpenters to assemble it.

Figure 6H.7 ▶ Post–World War II Homes Many Americans live in (a) split-level or single-level *ranch*-style homes. These smaller styles flourished in the baby boom era of the 1950s and 1960s. (b) By the 1970s, contemporary styles with unconventional shapes had begun to appear in large numbers, but today, home styles have returned to colonial and more traditional layouts.

6I   A Cultural Geography of Sports

Think about how important sports are in American society. Sports are intricately entwined with our cultural lives. In this section, as a case study, we explore the geography of sports and how the landscapes of sport reflect our cultural values.

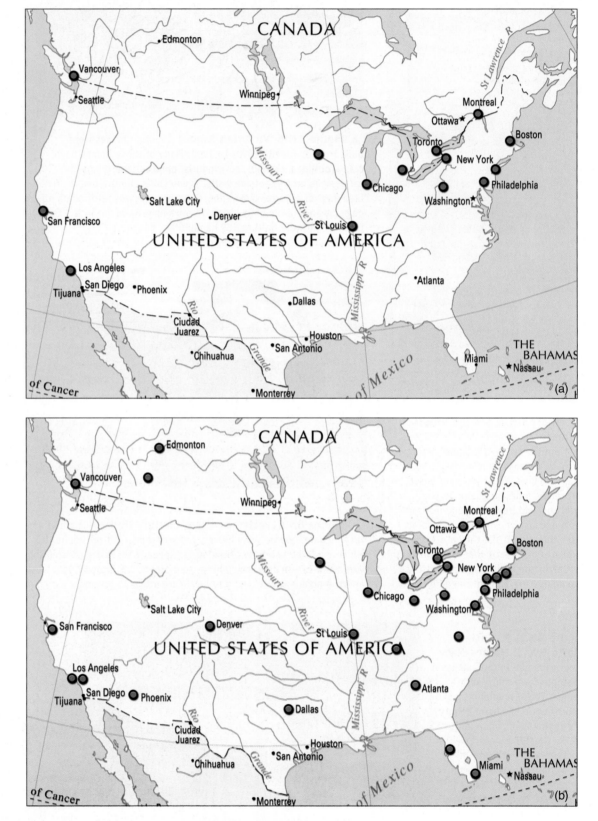

Figure 6I.1 ▶ Location of Pro Hockey Teams, 1971 and 2010 Geographers recognize that certain sports have specific patterns. Look at the maps of hockey teams in (a) 1971 and (b) 2010. In 1971, nearly all the hockey teams were in the northern United States or Canada. Why? Climate plays a large part. Hockey was traditionally played outdoors in cold environments. You simply could not play hockey in the southern United States until modern refrigeration technologies became available. And certainly not enough rinks existed in the South to support a fan base for a pro team. But what changed in the past decades that caused a southward migration of the sport? First, technology allowed indoor rinks to be more practical. But more importantly, the U.S. population shifted southward and westward. These areas of the country now have enough people to support major sports teams, and their populations are made up of transplanted northerners who grew up playing and watching hockey. So, in this case, demographic change spawned cultural change.

NASCAR is another sport that has expanded its area of cultural influence. Forty years ago, most NASCAR drivers were from the Southeast, but national television coverage of racing beginning in the late 1960s brought knowledge of stock-car racing to other areas.

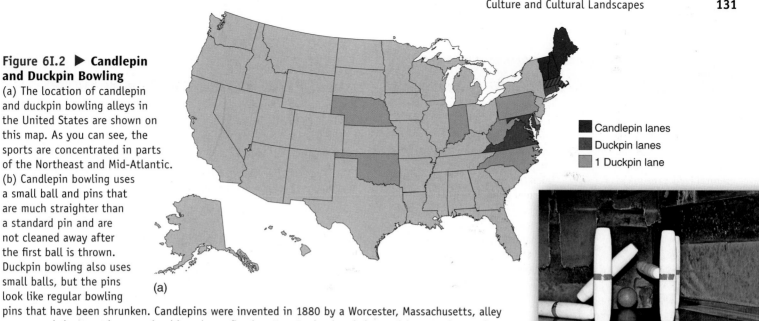

Figure 6I.2 ▶ Candlepin and Duckpin Bowling
(a) The location of candlepin and duckpin bowling alleys in the United States are shown on this map. As you can see, the sports are concentrated in parts of the Northeast and Mid-Atlantic.
(b) Candlepin bowling uses a small ball and pins that are much straighter than a standard pin and are not cleaned away after the first ball is thrown. Duckpin bowling also uses small balls, but the pins look like regular bowling pins that have been shrunken. Candlepins were invented in 1880 by a Worcester, Massachusetts, alley owner, and the sport has remained largely confined to New England and the maritime provinces of Canada. If you grew up outside this area, you may have never even seen the sport. Duckpins were probably invented in eastern Massachusetts as well in the 1890s but were introduced to the Baltimore area around 1900. Notice the pattern on the map. Because the sports are isolated in these areas and are not widely known, candlepin and duckpin bowling might be considered a folk culture sport. Can you think of other sports that are found in some areas of the country but not others?

It's obvious from our examples that the location of a sport on the landscape reflects the culture and people of the area to some degree. If you've been to a large US city, you've probably seen recent immigrants playing soccer on weekend mornings in parks where nobody played soccer 20 years ago.

Earlier in this chapter, we discussed the social construction of space. In other words, cultural geographers believe that what we build and how we organize our cities and towns reflects our culture. In modern American cities and towns, sports facilities are often given prominent locations. Large stadiums for professional teams are often given more priority than affordable housing or other infrastructure improvements. Sometimes these projects are justified because they generate economic revenue that helps the city, but other times sports stadiums are supported because they help the morale of the community. We want to rally around the home team, even if the economy is bad. In American culture, rooting for the home team is valued. Think about how many people have Super Bowl parties and you have a good idea of how important sports can be to Americans.

There's another way of looking at the cultural landscape of sports. Picture in your mind the inside of a major league sports stadium. Trying to understand a society's cultural values by observing the built environment is referred to as "reading the landscape."

Figure 6I.3 ▶ Pro Baseball Stadium Sports landscapes often indicate more about our society than just our entertainment or recreational preferences. Look carefully at the photo of Fenway Park and make a mental list of all the different things in this photo that indicate something about modern American or global culture. What do these say about American values? Do you see nationalistic or patriotic symbols? Economic symbols? Do you see indicators of social differences? If you had to analyze American society just from inside a major league baseball stadium, what would you conclude?

Key Terms

artifact (6C)
barriers to diffusion (6D)
contagious diffusion (6D)
cultural convergence (6C)
cultural diffusion (6D)
cultural landscape (6F)
culture (6A)
culture complex (6B)
culture hearth (6E)
culture realm (6A)
culture region (6A)
culture trait (6A)
diffusion (6D)
folk culture (6G)

foodways (6G)
hearth (6D)
hierarchical diffusion (6D)
ideological subsystem (6C)
innovation diffusion (6D)
mentifacts (6C)
popular culture (6G)
relocation diffusion (6D)
reverse hierarchical process (6D)
social construction of space (6F)
sociofact (6C)
sociological subsystem (6C)
technological subsystem (6C)

Basic Review Questions

1. Define *culture*.
2. What is a culture trait? Give a few examples.
3. Is culture inherited?
4. What is a culture region?
5. How are culture traits related to a culture complex?
6. Define and give examples of artifacts, sociofacts, and mentifacts.
7. What parts of our lives are included in the sociological subsystem?
8. What is the ideological subsystem?
9. What is cultural diffusion?
10. Explain the differences between expansion diffusion and relocation diffusion.
11. What is hierarchical diffusion?
12. Why is migration diffusion a type of relocation diffusion?
13. Describe some barriers to diffusion.
14. What is meant by *culture hearth*?
15. What are some important world culture hearths?
16. Where was the Mesopotamian civilization?
17. Where was the Harappan civilization?
18. Where was the culture hearth in ancient China?
19. What were some important culture hearths in sub-Saharan Africa?
20. What were some important culture hearths in the Americas?
21. What is environmental determinism?
22. Explain what is meant by the social construction of space.
23. Compare and contrast folk culture and popular culture.
24. What is a foodway?
25. What is a Georgian-style home? A Gothic Revival house?
26. What are some differences between Classical Revival and Greek Revival homes?
27. When was the Victorian period?
28. Describe some geographic patterns of sports in the United States.

Advanced Review Questions

1. What is meant by *reading the cultural landscape*? What can be learned from this technique?
2. What are some key ways in which culture is passed along to young children?
3. What culture regions in the United States do you think are most distinctive? Is your school in a well-known culture region? If so, what are the boundaries of that region?
4. The text discusses the culture complex of the car. What other important culture complexes can you identify in US or Canadian society?
5. Identify examples of culture convergence in modern society. Specifically, what common elements of our culture are borrowed from other cultures?
6. What are the most important artifacts, mentifacts, and sociofacts in the culture of your country or region?
7. How does the Internet affect cultural diffusion in the world today?
8. What were the important contributions to world culture of the ancient culture hearths?
9. How are food patterns in the United States related to the country's cultural history?
10. Explain how house types can be used to date an area of the United States. Why are houses a good cultural artifact? In other words, why are homes so indicative of particular time periods and cultural attitudes at those times?

Further Study Topics

- What mentifacts in American or Canadian society are driving the primary political debates of this era? Have those critical ideologies changed with time? How? What were the important mentifacts in American culture at the time of the American Revolution?

- How is jihadist Islamic fundamentalism different from contemporary American culture from a perspective of the technological, sociological, and ideological subsystems of culture? Which subsystem is the most important to understanding the clash of cultures?

- Research the hierarchical diffusion of design in the fashion industry, focusing on how ideas generated in places such as New York, Paris, and Milan end up in "big box" stores in small towns.

- Are there culture hearths in the world today? Imagine you're a cultural geographer 2,000 years from now. What will you describe as the culture hearths of this era? Some would argue that the United States is the center of global culture. Do you agree or disagree?

- Examine how ancient African cultures were treated by European historians and scholars over time. Did Eurocentrism or racism lead to an undervaluing of the accomplishments of African society? Did European attitudes about African culture contribute to the slave trade? Do unfair stereotypes about Africa exist today?

- How do city governments socially construct space to change the culture of a city? Think about the renaming of places or roads, development projects, gentrification, and similar initiatives.

- Many scholars have argued that the United States has more and more "placeless" locations because of the proliferation of chain stores. For example, Home Depot, Barnes & Noble, and Walmart are common everywhere. Are we moving toward a country with no regional culture? Is there a single American culture without regional variations?

Summary Activities

Study the map below and discuss some of the cultural features that you see. How many different cultures are referenced? What does it say about this area and its history? Can you figure out what part of the country it is?

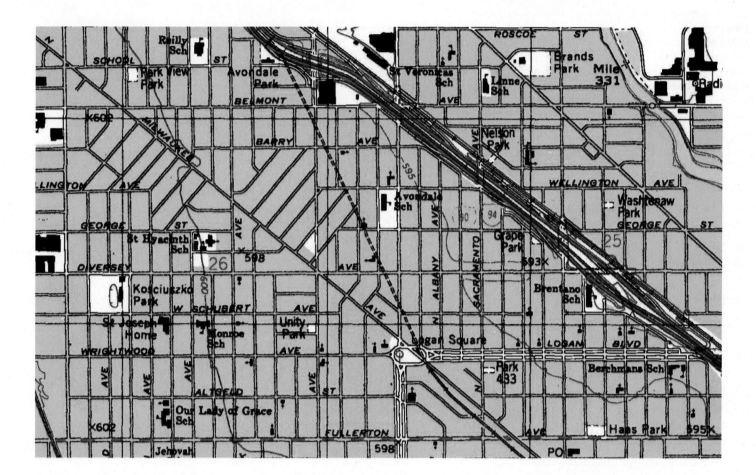

The Geography of Language

CHAPTER MODULES

Consider for a moment the following lines from a classic of the English language:

Ða wæs on burgum Beowulf Scyldinga,
leof leodcyning, longe Þrage
folcum gefræge (fæder ellor hwearf,
aldor of earde), oÞÞæt him eft onwoc
heah Healfdene; heold Þenden lifde,
gamol ond guðreouw, glæde Scyldingas.

Although confusing, this is English. Specifically, it is thousand-year-old English from the epic poem *Beowulf*. Here's the translation in modern English:

Now Beowulf bode in the burg of the Scyldings,
leader beloved, and long he ruled
in fame with all folk, since his father had gone
away from the world, till awoke an heir,
haughty Healfdene, who held through life,
sage and sturdy, the Scyldings glad.

Despite the odd sentence structure, it becomes a bit easier to figure out. But this is the reality of language. It is constantly changing in structure and content. If you watch a television show from the 1950s and someone says, "Swell," it doesn't really sound like the way we talk today, but back then it sounded normal.

Language changes over time, but it also changes across space. English has only been spoken in North America for about 500 years. The history of Spanish and Portuguese in Latin America goes back only about 500 years as well. In Australia, English arrived about 200 years ago. We hear geographic differences in language most often when we listen to people from other parts of the world speaking the same language as we do; not only does accent change, but vocabulary changes as well. In British English, the trunk of a car is a "boot," a cookie is a "biscuit," a truck is a "lorry," and a potato chip is a "crisp." Geographic concepts—in this case, distance—help create patterns of language across the globe.

In this chapter, we discuss what language is and how it is classified. We then talk about the development of the major language families around the globe and their spatial distribution. Finally, we discuss several ways in which language is visible in the cultural landscape and explore some examples of language-related conflict.

7A   Basic Components of Language

What is language? Spoken and written forms of communication quickly come to mind, but are these the only components of language? Can a language be considered such if it lacks a written component? **Language** can be defined as a system of communicating that involves sounds, gestures, marks, or signs. We commonly recognize certain sounds as spoken language, but listen to a language you don't speak or understand, and confusion is immediate. The English language has between 40 and 50 unique **phonemes**, or sounds. The language known as Rotokas, spoken on the island of Bougainville, part of Papua New Guinea, has only 11 phonemes. At the other end of the spectrum, some southern African languages, such as those spoken by the San peoples, may contain over 100 phonemes, including clicks, pops, and other noises not found in English or other European languages.

Gestures can also express ideas, and certainly you can think of a few that have an instant impact on someone. Less offensive gestures include putting the palm of your hand out to signal someone to stop and pointing at something. But gestures are not universal; they vary by culture or language. For example, if Americans want to signal to someone to come over to them, they might put out their hand with their palm in and fingers up in the air and move their fingers in and out. But in some parts of Asia, for example, this is considered rude and is used only to call animals, children, and subordinates. Fingers pointing down are considered more agreeable in these areas, but this looks odd to most Americans.

As you know by reading this, language can be depicted by a series of written marks as well. It is pretty remarkable that our brains can so quickly process certain combinations of lines and dots and interpret them as having meaning. English-speaking students who have tried to learn Arabic, Chinese, Japanese, or even Russian know how difficult it can be to learn a new writing system. It requires, for example, knowledge of between 1,800 and 4,000 characters to read a novel in Japanese.

Writing has its origins in ancient cave drawings. Early humans told stories by painting pictures on caves and cliffs. Paintings on the walls of a cave at Lascaux in southwest France have been dated to 17,000 years ago. But the origins of modern writing are only about 6,000 years old and can be traced to ancient Mesopotamia. One consequence of early trade was that the merchants and buyers learned how to keep track of what was being bought and sold. This led to the development of **cuneiform** writing.

Another early form of writing was the system of hieroglyphics developed by the ancient Egyptians. Like early Sumerian writing, the Egyptian system began by using tiny pictures, or pictographs, to represent entire words. But in time some symbols came to represent particular sounds. For example, the symbol of

◀ **Figure 7A.1** The earliest examples of Sumerian writing tend to be records of grain, beer, and other agricultural commodities. This form of writing, shown here on a clay tablet from 5,000 years ago, is referred to as cuneiform. Symbols were made in wet clay tablets using a wedge-shaped end of a reed. When the clay hardened, the letters were permanent. The word *cuneiform* means "wedge shape." At first, a cuneiform symbol was a tiny picture, or representation, of the object it was representing. This is known as **pictographic writing.** But over time the symbols became more abstract and did not resemble the things they represented. After the Sumerian civilization declined, groups that came later, such as the Babylonians and the Akkadians, adopted the cuneiform characters even though they spoke a different language. In doing so, they simply took the characters and made them each represent a different syllable in their own language, so each "letter" or symbol represented a different sound. This is the direct ancestor of modern sound-based alphabets.

◀ **Figure 7A.2** In 1799, French soldiers found a large tablet, known as the **Rosetta Stone** and originally carved in 196 BC, in the delta region of the Nile River. On the tablet was the same inscription written in three different scripts. One was in hieroglyphics and the others in different scripts of ancient Greek. Because scholars knew ancient Greek, they were slowly able to decipher the hieroglyphics by the 1820s. A Frenchman named Jean-François Champollion is the first to be credited with deciphering the pictographs, although several other scholars contributed important pieces to the puzzle.

a word beginning in "b" might come to represent the sound or letter "b" in a new word. The Egyptian word for mouth was *r'i*, so the symbol for mouth was often used to represent an "r" in other words. This is, in part, how alphabets began to be developed. A single character would represent various things depending on how it was combined with other characters. Egyptian hieroglyphics were so complicated that it wasn't until the early nineteenth century that modern scholars could even understand them.

Ancient cuneiform writing styles slowly changed as different groups adopted and changed them. Over time, they formed into many of the alphabets used today. The modern English alphabet originated with the alphabet of the Phoenicians, who lived at the eastern end of the Mediterranean in what is now mostly Lebanon. The Phoenicians were very active in trade, and their culture spread by relocation diffusion (see Module 6D) to other parts of the Mediterranean. The Greeks adopted the Phoenician alphabet and modified it a bit. In turn, the Greek alphabet was adopted and modified by the Etruscans, a people who lived in Etruria, an area of Italy to the north of modern Rome. When the Romans rose to dominance in Italy, they adopted the Etruscan alphabet and eventually spread it throughout their empire. Today, it is used throughout Western Europe and around the world. As geographers, we take note of the fact that alphabets change not only with time but also with location. As the concept of an alphabet was introduced to new areas, the writing system was modified to accommodate existing culture traits present there—most often, the spoken language.

Figure 7A.3 ▶ Signs and gestures can also be used for language. Modern **American Sign Language** developed out of a language that had developed in France. In 1816, a Yale graduate and Protestant minister named Thomas Hopkins Gallaudet traveled to France to learn about educating deaf children at a school founded for that purpose in Paris. Gallaudet learned French sign language and modified it to teach American students. This modified version of signing gradually mixed with more informal signs already used by deaf Americans to become modern American Sign Language, or ASL. Today, ASL is used by between 100,000 and 500,000 speakers worldwide, but most are in the United States and Canada. Over 100 other forms of sign language are used around the world.

7B   Dialects, Accent, Linguae Francae, Pidgins, and Creoles

Languages often have slight variations from place to place. American speakers of English hear this when watching movies or television programs that originated in Great Britain or Australia, for example. It is clear that the actors are using English, but occasionally a word is misunderstood or a meaning missed because of a difference in vocabulary or grammar. Scholars use the word **dialect** to refer to variations of sounds and vocabulary within a language. Dialects generally develop because geography, notably distance and isolation, allow common cultural traits to diverge. Dialects can differ from each other in vocabulary and the ways in which a word sounds or words or sentences are formed. For example, if you go to the movies, do you wait "on" line or "in" line?

The word **accent** can sometimes have the same meaning as the word *dialect*, but it should only be used to refer to differences in how a language sounds or is spoken. *Dialect* is a broader term and refers to vocabulary and grammar differences, as well as to how a language sounds. Other terms that can mean dialect are *idiom*, *patois*, and *vernacular*. **Idiom** is often used synonymously with *dialect* to refer to a language that is peculiar to a certain group of people or region. The word **patois** can also mean dialect, but it generally refers to rural or provincial speech or to a nonstandard form of a language, as in "He speaks English with a Jamaican patois." **Vernacular** also refers to a local form of a language, as in "We may call it a milkshake, but in the local vernacular it is called a frappe." *Vernacular* can also refer to local or nonstandard architecture or other culture traits that are common only in an isolated area. Note that, with nearly all of the dialect examples discussed, there is a distinct geographic component.

A **lingua franca** is a language used by people for purposes of cross-cultural communication or trade. In other words, it is a common language that people often learn as a second language, so that they can talk to other people in their area who use a different tongue. Kiswahili in East Africa is a well-known example of a lingua franca. Other linguae francae include Russian in countries that were once part of the former Soviet Union, such as Central Asia, and Hindi in India. In the past, Greek and Latin were the linguae francae of the Roman Empire. In more recent times, French was used by diplomats to conduct international political negotiations. The European Union, NATO, and the United Nations still use French as an official language. Perhaps you noticed announcements in French during the last Olympic Games. This is because French is an official language of the International Olympic Committee.

▲ **Figure 7B.1** Vocabulary can help distinguish between dialects. For example, what do you call this item? Americans refer to a "mailbox," but in Britain it is a "postbox." Many Americans say "store," but a Londoner might refer to a "shop." The spoken differences between countries do not rise to the level of being separate languages, but they are real nevertheless. In most case, dialects are considered to be mutually intelligible—that is, the differences should not be so great that speakers of different dialects cannot understand each other's general meaning. However, many dialects deviate so far from their "standard" versions that they have become difficult for outsiders to comprehend.

▲ **Figure 7B.2** In India, Hindi serves as a lingua franca for a country with over 20 official languages and over 400 total languages.

Today, English is the lingua franca of most of the world's business, scientific, and academic communities, and many see it as the likely global language of the future. As many as 750 million people worldwide speak English as a second language, and it is an official language in countries with populations of approximately 2 billion people. The rise of the Internet, dominated by English-language sites, is often cited as a reason for the rise of English, as is the fall of the Soviet Union, which left the United States as the dominant political power on the planet. Some thinkers worry that the rise of a single, global language could lead to the extinction of smaller languages.

A **pidgin**, like a lingua franca, is a simplified language that is used by people who speak different languages for common communication. What differentiates a lingua franca from a pidgin is that a pidgin usually is not the native language of anyone using it, and pidgins usually have simplified vocabularies and grammar, so that they can be learned quickly. The word originates from Chinese pronunciation of the word *business*. In the eighteenth and nineteenth centuries, Chinese, English, and Portuguese traders in Canton (now Guangzhou, China) developed a simple, unique language so that they could trade together. Pidgins are still used in the Caribbean, parts of Africa, and elsewhere.

Figure 7B.3 ▶ If a pidgin is adopted by a group of speakers as its first, or primary, language, then we refer to it as a **creole**. Examples include Jamaican Creole, based on English, Haitian Creole, which is derived from French, and Krio in Sierra Leone, which is also based on English. This woman is selling fish in a Jamaican village.

7C · Language Families

The history of modern linguistic study begins in colonial India. In 1786, Sir William Jones, a judge of the Supreme Court in Calcutta, gave a lecture in which he hypothesized that Latin, Greek, the Germanic languages, Sanskrit (the ancient language of much of India), and the Celtic languages, such as Irish, are all related. Jones noted that certain words in all the languages are surprisingly similar and thus must be related. For example, the word *father* in several different languages can be seen in table 7c.1. The similarities among the languages are fairly remarkable, even though the languages are spoken on opposite ends of the Eurasian landmass. So it would seem that all of these languages are related. But if that is the case, why are the first letters different? The letters "p" and "f" don't really sound the same. This, surprisingly, brings us to *Little Red Riding Hood*.

Table 7C.1 Words for "Father"	
Language	**Word for "Father"**
Latin	pater
Old English	fæder
Ancient Greek	pater
Old Norse	faðir
Sanskrit	pitar
Old Irish	athir

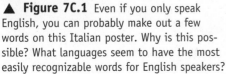

▲ **Figure 7C.1** Even if you only speak English, you can probably make out a few words on this Italian poster. Why is this possible? What languages seem to have the most easily recognizable words for English speakers?

In 1822, Jakob Grimm, one-half of the Brothers Grimm, collectors and publishers of the now-famous fairy tales, outlined a theory that modern German and English had experienced one or two shifts in the use of consonants since the time of ancient languages, such as Latin and Sanskrit. Specifically, consonants *k*, *t*, and *p* became *h*, *th*, and *f*, respectively. He also documented a change from the older Low German to modern High German. There is some controversy about whether these notions were Grimm's alone or whether he borrowed from contemporaries, but whatever the case, this consonant shift is now known as **Grimm's law**.

As the study of language progressed, scholars began grouping languages into families and tracing their geographic and structural changes through time. A **language family** is a collection of languages with a common ancestor, known as a **proto-language**. Languages are grouped into families through a method known as *genetic classification*. Think of an ancient proto-language as if it was a distant great-grandparent. A language that develops from it is akin to its child. Over time, the child language might develop into several additional languages and in time, there could be dozens or hundreds of languages descended from the same original ancestor. Researchers attempt to look at all languages that originated from the same source and classify them into groups that are most closely related, known as genetic nodes (also called branches). This process is often quite difficult. While scholars may be confident of which family a language is a member of, placing it in the proper branch can be quite difficult.

Overall, there are about 6,800 living languages spoken on the planet today. Many of these survive only in small areas and have only a handful of speakers, often less than 1,000. These 6,800 languages can be grouped into about 120 language families. Language families can be further divided into branches, or smaller groups of related languages. For example, in the Indo-European language family, English is in the Germanic branch of the family, but Kurdish, the main language of the Kurds, is in the Indo-Iranian branch. They have a common ancestor but developed along different paths. The major language families are highlighted in the series of maps on the following pages. You should spend time learning their basic geographic patterns before continuing. As you look at the maps, ask yourself how geography and history helped create the modern language pattern of the world.

Although two languages can share similarities to each other because they are from the same family, they may also share similarities because of geographic proximity. In other words, two languages from two different language families, or branches of a language family, can develop similarities because they are next to each other. Two or more languages that are geographically contiguous and have similar words or grammar are known as a **sprachbund**. Many of the most well-known sprachbund are in areas where several culture regions come together. One example is the Balkan region of Eastern Europe, well known for its cultural complexity. Languages such as Romanian, Albanian, Bulgarian, and Greek are all Indo-European languages, but they are from very different branches. Yet, they share unexpected similarities due to geographic proximity. In Southeast Asia, a sprachbund exists among languages from the very distinct Sino-Tibetan, Austro-Asiatic, and Mon-Khmer language families.

▲ **Figure 7C.2** The origins of runes are unclear, but they were probably developed by the Goths, a Germanic people who lived in Northern Europe. Runes were used from about the third century all the way to the sixteenth century in some areas. Over time, the Latin alphabet we use today superseded the use of runic scripts.

The **Afro-Asiatic** language family is a group of over 370 languages that are primarily spoken in North Africa and Southwest Asia (the Middle East). One of the most important subgroups of the Afro-Asiatic family is the large **Semitic** branch, which includes over 70 languages. The Semitic language with the largest global impact is probably Arabic, which has about 35 major dialects spoken throughout the Middle East and North Africa. Arabic is also, of course, the holy language of Muslims because it is the language of the Koran (Qur'an). Because the Koran was revealed to Muhammad in Arabic, only in Arabic can it be truly understood. Thus, even in Muslim areas of the world where Arabic is not the first language, many people learn the stylized, classical form of the language needed to read and recite the Koran. Spoken Arabic can vary greatly, to the point of being mutual unintelligible between some regional dialects. Major Arabic dialect groups can be found in North Africa, Egypt, the Arabian Peninsula, Syria, and Iraq.

▼ **Figure 7C.3 Major Language Families**

Language families

1 ☐ Indo-European
      a. Romance b. Germanic c. Slavic
      d. Baltic e. Celtic f. Albanian g. Greek
      h. Armenian k. Indo-Iranian
2 ☐ Uralic-Altaic
3 ☐ Sino-Tibetan
4 ■ Japanese-Korean
5 ▨ Dravidian
6 ☐ Afro-Asiatic
7 ☐ Niger-Congo
8 ■ Sudanic
9 ▨ Saharan
10 ☐ Khoisan
11 ☐ Paleo-Asiatic
12 ■ Austro-Asiatic
13 ■ Malayo-Polynesian
14 ▨ Australian
15 ☐ Amerindian
   ☐ Other
      16. Eskimo-Aleut 17. Papuan 18. Caucasian
      19. Basque 20. Vietnamese

16 ☐ Unpopulated

The **Indo-European** family, of which English is a member, includes over 440 languages spoken originally across the Euro-Asian landmass and now around the globe. This diverse and complicated family is worth a detailed look, both for its connection to our history and for the global importance of some of its languages.

The oldest surviving Indo-European branch is the Indo-Iranian subgroup. As the name suggests, these languages are spoken in modern-day India and Iran, among other locations. Farsi (Persian) and Hindi are among the languages in this region with the most speakers.

Another important branch of Indo-European is Greek, a language whose ancient history we know more about than almost any other language in the world. Greek is at least 3,400 years old.

The Romance subgroup is also important to modern English, even though it is now rather small in terms of the number of speakers. This is because Latin, the most influential Italic language, is no longer spoken by many people. But Latin is the ancestor of many of Europe's spoken languages, including Italian, Spanish, French, Portuguese, and Romanian.

Celtic languages were once spoken throughout a large part of Europe, but today they survive in only a few areas. Modern Celtic languages include Gaelic Irish, Gaelic Scots, Manx, Welsh, Breton, and Cornish.

The Baltic and Slavic subgroups include Russian, Ukrainian, Bulgarian, Serbo-Croatian, Czech, Slovak, Polish, and Macedonian.

The remaining important Indo-European language subfamily is the parent group of English, known as the Germanic subgroup. This large group includes English, German, Dutch, Swedish, Afrikaans, Norwegian, Danish, Yiddish, Icelandic, and many other smaller languages. The earliest evidence of Germanic languages is about 2,000 years old. Many of the earliest surviving texts are written with a **runic alphabet**.

The largest language family in terms of number of languages is the **Niger-Congo** group, which accounts for about 1,400 languages spoken in Africa by a total of 600 million people. The group contains nine major branches, including the important Bantu languages.

The large **Sino-Tibetan** family includes 250 or more languages. The prefix *Sino* refers to China, and the Sinitic languages include the many dialects of Chinese. The most important and most widely spoken is Mandarin, used by a staggering 870 million people in China alone. Another 10 million around the world use it as a first language and over 200 million as a second language. This easily makes Mandarin the most widely spoken first language on the planet. Standard Mandarin, known in China as Putonghua, is the official language of the People's Republic of China and is based on the dialect of Beijing, the country's capital.

But Standard Mandarin is not the only form of Chinese spoken in China. Various other dialects are used, and because of China's huge population—over 1.3 billion—some of the regional forms of Chinese have tens of millions of speakers. For example, people in Shanghai speak Wu, a language that has over 77 million speakers. Other important variants include Yue and Hakka, both used in southern China. Yue is often referred to as Cantonese because it is used in and around the city of Guangzhou, formerly known as Canton. Yue is also spoken in nearby Hong Kong. Yue has about 71 million speakers around the world, while Hakka can claim 33 million speakers worldwide.

The **Malayo-Polynesian** language family includes over 1,200 languages primarily spoken across Southeast Asia and the South Pacific. About 20% of the world's population speaks a Malayo-Polynesian language. One of the most unusual members of the Malayo-Polynesian branch is Malagasy, spoken by the people of Madagascar off the coast of Africa and thousands of miles across the Indian Ocean from its closest linguistic neighbors. Scholars believe that, about 2,000 years ago, seafarers from Southeast Asia made their way to the island, probably by traveling along the African coastline. Because Africans had not settled Madagascar, the settlers continued to speak their own Malayo-Polynesian tongue.

Map labels:
Norwegian, Swedish, Finnish, 1b, 2, 1c, German, Polish, Byelo-Russian, Ukrainian, 1d, 1c, 1a, French, 1e, 1b, 19, Portuguese, Spanish, Italian, 1c, 2, Turkish, 1f, 1g, Kurdish, 2, Berber, Arabic, Wolof, Fulani, Bambara, 7, Fulani, Akan, Yoruba, 9, 8, Amharic, 6, Cushitic, Congo, Ganda, Swahili, Luba, Mbundu, Bemba, 7, Shona, Hottentot, 10, Bushman, Zulu, Afrikaans, 1b, 1b, Luba, Malagasy, 13, Kazakh, Kirgiz, Uzbek, Turkmen, Farsi, Pashto, 1k, Hindi, 1k, Tamil, Telugu, 5, 12, 12, 1k, Mongol, Ulgur, Tibetan, Chinese, 3, Yakut, Tungus, Manchu, Chukchi, 11, Koryak, 1c, 1c, Korean, 4, Japanese, 2, 2, 2, 2, 1h, 18, 20, 13, 13, 17, 14, 1b, English, 1b, 1b

0° 20° 40° 60° 80° 100° 120° 140° 160° 180°

7D   Geography of English

Today, English is spoken around the world as a second language and in many places as a first tongue. Modern English has numerous dialects and accents. In England alone, there are several dialects. The "standard" form of English is known as RP, which stands for **Received Pronunciation**, and traditionally is the language of educated Britons in London and southern England. Because of radio and television broadcasts, this version of the language is propagated throughout the British Isles. But other dialects survive, and many are now commonly heard in the media as well. These include the form of English spoken in Wales, which has a lot of Celtic influence; Lowland Scottish; Cockney, a dialect traditionally spoken by the lower classes in and around London; and dialects used in Northern Ireland.

English as spoken in the United States and Canada began developing as soon as English speakers arrived in the Americas 500 years ago. Geographic differences in North American dialects began right from the start. In what is now the United States, the first permanent colonies were in Virginia and New England. Early Virginian settlers were largely from the West Country, the far southwestern part of England. This region of England had a unique accent, which scholars say can still be heard in rural Tidewater areas of Virginia, North Carolina, and Maryland. Early New England settlers, such as the Plymouth colonists who arrived on the *Mayflower*, were largely from eastern and central England and thus had a different accent. In time, the accents in the United States diversified, and today scholars identify four major dialect areas.

Geographically separated by an ocean from England, dialects and accents in the United States were able to develop on their own. U.S. English adopted countless words from French, Spanish, German, Native American, and other languages. *Chipmunk*, *moose*, *squash*, and *skunk* are Native American words. French has given us *cuisine*, *déjà vu*, and *finale*, and Spanish words in English include *alligator*, *cargo*, and *mosquito*.

Elsewhere in North America, Canadian English is very similar to U.S. English. The movement of many British Loyalists after the Revolutionary War helped ensure similarities among speakers in the two regions. Today, there is so much media overlap between the two countries that the differences in accent and dialect are not even noticeable to many people. In the Caribbean, a form of pidgin English formed among slaves who had originally come from different linguistic backgrounds. Pidgin forms of the language are used all across the region, and because Caribbean slaves were sold to plantations in what would become the U.S. South, elements of these pidgins are evident in traditional African American dialects of English. **Gullah**, also known as Geechee, a creole language spoken on islands off the South Carolina and Georgia coasts,

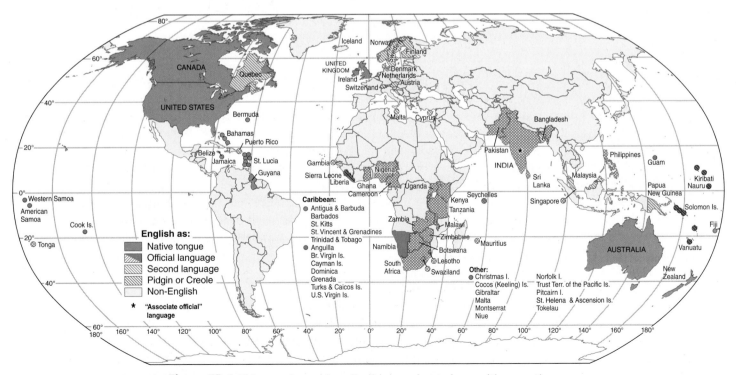

▲ **Figure 7D.1** This map shows where English is spoken today as either a native tongue, an official language, a second language, or a pidgin or creole.

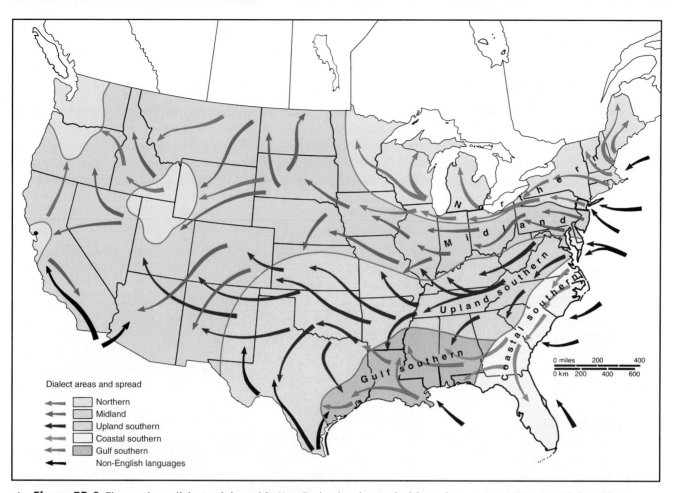

▲ **Figure 7D.2** The northern dialect originated in New England and spread with settlers across upstate New York and into the upper Midwest. The southern dialects spread along coastal areas and across the Deep South. The midland dialect is distinct because many of the settlers that went to Pennsylvania and New Jersey were not from England, but were Germans, Scots-Irish, or other non-English speakers. The English-speaking immigrants who did settle in the Mid-Atlantic were largely Quakers and drew their ranks from the central and northern areas of England, so their English was different still from the dialects spoken in New England and the South. The West was the last area to be settled, and the dialect of English spoken there reflects some pronunciation differences from the eastern regions. It is considered to be a very young dialect.

developed from a form of pidgin English with thousands of African loan words. In Gullah, the phrase "Get in here and sit down" becomes "In yah cah sid down."

Another well-known dialect of English is Australian English. Early settlement in Australia was largely in the form of penal colonies to reduce the stress on crowded British jails. Over 130,000 prisoners were transported to Australia between about 1790 and 1840. Free settlers also arrived on the continent, adding to the number of English speakers. Many of the convicts spoke the working-class Cockney dialect of the London area or with an Irish brogue (accent). These variations are still audible in modern Australian English.

New Australian settlers faced an interesting problem because there were a lot of plants and animals in the region that were completely different from anything they had ever seen. Because of the distance from Great Britain, new words were often created by the settlers that were different from anything spoken in England. In other cases, words that were used in England at the time settlers left continued to be used in Australia after they had become extinct in Britain. In other cases, words were adapted from indigenous aboriginal speech. *Kangaroo*, *boomerang*, and *dingo* are examples of Aborigine contributions. All of these factors led to the distinct Australian dialect of today.

Elsewhere, English is spoken in New Zealand, India, South Africa, and numerous other places. Basically, any place that was a British colony continues to use English to some extent. Tens of millions speak English regularly in India, making it the third largest user of English after the United Kingdom and United States. English is often used by the Indian government and armed forces, and thus it is necessary for many Indians to learn it. Along with Hindi, it serves as a lingua franca for the diverse country. English also has this role in some of Britain's former colonies in Africa, such as Nigeria, where half the population uses a creole or pidgin English as a second language.

7E Language Isolation and Language Extinction

As mentioned earlier, languages change over time and space. Languages can grow, change, merge with other languages, or even wither and die. You may have studied Latin in school. Latin was once spoken by millions as the lingua franca of the Roman Empire and the Catholic Church, but today there are only a handful of fluent speakers. But Latin survives in the 600 million speakers of the Romance languages, such as French, Spanish, and Italian. This section discusses how languages change and either become new languages or die.

▲ **Figure 7E.1** Languages such as Basque, spoken in some areas of the Basque Country in northern Spain, are known as isolates because they are unrelated to other languages.

If we think of languages as the branches on a tree, one way that new languages can be created is if a branch splits into two separate parts. This is called **language divergence**, the dividing of a language into many new languages. Often, this divergence occurs because language speakers become geographically isolated in two or more areas.

Speakers of Latin once covered much of Europe, but after the Roman Empire fell apart, isolation and distance allowed versions of Latin spoken far from Rome to become early forms of French, Spanish, and Romanian. The languages diverged and became something new. A more recent example may be Korean, which some scholars argue is diverging into North Korean and South Korean dialects because of the isolation of the north from the rest of the world.

But two different languages can also merge. This is known as **language convergence**. If an area has a high number of bilingual speakers, individual speakers may begin to use vocabulary and grammatical structures of one language when speaking the other. This has been documented, for example, in villages in India that straddle two major language regions.

A **language isolate** is a language that belongs to no known language family and is not related to any living language. In other words, these languages are unique, as far as we know. The most commonly cited examples of language isolates are Basque, Japanese, Ainu, and Burushaski. Basque is the language of the Basque peoples of northern Spain and southern France. Some scholars believe that it is the only surviving example of the language family used throughout southwestern Europe before the Roman Empire took control of the region. Other researchers suggest, based on some good evidence that it is related to languages used far to the east in the Caucasus region, but this has yet to be proven. About 600,000 people speak Basque today.

Japanese, spoken by about 125 million people, is also an isolate. Some scholars connect Japanese with nearby Korean, but others make connections to Austronesian languages farther south or to Altaic languages, such as Turkic and Mongolian. The isolate Ainu language is also spoken on the northernmost islands of Japan; the Ainu people are the aboriginal inhabitants of the islands. The language is now close to being extinct as Japanese replaces Ainu among younger generations. Burushaski is spoken in the Kashmir region of Pakistan. Although some scholars have connected Burushaski to Indo-European languages, which makes sense geographically, the connections are not accepted by all linguists.

While there are still nearly 7,000 languages spoken on earth, the past few centuries have witnessed a dramatic loss of languages, called **language extinction**. Since the year 1500, approximately 300 languages have ceased to be spoken by anyone. Since many had no written forms, some are truly lost. Others survive only through existing manuscripts. Over 90% of all languages are spoken by only 100,000 or fewer people, and a few hundred tongues have 50 speakers or less. Many of the languages that have been lost are in places that witnessed massive changes in their populations due to colonialism. Many Native American languages—over 50, by some estimates—have become extinct in the past four centuries.

Today, the *Ethnologue* database of languages classifies 473 languages as nearly extinct. The highest number is in the Americas, where 182 languages are on the verge of disappearing. The Ona language of Argentina, for example, had only one to three speakers in 1991. The Tuscarora language of Canada and the United States, a member of the Iroquois family, has fewer than 20 speakers. The Pacific region is also hard hit, potentially losing more than 152 languages. Even Europe, where language patterns are well established, is at risk of losing some of the traditional languages of the Saami people, formerly called Laplanders. Most of the languages on the verge of extinction are languages of native peoples, which highlights their isolation from the rest of the world and the pressure to adopt the culture traits of the majority population.

▲ **Figure 7E.2** This map shows languages that are nearly extinct. In most cases, the youngest speakers are older people, meaning that in a generation or two the language may cease to be spoken.

7F   Toponymy

Learning language patterns is an important way to understand the geography of language, but language can also be viewed on a much more local scale. From small towns to big cities, language provides clues to a location's history and the cultures that have influenced it. From our discussion of cultural landscapes in Chapter 6, we know that geographers believe that cultures leave an imprint on the landscape. A careful examination of a town, neighborhood, or community will reveal language on business signs, on monuments, and in the names that people give to places. The last item is the focus of this module.

Toponymy is the study of place names, and it is derived from the Greek words *topos*, meaning "place," and *ounouma*, meaning "name." Place names can indicate physical features, such as a river or mountain, or human features on the landscape, such as towns or roads. If a street is called Mine Street, it may mean that there once was a mine in that area. If there is no mine there currently, we may have learned something about that location without even opening a history book.

In Modules 6F and 6G, we discussed how the cultural landscape can reveal and contain the cultural residue of many different cultures. Often, toponyms reveal something about one or more cultures present in an area in the past. In the United States and Canada, for example, many towns and physical features have names that reflect the native heritage of the area. In the United States, Alabama, Alaska, Connecticut, Dakota, Hawaii, Idaho, and Texas are just a few state names derived from native languages. In Canada, itself a native word meaning "community," the provincial names Manitoba, Ontario, Nunavut, and Saskatchewan have native origins.

Other U.S. and Canadian place names reveal other influences. The Hudson Valley of New York was one of the first areas to witness significant Dutch settlement. Accordingly, Dutch place names still persist in the region, even though significant Dutch settlement in the area had stopped by the end of the seventeenth century. Yonkers, Peekskill, Catskill, the Bronx, and Staten Island all have names with Dutch origins. The suffix *-kill* on many town names in New York is a clue to a Dutch origin and means "stream."

Other toponyms are patriotic in origin. Examples include Independence, Colorado; Liberty, New York; and Freedom, California. Patriotic place names can also be names of important figures in a country's history, such as Washingtonville, New York, and Lincoln, Nebraska, which changed its named from Lancaster when it became a state in 1867. Although Lincoln is seen as a hero of the Civil War, the other side of the conflict is also represented. For example, Jefferson Davis County in Mississippi and Jeff Davis County in Georgia are named for the former president of the Confederacy during the Civil War. Countless other place names are memorials to important people of the past. Gainesville, Florida, is named for War of 1812 general Edmund Pendleton Gaines. Irvington in New York is named for writer Washington Irving, who wrote *Rip Van Winkle* and *The Legend of Sleepy Hollow*, which got its own place name in 1996 when North Tarrytown changed its name to Sleepy Hollow to attract more tourists.

Political change can also bring about place name changes for ideological reasons. When the Soviet Union took control of Bucharest, Romania, in 1948, it renamed streets to correspond with communist ideology. For example, Carol I Boulevard, named in honor of the first king of Romania, was renamed Boulevard of the Republic. After the fall of the Communist government in Poland

◀ **Figure 7F.1** Perhaps the most basic toponyms are descriptive. These place names tell us something about the physical character of the location, such as Stony Point, Pine Street, Sandy Hook, or Rocky Mountains. The description can also refer to what can happen to you at a place, such as Death Valley, California; Frozen Horse Creek, Montana; or Cold Shivers Point, Colorado. How do you think the famous Wall Street got its name?

in 1989, Warsaw, Poland, renamed a major road Jana Pawła II after the Polish pope. It had formerly been named for a prominent postwar communist named Julian Marchlewski. If we return to the notion of landscape as a source of meaning, these changes make sense. The citizens of Warsaw want their environment to reflect the people and ideals that they value, rather than a foreign ideology valued at some point in the past. Closer to home, many roads and schools have been renamed in the past three decades to honor figures in the civil rights movement, such as Martin Luther King Jr. and Rosa Parks.

Figure 7F.2 ▶ Some toponyms alert us that a place was likely named at a particular time in the past. Cultural geographer Wilbur Zelinsky demonstrated this by examining "classical" town names in the United States, places such as Syracuse, Rome, Ithaca, and Troy. Just after the American Revolution, the people of the fledgling United States developed a fascination with the cultures of ancient Greece, Rome, and the Near East. For decades afterwards, parents in large numbers named their children Ulysses, Alexander, Homer, and other names from the classical past. At the same time, they began building houses that looked like Greek and Roman temples. And Americans started naming towns after locations in ancient Greece and Rome. But you will notice that there are fewer of these names in New England or along the coastal regions of the East. Can you think why this might be?

◀ **Figure 7F.3** Place names can sometimes be just a bit odd. Some names seem unlikely choices for a place to live, such as Hell, Michigan, while others, such as Cookietown, Oklahoma, are much more appealing. Truth or Consequences, New Mexico, is named after a popular radio, and later television, show of the 1940s and 1950s. In 1951, the show's host, Ralph Edwards, offered publicity to any town that would change its name to that of the show. Thus, Hot Springs became Truth or Consequences. Snowflake, Arizona, is named not for frozen precipitation but for a Mormon land agent named William Flake and a Mormon apostle named Erastus Snow. The early settlers of the then-unnamed Peculiar, Missouri, having trouble deciding on a name for the town, sent a message to the postmaster general in Washington, asking him to give them any name he wanted, as "long as it is sort of peculiar," and a town name was born.

7G   Language Conflict

Beyond names, language has been or is at the heart of other conflicts around the world. Sometimes, the conflict is over what language should be used in a particular country or region, and other times the dispute centers on the cultural "pollution" of one language by another. Here we discuss conflicts over place names, language and national identity, and language "purity."

Political conflicts over place names can become serious at times. In the 1980s, the country of Yugoslavia broke apart. One part of the country, Macedonia, renamed itself the Republic of Macedonia. This did not go over well, however, in neighboring Greece, which claimed the name Macedonia as the northern part of its country and the ancestral homeland of the legendary Alexander the Great. Greece protested to the United Nations, and an international tribunal recommended changing the name to the Former Yugoslav Republic of Macedonia, or FYROM. Arabs often object to calling the body of water between Iran and Saudi Arabia the Persian Gulf, preferring the term *Arabian Gulf.* For decades, Israeli and Palestinian groups have fought over the names of places in the region. After gaining statehood in the 1940s, Israel renamed many places using traditional Hebrew names. For example, Nazareth was renamed Al-Nasirah. This attempt to change the cultural landscape has met with strong resistance from many Palestinian groups.

▲ **Figure 7G.1** Some of India's numerous official languages can be seen on its currency.

Often, people argue over what language should be spoken in a country because language is an important component of ethnicity (see Module 9A) and therefore national identity (see Module 10E). After the Soviet Union fell apart in the early 1990s, citizens of the nearly independent countries of Uzbekistan, Kyrgyzstan, and Kazakhstan sought to repress the use of Russian, which had been pushed on them by the Soviet leadership, in favor of traditional languages, such as Uzbek, Kyrgyz, and Kazakh. This was problematic, however, because in many areas the traditional languages were actually spoken only by a minority of the population. In the end, many of these countries declared the traditional tongue as the "state" language but continued to recognize that the other languages needed to be taught.

In the past few decades, some in the United States have advocated for making English the official language. In nearly every session of Congress, an amendment to the Constitution is proposed, calling for English to be declared the official U.S. language. Between 10% and 15% of Americans speak a language other than English, causing a great resource burden on governments to, for example, educate non-English speakers, print non-English versions of ballots and government documents, and train safety workers to handle emergencies in several languages. Opponents argue that the United States has always resisted attempts to declare a national language. As early as 1780, an attempt by John Adams to establish an academy devoted to English was declared undemocratic by his critics and rejected. Those opposed also argue that a law establishing an official language would interfere with a citizen's right to due process because courts

▲ **Figure 7G.2** This menu in French-speaking Montreal, Canada, shows the influence of loan words. Which words are obviously French and which are borrowed?

Figure 7G.3 ▶ In Quebec, legislation has been used to preserve the use of the French language. Quebec has both French and English speakers, and portions of the French-speaking Quebecois have long sought to break off from the rest of Canada, although attempts have so far been unsuccessful. In 1977, proponents of French were able to pass Bill 101, a measure that requires nearly all schoolchildren in Quebec to go to French-speaking schools. Today, almost 95% of Quebec's citizens use French in their daily activities, up from under 90% in the early 1990s. Quebec law states that French must be the predominant language on any sign and officials may measure the size of the letters to insure that French is given a great prominence. As geographers, note how an attempt is being made to cleanse not only the culture trait itself, the language, but also the cultural landscape. What does this indicate about the power of the cultural landscape? If, as discussed previously, culture is reflected in the landscape, can the rate of cultural change be slowed by slowing change to our daily environment?

might no longer provide interpreters or translators to non-English-speaking defendants. Proponents argue that exceptions could be made for public safety, and they tout savings to taxpayers as a main reason for their position. They also argue that making English an official language would encourage immigrants to learn English.

Many countries, of course, do have official languages. India, for example, has over 20 official languages. Switzerland has 4: French, Italian, German, and Romansh, a language spoken by only 0.5% of the population. Belgium has 3 official languages: French (Walloon-dialect), German, and Dutch (Flemish). For much of the twentieth century and into the present, tensions existed between the French-speaking Walloons in the south part of the country and the Flemish populations in the northern region of Flanders. To keep the state from falling apart, Belgium chose, in the early 1990s, to create a federal system that gives each ethnolinguistic group its own administrative area of the country. While the national government continues to handle issues such as defense, justice, and economic policy, most other concerns are handled by the regional governments. In the past decade, political parties that support independence for Flemish-speaking Flanders have gained power.

An interesting type of language-based conflict involves charges by certain cultures that their language is being "polluted" by words from other languages. **Loan words** are terms used by a particular language that have their origins in other tongues. For example, some in Germany have called for an end to use of "Denglish" (Deutsch + English = Denglish). Words such as *surfen* or *downloaden* have become common in German when referring to the Internet. Japan has adopted English words such as *elebeetaa* (*elevator*) and *suupaa* (*supermarket*). English, as discussed earlier, has countless examples of loan words. But English and Japanese generally welcome new words from foreign countries. Why are some cultures opposed to the incorporation of words from other tongues, while others are not?

Perhaps the strongest opposition to the use of English loan words has occurred in two French-speaking regions, France and the Canadian province of Quebec. For decades, English has been creeping into the French language, and vice versa. *Le weekend* and *le marketing* are examples of English loan words in French. Starting in 1975, however, the French government began passing laws banning English from advertising, scientific meetings, official government documents, publications, radio programs, and television. The Académie Française, founded in 1635, is the official agency tasked with maintaining the purity of French. In the past decade, over 15,000 companies have been fined between $100 and $1,500 for including English words in their marketing or packaging materials. The government has also required French websites to publish at least one version of their site in French.

Key Terms

accent (7B)
Afro-Asiatic (7C)
American Sign Language (7A)
creole (7B)
cuneiform (7A)
dialect (7B)
Grimm's law (7C)
Gullah (7D)
idiom (7B)
Indo-European (7C)
language (7A)
language convergence (7E)
language divergence (7E)
language extinction (7E)
language family (7C)
language isolate (7E)
lingua franca (7B)

loan words (7G)
Malayo-Polynesian (7C)
Niger-Congo (7C)
patois (7B)
phonemes (7A)
pictographic writing (7A)
pidgin (7B)
proto-language (7C)
Received Pronunciation (7D)
Rosetta Stone (7A)
runic alphabet (7C)
Semitic (7C)
Sino-Tibetan (7C)
sprachbund (7C)
toponymy (7F)
vernacular (7B)

Basic Review Questions

1. What is language? What are phonemes?

2. What are the oldest forms of writing?

3. What is meant by *pictographic writing*?

4. When was American Sign Language invented?

5. What is the difference between a language and a dialect?

6. How are accents and dialects different?

7. What is a lingua franca? How does it differ from a pidgin?

8. What is the difference between a creole and a pidgin?

9. What is a language family? What language family is English a part of?

10. What is a proto-language?

11. What are the largest language families in the world?

12. Where do you find the Sino-Tibetan language family?

13. Where do you find Celtic languages?

14. What is Received Pronunciation?

15. What is Gullah?

16. What is language convergence and divergence?

17. What is a language isolate? Give two examples.

18. What is an extinct language?

19. What is toponymy?

20. Why are classical town names concentrated in places such as Upstate New York?

21. What is language pollution?

Advanced Review Questions

1. What is the Rosetta Stone, and why was it important to scientists?

2. What major dialect regions exist in the United States? Why does Canadian English differ in dialect from American English?

3. What is the role of a lingua franca, and what are the most important linguae francae in the world?

4. What factors in the modern world make the extinction of languages more likely? What technologies might reverse the trend toward fewer languages?

5. What are the origins of English?

6. Hypothesize about how the Internet affects language convergence or divergence.

7. Describe the pattern of the major language families of the world and discuss the geographic factors that caused the families to become established in certain areas. What are some of the strongest barriers to language diffusion?

8. Describe the pattern of language extinction around the world and discuss what geographic factors might lead to a language dying out.

9. What languages are part of the Semitic language family?

10. What can place names tell us about the cultural history of an area?

11. Define and explain loan words and give a few examples from modern American English. Discuss how loan words can be a point of contention.

12. Discuss some of the ways that language or place names can lead to conflict.

Further Study Topics

- Analyze the street names of a particular part of your community. What are the origins of the names? Do they tell you anything about the history of the town? Can you find examples of place names that relate to something in the town that no longer exists, such as a former industry or ethnic community?

- Conduct more research about the Académie Française and its mission to keep French pure and free of loan word contamination. Do you think this effort is necessary to preserve French culture? Is it a battle that can never be won?

- Governments often change names for political purposes. Research how Israel and the Palestinians in the West Bank and Gaza have changed place names to suit political aims or to establish territorial claims. What types of features (towns, roads, historical sites) have been renamed?

- Should the United States make English the official language of the country and stop providing government documents and education in other languages, such as Spanish? What are the pros and cons of a single national language? What do other countries do?

- Research dialect differences between your part of the country and other regions. What are main differences, and why do the differences exist? Are there vernacular terms in your region that are not used elsewhere in the country?

- Why are some of the languages in the Middle East called "Semitic" and some of the languages in Africa called "Hamitic"?

Summary Activities

On the blank world map below, draw and label the major world language families.

The Geography of Religion

CHAPTER MODULES

Stop for a minute and think about all the good and bad things that have been done throughout human history in the name of religion: kindness and charity, war and hatred, huge monuments raised up toward the heavens and cities burned to the ground, heroism, and human sacrifice. Few things have the ability to motivate humans more, for good or for bad, than religious ideas. The Crusades of the Middle Ages, the sacrifice of thousands by the Aztecs, and the 9/11 terrorist attacks on the United States were all motivated, in part, by religious beliefs. Conversely, charity groups at the local, national, and international levels help suffering people every day in the name of the same religions.

Religion is perhaps the most influential component of human culture on our daily lives. Even if you are not religious, your life and culture have probably been shaped by religious ideas. For example, weekends in North America and Europe are Saturday and Sunday. Why? Well, the Jewish Sabbath is Friday night and Saturday, and the Christian Sabbath is Saturday night and Sunday. In Judeo-Christian societies, these days became the days to rest from work. But in many Islamic countries, Friday is a rest day because it is the day that many Muslims go to mosque for prayer services.

Naturally, there is a geography of religion. In this chapter, we explore several ways in which religion can be viewed spatially. At the most basic level, religions flourish in some places and not in others. This basic geography is vital for your understanding of the world, and we will address basic religious beliefs and their global patterns. But religions also change the landscape by creating buildings and other human-made features, or by declaring certain spaces as sacred. Often, you can see a church or temple from miles away as you enter a town or city. This is not an accident. In addition, religions can change a culture or cultural landscape by introducing or influencing social or political ideas. In the United States, for example, views on abortion, the death penalty, euthanasia, and premarital sex are all related to religious attitudes in a particular region.

8A   Classifying Religions

Scientists love to classify things, and geographers are no exception. Classification allows us to take a very complex set of things and group them together into manageable units by finding some commonalities among the items. A **religion** is a cultural system of beliefs, traditions, and practices often centered around the worship of a deity or deities. Each faith is unique. Even within religions there is great diversity. Take Christianity, for example. Catholic, Orthodox, and Protestant denominations are all Christian, but they are often very different in modes of worship, beliefs, values, and bureaucratic organization. So there is value in grouping diverse sects as "Christian" when comparing Europe to North Africa, for example, where Islam dominates, but there is also value in identifying the location of religious subgroups when looking at religious differences within Europe.

One common way that scholars group religions is to distinguish among religions that actively seek to spread their ideas to other areas and religions that do not. Religions that seek to convert nonbelievers to their ranks are known as **universalizing religions**. They are open to anyone who is willing to do what is required for acceptance into the religion. These religions often use missionaries to actively seek out new members. Christianity and Islam are both universalizing religions, and both continue to grow rapidly around the world.

▼ **Figure 8A.1** Religion affects the way we use space in our towns and cities. In addition to building churches, temples, mosques, and shrines, we allocate often valuable land for functions such as cemeteries. This Muslim cemetery in Poland has obvious religious symbology, such as the crescent and the use of Arabic script.

▲ Humans glorify and honor religion and religious figures by building dramatic work, such as cathedrals and statues. This Buddhist statue, the Daibutsu (Great Buddha) of Kamakura, Japan, is one of the most famous in the world and weighs over 120 tons.

Followers of other religions view themselves differently and feel that their beliefs are unique to their people or region of the world. To be a member, you must be born into the religion. Often, these types of religions are associated with a particular ethnic group, so they are classified as **ethnic religions**. Hinduism is essentially an ethnic religion confined to people of South Asian descent. Shinto in Japan and Judaism are also ethnic religions.

A subset of ethnic religions is what can be called **traditional religions**. These faiths are practiced by small groups of people who largely live in isolated or developing areas of the globe. Tribal groups in remote parts of Africa or the Amazon whose ideas have not spread much beyond their own people are examples. In the United States, Native American religions would be classified as traditional.

Religions can also be classified based on other characteristics. Some religions believe in one Supreme Being. These religions are called **monotheistic** because they worship one god. Judaism, Zoroastrianism, Christianity, and Islam are examples. Other faiths believe in multiple gods and are thus labeled **polytheistic**. Hinduism is polytheistic, as were the religions of the ancient Greeks, Romans, and Norse peoples. The Romans, for example, worshipped Jupiter, Mars, Venus, Neptune, and countless other deities, while the Norse peoples of Scandinavia worshipped gods such as Odin, Thor, and Freyr. Many traditional religions are also polytheistic because they are what is known as animistic. **Animism** is the belief that souls and gods inhabit all or most objects—especially natural objects, such as trees, stones, and bodies of water. Shinto, the traditional religion of the Japanese people, is animistic.

▼ The most important moments of people's lives are often influenced by religion. Many holidays, weddings, funerals, and other ceremonies are based in religion. Here, a young boy plays with a *dreidel* during the Jewish holiday of Hanukkah.

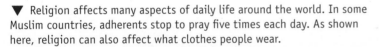

▼ Religion affects many aspects of daily life around the world. In some Muslim countries, adherents stop to pray five times each day. As shown here, religion can also affect what clothes people wear.

8B   Major World Religions

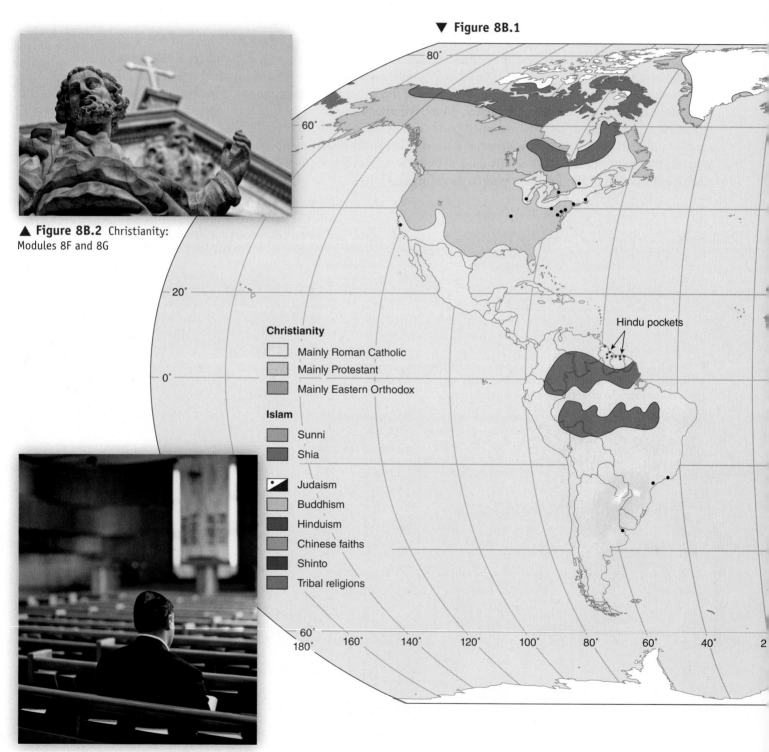

▲ **Figure 8B.2** Christianity: Modules 8F and 8G

▲ **Figure 8B.3** Judaism: Module 8E

▼ **Figure 8B.1**

Christianity

☐ Mainly Roman Catholic

☐ Mainly Protestant

☐ Mainly Eastern Orthodox

Islam

☐ Sunni

☐ Shia

☐ Judaism

☐ Buddhism

☐ Hinduism

☐ Chinese faiths

☐ Shinto

☐ Tribal religions

Hindu pockets

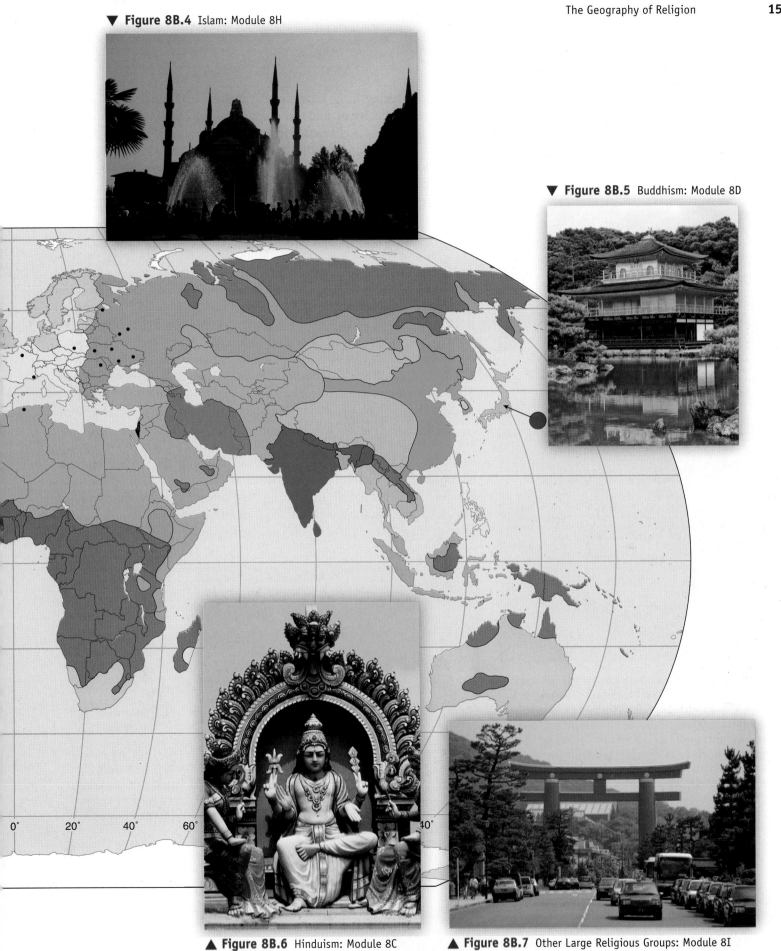

▼ **Figure 8B.4** Islam: Module 8H

▼ **Figure 8B.5** Buddhism: Module 8D

▲ **Figure 8B.6** Hinduism: Module 8C

▲ **Figure 8B.7** Other Large Religious Groups: Module 8I

0°   20°   40°   60°   40°

8C   Hinduism

Hinduism is at least 4,000–5,000 years old, making it the oldest of the major world religions. The word *Hindu* is derived from the Persian word for the Indus River, and this emphasizes how closely connected this religion is to the historical region of India, which now is covered primarily by the countries of Pakistan and India. Many argue that to be Hindu you must be Indian, and thus Hinduism is generally considered to be an ethnic religion. Its origins are in what is now Pakistan along the Indus River. Sometime between 2000 and 1000 BC, this civilization, probably already in decline, was invaded by a Central Asian people known as the Aryans. The Aryans brought their own religious ideas with them, and it is generally believed that Hinduism arose as a combination of indigenous Indus valley ideas and Aryan mythology.

As shown on the world map in Module 8B, the vast majority of Hindus live in India. According to the 2001 Census of India, over 827 million Indians, about 81% of the population, were Hindu. In neighboring countries, there are perhaps 20 million Hindus in Nepal, 2–3 million in Pakistan, over 12 million in Bangladesh, and about 3 million in Sri Lanka. Another 4–5 million live in Indonesia, 2–3 million in Malaysia, over a half million in Mauritius, as well as a few hundred thousand in Fiji. In Europe, Great Britain has the most Hindus, with about 500,000. South Africa has about the same. The United States can claim about 1 million Hindus, and there are significant populations in Canada as well.

At the root of Hinduism is the notion that a person's soul has existed since the beginning of time and that it passes from one being to another in a cycle of "rebirth" and "redeath." Commonly referred to as **reincarnation**, this cycle of repeated birth and death is called *samsara* by Hindus. A soul inhabits a organism, and when the being dies the soul passes to another life form. The type of life form the soul will inhabit after death is determined by the actions of the being in previous lives.

▲ **Figure 8C.1** The notion that each person has a place in society, and thus obligations to uphold (**dharma**), is a basic concept supporting India's **caste system**, a complex division of society into thousands of different economic classes. If you're born to be a blacksmith, many Hindus believe that you are violating your dharma if you desire instead to be a scientist, a truck driver, or an artist. Below all the castes are the **untouchables**, also called *Harijans* or *dalits*. Untouchables perform jobs that Hindus consider to be spiritually and physically unclean. For example, most Hindus are vegetarians, so any job that requires handling animal carcasses, bodily fluids or waste, or skin is considered very unclean. After India became an independent country in the 1940s, laws were gradually implemented that outlawed the caste system and tried to help untouchables and lower castes through affirmative action programs for government jobs, education, and political representation. Although the caste system has technically been outlawed in India, it is still a very strong reality in many areas of India, especially rural areas.

◄ **Figure 8C.2** In addition to important figures such as Shiva and Vishnu, the elephant-headed deity Ganesh is very popular and is believed to be a remover of obstacles in a follower's life. The symbolism of Hindu icons is complex to non-Hindus, but each element has a meaning. For example, the raised, open hand means that the deity is willing to bestow blessings on a believer.

This is the notion of **karma**, that every action a person takes has a consequence at some point in the future. Good or bad, everything we do, according to Hindus, matters.

But Hindus also believe that the cycle of birth and death can be broken, and this is the primary goal of the Hindu religion. The release from the cycle of birth and death is known as *moksha*. Also crucial to Hindus is the concept of *dharma*. The term *dharma* generally is translated as "duty." It means that every Hindu, every member of a society, has certain obligations that he or she should respect and fulfill. For example, a king has an obligation to take care of his people. Failure to do this is a violation of his dharma and thus brings bad karma (and bad consequences in the future).

Hindu Worship

Hinduism is polytheistic, and most Hindus worship one or more of the religion's thousands, or by some accounts millions, of gods and goddesses. Hindu cosmology has a trinity of gods that stand above the others. These are Brahma, the creator; Vishnu, the preserver; and Shiva, the destroyer. Of these three, Vishnu and Shiva have large sects of adherents devoted to them.

Stories of Hindu gods and goddesses are contained in what is collectively known as the **Vedas**, the Hindu holy books. The Vedas as a whole contain theological writings, poems, songs, myths and stories, and straightforward directions for conduction ceremonies and rituals.

Hindu worship is centered on prayer and homage for a particular god or goddess. Hindus may take flowers, sweets, or rice to a temple or shrine devoted to the god. They may also repeat the deity's name or chant mantras—a series of syllables, words, or phrases—to the god or goddess. Most of the time, Hindus worship individually. Communal ceremonies are relatively rare compared to other religions.

(a)

(b)

◀ **Figure 8C.3** (a) Hindu temples can be quite small, just a rough covering over an image of a deity, or very large. (b) Larger Hindu temples are often covered with statues of deities, often brightly painted. Inside the temple, there is one or more small rooms where a representation of a deity is kept. Festivals in honor of a particular god or goddess are also an important part of Hindu worship and are usually seasonal. Many of the larger festivals attract large numbers of pilgrims. The most well known is the Kumbh Mela festival, which rotates among four Indian cities, one city every three years. Hindus also celebrate numerous holidays during the year—such as Diwali, which is celebrated in the fall. It is the festival of lights and marks the start of the new year.

8D   Buddhism

Buddhism is an important world religion practiced by about 400 million people worldwide. Buddhism has its roots in Hindu India during the sixth century BC, or about 2,500 years ago. According to legend, in 566 BC a boy named **Siddhartha** was born in the foothills of the Himalayas, an area that now would be considered part of Nepal. Born into an important family in the region, Siddhartha was given a privileged upbringing that ensured him every possible luxury and protection. But he became disillusioned after witnessing the suffering and death of people outside his palace. For six years, Siddhartha wandered northern India in search of a spiritual system that would help him achieve the peace of mind he had witnessed in a holy man. Finally, after a long night of meditation, the path to enlightenment became clear to him, and he awoke, according to Buddhists, not as Siddhartha but as the Buddha, meaning "One who is awake" or the "Enlightened." Armed with his revelations, the Buddha began a 45-year career as a wandering teacher/prophet traversing the Ganges valley of northern India. At about the age of 80, around the year 486 BC, the Buddha died not far from his birthplace.

Like Hindus, Buddhists believe that humans and all other living things are reborn time and time again. Furthermore, Buddhists also believe in the notion of karma, that good deeds in life can move a person to a higher life form or existence in a future life, and vice versa.

▲ **Figure 8D.1** Buddhist temples often contain statues of the Buddha. These statues typically come in three forms: sitting, standing, and lying down. This large Buddha is in Nara, Japan. The small figures of an overweight, happy man that many people call "buddhas" are not typically depictions of the Buddha but represent Budai, a tenth-century monk popular in East Asian folklore.

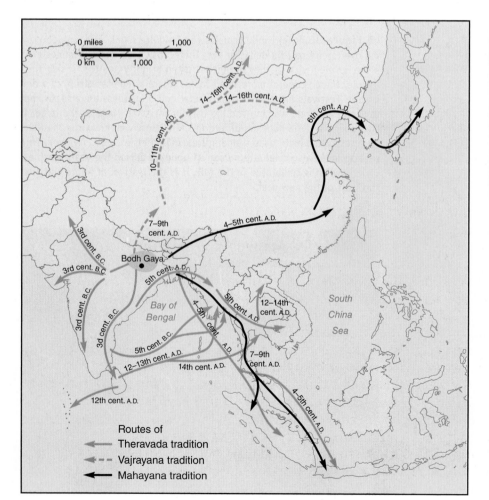

◀ **Figure 8D.2** This map shows the diffusion of Buddhism from its origin in South Asia into Southeast and East Asia. As you can see, Theravada, Mahayana, and Vajrayana forms of the religion developed along different paths of diffusion.

Breaking the cycle of birth and death is one of the two major goals of a Buddhist. The other is to escape the suffering of life. The Buddha taught that there are **Four Noble Truths**:

1. Life is suffering (*dukkha*).
2. Suffering is caused by human desire or craving.
3. Suffering can be ended.
4. The way to eliminate desire is through the **Eightfold Path**: Right Understanding, Right Thought, Right Speech, Right Action, Right Livelihood, Right Effort, Right Mindfulness, and Right Concentration.

If a Buddhist achieves a cessation to suffering by following the Eightfold Path, he or she can attain *Nirvana*. Although this term is often crudely translated as "heaven," the word literally means to "quench" or "blow out," as in a flame. With Nirvana, according to Buddhist beliefs, comes the end of greed, hatred, and similar sources of suffering.

After the Buddha's death, his teachings were kept alive by oral tradition and eventually written down to constitute what is called either the **Pali Canon** or the *Tripitaka*. *Pali* refers to a dead language that was used at the time to record the teachings. *Tripitaka* means the "Three Baskets" because the writings contained three main sections.

In the third century BC, the Indian ruler Ashoka, after witnessing the carnage of a military campaign, promoted Buddhism throughout what is now most of India. He also encouraged missionaries to spread Buddhism to Sri Lanka, where even today the majority of the population is Buddhist. In time, Buddhism spread beyond Sri Lanka to Burma, Thailand, Laos, and Cambodia in Southeast Asia. This form of Buddhism is today referred to as **Theravada Buddhism**, and it is considered more conservative than other sects, meaning that it most closely represents the teaching of the Buddha with very little interpretation. Theravadans are today found primarily in Sri Lanka, Burma, and Thailand, as depicted in the map. Note that Buddhists are no longer found in India in large numbers. After about 500 AD, the religion began a slow decline in India as Hinduism, and later Islam, rose to prominence in the region.

▲ **Figure 8D.3** Monks are common in many Buddhist societies. Young men, and sometimes women, commonly become monastics for a period of time, such as a few months or a year, before returning to their secular lives.

Buddhism also diffused out from India to the north. Buddhist teachings first took hold among peoples living in what is now northern India and Pakistan, Afghanistan, the countries of Central Asia, and far western China. Historically, the great Silk Road—actually, several major trade routes—passed through this area, connecting it with the Middle East, eastern Europe, and the heart of China. By about the first century AD, Buddhism had moved into China, where it began to catch on. During the second half of the first millennium (AD 500–1000), Buddhism thrived in China. The form of Buddhism that took hold there is known as **Mahayana Buddhism**. This sect has more spiritual and mystical components than Theravada sects, and in time Mahayana sects spread to Korea, Japan, and Southeast Asia.

The final Buddhist region that should be mentioned is Tibet and Mongolia. Because Tibet is mountainous and largely inaccessible, Buddhism did not enter the region until the eighth century, or 1,300 years after the religion was founded. The **Vajrayana** tradition of Buddhism that took hold there, and later spread to Mongolia, shares a lot of elements with Mahayana sects, but it contains a variety of esoteric elements, including magic formulas known as mantras and complex mystical diagrams called mandalas.

Today, Buddhists number about 400 million worldwide. Of these, about 100 million or more are Theravada Buddhists living primarily in Burma, Thailand, Cambodia, Laos, and Vietnam. Mahayana Buddhists number about 200–300 million and are found mostly in China, Japan, Vietnam, and South Korea. The remaining Buddhists are the 10 million or so Tibetan and Mongolian Buddhists of the Vajrayana tradition. In North America, there are perhaps a million Buddhists in the United States and 300,000 or so in Canada. Decades of immigration to both countries from Asia has naturally increased the number of Buddhists.

Buddhist houses of worship are known as temples. Because of the diversity of Buddhism, the look of Buddhist temples varies greatly. But a very common element is the presence of *stupa*, an often bell-shaped structure that has origins before Buddhism even began. The stupa symbolically represents both the universe and the Buddhist path to enlightenment that leads upward toward Nirvana.

8E   Judaism

Compared to the other four major world religions, **Judaism** is a much smaller faith. Worldwide, only about 14–15 million people practice the religion. But size alone is no way to judge the importance or impact of a religion. As the spiritual foundation of Christianity and Islam, Judaism has changed the world in indescribable ways. To understand the other two faiths, you must understand Judaism. Furthermore, because of its age, over 2,500 years old, Judaism has long influenced many of the world's civilizations. Our values, beliefs, customs, and laws often bear the imprint of ideas that began with a small group of nomads thousands of years ago.

Judaism is the religion of the Jewish people, an ethnic religion, so the history of Judaism is largely tied with their story. The ancestors of the Jews, the Hebrews, were a small, tribal group that lived in the Middle East in what is now Iraq, Syria, Jordan, Saudi Arabia, and Israel. According to Jewish history,

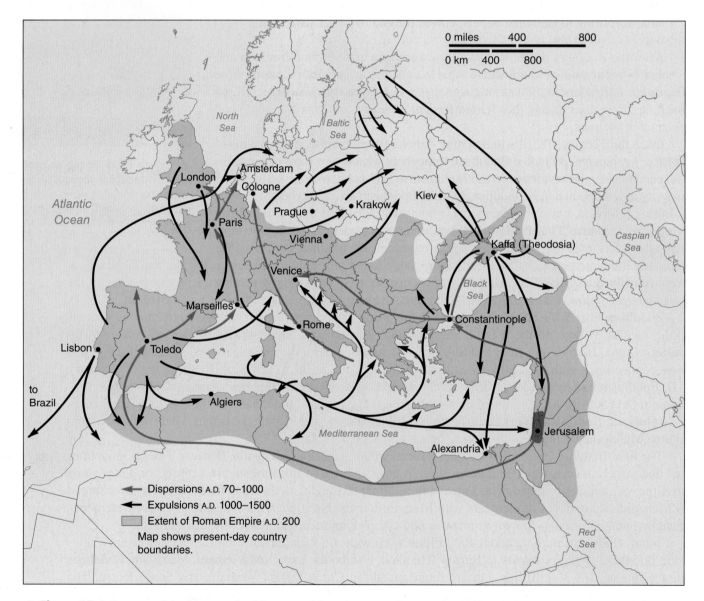

▲ **Figure 8E.1** Because of the Diaspora, Jewish communities are scattered across the globe, settling primarily in Europe, North Africa, and other areas of the Middle East. This map shows the movement of Jewish populations during the years 70–1500. Centuries later, many European Jews fled the horrible genocide of the Nazi Holocaust during the 1930s and settled in the United States, adding to existing Jewish communities that date back to 1654, when a group of 23 Sephardic Jews fleeing from persecution in Spain during the Inquisition settled in New Amsterdam, now New York City. Today, the United States has the largest Jewish population on the planet, with nearly 6 million Jews. Israel has between 4 and 5 million Jews. Russia, France, Canada, Great Britain, and Argentina also have sizable Jewish populations, as do South Africa and Argentina.

about 1900 BC, Abraham, then living in a city in northern Mesopotamia (modern Iraq), was visited by God and told to take his family and move to the west. Abraham obeyed, and as he moved west he was visited by God again and told that someday the lands of that area, now modern Israel, would be his.

While the history is a bit uncertain, between about 1500 and 1250 BC many Hebrews settled in ancient Egypt. Around 1250 BC, a man named Moses, according to Jewish and Christian history, was chosen by God to lead a large group of the Hebrews out of Egypt and to the East. During this exodus, Moses gave what might have been a variety of peoples a unique identity, that of *bene yisrael*, or "Children of Israel." The Ten Commandments, according to tradition, were revealed to Moses during this time. Eventually, the *bene yisrael* settled in Canaan, the land between the Mediterranean Sea and the Jordan River. But over the centuries, the peoples of the area were torn by alternating periods of division, unification, and even exile to the Mesopotamian kingdom of Babylonia.

Eventually, the Greeks and then the Romans became the rulers of the region. It was under the Romans that Jewish history changed forever. In AD 70, after a revolt against them, the Romans expelled the Jews from the region. A courageous holdout, and later mass suicide, by some revolutionaries at the mountain fort of Masada in AD 73 is an important event in Jewish history, and Masada remains a sacred place for modern Israeli Jews.

The expulsion of the Jews from the region is known as the **Diaspora**, or scattering (see Module 10F). Jewish populations moved away from their territory and settled throughout the Middle East, North Africa, and southern Europe. In time, Jewish communities migrated even farther.

Jewish Worship

Judaism is a monotheistic religion. God is seen as an all-powerful being who granted humans free will. Humans are able to communicate with God through prayer and God can appear to humans in revelations. This communication between a Supreme Being and humanity is not present in all religions. Often, deities are distant and aloof.

Jews believe that God gave humans his law through the **Torah**. In its most basic sense, the Torah is the first five books of the Hebrew Bible, later called the Old Testament by Christians. But there is a broader meaning of Torah that also includes oral explanations of the laws in these five books. These oral explanations were passed down through the generations by teachers and rabbis, the spiritual leaders of the Jewish community. When Jewish children symbolically pass into adulthood, knowledge of the Torah is an essential part of their passage.

Holy days and festivals are a central part of Jewish life. Because they are based on a lunar calendar, the holy days fall at different times each year. The Jewish Sabbath begins at sundown on Friday evening and lasts until Saturday evening. This is symbolic of God resting on the seventh day of creation, as portrayed in the book of Genesis, the first book of the Torah (and Christian Old Testament). Jews are not supposed to work on the Sabbath, and in conservative Jewish communities this is strictly obeyed. Other Jewish holy days fall throughout the year. Some of the more important are Rosh Hashanah, Yom Kippur, Pesach, Shavuot, Sukkot, Purim, and Chanukah.

Observant Jews are required to eat food that is **kosher**. To be kosher, food must be prepared in accordance with a long list of dietary laws. Animals must be killed in a specific way, or the meat cannot be consumed. Only animals that have a cloven hoof and dual digestive tracts can be eaten. This means that cows, goats, and sheep can be eaten, but pigs and horses are forbidden. Seafood must have scales and fins, so lobster, crab, and eels are not kosher.

▲ **Figure 8E.2** Jewish life is full of traditions and religious practices almost from birth. Jewish children are supposed to receive religious training after about age five. This is usually conducted at the local **synagogue**, a Jewish place of worship. Each synagogue has an ark, a cupboard, on the wall that faces Jerusalem and contains a copy of the Torah. A boy becomes an adult (*bar-mitzvah*) in the Jewish community at age 13 and a girl at age 12 (*bat-mitzvah*).

8F   Christianity

The largest religion, with over 2 billion adherents, **Christianity** is an important religious force in the world today. The prehistory of Christianity is the history of Judaism—Christianity is an offshoot of the earlier religion. Judaism taught that a Messiah from the descendants of David would come forward to end the oppression of the Jewish people and establish a Kingdom of God. Christians believe that this Messiah was a Jewish man named **Jesus**, who was probably born about 4 BC. The word *Christ* is Greek for "anointed one" or Messiah.

Many Christian beliefs naturally stem from Judaism. Monotheism, obedience to God's commandments, and acknowledgment of an afterlife are all central elements of both Christianity and Judaism. To Christians, God is an all-powerful, perfect being who loves everyone unconditionally. But Christianity naturally adds to these core Jewish beliefs a variety of values that stem from Jesus's life and teachings. Basically, Jesus taught his followers to love God and each other. Christians also believe that Jesus, by allowing himself to be crucified, gave humans the opportunity to be forgiven by God for their sins. Thus, everyone can attain salvation and go to heaven. Another central idea of Christianity is the belief in a trinity comprised of God, Jesus, and the Holy Spirit. The Holy Spirit is conceived as the active presence of God in believers.

Christian Worship

Christians believe that they can communicate with God through prayer. Prayer can be formal, conducted in a group or an organized religious service, or personal. Some sects of Christianity also believe that prayer to Jesus's mother, Mary, or to saints can also be received by God.

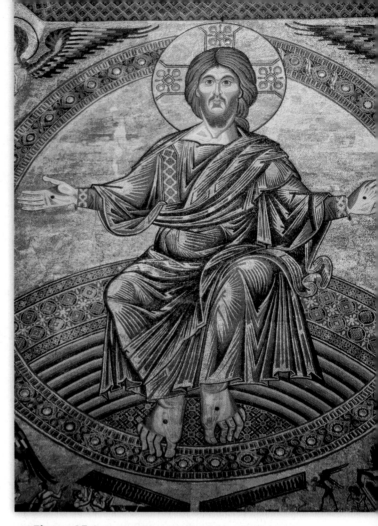

▲ **Figure 8F.1** Most of the details of Jesus's life are unknown. Some scholars believe he lived a humble life as a tradesman, but others feel he may have been a rabbi before beginning his public ministry. At about age 30, Jesus began preaching throughout Palestine and attracting followers. Jesus's claim to be the Messiah was welcomed by many because a lot of Jews were expecting a savior to release them from their oppressive Roman rulers. Jesus's message, one of salvation for all regardless of status in society, including slaves and sinners, directly confronted both Roman rule and the Jewish hierarchy. In about AD 29, Jesus was executed by the Romans and his disciples and followers were scattered.

Christians worship as a community on Sunday, considered the Christian Sabbath, but there is evidence that the Jewish Sabbath was also observed for centuries after Christ's death. The nature of Christian communal worship, however, varies widely. In some sects, such as Roman Catholic, Orthodox, and Episcopal (Anglican) churches, worship services are very structured and ritualized. In other sects, such as among the Quakers, services are quiet and simple. In modern evangelical churches, services are often loud, festive occasions. Sunday services for some Christians can be as short as 20–30 minutes. For others, all-day services are common.

Christians celebrate several major holidays. For most, the most important holiday is Easter, which celebrates Jesus's resurrection from the dead. Christmas, commemorating Jesus's birthday, is also widely practiced and has become a secular holiday as well. Some sects of Christianity, such as Catholicism and Eastern Orthodoxy, also celebrate days in honor of various saints, persons declared by the Church to be models of proper Christian action.

▲ **Figure 8F.2** Most Christians practice the ritual of baptism either in infancy or in adulthood. Baptism involves cleansing with water as a symbol of the believer's commitment to God. Here, a baby is baptized by a priest of the Ukrainian Orthodox Church. Another Christian ritual is the Eucharist.

▲ **Figure 8F.3** The United States is the largest Christian country in terms of population, with about 225 million Christians. Brazil, Mexico, Russia, and China are the next in line, although Christianity in China is tightly controlled. This image shows the Cathedral of Brasilia in the Brazilian capital. Worldwide there are about a billion Catholics, 400 million Protestants, 225 million Orthodox Christians, 70 million Anglicans (Church of England/ Episcopalians), and nearly 300 million other Christians who do not fall into one of these categories.

8G   The Spread and Distribution of Christianity

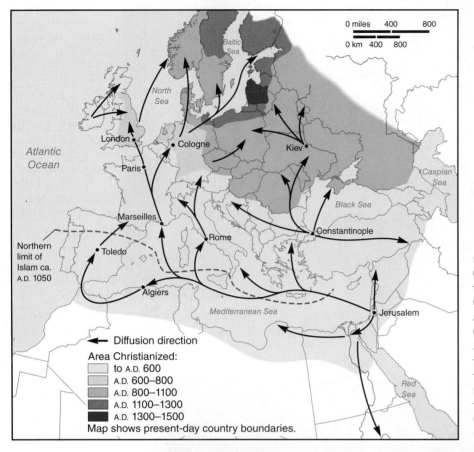

◄ **Figure 8G.1** After Jesus's death, his disciples moved out into the wider Roman Empire. In general, Christians were seen as a sect of Judaism, and at first Christians were mostly Jews by birth. But soon, Christians decided that their message was appropriate for a wider audience, and they began converting Gentiles (non-Jews). Geographically, the Mediterranean area was a good one for missionary work because travel was relatively safe compared to other areas of the world. Boats criss-crossed the Mediterranean Sea regularly, allowing ideas to flow from one country to another. By the end of the second century AD, Christianity had spread as far west as Spain, as far north as Britain, and as far east as India.

Figure 8G.2 ▶
Christianity took hold early on in Egypt and diffused to the south. The **Coptic Christians** of Egypt and Ethiopia are descendants of these early Christians. Here, a Coptic monk participates in a Christmas service in Cairo, Egypt.

◀ **Figure 8G.3** Persecutions of early Christians in the Roman Empire continued until they were stopped by the Emperor Constantine in AD 312. The next year, Constantine conquered his rivals and felt that the victory had been aided by the Christian God, and he decided that the persecution of Christians should cease. The 313 Edict of Milan called for tolerance of all faiths in the Roman Empire. Soon, Christianity became the official religion of the empire, and this meant that it spread rapidly throughout Europe. Over time, the Roman Empire split into two parts. One had a capital at Rome and the other at Constantinople, now Istanbul. This division affected the Christian Church as well, and in time, theological and administrative differences began to split the religion. This culminated in what is commonly known as the **Great Schism** of 1054. Christianity split into two major groups, and the split between Roman Catholics and Eastern Orthodox Christians exists to this day. This church is Greek Orthodox.

▲ **Figure 8G.4** By the sixteenth century, many Christians also felt that the Catholic Church had grown greedy and bloated. The decisive moment came in 1517 when a disaffected priest named Martin Luther wrote and began to distribute his *95 Theses* in what is now Germany. This short work was a criticism of corruption in the Church, particularly the sale of indulgences, the practice of forgiving sins in exchange for money. Luther was one of a number of thinkers who argued that salvation could be achieved without the rituals required by the Catholic Church. This break from Rome and the ideas of the Catholic Church is known as the **Protestant Reformation**.

Within a few decades, many kingdoms of northern Europe had broken from Rome. Thinkers such as Zwingli and John Calvin also contributed to the spread of the Reformation. Calvinism is the origin of such Protestant denominations as the Presbyterians, Congregationalists, and Baptists. This Protestant Church in Polynesia represents the global diffusion of the ideas of the Reformation.

▲ **Figure 8G.5** Protestant ideas spread to North America with early English, Dutch, and German settlers. As successive waves of immigrants arrived in the United States, they brought or reinforced religious ideas. Lutheran churches, such as this one in North Dakota, represent the millions of German migrants who settled in the American heartland.

▲ **Figure 8H.1** The oldest stones of the Quba Mosque in Medina, Saudi Arabia, were laid by Muhammad, and the first structure on the site was completed in the year 622. It is one of several holy sites for Muslims in Medina.

8H Islam

Given the global situation today, perhaps no religion is more misunderstood by nonbelievers than Islam. The youngest of the world's major religions, **Islam** has quickly grown to become the second largest religion on the planet.

Islam starts with the AD 570 birth of **Muhammad** in the city of Mecca, now in Saudi Arabia. Muslims believe that Muhammad is the last, and therefore greatest, prophet of God, or Allah. Muhammad's father died before he was born, and his mother when he was just a boy, so he was raised by an uncle, Abu Talib, an important man and leader of his clan. When he was in his twenties, Muhammad married a woman named Khadija, and together they had three sons and four daughters; but all three sons died while still very young. His daughter Fatima grew to marry a man named Ali, the son of Muhammad's uncle, Abu Talib.

At some point after his marriage, Muhammad began meditating for days or even weeks at a time at a location known as the Cave of Hira, near Mecca. Muslims believe that one night, when Muhammad was 40 years old, he received a visit at the Cave of Hira by the angel Gabriel, who instructed him to preach God's message. From this point on, Muhammad began a public ministry to teach others.

Beginning with his family, he was soon preaching to the poor and troubled of Mecca, a city with a large lower-class population. This made him unpopular with local authorities, who wanted to keep the lower classes in line and who feared that Muhammad would ruin an annual and popular pilgrimage that brought people to Mecca to worship idols located there. In 622, he preached to a group of pilgrims from the town of Yathrib, located about 250 miles north of Mecca. They agreed to allow

◀ **Figure 8H.2** How Muslims are expected to live can be summarized by the **Five Pillars:**

1. A confession of faith, known as the *Shahadah*. It is, simply, "There is no god but God, and Muhammad is His Prophet."
2. Prayer. Muslims are expected to pray five times a day. The times of the five prayer sessions are when a Muslim wakes up, at noon, midafternoon, sunset, and before going to bed. During prayer, Muslims face in the direction of Mecca, no matter where they are in the world.
3. Charity. Muslims, except the poor, are expected to give one-fortieth of their income and possessions to the poor each year.
4. Observance of the holy month of Ramadan. During Ramadan, Muslims fast during the day and only take food or drink in moderation at night.
5. Pilgrimage, or the **Hajj**. Every able-bodied Muslim who can afford the journey is expected to make a pilgrimage to Mecca once during his or her lifetime.

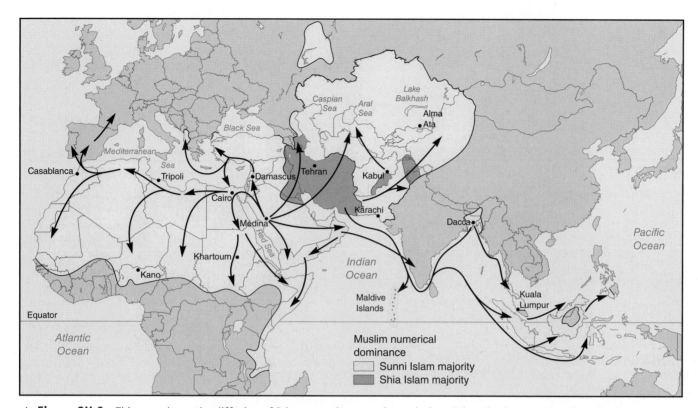

▲ **Figure 8H.3**   This map shows the diffusion of Islam over the centuries and where Islam dominates today. Overall, there are about 1.2 billion Muslims in the world. Of this number, about 90% are Sunnis and 10% Shi'ites. Shi'ites live primarily in Iran and southern Iraq. The most populous Muslim country is Indonesia, with over 170 million Muslims, highlighting that many Islamic countries are not Arab countries. For example, Pakistan, Bangladesh, and India each have over 100 million adherents. Turkey and Iran, both non-Arab Middle Eastern countries, also have over 60 million Muslims each. Note, as well, the spread of Islam into areas south of the Sahara Desert. This is one of Islam's frontiers.

Muhammad and his followers to move to their city and establish a community there. The move of Muhammad and his followers to Yathrib, renamed Medina, is the start of the Islamic calendar and is known as the *Hijra*. Muhammad built a mosque in Medina as a place of worship and, over time, followers came and the community grew.

But Muhammad's flight to Medina made him a traitor in the eyes of Mecca's leaders, and they declared that he and his followers be destroyed. Conversely, Muhammad considered Mecca to be the home of the Arabs, and thus he wanted his followers to take the city someday. Between 2 AH (*Anno Higrae*) and 8 AH, the Muslims and forces from Mecca battled several times. In 8 AH, Muhammad's followers captured Mecca and took control of the city. Muhammad declared an amnesty and destroyed the idols that pilgrims had prayed to for centuries. About two years later, in 10 AH, or 632, Muhammad died in Medina.

Islam builds on the monotheistic ideas of Judaism and Christianity before it, and many of the traditions and stories of those religions are present in Islam. The primary source of Islamic beliefs is the **Qur'an**, sometimes spelled Koran, which Muslims believe contains the actual words of God as revealed to Muhammad, the Prophet, during a period from 610 until Muhammad's death. Because it is considered to be the word of God, Muslims believe that the Qur'an must be read in Arabic, the language in which it was revealed to Muhammad. The book is arranged into 114 sections, called *suras*, by length. The shortest passages are first, the longest last.

The most important Islamic belief is in a single, all-powerful God who created the world out of mercy and kindness. To accept God's laws is to submit, or *islam*. *Muslim* means "that which submits." Humans, given free will by God, must choose to surrender to his laws. Humans, according to Muslims, are God's greatest creation. In return for creation, humans are expected to be thankful to God and to surrender to God's laws.

▲ **Figure 8H.4** The Muslim house of worship is the **mosque**. Mosques are really community centers, places for local Muslims to go for prayer, community gatherings, quiet contemplation, or school. They can be large and grand, such as these side-by-side mosques in Cairo (a), or simple, like the local mosque in eastern Poland (b). Muslims have no real Sabbath, but Friday is the closest thing. On this day, large services are held at many mosques, and a religious teacher or leader, called an *imam* by the majority Sunnis, leads prayers and often gives a sermon. Imams in the Sunni faith also often serve as judges in matters of **Sharia**, or Muslim law. In the Shi'ite branch of Islam, the term *imam* refers to one of the direct successors of Muhammad, an infallible interpreter of the Qur'an, and is thus much different than a Sunni imam, who holds a position relatively equal to a Jewish rabbi or Christian priest or minister.

The most important event in Islam happened soon after the death of Muhammad. Because he had no sons, the fledgling Muslim community had to answer the question "Who will lead us?" Sunnis, who now account for about 90% of all Muslims, believed in a community-chosen leader, while the Shi'ites supported a member of Muhammad's family. More specifically, Shi'ites supported the leadership of Ali, Muhammad's cousin and the husband of his daughter Fatima. But Ali was murdered in 661 and his son, Husayn, died violently in 680. Husayn's death occurred in what is now the city of Karbala in Iraq, and a shrine there is one of the holiest places for Shi'ite Muslims.

In the seventh and eighth centuries, Islam spread rapidly and often by military conquest. By the mid-eighth century, Islam had already spread as far west as Morocco and Spain and east into Persia (Iran) and Central Asia. The first Muslims had also already visited China by this time. By the twelfth century, Islam had spread across the Sahara Desert and down the eastern coast of Africa. It had also crossed the Indus River into what is now India, and from there Islam moved with trade routes into Southeast Asia. In the six-teenth and seventeenth centuries, Muslim armies under the Ottoman Empire moved into the southwestern European region of the Balkans, such as modern Greece, Serbia, Croatia, Bosnia, and Herzegovina, and into parts of Hungary.

▲ **Figure 8H.5**   The status of women in Islam has received a lot of attention in recent years. The Qur'an itself generally calls for equality between men and women. Women have the right to marry freely, own property, have a job, and get an edu-cation. There are some passages in the Qur'an that favor men, but few justify the harsh treatment of women found in many Islamic countries. For example, the Qur'an calls on Muslims to dress modestly, but it does not require women to cover them-selves completely. One passage refers to Muhammad's wives hiding behind veils when his male friends are talking to him, but this is not interpreted by many Islamic scholars as a requirement for women to always be veiled in public. Most of the harsh treatment women are subjected to in the Islamic world is more a matter of a cultural history of mistreatment rather than the laws set forth in the Qur'an. Because of this, there are great differences in the status of women's rights in Islamic countries. In Saudi Arabia, Afghanistan, and other Muslim fundamentalist countries, women clearly are denied even the most basic civil and political rights. But in other Muslim countries, such as Turkey and Indonesia, women have access to the same education as men and can hold great power. In fact, Indonesia has had a female head of state.

8I   Other Large Religious Groups

Now that we have introduced you to the major world religions, let's take a brief look at other religions that have large followings. Some have a global presence and others are more localized, but all influence the lives of millions daily. Refer to Module 8B to see the location of these religions.

◀ **Figure 8I.1** Chinese folk religion (labeled "Chinese faiths" on the map in Module 8B), practiced by over 200 million people, is a combination of Chinese Buddhism, **Confucianism**, and **Taoism**. Confucius lived from 551 to 479 BC in what is now China. The philosophy put forward by him and his followers emphasizes the importance of loyalty to one's parents, family, and government. As such, it supports an orderly state. Taoism is much more mystical and esoteric than Confucianism, focusing on individual morality, self-restraint, and humility. The combination of these two philosophies with Buddhism creates a complex web of ideas that are unique to Chinese culture. Geographically, Chinese Traditional Religion is found wherever Chinese are found. Outside of China, Southeast Asia and North America are likely the largest areas for this religion.

◀ **Figure 8I.2 African Traditional Religion** is actually a catch-all term that refers to many individual religions in Africa that have some commonalities. Most traditional African religions can be classified as forms of animism (see Module 8A). Rather than eternal salvation, the focus of most African religions is on maintaining the order of society and life. Failure to properly respect the gods might bring a bad harvest or infertility, thus upsetting the life cycle. Many traditional African religions also include ancestor veneration, the respect and worship of one's deceased relatives. It is estimated that about 100 million people or more practice some aspect of this religion. Most are in Africa, but many traditional African religious ideas are the foundations of North and South American religions such as Voodoo and Santería. Both of these combine traditional African ideas with Catholic teachings.

◀ **Figure 8I.3 Sikhism** was founded by Guru Nanak, who was born in 1469 in what is now northern India. Nanak received a vision at age 30 and began teaching in the region. After his death, a succession of gurus added to his ideas. A reaction to perceived problems with both Islam and Hinduism, Sikhism is a monotheistic religion that preaches equality for men and women among all classes. In this regard, it rejected the Hindu caste system but retained a belief in karma and reincarnation. Monotheism and daily prayer represent more Islamic traditions. Sikh men are distinctive because they do not cut their hair, keeping it in neatly wrapped turbans. The majority of the world's roughly 20 million Sikhs are in India, especially the northwestern state of Punjab, the traditional Sikh homeland. The holiest temple of the Sikhs, the Golden Temple, can be found at Amritsar in Punjab. This smaller temple is in northern India. Emigration has resulted in Sikh populations in both the United States and Canada.

▲ **Figure 8I.5** **Jainism** developed as a reaction to Hinduism at about the same time that Buddhism did the same thing, in the sixth century BC. Most of the world's Jains are in India or countries settled by Indians. Jains, who number about 4 million worldwide, believe that the only way to escape the cycle of rebirth is to cease all activity that might accumulate bad karma. Thus, Jains see extreme asceticism and a roving, monastic lifestyle as the only true way to salvation. Jain monks and nuns renounce all possessions and wander on foot for much of their lives, begging for food and other necessities and refraining from harming any living thing.

▲ **Figure 8I.4** The **Bahá'í** faith was founded in the nineteenth century in what is now Iran and Iraq. The main message of Bahá'í is that all peoples are the same regardless of background or religion, although Bahá'í is considered preferable to other religions because it was revealed to humans after other religions. Bahá'í thus seeks to unite the peoples of the world, and because it is a universalizing religion by its very nature, Bahá'í has spread to nearly every country. The total number of Bahá'í adherents is roughly 6 million. The Shrine of the Báb, shown here, is located in Haifa, Israel, and is considered one of the most holy places in the religion.

◄ **Figure 8I.6** **Shinto** is the ancient, animistic religion of Japan. Shinto believers acknowledge that gods, *kami*, are present in all natural objects. People pray to and honor the gods to ensure that good fortune will fall on them. This shrine is to Hachiman, Shinto god of war. Shinto shrines are marked by the presence of a *torii*, a distinctively shaped gate (see Module 8B). While only about 4 million people are devout followers of Shinto, nearly everyone in Japan makes regular trips to a shrine to pray for good fortune. In addition, marriages and other happy occasions are often marked by a service at a shrine. Festivals are common Shinto celebrations, bringing large populations to shrines for entertainment and worship. Shinto can certainly be considered an ethnic religion because it is intimately tied to being Japanese. Most Japanese also practice elements of Buddhism in their lives, making Japanese society an interesting study in religious coexistence. For example, most Japanese families choose Shinto weddings but Buddhist funerals.

8J   Landscapes of Religion

Examining the spatial distribution of particular religions, as we have done in the previous modules, is probably the most common way to examine the geography of religion. If we think back to the concepts of pattern and process, there is a pattern to where religions are found around the globe, and there are processes that account for that pattern. But geography is more than just learning where things are. In this section, we explore some other ways in which geographers have looked at the geography of religion and religious ideas.

Religious Landscapes

In Module 6F, we explored the idea of the cultural landscape. As conceived by Carl Sauer (see Module 2E) and others, the natural landscape is modified by a human culture to produce a cultural, or human, landscape. Religion, as a primary component of many cultures, is certainly present on the landscape. The most obvious examples of this are basic religious structures, be they churches, temples, shrines, mosques, or synagogues. Each religion, and usually denominations within religions, has unique design elements that affect the physical structure and look of their houses of worship. A traditional Protestant church in New England generally looks different from a Catholic church, even though worshippers at both are Christian. Muslim mosques almost always have a *minaret*, or tower, which provides a place for a *muezzin*, or caller, to make a call for prayer over the surrounding neighborhood. Many Christian cathedrals have a cross-shaped floor plan. Hindu temples vary in shape and form based on the primary deity that the temple honors. Japanese Shinto shrines are immediately identifiable by the presence of a *torii*, or gate.

▲ **Figure 8J.1** Religious buildings are often a clue to the ethnic history of an area. The presence of Orthodox Christian churches, with their onion-shaped towers, is a strong sign of an Eastern European heritage. In Pennsylvania, German churches were often the most ornate, so old, elaborate churches are generally a sign of German settlers rather than Irish or Scottish settlers, who preferred simpler designs.

Religion can also be seen in the way some societies organize their cities. In the Spanish Catholic settlements of Middle and South America, the main square nearly always has a large church. Mormon communities also have the local temple in the middle of the town. The surrounding town was laid out in a gridlike pattern, as envisioned by The Church of Jesus Christ of Latter Day Saints' founder Joseph Smith. Houses were to be set a particular distance from the road, front yards were to be landscaped, and backyards were to have gardens. Many Indian Hindu villages also have a temple in the middle of the community. The plain, agricultural landscapes of the Amish are also inspired by their religious belief that a simple life brings them closer to God.

Another type of religious landscape is the geography of religious administrative areas. For example, in the Catholic Church, which is very hierarchical, regions of a country are divided into dioceses. A diocese is then further subdivided into parishes, or local church communities. The Orthodox and Episcopalian Churches use similar hierarchical structures with defined territories.

◀ **Figure 8J.2** There is great diversity in the size of religious buildings. At the smallest end, tiny roadside shrines and home-based altars are often personal tributes to religious beliefs, but there are spatial patterns as well. For example, several studies have shown that in Christian areas, Catholic families are much more apt to display a small shrine or grotto on their property than are Protestant families. In Thailand, although most people practice Buddhism, old, animistic traditions persist in the prominence of spirit houses. These tiny shelters are erected when a family moves into a home, in case the property is occupied by the spirits of past residents. If so, according to Thai beliefs, the phantoms will be able to move into the smaller spirit house, which the family stocks with food and water. Shrines or altars in the home are common in many cultures, including the Japanese, some Hindus, and Mexican Americans in the U.S. Southwest. At the other end of the spectrum, some religious buildings are very large. The Basilica of Our Lady of Peace in Côte d'Ivoire, with 300,000 square feet of space, is the largest church in the world.

Many religions believe that certain places hold special religious significance. As geographers, we can study not only the location and distribution of these holy/sacred places but also their meaning. In general, this is a dichotomous distinction between **sacred** and **profane landscapes**. The word *profane* means "unconsecrated" or "ordinary." The word comes from the Latin *pro fanum*, meaning "before the Temple." People who were not admitted in because of their behavior or character were *pro fanum*, or outside of the Temple. Thus, profane places are the ordinary, unholy places of the world, while sacred places have religious or spiritual meaning. Why certain places take on sacred qualities is debated by scholars, but geographer Yi-fu Tuan (see Module 2F) has emphasized that many sacred spaces seem to have qualities that make them different from other places. Thus, these locations may have a uniqueness that makes them seem otherworldly, separated from the profane world. Tuan also argues that sacred places have order and are whole, self-contained environments that radiate power. Theorists also debate whether sacred spaces are created by humans or have intrinsic qualities that people naturally consider sacred.

There is great variety in the types of places considered sacred by peoples around the world. The scholars Jackson and Henrie put sacred places into three categories.

▲ **Figure 8J.3** Cemeteries, and related places for the dead, are another common landscape element that varies from religion to religion. The pyramids of ancient Egypt might be the most well known landscapes of the dead, and they are certainly the largest. At the other extreme, Hindus have almost no burial sites or memorials because the dead are cremated and their ashes scattered. This contrasts greatly with large, permanent Christian cemeteries—such as this one in Florence, Italy— which utilize a great deal of prime real estate in most communities. The Parsis of India, practitioners of the ancient religion of Zoroastrianism, do not bury their dead. Instead, when possible, they leave the deceased in the open air on what are known as Towers of Silence, or dakhmas. In time, the body is eaten by birds and decays.

◄ **Figure 8J.4** The Western Wall in Jerusalem, a sacred place for Jews, is within meters of the Dome of the Rock, the third most sacred place for Muslims.

First, some places are sacred because they are historical sites important to a religion. For example, Jerusalem's Western Wall, also called the Wailing Wall, is sacred to Jews because it is the only remaining part of the Second Temple of Jerusalem, which was destroyed by the Romans in AD 70 and was an important catalyst for the Diaspora. In the United States, South Royalton, Vermont, is not considered sacred space by most Americans, but for Mormons it is revered as the birthplace of the religion's founder, Joseph Smith. What is sacred for some is not for others. For Shi'ite Muslims, the city of Karbala in Iraq is sacred because it is the site where the Shi'ite leader and Muhammad's grandson, Husayn ibn 'Ali, was killed in AD 680. For many Christians, sites in and around Jerusalem believed to have been visited by Jesus hold sacred status.

Second, some places are sacred because they are a homeland, the origin area of a particular religion or sect. The Chaco Canyon area of New Mex-

▲ **Figure 8J.5** Many sacred spaces around the world have, or had, the common connection of being healing sites. One of the most well known is Lourdes in France, shown here. In recent decades, Medjugorje in Bosnia has become internationally known to Christians because it is believed that the Virgin Mary has appeared almost daily to a group of locals since 1981. Tens of thousands flock to the site every year, and many claim to have seen the Virgin Mary in the sky. In ancient Greece, the city of Epidaurus was renowned for its temples to Asclepius, the god of healing.

ico was home to the ancient Pueblo Indians, but it is now deserted. Local Native American peoples, such as the Navajo and Hopi, continue to consider this space a sacred homeland because of its past significance.

Third, some places are sacred because they are **mystico-religious sites**, places in which God, or another deity, comes into direct contact with humans. For Muslims, the Dome of the Rock in Jerusalem is believed to be the site where Muhammad ascended to heaven to speak with Allah (God) before returning to earth. For Buddhists, the site of the Bodhi Tree, in modern India, is sacred because it is the place where the Buddha attained enlightenment, thus making a connection between the mystical universe and the human world.

Key Terms

African Traditional Religion (8I)
animism (8A)
Bahá'í (8I)
Buddhism (8D)
caste system (8C)
Christianity (8F)
Confucianism (8I)
Coptic Christians (8G)
dharma (8C)
Diaspora (8E)
Eightfold Path (8D)
ethnic religions (8A)
Five Pillars (8H)
Four Noble Truths (8D)
Great Schism (8G)
Hajj (8H)
Hijra (8H)
Hinduism (8C)
Islam (8H)
Jainism (8I)
Jesus (8F)
Judaism (8E)
karma (8C)
kosher (8E)
Mahayana Buddhism (8D)
monotheistic (8A)

mosque (8H)
Muhammad (8H)
mystico-religious sites (8J)
Pali Canon (8D)
polytheistic (8A)
profane landscape (8J)
Protestant Reformation (8G)
Qur'an (8H)
reincarnation (8C)
religion (8A)
sacred landscape (8J)
Sharia (8H)
Shinto (8I)
Siddhartha (8D)
Sikhism (8I)
synagogue (8E)
Taoism (8I)
Theravada Buddhism (8D)
Torah (8E)
traditional religions (8A)
Tripitaka (8D)
universalizing religions (8A)
untouchables (8C)
Vajrayana (8D)
Vedas (8C)

Basic Review Questions

1. What is the geography of religion?
2. What is a universalizing religion? Provide two examples.
3. What is an ethnic religion? Provide two examples.
4. What is a traditional religion?
5. Distinguish between monotheistic and polytheistic religions.
6. What is animism?
7. What are the basic beliefs of Hinduism?
8. What are the basic beliefs of Buddhism?
9. What are the basic beliefs of Judaism?
10. What is kosher food?
11. What was the Great Schism, and what were the geographic consequences?
12. Where do you find most Coptic Christians?
13. When was the Protestant Reformation, and what caused it?
14. When was Islam founded? What were the key events in the early days of the religion?
15. What are the Five Pillars of Islam?
16. What is Sharia?
17. What are the differences between Confucianism and Taoism?
18. What are some examples of animistic religions?

19. What is Bahá'í?
20. What is Jainism?
21. Explain the difference between a sacred and a profane landscape.
22. What is a mystico-religious site?

Advanced Review Questions

1. What are the pros and cons of a religion being universalizing? Can you think of examples where it would not be beneficial to be universalizing? Is there a danger to being part of an ethnic religion that does not seek to take in new members?
2. How does the caste system relate to Hindu religious beliefs?
3. How does suffering relate to Buddhist beliefs?
4. Describe the geographic extent and ideological differences between Mahayana and Theravada Buddhism.
5. What historical events led to the division of Christianity into Catholic, Protestant, and Orthodox branches?
6. Where and how did Islam spread beyond its beginnings in the Middle East?
7. In what ways does religion change the cultural landscape? What are some typical buildings in each of the major world religions?
8. Why do some places become sacred spaces?

Further Study Topics

- India has officially made caste discrimination illegal, but caste continues to influence Indian society in many ways. Research the steps that the Indian government has taken to reduce caste discrimination, and discuss whether the caste system is still a major force in Indian society.

- Research the Jewish Diaspora, and describe how the scattering of the Jewish people led to the geographic pattern of Judaism in the modern world. What are the differences between Jewish communities in different parts of the world? What role did the history of the Diaspora play in modern Zionist movements that sought to create a homeland for Jews, eventually leading to the creation of the state of Israel?

- In addition to Jewish kosher laws, what other food taboos have their origins in religion? Consider including Hinduism, Buddhism, Christianity, and Islam in your research.

- In the past decade, there has been a lot of discussion about the Islamic concept of jihad. Conduct an objective study of the Koranic origins of the concept and how it has been interpreted by Islamic leaders in different parts of the world and in different sects of the religion.

- Where in the world do you find Sharia law being practiced as the primary legal system? Are these areas growing or contracting? Why?

- Research the importance of a major sacred site, such as Lourdes to Christians or Hardiwar to Hindus.

Summary Activities

On this blank world map, sketch the geographic distribution of the following religions: Christianity, Hinduism, Islam, and Buddhism. Indicate the boundary between Mahayana and Theravada Buddhism and between Sunni and Shi'ite sects of Islam.

Race, Ethnicity, and Gender

CHAPTER MODULES

In the discussion at the beginning of Chapter 6, we asked, "Who are you?" and many of the possible answers were related to culture traits. "I'm a Christian," for example, is an answer that is primarily rooted in culture traits. However, if a person answers, "I'm African American" or "I'm Hispanic," the situation gets more complicated. What do these terms mean? Does being an African American refer only to historical ties to Africa? Does it mean being racially black? Is a white Kenyan who immigrates to the United States an "African American"? Do African Americans share culture traits? When race, history, culture, and identity come together, we move from the realm of culture to that of ethnicity.

In addition to ethnicity, this chapter explores how geographers look at the issue of gender in societies around the world. Whether we are male or female certainly influences our lives, but does it affect our spatial lives? Does it affect where we go and what we do? Geographers would argue that it does, and that society often creates spaces or limits access to spaces based on gender.

ETHNICITY

Religion

Language

Racial characteristics

Geographic origin

Common history

▲ **Figure 9A.1 Components of Ethnicity** Ethnicity includes culture traits (such as religion or language), historical or geographic origins, and physical characteristics due to race.

9A   What is Ethnicity?

Ethnicity is a concept that is often confused with culture. While ethnicity does include elements of culture, it also encompasses many other ideas. Since we will be talking about both culture and ethnicity in subsequent chapters, it will be helpful to move forward with a solid understanding of the differences between the two. Remember first that *culture* refers to shared patterns of learned behavior, such as religious views, language, the types of clothing people wear, and societal beliefs about political ideas. It does not include racial or biological characteristics, and it does not necessarily refer to where you are from originally. You can be born in Nigeria but raised in Chicago and end up being culturally American rather than Nigerian, depending on how you were raised and who raised you.

Ethnicity differs from culture because it is based on how people choose to identify themselves. The word *ethnos* is Greek for "people," and we see the root in words such as *ethnography*, literally "writing about people." While there is no single accepted definition of *ethnicity*, a good working definition of an ethnic group is a social group that defines

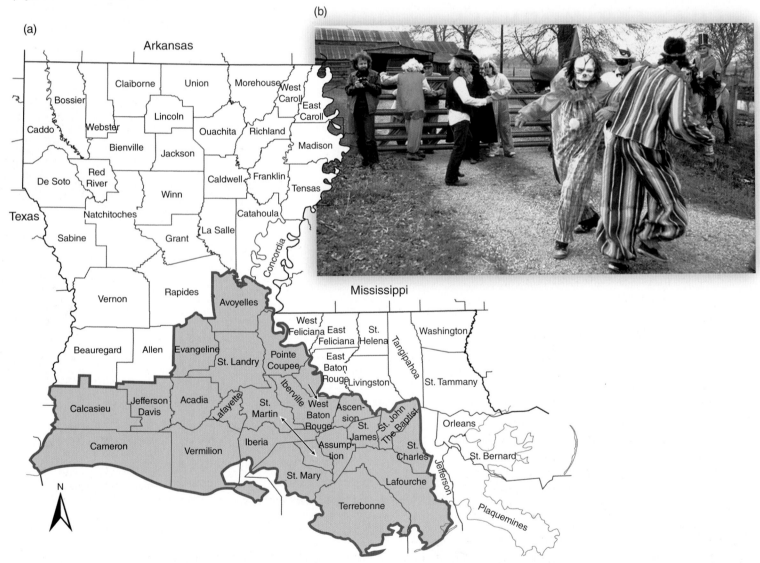

▲ **Figure 9A.2 Cajuns** Many Cajuns identify themselves as an ethnic group, and the government considers them as one. **Cajuns** share a historical origin in eastern Canada (Acadia) in what are now parts of Prince Edward Island, Nova Scotia, and New Brunswick. Between 1755 and 1763, the Acadians were forced to leave Canada after being deported by the British, and many settled in French-speaking Louisiana. (a) This map shows the parishes (counties) of Louisiana that have the highest percentage of residents who identified themselves as Cajun in the 2000 Census. Today, Cajuns share not only their history but also a unique dialect (Cajun French), religion (Roman Catholicism), food, and music. (b) In this photo, Cajuns in the town of Mamou celebrate Mardi Gras.

itself based on factors such as common culture traits or a common history, race, or geographic origin. An example of an ethnic group that defines itself on culture traits is the Jewish peoples of the world, who share religious ideas and in some cases dietary and other lifestyle choices. Many also share a common history of persecution and migration. African Americans in the United States certainly include race as part of their self-identity as an ethnic group. How many racially white African Americans do you know? Geographic origins are important to many ethnic groups that have recently arrived in the United States, such as Chinese Americans and Mexican Americans. Even though there are cultural differences within their countries of origin, they often band together to support one another when they arrive in the United States.

Note that ethnicity can include culture (language, religion), but culture cannot include ethnicity because ethnicity is a broader concept. For example, African Americans may share culture traits, but they also share the history of slavery, racial characteristics, and their origins on a different continent. If a white person acts like an African American, he or she is very unlikely to be accepted as an African American because for lack of a common history and common racial characteristics (such as darker skin).

The ethnic group itself defines what constitutes membership in the group. There is, therefore, a built-in sense of inclusion and exclusion. You are either "in" or "out" of the ethnic group. But why do groups organize themselves into groups? Often, group identity is related to the status of the group within society. Groups that are a minority within a society tend to emphasize their distinct identity more than do majority groups. Many majority groups focus more on class issues than ethnic identity. Think about the United States or Canada. Very few white Americans still strongly identify with their European roots unless they are recent immigrants. They may be proud of their heritage, but they do not necessarily have a strong group identity or affiliation with others of a similar background.

Several theories exist concerning why humans organize themselves into ethnic groups. Some scholars believe that people are born with an instinctive sense of ethnic identity, that there is a natural kinship with one's kind. Some have hypothesized that the pervasiveness of **ethnocentrism**, an attitude of cultural superiority, around the world and throughout time is related to these natural tendencies to favor people who are similar. Other scholars disagree strongly with this idea, arguing instead that ethnicity is socially constructed. They argue that ethnic identity is a result of the interaction among different groups of people. If a particular group of people see themselves as distinct from another group, they may perpetuate and amplify their differences through self-identification as an ethnic group. In other words, by identifying ourselves as being different, we establish that we are different.

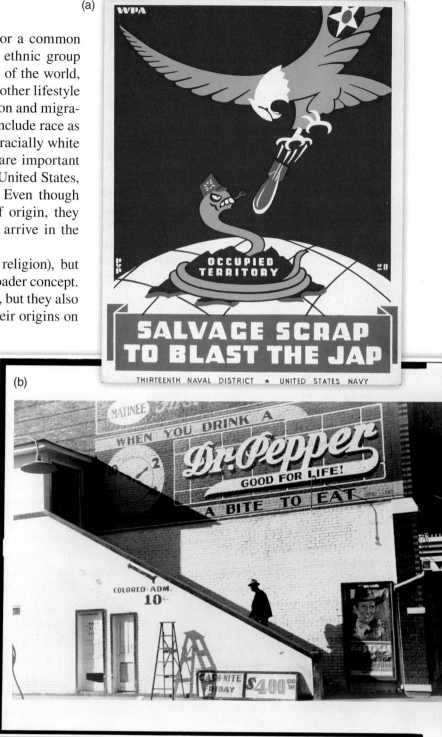

▲ **Figure 9A.3 In vs. Out** Here we have (a) a World War II anti-Japanese poster and (b) a 1939 photo of a movie theater in Mississippi. What do these images or graphics say about which group is "in" and which is "out" at the time? How does the poster use racist stereotypes to demean the Japanese? Do Americans do this today with any ethnic groups? If so, which groups?

▲ **Figure 9B.1 Manzanar** One example of a resurgent ethnic identity is the Japanese American community in the United States. With the outbreak of World War II, Japanese Americans, despite a long history in the United States, suddenly faced waves of discrimination from their neighbors and the government. Thousands were immorally and irrationally imprisoned in internment camps throughout the West, such as this one, Manzanar. After the war ended, many Japanese American internees downplayed their imprisonment and cultural heritage to distance themselves from a difficult and trying time in their lives. But decades later, in the 1980s, survivors began to demand that the U.S. government pay reparations and publicly apologize for the camps. This effort led many young Japanese Americans to embrace their heritage and history, leading to a resurgence in the cultural life of the Japanese American community. A legacy of this resurgence is the Japanese American National Museum in Los Angeles, which started as an idea in the early 1980s and opened in 1992.

9B   The Life of an Ethnic Group

How do ethnic groups form, and what happens to them when they move to a new society? Some scholars note that governments and other societal groups with power can cause ethnic groups to form. The United Nations decision to create the state of Israel in the 1940s is seen by some to have created a Palestinian identity among peoples who previously had not identified themselves as one group. For example, Christian and Muslim Palestinians were more apt to see themselves as part of the same group after the creation of Israel than before it. Most Americans don't even know that some Palestinians are Christian, assuming that all are Muslims, but this is not the case. This example is a form of **emergent ethnicity**, the creation of an ethnic identity not common in the past. As opposed to emergent ethnicity, there can also be cases of **resurgent identity**. Ethnic identities common in the past can fade and then reemerge. For example, in the United Kingdom, proponents of Welsh nationalism have fought to increase the teaching of Welsh in nursery and elementary schools in the past 40 years. Because of this, more young children in Wales can speak Welsh than can those over 60 years of age.

Ethnic group identity is strongest at times of change or chaos. At the most violent end of the spectrum, invasion can strengthen group identity. Invasion, however, does not have to come in the form of a military occupation. After the end of the Vietnam War, Vietnam's population boomed, increasing from 53 million in 1979 to nearly 82 million in 2004. This increase has elevated Vietnam to one of the most densely populated countries in Asia. Cities have grown too crowded to adequately support the rising population, so increasingly people have been moving from the most densely populated lowland areas into the less populated mountainous regions. These regions, however, are home to many of Vietnam's minority groups. In 2001, minority groups in Daklak province organized an armed uprising to protest the incursion of people into their region.

Ethnic identity can also change with current events. In our own recent history, think about how much American patriotism rose in the months after 9/11. Suddenly, American flags were everywhere, and most Americans identified themselves as Americans. This happens on a lesser scale during the Olympics. But at other times, we are less likely

Figure 9B.2 ▶ **Warsaw Ghetto Uprising** Eastern European Jews rallied together to rise up in 1943 against their German captors in the ghettos of Warsaw, where 500,000 Jews had been forced to live in a small, poorly serviced area. Many had already been sent to death camps, such as Treblinka, and news of their fate there solidified the resolve of resistance groups to rise up against the Germans. Tragic moments in a group's history can help solidify ethnic identity. Today, the uprising is commemorated in monuments such as this one in Warsaw.

◀ **Figure 9B.3 Tibet Riots** In 2008, Tibetans rioted against the Chinese government, in part because they felt that their culture was being eroded by decades of non-Tibetan Chinese migration to the area. The Chinese, argue many critics, are attempting to reduce ethnic identity in areas that are likely to oppose the government by watering down the population with outsiders of the more common Han Chinese majority.

to see ourselves as Americans, such as during a divisive election or some national debate. Ethnic identity is also commonly stronger during periods of migration and settlement. When a new people arrived in Canada or the United States, they had nothing vis-à-vis the rest of society except their common identity. Discrimination, lack of appropriate job skills, the language barrier, and poor social services tend to encourage new immigrants to stick with their own ethnic group.

Eventually, many ethnic groups do become part of the majority. This process often begins with **acculturation**, the process of learning how to operate within a new culture. Essentially, it is the adopting of a second culture. This might include learning a new language, adopting some new foods into the diet, or learning how to dress for particular social occasions. A person may be acculturated to a new society but not assimilated. A Russian immigrant may learn English and American customs on arrival in New York City, so that he or she can work, but at home still speak Russian, eat Russian food, and interact with family members as is common in their homeland.

Acculturation can lead to **assimilation**, the adoption of a new culture and the abandonment of most aspects of an original culture. If this occurs, ethnic identity may lessen as individuals associate with the majority. Assimilation can be thought of as having two stages. First, there is **cultural (behavioral) assimilation**. This refers to the situation in which an ethnic group maintains a strong self-identity yet has adopted enough of the culture traits of the host society to be a functioning member of it. In other words, the minority group has learned the cultural norms of the host society, and uses them when interacting with the majority, but maintains unique cultural lives, to some degree, within the ethnic community. A more complete form of assimilation is **functional assimilation**, which is the fusion of an ethnic group with the majority society. Although people may still identify with their cultural heritage and hold on to a few culture traits, in nearly all aspects of their lives they behave as the majority behaves. They may give up speaking the language of their parents and take up the language of the majority. They are also economically and socially integrated into society and have increased political clout. Intermarriage is a very common path to assimilation in many countries. Marriage outside the ethnic group tends to weaken the ethnic identity of both spouses.

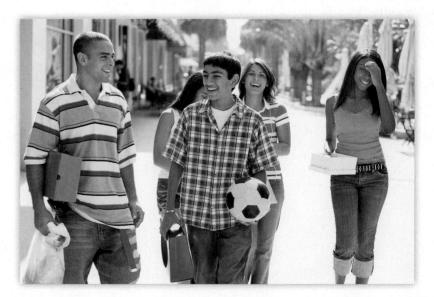

▲ **Figure 9B.4 Assimilation** The children of immigrants are often more assimilated than their parents, even if they were born elsewhere. Why might this be true?

9C   The Geography of Ethnicity

Geographers have approached ethnicity from a variety of angles. Staying with the themes of pattern and process, we can look at both the geographic distribution of ethnic groups and the mechanisms that contribute to the observed geography. It is important as well to remember the issues of scale that were discussed in Chapter 1: Ethnicity can have very localized geographies or national, and even international, distributions.

Ethnic Neighborhoods

At the smallest geographic scale, we can identify **ethnic neighborhoods** in many towns and cities. These are areas within cities that have concentrated populations of a particular ethnic group. For example, many cities around the world have a Chinatown. In the United States, urban areas with Chinatowns include New York; Washington, DC; Los Angeles; and San Francisco. But numerous other ethnic neighborhoods are well known in the United States. New York City has Little Italy, Harlem, and Brighton Beach, known today for its strong Russian character. In Los Angeles, Boyle Heights, formerly the center of the city's Jewish community, is now the center of the Latino community. Los Angeles also has a large Asian population, with corresponding neighborhoods. In addition to Chinatown, Los Angeles has a Little Tokyo, with a concentration of Japanese businesses, art, and cultural displays.

Like the Boyle Heights area of Los Angeles, an interesting reality of many ethnic neighborhoods is that they change their ethnic identity over time. This is often related to the availability of low-income housing. As new migrants enter a city, they are generally without jobs or another steady

▲ ▼ **Figure 9C.1 Ethnic Neighborhoods** What elements in these photos indicate the primary ethnic groups in the neighborhood?

▲ **Figure 9C.2 Lower East Side, New York City** Before the arrival of large numbers of Italians, New York's Lower East Side was also home to large numbers of Germans and Jews. Before them, Irish immigrants and freed black slaves lived in the same area. How does this relate to our earlier discussion about the cultural landscape?

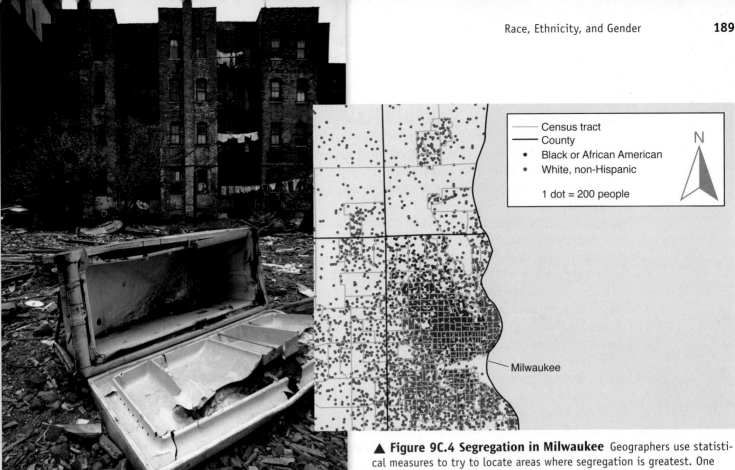

▲ **Figure 9C.4 Segregation in Milwaukee** Geographers use statistical measures to try to locate areas where segregation is greatest. One such measure, and there are many more, is the **index of dissimilarity**. This measure is used to compare how isolated two groups, such as blacks and whites, are from each other by looking at how similar the proportion of each group found in a neighborhood is to the overall proportion of the two groups in a city. The index produces a number that ranges from 0 to 100, which can then be mapped. A number closer to 100 represents a greater level of segregation. In 2000, the Milwaukee, Wisconsin, metro area had the highest index of dissimilarity in the United States for blacks compared to whites, 84.4. This map showing where whites and blacks live in Milwaukee clearly shows that blacks (blue) are quite segregated from whites (red).

▲ **Figure 9C.3 Ghettos** Today, of course, the word *ghetto* is used to refer to poor, minority areas of a city. These are essentially poor ethnic neighborhoods, but the term also introduces a notion of discrimination, that the minority group in the neighborhood is trapped there by society and cannot live among the majority. Because of its inherently spatial nature, geographers have long been interested in **segregation**, the separation between different social or ethnic groups. Is there a link between ethnicity and poor neighborhoods in the developed world?

source of income. Thus, they need to find affordable housing. In time, however, as their incomes increase and they assimilate into society, ethnic groups tend to move from the city to the more affluent suburbs. Meanwhile, the next wave of immigrants moving to the city is drawn to the area for the same reason (see Module 14E for a discussion of urban housing). In New York City, much of Chinatown today is in the same location as Little Italy was 50 years ago. As Italians left the city for the suburbs of Long Island, New Jersey, and upstate New York, more and more Chinese moved into the area. Other Asian and Hispanic groups now live in the area as well.

Of course, if an ethnic group does not assimilate into the majority society, or if the larger society puts up barriers (such as racism or class discrimination) that keep a group from assimilating, the group may be locked into a distinct geographic area. Historically, for example, Jews in many parts of Europe were restricted to certain areas of a city. These areas were known as **ghettos**, a word that is Italian in origin and refers to an area set aside by the government of Venice for Jews in 1516. European ghettos were often separated from the rest of the city with gates that were locked at night. This reflected both the mistrust and the ethnic hatred of Christian residents, but it also provided a degree of protection for Jewish residents, who were often attacked during Christian holidays because of the Christian belief that the Jews were responsible for the crucifixion of Jesus. Within the ghettos, local residents had a great deal of autonomy over their economic, political, and social lives. Jewish ghettos persisted in some countries, such as the predominantly Muslim country of Yemen, until after World War II. The Nazi ghettos were modeled on the ancient concept but, in reality, presented much poorer living conditions because of overcrowding.

In addition to mapping segregation, geographers can explore the spatial reasons segregation persists. For example, as ethnic groups assimilate, they often move out of urban ethnic neighborhoods to the suburbs. But sometimes social or legal barriers hinder this movement. For example, if a suburban community is concerned about minorities moving into town, it can pass zoning laws that prohibit the size of new home lots. By requiring that all new construction be on a 2-acre plot of land, a community assures that the price of any new home will be too expensive for lower-class home seekers. Racism can also play a role. Studies have shown that some landlords lie about the availability of an apartment or a house if they know that the prospective tenant is a member of a particular racial or ethnic group. This makes it more likely that some minority groups will remain in urban ethnic islands for longer than they would otherwise choose to do.

Segregation may also persist in some areas because members of the segregated group choose to live together rather than moving or assimilating. Maintaining a segregated ethnic neighborhood has several advantages. First, it allows culture traits, such as language or religion, to be maintained. A Russian Orthodox church, for example, might not survive if all its members move to different suburbs, but if they live near it, the congregation can continue to worship. Orthodox Hasidic Jewish communities often isolate themselves to ensure that the community follows the sect's strict laws. Second, self-segregation provides a measure of protection from outside challenges. We already mentioned that walled Jewish ghettos of Europe served as a protection against periodic attacks by majority Christians. Finally, self-segregation provides a social safety net in times of trouble. Local ethnic businesses, social institutions, and political institutions provide comfort in times of trouble. When minorities assimilate into the majority, it can be harder to find supportive and understanding institutions in diverse communities.

Despite the gains of the civil rights movement in the United States, segregation is still a reality in American cities. According to the U.S. Census Bureau, the prevalence of segregation fell for blacks between 1980 and 2000, but it remains higher in urban areas than in smaller cities. Cities in the Northeast and Midwest had the highest degree of African American segregation from whites, while western cities had the lowest. But despite the improvement in the degree of segregation between blacks and whites, blacks are still more segregated than most other minority groups. Compared to that of African Americans, Hispanic segregation generally did not improve between 1980 and 2000; it actually got worse on some measures. Asian segregation shows a similar trend of a slight worsening. Thus, despite gains in some areas of minority status in the United States, major problems remain.

Figure 9C.5 ▶ Ethnoburbs Nearly two decades ago, the geographer Wei Li noted that many urban areas were beginning to show strong pockets of ethnic concentration in suburban areas. In the 1990s, she coined the term **ethnoburb** to refer to these areas. Originally, she was researching Chinese settlements in the San Gabriel Valley near Los Angeles, shown here during a celebration for a business opening, but since her research has been published, numerous ethnoburbs have been identified in the United States and Canada. The Dearborn, Michigan, area, a suburb of Detroit, is a center of the Arab American community. The Vancouver, British Columbia, suburb of Richmond is now 40% Chinese and has sizable populations of South Asians. This trend is changing the way geographers and social scientists look at ethnic assimilation. Traditionally, it was believed that suburbanization diluted ethnic identification, creating a relatively homogenous suburban culture. But the emergence of ethnoburbs seems to indicate that ethnic groups can maintain their identity while adopting the suburban lifestyle of larger houses and more affluent lifestyles. The cultural landscapes of towns such as Dearborn and Richmond are dotted with ethnic restaurants and stores, and the communities celebrate their heritage with festivals, public displays, and educational programs. Political landscapes are also changing as suburban ethnic communities earn seats in local government institutions, such as city councils and school boards.

▲ **Figure 9C.6 Amish** Throughout the Great Plains, groups such as the Hutterites, Amish, Mennonites, and Doukhobors settled areas through cluster migration. Here, Amish residents of Nappanee, Indiana, have left their buggies tied up as they shop.

Ethnic Islands

Larger than ethnic neighborhoods or ethnoburbs, **ethnic islands** are areas of ethnic concentration in rural, or non-urban, areas. In the United States and Canada, many of these areas are in regions settled after the mid-nineteenth century. Many late nineteenth-century immigrants chose not to settle in East Coast cities, opting instead to head west to farm newly available lands in the Midwest and Great Plains. Often, based on advanced scouting of available lands or the "advice" of a real estate broker, whole communities were settled by the same ethnic group, a process known as **cluster migration**. When groups settled a new area en masse, it was not uncommon for them to build towns similar to the ones they left behind in Europe. Thus, European town plans were often recreated on the American landscape.

Elsewhere, areas were settled by individuals but still became ethnic islands because of timing or chain migration. Recall that chain migration is the process in which a small number of settlers send information back to their homeland, thus encouraging others from that area to move to the new area. While these areas today are not exclusively of a particular ethnicity, they often maintain a strong ethnic character through festivals, personal and place names, and businesses.

Figure 9C.7 ▶ Pella, Iowa This town, with its strong Dutch heritage, is an example of an ethnic island. Founded in 1847 by a Dutch separatist, the town was settled by Dutch impelled to migrate because of persecution at home. Settling in Iowa on land purchased for $1.25 per acre, they built houses out of sod and established a community. Today, Pella's population is still about 50% Dutch, and the town actively celebrates its heritage as a tourist attraction. The centerpiece of the town is a large, authentic windmill crafted by Dutch carpenters and engineers.

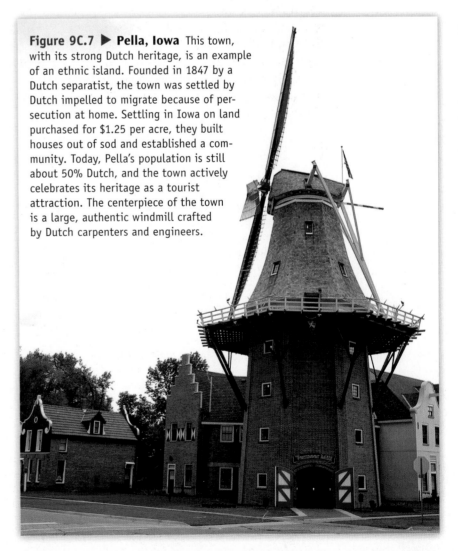

9D   Ethnicity in the United States

▼ **Figure 9D.1 Dominant Ancestral Groups in the United States** Look carefully at this map of the United States, based on the 2000 census, and try to explain the ethnic, ancestral, and racial patterns, given what you know about the geography and history of the country. Why are certain groups in each region?

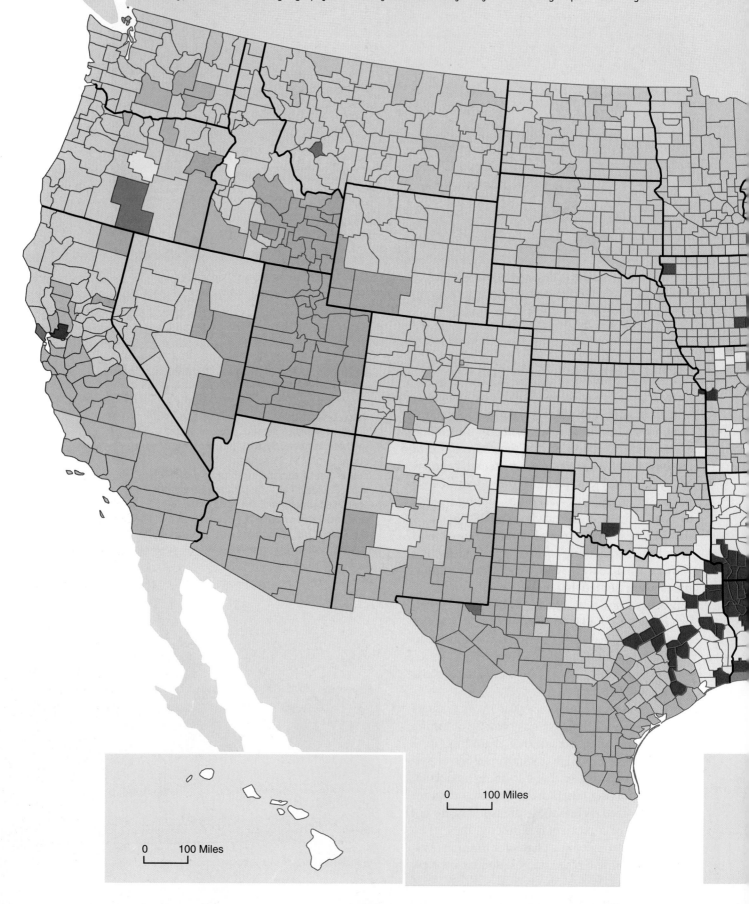

0   100 Miles

0   100 Miles

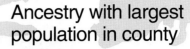

Ancestry with largest population in county

- African American
- Aleut/Eskimo
- American
- American Indian
- Dutch
- English
- Finnish
- French
- German
- Hispanic/Spanish
- Irish
- Italian
- Mexican
- Norwegian
- Puerto Rican
- Other

Other:
Chinese (San Francisco County, CA)
Cuban (Miami-Dade County, FL)
Dominican (New York County, NY)
Filipino (Kauai and Maui counties, HI)
French Canadian (Androscoggin County, ME)
Hawaiian (Kalawao County, HI)
Japanese (Hawaii State; Honolulu County, HI)
Polish (Luzerne County, PA)
Portuguese (Bristol County, MA and Bristol County, RI)

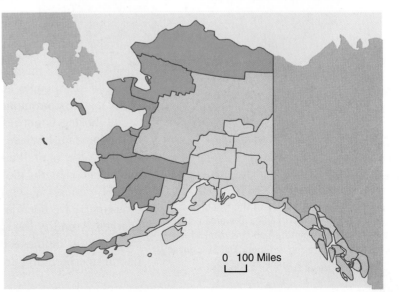

0   100 Miles

0   100 Miles

9E   Ethnic Provinces

Geographers also talk about **ethnic provinces**, large areas associated with a particular ethnic group. The French province of Quebec, for example, is largely associated with the French-speaking Quebecois ethnic group, while the Southwestern US is identified with Native Americans and Hispanics. In China, large areas of the country are ethnic provinces of non-Han Chinese, such as Xinjiang Province, which is home to millions of non-Chinese Uighurs and other ethnic groups with roots in Central Asia.

Ethnic provinces have often been related to political conflict (see Module 10G). Remember that part of the definition of *ethnicity* is an "in" versus "out" arrangement that includes only particular people. If a political arrangement arises such that a large ethnic province is included within the borders of a country, it is not a stretch to envision the possibility that the ethnic province might seek to establish more autonomy. Certainly, this is the case in Quebec, where the French-speaking population has repeatedly proposed secession from Canada. Around the world, similar examples abound. In Indonesia, the easternmost province of West Papua (formerly West Irian Jaya), inhabited by ethnic Papuans with great cultural and historical differences from most Indonesians, sought greater autonomy in the 1990s and a change of their state's name to West Papua.

Chinese Ethnic Regions and Hanification

China's relationship with its minority populations has been an interesting one. Traditionally, ethnic identity was discouraged by the Communist Party because it promoted differences within the population. But in recent decades, Beijing has encouraged ethnic groups to practice their own beliefs and celebrate their cultural differences. In addition, under China's One-Child Policy (see Module 3J), minorities were granted exceptions to have more than one child.

But skeptics see Beijing's positive treatment as a way for the government to keep ethnic groups from seeking greater autonomy over their regions, or even to seek independence. They point to a process that has been dubbed "Hanification" as evidence that China is trying to dilute ethnic provinces. **Hanification** refers to Beijing's giving incentives for ethnically Han Chinese, who make up 93% of China's population, to move into ethnic areas, notably Tibet and Xinjiang Province, home of the Uighurs.

The geopolitical realities of the world are also a factor when we look at Xinjiang and western China. Before 1990, China's western border was closed to almost all trade and migration because it was the frontier with the Soviet Union, with which China frequently had disputes. But when the Soviet Union fell apart, the borders became much more porous and caused a renewed flow of goods, people, and ideas. Ethnic minorities in China were now freer to communicate with ethnic brethren in newly independent neighboring countries. Some of these ideas, such as Taliban-style Islamic fundamentalism, are of great concern to Beijing. Almost immediately after the 9/11 attacks on the United States, China supported the U.S. war on terror and began using the global concern about terrorism to crack down on supposed Islamic radicals in Xinjiang. Critics, and Uighur activists, argue that tens of thousands have been jailed illegally by the Chinese government on terrorism charges. Amnesty International claims that many have been executed for their views. China defines a terrorist as anyone who has "separatist" views—a very liberal interpretation, to say the least.

▶ **Figure 9E.1 Tamil-Claimed Areas in Sri Lanka** In Sri Lanka, a violent civil war was waged from 1983 to 2009 between an ethnic minority, the Tamils, and the majority Sinhalese population. The Tamils claimed the eastern and northern parts of the island and sought to separate from Sri Lanka. The area claimed was almost exactly as pictured on this map, which represents the primary Tamil region. The Sri Lankan government defeated the Tamils in 2009.

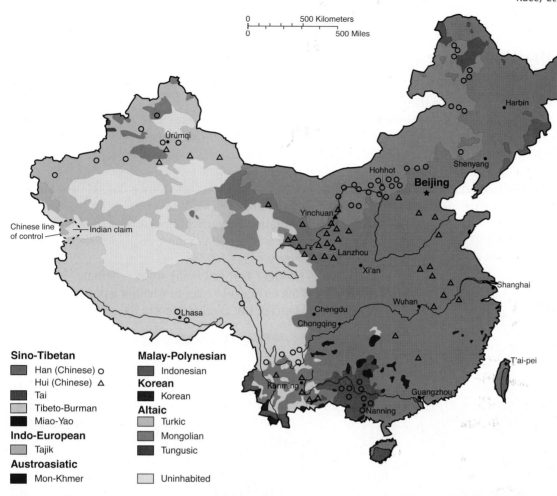

0   500 Kilometers
0   500 Miles

Chinese line of control — Indian claim

Ürümqi
Harbin
Hohhot
Beijing
Shenyang
Yinchuan
Lanzhou
Xi'an
Shanghai
Wuhan
Lhasa
Chengdu
Chongqing
T'ai-pei
Kunming
Guangzhou
Nanning

Sino-Tibetan
■ Han (Chinese) ○
  Hui (Chinese) △
■ Tai
■ Tibeto-Burman
■ Miao-Yao

Indo-European
■ Tajik

Austroasiatic
■ Mon-Khmer

Malay-Polynesian
■ Indonesian

Korean
■ Korean

Altaic
■ Turkic
■ Mongolian
■ Tungusic

■ Uninhabited

◀ **Figure 9E.2 Ethnolinguistic Regions of China** Take a moment to study the pattern of ethnic provinces of China. Do you notice anything about the location of China's ethnic minorities? In general, they are located on the periphery of the country, often in areas with topographic or climatic differences from China's central heartland. In the north and northeast, Mongols and Manchus can be found along the southern fringes of the Gobi Desert. Central Asian groups, such as the Uighurs, Kazaks, and Kirghiz, live in the arid far west. To the south is the large, isolated Tibetan Plateau, with its unique ethnic identity. Finally, mountainous southwestern China is home to myriad ethnic minorities, such as the Miao, Yao, and Tai. In total, China's minority population is roughly 90 million people, or about 7% of China's 1.3 billion total.

Figure 9E.3 ▶ Hanification In Urumqi, the largest city in China's western province of Xinjiang, the Chinese government fears that Islamic fundamentalism will fuel rebellion and calls for independence. To help reduce the cultural importance of the Uighurs and other Muslim groups in the region, the Chinese have moved millions of Han into the area. Population figures indicate that the Han population is rising in the west at twice the rate of the Uighur population. Slowly, Chinese stores and signs are replacing Uighur ones in many areas, as can be seen here behind these Han and Uighur senior citizens as they exercise in a public park. A similar situation has occurred in Tibetan cities, such as Lhasa, where Chinese culture is becoming more and more visible and traditional Tibetan culture less so. Many international advocates for Tibet cite these changes as evidence that China is trying to minimize problems with the minority Tibetans by making them into a minority in their own land.

9F   Gender and Geography

So far, we have examined identity in terms of culture traits and ethnicity, but, of course, a person's identity is based on a variety of factors. In the past three decades, human geographers have increasingly looked at gender as a source of identity. Geographers believe that society shapes spaces based on socially defined gender roles and that gender affects the way we interact with the world. **Feminist geography** focuses on gender relationships as being central to our understanding of how space is created and arranged (see Module 2H for more on feminist geography). Originally rooted in the movement for equal rights for women and men, feminist approaches today are much more likely to look not just at issues of men and women but also at differences among women. Not all women are the same, and issues such as age, cultural background, and sexual orientation may affect how a woman perceives and interacts with her world. Each of these characteristics can shape a woman's identity.

What is **gender**? Is it just being male or female? No, social scientists use the term *sex* to refer to whether a person is biologically male or female. But *gender* refers to the societal norms and

◀ **Figure 9F.1 Gendered Spaces** Does society create spaces that are gendered? Absolutely! On the simplest level, we have separate restrooms for men and women. Stores for women are often decorated differently than stores for men. There are still private clubs in the United States that allow only male or female members. Many gyms have a private workout area for women because they feel that women are more comfortable when not working out in front of men. In some Muslim countries, women are forbidden from being in many public places without a male family member or husband. What do the spaces pictured here say about accepted gender roles in these societies and how those roles may have changed over time? What types of spaces are designed primarily for men?

◀ ▼ **Figure 9F.2 Is Nature Gendered?**
In our society, do we think of nature and natural areas as being masculine spaces, feminine spaces, or something else? Do either of these images seem to be more masculine or feminine? Why? What is it about your culture that makes you classify each image the way you do? How are human-made spaces created to be masculine, feminine, or gender neutral?

behaviors that are expected of males or females. What passes as acceptable behavior for women in the United States would probably not be accepted in a country such as Saudi Arabia, where the status of women is much lower. Furthermore, some males adopt behaviors that are considered more feminine, and some females adopt behaviors that are traditionally masculine. What toys would you buy for a five-year-old boy? Would you buy the same for a five-year-old girl? Why or why not? Does your decision reflect biases in society? Is that good or bad?

Geographically, we know that boys and girls are not treated the same by their parents. Studies have shown, for example, that parents let boys wander and play farther from home than they allow girls. Why do you think this is the case? Some researchers think that this difference in "home range" may affect the way girls and boys navigate later in life. Namely, some researchers feel that boys learn to explore new environments more adeptly because they have more experience as children.

We've also seen societal spaces for men and women change over time. Certainly, 40 years ago the home was considered a woman's place, and magazines such as *Better Homes & Gardens* encouraged that stereotype. While Martha Stewart and others might perpetuate this attitude today, it is now much more acceptable for American men to stay home and care for children, cook, and do housework. Likewise, many work spaces, such as corporate boardrooms, were once forbidden to women by prejudice and societal barriers ("the glass ceiling"), but today, women are more accepted in business and leadership positions. While equality for men and women in business has not been achieved, global companies, such as Pepsi, have had female CEOs. Are there ways that men try to exclude women from certain spaces or place? Are there ways that women try to exclude men from certain spaces?

Another approach that some geographers take in examining gender and geography is to look at how men and women perceive environments. Think of your campus after dark. Do men and women perceive the safety of a dark campus the same? Why or why not? How we perceive the world is a function of biology, cultural norms, and life experience. Can you think of other places that men and women might perceive differently?

9G   The Global Geography of Gender

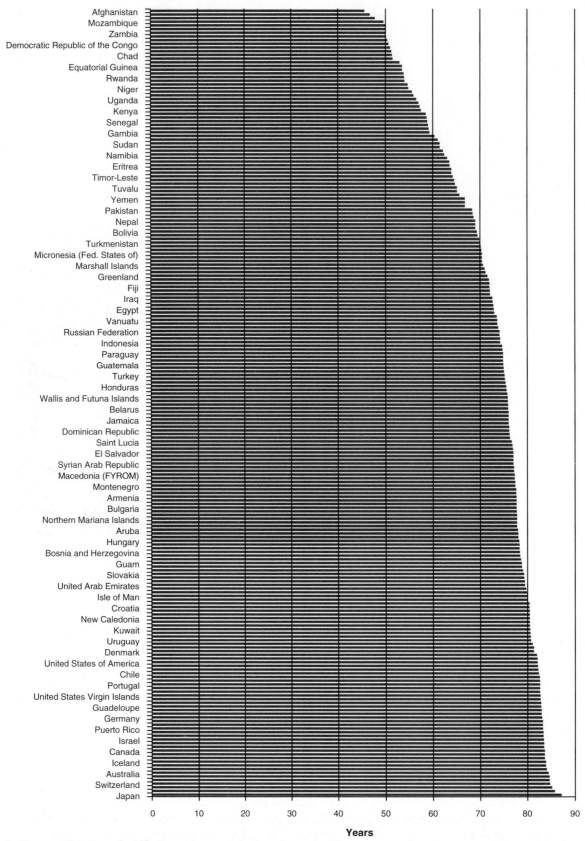

▲ **Figure 9G.1 Female Life Expectancy** This chart shows the life expectancy for women around the world. Why is there such a large discrepancy among countries? Is there a geographic pattern to the countries that have the lowest and highest figures?

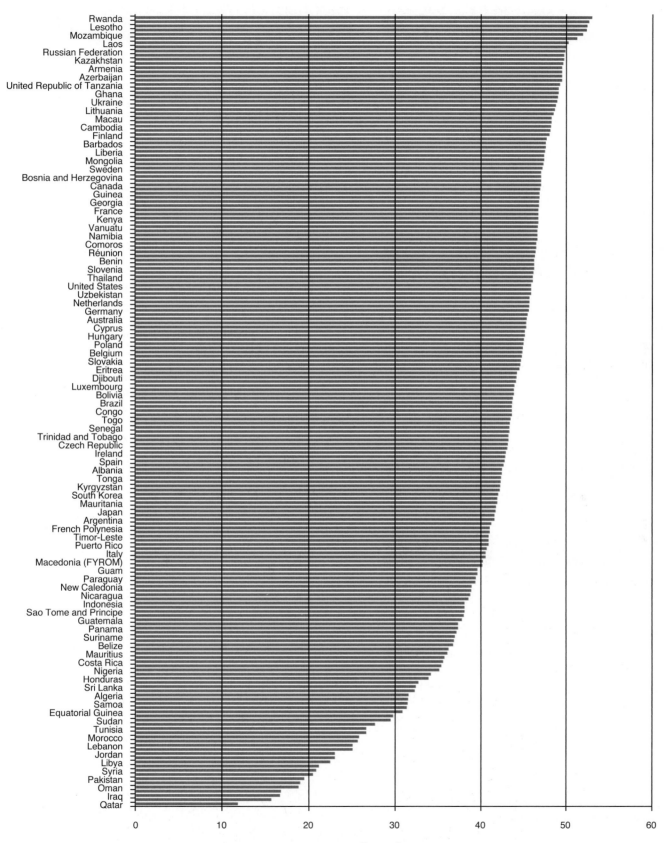

▲ **Figure 9G.2 Share of Women in the Adult Labor Force** Because women constitute about 51% of a normal human population, we would expect them to represent about half the workforce. This chart shows the share of the labor force that is women for the
countries of the world. Why is the percentage so low in many areas of the world, and is there a pattern to the data? What do many of
the countries with the lowest female labor participation have in common? Why might women be disadvantaged if they have low participation in the labor force?

Key Terms

acculturation (9B)
assimilation (9B)
behavioral assimilation (9B)
Cajuns (9A)
cluster migration (9C)
cultural assimilation (9B)
emergent ethnicity (9B)
ethnic islands (9C)
ethnic neighborhoods (9C)
ethnic provinces (9E)
ethnicity (9A)

ethnoburb (9C)
ethnocentrism (9A)
feminist geography (9F)
functional assimilation (9B)
gender (9F)
ghettos (9C)
Hanification (9E)
index of dissimilarity (9C)
resurgent identity (9B)
segregation (9C)

Basic Review Questions

1. What is ethnicity?

2. What are some common components of ethnicity?

3. What is ethnocentrism?

4. What is a ghetto?

5. What is acculturation? What is assimilation?

6. What is an ethnic neighborhood?

7. What is segregation?

8. What is an ethnoburb? An ethnic island?

9. What is cluster migration?

10. What is an ethnic province?

11. What is feminist geography?

12. What is the difference between gender and sex?

Advanced Review Questions

1. Describe the difference between culture and ethnicity. Why can ethnicity include culture but culture cannot include ethnicity?

2. How did Cajun ethnic identity develop?

3. Give some examples of ethnocentrism in American history.

4. What is the difference between an emergent ethnicity and a resurgent identity?

5. What is the difference between assimilation and acculturation?

6. What are the stages of assimilation? Can you identify groups in your country that are culturally assimilated but not functionally assimilated?

7. How is discrimination linked to the history of ghettos?

8. Explain the differences between ethnic neighborhoods, ethnoburbs, and ethnic islands.

9. Discuss the historical factors that led to the current ethnic pattern of the United States depicted in Module 9E.

10. What is a gendered space?

11. Discuss the geographic differences in the status of women around the world. What factors are related to better or worse conditions for women in some regions?

Further Study Topics

- In an era of globalization, are there any emergent ethnicities anymore?

- Do U.S. policies toward immigration speed or slow the process of assimilation? Think about public services, including education, in your answer. What role does communications technology, such as the Internet, play in the acculturation process?

- What services are provided by ethnic neighborhoods (but are not available elsewhere) to help immigrants assimilate? Travel to an ethnic neighborhood and conduct a survey of the types of businesses. Take note of the language and symbols on signs.

- Other than the index of dissimilarity, what statistical techniques do social scientists use to measure the degree of segregation in a city or region?

- Research ethnic and racial trends in the United States, and discuss what the ethnic map of the country might look like in 50 years.

- Is Hanification in China unethical or immoral, or is it just an inevitable part of China's history?

- Are spaces gendered on your campus or your community? What places are primarily male, and which are female?

- What can the global community do in the next few decades to improve the status of women around the world? What ideologies or conditions might hinder such efforts?

Summary Activities

Consider an immigrant who arrives in your country, speaking a foreign language and having almost no knowledge of your culture. Make a list of the various skills and social norms that the immigrant must learn before he or she can be a fully functioning member of society. What skills are most important to be able to hold a basic job? Where might he or she work? Where do you think this immigrant might live in your community, and why?

_____

_____

_____

_____

_____

_____

_____

_____

_____

_____

A World of Nations and States

One of the key concerns of human geography relates to the ways in which people organize and govern themselves politically. *Political* is a very broad term, but it most generally refers to the exercise of power, control, and authority. As it is related to the study of *politics*, political geography examines how human beings govern themselves, what facilitates governance, and what either impedes or aids the ability to get things done. Because it is *geography*, political geography is particularly concerned with how the exercise of political power, political identity, and political resistance is reflected spatially. Political geography also seeks to understand how the construction of political units themselves, at different scales, can have an impact on governance, identity, and the potential for individual political action.

This chapter surveys the geography, history, and functions of political forms, focusing especially on the concepts of state and nation—two key players in the modern world. It also examines the relationships within and between states. Chapter 11 is more focused on the operations of the modern state, subdivisions within the state, and electoral geography.

10A Sovereignty, Legitimacy, and Territoriality of Political Units

Political geography begins with the **political unit**. As human beings, we are constantly organized in a variety of political units at several different spatial scales. A country, or **state**, is the most important of these units, but many others exist and influence our actions. At a small scale, for example, a geography class is a political unit. There is an organization, clearly defined boundaries, and a form of governance—the teacher. While a class is not necessarily spatial, it is much easier to hold a class in a specially designed classroom that provides the class with definition and boundaries. Certainly, a town or city is a political unit. There is a government and a population that is governed. There are actions that the government can and cannot take. Depending on state law, for instance, cities and towns may raise taxes or float bonds; however, they are never empowered to establish an army. There are various political institutions that belong to the town government, as well as a clearly defined territory within which the government exercises some form of control.

Political units can also exist at the largest scales, larger than the scale of a country or state. One good example of this is the European Union (EU), composed of 27 countries but with its own governance, rules, institutions, and territory. The EU represents an exceptionally well-integrated bloc, with a parliament, a common currency, and open borders between many member states. At the largest scale is the United Nations (UN), an association of 192 members—almost every country in the world—but which operates as a political unit as well. While the UN does not prevent all conflicts from occurring, it has been a forum for discussion and a means for the international community to cooperate on a variety of goals.

Three guiding principles help us understand the nature of these political units: sovereignty, legitimacy, and territoriality. It is often said that the world is made up of sovereign states. **Sovereignty** indicates that a particular government has complete control and jurisdiction over a defined area. This is unrelated to how the government is constituted. Sovereignty indicates power, and full sovereignty allows a government to determine exactly what goes on within its territory. Most political units exercise something less than complete sovereignty. Even states are limited by agreements, international law, and sometimes powers that are left to subdivisions. In such a case, we speak of partial sovereignty; the government or other controlling authority has less than complete control, although it may have authority over many aspects.

In addition to sovereignty, each political unit is expected to have **legitimacy**. This term defines whether the government of the unit is considered to have the standing or right to rule a state's people and territory. Legitimacy can be conferred externally and internally. Outside recognition by all other governments gives a government external legitimacy. In the case of a state, this recognition is marked by the establishment of **diplomatic relations**, which includes sending out an ambassador, establishing an embassy, and signing treaties.

The consent of the people gives a government internal legitimacy. Legitimacy is marked by whether the people in the state have some say over how the government is constituted, the types of laws and rules it passes, and the ways in which these laws are implemented. There should also be a means to make changes to the government in a periodic way. This type of legitimacy can be measured through the nature of governance. Often, a **democracy** is a government that is considered to rule with the consent of its people and, so, is internally legitimate. This may have nothing at all to do with whether that government is considered legitimate to other governments.

Table 10A.1	Countries That Do Not Recognize Israel as a State

Israel is a fully functioning democracy that has a robust set of political parties, free elections, and an opportunity for Israeli citizens to determine the constitution of the government. However, Israel is not recognized as legitimate by a number of its neighbors.

Afghanistan	Lebanon
Algeria	Libya
Bahrain	North Korea
Bangladesh	Pakistan
Cuba	Republic of China (Taiwan)
Indonesia	Saudi Arabia
Iran	Sudan
Iraq	Syria
Kosovo	United Arab Emirates
Kuwait	Yemen

The world's division into states also demarcates political entities, each assumed to have complete sovereignty within its borders. Political units below and above the state level are likewise spatial units. In other words, sovereignty occurs within a particular **territory**. Inside the boundaries of that territory, a government has some measure of sovereignty. Outside the boundaries of that territory, a government does not have sovereignty. In political units that are not states, sovereignty can be nested. The government of the city of Milwaukee enjoys certain authority, but that is superseded by the authority enjoyed by Wisconsin's government, which in turn is superseded by the sovereignty exercised by the United States. This sovereignty is not superseded by any other entity. Power and authority end at the level of the United States.

There are some parts of the world for which no government exercises sovereignty. The ocean is one such area. Most governments claim sovereignty a certain distance away from their coastlines. These distances vary depending on the level of sovereignty. But no government has sovereignty over some parts of the ocean, described as the **High Seas**. The Antarctic continent is another area without sovereignty or jurisdiction. While various countries have bases in Antarctica by way of international treaty, there is no single country that controls Antarctica. In fact, the entire continent is considered to be outside of state sovereignty.

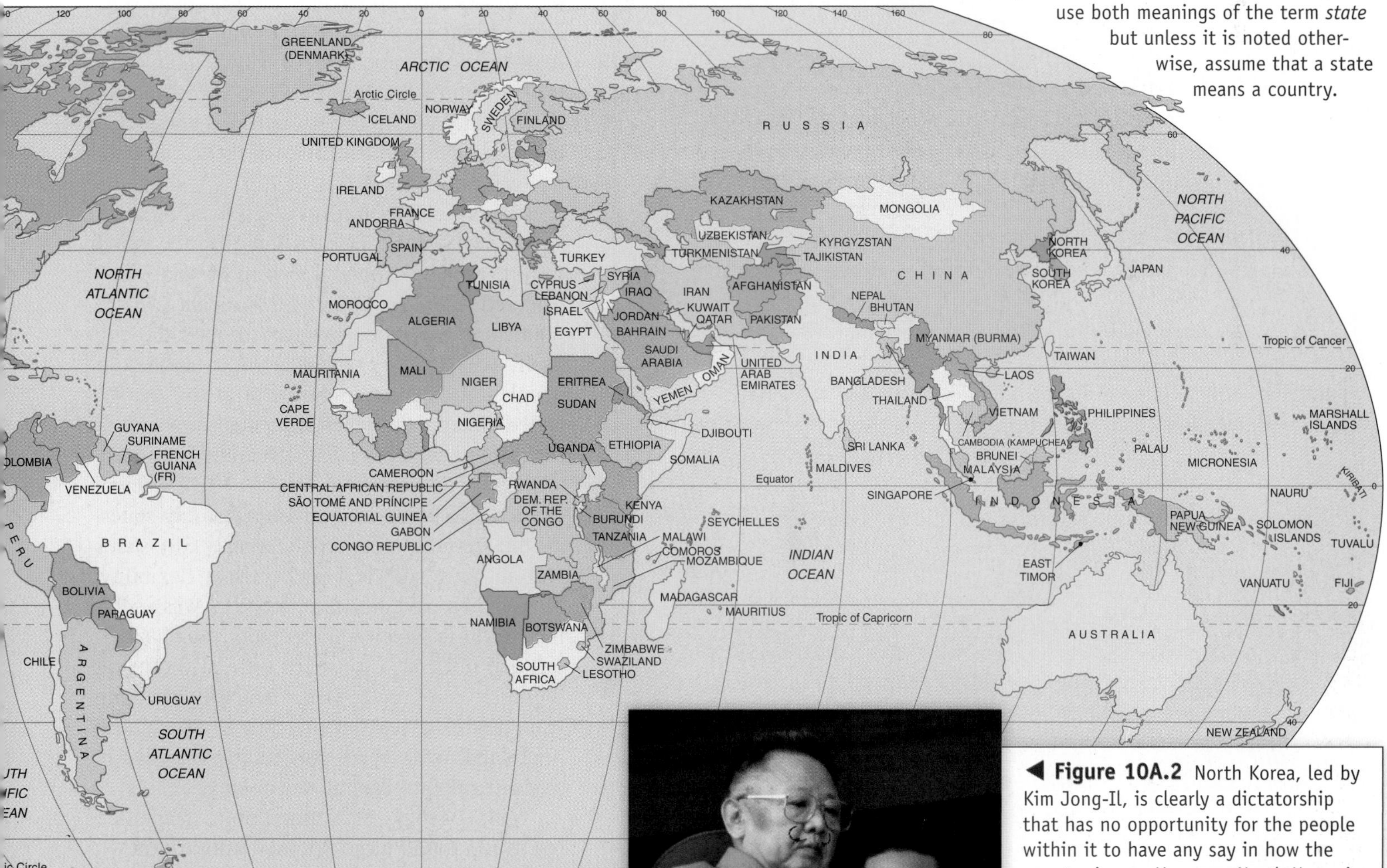

▼ **Figure 10A.1** If you look at a political map of the world, you can see the familiar, color-coded division of different countries. This reflects the division of the world into what political scientists and political geographers describe as states. Unfortunately, the word *state* is used to describe different things. In the United States, it refers to divisions such as Ohio or Alabama. Several other countries use the same terminology for their regional subdivisions. In this textbook, we use both meanings of the term *state* but unless it is noted otherwise, assume that a state means a country.

◄ **Figure 10A.2** North Korea, led by Kim Jong-Il, is clearly a dictatorship that has no opportunity for the people within it to have any say in how the country is run. However, North Korea is recognized by most other countries as a legitimate country or as having a legitimate government.

10B History of Political Forms

The political map that we see today is simply one pattern in the never-ending series of patterns that have defined the political organization of the world. Historically, there have been many types of political entities, all of which had some measure of sovereignty and perhaps a lesser extent of legitimacy.

Unlike the modern state, not all of these political entities were exclusively territorial. For example, tribal groups, or **chiefdoms**, inhabited particular places but at the same time were less likely to demarcate rigid boundaries. Certainly, tribal populations had a sense of familiar ground and resources over which they sought control. But territories were not mutually exclusive and did not have clearly defined boundaries, and the tribal organization was vested within the group, the chief, and the specific places the group occupied. Moreover, the periodic migrations of tribal groups, either seasonally or as their original settlements became less fertile, fostered a different conception of territory.

▼ **Figure 10B.1** In a feudal system, each lord possessed control—not necessarily ownership—over a manor. Each king had control over the lords and granted the use of these manors to the lords, who were vassals of the king. There could be several levels of vassalage, all the way down to the lowly peasant or serf, who was forced to till the lord's estate in exchange for the use of some land for himself and his family.

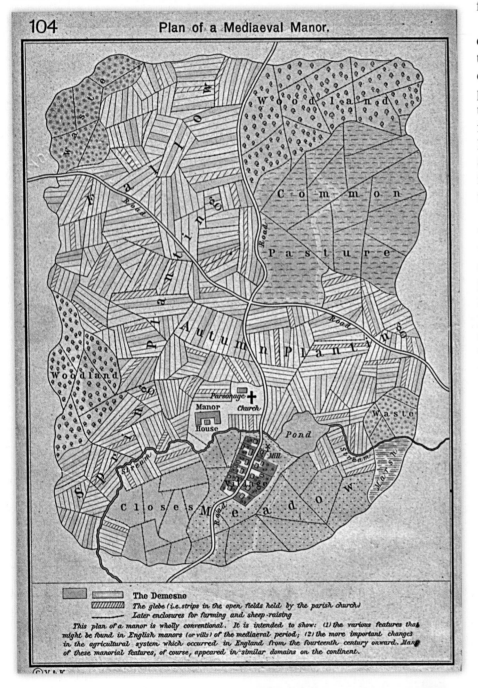

While involving many more people, a **feudal system** also results in a political organization not necessarily tied to complete territorial control. This system was based on the principles of personal allegiance and vassalage. The term **vassal** means someone who must show fealty and pay some form of tribute to an overlord in return for being able to use the land. Sovereignty within this system was conducted in a personal way, and lines of territorial control were often fluid.

A very common form of political territory was the **city-state**. The first cities in the world were organized around a system of small city-centered states. Essentially, this meant that the political organization revolved around the city itself, which was composed of a number of people not engaged in agriculture, and the so-called hinterlands, which were made up of all of the farmers who provided agricultural products to the city dwellers (see Module 13B). Ancient Greece also comprised a number of city-states, as did several other civilizations. City-states had an advantage of high levels of flexibility, as well as a political simplicity that was useful in a world in which transportation was hazardous and difficult. City-states were also often at the forefront of trade. Their flexibility, resulting from not being held back by a large agricultural hinterland, made them particularly effective in participating in a capitalist economy.

The history of humankind has often revolved around large political entities known as **empires**. Empires rapidly became politically prominent and have played a huge role in the history of the ancient, medieval, and modern worlds. An empire is made up of several

Figure 10B.2 ▶ In medieval Italy, a city-state such as Venice prospered because of its placement between rich sources of raw materials and larger markets eager to purchase those materials. Other cities in medieval Europe also grew rich from trade, and for a time the city-state became the most economically vital entity in the world. This map shows the location of Venice itself, along with the fairly small territory that surrounded it (in green). It also demonstrates that, for Venice, the most significant aspect of its prosperity lay in the trade routes and markets that connected it to places throughout the eastern Mediterranean. Territory was held not as a source of raw materials but as a means to facilitate the deployment of merchant ships. Source: From Dennis Sherman and Joyce Salisbury, *The West in the World, Third Edition,* © 2008 by The McGraw-Hill Companies, Inc., page 315. Used by permission.

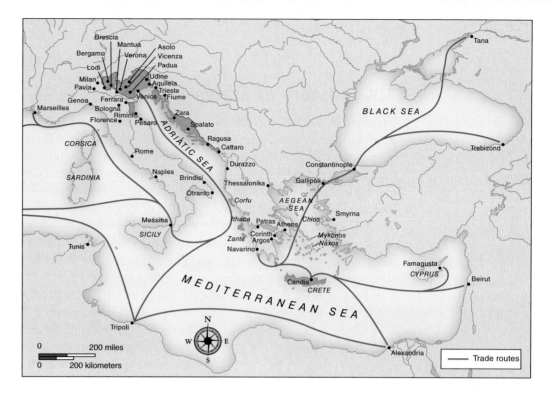

culturally distinct regions that are held together by force, under the control of a single dominant region. Most empires are not formed on the basis of mutual consent but, rather, are products of coercion as a result of the expansion of a particularly successful state. Empires came in several different flavors but most were ruled autocratically, by an emperor and his retinue. They generally favored a dominant culture and cultural group. Political geographers distinguish between the dominant part of the empire, sometimes termed the **metropole**, and the parts of the empire that are subordinate and have very little right to self-determination, sometimes termed **colonies**.

Within the last two centuries, many European countries have sought to create a series of sea-based empires, which included colonies that stretched around the world. The British Empire was the largest of these, covering nearly a quarter of the world's land surface. France, Spain, Portugal, the Netherlands, and Belgium controlled broad swatches of territory many times greater than their own size. While several of these empires lasted for well over a century, they eventually succumbed to the modern view that all peoples should enjoy the right of self-determination, and that colonies are not a desirable form of political organization.

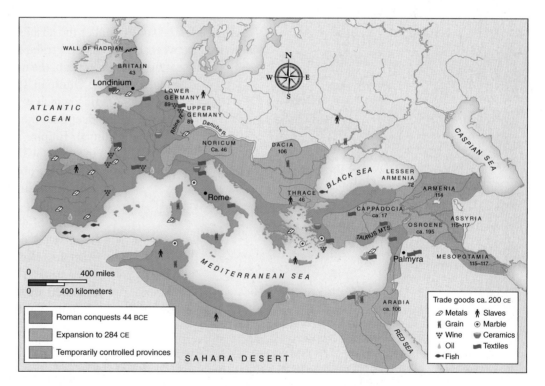

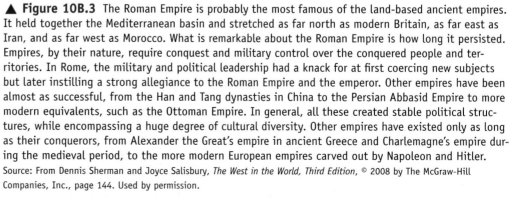

▲ **Figure 10B.3** The Roman Empire is probably the most famous of the land-based ancient empires. It held together the Mediterranean basin and stretched as far north as modern Britain, as far east as Iran, and as far west as Morocco. What is remarkable about the Roman Empire is how long it persisted. Empires, by their nature, require conquest and military control over the conquered people and territories. In Rome, the military and political leadership had a knack for at first coercing new subjects but later instilling a strong allegiance to the Roman Empire and the emperor. Other empires have been almost as successful, from the Han and Tang dynasties in China to the Persian Abbasid Empire to more modern equivalents, such as the Ottoman Empire. In general, all these created stable political structures, while encompassing a huge degree of cultural diversity. Other empires have existed only as long as their conquerors, from Alexander the Great's empire in ancient Greece and Charlemagne's empire during the medieval period, to the more modern European empires carved out by Napoleon and Hitler.

Source: From Dennis Sherman and Joyce Salisbury, *The West in the World, Third Edition,* © 2008 by The McGraw-Hill Companies, Inc., page 144. Used by permission.

10C History of States

The map in Module 10A shows a pattern of what appear to be sovereign, independent countries. As with all geographical patterns, this represents a particular point in time, resulting from a series of processes. This map reflects the rise and dominance of the **modern state system**. With only a few exceptions, the modern world is made up of territorial states—political units that are supposedly independent and contain a fair amount of area.

Figure 10C.1, from 1491, shows particular aspects of the world system a little more than 500 years ago. The world is composed of a combination of large land empires, several city-states, areas of feudalism, and a number of zones where small tribal groups reside. Contact has not been made between the new and old worlds. South America includes a combination of small chieftains and large empires. The Incan Empire stretches along the western Andes. The Aztec Empire flourished in what is now southern Mexico, and far-ther north the North American continent exhibits a primarily chieftain-oriented culture or political system, often made up of various confederations and loosely shifting alliances.

▼ **Figure 10C.1**

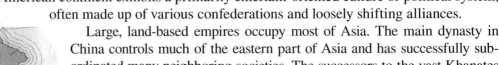

Large, land-based empires occupy most of Asia. The main dynasty in China controls much of the eastern part of Asia and has successfully sub-ordinated many neighboring societies. The successors to the vast Khanates established by Tamerlane continue to persist but are drained of much of their power. By 1523, the Mughal Empire will have started to successfully stretch over what is now northern India and Pakistan. Smaller kingdoms are found in Southeast Asia, with some very significant trading sites. Japan is a loosely aligned feudal society under the auspices of an emperor. Africa south of the Sahara is divided between kingdoms and tribal societies. In the Middle East and along the entire eastern Mediterranean, the dominions of the Byzantine Empire have been conquered by the Ottoman Turks, who are beginning consolidate control over vast domains, which will eventually extend from the Caspian Sea to Algeria and deep into the heart of Europe. The eastern advance of the Ottoman Empire is checked only by a significant new empire in Persia, which itself is able to expand into Central Asia.

Europe has largely shed the economic and politi-cal system of feudalism. It is composed of a combi-nation of newly centralized kingdoms and empires, some of which stretch over large disparate territories, as well as continually impressive city-states. New states have also begun to appear. By the fifteenth century, France has emerged as a strongly consoli-dated state, as has England and Spain. Italy and Ger-many, on the other hand, are still very much divided between kingdoms and cities.

How did the map of 1491 turn into the map of 2012? To take a long perspective, we can point to four major changes that occurred:

1. The growth of the **Westphalian state system**. This dates from the Treaty of Westphalia in 1648 and is based on the idea of a world composed of autonomous, clearly bounded, sovereign territo-rial states. The modern state system is composed of territories that are far more closely controlled and integrated than political territories had been up until this point. The fact that this system eventually replaced many different types of political forms speaks to the appeal and enduring power of the Westphalian concept.

2. The growth of nationalism and the nation-state ideal (discussed more fully in Module 10G). This rep-resented a sea change in attitudes toward what constitutes the state, the role of residents (often trans-formed from mere subjects to fully enfranchised citizens), and the role of a government assumed to have national legitimacy.

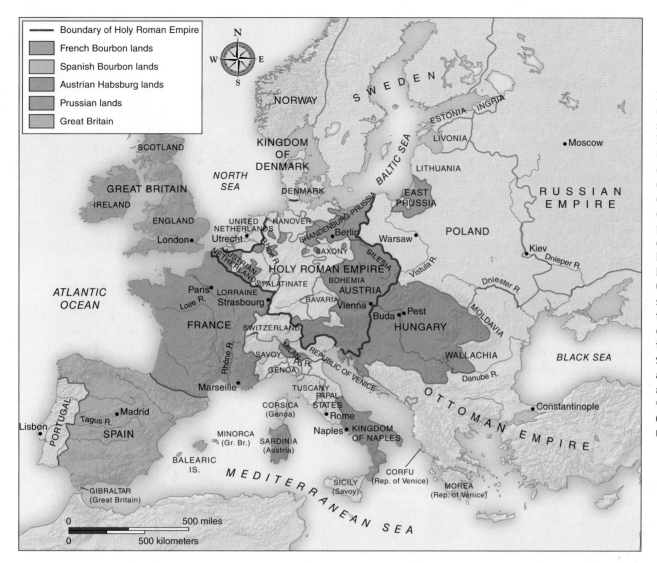

3. Europe's impact on much of the non-European world. The European legacy includes the shape of many modern countries; the balance of political, economic, and cultural power; and diffusion of the Westphalian state system and the nation-state ideal. The reasons for Europe's global influence are complex, but they are also partly coincidental. Spain, Portugal, France, England, the Netherlands, and others developed a series of overseas empires. When these empires eventually dissolved, they left a huge legacy.

4. **Decolonization** (particularly in the last two centuries). The United States was the first colony to declare its independence. But following that, several other New World colonies also declared themselves independent. In the nineteenth century, the Spanish colonies in Central and South America became separate states, Brazil gained independence from Portugal, Haiti threw off its French overlords, and Canada obtained independence from Great Britain. By the second half of the twentieth century, nearly all the colonies in Africa and Asia had become independent. Moreover, dozens of new states had emerged from the dismantling of the Austro-Hungarian, Ottoman, and Russian Empires. As the era of formal empires passed, we are now left with a proliferation of new states. There are more than four times as many states today as there were in 1939.

◀ **Figure 10C.3** In 1405, the emperor of China sent out a great admiral, Zheng He, to explore the regions of the Indian Ocean and beyond. Given its technology, China could have readily conquered and colonized much of the world. But the Ming emperor decided not to go any farther, and these Chinese vessels were called back in 1433. Ironically, about four centuries after China ceased explorations, the country was humiliated and subjugated by the same European powers it could once have easily destroyed.

10D Variations in Modern States

The modern world is made up of about 195 states. Officially, these states are considered to be equally sovereign and equally legitimate (see Module 10A). Moreover, each state is expected to have control over a fixed territory, with clear boundaries that separate that state's territory from its neighbors'.

But not all states are created equally. Individual states exhibit vast differences in levels of sovereignty and legitimacy. Some governments have little control over their state's territory. Other states exert effective control but are not recognized by other countries. Beyond this, there are enormous variations in the size of states.

The term **satellite state** is often used to describe states with less actual sovereignty. When the Soviet Union existed, several countries in Eastern Europe were satellite states. They did not have the freedom to exercise their own foreign policy or even to make internal changes.

▲ **Figure 10D.1** In 1968, the new leader of Czechoslovakia initiated a series of reforms and new freedoms in that then-Communist country. These included greater freedom of speech. The reforms alarmed the Soviet Union, which feared that its "ally" was overstepping its bounds. After unsuccessfully warning the Czech government to change course, the Soviets and other Warsaw Pact members intervened with tanks and troops.

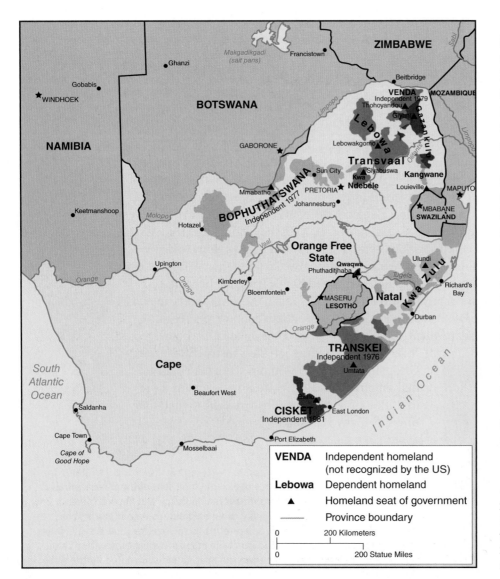

▲ **Figure 10D.2** During the era of apartheid, South Africa established a network of African homelands for the black African population, yet these areas were recognized as "states" only by South Africa. Maps published in South Africa showed the homelands, while outside maps did not.

The legitimacy of states also varies. Some states are recognized only by a few countries, or even just a single country. Maps made in different countries of a particular territory may vary if a country does not recognize the legitimacy of a state or the boundary demarcating one state from another.

Even though these states might exist only at a particular scale of operation, there are huge variations in the size and the population of each state in the world. From the map, it is obvious that the largest states by area are Russia, Canada, the United States, Brazil, Australia, and several others. Other states, such as India, Indonesia, and Japan, have very large populations. On the other side, the map of the world includes even the tiniest states. Monaco, San Marino, the Maldives, Bahrain, Barbados, Grenada, Nauru, and Vatican City are what we might describe as **micro-states**. These states are very small but are still considered to possess a certain degree of sovereignty, legitimacy, and territory.

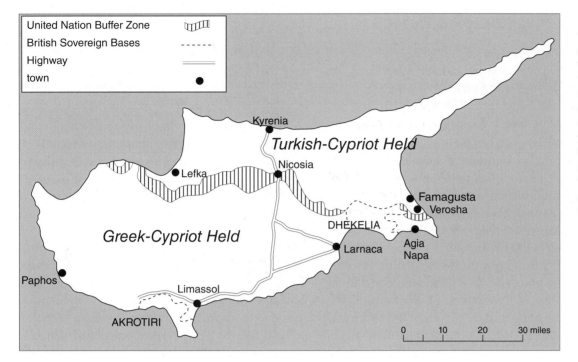

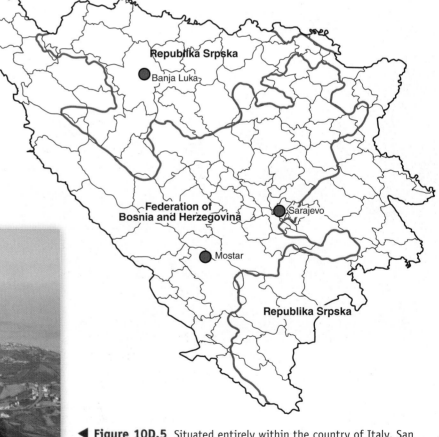

◀ **Figure 10D.3** Today, Cyprus is divided between a Turkish-speaking zone in the north and the remainder of the island, which is Greek speaking. Greek Cypriots do not recognize the legitimacy of the Turkish zone; nor does much of the rest of the world. But this zone and the boundary within Cyprus is recognized as legitimate by Turkish Cypriots and by Turkey itself. Depending on where maps are published, these territories may or may not be indicated.

Figure 10D.4 ▶ Bosnia and Herzegovina, forged by the bloody and bitter wars that racked Yugoslavia in the 1990s, appears on the map to be a single country. In fact, Bosnia is divided into two distinct entities: One is controlled primarily by Bosnia's Muslim population and the other is controlled by Bosnia's Serbian population. Unlike Cyprus, which has no overarching government, Bosnia has an institutional structure. However, this structure is extraordinarily weak and has little bearing on the day-to-day lives of residents.

◀ **Figure 10D.5** Situated entirely within the country of Italy, San Marino is an independent state with 24 square miles of territory and 30,000 people—the third smallest in Europe after the Vatican City and Monaco. Its transportation system consists of some roadways and a cable car to its capital. It has adopted the euro as its currency, shifting from the Italian lira. San Marino makes a good living from tourism and the sale of postage stamps.

10E Four Markers of a Nation

The term *nation* is often incorrectly used to describe a country. **Nation** is not a synonym for *country*; rather, it is meant to represent a group of people who feel that they belong together as a polity for a number of reasons. Unlike a state, which is clearly defined in most cases, a nation can be somewhat amorphous. This can be a somewhat difficult concept to grasp, but a few markers can help define a nation:

1. The first marker is a shared cultural heritage or shared belief that helps unite a group of people and distinguishes them from their neighbors. Nations are generally large, including sometimes millions or even hundreds of millions of people. What makes these people feel that they owe their first loyalty to each other? There needs to be some element that promotes this feeling of solidarity. Often, it is something cultural, such as a shared language or religion. Or solidarity can be based on a historical legacy, a series of events that members of the nation hold in common regard. Sometimes, the notion of nationhood or national identity can be related to a distinct set of ideas.

2. The second marker is loyalty. Loyalty to a nation is distinguished by the primacy it holds on people's allegiance. It is so powerful that people are willing to give their lives to ensure the continued existence of the group members and territory that make up their nation. This loyalty is expressed toward all the people of that nation; in other words, it is a **horizontal loyalty**. Prior to the development of nations and nationalism, the ruler did not necessarily need to have anything in common with the people he or she ruled. Political structures were hierarchical and the people were considered subjects. The people were expected to owe allegiance to the ruler, a **vertical loyalty**. In the eighteenth century, Enlightenment philosophy stressed that loyalty and allegiance should be to all those who constituted a "nation" because of a shared culture and shared ideas. The idea of loyalty to the nation is an extremely powerful aspect of nationhood. One would expect people to have loyalty to all sorts of political and social units. But the nation expects a **primary loyalty**, which transcends that of other allegiances. This is necessary to persuade individuals to die for the national cause. It also expects an implicit

(a)

(b)

◀ **Figure 10E.1** Scholars often distinguish between so-called **ethnic nations**, which are based more on cultural commonalities, and **civic nations**, which are based on shared principles. (a) The Japanese nation is clearly ethnic, tracing its descent from a distinct group of people. (b) The American nation is made up of many different peoples and, instead, is based on a shared set of ideas.

▲ **Figure 10E.2** In any country, service in the military represents a sacrifice that people make for the good of the nation. By serving, soldiers put themselves at risk of making the ultimate sacrifice. These coffins are for soldiers who died in the current conflict in Afghanistan.

▲ **Figure 10E.3** A nation's territory is expressed in its national landscape. Much of the work in political geography has tried to decipher and uncover different aspects of **national landscapes**, particularly through various landscape elements such as houses, churches, parks, monuments, and all manner of things that help determine the national flavor of the place (see Module 6F, on reading cultural landscapes). Finland's beautiful national landscape of forests and lakes represents a strong element of the Finnish national identity.

acknowledgment of **exclusivity**—that a person is loyal to only one nation. Individuals who claim two national loyalties are considered suspect.

3. Another marker of a nation is its territorial expression. Like a state, a nation has a distinct territory, which it considers to be its natural **homeland**. Unlike a state, the members of a particular nation may not be found in a territorially demarcated and contained place. In fact, members of a nation can be strewn about in several different places. But there persists a strong sense of a distinct space and of places enshrined in national memory. The importance of the soil to national mythology is witnessed by some of the bloodiest battles between two different national groups who claim the same land.

4. The fourth marker of a nation is based in its political goals. Being a defined nation means that members of the nation seek **self-determination**. This idea of self-determination—whereby members of a nation are allowed to form their own sovereign state—is what animates the ideology of **nationalism**. At different times, nationalism has resulted in a lot of grief as well as hope. But without nationalism, the idea of a nation would be impossible.

▲ **Figure 10E.4** In 2002, East Timor finally gained independence from Indonesia, achieving its self-determination after a protracted and violent struggle.

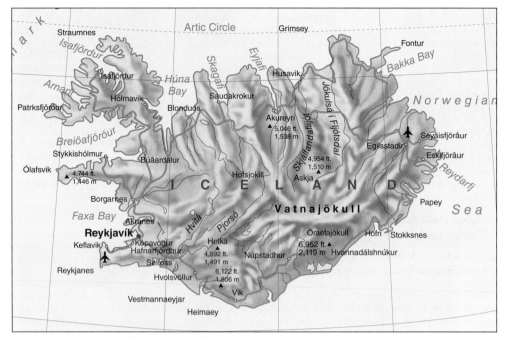

▲ **Figure 10F.1** Perhaps the best example of an undisputed nation-state is Iceland, a very small country with about 300,000 people. It was settled by Scandinavians centuries ago and contains no indigenous people. Iceland also benefits from being an island.

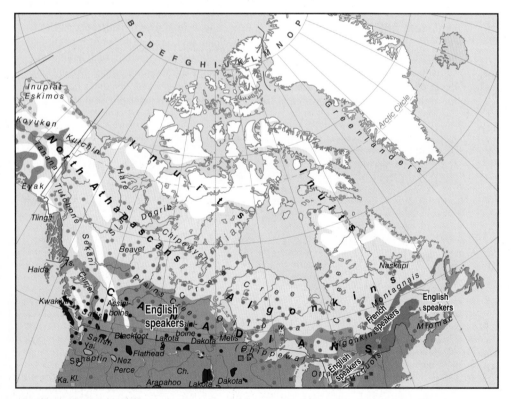

▲ **Figure 10F.2** Canada includes at least two nations: the numerically dominant English-speaking Canadians and the smaller but historically prominent French-speaking Canadians. French-speaking Canadians are found throughout the country, but they are clearly concentrated within the province of Quebec. A variety of accommodations have been attempted over the 130 years of Canada's existence. Since 1960, Quebec has pushed for greater political sovereignty and in 1995 came quite close to approving a referendum requesting secession. More recently, Canada has begun to acknowledge the presence of other distinct nations made up of indigenous peoples, or what Canadians call First Nations.

10F The Relationship between Nations and States

The ideal arrangement under nationalist ideology is that every nation should have control over a state. Conversely, every political state should embody a specific nation. Therefore, the German people should live within the country of Germany, be governed by German leaders, and partake of German institutions. This correspondence between nation and state is what informs the **nation-state ideal**.

While the nation-state is certainly an ideal in our modern world, it is not a reality for most countries. There are approximately 195 states in the world today. How many nations are there in the world? It is hard to say, because it all depends on what you consider to be a nation. One group's nation may be considered merely a tribe by outsiders, or even less. Taking an expansive view, some scholars argue that as many as 4,000 to 5,000 nations exist today. Even conservative estimates are far higher than the existing number of states. Thus, the goal of self-determination conflicts with the limited number of states existing in the world. This makes for a number of state and nation forms.

One form is the true **nation-state**. Several countries come very close to this ideal, where the state contains a single nation that is not disputed by anyone inside or outside. Some people consider Japan, with 128 million people, close to the nation-state ideal. Certainly, the Japanese feel a distinct sense of their national identity in the state of Japan, which is made up primarily of ethnic Japanese. However, some people do not fit into this Japanese type. Japan still includes the Ainu, a distinct ethnic group who some have suggested constitute another nation. Another aspect of modern Japan has been the growth of its immigrant population, many of whom are originally of Japanese ancestry but returned as immigrants from other countries.

Another form is a **multinational state**, in which a country contains more than one nation. Most countries are multinational, at least to some extent. Often,

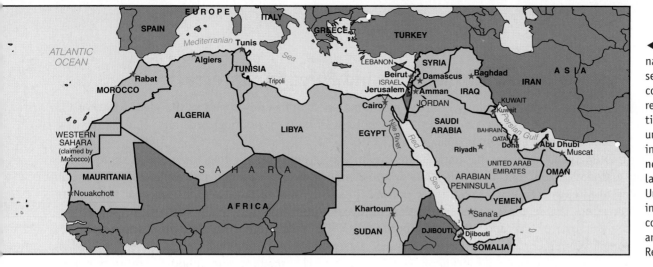

◄ **Figure 10F.3** The Arab nation is divided among several states, which share commonalities of language, religion, and sense of identity and history. Attempts to unite these disparate states into a single country have not succeeded, however. The last attempt was that of the United Arab Republic, which included the present-day countries of Egypt, Syria, and Libya. The United Arab Republic disbanded in 1964.

there is a dominant nation that is in control of the state apparatus and that historically has been identified with a particular state. But the country also includes one or more other nations. These nations may be recognized as such by the state, or they may be ignored or even actively repressed. The extent to which the state and the dominant nation are able to negotiate with the other nations within the state determines the level of political discourse and overall political stability.

A third form occurs when a nation encompasses more than one state: a **multistate nation**. These nations may or may not have control of the state. Instead of wanting to break the country apart, some politicians and residents of a multistate nation may seek ways to join the pieces together. Dictators with grandiose ambitions often use the presence of co-nationals across the border as a pretext for invasion. In 1990, Saddam Hussein attacked Kuwait, claiming it to be a part of the Iraqi nation.

Another form occurs when a nation has no state to call its own: we call this a **stateless nation**. In this case, the nation may straddle several states or even be contained within the boundaries of a single state.

A final form occurs when a group of people who consider themselves to be part of a nation are not consolidated spatially. In such a case, there is almost always a particular homeland or territory that the group identifies with, but now the group members are dispersed. We call this kind of national group a **diaspora**. Members of a diaspora feel a sense of national commonality, but without any form of spatial connections. A diaspora group has at some point left its homeland—although this may be more legendary than historical. These people then become a minority population in another country or countries, but they never really assimilate or adopt another national identity, instead choosing to maintain transnational contacts with other members of the diaspora.

▼ **Figure 10F.4** Kurdistan stretches across Turkey, Iraq, and Iran. Kurds have been prosecuted in all three countries and have been denied the right to a single state of their own. Recent events have allowed a Kurdish enclave to be formed in northern Iraq. While this enclave has no recognition as an independent state, it has been able to maintain a degree of control over a loosely defined territory.

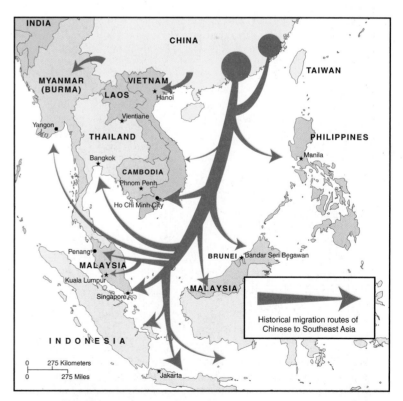

▲ **Figure 10F.5** The most well-known example of the diaspora population is that of the Jews, but *diaspora* also describes other groups, including the Chinese in Southeast Asia, shown in this map, Indians throughout the world, and even smaller groups, such as Mauritians, who have been able to develop a very strong sense of national identity outside their home territories.

10G Nationalism as an Ideology and Force in Statecraft

Although few countries have actually realized it, the nation-state has developed as the ideal form for the modern state. This makes nationalism a critical ideology in modern political relations. But nationalism means different things to different people.

Primordialism is the view that nations are organically grown entities, that the world is divided into different national groups that have persisted for some time, and that nationalist movements represent an awakening of already significant identities. Opposed to this is **constructivism**—the view that nations are artificial creations that result from modernization, elite aspirations, or a series of events that makes nation-building a much more viable approach than anything else. The third view is **instrumentalism**, which sees nations as emerging for a particular purpose, to meet the demands of a situation. Each of these views, when taken to the extreme, can seem a bit ridiculous. Clearly, there is something to a national identity that goes beyond the imperatives of the moment, yet we know that national identities shift over time and that old identities can expire and new ones emerge.

Centripetal forces unify and bring together. Nationalism can be a centripetal force because it bonds together individuals within a nation. People in the nation-state, who subscribe to the nationalist idea, are less likely to be rebellious and are more likely to make greater personal sacrifices for the good of the nation. Leaders who are charismatic and successful enough to epitomize this type of nationalism are granted a great deal of power and loyalty. This type of emotional bonding often translates into a greater degree of citizen mobilization, particularly where the military is concerned.

Economically, the nation-state offers a number of advantages over other forms. People are more honest about taxes, because people are willing to give up some of their money to benefit the nation. They are more receptive to appeals to buy goods produced within the nation and to respond to charitable appeals to fellow nationals in need. A strong national identity develops a sense of "us-ness," which is opposed to others who are outside of this group.

The state fosters a sense of nationalism among its people through the creation of governing structures that are representative of a distinct people. **Unifying institutions** help promote nationalist ideology and bring members of the nation together. Education, usually compulsory, instills a sense of national history and mission. A national military or compulsory national service—as practiced in several countries, such as Germany, Israel, and Switzerland—can bring together all young men and women toward a common purpose. Some countries designate a national church, which unites all members in faith. Excellent transportation and communication networks—roads, decent phone systems, strong banking networks—integrate the state, which can also benefit national integration.

Centrifugal forces tend to pull apart and disperse. Several factors can make nationalism into a strong centrifugal force. **Ethnoregionalism** occurs where a **minority national group** (a group that considers itself a nation but does not have control of the state) is concentrated in a particular region of a country. In several cases, this national group is too small to pose a threat to the entire state,

◀ **Figure 10G.1** The Soviet Union relied heavily on posters to try to unify its people. This "Motherland Is Calling" poster was created in July 1941 during the first days of the war between Nazi Germany and the Soviet Union. This war helped catalyze a feeling of Soviet consciousness of themselves as a nation, despite the fact that the country was made up of dozens of nationalities. Joseph Stalin was particularly fond of this poster and had it reprinted thousands of times.

although they may create a variety of difficulties. In other cases, the national group is substantial and may constitute the numerical majority of the country. These ethnoregional or subnational movements can be manifested in a couple of different ways. People who feel unfulfilled are likely to demand some sort of autonomy, although the level of autonomy desired may vary. Throughout the world, there are separatist movements looking to become independent, and a few of these are successful.

Complete independence does not always need to be the goal. Sometimes, a region simply seeks more power, as well as more autonomy. Devolution movements, as have been practiced most recently by Scotland within the United Kingdom, can be successful in satisfying a peoples yearning for some control over their own destiny. It can be a delicate balancing act among the interests of the central state, the interest of the dominant national group, and those of groups seeking more autonomy.

Sometimes, ethnoregional movements do not seek to create their own independent country but, rather, to separate from their existing state in order to join a neighboring state. Such **irredentist movements** are different from a simple boundary dispute, which often has to do with historical claims or a desire to capture certain resources. Most of the time, the impetus for change comes from the people who inhabit a particular region. The danger with irredentist movements is that they automatically involve a neighboring country, which broadens the potential conflict considerably.

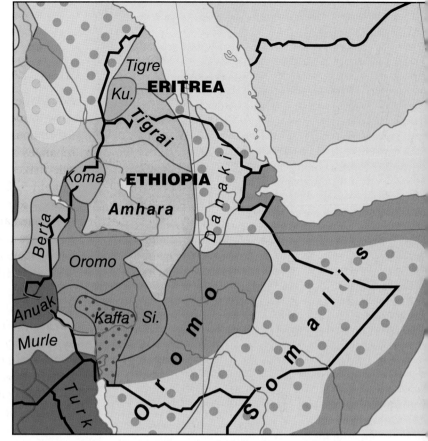

▲ **Figure 10G.2** The country of Eritrea was able to secede from Ethiopia after a long conflict. Eritreans felt that they were very distinct from the general Ethiopian national identity and had no wish to remain in that country. However, as this map indicates, ethnic groups spilled across the boundaries between the two countries, making secession difficult. Most countries are reluctant to allow a portion of that country to simply secede, so secessionist movements often result in bloody civil wars.

◀ **Figure 10G.3** The South Tyrol was acquired by Italy after World War I, but it includes a predominantly German-speaking population that identifies more with the North Tyrol and East Tyrol, located in Austria. This population wished to rejoin with Austria and developed a strong irredentist movement. Disputes between Italy and the South Tyrol region broadened into a dispute between Italy and Austria itself, leading to adjudication by the United Nations in 1961.

▲ **Figure 10H.1** In 1995, several European countries lifted all border controls between them, allowing for unimpeded access across international boundaries. The **Schengen Agreement** now includes most Western and Central European countries and has spread to include many Eastern European countries as well. While there is a great deal of correspondence between the Schengen Zone and the European Union, it is far from complete. Switzerland, as in the example here, is part of the Schengen Zone but not part of the European Union. Crossing from Germany to Switzerland is no more difficult than crossing from Iowa to Nebraska. On the other hand, the United Kingdom is not part of the Schengen Zone, although it is a member of the European Union.

10H Boundaries and Borderlands

Boundaries are an essential aspect of any political unit. This is particularly so with modern states. Nearly every state in the world has clearly established boundaries. An **international boundary** is recognized as a line that separates one state from another. Where there are boundary disputes, each side makes specific claims as to where the boundary *should* be located. Moreover, it is rare to find an unattended boundary between two sovereign states—some countries in the European Union are the single exception.

Boundaries are also a focus of national concern. While nations are not as clearly defined geographically as states, most nations have a sense of where their territory ends. The problem is often that national territories overlap or that a national territory does not coincide with a state boundary.

The area that surrounds the boundary is termed a **borderland**, or border region. These vary in width, depending on the criteria employed. The **border** is thus a region, while a boundary is simply a line. Border regions appear different, depending on the nature of the boundary.

The notion of **effective national territory** relates to the fact that the legal area, or **de jure area**, of a state is not coincident with the territory that it effectively controls, the **de facto area**. In many states, these are one and the same, but often they are not. **Frontier** describes an area at the edge of any type of effective political control or at the edge of settlement. The frontier's edge shifts frequently with settlement advances or increasing military control.

Traditional approaches have classified boundaries according to natural features, cultural aspects, and geometric shapes. **Natural boundaries** occur where there are natural features that divide one country from another. An island is a perfect example of a natural boundary, since it is always surrounded by ocean. It is important to note, however, that there is no such thing as a truly natural boundary. All boundaries are constructed as a means of defining a state's power and level of sovereignty. To increase state territory, countries throughout history have routinely passed over so-called natural boundaries and expanded to include as much area as they could, given their military strength or their capacity to govern.

▼ **Figure 10H.2** Geographers refer to boundaries within a country as **internal boundaries**. These separate substate units. This famous boundary line, called the Four Corners, separates Arizona, Utah, Colorado, and New Mexico.

▲ **Figure 10H.3** This border region in Slovenia lies near the Italian boundary. Often, border regions exhibit a great deal of cultural diversity, including national groups from both sides of the boundary. They may also contain items that are prohibited or much more expensive across the boundary: liquor stores, cheap gasoline, or casinos.

◀ **Figure 10H.4** The area in northwest Pakistan is a frontier where Osama bin Laden and many members of Al Qaeda were suspected of hiding. It is still a hotbed of terrorist activity and virtually no government control.

▼ **Figure 10H.5** The way in which boundaries are formed can be significant, because boundary disputes can result from differing interpretations of a particular natural feature. For instance, the Sarda River functions as a boundary between India and Nepal, yet these countries disagree about which stream constitutes the source of the river and, so, where the correct boundary should be drawn. Disputes can also arise as a river or other natural feature changes its course.

▲ **Figure 10H.6** In 1494, two years after Columbus landed in the Western Hemisphere, the pope created the boundary of Tordesillas, which divided lands in the New World belonging to Portugal from lands belonging to Spain. In so doing, he ignored the native Amerindian populations living there. The impact of this antecedent and geometric boundary continues today, as Brazil (lying partly east of the line) is Portuguese speaking, while most of the rest of South America is Spanish speaking. Source: From Dennis Sherman and Joyce Salisbury, *The West in the World, Third Edition*, © 2008 by The McGraw-Hill Companies, Inc., page 378. Used by permission.

▲ **Figure 10H.7** The creation of the subsequent boundary between India and Pakistan in 1946 was followed by mass migrations on both sides. Hindus fled the newly created state of Pakistan, and Muslims left India to find a more hospitable environment in Pakistan.

▲ **Figure 10H.8** In the demilitarized zone between North Korea and South Korea, each country deploys a massive number of troops along a narrow "no man's land" to ensure that no person breaches this boundary.

▲ **Figure 10H.9** Some towns—such as Stanstead, Quebec, and adjacent Derby Line, Vermont—contain a few unguarded boundaries, including some that intersect public libraries! Such towns have bristled at proposals to put up fences and other barriers.

The decision to establish a clear break between countries may not take place so much on the ground as on a map. **Geometric boundaries** are drawn up as lines on a map without much interest in whatever natural or cultural features are present. The line dividing the United States and Canada at the 49th parallel is a good example of a geometric boundary. However, portions of the US-Canadian boundary are also natural, running through the Great Lakes, several ocean inlets, and river systems. The boundary between the United States and Mexico is likewise a mixture of geometric boundaries and the extensive natural boundary of the Rio Grande.

Boundaries can also be considered relative to human settlement. An **antecedent boundary** is created before an area is known or populated. Many so-called antecedent boundaries, of course, were drawn with no recognition of the populations living there.

Subsequent boundaries are created after recognized settlement. They are meant to separate existing cultural groups and may signify an attempt to align the boundaries that exist between nations, which are cultural and not always visible, with the boundaries that exist between states. Sometimes, the presence of state boundaries alters the boundaries between nations. This is especially true when a particular group of people feel uncomfortable in a neighboring country.

All international boundaries share the same basic purpose, separating one state from another, but in so doing they play several distinct functions. First, *boundaries disrupt traffic*, be it of people, goods, or information. The Cold War was marked by the creation of heavily **militarized boundaries** that discouraged crossing. During that period, East German guards were told to shoot at anyone trying to cross into the west. Such heavily fortified boundaries are still found today.

At the other extreme are **open boundaries**, where crossing is unimpeded. As noted before, the Schengen Agreement allows for completely unrestricted and uncontrolled crossing between several European countries. Between these two extremes are a number of security levels. The militarization of a boundary reflects the political relationship between two countries, as well as concerns about immigration, flows of goods, or any number of other concerns. The level of security along the US-Canadian border has fluctuated with these concerns. During Prohibition in the 1920s, the boundary was a site for bootlegging illegal liquor. Today, despite increased security since 9/11, this is considered a fairly relaxed boundary.

Figure 10H.10 ▶ The development of new boundaries can disrupt the rhythms of ordinary life. After World War II, the boundary between Italy and the former Yugoslavia shifted and crossed some major population centers. This was especially true near the city of Gorizia. Some villages were cut in two, and transportation links were severed. In response, the Yugoslav government built the city of Nova Gorica (New Gorizia) to serve the population that had previously shopped and worked in Gorizia.

Second, *boundaries may represent division* between two realms of governments, two economic systems, and even two different levels of welfare. These divisions can be apparent on the landscape as a particular set of settlement patterns, housing developments, cities, stores, and streets give way to a landscape that is quite different. The Iron Curtain was such a series of international boundaries, which divided Communist Eastern from capitalist Western Europe. Boundaries may divide very different societies with different social mores or divide prosperous from more impoverished societies. In these cases, illegal immigration can be an issue. The poor country sends out immigrants or potential immigrants, which the rich country may either welcome or reject, depending on its current labor needs.

Third, *boundaries help embody the edge of national identity.* Although the nation-state is rare in reality, it does represent an ideal. In many cases, the boundary is clean and the limit of state sovereignty coincides with the edge of a nation's territorial identity. Crossing an international boundary entails a movement, not just from one country to another but also from one national region to another. When a political boundary does not coincide with the national boundary, the break is messy. The boundary and the region that surrounds it become far more confusing and more contentious. In some cases, people on each side of the state boundary have more in common with each other than they do with their respective countries.

Geographers find borderlands to be interesting objects of study in their own right. While international boundaries can divide people, they also create common issues and interests. Border regions, often at the margin of national life, can be zones of political, economic, and cultural overlap, and they may develop their own identity distinct from that of either state.

Figure 10H.12 ▶ There now exist over 40 Euroregions, of which 12 are depicted on this map, and they are designed to enhance the significance of border areas. They help promote interactions between people, they often develop particular institutions, and in some cases they have even developed their own councils. In an increasingly globalized world, where boundaries can be readily crossed, it is possible to think that these Euroregions will become ever more important.

▲ **Figure 10H.11** Industries in a prosperous country may locate across the border in order to take advantage of cheaper labor and looser regulations in a poorer country. This is the case in the *maquiladora* factories that populate the US-Mexico border.

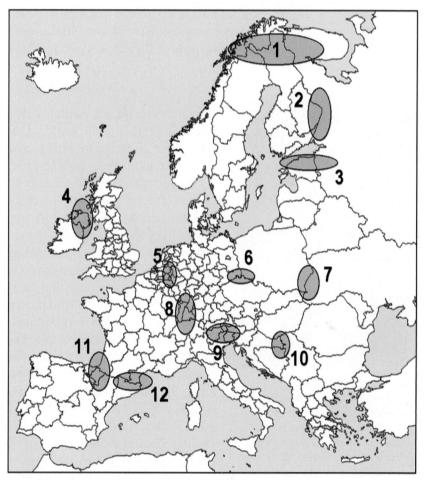

1. Nordic countries and Northwestern Russia
2. Karelia
3. Northeast Estonia
4. Northern Ireland
5. Euregio Meuse-Rhin
6. Euroregion Nysa
7. Galicia
8. Regio TriRhena
9. Northern Italy
10. Eastern Slavonia
11. Basque country
12. Catalonia

10I Geopolitics and the Global Order

Political territory and space are clearly intertwined. Both states and nations have a spatial expression. Political considerations affect how states exercise power geographically and how the national space is represented internally and externally. But we can also think about how space itself may affect global politics. This is a concern under the umbrella of geopolitics. **Geopolitics** is the study of how geographical space—including the types of interrelationships between states, the different functions of states, and the different patterns of states—affect global politics.

▲ **Figure 10I.1** Mackinder's map showing the geopolitical relations between regions in the world. For him, *World-Island* denoted the Eastern Hemisphere continents of Europe, Asia, and Africa. The Heartland was the pivot region from which it was possible to control the World-Island.

Geopolitics has a long and checkered history. The term *geopolitics* was first coined in 1904 and popularized by a man named Halford Mackinder. Mackinder's view was that the world is divided between a world island, composed of Eurasia and Africa, and the surrounding areas, termed the Outer Crescent. The pivot area was the lands of Eastern Europe and Russia. According to Mackinder,

> *Who rules East Europe commands the Heartland; who rules the Heartland commands the World-Island; who rules the World-Island controls the world.*

One other theory, written a decade earlier by Alfred Mahan, examined the influence of sea power and, in some ways, serves as a counterpoint to Mackinder. Later on, a theory by Alexander De Seversky used a polar projection map to define areas of US air dominance, Soviet air dominance, and the zone of overlap where both faced off.

Unfortunately for Mackinder's theory and for geopolitics as a field of study, the most influential early proponents were German Nazis. They sought to apply this theory in their grab for Eastern Europe and Russia. The Nazis were not shy in utilizing a number of theories from geopolitics, notably the ideas of nineteenth-century German geographer Friedrich Ratzel, who wrote about the biological nature of states and tied the health of a state with its expansion. The German term *Lebensraum*, meaning "living space," became associated with territorial aggression and the subjugation of conquered peoples.

After World War II, American foreign policy experts adopted geopolitical principles to fashion a view of the world. In their minds, the world was composed of the capitalist free world, led by the United States, and the Communist world, led by the Soviet Union. This notion guided a couple of important policies. One was the policy of **containment**, which sought to limit any Soviet advance to any **nonaligned countries**—countries not allied with either the Soviet Union or the United States—thereby containing Communist expansionism. The 1949 defeat of Chiang Kai-shek in China was a major blow for containment. The other policy addressed the **domino theory**, which looked at every political change in a country's government as a domino that causes other dominoes to follow in a chain reaction. In this case, the fear was that one new Communist country in a region could tip the other countries in the region to communism. Taken to its extreme, the last domino could be the United States itself. During the Cold War era, the leaders of the Soviet Union also adopted geopolitical strategies, in particular the idea that they would need to expand as much as possible and control their borders through the creation of a series of satellite states. Various

▲ **Figure 10I.2** George Kennan was a career Foreign Service officer who introduced the policy of containment. In an anonymous article in *Foreign Affairs*, Kennan wrote, "The main element of any United States policy toward the Soviet Union must be that of a long-term, patient but firm and vigilant containment of Russian expansive tendencies."

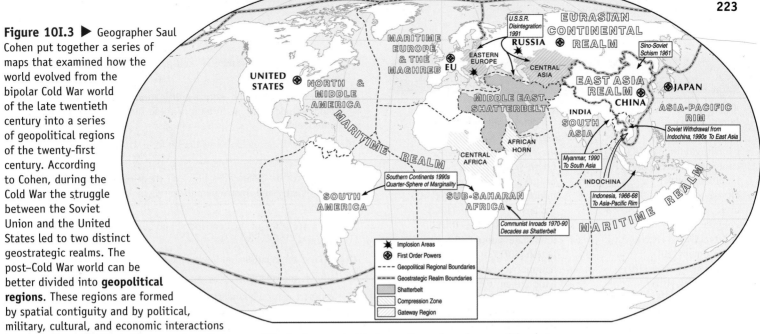

Figure 10I.3 ▶ Geographer Saul Cohen put together a series of maps that examined how the world evolved from the bipolar Cold War world of the late twentieth century into a series of geopolitical regions of the twenty-first century. According to Cohen, during the Cold War the struggle between the Soviet Union and the United States led to two distinct geostrategic realms. The post–Cold War world can be better divided into **geopolitical regions**. These regions are formed by spatial contiguity and by political, military, cultural, and economic interactions between them. **Shatterbelts** are regions that are politically fragmented and are often areas of competition between two ideological or two religious realms. Southeast Asia used to be a shatterbelt, because it was an area of conflict between the Soviet Union and the United States.

Today, Southeast Asia is no longer an area of Cold War competition but, instead, has become a rapidly industrializing member of the East Asian trading network. The Middle East, however, is still a shatterbelt. During the Cold War, it was buffeted by the ideological power plays between the Soviet Union and the United States. These have largely dissipated, but the religious differences that divided it then still divide it now. Moreover, the intrusion of various outside powers, whether well meaning or not, keeps tensions and conflicts at a boil.

democracy movements in Hungary and Czechoslovakia were brutally put down by the Soviet Union because of the fear that they would open the way to a breach of the Soviet motherland.

Newer ideas of geopolitics can be useful in analyzing the world today, particularly if stripped of their imperialist motivations.

ALL I WANT FOR CHRISTMAS iS... TO WRAP IT UP!!

FOR YOU, AMERICA! LOVE, YOUR TROOPS!

© 2001 Chris S. Patterson

▲ **Figure 10I.4** Cartoons can be powerful reflections and shapers of how people view the world. In the wake of the 9/11 attacks, this cartoon expressed the view that the United States had had enough and was poised for retribution. Source: www.CartoonStock.com

We use the term **critical geopolitics** to dissect the ways state boundaries are perceived, relationships between states, and the ways the world is portrayed. Any political view of the world, such as the domino theory, is framed by a particular set of beliefs. These beliefs can also be shaped by individual actors, who try to mobilize populations through a particular set of geographical understandings. The creation of geopolitical visions can be intentional, as when a country seeks justification for going to war. These visions can also develop over a long period of time. A famous book written by Edward Said, entitled *Orientalism*, examines how the Middle East has been imagined in a particular way by the West. We can cite other examples. Terms such as *axis of evil*, *Third World*, and even *Eastern Europe* conjures up distinct and powerful geographical visions.

Key Terms

antecedent boundary (10H)

border (10H)

borderland (10H)

centrifugal forces (10G)

centripetal forces (10G)

chiefdoms (10B)

city-state (10B)

civic nations (10E)

colonies (10B)

constructivism (10G)

containment (10I)

critical geopolitics (10I)

de facto area (10H)

de jure area (10H)

decolonization (10C)

democracy (10A)

diaspora (10F)

diplomatic relations (10A)

domino theory (10I)

effective national territory (10H)

empires (10B)

ethnic nations (10E)

ethnoregionalism (10G)

exclusivity (10E)

feudal system (10B)

frontier (10H)

geometric boundaries (10H)

geopolitical regions (10I)

geopolitics (10I)

High Seas (10A)

homeland (10E)

horizontal loyalty (10E)

instrumentalism (10G)

internal boundaries (10H)

international boundary (10H)

irredentist movements (10G)

legitimacy (10A)

metropole (10B)

micro-states (10D)

militarized boundaries (10H)

minority national group (10G)

modern state system (10C)

multinational state (10F)

multistate nation (10F)

nation (10E)

national landscapes (10E)

nationalism (10E)

nation-state (10F)

nation-state ideal (10F)

natural boundaries (10H)

nonaligned countries (10I)

open boundaries (10H)

political unit (10A)

primary loyalty (10E)

primordialism (10G)

satellite state (10D)

Schengen Agreement (10H)

self-determination (10E)

shatterbelts (10I)

sovereignty (10A)

state (10A)

stateless nation (10F)

subsequent boundaries (10H)

territory (10A)

unifying institutions (10G)

vassal (10B)

vertical loyalty (10E)

Westphalian state system (10C)

Basic Review Questions

1. Describe some of the scales of a political unit.

2. What is the relationship between sovereignty and authority?

3. Contrast external legitimacy with internal legitimacy.

4. How does sovereignty work within a territory?

5. Name the different types of political entities that existed in the history of the world. Which of these are territorial?

6. What is the relationship between an empire and its colonies?

7. When did the modern state system come into effect? How is this related to nationalism and the nation-state ideal?

8. How has Europe impacted the non-European world in terms of political geography?

9. What has been the role of decolonization in creating new countries?

10. How does legitimacy of states vary? What is a micro-state?

11. What are the four markers of a nation?

12. What is the difference between an ethnic nation and a civic nation?

13. How did nationalism help change allegiance from vertical loyalty to horizontal loyalty?

14. What is the importance of self-determination to the ideology of nationalism?

15. Compare a true nation-state, a multinational state, a multistate nation, and a stateless nation. Which of these fits better within the nation-state ideal?

16. What is a diaspora, and how does it fit in with the notion of homeland and nation?

17. What are the differences between theories of primordialism, constructivism, and instrumentalism when considering how nations emerge?

18. What are some of the centripetal and centrifugal forces that affect a nation?

19. What is the relationship between ethnoregionalism and irredentism?

20. What is the relationship between a border region and a boundary?

21. Compare natural boundaries, geometric boundaries, antecedent boundaries, and subsequent boundaries.

22. How did the Schengen Agreement in the European Union affect boundary crossings?

23. What are some of the functions of international boundaries?

24. How does the role of effective national territory relate to the idea of a frontier?

25. How are Euroregions a good example of borderlands?

26. How did American foreign policy utilize geopolitical principles, especially after World War II?

27. How do shatterbelts function within the geopolitical viewpoint?

28. How is critical geopolitics used to dissect the way in which the world is portrayed?

Advanced Review Questions (Essay Questions)

1. Describe the relationship between legitimacy and sovereignty in the creation of states. Is a democracy more legitimate than another form of government? How would sovereignty work under a system in which there was a large, supranational entity, such as the European Union?

2. Describe the development of political entities over the course of world history. How did territoriality begin to influence the creation of some of these entities? What allowed an empire to maintain stability for a long period of time?

3. What is the Westphalian state system, and how has it been responsible for creating our modern world? What is the relationship between the development of states and the growth of nationalism? How has the growth of new states as a consequence of decolonization been affected by nationalism?

4. What are some of the differences between states in the world today? How does a satellite state enjoy less sovereignty? How might micro-states also find their sovereignty hampered by their size and geographical location?

5. Describe the four markers of a nation. How is an ethnic nation different from a civic nation? Would you consider an ethnic nation to command greater loyalty than a civic nation?

6. How might a multinational state result in an ethnoregional movement? What are some of the centripetal forces that can be used to

keep a multinational state together? Give an example of a multinational state that seems to work cooperatively, as well as one that is falling apart.

7. Compare the primordialist and constructivist views of national identity. How might somebody who considers national identity to be primordial view national unity in a different way than somebody who thinks of national identity as something constructed?

8. What are some of the functions of international boundaries? How would a militarized boundary create a different borderland environment than an open boundary? How do boundaries fit into the notion of a frontier?

9. What is the role of geopolitics in looking at the relationships between countries in the world today? What specifically was the Mackinder theory of geopolitics, and how was it discredited before World War II? How has geopolitics been used after World War II in regard to the policies of containment?

- Members of a diaspora feel that they belong to one nation while living among members of another nation within another state. The best-known diaspora population is the Jews, but there are several others in the world today. Consider the populations of Cubans in the United States (or another population). Would this population be considered a diaspora or just another ethnic group? What is the difference?

- There is a huge variation in how well states can control their own boundaries. In the United States, there has been a debate over how effective the government is in controlling its boundary with Mexico. Examine some of the factors that might make it difficult to control boundaries such as that between the United States and Mexico. How would an open boundary alter the nature of US-Mexican relations?

- Critical geopolitics analyzes the understandings that people have of the world, how these perceptions are shaped, and how new perceptions are created. How might critical geopolitics help us understand the way in which the United States has dealt with countries such as Vietnam, Iraq, and the Dominican Republic? How have our geopolitical images of Russia changed over the last 25 years?

- In the world today, there are approximately 200 states, but many more nations are striving to become their own states. This has had a major impact on international relations and world peace. Consider a current ethnoregional movement. How successful has that movement been in facilitating autonomy or even independence for its people? What determines whether this movement is peaceful or violent?

Further Study Topics

- The European system of empires existed for a long time before eventually dissolving during the twentieth century. How did events during the twentieth century cause this to occur? Choose a European empire from the twentieth century, such as the British, Portuguese, Dutch, or French empire, and discuss the factors that would have caused the empire to break up.

Summary Activities

On the following map of the world, identify five nations that, as yet, do not have full self-determination.

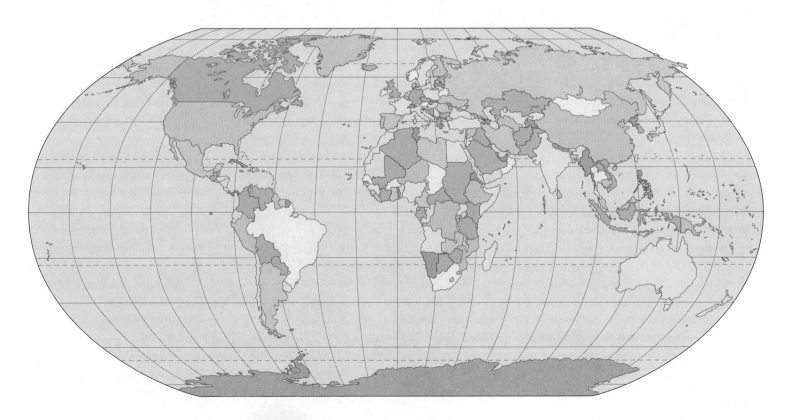

CHAPTER 11

Geography of Governance and Representation

CHAPTER MODULES

The modern political state is a complicated thing. Most states include large swaths of area, millions of people, and significant physical and human diversity. Moreover, governments nowadays take it upon themselves to perform a wide array of functions. The modern welfare state is responsible for its residents' education, health, welfare, infrastructure, safety, arbitration, environmental protection ... the list goes on. This is way beyond what was expected in the past, when most states were primarily involved in defense. This also means that the government has to raise money to pay for all of these programs.

Geography plays a huge role in the administration of these functions. Countries manipulate space to make governance easier and to recognize a country's diversity. Nearly every state is divided into political subunits, and many of the previously mentioned functions are provided at these levels. The national government may provide additional funding but often expects regional and local governments to deliver the services. In the United States, each of the state governments (using *state* to refer to the subunit) provides for transportation, welfare, public higher education, many aspects of environmental protection, and prison services. Below that, city and other local governments provide safety functions, such as fire control and police; infrastructural functions, such as responsibility for water systems, support systems, and power plants; transportation and communication functions, such as traffic control and some road construction and maintenance; and educational functions, including the establishment and maintenance of public schools. In multicultural states, political subunits can be a way to acknowledge and even promote cultural differences. A government may even establish autonomous regions that grant a regional population special rights and even self-governance.

Geography is also used to pick a country's leaders. The most popular way of determining representation at the national level is through regions, with each subunit granted one or more representatives. Subunits are often also allowed to elect their own governments, many times leading to wide variations in policy within a single country.

11A Territoriality

How do institutions use space to administer and govern effectively? Most use space—in particular, the subdivision of territory—to accomplish their aims. A company may divide its overall market into various marketing districts. Teams of salespeople are assigned to work within each of these sales districts. In this way, the company uses a simple tactic of dividing its overall territory into smaller, more manageable pieces, or **political subunits**.

▲ **Figure 11A.1 Toyota Manufacturing Plants around the World** Multinational companies, such as Toyota, subdivide territory to administer their far-flung corporate businesses. For the most part, the spatial organization of such a company may devolve to country or continental units. So the company will be headquartered in Japan but will subdivide its territory into a North American headquarters, a European headquarters, and an Asian headquarters. These subdivisions may enjoy a considerable degree of autonomy and often market different products. Nonprofit institutions and charitable organizations may do the same. Especially if they are large, it makes more sense to try to administer their organization in a territorial manner.

In all of these examples, territory is being used as a means to manipulate space and make the administration of the institution more efficient. We can point to a few basic reasons for this:

1. Basic *efficiency*: Administering a large territory with a lot of people, resources, and other things can be exceptionally difficult. Problems can arise in lots of different places. Subdividing this large territory into a number of smaller subunits makes administration far more efficient and allows greater ease in determining where some of the potential trouble spots are.
2. Greater *flexibility*: An institution that controls a large territory can run into trouble if it treats all places within this territory in the same way. Subdividing the territory into appropriate spatial units provides a greater flexibility in administering some units differently than others. For business, this may entail marketing different product lines or adjusting advertising for different markets. For government, this can be related to the establishment of different traditions, or even different languages found within different regions of a state.
3. Greater degree of *responsiveness*: Administration can be more responsive to demands placed on it by its stakeholders within smaller units. Directors or governors of subunits are more likely to be able to react to a particular situation or need than administrators who are far removed in some distant headquarters or capital.

Beyond these three positive reasons are two negative reasons:

4. Subdividing territories can more easily *restrict access* to only certain people. Some societies rigidly control the movement of people between districts as a way to keep better tabs on them. In other societies, access may not be formally restricted, but territorial markers act as barriers for people who belong to the "wrong" group.

5. A *mismatch* between the actual scope of a problem and the ability to effectively deal with the problem may result from the proliferation of subdivisions. Problems such as effective land use are usually best handled on a fairly large scale, often at the scale of a metropolitan area. However, the only avenues to address this issue may be at the local scale, through such devices as zoning. Because land use issues spill over several smaller and competing jurisdictions, however, it's much harder to get anything done when possible solutions are available only at the local level.

The territorial development of the Roman Catholic Church exemplifies how territory evolved as a strategy. The early Church was composed of hidden communities of people who sought to avoid the sort of structure and hierarchy they witnessed in the Jewish religion—from which most early Christians converted. Within the Roman Empire, Christianity was still illegal, and it would have been difficult to establish a territorial structure, but earlier Christian theology also avoided marking off specifically "sacred" spaces. Once Christianity was recognized by the Roman Empire and became the state religion, however, the territorial precepts of the Church changed considerably. After the Roman Empire collapsed, the logic of the Church's territorial organization remained.

Over time as well, the Pope acquired the power to appoint bishops and to determine diocesan boundaries, and to elevate some dioceses to archdiocese status. The development of Church territoriality was useful in the administration of a huge, global institution, but it also heralded a far more bureaucratic and hierarchical structure. The identification of a community with a parish and the power of the parish priest in the lives of his parishioners is quite pronounced in some societies.

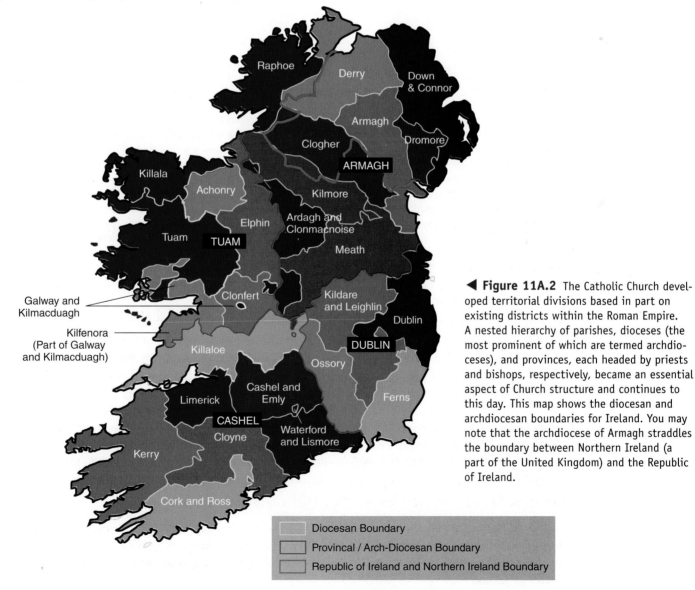

◀ **Figure 11A.2** The Catholic Church developed territorial divisions based in part on existing districts within the Roman Empire. A nested hierarchy of parishes, dioceses (the most prominent of which are termed archdioceses), and provinces, each headed by priests and bishops, respectively, became an essential aspect of Church structure and continues to this day. This map shows the diocesan and archdiocesan boundaries for Ireland. You may note that the archdiocese of Armagh straddles the boundary between Northern Ireland (a part of the United Kingdom) and the Republic of Ireland.

Diocesan Boundary

Provincal / Arch-Diocesan Boundary

Republic of Ireland and Northern Ireland Boundary

0 10 20 40 60 80
Kilometers

11B Political Economy and Functions of the Modern State

As we discussed in Chapter 10, states assume several roles. How do the institutions within the state apparatus protect and maintain the society? How do the residents of the state determine the government and the laws that the government passes?

To answer these questions, we must look at the political economic nature of the state itself. **Political economy** refers to the relationship among the state, the members of the state, and the economic activities contained within the state.

Throughout most of the world, states practice a more or less mixed economy, which includes both private and public sector functions. While most **private sector** factories, firms, and offices in a capitalist society are responsible for producing goods and providing services, there are still some things left for the **public sector** to do. The state has traditionally carried out functions related to its external relations, such as diplomacy and defense. It has also been involved in providing a system of adjudication or arbitration, often through a judicial system. Finally, the state has been responsible for collecting taxes.

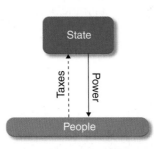

▲ **Figure 11B.1** Early modern states, often fashioned as kingdoms, were clearly more interested in bleeding their subjects than in providing services to citizens. This political economy was an **extraction economy** that sought chiefly to enrich the ruler and the aristocracy and to maintain its armies.

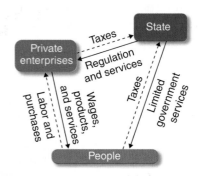

▲ **Figure 11B.2** With the development of a **capitalist economy** (see Module 15B), a wide variety of private concerns took control of the economy, and the state assumed a very different role. Certainly, it still required some measure of taxation in order to ensure that it could perform those services that only a state could—such as foreign relations, defense, and a judicial system—but the state acquired other functions as well.

Beyond these basic functions, many modern states take on additional roles. Some are related to caring for the population:

1. *Education.* This used to be a private concern, available to the wealthy. But as the capitalist economy developed, it required people to be literate and numerate. By the end of the nineteenth century, free compulsory education had been introduced in many countries.
2. *Social welfare.* Private capitalism did not necessarily worry about those people who were unemployed or otherwise falling between the cracks. In the early days of capitalism, the state was more intent on punishing those unfortunates who got into debt or found themselves without shelter. Increasingly, the state sought to care for people unable to care for themselves. Later, states began to take over the obligations not otherwise covered by the private sector. A pension system for the elderly is one example; a welfare system for those living below the poverty rate is another.
3. *Health care.* Most industrialized societies also provide a national system of health care. Even those that do not, such as the United States, provide some health care for the elderly and poor (see Module 4G).

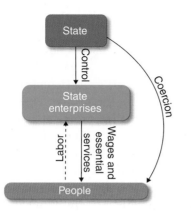

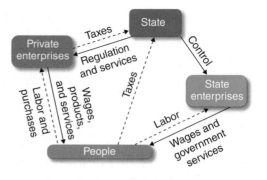

▲ **Figure 11B.3** The development of a **communist economy** in the twentieth century brought about a different view of state governance, as communist states assumed nearly all economic and social functions and tried to impose comprehensive control over economic activities.

▲ **Figure 11B.4** While the capitalist model of political economy has clearly prevailed in much of the world, no states can be considered exclusively capitalist. Rather, many states are what we call **mixed economies** (see Module 15B): The government controls certain economic activities it considers key or appropriate to the public trust while leaving others in the hands of the private sector.

Governments also have other functions to ensure that the economy operates as smoothly and fairly as possible:

4. *Currency.* There needs to be some form of legal tender, so that transactions can be conducted in a standard way. A country's currency has to be established, printed, and regulated.
5. *Business regulation.* The state must be able to regulate and police private companies and make sure that they follow an agreed-upon set of standards and rules, that they deal fairly with their employees and their customers, and that they limit the amount of pollution discharged into the land, air, and water.
6. *Infrastructure.* The state may also be responsible for establishing and maintaining various systems of communication, transportation, and other infrastructure that facilitate the conduct of business. Many of these items, such as the construction of highways and the maintenance of ports, serve everybody and, so, are considered the state's responsibility.

◀ **Figure 11B.5** Governments are normally responsible for the development and maintenance of ports, such as the port of Los Angeles and Long Beach, which occupies over 10,500 acres of land and water and is the busiest container port in the United States.

11C Theories of the State

Geographers and other scholars use a few well-known **theories of the state** to discuss how states operate, particularly those within democratic, capitalist systems.

A **pluralist theory of the state** views government as a neutral arbiter of all the different stakeholders. The government is elected by the people, and it creates and enforces laws for the people. There is no real bias toward a particular group of people within the state, and elections determine exactly what kind of political philosophy prevails. An election that favors a government from the left is likely to provide more services and regulate business more tightly. Such governments are often described as democratic socialist, or in the United States, liberal. An election won by a government on the right is likely to favor business interests and looks to reduce the scope of state power. More recently, the term **neoliberalism** (not to be confused with *political liberalism*) has been used to describe a set of policies that favor minimal government interference in markets and the promotion of free trade. Many argue that such neoliberal policies apply, no matter what the outcome of an election.

Elite theories of the state see governments, no matter what their political ideology or their constitution, as likely to support an elite class of people. Every society is made up of an elite who controls the economy and the society and who are favored by the government itself. While elite theories are not necessarily the same as Marxist theories, they share the idea that the state is not a neutral entity, but promotes the interests of a particular group.

▲ **Figure 11C.1** In many countries, several political parties put up candidates for election, ranging all the way from the extreme left to the extreme right. According to the pluralist theory of the state, these elections decide the direction of government.

Marxist theories of the state look at the state as a vehicle promoting capitalism and the capitalist class—in other words, those who control the means of production. The state serves capitalism, either through various key figures who represent the capitalist class and its interests or through the state's embeddedness within the capitalist mode of production.

In a nondemocratic, noncapitalist society, the state serves a very different role than these theories would imply. **Authoritarian**, or **autocratic**, **states** concentrate political power in a single individual or a clique

Figure 11C.2 ▶ The influence of media barons, such as Rupert Murdoch, is controversial. Murdoch owns major newspapers and television networks in the United Kingdom, Australia, and the United States. He enjoys immense influence through these media outlets, and some have complained that he manipulates the political systems in all three countries to favor his interests.

Figure 11C.3 ▶ China's Communist Party created a totalitarian form of government. All power was vested in the party apparatus. People who challenged the government were imprisoned. Many people were sent to "re-education camps." And all aspects of society—from theater to education—were expected to uphold the party line. Included in this was a vision of Party Leader Mao Zedong as an all-knowing presence. This color lithograph is titled "Chairman Mao is the Red Sun in our Hearts."

(termed an **oligarchy**). Most premodern states were autocracies or oligarchies, and several survive today. **Totalitarianism** is one type of autocracy that has been associated with ideologies of fascism, communism, and religious fundamentalism.

Clearly, in a totalitarian society, the state serves the structures in power. The state represents a particular party, no opposition to that party is allowed, and no popular dissent is permitted to challenge the government or its laws. Ironically, many modern totalitarian states attempt to create a patina of democracy by establishing institutions—parliaments, elections, a judiciary, and sometimes even a constitution—that mimic those found in democratic states. The difference is that these institutions are toothless. Elections support the ruler or the ruling party with 99% of the vote.

The difference between a totalitarian and an authoritarian type of government is sometimes murky but often has to do with the degree of control vested in the government and the conformity demanded of the people. A totalitarian government is generally directed from a single political party and an official ideology. It requires total adherence to this ideology and enforces it through state control of education, businesses, and institutions such as secret police. The justification for this, as with all types of autocratic rule, is that there is a correct ideology, which supersedes the opinion of the people (who may be swayed by a false consciousness). In any event, it is clear that all autocratic states give their people little say in governance.

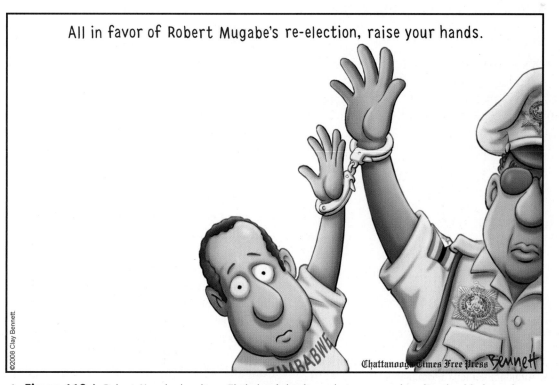

All in favor of Robert Mugabe's re-election, raise your hands.

▲ **Figure 11C.4** Robert Mugabe has been Zimbabwe's leader and strongman since it gained independence in 1980. While elections have been held, there have been consistent reports of voter intimidation, which have made it all but impossible for voters to exercise their rights.

▲ **Figure 11D.1** In Israel, all Jews—at least those with Jewish mothers—are granted automatic citizenship in Israel based on the Law of Return of 1950. This is a potent example of jus sanguinis, where instant citizenship is offered on the basis of ethnic descent. This photograph shows Jewish immigrants from France arriving at the Ben Gurion International Airport in July 2007.

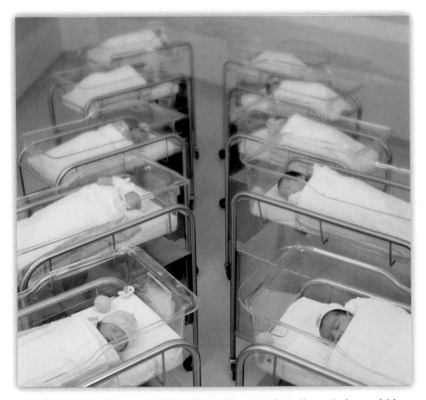

▲ **Figure 11D.2** The principle of jus soli means that all people born within a country's territory are automatically granted citizenship. This also applies to the children of people who enter illegally.

11D Citizenship

In many types of monarchical, feudal, or imperial settings, the residents of a state were considered to be merely **subjects**. They were given few rights, despite their many obligations for military service, labor, and taxation. By contrast, the notion of **citizenship** embodies the responsibilities and rights that (some) residents of a state possess. *Citizenship* is an old term, rooted in ancient Greece and Rome, and it came into widespread use in a number of European trading cities during the Middle Ages. But it is only with the growth of the modern state that citizenship has become universal, at least as an ideal. Citizens are able to decide who should be in the government through voting (political rights). And they are entitled to a certain level of justice, free speech, and association (civil rights). In some societies, they are also accorded some social and economic guarantees, such as the right to health care, education, or a pension (economic and social rights).

In ancient and medieval societies, most residents were not citizens: Women, slaves, foreigners, and the poor did not count. Even in modern countries, many residents may not be citizens. They may be immigrants who have yet to or may be unable to become citizens. Or they may be members of a particular class or ethnicity denied citizenship altogether. It is important to remember that just because people are said to be citizens does not necessarily mean that they enjoy full participation in the political process. African Americans in the South before 1960 were formally citizens but had few political or civil rights.

The manner in which citizenship is determined varies by state, but there are two main systems. **Jus sanguinis** (Latin for "right of blood") applies when your citizenship is based on that of your parents. In Germany, for instance, a person gains citizenship by virtue of her parents' citizenship. She can be born in Russia, but parental status applies. Variations of this exist in other countries. At the same time, jus sanguinis discriminates against children of foreign immigrants. A child born in Germany of Turkish parentage does not automatically gain citizenship. This system can result in generations of people residing in a country but not allowed to be citizens.

Jus soli ("right of the soil") applies whenever citizenship is acquired through birth within a state's territory. In the United States, children of immigrants, even illegal immigrants, are granted automatic citizenship rights by virtue of birth on US soil. This

Table 11D.1	Countries Providing External Voting
Here is a list of the several countries that allow emigrants and other conationals to participate in their electoral process.	
Region	**Country**
Africa (28)	Algeria, Angola, Benin, Botswana, Cape Verde, Central African Republic, Chad, Côte d'Ivoire, Djibouti, Equatorial Guinea, Gabon, Ghana, Guinea, Guinea-Bissau, Lesotho, Mali, Mauritius, Mozambique, Namibia, Niger, Rwanda, São Tomé and Príncipe, Senegal, South Africa, Sudan, Togo, Tunisia, Zimbabwe
Americas (16)	Argentina, Bolivia, Brazil, Canada, Colombia, Dominican Republic, Ecuador, Falkland Islands, Guyana, Honduras, Mexico, Nicaragua, Panama, Peru, United States, Venezuela
Asia (20)	Afghanistan, Bangladesh, India, Indonesia, Iran, Iraq, Israel, Japan, Kazakhstan, Kyrgyzstan, Laos, Malaysia, Oman, Philippines, Singapore, Syria, Tajikistan, Thailand, Uzbekistan, Yemen
Western, Central and Eastern Europe (41)	Austria, Azerbaijan, Belarus, Belgium, Bosnia and Herzegovina, Bulgaria, Croatia, Czech Republic, Denmark, Estonia, Finland, France, Georgia, Germany, Gibraltar, Greece, Guernsey, Hungary, Iceland, Ireland, Isle of Man, Italy, Jersey, Latvia, Liechtenstein, Lithuania, Luxembourg, Moldova, Netherlands, Norway, Poland, Portugal, Romania, Russia, Slovenia, Spain, Sweden, Switzerland, Turkey, Ukraine, United Kingdom
Pacific (10)	Australia, Cook Islands, Federated States of Micronesia, Fiji, Marshall Islands, Nauru, New Zealand, Palau, Pitcairn Islands, Vanuatu
Total 115	

Source: Data from The Electoral Knowledge Network http://aceproject.org/ace-en/topics/va/comparative-review/onePage.

aspect of the law has become quite controversial. Jus soli also applies to those born within American diplomatic and military facilities abroad.

Citizenship is not necessarily exclusive to a single state. In many countries, multiple or **dual citizenship** is allowed. In this case, a person can be a citizen of two countries. This often occurs because of the different ways in which citizenship is acquired, so it is possible for somebody to be a citizen of both the United States and Germany.

▲ **Figure 11D.3** Valdas Adamkus, president of Lithuania from 1998 to 2003 and from 2004 to 2009, was also a US citizen. American citizens often participate in foreign elections as citizens and have held political office in another country.

▲ **Figure 11E.1** Like all countries, the United States contains a hierarchy of subunits. First-order subunits are called states and second-order subunits are called counties, except in Alaska (where they are called districts) and in Louisiana (where they are called parishes). Below this subunit is often another order that involves some form of municipality or local government. And these local governments can be further divided—into wards, districts, and precincts—in administering their own polity. This graphic shows the subdivision from country to state to county to city to ward in Cleveland, Ohio.

11E Subdividing the State

Every state further divides its territory into political subunits. In fact, most states divide and subdivide their territory into a hierarchy of units. These political subunits are known by many different names. The first order of subdivision, for example, may be known as a state, a province, a prefecture, a district, or any number of names. The name for this subunit is actually less important than its functions, and these can vary widely. Below this first-order subunit is usually a second-order subunit that is allocated particular powers.

The development of political subunits demonstrates the use of territoriality, as described in Module 11A. They are developed in order to promote greater efficiency, flexibility, and responsiveness. Another reason is that subunits can be used to recognize the substantial diversity within a state. Subunits may develop over time, arising from historical domains and tied to existing sociocultural divisions. We can think of this as subsequent development of political subunits.

In other cases, subunits are established before there has been substantial settlement (at least of the dominant population). Over time, these political units might begin to acquire a distinctive personality and may even press for greater rights.

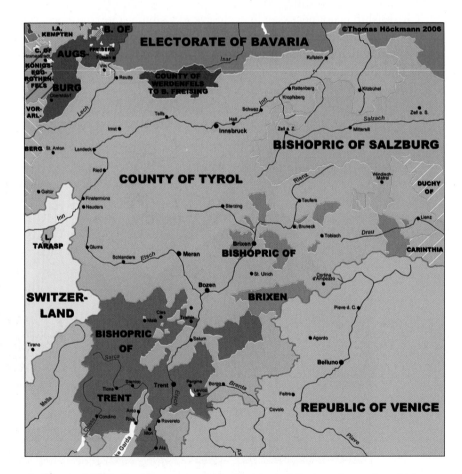

▲ **Figure 11E.2** Tyrol is a state within Austria, but it stems from a long history. The County of Tyrol was a feudal territory established in the thirteenth century. It formed a coherent identity long before the modern country of Austria. Such historical regions constitute the subdivisions of many countries in Europe and Asia. Even within newer settlements, such as the United States, political subunits were developed from existing colonies.

Two types of systems define the relationship between the central government and its first-order subunits: unitary states and federal states. It is important to remember that what these are called may be much less important than the real relationship that exists between the center and the subunits.

In **unitary states**, nearly all of the sovereignty and power reside with the central government. First-order subunits, such as states or provinces, have little independent authority of their own. In unitary states, the central government may determine how each subdivision is governed, even going so far as to appoint an administrator. District boundaries may be easily altered by the central government. Districts may not have a legislature or any other sort of independent decision-making power, and they likely have no constitutional rights. Such unitary states may be perfectly democratic; it is just that the decision-making process resides at the center. There are considerable variations to this form.

▲ **Figure 11E.3** Western Australia was settled by Europeans in 1826 and has been an Australian state since 1901. Perth is its capital city and home to nearly three-quarters of its population. Western Australia has acquired a distinct personality, fostered by its environmental conditions and its remoteness from Australia's main population centers.

▲ **Figure 11E.4** France's historic provinces were abolished after the French Revolution of 1789. New départements were established that were considered to be generally powerless or creatures of the central state. In this system, the central government appointed the prefect but allowed each département to elect its own legislature.

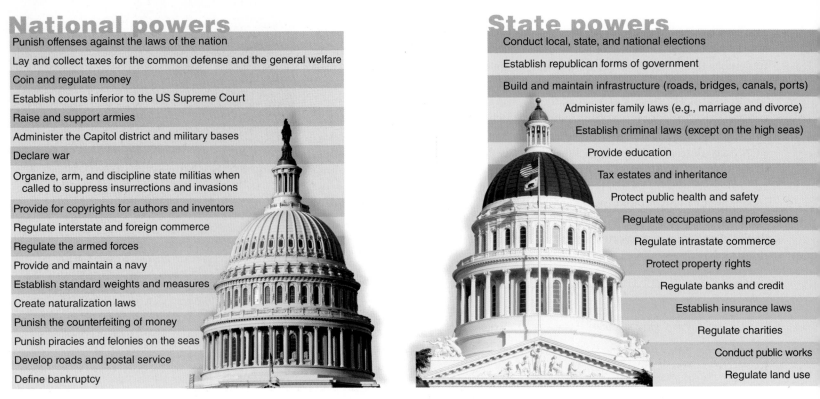

National powers

Punish offenses against the laws of the nation

Lay and collect taxes for the common defense and the general welfare

Coin and regulate money

Establish courts inferior to the US Supreme Court

Raise and support armies

Administer the Capitol district and military bases

Declare war

Organize, arm, and discipline state militias when called to suppress insurrections and invasions

Provide for copyrights for authors and inventors

Regulate interstate and foreign commerce

Regulate the armed forces

Provide and maintain a navy

Establish standard weights and measures

Create naturalization laws

Punish the counterfeiting of money

Punish piracies and felonies on the seas

Develop roads and postal service

Define bankruptcy

State powers

Conduct local, state, and national elections

Establish republican forms of government

Build and maintain infrastructure (roads, bridges, canals, ports)

Administer family laws (e.g., marriage and divorce)

Establish criminal laws (except on the high seas)

Provide education

Tax estates and inheritance

Protect public health and safety

Regulate occupations and professions

Regulate intrastate commerce

Protect property rights

Regulate banks and credit

Establish insurance laws

Regulate charities

Conduct public works

Regulate land use

▲ **Figure 11E.5** The United States was the first state to be organized as a federation. The US Constitution gives the powers that are not explicitly tied to the federal government to the states, which has given the states a great deal of sovereignty over a number of aspects of governance. This graphic outlines the traditional division of responsibilities within the US federal system. The regulation of the Interstate Commerce Clause has been one of the sticking points between those who feel the federal government should have more power and those who believe more power should be vested in the states. Source: From Brigid Callahan Harrison and Jean Wahl Harris, *American Democracy Now, Second Edition*, © 2011 by The McGraw-Hill Companies, Inc., pages 89 and 91. Used by permission.

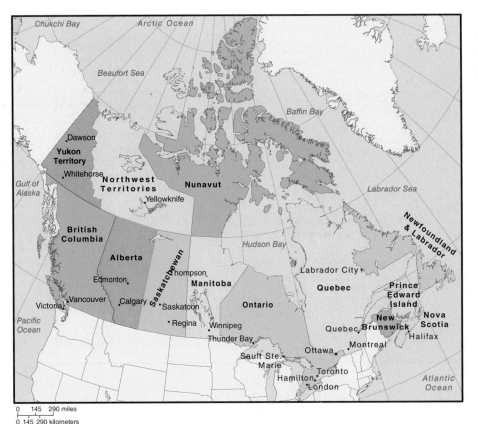

◀ **Figure 11E.6** In Canada, some of the trappings of a confederation system remain, albeit as part of a federation. The British North America Act set up two systems of sovereignty: one for the central government and one for each province. As a result, Canadian provinces were able to establish property and civil rights, labor laws, and transportation and communications systems. This gave the provinces a substantial degree of authority. What ultimately made this a federal system is that individual provinces in the Canadian system do not have any right of veto over federal rules and Canada has a proportional system of representation.

Figure 11E.7 ▶ The former Soviet Union is a good case of confederation in name only. The USSR was composed of 15 republics that were considered to have a fair degree of sovereignty. In fact, two of these republics—Ukraine and Belarus—were represented in the United Nations as member countries! According to the Soviet constitution, each republic was free to establish its own rules and even to secede if it wished. But, in fact, the Soviet system was very tightly controlled under the auspices of the Communist Party, and individual republics had very little real power.

In other cases, unitary governments provide a great deal of internal autonomy. In these cases, the central government grants powers to the lower administrative units through a process of **devolution**.

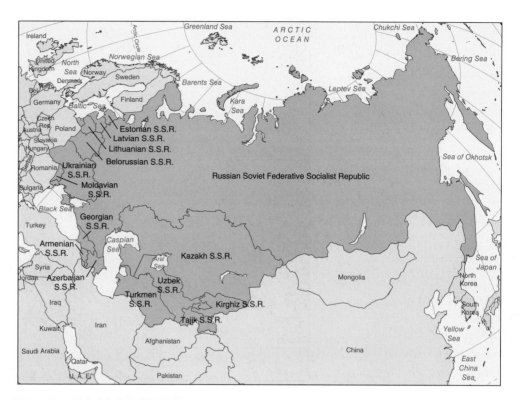

◀ **Figure 11E.8** In the United Kingdom, the situation is complicated by the presence of two ancient kingdoms that have successively demanded greater autonomy, each with a vigorous national party. Finally in 1997, both Scotland and Wales were empowered to determine much of their own internal affairs. Northern Ireland also has a special arrangement, although conflict there has prevented greater autonomy. So while the United Kingdom is ostensibly a unitary state, in fact, several components within it have a degree of autonomy far surpassing that of many federal states. However, these rights are not constitutionally enshrined and can be taken back by the central government at any time.

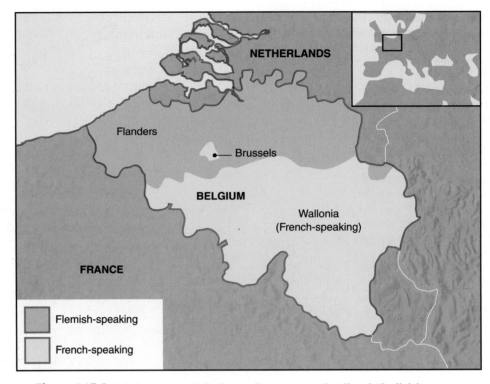

▲ **Figure 11E.9** Belgium was technically a unitary system. But linguistic divisions between its French-speaking Wallonia and its Flemish (Dutch) speaking Flanders provoked the creation of a tripartite regional federal system in 1994. Wallonia and Flanders operate as autonomous districts, which have obtained more authority over their internal affairs and conduct official business in French and Flemish, respectively. Each district includes separate political parties. The capital region of Brussels represents the third region. While mostly French-speaking, it is contained within Flanders and considered to be a more bilingual zone.

In **federal states**, each of the subunits is granted an independent constitutional authority, which defines its level of power. The central state is still considered to have greater sovereignty and is expected to conduct foreign affairs, but the subunits are allowed a great deal of latitude in passing and enforcing laws and regulations. Federal states always have their own independent governments and legislatures, as well as the ability to make their own laws, which may be quite different from those of other subunits in the country.

In these cases, as in the former Soviet Union (and in its successor state of Russia), federalism is a method of ensuring that each of the different national groups within these multinational states are given possession of some sort of territory. In this way, federalism attempts to fashion stability between rival ethnic and national groups. Federalism is also a good way to manage large countries. Seven of the eight largest countries by land area—Argentina, Australia, Brazil, Canada, India, Russia, and the United States—are organized as federal states. Only China continues as a unitary state.

In **confederations**, sovereign states agree to abridge some of their independent powers in order to work together as a group, but each state retains a great deal of sovereignty. The United States began as a confederation, but it grew to be unworkable because there was no overarching central authority. Switzerland and Canada also were confederations, but both have adopted a more federal system. More recent confederations that were attempted include the United Arab Republic (a union between Egypt and Syria), which eventually dissolved; the United Arab Emirates, which has become more centralized since the 1970s; and Serbia-Montenegro, which ended with Montenegro's secession in 2006.

Just how meaningful is the formal relationship established between the central state and its subdivisions? The formal relationship may be in name only and obscure the true power dynamics.

Many countries grapple with the relationship between their central government and its political subunits. The United States has witnessed the development of political parties based upon a greater level of power for individual states, it has undergone a civil war based on the desire of a group of states to secede from the federal government, and it continues to try to determine exactly what the appropriate relationships should be.

Other countries are in similar straits. The territorial relationship between the central state and each of its subunits speaks to the way that regional interests can be accommodated. Multinational countries that include a number of ethnoregional groups, for instance, may seek to grant some of these regions more autonomy in the hopes of staving off secessionist movements. Conversely, some countries may seek to tighten up the relationship between the central state and its subunits. The development of the modern state involved the subordination of regions to a central authority. Contemporary states may find that the proliferation of many different legal systems, linguistic regimes, or even customs becomes increasingly inefficient in a modern political economy. Governments may feel that this sort of diversity represents a threat to national integration.

▲ **Figure 11E.10** In the Canadian system, some have spoken of an **asymmetrical federalism.** One province, French-speaking Québec, has obtained even more powers than other provinces with the establishment of a French-only language law, control over immigration, its own pension system, and the establishment of an independent foreign presence. In this photo, a marcher raises a sign in support of Québec's language law.

▲ **Figure 11E.11** Louisiana has a different set of traditions than other US states. It has parishes instead of counties, a different electoral system, and some major differences in the legal system, which is influenced by the Napoleonic Code and follows civil law as opposed to the English common law used in other states. This is a photograph of a Louisiana courthouse in Abbeville, Louisiana.

11F   Cores and Capitals

Many states include a clearly defined **core region**. This core region can represent the place where the state and the dominant nationality emerged. From this core, the state expanded through a process of accretion, leading eventually to a larger and larger territory. This is not true of all states. Some states emerged from multiple cores that at some point merged together either voluntarily or through conquest. Often, the population, economic, and cultural focus of the country is still found in the core.

In the developing world, many states that emerged from colonialism may be hard put to define a core area apart from that imposed from abroad.

The state contains a **capital city** as well as a **capital region**. The capital of the country—as the political center—may or may not be in the core, depending on the logic of capital location. Some states contain more than one capital, each having separate political functions, such as legislative, executive, or judicial.

Because of its important nature as the headquarters for government and a symbol of the state's power, the capital region is accorded a special status. In many cases, such as in the United States and Australia, the capital is located in a territory completely independent of any other subunit.

In approximately half of all countries, the capital is the largest, most important city. In Mexico, for example, Mexico City serves as both the capital of the country and the clear center of the country's economic and cultural life.

The location of the capital can be powerfully symbolic. And it can be quite controversial.

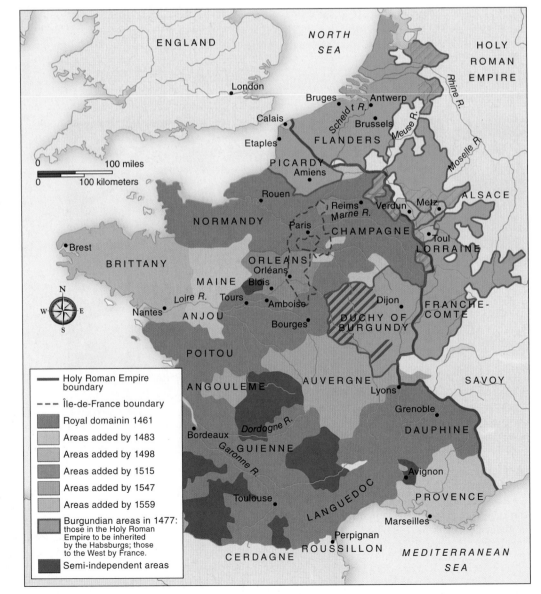

Figure 11F.1 ▶ The Île-de-France is the undisputed core region of France. It includes the capital, Paris, but also is the origin of the French state. This map shows how the French state grew over several decades. This is distinct from the growth of French culture or language, but the rise of a powerful state was vital in the diffusion of French to places that were not yet French-speaking. Source: From Dennis Sherman and Joyce Salisbury, *The West in the World, Third Edition*, © 2008 by The McGraw-Hill Companies, Inc., page 330. Used by permission.

Map legend:

★ Battle Site
☐ Fortress
▪▪▪ German Confederation Boundary in 1815
Prussia in 1815
Annexed by Prussia by 1866
Joined with Prussia in North German Confederation in 1867
━━ North German Confederation Boundary in 1867
States Added to Form German Empire in 1871

(a)

(b)

◄ **Figure 11F.3**
Like some other countries, Bolivia contains two capitals. (a) La Paz is the administrative and legislative capital. (b) Sucre is the constitutional capital and seat of the Supreme Court.

▲ **Figure 11F.4** Some residents of the capital region may not even enjoy the same privileges as the residents of other districts. In the District of Columbia, for example, residents do not have representation. DC residents were granted the right to vote for president only in 1961, by virtue of the Twenty-third Amendment to the US Constitution.

◄ Figure 11F.5 Capitals may be chosen from the historic center of the country. The city may not have always been the capital city, but it represents a core area from where the state and nation evolved. Many European capitals fit into this category. However, even in these cases, there have been shifts in the location of capitals. While Rome has long held a central place as capital of the Roman Empire and then the headquarters for the Catholic Church, it became a modern capital only in 1867 with the unification of Italy.

Figure 11F.6 ► In former colonies, many existing capitals emerged from the former colonial capitals. While they may not have been important settlements before European conquest, these cities served as the center of the colony and after independence became the center for the new country. Jakarta, Indonesia, developed from the colonial capital of Batavia.

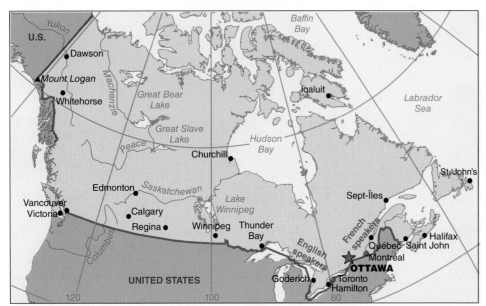

◄ Figure 11F.7 Rather than use existing cities to form a capital region, several countries have attempted either to introduce a new city that can serve as a capital or to designate an existing smaller city as the new capital city. The reasons behind the selection of **introduced capitals** differ but often reflect a break from regional interests and an orientation toward the future instead of the past. Both Ottawa, Canada, and Washington, DC, were cases of a **compromise capital** between different sectional interests within the country. Ottawa was introduced as a capital in order to serve at the boundary between French-speaking Lower Canada (Québec) and English-speaking Upper Canada (Ontario).

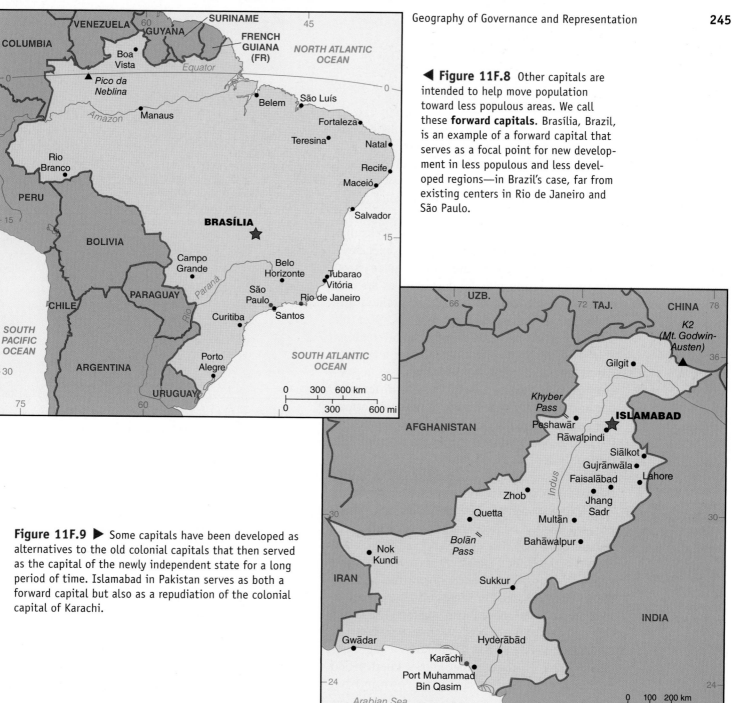

◀ **Figure 11F.8** Other capitals are intended to help move population toward less populous areas. We call these **forward capitals**. Brasília, Brazil, is an example of a forward capital that serves as a focal point for new development in less populous and less developed regions—in Brazil's case, far from existing centers in Rio de Janeiro and São Paulo.

Figure 11F.9 ▶ Some capitals have been developed as alternatives to the old colonial capitals that then served as the capital of the newly independent state for a long period of time. Islamabad in Pakistan serves as both a forward capital but also as a repudiation of the colonial capital of Karachi.

◀ **Figure 11F.10** Capitals may be established in the most central area of the country. Such is the case when Turkey chose its capital of Ankara, which is in the center of the Anatolian peninsula, instead of the more important and populous city of Istanbul.

11G Peripheral and Special Regions

In contrast to core areas, states also include areas that are **peripheral** in some respect. (This is a little different than the discussion of core and periphery found in Module 18C.) They may be peripheral because they are at the edge of effective political control. They may be areas recently integrated into the state. They may be areas that are culturally distinct. Or they may be exclaves.

Peripheral regions are often given special treatment and may be described as **special regions**, political subunits that are granted different powers than regular subunits. Not all special regions are peripheral; capital regions discussed in the previous module are a type of special region as well. But in many cases, a government will treat peripheral regions differently because it has to work harder to maintain effective control, as in the case of a frontier region. Or it has to accommodate a region that is culturally distinct in some way.

Special regions are given a status that marks them as distinct from other units within the state. The United States has several such units, which are accorded a variety of powers, while still remaining under the sovereignty of the United States. In the United States, the term *territory* has defined a transitional zone prior to the achievement of a full-fledged substate unit status, or it can indicate a special subordinate or alternative status that will persist for quite some time. Another special region is Puerto Rico, defined as a commonwealth. This is a status that allows Puerto Rico to have a great deal of say over its own internal

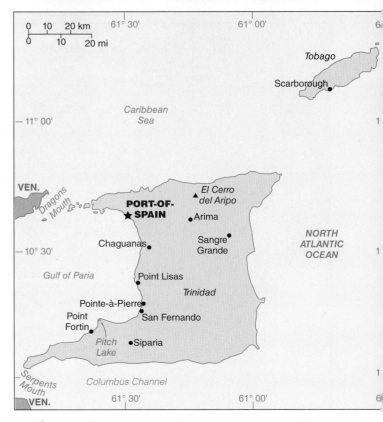

▲ **Figure 11G.1** Peripheral territories may be geographically removed, perhaps separated by another country or an ocean. The island of Tobago is separated from the main island of Trinidad, which includes the bulk of the country's population, as well as its capital.

▲ **Figure 11G.2** When a part of a state's territory is geographically separated by another country, it creates an **exclave**. There are many full or partial exclaves in the world. The breakup of the Soviet Union left the Russian area of Kalingrad as an exclave surrounded by Lithuania, Poland, and the Baltic Sea.

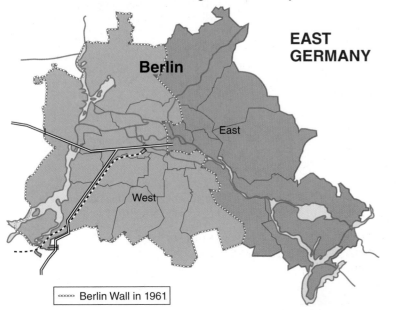

◀ **Figure 11G.3** An **enclave** is a part of or an entire country surrounded by another country. During the Cold War and the division of Germany, Berlin was a very well-known West German enclave bounded completely by East Germany. In the late 1940s, the Soviet Union blocked access to this Western-held area, prompting a series of airlifts.

◀ **Figure 11G.4**
Sometimes a country will make a distinction between a regular substate unit and other units with different authorizations. For example, Canada distinguishes between a province and a territory. While provinces are vested with a host of constitutional prerogatives, territories in Canada—Yukon, Northwest Territories, and Nunavut—lack any inherent jurisdiction and are essentially wards of the central government.

◀ **Figure 11G.5**
The Aland Islands, located between Sweden and Finland, is another type of special region. While a part of Finland, the islands joined the European Union as a separate entity and do not need to participate in the EU tax system.

◀ **Figure 11G.6** Italy's five **autonomous regions** are meant to account for cultural distinctiveness or certain special circumstances. In the north, three border regions—Trentino Alto-Adige, Friuli-Venezia Giulia, and Val d'Aosta—contain culturally distinct populations. The islands of Sicily and Sardinia share differing historical circumstances.

Figure 11G.7 ▶
The Sami people, sometimes called Laplanders, occupy the far northern reaches of Scandinavia. While considered a single ethnicity, like the American Indian, the Sami have very distinct cultures and language groups. In northern Finland, they have been granted domicile areas that are now home to about half of all Finnish Samis.

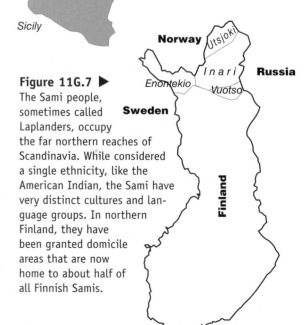

affairs. Puerto Rico is not subject to federal taxation, but it also does not enjoy any formal representation in the US Congress. The United Kingdom similarly has a number of territories or regions that are distinct from its formal subdivisions. The Isle of Man and the Channel Islands are examples.

Interestingly enough, some special regions clearly belong under the sovereign umbrella of a country and yet are outside the organizations to which that country belongs. Greenland, for example, is a self-governing region of Denmark. Yet while Denmark is a part of the European Union, Greenland is not. The same is true of the Danish Faeroe Islands.

The examples given come from outside the land boundaries of a particular country. However, many countries include regions that they feel ought to have a special status partly because of their cultural distinctiveness. Québec, Canada, discussed earlier, enjoys special powers, although nothing in the Canadian constitution mandates this. In some countries, the constitutions do designate that certain regions have significantly more autonomy. Spain designates the Basque region and Catalonia for special levels of sovereignty. Both of these regions have vigorous secession movements, and the idea is that greater regional autonomy will help quell these movements.

One special region common in the Americas but found throughout the world is the **reservation**. These are established as a territory for indigenous peoples. They usually represent just a fraction of the land that these peoples had previously occupied and, in many cases, was land that the arriving European settlers did not want. The levels of autonomy and self-rule vary, depending on the country. The relationship between American Indian reservations and the US federal government is somewhat complex. These regions are considered to be separate legal entities and are allowed a measure of self-rule. Many have created their own constitutions and can make laws distinct from those outside reservations. At the same time, residents of reservations are also citizens of the United States, and must abide by federal laws as well. Most recently, several Indian reservations have established gambling casinos, exploiting their ability to make separate laws.

11H Electoral Geography

In all democratic societies, and even in several that are not really democratic, there is a system in place whereby citizens of a country are able to translate their political preferences into electoral action. The notion of a **pure democracy**, in which all citizens have a say in all the issues pertaining to their community, has given way to a **representative democracy**, a more complicated structure in which people elect representatives who are supposed to take the time to understand the issues and to represent their interests. The citizenry's main responsibility, then, is to vote for these representatives during scheduled elections.

Figure 11H.1 ▶ The US presidential election of 1948, known best for the surprise victory of President Harry Truman, was also a pivotal election for both major parties. On one hand, Republican Thomas Dewey continued to hold many of the well-developed and economically integrated states in the Northeast that had long voted for Republican candidates. Truman held many of the Democratic Party bulwarks of states in the South and West. But the changes that are so familiar today began to appear at this time. Dewey captured four of the states in the Great Plains, and Truman made inroads in some eastern and Industrial Belt states. What's more, the candidacy of Dixiecrat Strom Thurmond, waged as a protest against the civil rights tendencies of some Democrats, showed the beginnings of the South's political movement away from the Democratic Party.

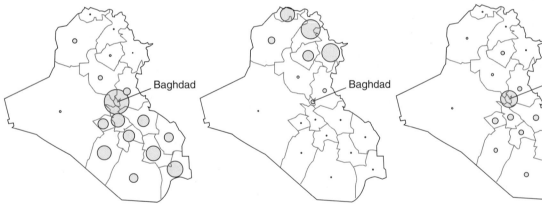

United Iraqi Alliance   Kurdistan Alliance   Iraqi List

◀ **Figure 11H.2** This map, reflecting Iraq's first free election, shows the sectionalism based on national group. The United Iraqi Alliance, dominated by Shi'ites, is focused in the south of the country. The Kurdistan Alliance is concentrated in the north. The more secular Iraqi List was based around Baghdad. From all accounts, Sunni Arabs did not participate as much in this election. But the election shows a strong degree of religious sectionalism.

Figure 11H.3 ▶ Some elections are so significant that they create a whole political vernacular. After the election of 2000 in the United States, the division of the country into "red" states, which went to the Republican candidate, George Bush, and "blue" states, which went to the Democratic candidate, Al Gore, became a metaphor for culture, politics, and the wider societal divide between regions. Our political vocabulary has been shaped by these mapped phenomena, and we understand terms such as the *solid South* or *bellwether state* and now *red states* and *blue states* or the phrase that a state is becoming *increasingly purple*.

◀ **Figure 11H.4** The use of *red* and *blue states* can be very misleading. Plenty of conservatives live within so-called blue states, and red states usually contain a number of liberal enclaves. Texas has consistently voted for the Republican nominee for president since 1980 and is clearly marked as a red state. But Texas also contains several areas that tend to be more liberal. Austin is one such area. Counties along the Mexican border are among the most Democratic in the country.

Electoral geography examines how people's political preferences are manifested in representation. Along with weather maps, electoral maps are probably the closest most people come to observing geographic patterns. After the polls close, maps are displayed, showing the winners in each of the designated districts, and pundits offer their opinions on what produced these patterns and how the outcomes are going to reshape the politics of the country. Electoral geographers do engage in that type of analysis, generally at a deeper level, but they are also interested in how geography affects electoral outcomes, why context is important, and how manipulating electoral districts can benefit one political interest over another.

One aspect of electoral geography lies in the *interpretation of election outcomes*. Where is party support strongest and where is it weakest? Which district shows the greatest degree of change from one election to the next? Which districts best reflect the preferences of the country as a whole? Political geographers may look at these spatial variations and examine how they line up with other indicators: religion, economics, language, ethnicity, or particularly important local events. More comprehensive explanations can tie long-standing electoral patterns to major regional differences or to difference in the levels of development

This sort of exercise can be done at a wide variety of scales, from the country down to the locality. And while the factors at play may vary a bit, the exercise remains the same. An additional twist is to examine elections over time. These may suggest sectional splits between regions, as well as how these different sections have stabilized or changed.

Geographers have long wondered whether people's electoral behavior is shaped by the others in their community. In other words, is there an independent **neighborhood effect**, or **contextual effect**, in which the characteristics of people in a local area help determine their political preferences? This ties into a major geographic question about the overall importance of place in shaping people's attitudes and behaviors. There has been some support for this neighborhood effect, and some studies indicate that where people live can be as important as who they are and where their other interests lie. Much of this has to do with the importance of the local community as a place of interaction, affiliation, and particularity. People are influenced by whom they know and by the local political culture.

Figure 11H.5 ▶ In some countries, the examination of elections may also be helpful in gauging support for strong regional movements. In Italy, the Lega Nord has been very successful in capturing political support in certain parts of Lombardy and Veneto; less so in other northern provinces. Interestingly, in the province of the Alto Adige, the Lega Nord loses much of its support to the German-language SVP party, which is supported primarily by the German-speaking South Tyrolean population. There are also variations in support depending on the distinction among small towns, rural areas, and bigger cities. The Lega Nord has found its greatest strength in a string of densely industrialized regions made up primarily of small towns with both low unemployment and low urbanization. Support is lower within the biggest cities of the region, such as Milan and Turin.

30+%
25 to 29.9%
20 to 24.9%
15 to 19.9%
10 to 14.9%
5 to 9.9%
1 to 4.9%
0 to 0.9%

11I   Electoral Systems and Manipulation

Geographers are interested in the nature of different electoral systems—specifically, the geographic relationship between constituents and their representatives.

Both the single member and majoritarian systems generally lead to the predominance of strong major parties and the marginalization of minor parties. They produce disproportional results, allowing the winning party to gain far more seats than the percentage of its overall vote would suggest. Unless they have some regional support, small parties have a hard time gaining any representation at all. The value of these systems, however, is that they create a strong correspondence between a representative and her district and ensure that all parts of the country are represented.

The value of the list system is that it allows many smaller parties to have some representation, even if they are not regionally based. Often, the percentage of the vote a party receives translates more readily into the number of representatives it elects. So a party that receives 30 of the overall vote gets 30% of the seats. Small parties, such as the environmentalist Green Party, which is popular in Europe, can thrive under this system. But there are two problems with this system. First, because there are so many parties, it is very difficult for any single party to command an outright majority of the seats in the national legislature and, so, must forge coalitions between themselves and a number of minor parties. These coalitions can and do come apart between scheduled elections. The second problem is that there is much less affinity between a legislator and the constituents—the politician is more connected to the party than the district. Some regions may be underrepresented or even unrepresented.

Electoral districts can be manipulated to produce results that favor one political party or political interest over another. One form of manipulation is through **malapportionment**, in which some electoral districts vary in size although they are equal in representation. The 100,000 people in one district essentially have the same degree of representation as 30,000 people in another district. This used to be a fairly common occurrence around the world because electoral districts were initially based not on population but on historic tradition. In the past, US electoral districts varied substantially by population. The movement from rural to urban areas without any change in the size or shape of districts meant that urban areas had fewer representatives than their population warranted. Rural areas were reluctant

Single member plurality system
or "first past the post" system.
The entire country is divided into electoral districts, which elect only one representative. That person is elected because he or she gained the most votes, even if not a majority.

Electoral district 1 of 100

Candidate A	40%
Candidate B	35%
Candidate C	25%

United States
Canada
United Kingdom
India

Majoritarian system.
In this system, the winner must have a majority of the overall votes. One way to achieve this is to have consecutive elections where the first stage weeds out all but the top two vote-getters and the second stage permits only those two on the ballot. A second method is to allow people to designate their second choice, so that these votes can be allocated later.

Electoral district 1 of 100

Candidate A	40%
Candidate B	35%
Candidate C	25%

↓

Candidate A	45%
Candidate B	55%

France
Australia

List system of proportional representation.
Electoral districts are marked off but may have any number of representatives. In Israel and the Netherlands, the entire country constitutes an electoral district. Each party draws up a list of candidates in each electoral district, and people tend to vote for the parties rather than the candidates themselves. There is often a minimum threshold, so the smallest parties do not get in.

Percentage in entire country or in large district

Party	Percent	Seats
A	40	50
B	20	25
C	20	25
D	9	none
E	6	none
F	5	none

Israel
Netherlands
Italy

Mixed system
includes both proportional voting and a plurality system. This allows stability but also allows for representation by some smaller parties. The system has worked well in Germany and has given it more stability than a number of countries that rely on proportional systems alone.

For 40 districts

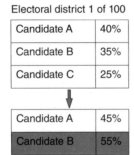

Candidate A	40%
Candidate B	35%
Candidate C	25%

+

Remaining 60 districts

Party	Percent	Seats
A	40	30
B	20	15
C	20	15
D	9	none
E	6	none
F	5	none

▲ **Figure 11I.1** While there are many variations, most electoral systems can be categorized into four basic types.

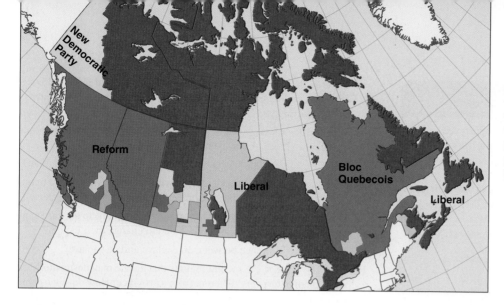

◀ **Figure 11I.2** Regional parties can do quite well in the single member plurality system. In Canada, the Bloc Québécois has turned its strength in Québec into a powerful presence in the Canadian parliament. The Conservative Party of Canada has become a national party. But it began as the Reform Party, based primarily in the Western Provinces.

to give up their power, and party identifications made it difficult to change until the Supreme Court ruled in 1962 (*Baker vs. Carr*) that "the one person, one vote" principle made these forms of malapportionment illegal. Constitutional malapportionment still exists, however—the US Senate is based on small states having the same representation as large states—and some forms are unavoidable, since congressional districts cannot straddle state lines, but malapportionment has been considerably minimized.

Another tactic is to concentrate the support of one party or one group of people in one district and dilute their support throughout a number of other districts. This type of manipulation, known as **gerrymandering**, is possible only in a plurality or majority system, since proportional systems would not shut out a second or third party with support in a district.

Gerrymandering has been a very popular strategy for whichever party is in power. Gerrymandering has been used to serve the purposes of political parties who decide exactly how districts are drawn. It has also been used to enhance the electoral prospects of particular ethnic and racial groups. Geographic information software, with access to electoral databases and party registration information, can be especially useful in drawing precise boundaries. It used to be that electoral districts were drawn only once every 10 years after the census results, but recently some politicians have decided that nothing stops them from redrawing electoral boundaries whenever the time seems right.

While there have been accusations of gerrymandering in other countries, it does not seem to be nearly as common as in the United States, in many cases because of a proportional system and in other cases because districts are drawn by independent commissions.

▲ **Figure 11I.3** Some fairly extreme smaller parties can have a strong influence under a list system of representation. Israeli politics has had to accommodate the concerns of highly religious parties that have prevented a relaxation in rules regarding when stores and businesses can be open. Rabbi Ovadia Yosef is the spiritual leader of Israel's ultra-Orthodox Shas party, which draws a great deal of support from Israel's Sephardic community (Jews that originate from the Middle East and North Africa).

Figure 11I.4 ▶ In the United States, the Voting Rights Act was intended to ensure that minority groups also got adequate representation. This has been used as a way to try to concentrate minority representation in just a few districts. For this reason, many conservative politicians have been enthusiastic about using this as a tool to maximize liberal-leaning minority voters in one place while minimizing the influence of such voters in many other districts. These oddly shaped districts represent such attempts over the last twenty years.

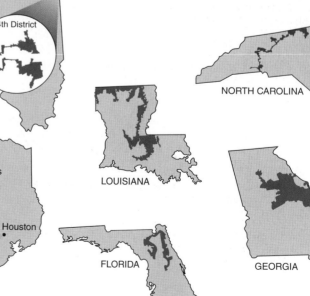

Key Terms

asymmetrical federalism (11E)
authoritarian states (11C)
autocratic states (11C)
autonomous regions (11G)
capital city (11F)
capital region (11F)
capitalist economy (11B)
citizenship (11D)
communist economy (11B)
compromise capital (11F)
confederations (11E)
contextual effect (11H)
core region (11F)
devolution (11E)
dual citizenship (11D)
electoral geography (11H)
elite theories of the state (11C)
enclave (11G)
exclave (11G)
extraction economy (11B)
federal states (11E)
forward capitals (11F)
gerrymandering (11I)
introduced capitals (11F)
jus sanguinis (11D)
jus soli (11D)

list system of proportional
   representation (11I)
majoritarian system (11I)
malapportionment (11I)
Marxist theories of the state (11C)
mixed economies (11B)
mixed system (11I)
neighborhood effect (11H)
neoliberalism (11C)
oligarchy (11C)
peripheral (11G)
pluralist theory of the state (11C)
political economy (11B)
political subunits (11A)
private sector (11B)
public sector (11B)
pure democracy (11H)
representative democracy (11H)
reservation (11G)
single member plurality
   system (11I)
special regions (11G)
subjects (11D)
theories of the state (11C)
totalitarianism (11C)
unitary states (11E)

Basic Review Questions

1. What is a political subunit? What is the relationship between subunits in the state?

2. What are the advantages of utilizing territory to administer a state? What are the disadvantages?

3. Beyond the state, how do other institutions utilize territory to achieve their aims?

4. What is the political economy of a traditional kingdom? What is the political economy found within a capitalist economy? What is the political economy of communism?

5. What makes a mixed economy a balance between private and public sector activities?

6. What are some of the functions of the modern state?

7. How does a pluralist theory of the state view government? How does the elite theory of the state see the government? What is the role of the government in the Marxist theory of the state?

8. What is the role of the state in an authoritarian or a totalitarian regime? What is the difference between totalitarianism and authoritarianism?

9. What is the difference between a subject and a citizen? How does citizenship relate to political rights?

10. Describe the difference between the systems of jus sanguinis and jus soli.

11. How does dual citizenship work?

12. How can political subunits be used to acknowledge cultural diversity within a state?

13. What is the difference between a unitary state and a federal state? How do confederations work? How does sovereignty work in each of these systems?

14. What is the process by which a state can grant powers to lower political subunits?

15. What are some of the problems involved in a system of federalism?

16. Give some examples of core regions within a state. Must a core region contain the capital? What are some of the ways a capital is selected?

17. Compare introduced capitals to compromise capitals to forward capitals. Why have some countries decided to change their capital?

18. What is the difference between an enclave and an exclave?

19. Describe some of the special regions that a state may designate. How is a Canadian territory different from a province? How do some countries use reservations to provide territory for indigenous peoples?

20. What is the difference between a representative democracy and a pure democracy? How is a representative democracy depicted geographically?

21. How can electoral geography help show spatial patterns of representation?

22. How did the terms *blue states* and *red states* reflect a specific electoral geography? Why are the terms *blue states* and *red states* misleading, especially when scale is considered?

23. How does the neighborhood effect shape people's political preferences?

24. Describe a basic system of representation. What are some of the differences among these systems? What system is found in the United States?

25. How can electoral districts be manipulated to benefit one political party? Describe the difference between malapportionment and gerrymandering.

Advanced Review Questions (Essay Questions)

1. Describe the strategies that institutions can use to manipulate space through territoriality. What are some of the positive aspects of the strategies in encouraging greater efficiency, flexibility, and responsiveness? What are some of the negative aspects in terms of restricting access and creating a problem of spatial mismatch? How have international corporations and the Catholic Church used territoriality in this manner?

2. Describe how political economy can regulate economic activities within a state. How is a capitalist economy different from a communist economy in regard to their views of private sector and public sector activities? What is the role of the mixed economy in balancing these different types of activities?

3. How might a pluralist theory of the state create a number of different outcomes, depending on the elections? How does this differ from an elite theory of the state in regard to the level of power exercised by the people? How would a neoliberal regime fit within these two theories?

4. What is the value of citizenship? Compare the two main ways in which citizenship is determined, and provide examples from existing countries. How would these different forms of determination affect the status of immigrants to a country?

5. Compare the unitary state system with a federal state system in regard to how central governments treat their political subunits. What would some of the advantages of federalism be in dealing with cultural diversity? How might federalism also create some problems related to asymmetrical federalism? How meaningful would be the formal relationship established between the central state and subdivisions?

6. Describe those cases where the selection of the capital may be used to mediate between two distinct regions. How might former colonies use the selection of the capital to show their independence from the mother country? What is the relationship between capitals and a country's core region?

7. Many states use special regions as a way to acknowledge cultural diversity within the country. What are a few examples of these special regions, and what are some of the powers and rights these special regions have that are not found in other regions? In the United States, how have reservations been used in relation to the American Indian population?

8. How is electoral geography sensitive to geographic scale? How might apparent patterns in one scale obscure certain differences found at another scale? To what extent is electoral geography indicative of representative democracy? Give an example that shows how electoral geography may help shape the vernacular of different regions in the United States.

9. What are four different electoral systems, and how do they create a different balance of power between major parties and minor parties? What system is the best for a strong regional party? What system is the best for a special-interest party that is dispersed countrywide? How can geography be used to help manipulate different electoral outcomes?

Further Study Topics

• The children of undocumented immigrants born in the United States are considered to be citizens based on how the United States determines citizenship. Some legislators have suggested changing the Fourteenth Amendment to prevent this type of activity. Discuss some of the problems and some of the advantages that can be found in altering the US system of citizenship to prevent the children of undocumented immigrants from becoming citizens.

• Modern states can use territory to accomplish a number of goals, some of them negative. Think about some of the territorial strategies that have been utilized by various governments as a strategy to marginalize certain populations. How does the creation of Indian reservations in the United States deploy territorial strategies?

• Discuss the importance of the variety of capitals for various states in the world today. Consider the selection of Ottawa in Canada, Brasília in Brazil, Islamabad in Pakistan, and New Delhi in India. What were each country's goals in selecting these capitals? How were these choices successful in meeting these goals, and why?

• Gerrymandering is a very common strategy by which one political party attempts to maintain its advantage in electoral cycles. Describe a case in which gerrymandering has been used. What has been the effect of this in terms of the political process? How have governments sought to avoid some of the bias inherent in gerrymandering? How has the desire for minority representation in some cases created what are effectively gerrymandered districts?

• Multinational states have sought to use special districts as a way to assuage the demands of different national groups. Take an example of a special minority region, and describe to what extent this strategy has been effective.

Summary Activities

Assume you are the campaign manager for a national political party and need to allocate $100 million to try to win the election. Using the electoral college map, how would you try to divide the money among the 50 states in order to secure the 270 electoral votes needed to win?

Here are the following items to consider in your strategy:

• It costs $1 million per electoral vote in competitive or uphill states.
• It costs less for states that generally are with that party.
• You will need to decide where best to spend your money.

In doing this exercise, you can choose to be the campaign manager for the Democratic Party or the Republican Party. However, you might also choose to manage the campaign for a third party. This could be a Libertarian, Green, or Centrist party. In this case, your strategy might be to make the best possible showing, depending on what you consider to be your areas of strength. Please produce a map of your electoral strategy and then explain why you chose to invest money in some states and not others.

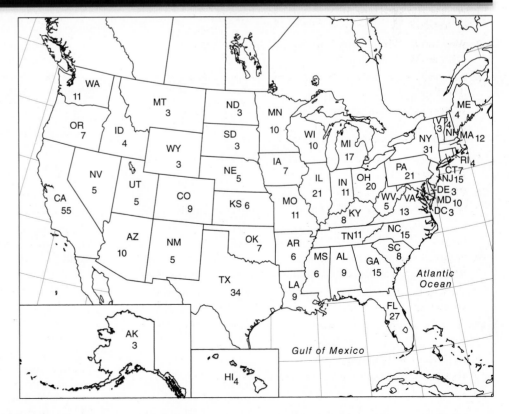

37L

Environment and Conservation

Human-environment interaction has long been a central theme of geography. *Physical geography* refers to the subdiscipline of geography that focuses on physical patterns on the earth's landscape, such as how mountains and beaches form, what happens to a landscape during glaciations, the flow of water on the landscape, vegetation patterns, and climates. But human geographers also have a stake in the environment. Nearly everything that humans do is affected by or affects the environment, and thus human geographers must have a basic understanding of environmental issues.

Think about what happens when a city grows. Yes, the population rises, but that rise means countless new buildings, roads, parking lots, and schools. Each new building or transportation link that is added to the city destroys or alters a field, a forest, or a wetland. When something as simple as a parking lot is created, for example, it can dramatically alter rainfall runoff. Instead of the water soaking into the ground, it runs off in specific directions, often causing unexpected erosion or pollution from the oil and other chemicals in the parking area. In this chapter, we explore the ways in which humans modify the natural environment, as well as ways the environment might alter human activity.

12A How Geographers See the Environment

Before we can adequately discuss the relationship between human geography and the environment, we should first look at the different ways geographers have explored the human-environment relationship.

The most common use of the word **environment** refers to the physical or natural environment—in other words, trees, wetlands, mountains, oceans, and so on. Basically, geographers use the term *physical* or *natural environment* to refer to everything that is not human-made. Much of the discussion of environment in the press focuses on human modification of the natural environment.

If you recall from Module 2D, at the beginning of the twentieth century the prevailing notion of human-environment interaction was the idea of environmental determinism. Followers of this idea believed that the physical environment controlled the culture of a society. So, for example, people from mountainous areas might be heartier and stronger than people from flat areas, according to the determinists, because their environment is "tougher." The danger of this belief was that people were stereotyped, often along racial lines. So, for example, some environmental determinists believed that all peoples of tropical areas were lazy and morally bankrupt because of the heat and humidity.

In time, environmental determinism began to be challenged by a new breed of scholars. In the 1920s, geographer Carl Sauer at the University of California, Berkeley, began to write about the cultural landscape. He disagreed with the environmental determinist position and believed that the human landscape was a result of human culture modifying the natural landscape. He wrote, "The cultural landscape is fashioned from a natural landscape by a cultural group. Culture is the agent, the natural are the medium, the cultural landscape is the result." Of course, successive generations of human impact and different cultures can create complex human landscapes. If you look at the American West, you have to understand the effects of various native cultures, as well as the Spanish and later European American impacts, in addition to recent immigration. Sauer's view of the cultural landscape is still important today among cultural geographers.

Starting in the 1940s with early work on natural hazards (see Module 12B), some geographers began focusing on the psychological aspects of the human-environment relationship. At first, research focused on

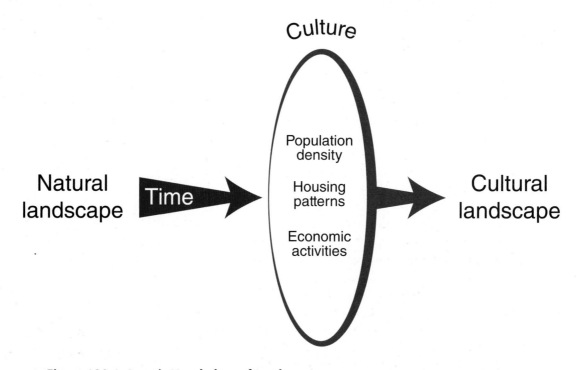

▲ **Figure 12A.1 Sauer's Morphology of Landscape** As shown in this diagram, Sauer believed that the physical landscape was modified by culture to produce a human landscape. Thus, if we understand what the physical landscape looked like before human contact, and we can observe the human landscape today, then we can begin to deduce what a particular culture values. Was the natural environment destroyed or preserved? Was the landscape modified to suit particular goals of a society?

Figure 12A.2 ▶ Cultural Ecology Sauer's ideas were widely adopted by other geographers, but not universally accepted. Some criticized the approach for not being scientific enough and began to adapt ideas from biology and ecology to create what is known as **cultural ecology**. Cultural ecologists study how human societies adapt to the local habitat and often focus on traditional societies engaged in farming or other primary activities. The focus is often on humans as biological entities in a larger ecosystem. Like other organisms, humans will often change based on environmental conditions. Cultures with great technological knowledge might adapt to their environment differently than a society with less scientific expertise. Of course, there is the danger of reverting back to the ideas of environmental determinism to say that the environment causes cultural change, and this has been a criticism of cultural ecology, but the field has continued within human geography for decades with much of the research focused on small communities and agriculture in developing parts of the world.

why humans did or didn't react to certain natural disasters. In the face of a hurricane, for example, some people choose to evacuate and others board up their houses and stay to ride out the storm. Why doesn't everyone react the same way when faced with environmental danger? The answer to this question helps explain our views on the natural environment: Can we conquer nature or not?

In time, this psychological work by geographers developed into behavioral geography, a broad term that includes researchers working in various subfields of geography (see Module 2F). Some behavioral geographers tried to develop statistical models that would help explain human behavior, including how we interact with our environment. But others took a more humanistic and less statistical approach and began to research individual attitudes toward the natural environment. For example, research by behavioral geographers and psychologists has shown that some people are naturally risk-takers when it comes to the environment. These individuals feel that nature can be conquered by humans. Think about a BASE jumper who admires the natural environment but also wants to conquer it by jumping off a 500-foot cliff. Similarly, some people have no qualms about logging a forest because they believe the natural landscape is meant to support humans, while others feel that humans should do everything to conserve the natural environment. Can you think of how these differences in the way that humans perceive the natural environment could affect the decisions made by a whole society? Do humans see the natural environment the same way now as we did hundreds of years ago?

▲ **Figure 12A.3 Nature in Fairy Tales** Think about classic fairy tales like *Little Red Riding Hood* or *Hansel and Gretel*. How do these stories portray the natural environment, forest, or wilderness? Do children's stories today portray nature the same way? Why or why not?

12B Natural Hazards

Think about the 24-hour news channel coverage every time a major hurricane strikes the coast of the United States. There are nearly always two types of person-on-the-street interviews. The first is with the person sitting in a long line in a car, trying to leave the area. They say something like, "We just don't want to take any chances." Conversely, there is the interview with the resident who is refusing to leave. "We've been here 50 years," he or she says, "And nothing is going to make me leave my house." What you are seeing is how humans react to hazards in the environment in very different ways. Geographers have extensively researched natural hazards and the human response to them.

Natural hazards are environmental events such as floods, hurricanes (also known as cyclones or typhoons), earthquakes, tornados, tsunami, mudslides, volcanic eruptions, and droughts. No matter where you choose to live on the earth, there is a certain risk involved that comes naturally from being a living organism within a larger ecosystem. But some areas are known to be more risky than others, yet people choose to live there. Residents of Tokyo know that they are periodically going to face a devastating earthquake, as do residents of parts of California, yet these two areas remain densely populated.

Geographers working in the field of **environmental perception** have explored this issue. At its simplest, some people feel that the benefits of living in a hazardous place—a good job, nice weather, and other factors—outweigh the dangers. Cognitive dissonance theory explains the situation in which a person has two conflicting ideas about something. On one hand, people living in a hazard zone know the place might be dangerous, but they also want to live a long life. So they need to mentally deal with this disparity. Some might react by moving. Others might try to earthquake-proof their homes or take protective measures. Or they might simply convince themselves that the threat is not as great as they are being told.

The pioneering geographic work on natural hazards was undertaken by **Gilbert White** in the middle of the twentieth century. White spent years studying human adjustment to flooding, especially along the critical Mississippi River system. He concluded that human responses to flooding or to the rise of floodwaters are either structural or nonstructural. **Structural responses** include the building of levees, walls, or other engineering systems to protect humans from floods or to modify the flooding risk. **Nonstructural responses** are actions taken by a society, a political body, or individuals to reduce the risk. For example, in some areas, people are simply not allowed by law to live in an area where flooding is a risk, thus minimizing the potential damage of a large flood.

White concluded that structural responses actually increased risk because they encourage more development of homes and businesses in flood-prone areas and because they create a greater sense of security among residents. Can you apply the same ideas of structural and nonstructural responses to areas where hurricanes or earthquakes are common? What

▲ **Figure 12B.1 Mount Saint Helens** Perception of natural hazards came to national attention in 1980, when it became clear that Mount Saint Helens in Washington State was about to erupt. Harry Truman, the 84-year-old, somewhat cranky operator of a tourist lodge near the mountain, refused to leave his lodge and was the focus of national media attention. He believed that there was no way the mountain could erupt with enough force to kill him. In the end, he was wrong and was killed in the blast, which traveled at up to 700 miles per hour at temperatures as high as 900 degrees centigrade. Some considered him a hero, others a fool.

(a)

(b)

▲ **Figure 12B.2 Structural Failures and Natural Disasters**
Structural steps taken by societies to protect themselves from
natural hazards often fail. Two modern examples are the levees of
New Orleans and the roadways and buildings in Kobe, Japan. In
New Orleans (a), the citizens believed they were safe, but levees
designed to protect the city from flooding were not adequate
against a strong, Category 5 hurricane, such as Katrina in 2005,
leading to devastating floods. In Kobe (b), structures such as "earthquake-proof" elevated roadways were powerless against
the magnitude 7.3, Great Hanshin earthquake that occurred in 1995. These failures caused both the United States and Japan
to rethink their plans to protect citizens against hazards. Unfortunately, the lessons learned were not enough in Japan to
save tens of thousands from perishing in March 2011, but undoubtedly more would have died had Japan not learned from the
1995 disaster.

structural steps have coastal homeowners taken to reduce the risk of their homes being destroyed during
an earthquake? What about nonstructural steps by the government?

Other scholars have examined how humans react to natural hazards in terms of **cognitive factors** and
situation factors. Cognitive factors include a person's personality and personal attitudes toward nature, risk,
and other related factors. Some people are risk takers; others are not. Situation factors are where people are
located, how old they are, their financial resources, and other factors that might affect their actual or perceived
ability to deal with a possible hazard. The interaction between these two types of factors affects a person's
final response. For example, a risk taker with no money might react differently than a risk taker who is rich.

◀ **Figure 12B.3 Flood Insurance** The
US government created a program in 1968 to
help provide flood insurance to people living
in flood zones. Is this program a good use
of government resources? What do you think
are the pros and cons of protecting people
in flood zones from financial loss?

12C Natural Disasters

Natural disasters challenge our notion that humanity can conquer nature. Most of the time, other than the daily weather, most people pay little attention to the physical environment around them. We certainly rarely think about the geologic activity under our feet or the potential danger of a volcano hundreds or thousands of miles away, but catastrophic natural disasters can certainly impact humans in dramatic and deadly ways.

Earthquakes

An **earthquake** is caused by any event that releases seismic waves. Usually, this is caused by the movement of faults beneath the earth's surface, but volcanoes, nuclear tests, and underground explosions can also cause earthquakes. The size of an earthquake (in terms of energy released) is measured with a seismometer and reported using the **moment magnitude scale**, which uses numbers on a logarithmic scale. Thus, a 6.0 earthquake is about 32 times more powerful than a 5.0 earthquake. You probably have heard of the Richter scale, developed in the 1930s, but this measure is rarely used anymore and is considered outdated. The values of the moment magnitude scale are similar to those of the Richter scale, but they are calculated differently. The intensity of an earthquake in terms of shaking is measured using a different scale, known as the Mercalli scale.

Earthquakes cause structural damage through shaking and openings in the ground, and they are particularly dangerous when they occur at night because more people are inside. In poor areas of the world prone to earthquakes, such as Iran, Pakistan, and China, buildings are often not able to withstand the effects of a powerful quake, so the more people who are inside at the time of the disaster, the higher the death toll. In the aftermath of a powerful earthquake, disruptions in food and water supplies often kill more people, and diseases such as cholera are always a concern in any natural disaster in which water and sewage systems are compromised.

Table 12C.1	Top 10 Deadliest Earthquakes		
Year	Location	Magnitude	# of Deaths
1556	Shaanxi, China	~8	830,000
1976	Tangshan, China	7.5	255,000
1138	Aleppo, Syria	Unknown	230,000
2004	Sumatra, Indonesia	9.1	227,898
2010	Haiti	7.0	222,750
856	Iran	Unknown	200,000
1920	Haiyuan, China	7.8	200,000
893	Iran	Unknown	150,000
1923	Tokyo area, Japan	7.9	142,800
1948	Ashgabat, Turkmenistan	7.3	110,000

The deadliest earthquake in recorded human history is probably the 1556 Shaanxi earthquake in China, believed to have killed 830,000 people. The 2004 Indian Ocean tsunami (Great Sumatra-Andaman tsunami), caused by an earthquake, killed at least 227,898 people and injured tens of thousands of others, and a 1976 earthquake in Tangshan, China, killed 255,000 people. Recently, the 2010 earthquake in Haiti was responsible for 222,750 deaths. The relatively recent dates of two of these events should make you think twice about the notion that we are immune to disasters in the modern, technological age.

Hurricanes/Typhoons/Cyclones

Hurricane, **typhoon**, and **cyclone** all refer to the same thing: a strong cyclonic storm system with low pressure, strong thunderstorms, high winds, and rain that is generically called a tropical cyclone. The term

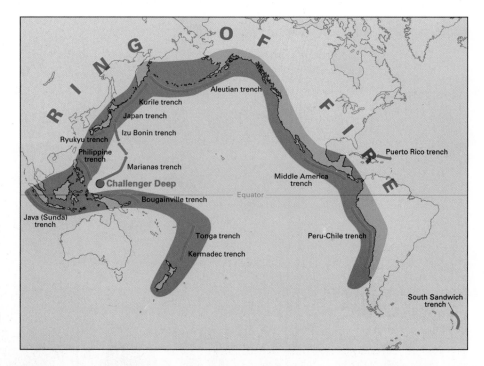

Figure 12C.1 ▶ Ring of Fire Earthquakes can and do occur continually around the world. Most are imperceptible to humans but are easily recorded by seismologists. Annually, there are about 18 earthquakes of magnitude 7.0–7.9 somewhere on the planet and usually one earthquake that exceeds 8.0. About 9 out of 10 of the world's earthquakes take place along the **Ring of Fire**, a horseshoe-shaped zone in the Pacific Ocean that is over 40,000 kilometers long and essentially follows the edge of the Pacific Plate. Note that many densely populated areas coincide with areas of significant earthquake activity (see population distribution maps in Modules 3B, 3C, and 3D).

◀ **Figure 12C.2 Tsunami** The word **tsunami** comes from Japanese and means "harbor wave." They are caused whenever there is a massive displacement of water, usually in an ocean, as a result of an earthquake or a volcanic explosion. It is generally incorrect to refer to tsunami as tidal waves because they are not caused by tides. *Seismic sea wave* is a term some scientists use. Eight out of 10 tsunami occur in the Pacific Ocean. As demonstrated by the Sendai, Japan, tsunami of March 2011, shown here, the effect can be devastating for coastal areas because the waves can be tens of meters above normal sea level, and thus massive flooding and physical destruction of buildings can occur. In the aftermath of a tsunami, food shortages, lack of fresh water to drink, and disease can cause additional deaths. In the Great Sumatra-Andaman tsunami of 2004 in Southeast Asia, the waves were as high as 30 meters. Tsunami in Europe killed about 100,000 in Portugal in 1755 and 100,000 in Italy in 1908.

hurricane refers to storms in the Atlantic Ocean, *typhoon* to Pacific Ocean storms, and *cyclone* to Indian Ocean storms. Hurricanes peak in later summer months in tropical areas near the Equator and are damaging because of wind and water. Winds can reach over 150 miles an hour in the strongest storms and can spawn tornados with winds over 200 miles per hour in localized areas. Obviously, buildings and other structures are often destroyed by high winds.

Beyond high winds, water can be a major destructive factor for human populations when a tropical cyclone hits. In addition to intense rainfall, hurricanes can also cause **storm surges**, a wall of wind-driven water that can be meters or tens of meters higher than sea level. In low-lying coastal areas, this wall of water can cause massive flooding and destruction of roads, bridges, and other structures. In the 2008 cyclone that hit Burma, the storm surge inundated much of the country's coastline. Unfortunately, this area is also a major agricultural production area, so the loss of rice and the disruption of food and drinking water systems led to tens of thousands of deaths.

Table 12C.2	Deadliest Cyclonic Storms	
Year	**Location**	**# of Deaths**
1970	Bangladesh	500,000
1839	India	300,000
1737	India	300,000
1975	China	210,000
1876	Bangladesh	200,000
2008	Myanmar (Burma)	~146,000
1991	Bangladesh	138,866
1882	India	100,000
1922	China	60,000
1864	India	60,000

This table shows the years and modern locations of the 10 deadliest cyclonic storms (hurricane, typhoon, or cyclone) in recorded human history. The 1970 Bhola Cyclone, which tops the list, helped spark the Bangladesh Liberation War, which led to the country's independence. At the time, the country was East Pakistan and was part of a divided country, which also included West Pakistan, the area that is now known as just Pakistan.

Tornados

Tornados are fast-moving, short-lived columns of air that can sustain winds of up to 300 miles per hour, although most have winds between 40 and 110 miles per hour. Tornados have a unique spatial pattern on the earth's surface. Although few places are immune from the threat of a tornado, most tornados occur in just a few small zones. The United States has the most tornados by far, about 1,200 a year, which is about four times as many each year as in all of Europe. Within the United States, Tornado Alley is the leader in tornado frequency. Florida also experiences a very high number of tornados, but these tend to be weaker than the massive funnels often seen in Tornado Alley.

Figure 12C.3 ▶ Tornado Alley Each green dot on this map represents the touchdown point of a tornado between 1950–2009. Tornado Alley has unique characteristics that make it ideal for the development of tornados. Comprising a large area between the Rockies and the Appalachians, the region is perfectly suited for the formation of tornados because cold air masses from the north can mix with warm, often humid air masses from the south without being blocked by mountains or other barriers. The area known as Dixie Alley, which spreads across the Gulf states into the Tennessee Valley is also prone to long-distance, violent tornados and is actually deadlier than Tornado Alley.

12D Human Geography and Water

Water is obviously vital for human survival, and the human landscape is intertwined with water patterns. A human simply cannot survive more than a couple of days without water; therefore, where we are able to live is almost entirely based on access to water. So on one hand, human patterns on the earth's landscape are strongly influenced by water. But water is also affected by humans, so we must look at the interaction of the human environment with water in the physical environment.

The first way to think about the human geography of water is our proximity to this vital substance. About 40% of the world's population lives within 100 km (60 mi) of a coast. This means about 2.5 billion people. In the United States, a full 50% of the population lives within 80 km (50 mi) of either an ocean or one of the Great Lakes. This gives you a rough idea of how strong our relationship with large bodies of water actually is. A change in the quality of water along those coastal areas is certainly going to impact human settlements, and conversely, changes in human settlement patterns can positively or negatively affect coastal regions.

But in some parts of the world, people have chosen to live in places that don't have a lot of water, so another way to think of the geography of water is to look at human modification of waterways, specifically **water diversion**. Humans divert water to places that are dry to serve those living in areas with inadequate supplies. In the western United States, aqueducts and dams divert and store water from the Colorado River and take it all the way to Southern California, where it sustains the vast agricultural zone of the Imperial Valley. The All-American Canal alone irrigates 500,000 acres of cropland. The canal also supplies hydroelectric power for cities along its path. But the environmental consequences are real as well. Diverting water into California means that less water flows to the lower reaches of the Colorado River, causing areas across the border in Mexico to almost dry up. Also, water taken into California to irrigate cropland has led to runoff in the area of the Salton Sea, which now has a high concentration of fertilizer and pesticides, resulting in **water pollution**. Human modification of water systems can often be dramatic. The massive Three Gorges Dam in China has changed a portion of the Yangtze River into a reservoir over 600 km (375 mi) long. The failure of the Banqiao Dam in China in 1975 killed 25,000 people outright and over 145,000 more in the aftermath because of diseases, as well as destroyed over 5 million buildings.

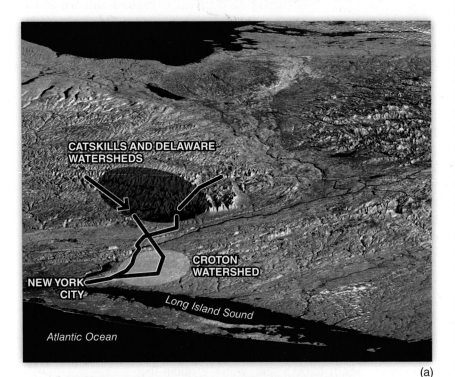

(a)

(b)

◀ **Figure 12D.1 New York City Water System** Human geography also helps us understand how humans use (and abuse) water resources. Drinking water alone requires massive alterations of the physical landscape. One hundred miles north of New York City (a), water is collected in four large reservoirs and taken through aqueducts, many constructed in the early twentieth century (b), south and under the Hudson River to another system of reservoirs in Westchester and Putnam Counties. From there, water flows through more aqueducts to New York City. In total, the city uses about 1 billion gallons of water each day! Imagine what type of sewer system is needed to handle that much use.

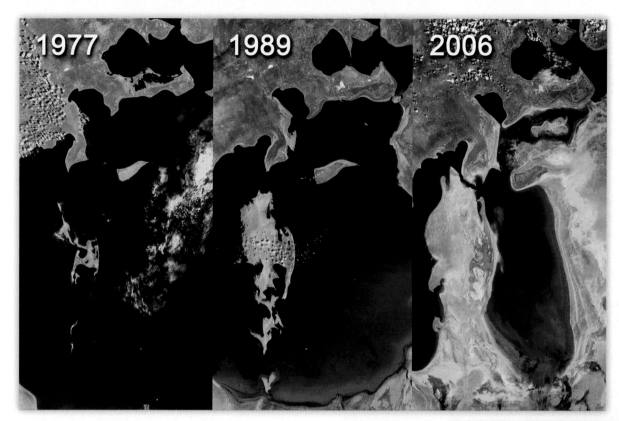

**Figure 12D.2 Aral Sea** In some cases, human modification of water systems can be dramatic. The Aral Sea along the border of Uzbekistan and Kazakhstan in Central Asia was once the fourth largest freshwater lake in the world. Today, it is just 10% of its original size, and much of the remaining water is too salty to support fish. Diversion for irrigation of cotton fields is responsible for much of the decline. The water that runs off the fields and back into the Aral Sea is polluted and salty, and the ecosystem and even the climate of the region are damaged beyond repair.

Figure 12D.3 ▶ Southeastern Anatolia Project While there are certainly serious environmental and lifestyle concerns to overuse of water resources, water can sometimes lead to conflict as well. The fact that much of Israel's water comes from areas under the disputed West Bank causes tensions between Israel and its neighbors. Wells and aquifers divert water from outside Israel's borders to inside. Much of Syria's and Iraq's water comes from Turkey, which is constructing a series of 22 dams and 19 hydroelectric plants in the Tigris and Euphrates river basins as part of the Southeastern Anatolia Project (GAP, from the Turkish name). Here, cotton fields in Turkey south of the large Atatürk Dam can clearly be seen. This area once relied on wells and local water sources, but now irrigation channels allow greater cultivation. But increased water use in Turkey reduces water supplies to Syria and Iraq, causing tension among the countries.

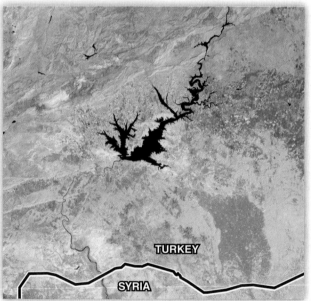

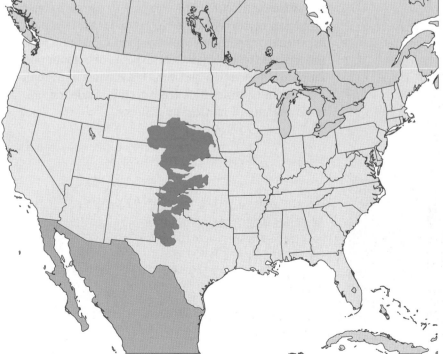

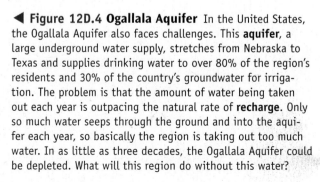

◀ **Figure 12D.4 Ogallala Aquifer** In the United States, the Ogallala Aquifer also faces challenges. This **aquifer**, a large underground water supply, stretches from Nebraska to Texas and supplies drinking water to over 80% of the region's residents and 30% of the country's groundwater for irrigation. The problem is that the amount of water being taken out each year is outpacing the natural rate of **recharge**. Only so much water seeps through the ground and into the aquifer each year, so basically the region is taking out too much water. In as little as three decades, the Ogallala Aquifer could be depleted. What will this region do without this water?

12E Human Geography and Air Pollution

Air pollution is the introduction of chemicals, biological matter, or particulates (small solids) into the atmosphere, and there is most certainly a geographic pattern of unhealthy or abnormal air. For example, where are you most likely to find smog, an urban area or a rural area? Urban areas, right? Why? Automobiles, industry, and other sources of pollution are more likely to be concentrated there. Truly understanding the pattern of air pollution on a local, regional, or global level requires knowledge of human geography. The leading causes of air pollution are engines, industry, and power generation.

Engines create pollution by burning gasoline and diesel, which produces pollutants such as carbon monoxide, nitrogen oxides, and hydrocarbons. Motor vehicles are a major source of engine-produced pollution, and there is certainly a geography of automobile use. Urban areas are often plagued with smog caused largely by cars.

▲ **Figure 12E.1 Smog Smog** is produced by sunlight reacting with ozone released from cars, factories, and power plants. Los Angeles, shown here, is plagued by poor air quality despite efforts made in recent years to reduce particulates in the air through stricter controls on cars and other sources of pollution.

Reducing American dependence on the automobile is difficult, but car use is not only an American challenge. Across Asia, rising car use coupled with industrial expansion has created often noxious conditions. A 2008 United Nations report warned that pollutants are blocking out the sun across Asia and reducing crop yields in places such as India as less sunlight reaches plants. In Guangzhou, a large city in southern China, natural light levels have declined by 20% in the past three decades. Rain washes pollutants out of the atmosphere, but when soot lands on glaciers, the darker color can cause them to melt faster.

Air pollution can take a high toll on human health. It is estimated that nearly 350,000 people a year die in India and China alone from air pollution–related diseases. Diesel-powered cars and trucks, coal-burning factories, and the use of coal- and wood-burning stoves inside homes are the main causes of this increased mortality. The World Health Organization is predicting that chronic obstructive pulmonary disease (COPD) will continue to rise as a cause of human mortality in the next two decades. In poor areas of the world, the use of wood for cooking food indoors also compounds the problems of outdoor pollution from factories and vehicles. Living in a small room with constant fires leads to the inhalation of a large quantity of particulate matter.

◀ **Figure 12E.2 Asian Pollution** In China, rising incomes have led to a boom in auto use as middle-class Chinese workers are now able to afford a small car. Approximately 80% of all new car buyers in China are first-time buyers. Beijing alone now has over 3.5 million cars, and their emissions are creating pollution challenges for the growing country. Here, smog hangs over tourists in Beijing's Tiananmen Square.

Figure 12E.3 ▶ Lawn Mowers When we think of local air pollution, we generally assume that cars are the worst culprit, but other machines can have a dramatic impact on air quality. Lawn mowers are notorious polluters. The tiny machines utilize over 800 million gallons of gasoline per year, and the Environmental Protection Agency estimates that 17 million gallons of that are spilled by operators. This is more spilled fuel than occurred with the *Exxon Valdez* tanker accident in 1989. Annually, a lawn mower can produce the same amount of greenhouse gases as 43 new cars, each driving 12,000 miles.

Human-induced air pollution can affect us in ways other than just health. As mentioned before, reduction in daylight levels in areas of India and China have reduced crop yields. Environments can also be altered due to the creation of acid rain. **Acid rain** refers to elevated levels of nitric and sulfuric acids in rain or other atmospheric deposition. It is primarily caused by the emission of sulfur dioxide and nitrogen oxides by power plants and factories that burn fossil fuels, such as coal. Once in the atmosphere, the chemicals react with water, oxygen, and other components to produce acids. When the acids fall to earth in rain, snow, or fog, they can have a negative impact on the local ecosystem. Streams and lakes can become too acidic to support some or all life forms. Furthermore, some trees are sensitive to acid and die if acid rain is persistent.

▲ **Figure 12E.4 Acid Rain** These trees in North Carolina have been killed by acid rain. In the 1980s, many lakes in the Adirondack Mountains of upstate New York were found to have pH levels of 4.2–5.0. This is about as acidic as tomato juice and close to some forms of orange juice. Some lakes were so acidic that fish could no longer live in them. Government intervention has improved the situation a bit, but there have been other effects as well. For example, maple trees are replacing oaks and other species in many parts of the East because they are more tolerant of acidic conditions.

12F Solid Waste

Stop for a moment and do a mental tally of how many items you ate, bought, or used today that came in a wrapper, package, box, can, or bottle. In industrialized, consumption-oriented societies like ours, nearly everything we buy has packaging that gets used and thrown away. With over 6 billion people on the planet, garbage and waste have become a significant challenge for many countries.

The amount of waste generated in a country such as the United States is simply staggering. In 2009, Americans generated over 243 million tons of municipal **solid waste** (garbage), and American factories generated 7.6 billion tons of industrial waste. Consider the following:

- Americans throw out 20 million televisions each year.
- The US Post Office delivers nearly 90 billion pieces of "junk mail" each year.
- The average American produces about 4.6 pounds of solid waste per day, but only 1.5 pounds get recycled or composted.
- Paper and cardboard account for 33% of all garbage produced in the United States, and lawn trimmings or food scraps make up an additional 25%.

There is some good news in solid waste management. Recycling and composting of waste has risen dramatically in the United States in recent years. In 1960, only about 6.4% of US municipal solid waste was recycled. By 1985, the percentage had risen slightly, to 10.5%. But the 1990s and 2000s saw a significant public interest in recycling and suddenly bins were appearing on curbsides and in public buildings. By 2007, 33.4% of garbage was being recycled. Although Americans produce more garbage per person than they did in 1960 (4.6 pounds versus 2.68 pounds), the stress on landfills would be by 2007 much greater had recycling not taken hold on some level. But recycling has great benefits.

Where does all the garbage go? Although you rarely see them, **landfills** are a common part of our cultural landscape and will undoubtedly prove an interesting find for future archeologists. The number of landfills in the United States has actually declined in recent decades. In 1988, according to the EPA, there were nearly 8,000 landfills in the United States but that number had dropped dramatically to just 1,754 sites. However, landfill size has increased to meet demand, so there are fewer landfills but larger ones. With fewer landfills and growing cities, there are not always landfills close to major metropolitan areas. Therefore, many cities need to transport their garbage hundreds of miles away for disposal. For example, some garbage from Brooklyn in New York City is loaded onto train cars and shipped all the way to Virginia.

Landfills, of course, are not without controversy. No matter how well managed they are, there is always the risk that chemicals or other pollutants in the garbage can pollute the surrounding area. Companies use sophisticated liners to try to prevent leaks, comprised of a couple of feet of low-permeable clay with a

▲ **Figure 12F.1 Chinese Plastic Bags** As China became more capitalistic in the 1990s and 2000s, it became common for stores to give customers free plastic bags for their groceries and other purchases. In time, however, the amount of bags being used rose to approximately 12 billion a day. Many of these bags ended up discarded in the street and were choking landfills. As of June 2008, China banned the thinnest plastic bags and began to require that stores charge for other plastic bags. This is the second major phase of China's fight against "white pollution." Before the campaign against plastic bags, the Chinese government targeted the white foam containers food vendors used for take-out orders. Buying food from street vendors is very common in China, but the containers would often end up on the street as litter. The problem of plastic bags is not a uniquely Chinese problem, of course. The Sierra Club estimates that Americans throw out 100 billion plastic bags each year!

(a)

◀ **Figure 12F.2 Fresh Kills Landfill** (a) The problems of urban waste disposal were highlighted in the controversy over the Fresh Kills Landfill on Staten Island, part of New York City. After opening in 1948, the landfill grew to become the largest in the world at 2,200 acres (almost 96 million square feet), causing some to declare it the largest human-made object on the planet. Public pressure resulted in its closure in March 2001, but it was reopened to handle debris after the terrorist attacks of September 2001. (b) Fresh Kills is now being converted into public parkland, and when the project is complete it will be three times as large as Central Park. This methane well at the site today gives a clue to the existence of the tons of trash buried below.

(b)

layer of polyethylene (plastic) on top, but environmental activists dispute the ability of liners to prevent all leaks. But people who live near a landfill rarely want a facility expanded, and opening a new landfill is even more controversial. Landfills are certainly part of the **NIMBY** ("Not In My Back Yard") phenomenon, in which people oppose unpleasant land uses near where they live. In other words, people need landfills, but nobody wants to live near one.

Reducing the need for landfills is obviously the best choice for most societies, but this requires significant cultural and economic effort. Culturally, people need to change habits, such as taking reusable bags to the grocery store or using cloth napkins instead of paper. While some groups in a society will change, to get widespread cultural change often requires significant public and private effort. The bulk of items put into landfills can be reduced significantly using incinerators to burn garbage, but incinerators must be financed, can result in additional air pollution, and often face local opposition to their construction.

Figure 12F.3 ▶ Recycling Cans Recycling just 1 ton of aluminum soda cans saves the equivalent of 1,665 gallons of gasoline. The amount of carbon dioxide emissions saved each year in the United States by our current solid waste recycling efforts is equivalent to pulling 35 million cars off the road.

12G Hazardous Waste

Hazardous waste, also known as **toxic waste**, is waste that poses a risk to either the environment or human populations. In the United States, hazardous waste includes substances that have the potential to increase mortality or illness if improperly treated, handled, stored, or transported. In general, hazardous wastes include those that are flammable, corrosive, radioactive, explosive, oxidizing, or biologically toxic. Geographically, toxic waste can be a local, regional, national, or international issue.

On the local level, businesses and even homes generate hazardous waste materials. Businesses that generate or use hazardous waste include auto repair shops, photo developers, dry cleaners, hospitals and medical offices, and exterminators. Gas stations, for example, have to be particularly careful to prevent gasoline from seeping into soils. The disposal of oil at mechanics' garages and oil-change chain stores is another area of concern. Medical offices, too, cannot simply throw biological materials into the local garbage. Fortunately for workers at small businesses, government regulations for the handling and disposal of dangerous materials is stronger than in the past, and even small businesses are required to have substantial training for workers.

The impact of local businesses on pollution is clearly seen through the US government's **Superfund Program**. Officially known as the Comprehensive Environmental Response, Compensation, and Liability Act, the Superfund Act became law in 1980 in response to the very public pollution nightmare at Love Canal and places such as Valley of the Drums in Kentucky. The program allows the government to assess the magnitude of a pollution site, to prioritize its cleanup compared to other sites, and to develop and implement cleanup programs. About 1,300 sites are currently listed as Superfund sites, and many of these are the

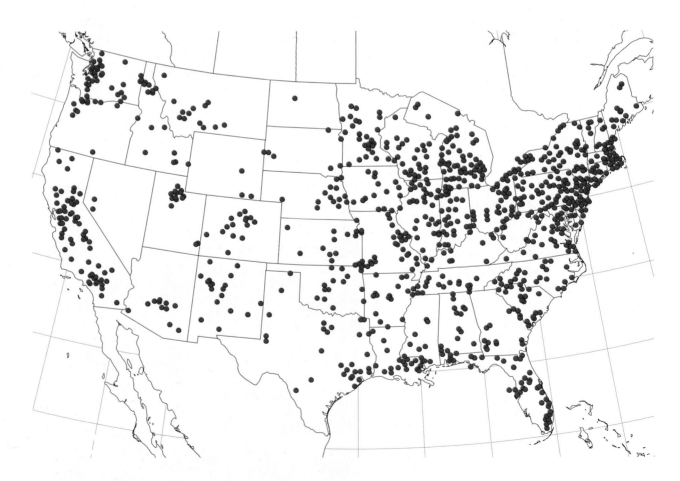

▲ **Figure 12G.1** Can you detect a pattern between the location of Superfund sites, indicated by the red dots, and any other economic patterns in the United States?

◀ **Figure 12G.2 Valley of the Drums** One of the pollution sites most responsible for spurring the government to action with the Superfund Program was known as the Valley of the Drums. Located in Bullitt County, Kentucky, the site began to be used as a dumping site for barrels of toxic waste in the 1960s, but at the time few laws were in place to govern the management of waste sites, even when some of the barrels burned for weeks in 1966. By the late 1970s, however, it had become clear that many of the barrels were leaking and that the scope of the problem was beyond the ability of local officials to cope with the matter. The dramatic photos of thousands of barrels on the 23-acre site were used by congressional representatives and environmental activists to help win support for the Superfund Program.

result of pollution by a single small polluter, not the work of a global multinational company. In most cases, the cost of cleaning up a Superfund site is borne by the polluter, but when that is not possible, the government covers the costs. But the amount of government money to support the program has shrunk since the 1990s from over $4 billion to less than $200 million. Because of this, fewer sites are being cleaned up.

One of the particularly geographic aspects of toxic waste is its movement. Yes, the location of waste storage is certainly a geographic issue, but when dangerous substances have to be transported from one site to another, many more political jurisdictions get involved. Dangerous wastes are transported by trains, planes, and trucks, so the regulations governing their movement are complicated. This has been most publically discussed in relation to the movement of spent nuclear fuels.

Another way geographers have been involved in studying hazardous waste is in the analysis of contaminated areas and notably the identification of waste-induced diseases. The term **cancer cluster** refers to an unusual concentration of cancer in a particular area. Sometimes, these clusters are the result of unseen chemicals in the local water or soil. But how do public health officials determine if a concentration of cancer cases is random or statistically unusual? Geographers are able to use spatial analysis techniques, basically specialized statistical methods, to determine with some certainty whether a cluster is unusual. In recent decades, the identification of high rates of mesothelioma among workers exposed to asbestos is a well-publicized example of how exposure to a dangerous substance can cause large-scale health problems.

Figure 12G.3 ▶ Yucca Mountain From 1987 to 2009, the government proposed storing nuclear waste from around the country in a large facility under Yucca Mountain in Nevada. In addition to concerns over the ability to safely store nuclear waste for long periods of time at the facility, there was great concern in some areas along major transportation routes that nuclear waste would be traveling through local towns. Critics of the program argued that an accident or a terrorist attack could contaminate areas far from where the waste was being produced.

12H Geography of Fossil Fuels

Fossil fuels are the source of much of the world's pollution. They are formed when organic matter deposited on the earth's surface is changed by pressure and time over thousands of years to form coal, oil, or natural gas. Understanding the geography of fossil fuels helps us understand why they are the source of so much conflict in the world. The maps and captions on these two pages will help you better understand the geography of these precious resources.

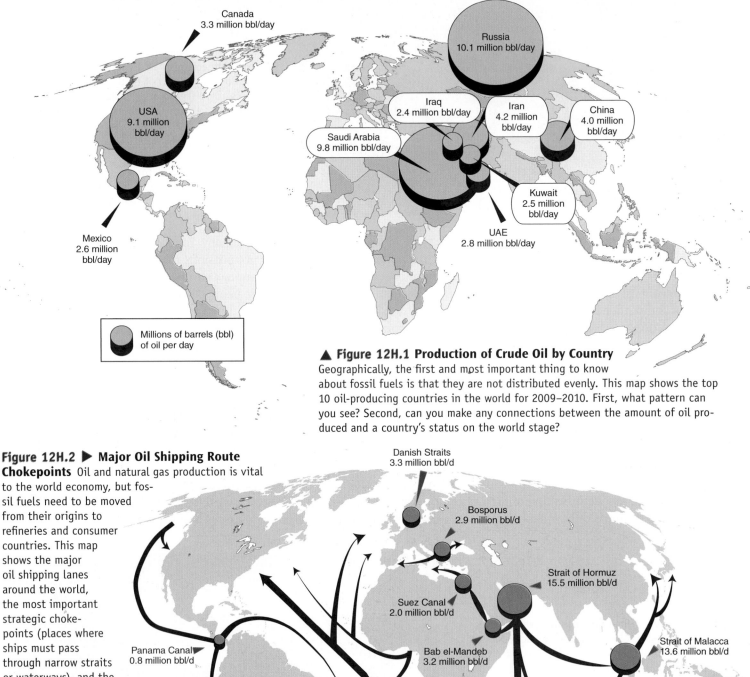

Canada
3.3 million bbl/day

Russia
10.1 million bbl/day

USA
9.1 million
bbl/day

Iraq
2.4 million bbl/day

Iran
4.2 million
bbl/day

China
4.0 million
bbl/day

Saudi Arabia
9.8 million bbl/day

Kuwait
2.5 million
bbl/day

Mexico
2.6 million
bbl/day

UAE
2.8 million bbl/day

Millions of barrels (bbl)
of oil per day

▲ **Figure 12H.1 Production of Crude Oil by Country**
Geographically, the first and most important thing to know about fossil fuels is that they are not distributed evenly. This map shows the top 10 oil-producing countries in the world for 2009–2010. First, what pattern can you see? Second, can you make any connections between the amount of oil produced and a country's status on the world stage?

Figure 12H.2 ▶ Major Oil Shipping Route Chokepoints Oil and natural gas production is vital to the world economy, but fossil fuels need to be moved from their origins to refineries and consumer countries. This map shows the major oil shipping lanes around the world, the most important strategic chokepoints (places where ships must pass through narrow straits or waterways), and the amount of oil that flows through each chokepoint on a typical day. What do you think are some of the security concerns regarding these major chokepoints? If one of them were closed because of war or an uncooperative government, what would the impact be on the global economy?

Danish Straits
3.3 million bbl/d

Bosporus
2.9 million bbl/d

Strait of Hormuz
15.5 million bbl/d

Suez Canal
2.0 million bbl/d

Strait of Malacca
13.6 million bbl/d

Panama Canal
0.8 million bbl/d

Bab el-Mandeb
3.2 million bbl/d

bbl/d = Barrels per day

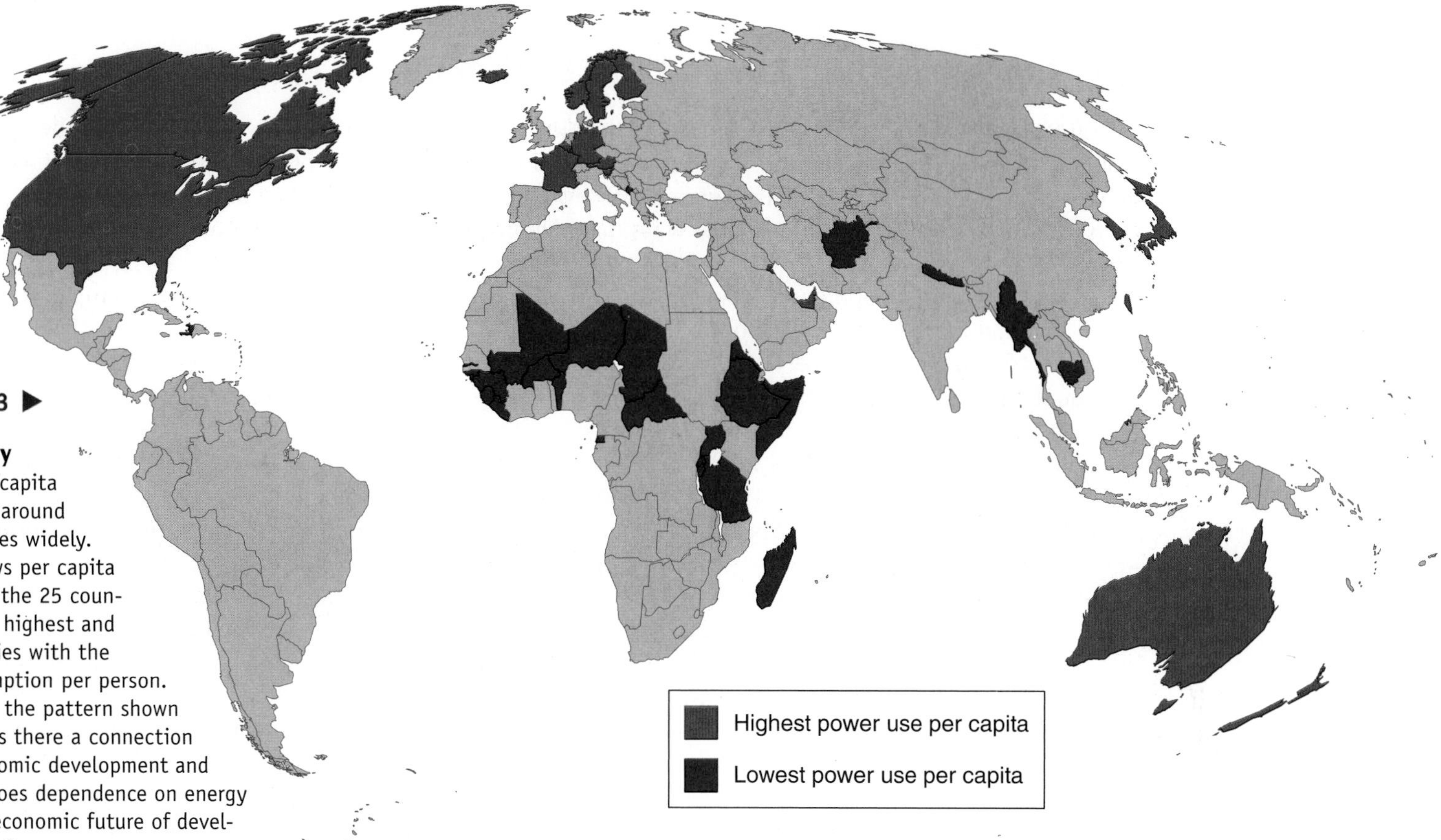

Figure 12H.3 ▶ Power Use per Capita by Country Per capita use of energy around the world varies widely. This map shows per capita power use for the 25 countries with the highest and the 25 countries with the lowest consumption per person. What explains the pattern shown on the map? Is there a connection between economic development and energy use? Does dependence on energy threaten the economic future of developed countries?

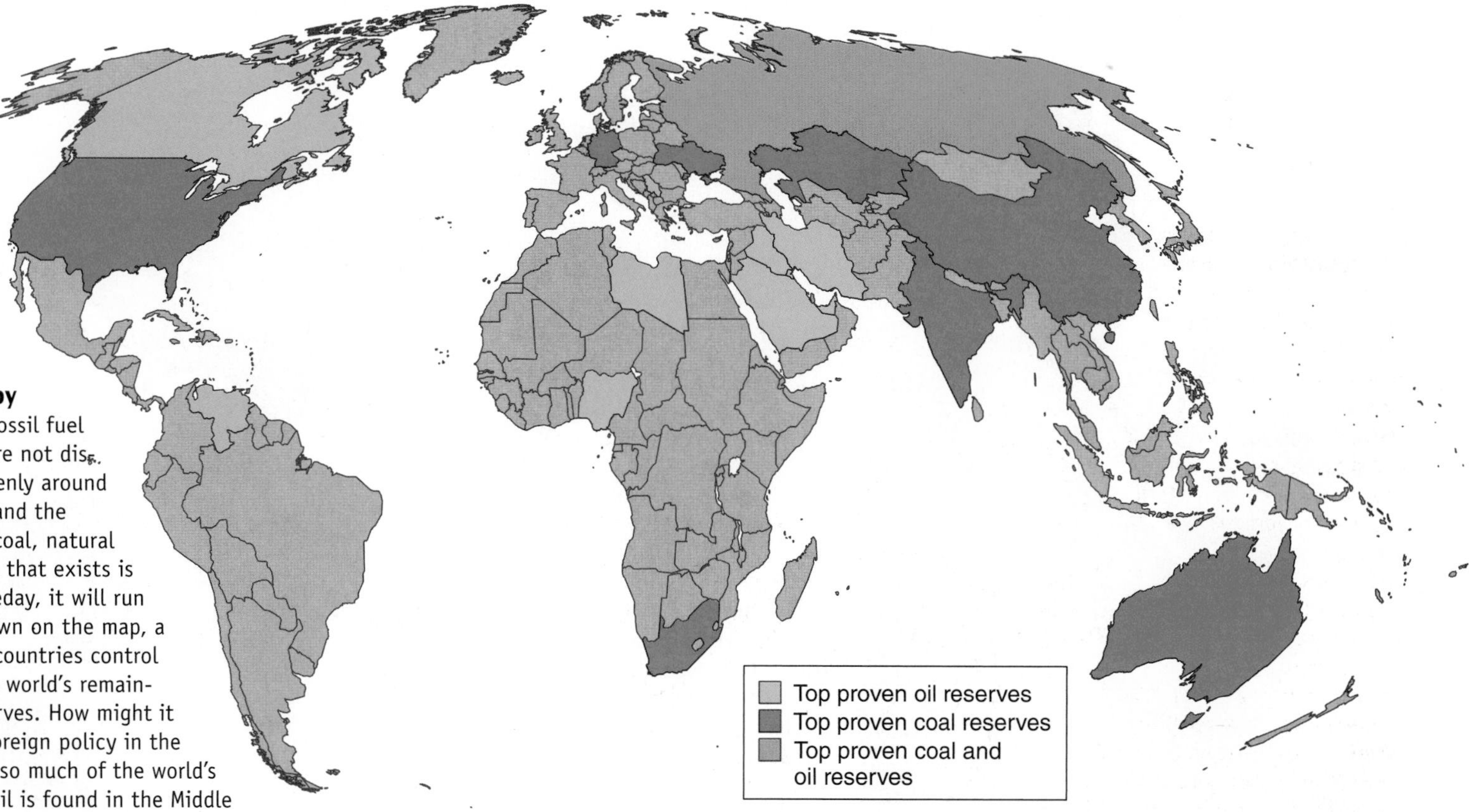

Legend:
- Highest power use per capita
- Lowest power use per capita

Figure 12H.4 ▶ Oil and Coal Reserves by Country Fossil fuel resources are not distributed evenly around the world, and the amount of coal, natural gas, and oil that exists is finite. Someday, it will run out. As shown on the map, a handful of countries control most of the world's remaining oil reserves. How might it affect US foreign policy in the future that so much of the world's remaining oil is found in the Middle East and Russia? Does the location of coal in the world help explain why the United States is one of the top consumers of coal?

Legend:
- Top proven oil reserves
- Top proven coal reserves
- Top proven coal and oil reserves

12I   Population Growth and the Environment

As you learned from Chapter 3, the world's population is increasing rapidly. By the year 2050, the world's population, currently at 6.7 billion people, is expected to increase to 9.3 billion people. This tremendous increase in only a few decades will put considerable pressure on the environment at both the local and global levels. In this section, we'll explore some ways in which growing populations alter our relationship with the natural environment.

Simply saying that population growth is bad for the environment is too simplistic. For example, if populations rise and more people move to urban areas, it can be easier for countries to control waste and water resources. It's easier to treat the waste of 1,000 people living in an apartment building than in hundreds of individual residences. But at the same time, urban populations living in high densities can produce concentrated air and water pollution if not managed properly.

Scholars have created several models to try to predict or explain the relationship between population and environmental change. In the 1970s, a publication entitled *The Limits to Growth* by Donella Meadows and several other scholars at the Massachusetts Institute of Technology argued that, in time, population and industrialization would continue to grow but then suddenly collapse as food and resources became scarce and pollution increased. This pattern was known as "overshoot and collapse" because the notion was that population and economic growth would overshoot their natural sustainability and then collapse. This concept of sudden environmental catastrophe is challenged by other experts, who argue that environmental damage will be more gradual as populations rise.

Other scholars have put forward other ideas to describe the human-environment relationship. Ehrlich and Holdren proposed a model of human impact on the environment (I) that was a function of population size (P), affluence (A), and technology (T), such as a society's ability to produce energy more efficiently. Their model proposed a relationship I = PAT. Population growth can cause environmental damage, but a relatively stable population can also have more impact on the environment if it becomes more affluent. As a society becomes richer, people tend to use more energy and produce more waste. Americans produce a lot more garbage and use more energy per capita, for example, than citizens of poor countries. This model has been discussed

◀ **Figure 12I.1 Health, Population, and Environment** Not only can growing populations affect the environment, but the environmental damage can then affect the health of the population and that of future populations. For example, increased air pollution caused by rising urban populations can lead to increased childhood mortality or illnesses due to respiratory problems.

widely by scholars, but it is not universally accepted. Some experts argue that it is too simplistic and does not account for factors such as cultural change. For example, in the United States, as we've seen, recycling has increased in recent decades as American culture has become less accepting of just throwing everything away. This increase in recycling has partially offset the environmental impact of a rising population rate.

Other researchers have added variables such as educational levels and unemployment to help better predict the effect of a population on the local environment. It can be argued, for example, that more education might lead to better management of natural resources. Of course, education can also lead to more affluence, which may increase resource use.

Regardless of the model, many geographers and researchers are concerned about increasing populations. Worldwide, urban populations are on the rise as people move from rural areas to cities. But city dwellers consume more food, energy, and goods than do their rural counterparts. In China, for example, pork consumption is much higher among city dwellers than among rural residents. Chinese urban residents also have more televisions, refrigerators, and other energy-consuming appliances and use three times as much coal per capita than people in the country. Cities can also produce air pollution that can travel to other regions of the world. So if the world population is rising and we are becoming more urbanized, can we expect a greater toll on the environment than if the population were growing without increased urbanization?

Rising populations can lead to numerous environmental concerns, including **deforestation** and **coastal pollution**. In the past 20 years, about 120,000 square kilometers of forest loss each year can be attributed to human activity. This is equivalent to an area about the size of the state of Ohio. Forests can be maintained with small human populations, but as populations increase or economic activities change, damage can occur rapidly. Deforestation results in increased air pollution, soil erosion and reduced soil fertility, flooding, and loss of biodiversity as plant and animal species are destroyed. Cattle ranching and timber operations have been major sources of deforestation in tropical areas. Growing populations can also affect coastal ecosystems. Worldwide, population densities near coasts are twice as high as the global average, and as populations rise, waste and other pollution can easily damage fragile marine ecosystems. Oil spills, such as that caused by the explosion of a BP oil rig in the Gulf of Mexico, kill untold numbers of birds and aquatic animals, pollute water and beaches, and affect coastal fisheries for years to come.

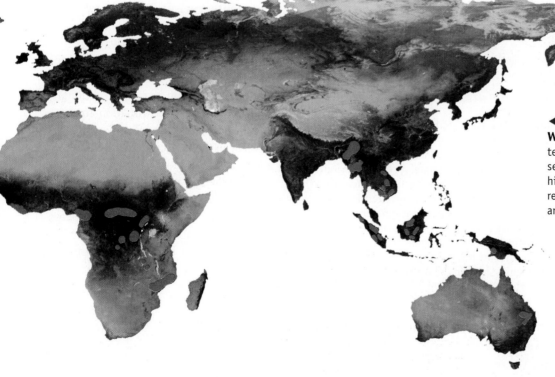

◀ **Figure 12I.2 Deforestation Worldwide** Geography is about pattern and process. What patterns can you see among areas of the world that have higher rates of deforestation, shown in red, and what processes do you think are causing the patterns?

12J Environmental Justice

It's a geographic fact that pollution and other environmental problems are not evenly distributed at the local, regional, national, and global levels. Some areas are simply more polluted than others. Why is this? In this section, we'll explore the concept of environmental justice and its geographic aspects.

In the 1980s, some activists began arguing that issues such as race and social status were responsible for the concentration of pollution in some areas. Perhaps as a result of the civil rights movements of the 1950s and 1960s, community organizers became more willing to challenge issues of discrimination in poor communities and had learned how to use grassroots campaigns to encourage participation by community citizens. At the same time, disasters such as the poisoning and sickness of residents at Love Canal in New York shone a bright light on the realities of industrial pollution in the United States. By the 1990s, these activists had coalesced into what was known as the environmental justice movement.

Environmental justice includes several principles. First and foremost, environmental justice means that environmental laws and regulations are implemented everywhere without regard to race, ethnicity, or socioeconomic status. It also means that information about the legislative and decision-making processes is available to all people. In poor or disadvantaged communities, it can be very difficult for residents to know how to participate in community or state government and how to fight governmental decisions they disagree with.

One common concern of environmental justice activists is known as **environmental racism**. The term refers to a situation in which polluters intentionally or unintentionally take advantage of a minority community because they feel the community is less likely to oppose the environmental hazard. Additionally, it can refer to discrimination in terms of the enforcement of environmental laws or in the appointment or election of citizens to positions that oversee community laws or regulations. Highly polluting industries, nuclear power stations, and waste storage or waste processing facilities are examples of activities that are located in poor, often minority locations.

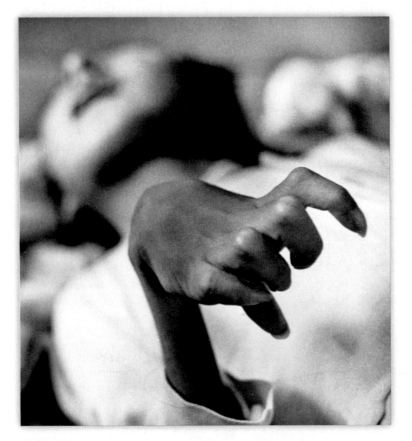

▲ **Figure 12J.1 Minamata Disease** Before the environmental justice movement, one of the best-known cases of industrial pollution was the widespread mercury poisoning of residents in Minamata, Japan. Between 1932 and 1968, the Chisso Corporation of Minamata, a chemical manufacturer, dumped methyl mercury into its wastewater, which then flowed into the local bays and contaminated seafood. Over time, residents were poisoned by the mercury, causing birth defects, muscle problems, weakness, and sight and hearing damage, a combination of symptoms that would come to be known as **Minamata disease**. While media coverage of Minamata disease began in the 1960s, it was a photo essay by famous American photographer W. Eugene Smith in the early 1970s that caught the attention of the world.

(a)

(b)

▲ **Figure 12J.2 Environmental Racism in Chester, Pennsylvania** One example of environmental racism can be seen in the case of (a) Chester, Pennsylvania, located about 25 kilometers south of Philadelphia. Housing discrimination, factory closures, and white flight combined to change this once-prosperous industrial town into a predominantly poor, African American community. In a county where the average black population is less than 10%, Chester is 60% to 70% African American.

During the 1980s and 1990s, the state of Pennsylvania issued five permits for waste processing facilities in Chester. In total, eight waste facilities, such as the trash incinerator shown here (b), are located within a half mile of each other. Because the city is poor and the residents relatively poorly educated, critics argue that the community was targeted because officials and companies felt that there would be less resistance to the siting of hazardous waste processing plants. In total, the waste plants process more than 2 million tons of waste a year, thousands of times the amount of waste processed anywhere else in the county. At first, residents were not prone to complain because the town needed jobs, but soon health problems emerged. By the mid-1990s, Chester had the highest child mortality rate in the state and a high rate of some types of cancerous tumors; 60% of children had high lead levels in their blood. Foul odors, noise, and dust were also common.

Chester residents began to fight back in the 1990s at public meetings, with protests, and in time with lawsuits. But activists found that the federal government was largely unwilling to help and that local politicians often supported the issuing of permits for more waste facilities. The public was required to be notified when waste facilities applied for permits, but small notices in newspapers are not as effective in poorer communities where literacy rates are often lower than average. In the late 1990s, residents were taking up legal action against the state and local companies, but these efforts have largely been unsuccessful, in part because of politics and the unwillingness of officials to go against businesses or powerful politicians who could deliver votes in a battleground state. Another problem is that many laws are very specific and do not take into account geographic factors. For example, each of the permits issued for waste facilities in Chester may have been legal and justified in terms of that one plant, but the laws and permitting processes often failed to consider that numerous other waste plants were already there. Because of this failure of the law, there can be a resulting geographic concentration of pollution-generating facilities. Today, the town continues to be a popular location for factories, and community organizers continue to fight for better environmental monitoring and health protections.

Key Terms

acid rain (12E)
air pollution (12E)
aquifer (12D)
cancer cluster (12G)
coastal pollution (12I)
cognitive factors (12B)
cultural ecology (12A)
cyclone (12C)
deforestation (12I)
earthquake (12C)
environment (12A)
environmental justice (12J)
environmental perception (12B)
environmental racism (12J)
fossil fuels (12H)
Gilbert White (12B)
hazardous waste (12G)
hurricane (12C)
landfills (12F)

Minamata disease (12J)
moment magnitude scale (12C)
natural hazards (12B)
NIMBY (12F)
nonstructural responses (12B)
recharge (12D)
Ring of Fire (12C)
situation factors (12B)
smog (12E)
solid waste (12F)
storm surges (12C)
structural responses (12B)
Superfund Program (12G)
tornados (12C)
toxic waste (12G)
tsunami (12C)
typhoon (12C)
water diversion (12D)
water pollution (12D)

Basic Review Questions

1. What is cultural ecology? What is behavioral geography?
2. What is environmental perception?
3. What is a natural hazard?
4. What was Gilbert White's primary contribution to geography?
5. How does cognitive dissonance relate to people-environment interactions?
6. What is the moment magnitude scale?
7. Where is the Ring of Fire located?
8. How are earthquakes and tsunami related?
9. How are hurricanes and storm surges related?
10. Where is Tornado Alley?
11. What happened to the Aral Sea?
12. Where is the Ogallala Aquifer?
13. What is acid rain?
14. What is classified as solid waste?
15. What qualifies as hazardous waste?
16. What does NIMBY stand for?
17. What is the purpose of the Superfund Program?
18. What is a fossil fuel, and where are most of them found?
19. What are the consequences of deforestation?
20. Define environmental justice.
21. What is environmental racism?

Advanced Review Questions (Essay Questions)

1. How were Sauer's ideas about landscape a break from environmental determinism?
2. How does environmental perception affect human-environment interaction?
3. Explain how cognitive and situation factors affect attitudes toward the environment.
4. What are the deadliest types of natural disasters in terms of human casualties? Is there a geographic pattern to certain types of disasters?
5. How is water use related to culture?
6. Discuss how human activities lead to air pollution. What are the worst types of human activities for the atmosphere? What are the effects of air pollution on human health?
7. How much garbage do Americans generate each year? Where does this end up, and what are the consequences?
8. Are Americans recycling more or less than in past decades? Explain. What factors have led to changes in recycling behavior?
9. Describe the major fossil fuel production areas in the world, as well as the location of major oil pipelines.
10. What models have been put forth to investigate the relationship between population growth and the environment?
11. What regions of the world have the greatest environmental problems? Does the developing world have the worst environmental problems?

Further Study Topics

- How is US foreign policy related to the locations of oil and oil pipelines? It was often said that the United States went to war in Iraq to protect strategic oil supplies. What does the evidence suggest to you?

- Is environmental pollution and other negative impacts a necessary result of development and industrialization?

- Is there evidence to support or refute the I = PAT model proposed by Ehrlich and Holdren?

- Is environmental justice an issue in the United States today? Was the response of BP and the US government to the 2010 Gulf of Mexico oil spill an example of environmental racism? What can governments do to prevent environmental racism?

- Do Americans have the right to criticize foreign countries for deforestation, given the US history of deforestation? As part of your research, investigate deforestation rates in the United States over the past century or more.

Summary Activities

On this blank map of the United States, indicate where you would find Tornado Alley and Dixie Alley. What causes the high number of tornados in these areas?

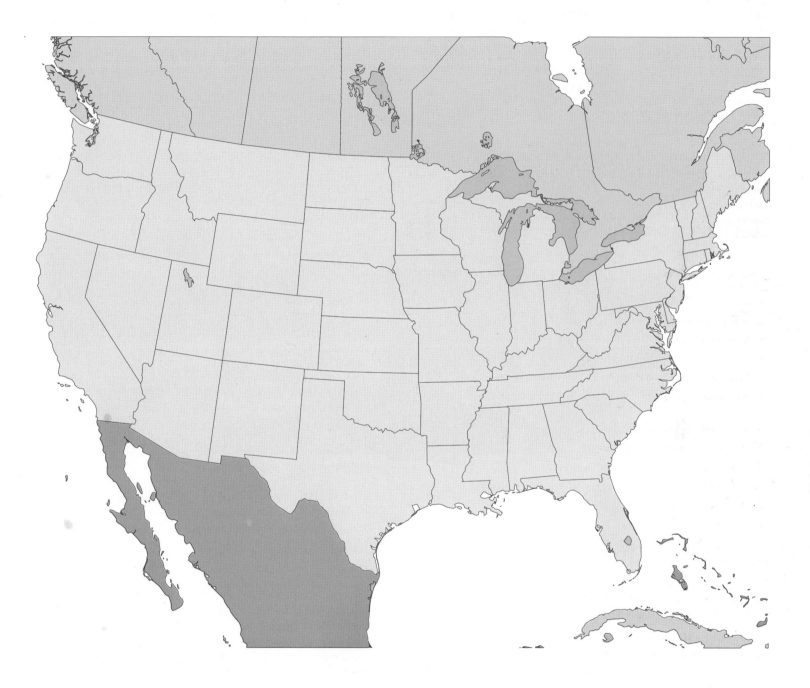

CHAPTER 13

Urbanization and Urban Networks

CHAPTER MODULES

We have now reached the point where half of humanity lives in cities. For most of you reading this book, this will not seem surprising. Westernized, economically developed countries became mostly urban long ago. A majority of people lived in British cities by 1850. Today in North America, Latin America, Europe, Japan, and Australia, about three out of four people live in cities or suburbs. Just as fewer people make their living from agriculture, as we discuss in Chapter 16, so fewer people live on farms or in the small towns that grew up to service farms. Cities make the most sense in an economy reliant on production and services. These jobs do not require abundant land but thrive instead on interaction and conglomeration. Cities also become more important as economies depend more on consumption. People enjoy being able to shop in a relatively contained area. They like the choices of restaurants and take-out places when they do not feel like cooking.

They like to have easy access to day care facilities, laundromats, repair shops, physicians and hospitals, lawyers, and accountants—all of the things that cities can provide. Companies, too, prefer the proximity to suppliers and to specialized services, like advertising, shipping, and commercial banks. Cities become indispensible in providing these in a smaller geographic space.

Still, large parts of the world are primarily rural. The bulk of people in Africa, South Asia, and Southeast Asia continue to work the land and to live in villages. But even these regions are experiencing tremendous rural-to-urban migration (see Module 5B) as cities become bigger and more numerous. As urbanization has spread, connections between cities have developed. The interactions of goods, money, and people are primarily urban-based, moving within a larger network of cities and creating an established urban hierarchy within countries and across the world.

13A Urban Beginnings

Up until a few thousand years ago, cities simply did not exist. Part of this was because cities were not economically practical. As we discuss in Module 15A, the prehistoric economy was based mainly on hunting and gathering. It relied on small groups of people, sometimes described as clans, who banded together to kill game and to gather useful plants. Hunting and gathering populations were itinerant, meaning that they followed their sources of food. Any settlements were temporary. Politically, clans operated in a fairly simple fashion with direct lines of authority from a head man or chief to the other members of the clan. Such a political system would not work at all in cities, with thousands of people to govern and regulate.

Table 13A.1	Ways to Distinguish Early Cities from Villages
Any discussion of early cities requires some type of definition, but this can be difficult to come up with. Geographers and other scholars have used various criteria.	
Population Size	While villages generally numbered under a thousand people, most cities had a population of thousands.
Population Density	Cities also included much higher densities, usually several thousand people per square mile, with the earliest cities having even higher densities.
Built Environment	Cities also contained many more impressive buildings, monuments, and streets than the countryside.
Centers	Once established, cities were important centers of economic, cultural, and political life, and this was reflected in these built structures.
Nonagricultural Population	Perhaps the most distinguishing feature is that, while cities sometimes contained a little bit of farmland, the vast majority of the city population was not engaged in farming. This meant that urban people needed to be fed by farmers in the countryside.
Occupational Specialization	All of these nonagricultural workers were involved in different types of trades and tasks, from metal workers to tanners to scribes. This was yet another hallmark of early cities and is a characteristic of modern cities as well.

The emergence of cities required complementary developments in both economic and political systems. The movement to an agricultural economy was a key component of this. When agriculture finally did get started—a process described in Module 15D—it set into motion a whole set of cultural changes that permanently altered the spatial and social organization of society.

First of all, agriculture required a settling down. **Settlements**, rather than being of temporary construction, were now built of more permanent materials. True villages could emerge near the farm fields. The land and the built community also represented a significant investment in labor and resources, so villagers were motivated to protect what was theirs.

Second, the overall density of population in agricultural areas increased substantially. The main advantage of agriculture over hunting and gathering is that agriculture allows people to obtain more food out of the same unit area of land. This density increased the number of people who came in close contact with each other. It probably led to more neighboring communities, especially in fertile areas. The chance for different populations of people to "rub shoulders" was therefore greatly increased.

Third, true food **surpluses** became possible, and they could be planned for, in some cases. This raised the issue of what to do with the food. Early domesticated species tended to be grains, because they provide a higher concentration of calories and they can be easily stored and transported. The storage of food allowed for distributions, trade, taxation—all of which would be much more difficult in an economy where food was consumed soon after it was hunted or gathered.

Fourth, the food supply was on a more regular **schedule**. Cycles of the day, of seasons, and of rain and drought became crucial. This brought intensified attempts to explain what was going on and to try to make the environment more favorable.

Fifth, agricultural development set into motion an even greater **division of labor**. This was particularly true in places where irrigation was required, since the construction of sluices, channels, and levees required coordinated efforts. People were given specific chores to do, with some prestige or value placed on certain tasks as opposed to others.

The leap from these agricultural villages to true cities required a far more complex political organization. This was essential in order to govern a larger, more differentiated population. Furthermore, some source of recognized authority was needed to distribute food to city-dwellers and to procure it from the surrounding farmers. Such redistribution may have been accomplished by trade, taxation, tribute, or a combination of all three. This also relates to the city's role as a center of political, economic, and cultural power. The development of cities was bound up with the development of more complex political forms—what is described in Module 10A as a state. The people in charge of these states almost always resided within the cities, and most of the political leaders were spiritual guides as well, pointing to the connection between religion and the growth of an elite.

▼ **Figure 13A.1**

Although agriculture was a precondition to city development, there was an enormous gap in time from the first agricultural settlements (9000 BC) to the first cities (4750 BC). However, it is interesting that, just as agriculture developed in several independent hearths (see Module 15D), so did cities. Most agree that "true" cities first showed up in Sumeria about 4750 BC.

There is distinct evidence for important cities in southern Mexico about AD 0.

Cities likely diffused from Sumeria to Egypt.

Cities later appeared in China, likely independently of Sumerian cities.

Cities likely diffused to the Indus valley in present day Pakistan.

All of these cities show evidence of a powerful ruling class with a theocratic orientation, literacy, and an advanced means of distributing the surplus and, with the exception of Meso-America, show substantial evidence of irrigation works.

13B Early Spread of Urbanism

The earliest cities emerged first in Sumeria, and then independently in northern China and Meso-America. Other hearths, such as the Indus valley and Egypt, could have emerged independently or as a process of diffusion from the Sumerian cities. While very different in appearance and culture, all of these ancient cities emphasized religion (see Module 6E).

Once established, the idea of the city diffused to other areas. In ancient times, cities needed to obtain food for their populations. Some ancient cities relied largely on trade, but most were situated in the midst of fertile environments, where sustained agricultural surplus was likely. The area surrounding a city from which it obtains its food is called the **hinterland**, and the range and fertility of the hinterland largely determines the size of the city.

▲ **Figure 13B.1** Iron allowed for better axes to clear more trees off more land, as well as better plows for digging up firmer, but more fertile, fields. This increased the amount of land that was usable and the amount of surplus food that could be extracted. The ancient Chinese were the first to develop iron moldboard plows, in the fourth century BC.

At first, cities were found only in river valleys with light, easily worked soil. Later, technological developments expanded the environments where cities could thrive and grow. Most important of these would be the transition from bronze (copper alloy) to iron beginning in 1000 BC.

All cities are constrained by transportation. Access to food sources, resources, and other cities is of critical importance, and transportation enables such access. This is one reason that cities are so often located on water bodies, since they have traditionally allowed easier and cheaper transportation access by boat. Cities began in places with good access, but transit improvements allowed cities to interact with a broader area. Iron allowed for better wheels for carts and for faster ships. In addition, cities began to initiate the development of road networks and sea lanes for easier travel and access to resources. All of these advances meant that cities could get bigger, since they could rely on a larger hinterland. These transportation routes also opened up new lands for the diffusion of new cities.

A final factor in the further development of a more urban world lay in the expansion of states. The earliest cities were likely in city-states (see Module 10B), composed of the city and its hinterland. But rulers aspire to bigger things, and many induced their followers to conquer other cities, or areas that were completely unurbanized. The urban-based societies then brought more territory under centralized control. Gradually, smaller city-states evolved into larger **territorial states**, which managed a number of cities and extended far beyond the hinterland of a single city. These states also helped establish cities in places that had none, as a means of extracting surplus from area farmers.

Eventually, the expansion of political states led to the emergence of large, stable empires in the ancient world. The most notable in the classical period were the Roman Empire in the Mediterranean and the Han Empire in China. There

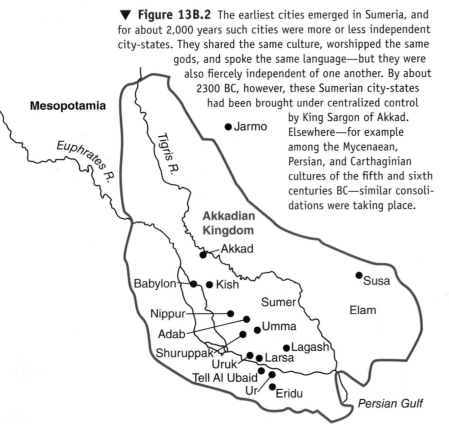

▼ **Figure 13B.2** The earliest cities emerged in Sumeria, and for about 2,000 years such cities were more or less independent city-states. They shared the same culture, worshipped the same gods, and spoke the same language—but they were also fiercely independent of one another. By about 2300 BC, however, these Sumerian city-states had been brought under centralized control by King Sargon of Akkad. Elsewhere—for example among the Mycenaean, Persian, and Carthaginian cultures of the fifth and sixth centuries BC—similar consolidations were taking place.

Imperial Park

Imperial Park

Ch'ung-hsuan Gate

Daming Palace

Imperial City

Ch'eng-tien Gate

Hsing-Ch'ing Palace

Administrative City

West Market

Ch'un ming Gate

East Market

Yen-hsing Gate

Ming-te Gate

Hibiscus Gardens

Chu-chiang Lake

0   1   2 kilometers

Chang'An City

o Taoist monasteries
□ Buddhist monasteries
⚓ Other churches
▭ Walled quarter
▬ Walls

◀ **Figure 13B.3** The Chinese civilization is notable for its continuity, punctuated by a series of dynasties, and for its large population and territory. The various capitals of China achieved a size and splendor that surpassed everywhere else in the world. This map of Chang'An shows a city developed as a rectangle oriented to the north, with regularly spaced streets. The imperial palace along the northern quadrant adjoins the imperial park. During the T'Ang dynasty, the city included several large marketplaces, numerous temples, and monasteries of many different faiths.

were several other empires that waxed and waned, including ancient India, the Sassanian Empire of Persia, and the Axum Kingdom in Ethiopia.

Within these large empires, urban development was transformed in two major ways. First, the imperial capitals attained a truly heroic size. Rome is estimated to have reached a million people by AD 150. Chang'An, which was the capital of several Chinese dynasties, was called a million people's city by AD 750. Baghdad, as the capital of the Islamic Caliphate, would grow past 1 million people as well.

The second important consequence of these large empires was that they functioned as major engines of urban development. All empires were subdivided into provinces, and each province was governed from a capital. Further political subdivisions led to even greater elaboration of towns and cities. Beyond politics, some cities could emerge for economic reasons, such as trade or access to a major resource, or as centers for churches or universities.

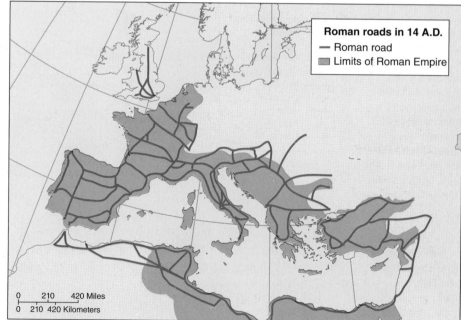

Roman roads in 14 A.D.
— Roman road
▨ Limits of Roman Empire

0   210   420 Miles
0   210 420 Kilometers

▲ **Figure 13B.4** In the Roman Empire, the establishment of cities was a means of securing Roman territory. The idea was that colonial cities would be attractive to Roman citizens because even rural Romans considered themselves to be "urban" people. And the establishment of cities also effectively projected Roman power and grandeur. All cities and towns were linked to Rome by roads, aiding in the development of commerce and making it easier for government and military officials to get around. These cities were also important because they allowed for the efficient collection of taxes.

13C Urbanization in an Era of Capitalism

Urbanization refers to the increase in the percentage of people who live within cities. Eventually, the number of people living in cities outstrips the number of people living in rural areas. The population goes from being mostly rural to being mostly urban. You should not confuse this with urban growth or city size. Some societies can see a tremendous expansion in some of their largest cities, but they are not truly urbanizing. Despite the presence of some truly great cities in the past, up until 200 years ago, the mass of humanity continued to live in the countryside. Cities generally contained society's elite, the people needed to support the elite, and a relatively small number of merchants, artisans, and tradespeople. Great cities were primarily political capitals—centers of governments, large and small. By and large, the population within these cities was supported through taxation and tribute from the much larger numbers of farmers in the countryside. In a number of cases, elite residents of cities also owned huge swaths of land in the countryside.

Another concept you should keep in mind is that of **situation**, as discussed in Module 1C. As cities evolved, the logic of their situation changed. The original cities were surrounded by a smaller hinterland. The ability to transport surplus from the farms in the hinterland to the residents of the city was key. Imperial cities were interested in political control of their empires. The best location for an imperial city was where such control could be more easily exercised. Empires expended a lot of time, money, and manpower to control sea lanes, build canals, and develop road networks to facilitate this control.

The nature of urbanization changed with the introduction of a capitalist economy (see Module 15B). In Europe, a type of urban settlement emerged that was different from anything else that had existed before. Of most significance is that these new towns relied more on the activities of merchants and artisans than on

Figure 13C.1 ▶

After the fall of the Roman Empire, shown by the series of invasions on this map, there simply was no economic basis for the continued existence of large Roman cities. The entire basis for civilization was swept away. Isolated communities lived on far-flung estates ruled by German tribesmen separated by tracts of wilderness. Rome itself lost 80% of its population in the first century and, by AD 1000, had only 35,000 people remaining. But at least Rome continued as the center of the Roman Catholic Church and retained some urban functions. Other cities, which depended on the Roman Empire for their economy, declined even more precipitously.

Source: From Dennis Sherman and Joyce Salisbury, *The West in the World, Third Edition*, © 2008 by The McGraw-Hill Companies, Inc., page 179. Used by permission.

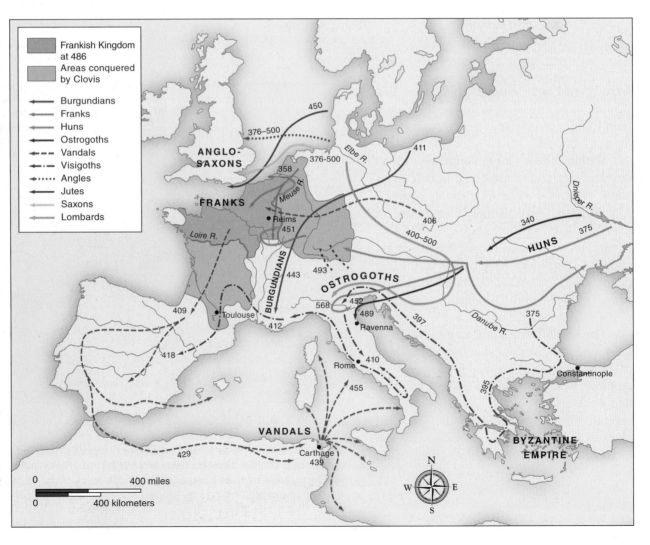

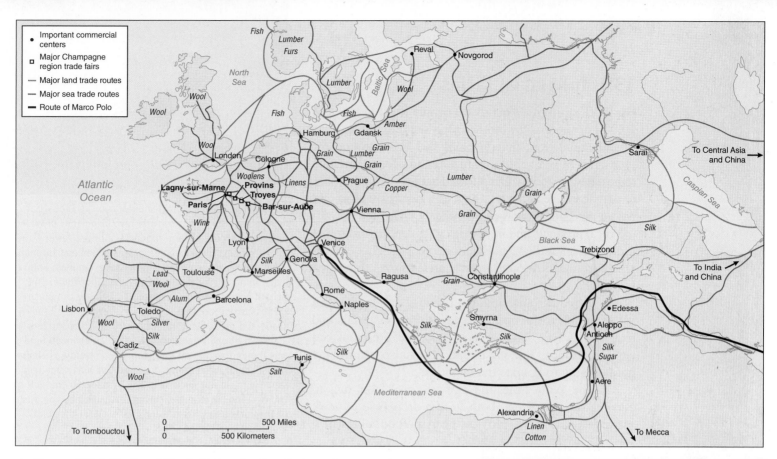

▲ **Figure 13C.2 Medieval Trade Networks** Two distinct urban networks emerged in Europe beginning around AD 1100. In the north, along the Baltic and North Seas, there was a group of trading towns. Many of these were part of the Hanseatic League and were involved in trade in bulk goods: fur, wool, beer, herring, and salt. In southern Europe, there was a collection of towns anchored by Venice and Genova. These cities were involved in a larger Mediterranean trade and were predominantly involved in luxury goods.

▲ **Figure 13C.3** Many of the emerging marketplaces witnessed the exchange of bulk products, such as wine.

any political leaders. This reliance on commerce altered the situation of new capitalist cities. In the new cities, economic integration took place in an era of fragmented political strength. Economic activity no longer required political power centralized in a leader or a strong central government. Access to raw and agricultural materials, markets, and the trading routes between goods and markets was the most important consideration and changed the logic of urban location. These new cities needed to be at the nexus of economic exchange.

These newer capitalist cities were significant primarily because of the way they helped form distinct urban networks. **Urban network** is a term that comes up repeatedly in discussions of urbanization. It refers to cities that are tied together in some meaningful way, what geographers and other urban researchers may describe as **functional linkages**. These ties were historically political and administrative, as particular cities operated as capitals for subunits within a kingdom or a state. Yet under this new capitalist system, the linkages between cities were based on trade, and the cities themselves were located along key trading routes. The growth of trade requires more specialization, and the economic connections between cities only grew with time. Merchants from one city, for instance, would foster business relationships with suppliers and distributors in other cities. The Hanseatic League was a good example of how these economic relationships could be formalized, providing safe harbor for out-of-town merchants, a basis for standardization, and other features that could ease the conduct of trade. Later, bankers in cities such as Genova would help underwrite merchant and artisan activities in cities throughout Europe. Late Medieval capitalist cities often hosted "visitors" from different places, who inhabited distinct neighborhoods, a precursor to later ethnic divisions within cities (see Module 9C).

13D Industrial Cities

By 1800, still only 1 out of 40 people lived in cities of 20,000 or more. This did not represent any large-scale urbanization, even though cities had been around for thousands of years. For urbanization to occur, there had to be a new economy that allowed a much larger number of people to live and work in cities. Capitalism alone did not do this, since it was still primarily interested in trading rural products and in small-scale manufacturing that did not employ large numbers of people. This change was introduced through industrialization, as described in Module 16A.

With industrialization, the urban situation changed yet again. Factories needed access to raw materials and markets, as had been the case with the pre-industrial capitalist cities. But industrialization also required a pool of labor to operate the factories.

At the same time, the agricultural sector had to become more efficient, both to free up people to work in the factories and to provide the extra food for the new

▲ **Figure 13D.1** Complementary to the Industrial Revolution was an agricultural revolution that provided a greater surplus of farm products, allowed fewer farmers to support more people, increased demand for manufactured goods among wealthier farm families, and made unnecessary much of the rural labor force. The British enclosure acts, as depicted here by the placement of stone walls, had a major effect on the landscape and on agricultural productivity. They shifted a system of open fields to one in which common land was divided among all local farmers, creating a familiar landscape of walls and hedgerows. But many smaller farmers could not make it in this system. So the pull of the new industrial cities was accompanied by the push of the rural areas. As these cities swelled, the rural areas lost population.

Figure 13D.2 ▶
Industrialization allowed some cities to become enormous, allowing them to meet and surpass the sizes of the greatest ancient cities. By 1850, London had a population of 2.5 million and Paris contained 1 million. By 1900, there were eight cities with populations over 1 million, topped by London with 6.5 million. This chart shows how industrialization affected the growth of several British cities during the 19th century. Note how the city of Bath, which was not a part of the industrial belt, barely grew at all during this period.

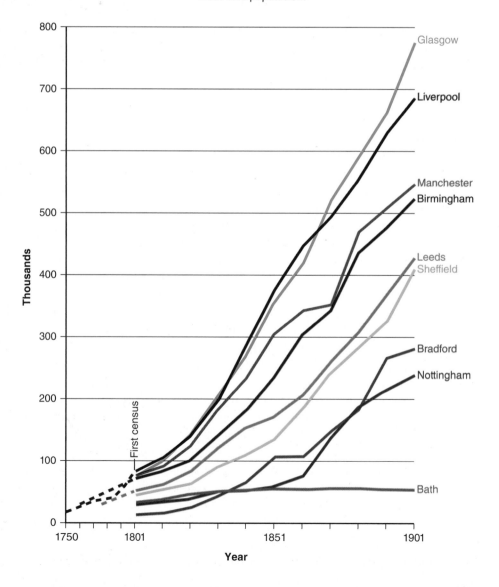

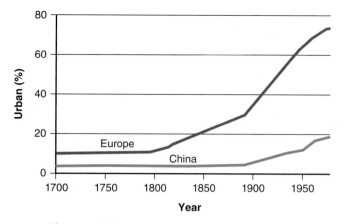

▲ **Figure 13D.3** Urbanization in nineteenth-century Europe was tremendous. While population doubled, urban population grew sixfold. Great Britain was the first society to become urbanized, owing to its leadership in the new industrial economy. England was 20% urban in 1800, 40% in 1850, and over 60% in 1890. The United States did not become a majority urban society until the 1920s.

urbanites. Moreover, the factories required easy access to fuel and sources of running water to operate the steam engines and for waste disposal.

With better transportation, cities got food from wider and wider areas. London got its staples from anywhere in the world: rice from India, wheat and beef from the United States and Canada. The sorts of raw materials needed for industrial goods could be obtained from around the globe. Products from North America, South America, and Asia found their way into British factories. The American South had become the major supplier of cotton by the mid-nineteenth century.

Industrialization had four major effects. First, it allowed some cities to get enormous, far larger than cities had ever grown. Second, it enabled the proliferation of cities, so more people could live in cities. Third, it led to more concentrated settlement patterns. And fourth, it altered the logic of urban location.

Figure 13D.5 ▶ The logic of location shifted with industrialization. Early factories consumed a great deal of coal, and because coal was a bulky commodity, many of these early factories were located near or on coalfields, such as this coalfield in Pennsylvania. And towns grew around these factories, so there was much urban growth in coal-rich areas. In addition, some cities benefited by being at the center of industrial trade. London, though not located on a coalfield, benefited because it was the commercial center for Great Britain. Many smaller industries and services that emerged as a consequence of the Industrial Revolution—industries such as food processing and refining, leatherworks, boot and shoe making, clocks and jewelry, and trading and banking service—also concentrated there. This, combined with the concentration of people, led to a massive redistribution of population in Britain. Later, every other country that industrialized would experience similar transfers in population.

▲ **Figure 13D.4** The factory system required a **concentration of labor** in one place. For this to occur, there had to emerge some form of **mass production** (see Module 16A). This favored concentrated settlement in a few places. Mass production of a particular good in a factory replaced the small-scale production in workshops scattered over several locations. The factory owners sought to erect cheap, concentrated housing for workers, like these buildings constructed in Glasgow in the 1840s. These tenements housed 40,000 people, with up to 8 people in a room and 30 residents to a toilet.

13E The Urbanization Curve

As we noted in Module 13C, urbanization is the process in which a larger percentage of people in a society come to live in cities. This is different from plain urban growth, which can occur if the growth in the rural population keeps pace with growth in the urban population. While cities were long the defining feature of most civilizations, the vast majority of the population continued to live in the countryside. Moreover, even when a society's population increased, often due to greater food production, this did not signify a general shift in population from rural to urban.

The **urbanization curve** is a way to describe the process by which a society becomes more urban. This curve is a general model of change based on time. There is no single year when the urbanization curve begins, since every society goes through each of these stages at different times. However, before 1800 all societies, from the most to the least economically advanced, were at the initial stage of urbanization.

The general shape of the model resembles the letter *S*. This indicates that most of the urbanization takes place in a short period of time during the acceleration stage. One of the reasons this curve is shaped this way is because of the nature of economic change. Foremost is the change from an agricultural society with little or no industry—much like Europe before 1800. Then the onset of industrialization opened up an entire urban economy and a market for urban products. That explains the intensity of acceleration. Usually, the acceleration stage does not take a very long time. In Great Britain, urbanization occurred primarily in the nineteenth century. It occurred in the United States a bit later. Despite early industrialization and the growth of industrial cities such as Lowell, Massachusetts, in the 1820s and 1830s, rapid urban development did not really take place until after the Civil War.

▼ **Figure 13E.1**

The next stage of urbanization is the saturation level. In this stage, the urban population no longer has any reason to grow. The society is primarily urban already and, since there is always a need for some percentage of rural and small-town population, it is difficult to conceive of a society where virtually everybody lives in cities. In contrast to the acceleration stage, where the bulk of migration is from rural to urban areas, in the saturation stage most migration is from urban metropolitan areas to other urban metropolitan areas.

Once conditions for urbanization are met, and a country becomes more industrialized, urbanization accelerates. As industry takes off in the cities, agriculture becomes more efficient, and more labor is available to work within the cities. In addition, a general current of modernization makes cities much more desirable places for people to live. In this period, the urban population increases to well over 50% of a state's total population, finally achieving about 70% or more urban population.

It is possible to consider a counterurbanization stage as people move out of metro areas into small towns and the countryside. This has not happened anywhere yet. But there have been a few glimmers suggesting a possibility. Nearly three out of four rural counties gained population in the 1990s, and fewer rural people left for the cities. However, this represented a slow-down of urbanization, not a reversal, since the overall US population grew by about 13%. Still, large numbers of Americans continue to insist that they prefer country living. In the future, perhaps economic conditions and the ability to act on these preferences will make counterurbanization a reality.

Initially, the population is dispersed, agricultural, and rural. Even within the most urbanized regions of the world, less than one-fifth of the population resides in cities, which were centers of administration, and later trade. This stage occurred the world over before industrialization. Prior to World War II, most countries in Africa and Asia (except Japan) were also at this stage.

Y-axis: Urban (%) — 0, 50, 100
X-axis: Time

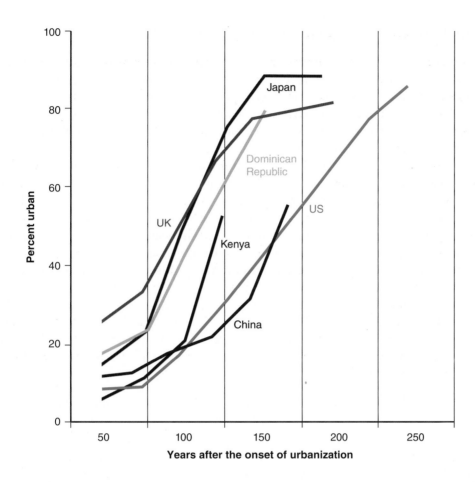

▲ **Figure 13E.2** Different countries go through the urbanization process at different times. Here the experience of a few countries is considered, comparing different time periods, but at 50-year intervals. In the United Kingdom (UK), urbanization occurred early once in the nineteenth century. The percentage of urbanization in the UK continued to climb throughout the 1800s until the UK became the first truly urban country in around 1860. In the US, the percentage of urban population doubled between 1860 and 1900. At this point in time, large-scale industries took off and began to employ a substantial number of people. Due to the multiplier effect (see Module 16D), each industrial job spurred even more jobs in the factories and in the service sector. By 1920, just over half the population lived in cities. For Japan, the urbanization occurred very rapidly in the twentieth century as Japan sought to modernize quickly and efficiently. Developing countries in Latin America, such as the Dominican Republic, urbanized after World War II but did so quite rapidly; now their urban percentage equals that of the developed world. Kenya has taken off more recently, along with much of sub-Saharan Africa. China, among the world's first urban civilizations, is urbanizing steadily but continues to hold a massive rural population.

In an era of Internet communication, global outsourcing, Amazon.com, and the fact that most jobs involve computers, are cities still indispensable? That question cannot be answered just yet, though experts have come up with diverging forecasts. All we know is that the global trend continues to be for people to move from the countryside to the city. Cities continue to attract people because they appear to provide the economic opportunities that cannot be matched in the countryside or in small towns. There is no counter-trend of people moving the other way. Suburbanization (see Module 14D) is not a movement out of cities but, instead, is an expansion of existing cities—a trend as old as cities themselves. So far, the overall number of people and the percentage of people living in cities continue to increase in every society, although certainly the urbanization trends are much sharper in less developed societies.

13F Urbanization Patterns around the World

While the world as a whole has reached a point where over half of the population live in cities, there continue to be wide variations in urbanization among different countries. Broadly speaking, those countries considered to be economically developed (more developed countries) are at the saturation stage of the urbanization curve and have at least 70% of their population living in cities. Those countries that are still developing economically (less developed countries) have a lower proportion of their population living in cities.

Most of these less developed countries are at the acceleration stage of the urbanization curve. This means that they are experiencing tremendous rural-to-urban migration (see Module 5B). This along with high rates of population growth (see Module 3G), can create explosive urban growth. Cities that had populations of a few hundred thousand people 30 years ago have doubled, redoubled, and redoubled again to become huge megacities of 5 to 10 million.

Urbanization generally corresponds with economic development. This is not surprising when one considers that wealthier countries usually enjoy a more dynamic economy and are more likely to undergo structural transformations that spur rural-to-urban migration. But there are a number of local peculiarities.

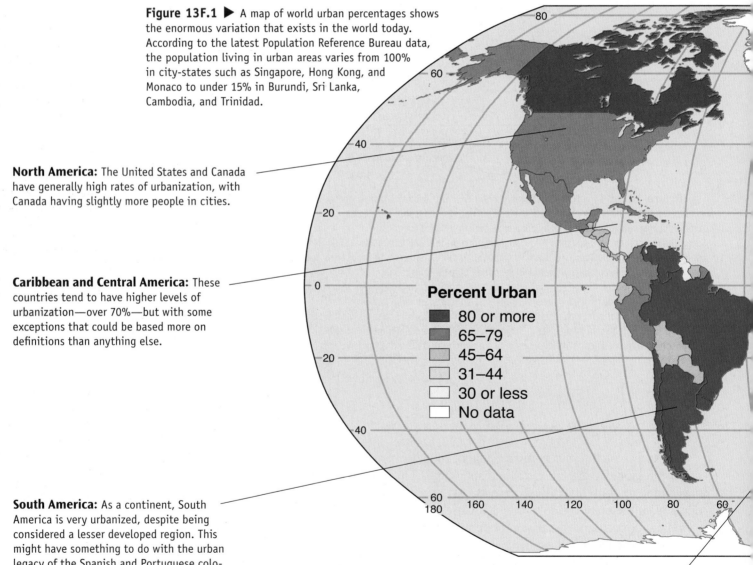

Figure 13F.1 ▶ A map of world urban percentages shows the enormous variation that exists in the world today. According to the latest Population Reference Bureau data, the population living in urban areas varies from 100% in city-states such as Singapore, Hong Kong, and Monaco to under 15% in Burundi, Sri Lanka, Cambodia, and Trinidad.

North America: The United States and Canada have generally high rates of urbanization, with Canada having slightly more people in cities.

Caribbean and Central America: These countries tend to have higher levels of urbanization—over 70%—but with some exceptions that could be based more on definitions than anything else.

Percent Urban
- ■ 80 or more
- ■ 65–79
- ▨ 45–64
- ▨ 31–44
- □ 30 or less
- □ No data

South America: As a continent, South America is very urbanized, despite being considered a lesser developed region. This might have something to do with the urban legacy of the Spanish and Portuguese colonies. Argentina and Uruguay have over 90% urban population.

Sub-Saharan Africa: There are many exceptions, but sub-Saharan Africa is the second least urbanized region in the world. Most countries have fewer than half of the population in cities, several with under 25%. Not surprisingly, the more economically advanced country of South Africa is the most urbanized large country in the region.

Some giant countries, such as India, have a lower urban percentage than economic progress would dictate. At the same time, several Latin American countries sport very high urban percentages, despite lagging in economic development when compared to North America and Western Europe.

It is important to remember that urbanization is different from population density. Some of the densest countries in the world have surprisingly high rural percentages. Bangladesh and even the Netherlands exemplify this. By contrast, sparsely settled countries, such as Canada and Libya, have fairly high urban percentages.

Western Europe: As the first region in the world to urbanize, Western Europe continues to be the most highly urbanized part of the world. At the same time, there are some surprises. The Netherlands, despite its high population density, contains a large rural proportion. So do Switzerland, Ireland, Finland, and Austria.

East Asia: Japan and South Korea are highly urbanized developed countries. China, which has the lion's share of the population, used to be massively rural. But rapid economic growth and the freedom to move have altered the equation. Today, China is close to having an urban majority.

South Asia: The demographic giant India contains some of the world's largest cities—Kolkata, Mumbai, and Delhi—but the vast majority of its population lives in rural villages. Other countries are similar. In fact, no country in this least urbanized region contains a majority urban population, despite very high population densities throughout. Bangladesh, for instance, is only 24% urban but has a population density of over 1,600 people per square mile.

Southeast Asia: Outside of the all-urban Singapore, this region is still primarily rural. Indochinese countries are less than 30% urban. Even Thailand and Indonesia, despite sporting enormous cities, are still primarily rural.

Oceania: The countries of Oceania vary widely, from the highly urbanized countries of Australia and New Zealand to many of the island countries with very small urban populations.

Middle East: By and large, the Middle East and North Africa are highly urbanized. There are several exceptions, however. Egypt still has less than half of its population living in cities. Syria and some of the Caucasus states also have fairly low urban percentages. Many of the Gulf States are over 90% urban, as is Israel.

Eastern Europe: This region is slightly less urbanized than Western Europe, but only Moldova has more rural than urban residents. Several of these urban populations, notably Russia, are actually declining in absolute terms as the population in general declines.

20   0   20   40   60   80   100   120   140   160   60
                                                   180

13G Agglomeration Economies and Urban Functions

With the advent of industrial cities, **agglomeration economies** became more significant. In agglomeration economies, different economic activities tend to locate next to each other and act as a powerful magnet, attracting other activities. These include different kinds of factories, infrastructure, and services. Markets might also be included in this. (Agglomeration economies are described in Module 16E in relation to industrial location, but help to explain why cities grew in densely packed networks.)

The cities that emerged contained many of the ingredients needed for modern industrial production. They often included suppliers that provided essential materials, good transportation facilities (such as harbors and railroad terminals), easy access to financial services in order to obtain credit, and other producer services (such as printing shops and advertising). These cities also became major markets. So many people and other industries located in one area that it was possible to sell products only to them. This seriously complicated the relationship between a city and its hinterland.

The linkages between **urban functions** within a city were complemented by the expanding connections between cities. An interurban network developed, in which cities took on specialized functions. These areas were generally the wealthiest and most integrated regions—and they were structured largely along transportation routes. The creation of an American Manufacturing Belt (see Module 16C) was a clear result of this. Not only were cities clustered together to facilitate manufacturing, but clear districts were defined.

The development of a modern urban economy has also spearheaded the specialization of cities today. Of course, cities are involved in many functions. They all serve as marketplaces, as manufacturing locales, as places of recreation and entertainment, and as administrative centers. However, one or two of these functions are more heavily promoted in some cities than in others. In the United States, some of this specialization is well known. We are all aware that Los Angeles is the center of the film and television industry, that Las Vegas depends heavily on tourism and conventions, and that Boston includes a disproportionate number of colleges and universities. These specializations, while not absolute, help distinguish cities from each other and contribute to a complementary urban network.

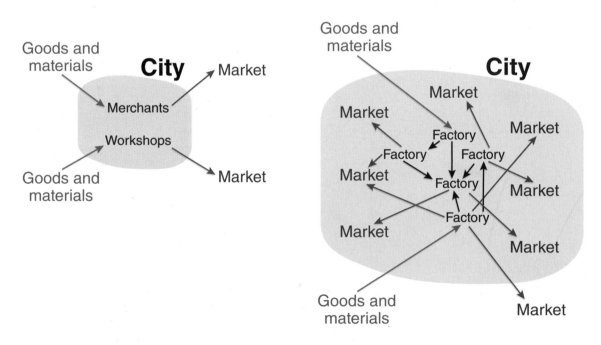

▲ **Figure 13G.1** Before industrialization, the city had been involved only in the exchange and distribution of materials from outside the city, with the lion's share of the market also located outside of the city. But with agglomeration economies, it was possible for a factory to get many of its inputs from other factories in the city itself (or from other nearby cities), and much of its market was located within the city. The old rural hinterland remained as the original source of materials and as a part of the overall market, but the industrial city was much farther removed from its rural base than it had ever been before.

Table 13G.1 Functional Concentrations of US Cities

This table shows some of the major US cities classified according to their dominant economic function. Cities serve many functions but are often distinguished by a few industries. The major categories in the table are Food Processing, Motion Picture and Sound, Accommodations, Arts, Entertainment, and Recreation, Beverage and Tobacco, Primary Metal, Textiles, Computer, and Finance and Insurance. Within these broader categories there are, of course, many specializations. These help point out areas of potential strength and vulnerability. Detroit, Michigan, continues to serve as a manufacturing center—with an economy based on the production of automobiles. Recent difficulties in the US auto industry, particularly the bankruptcies of Chrysler and General Motors, have had a profound influence on Detroit's regional economy. Washington, DC, as the country's preeminent administrative center, has benefited tremendously from the expansion of the federal government during the most recent recession.

Food Processing	Motion Picture and Sound	Accommodations	Arts, Entertainment, and Recreation
Chattanooga	Los Angeles	Honolulu	Cape Coral
Fayetteville	Nashville	Las Vegas	Orlando
Fresno	New York	Reno	Riverside
Harrisburg		Sacramento	Salt Lake City
Lancaster		San Diego	
Omaha		Virginia Beach	

Beverage and Tobacco	Primary Metal	Textiles	Computer	Finance and Insurance
Birmingham	Birmingham	Charleston	Albuquerque	Bridgeport
Charlotte	Charleston	Charlotte	Austin	Charlotte
Des Moines	Chattanooga	Chattanooga	Boise City	Cincinnati
Fresno	Chicago	Columbia	Boston	Columbus
Greensboro	Cleveland	Durham	Colorado Springs	Des Moines
Jacksonville	Fort Wayne	Greensboro	Durham	Hartford
Oklahoma City	Lancaster	Greenville	Fort Wayne	Jacksonville
Richmond	Milwaukee	Providence	Lexington	Madison
Syracuse	New Haven	Richmond	Milwaukee	New York
Winston	Pittsburgh	Scranton	Minneapolis	Omaha
	Portland OR	Winston	Oxnard	Philadelphia
	Syracuse	Worcester	Phoenix	Richmond
	Tulsa		Portland OR	Tampa
	Youngstown		Poughkeepsie	
			San Diego	
			San Jose	
			Winston	

Figure 13G.2 ▶ These functional specializations have a great bearing on the overall economic fortunes of particular cities. They also are subject to change—often with the foresight and targeted investment of city leaders. Akron, Ohio, was at one point the rubber and tire capital of the world. Nearly all of the major tire manufacturers—Goodyear, Goodrich, Firestone, and General—were located there. Over time, many of the headquarters and production functions for tire manufacturing left Akron (although Goodyear Tire still remains). Now the city has attempted to shift its focus to polymers.

13H Urban Hierarchies and the Rank-Size Relationship

Within an urban network, there also exists a particular kind of **urban hierarchy**. This reflects the idea that cities are rarely equal in size and importance to each other. Most are comparatively small within a system, while a few are much larger. In imperial urban systems, the size and importance of a city reflected its administrative position. Provincial capitals were larger and more important than district capitals, and the imperial capital was the largest city by far. Within an urban system regulated more by economics, this does not apply. Capitals can be large and important cities, but not always, and if they are, it is due to additional economic functions.

One relationship that seems to typify the overall urban hierarchy within a country is the **rank-size relationship**. A relatively even distribution of cities is determined by a very simple formula:

$$\text{Population of City}_r = \frac{\text{Population of City}_1}{r}$$

What this means is that the population of the second largest city in an urban system is equal to the largest city divided by 2. The third largest city is equal to the largest city divided by 3. The fourth largest city is one-fourth the size of the largest city and so on.

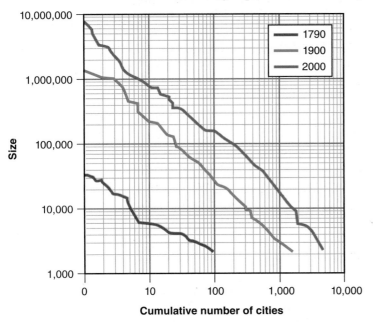

▲ **Figure 13H.1** This general city size distribution has persisted for most of US history, with individual cities moving up or down in rank. For population distributions from about 1850 to 1980, the same basic relationship applies. However, Los Angeles was virtually nonexistent in 1850; now it is second. Other cities that had a much higher rank in 1850, such as Boston and Charleston, now have a lower rank.

Figure 13H.2 ▶ In France, Paris has a city population of about 2.5 million; the next largest city, Marseilles, has a population of only about 800,000. An analysis of metro areas would yield an even greater difference. This gap has more than just demographic significance. Paris exerts an extraordinary influence on France, including politics, culture and economy. This map shows another manifestation of this influence—the number of university students in each city. Paris far surpasses any other city. Paris is also home to the Grand Écoles, very competitive institutions, which help train the French elite.

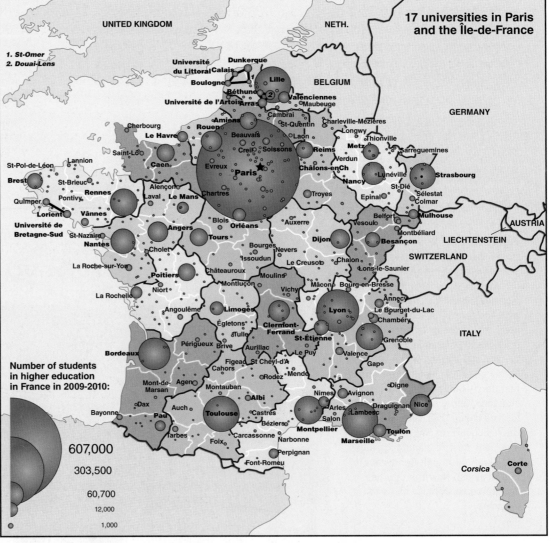

While the United States has a relatively even rank-size relationship, certain countries are more skewed. In these cases, the largest city is much greater than the second largest. This is what we call a **primate city**. A primate city overwhelms the rest of the country in terms of population, as well as cultural and economic importance.

What are the factors creating primate cities? One type of primate city results because of its former position as the capital of a much larger empire. In this case, the city grew to administer many more people and functions. When the empire was truncated, as has been true of many European countries, the capital city continued to have a disproportionate size.

The second type of primate city reflects uneven development among regions of a country. In a much less developed economy, many of the resources are swallowed up by the primate city. This also causes many of these cities to grow at a tremendous rate, overwhelming them with a population that is growing much faster than employment or services can. In such cases, the government may try to redirect population away from the primate city and toward secondary urban centers.

Some countries also have **binary** or **trinary rank-size distributions**, in which the top two or three cities overwhelm the rest. In Canada, Toronto numbers about 5.5 million and Montreal is close to 4 million, while Vancouver totals 2.5 million (but it is catching up). This is because Canada is not well integrated—perhaps reflecting a political and economic division between English and French Canada. Other political and economic divisions within a country may be demonstrated in that country's city size distribution.

Studying rank-size distributions has a significance beyond just how the cities are arrayed. It tells you something about the extent to which a country is economically and politically integrated, a little about its past, and a lot about the problems it may have in the future.

Table 13H.1 Populations of the Largest US Metropolitan Areas

Let's use the rank-size formula for the United States using metropolitan areas. This does not work out perfectly. US cities tend to be a bit more bunched up and closer in size to the largest city, New York. Still, it is pretty regular. An even distribution indicates a well-developed urban structure and reflects the huge size of the country.

	1980	1990	2000	2007	Rank
New York	16.5	16.8	18.7	18.8	1.0
Los Angeles	10.9	13.5	14.7	12.9	1.5
Chicago	7.3	7.4	8.4	9.5	2.0
Dallas/Fort Worth	2.7	3.3	4.4	6.1	3.1
Philadelphia	4.8	5.0	5.4	5.8	3.2
Houston	2.8	3.1	4.1	5.6	3.4
Miami	2.6	3.9	4.9	5.4	3.5

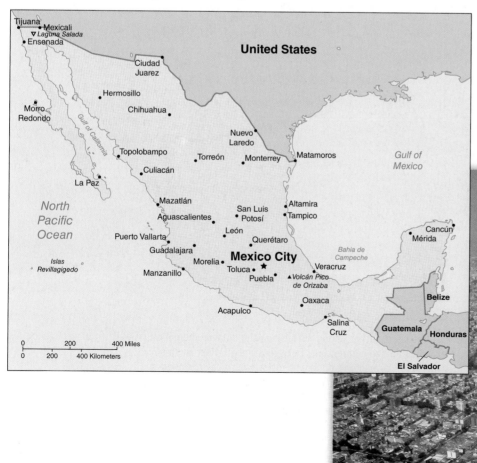

◀ **Figure 13H.3** Less developed countries that are less well integrated can demonstrate some great disparities in city size. Mexico City, for example, contains 15 million people; the next largest city, Guadalajara, contains only 2.5 million—about one-sixth of Mexico City's population. Montevideo is 10 times greater than the second largest city in Uruguay. In fact, the largest cities in Latin America often contain over a quarter of the population of their entire country.

13I Globalization and World Cities

Just as we can discuss the presence of urban hierarchies within a society, we can also examine a system of cities across the world. **Globalization** is an ever greater integration of people, companies, and governments across the world (see Module 16F). This is also true of cities and urban economies.

Not too far in the past, there was no such thing as a world system of cities. Cities operated within separate political, and later economic, spheres. Their size and function were dictated by the needs of their country, kingdom, empire, or whatever political unit contained them. The development and vitality of Kyoto had nothing to do with events in Chang'An, Rome, or Tenochtitlan. Within an empire, of course, urban networks and hierarchies developed. The conquest of the Americas set up a network of colonial capitals subservient to the main European capital. Santo Domingo, Mexico City, Lima, Quito, Santiago, and Buenos Aires were all linked to Madrid as part of the Spanish American Empire. As economics became a more important feature in the development of cities, urban interactions became cross-national. The fortunes of one city in an economy depended on that city's interactions with other cities. With the growth of a truly global economy, this meant that each city was tied, to some extent, to every other city in the world.

The urban system that develops out of globalization invokes a particular hierarchy. While all cities in the world have some global connection, the term **world cities** describes those cities that are at the top of the global hierarchy. World cities can be defined in two basic ways. The first has to do with the attributes of the cities themselves. Attributes that show economic prominence, such as the presence of corporate

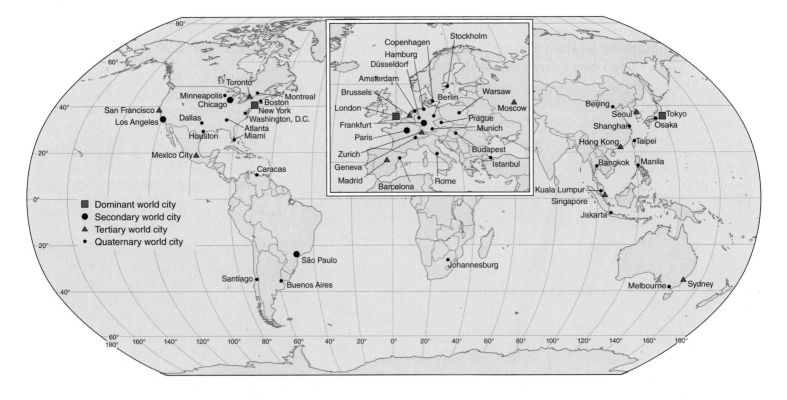

▲ **Figure 13I.1** Putting all of the data together, along with a healthy dose of judgment, we can establish a world city hierarchy and the connections between these cities. In this example, Tokyo, London, and New York are considered dominant cities with heavy connections between them. Each dominant city then enjoys influence with a set of secondary world cities. New York ties together with Los Angeles, Chicago, and São Paulo. Interestingly, none of these secondary cities are political capitals. A number of other cities in the Americas, such as Toronto, Washington, Miami, Mexico City, Rio de Janeiro, and Buenos Aires, are considered tertiary or quaternary world cities. Similar networks apply elsewhere.

headquarters, stock markets, industrial capacity, and large banks are often represented here. Population in and of itself does not make for a world city, though many cities that score highly in economic categories tend to have a very large population. The second definition has to do with the interactions between cities. This is more difficult to establish, but trade, financial transactions, air traffic, and other factors are indicators of a world city.

New York, London, and Tokyo have traditionally been considered the "big three" world cities. This is because of their preeminence on so many spheres of economic life. It also suggests a partition of the global economy into American, Euro-African, and Asian spheres. Beyond these three, however, there is room for debate, depending on what criteria are used. Looking at corporate offices gives more weight to Hong Kong, Singapore, Milan, and Paris. At one point, Detroit would have made some short lists as the headquarters of three major automobile companies. Looking at banks brings up another set of cities, including Frankfurt, Beijing, Munich, and Brussels. Advertising agencies and media centers would introduce Chicago, Los Angeles, and even Miami into the mix.

Examining world cities as part of an interurban network makes a great deal of sense, though it is difficult to do. We can assess global financial transactions, though they may not pick up all of the important interactions. Likewise, a stock exchange is an important barometer of connectivity, though many important cities do not have a major exchange. One approach would be to use air travel connectivity to come up with a hierarchy of cities. In this scheme, Paris fits in with the "big three" of London, New York, and Tokyo, followed by Hong Kong, Amsterdam, Singapore, and Frankfurt.

Outside of possibly the big three world cities of London, New York, and Tokyo, the relative status of a given city is up for debate, and clearly the status changes with time. Also, many cities in less developed countries are left out, despite enormous populations. Where are Cairo, Delhi, and even Beijing in these schemes? World city status is more than simple demographics. A city has to be at the forefront of the global economy. A map produced 10 years from now will have totally different configurations. But some sort of world city hierarchy will continue.

Table 13I.1　Number of Global 500 Corporations, by City

The corporation is an economic entity that operates in many countries through production and distribution channels. Yet corporations are all headquartered somewhere, and these represent the command and control functions for the company. Such businesses require the highest level of services as well. Cities containing many large corporate headquarters are assumed to direct operations in cities throughout the world. New York City traditionally has contained the most corporations, followed closely by Tokyo and London. New York's position reflects the overall dominance of the United States in regard to corporate headquarters, with about a third of the total. This table from 2009 has changed, depending on the fortunes of national economies and corporations. In the 1990s, Tokyo's position became stronger, but with the decline of the Japanese economy, many of its corporations have also fallen in value. London, while still a major financial center, has fewer corporate headquarters. Paris has assumed a commanding position in continental Europe. But the big story is in the rise of Beijing and to a smaller extent Seoul as dominant centers for world corporations. The growth of Mumbai, India, also bears watching. As other countries begin to develop more indigenous industries, this table should change as well.

Rank	City	Country	No. of Global 500 Companies
1	Tokyo	Japan	51
2	Paris	France	27
2	New York	US	27
4	Beijing	China	26
5	London	United Kingdom	15
6	Seoul	South Korea	11
7	Chicago	US	10
8	Madrid	Spain	9
8	San Francisco	US	9
10	Toronto	Canada	8
11	Zurich	Switzerland	7
11	Osaka	Japan	7
11	Moscow	Russia	7
11	Munich	Germany	7
11	Minneapolis	US	7
16	Houston	US	6
17	Mumbai	India	5
17	Amsterdam	Netherlands	5
17	Atlanta	US	5
17	Dallas	US	5
17	Los Angeles	US	5
22	Melbourne	Australia	4
22	Sydney	Australia	4
22	Calgary	Canada	4
22	Shanghai	China	4
22	Essen	Germany	4
22	Frankfurt	Germany	4
22	Düsseldorf	Germany	4
22	Rome	Italy	4
22	Stockholm	Sweden	4
22	Taipei	Taiwan	4
22	Boston	US	4
22	Philadelphia	US	4

Key Terms

agglomeration economies (13G)

binary rank-size distributions (13H)

built environment (13A)

concentration of labor (13D)

division of labor (13A)

functional linkages (13C)

globalization (13I)

hinterland (13B)

mass production (13D)

nonagricultural population (13A)

occupational specialization (13A)

population densities (13A)

population size (13A)

primate city (13H)

rank-size relationship (13H)

schedule (13A)

settlements (13A)

situation (13C)

surpluses (13A)

territorial states (13B)

trinary rank-size distributions (13H)

urban functions (13G)

urban hierarchy (13H)

urban network (13C)

urbanization (13C)

urbanization curve (13E)

world cities (13I)

Basic Review Questions

1. What are the different ways in which a city can be defined?

2. How does an urban definition depend on different criteria?

3. What is the relationship between the origins of an agricultural economy and the emergence of cities?

4. When did the first true cities develop? Where?

5. What is the importance of a hinterland in the development of cities?

6. How did the hinterland figure into the emergence of the first city-states?

7. What is the importance of transportation, technology, and fertility in the development of cities?

8. How did territorial states and later empires help spread urbanism to other places?

9. What does urbanization refer to?

10. How is the situation of a city related to its location as well as its size?

11. How did a traditional agricultural economy as found in all parts of the world up until AD 1000 affect the development of cities?

12. What was the role of capitalism in changing the logic and situation of cities?

13. What were the two urban networks that emerged in Europe beginning about 1180? How did these two networks differ?

14. What was the role of the Industrial Revolution in urbanization?

15. How did the Industrial Revolution change the urban situation?

16. What were the four major effects of industrialization on cities and urbanization?

17. Describe the urbanization curve, and discuss its stages.

18. How is the urbanization curve related to the nature of economic change?

19. How do world urbanization levels vary between countries in the world?

20. How does the level of urbanization depend upon how urban is defined?

21. How does urbanization correspond with economic development? What are some of the exceptions to this relationship?

22. How is urbanization different from population density?

23. How do agglomeration economies work in a system of cities, particularly in the industrial era?

24. How did an interurban network develop in the United States?

25. What is the role of certain urban functions? How might you classify different US cities based on their dominant economic function?

26. What is an urban hierarchy, and how might this be reflected by the rank-size relationship? What does it mean to have a relatively even rank-size relationship? What does it mean when there is a primate city? What is a binary or trinary rank-size distribution?

27. How has globalization created a set of world cities? How would world cities be defined under this scheme?

28. What are the primary world cities? What are a few of the secondary world cities?

Advanced Review Questions (Essay Questions)

1. Describe how the development of cities depended on the development of agriculture. Why do you think it took so long for the first cities to develop after agriculture first emerged? Where did the first cities emerge, and what were some of their characteristics?

2. How does the environment, technology, and transportation determine how large a city can be? Why do you think so many of the early states were city-states, and how does this relate to the notion of a hinterland? How did urbanism advance with the development of territorial states and empires?

3. Why did imperial cities, such as in the Roman Empire, rely on a particular political system to survive? What happened when that system disappeared? How was a new capitalist economy responsible for the development of a new type of city? How did this change the logic of urban situation? Compare the Hanseatic League and the cities in northern Italy in terms of how they facilitated the development of cities.

4. Why did cities remain a small percentage of the overall population until the Industrial Revolution, and how did industrialization allow cities to grow in size but also as a proportion of the overall population? What were the four effects of industrialization? How did industrialization allow for a much larger hinterland?

5. Draw and label the urbanization curve, and discuss its stages. Why is the urbanization curve related to economic change? How does it help explain some of the differences between countries in the world today? What may be some of the exceptions to the correspondence of urbanization with economic development?

6. What are agglomeration economies? How do agglomeration economies help cities develop in a relatively concentrated area? What are urban functions, and how would these help create an interurban network between cities? What were some of the major urban networks that developed in the United States?

7. Describe the rank-size relationship. How does the rank-size relationship indicate urban hierarchies within a society? How does the rank-size relationship work in the United States? How would a primate city operate as an exception to this rank-size relationship?

8. How does a global urban hierarchy as developed under a globalization system create a series of world cities? What are two basic ways in which world cities can be defined? What are some of the primary world cities in the world today, and what are some secondary world cities?

Further Study Topics

- Discuss some of the criteria that make the city different from the countryside. What are some of the factors used to define the city, and why might these not work in all cases? What are some of the cultural and sociological factors that help distinguish between city life and rural life? Do you see these distinctions as still important today?

- Both the Roman Empire and the Chinese Empire were able to establish a vast network of cities within their borders. These cities were situated in order to serve the empire. Look through some historical atlases and examine the distribution of cities in both the Han Chinese Empire and the Roman Empire. Research some of the functions of the main cities. How did these serve their empires with regard to military, trade, or agriculture?

- Select three developing countries (perhaps a country in Latin America, a country in Africa, and a country in Asia). How do the urbanization levels and changes vary among them? What might account for some of these variations?

- The American Manufacturing Belt described encompassed a set of linkages between American cities in the Northeast and Midwest. While these links still exist, other networks have also developed in the United States. Try to identify some of these other networks and some of the roles that are played by various cities within these networks.

- Examine how the rank-size relationship has worked for the United States over the course of its history. Why do you think it has been consistently successful in predicting the size of cities? What is the geography of the American urban hierarchy, and how has it changed over this period of time?

- Most of the world city literature is based on a fairly narrow view of what an urban hierarchy consists of. What are some of the other ways in which a world city hierarchy might be established? How might the map of world cities change in the next several decades?

Summary Activities

There are many ways to define world cities. Figure 13I.1 shows one way to categorize cities on the basis of financial strength. Using the same map and reference materials, look over some other ways in which world cities can be determined. Would these be the same cities pictured on the map or different cities?

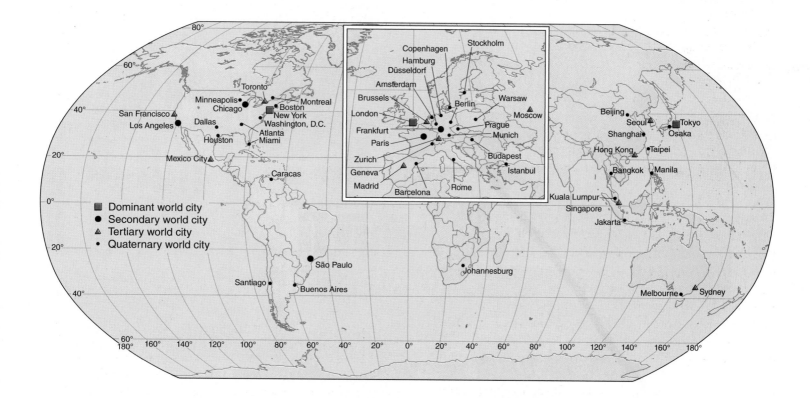

CHAPTER 14

The Changing Structure of the City

CHAPTER MODULES

The internal form of the city includes some basic elements that have remained constant since the first cities emerged. This reflects the fact that cities essentially separated people from their agricultural livelihood and created a concentrated and ordered community. However, a city from 5,000 years ago is nothing like a city of today. Indeed, there exist enormous variations in how cities are shaped and how they feel. Each region has some distinctive urban forms. And even within the same country, you can find some large differences. An American tourist will experience something completely different in San Francisco than in Los Angeles.

What makes for these differences, and how do cities provide for their residents? We address these questions in this chapter. When cities emerged, they were composed of a few basic elements, which would continue to shape the city. The changing morphology, or form, of the city represented changes in some of these basic elements, but the elements remained. How these elements vary, and how city shape varies, is a clear reflection of urban economics, culture, and technology. Transportation, in particular, has been instrumental in creating the type of city we see today, and in explaining differences between cities. At the same time, the city form has the potential to influence social and economic relations. In addition to the obvious cultural differences, the sprawling cities of America's Sunbelt create different constraints and opportunities than do the closely packed cities of Japan.

Cities in the United States are emphasized in this chapter, but we also want to examine some of the distinctions found in regions across the world. City forms vary substantially, even among other developed countries. We can only touch lightly on some of the specific challenges faced by cities in developing countries, for they are voluminous. But they are important to consider, since they are the fastest-growing cities in the world.

14A Early Urban Morphology

What are some of the most significant elements making up the form, or **morphology**, of a city? While there are many variations, all cities share an urban population, a center (node), a perimeter (outside boundary), and an internal transportation network. The first element was the **urban population** itself. As discussed in Module 13A, this is a population composed of individuals who were not themselves engaged in agriculture, yet they had to be fed and housed. So providing food and shelter for the urban population would be an ongoing challenge to the urban economy.

▲ **Figure 14A.1** In the most ancient cities of Sumeria, the housing stock was comprised primarily of mud brick—a mix of clay, sand, and water set out in the sun. These structures, still in use in Morocco, provide a feeling for what these dwellings looked like. In later cities, housing was built of more durable substances, but the fact of having a concentrated set of dwellings—far beyond what was found in a village—was important in distinguishing cities from the countryside. Early density levels in these places were phenomenally high.

The second element is the **urban center**. The center represents the organizing principle of the city and reflects the vital concerns of the population. The main items that comprised the center have changed over time. In ancient cities, the center was where the elites lived. In a medieval capitalist city, the center surrounded a marketplace. In a modern city, the center is the "downtown," where land value is at its peak and where office, banking, and retail functions are located, often in tall skyscrapers.

The third element defining a city is the **perimeter**—the manner by which a city is separated from the country. Today, the separation is often blurry, but for most of history this separation was critical. The separation represented a means of defense, since cities often provided safe haven for their residents and for the surrounding rural population. The perimeter also represented a social division. Living in cities was something of a privilege, and access was not automatically granted to everybody. From ancient times, most cities of any importance surrounded themselves with a wall, with access permitted or denied by a series of gates. In

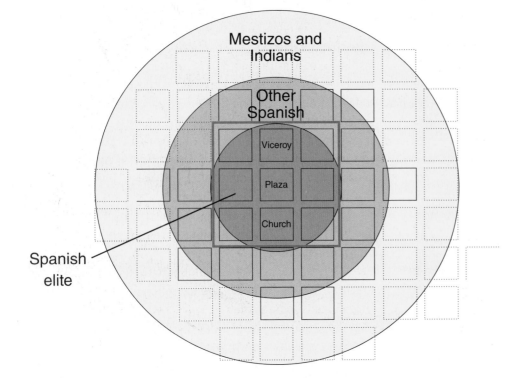

◄ **Figure 14A.2** With planning, many centers were established from the outset. One of most famous systems for planned cities was promulgated by Philip II of Spain and was known as the Law of the Indies. This applied to all of Spanish America. The law stated that "the plan of the place begins with the main square from which streets are to run to the gates and principal roads and leaving sufficient open space so that the town can spread out in a symmetrical manner." The plaza was primarily an empty block used for periodic markets, public gatherings, or military possessions. Around this plaza were located the main public buildings, the mansion of the viceroy, and the cathedral. This area and adjacent blocks marked the first zone, which was generally the only part of the city that was paved and well lit. The surrounding zone was inhabited by a rudimentary middle class of artisans, clerks, and small proprietors. This zone was not nearly as well serviced. Beyond this were settlements inhabited by menial workers.

Figure 14A.3 ▶ Medieval European cities were well known for their walls. Wall construction and maintenance were extremely expensive, consuming most of the municipal budget. The walls were vital for defense, and they served a social function. Medieval urban society, with its more achievement-oriented ethos and reliance on the market, became more remote from the traditional, agrarian life of rural Europe. A medieval saying that "city air makes men free" underlines this difference, as did the apocryphal ruling that a serf would be set free of his obligations if he managed to stay in a city for a year and a day. In Bruges, Belgium, the moat surrounding the wall afforded an additional layer of protection.

modern times, perimeters are defined in different ways. In the late nineteenth century, Vienna took down its old walls and replaced them with an enormous ring road, which helped encapsulate the interior city and serves as a boulevard for all of the most important buildings and monuments. Other cities marked themselves off by a system of parks or greenbelts (see Module 14F).

The fourth element is the **transportation network** that moves people and goods around. In most cases, this transportation network has been composed of surface streets, but several cities also adopted canals as a means of carrying heavy freight. The street or canal network also determined the design principles by which the city was shaped.

In an **organic city**, the street network developed by accretion. Streets varied in width, they were usually sinuous, and they could resemble labyrinths. Many ancient and medieval cities were organic. Even some US cities, such as Boston, are essentially organic with an odd street pattern.

Some streets were laid out along more symbolic lines. Many **planned cities** were rich with symbolic elements, but major cities in China, India, and Meso-America had a street pattern that followed cosmological principles.

The type of street pattern with the greatest impact is the **grid**. The first grid as a conscious design was developed by an ancient Greek—Hippodamus—who saw the grid as the rationality of civilized life. The grid's advantages are that it is regular, simple, and repeatable for as far as the city aspires to go.

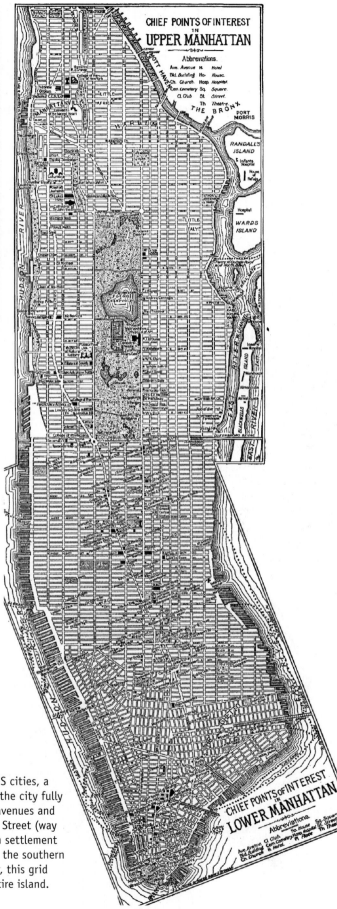

Figure 14A.4 ▶ In many US cities, a grid was imposed long before the city fully developed. In New York City, avenues and streets were laid out to 155th Street (way up past Harlem) in 1811, when settlement ended at Canal Street close to the southern tip of Manhattan Island. Later, this grid was extended to cover the entire island.

14B Three Historical Urban Types

As discussed in Modules 13B and 13C, the political economic system determined the extent of urbanization, as well as the logic of where cities were situated. The political economy also had a big impact on the internal form of the city. The earliest cities were marked by many of the same elements that would persist for a long time. These forms reflected the needs of the urban population, the city's position as a spiritual and political center, but also its role in the storage and redistribution of surplus grain.

With the growth of empires, the traditional city became larger and more complex, but many of the same elements applied. Cities could get bigger because of a larger area from which to extract surplus food. This had less to do with agricultural efficiency and more because empires controlled large hinterlands. The second factor that allowed for greater size was improved methods of distribution. Empires built up impressive transportation infrastructures, which enabled them to get food into the mouths of urban residents.

Within the new trading cities, many of these elements continued to be important. Most such cities had a prominent wall. The few that did not, such as Venice, were surrounded by water. Many also had some prominent churches and urban palaces (such as the palaces of the Medici family in Florence). What made these cities distinct was the importance placed on trade and artisan production.

The industrial city that emerged in the nineteenth century was the first urban form that generally came about without a wall. This was due mostly to the fact that these cities were located within larger countries, and military technology had long surpassed the point where wall defenses were practical. It was also the first urban form in which the elite did not necessarily inhabit the center of the city. This is because the city was based on mass production, and at that time, mass production was a dirty, sooty process.

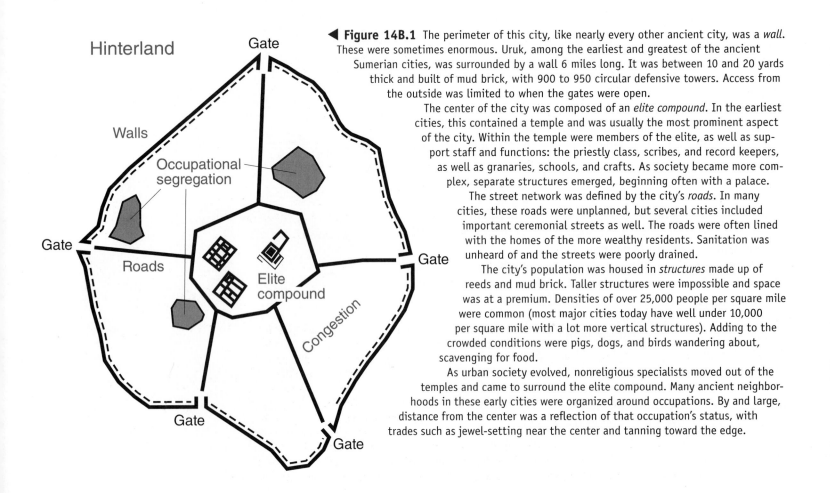

◀ **Figure 14B.1** The perimeter of this city, like nearly every other ancient city, was a *wall*. These were sometimes enormous. Uruk, among the earliest and greatest of the ancient Sumerian cities, was surrounded by a wall 6 miles long. It was between 10 and 20 yards thick and built of mud brick, with 900 to 950 circular defensive towers. Access from the outside was limited to when the gates were open.

The center of the city was composed of an *elite compound*. In the earliest cities, this contained a temple and was usually the most prominent aspect of the city. Within the temple were members of the elite, as well as support staff and functions: the priestly class, scribes, and record keepers, as well as granaries, schools, and crafts. As society became more complex, separate structures emerged, beginning often with a palace.

The street network was defined by the city's *roads*. In many cities, these roads were unplanned, but several cities included important ceremonial streets as well. The roads were often lined with the homes of the more wealthy residents. Sanitation was unheard of and the streets were poorly drained.

The city's population was housed in *structures* made up of reeds and mud brick. Taller structures were impossible and space was at a premium. Densities of over 25,000 people per square mile were common (most major cities today have well under 10,000 per square mile with a lot more vertical structures). Adding to the crowded conditions were pigs, dogs, and birds wandering about, scavenging for food.

As urban society evolved, nonreligious specialists moved out of the temples and came to surround the elite compound. Many ancient neighborhoods in these early cities were organized around occupations. By and large, distance from the center was a reflection of that occupation's status, with trades such as jewel-setting near the center and tanning toward the edge.

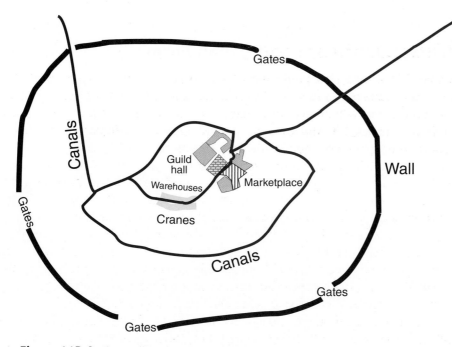

▲ **Figure 14B.2** The trading city was centered on a *marketplace*. Major cities had several marketplaces: a central square and a market near the town gates. The street system, particularly near the market, was also set up for commerce and production rather than for transportation. Street frontage was valuable land. The focus of activity was tied to ports and waterways. *Warehouses* were built nearby to store the goods. Harbors were dredged to allow for more and larger ships. The *guild halls*—major centers of artisan production—were found around the central marketplace. These began to take the role of power brokers, reflecting the guild influence in city government.

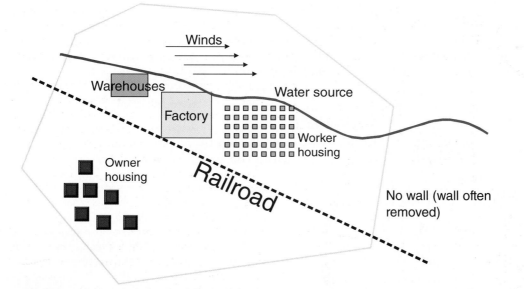

▲ **Figure 14B.3** Industrial cities were focused around their *factories*. These factories had to be located next to the *water*, since steam-powered mills drew in the water for their boilers. Water was also important as an outlet for sewage. Manufactured goods were stored in *warehouses*. These were often located near inns and hotels, where outside buyers stayed. The *railroads* were the factories' connection to the main ports. They were like factories on wheels and spread the pollution into all parts of the city and into the countryside. Finally, with the rise of the factory system, workers no longer lived in the same place they worked. Huge amounts of immigration meant that housing had to be constructed in a hurry, often by the factory owner. Long rows of *tenements* were hastily slapped back to back, so as to save space (and ventilation). These slums contrasted with the housing of the factory owner's estates placed on hillsides away from the soot and noise of the factory. Less wealthy but respectable citizens lived closer in.

14C Land Values, Densities, and Urban Form

What are the functions of the modern city, and what determines their distribution? Much of this can be traced to how urban land is valued. In other words, how much are people willing to pay for a particular parcel of land in a particular part of the city? We all know the importance of land value. It is reflected in how much a house might cost. Exactly the same house can be twice as expensive in one part of the

Figure 14C.1 ▶
Land Values in the City (values displayed in this graphic by height). There is a point in a city with the greatest degree of access. The city center might be defined as the **central business district (CBD)**. This is the point with the greatest access to offices, banks, stores, and other activities. In fact, because the CBD is an area, there is often designated a single intersection with the greatest access. This is called the **peak value intersection**, or the **prime value intersection (PVI)**. Usually, the PVI is located at the intersection of two main streets. In traditional small towns, this is where the main banks are located and other important stores. In big cities, there may be multiple PVIs, but they are often clearly marked by exceptionally tall buildings and a great deal of foot traffic. When considering a simple model of land value, we can see that it is based primarily on distance to the PVI. However, different functions have a greater stake in being close to the PVI and in having a greater degree of access. In this graphic, you can also see that land values are higher along major streets (like ring and radial roads), and especially where major streets intersect.

modern metropolitan area as it is in another neighborhood. The same is true with all sorts of things. Parking can cost a great deal in the center city but be free in most of the suburbs. In big cities such as New York, people pay as much to park their cars as people in other cities pay for rent!

While functions in the public domain are located based on public need, the private functions are determined by market principles. These market principles are based on the following equation.

$$\text{Land value} = f(\text{site, internal situation})$$

The f in the equation denotes *function*, specifically land value is a function of site and internal situation. *Site* and *situation* are terms defined in Module 1C. The *site* has to do with the physical attributes of the location. For instance, factories need flat land, while most people prefer to live in hilly areas. A view of water is generally quite nice, while a view of a factory is not. The *internal situation* defines the location relative to other parts of the city. In a word, situation boils down to **access**. How accessible are the workplaces, stores, and factories? Obviously, access has a different meaning for a factory owner than for a resident.

If we ignore site considerations for now and consider only internal situation, we can start to develop a model of land value that makes some sense.

Table 14C.1 Functions Found in Cities

The concept of **land value** begins with the different functions found within the city. Parts of the city are used for the exchange of goods and services (retail functions), some parts are used for offices and company headquarters, some parts are used for factories (industrial functions), and some parts are used for houses and apartments (residential functions). In addition to this, we have to add other parts of the city that are in the public domain: streets, landfills, and parks, as well as government buildings and schools (administrative and educational functions). These constitute a great deal of land in the modern city. There is also land that is under water, that is undevelopable (e.g., too hilly), or that is just left vacant.

PRIVATE FUNCTIONS
Residential
Commercial
Industrial
Railroads
Undevelopable
Vacant
STREETS
UTILITIES
PUBLIC FUNCTIONS
Parks
Government buildings
Schools and colleges
Airports
Cemeteries
Public housing
Other

Land value also determines the intensity of use within the city. The higher price for a parcel of land near the center means that it is more economical to use land more intensively and build upward. Fifty-story buildings become feasible when the price of land is millions of dollars an acre. Out toward the edge, tall buildings are not worth the lower land values. Because expensive land entails intensive use, there is a distinct relationship between land value and land density. Those office functions at areas of high value will be set in skyscrapers. Similarly, residential areas of high value will also be set in multistory buildings. Even the wealthiest resident of a big city could not afford to plunk down a detached single-family house in the middle of downtown.

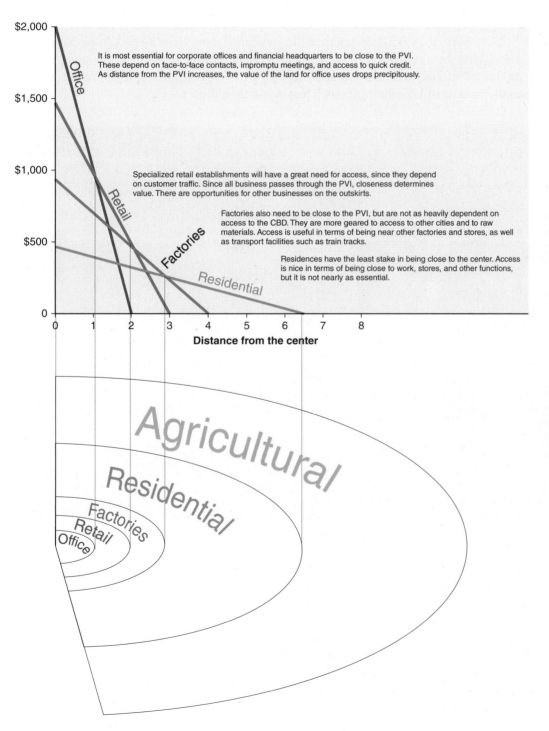

It is most essential for corporate offices and financial headquarters to be close to the PVI. These depend on face-to-face contacts, impromptu meetings, and access to quick credit. As distance from the PVI increases, the value of the land for office uses drops precipitously.

Specialized retail establishments will have a great need for access, since they depend on customer traffic. Since all business passes through the PVI, closeness determines value. There are opportunities for other businesses on the outskirts.

Factories also need to be close to the PVI, but are not as heavily dependent on access to the CBD. They are more geared to access to other cities and to raw materials. Access is useful in terms of being near other factories and stores, as well as transport facilities such as train tracks.

Residences have the least stake in being close to the center. Access is nice in terms of being close to work, stores, and other functions, but it is not nearly as essential.

Distance from the center

◄ **Figure 14C.2** This graph shows how different functions might value different parcels of land. The land goes to the highest bidder, and the value of each piece of land, depending on the distance from the PVI and the function for which it will be used. That means that land has different uses, depending on how far it is from the center. From the PVI to 1 mile away, land will be used for offices. From 1 to 2 miles, it will be used for retail; from 2 to 3+ miles, it will be used for industry. And from 3+ to 8 miles out, it will be used for residences. After 8 miles, the effective urban use of the land ends.

◄ **Figure 14C.3** We can convert this graph into zones surrounding the PVI, and describe the dominant land uses within each of these zones. Like the model of rural land use discussed in Module 15G, this is an abstract picture. It also tends to be a more accurate depiction of the city from 50 years ago. With the rise of suburbanization, many of the office, retail, and industrial functions have fled to the suburbs. Edge cities, as discussed in Module 14D, often cluster these functions together.

As we have seen from historical examples of urbanism, the center of every city has served to anchor that city, and it has helped reflect the city's priorities. In cities within the United States and in other parts of the world, the CBD reflected the primacy of commerce and the organization of the city based on land value. Land values in the CBD were generally prohibitively high for residential uses, so as the city expanded, most of the residential functions moved beyond the CBD.

The nature of land value also plays a big role in the density patterns found in cities. *Density* generally refers to the number of people per unit of land, such as a square mile. In looking at a city, it is important to distinguish between daytime and nighttime density. For example, the CBD itself has a very low **nighttime density** because most of its space is reserved for employment, but its **daytime density** (when people are at work) is high.

In general, American cities are the least dense in the world. Other cities have much higher densities: Hong Kong (271,000 per square mile, or 423 people per acre), Shanghai/Cairo (85,000 per square mile), São Paulo/Mexico City (33,000 per square mile), and Paris (20,000 per square mile). One of the densest cities in the United States is New York at 24,000 per square mile, or a little more than 37 people per acre. This higher density is made possible by a profusion of high-rise apartment buildings, which allow many people to live comfortably on limited ground area. Boston and Chicago are far less dense, with an average density of 12,000 per square mile, and most US cities are much less dense than this.

▲ **Figure 14C.4** The most distinguishing feature of a city is the central business district. In large cities, this downtown area can encompass a couple of square miles. Centrality is critical to the placement of the CBD and the kinds of functions it contains.

- It serves as a *central marketplace*. This means extremely specialized stores, the flagship stores of large department stores, large banks, and brokerage houses.
- It serves as a *major transportation node*. The CBD acts as a **nodal point** for all transit routes (except airports, which require lots of land). Large city CBDs still contain the major train depots, intercity bus stations, and a focal point for intracity transportation, such as streets, subways, and elevateds. It is an *administrative center* where government offices are located.
- It is where you find *high-level services*. Often, company headquarters are located there.
- There is *heavy pedestrian traffic,* since density causes people to walk and makes automobile use less convenient.

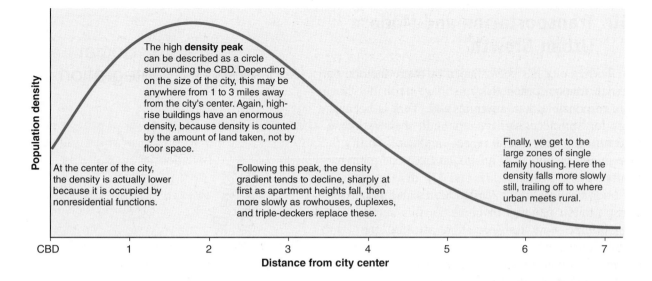

The high **density peak** can be described as a circle surrounding the CBD. Depending on the size of the city, this may be anywhere from 1 to 3 miles away from the city's center. Again, high-rise buildings have an enormous density, because density is counted by the amount of land taken, not by floor space.

At the center of the city, the density is actually lower because it is occupied by nonresidential functions.

Following this peak, the density gradient tends to decline, sharply at first as apartment heights fall, then more slowly as rowhouses, duplexes, and triple-deckers replace these.

Finally, we get to the large zones of single family housing. Here the density falls more slowly still, trailing off to where urban meets rural.

▲ **Figure 14C.5** The **density gradient** indicates the change in density over distance. This graph shows the nighttime density gradient, when people are at home.

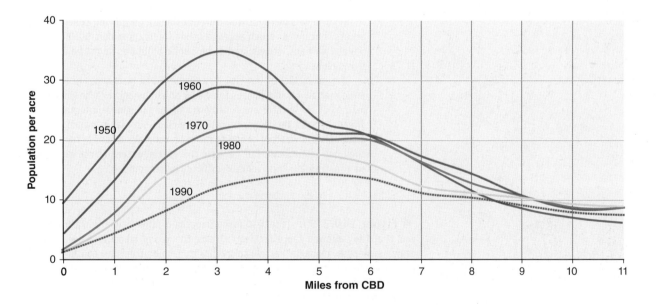

▲ **Figure 14C.6** This graph shows the changing density patterns for Cleveland between 1950 and 1990. In 1950, density levels in Cleveland were reasonably high and the city's population was at its peak of close to 1 million. By 1990, the city population had declined to half of that. Also evident was the shift in population away from the inner city, about 3 miles away from the CBD, into the outer city. The decline in this density peak shows the inner city losing almost two-thirds of the overall population.

14D Transportation and Modern Urban Growth

The modern city has been shaped by many factors, but internal transportation systems have probably been more responsible than anything else. That is because cities rely on accessibility—after all, their rationale is to function as a central place—and accessibility is determined by how easy it is to get from one point to another point. Modules 17E and 17F discuss transportation changes in the United States and modern transportation patterns in cities. In this section, we examine how transportation affected the shaping of American cities.

In looking at transportation and cities, it is helpful to consider them as a series of stages. The first stage was the **walking city**, in which the majority of people walked to get from one spot to the other (although wealthy people often had access to horse-drawn coaches). Before 1850, every city was a walking city. The US cities that were the biggest and grew the fastest in this period—New York, Boston, and Philadelphia—were only about 2 miles in overall radius.

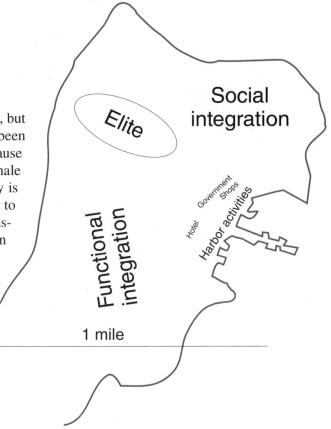

▲ **Figure 14D.1** The "center" of the walking city was at the port itself, where we would find wharves, warehouses, and trading offices. For these items, the friction of distance (Module 1F) was at its most acute and waterfront access was crucial.

Beyond this were located other businesses requiring central access, but not as much access as the directly commercial functions. Specialty shops, hotels, and some public buildings might be found in this second ring.

The remainder of the city was composed of residences of the middle and working classes joined by all shops and workshops. The mixing of these different functions caused functional integration. There was also relative integration by class—social integration—although the wealthy began to move to separate districts here as they had in England. But because the spatial extent of the city was so constrained, this could be difficult to accomplish.

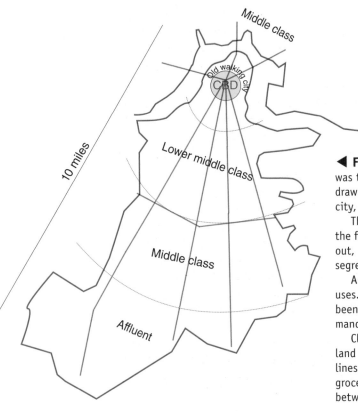

◀ **Figure 14D.2** Streetcars had many impacts on the city. The main impact was that they allowed the effective city size to expand tremendously. Horse-drawn streetcars made it feasible to live up to 5 miles from the center of the city, and electric trolleys expanded the radius to 10 and sometimes 20 miles.

Those who could afford to leave took advantage of this mobility. Since the fares were based on distance, the wealthiest could afford to live farthest out, while the middle class lived closer in. This tended to create more social segregation.

As the city expanded, the center of the city opened up to nonresidential uses. The new central business district emerged to include most of what had been the previous walking city, and it specialized in functions that could command the highest rents.

Closeness to a transit line affected access and thus land values. Prices for land along the transit lines soared, and the intersection between two major lines often became the nodes for newly decentralized functions: bank branches, grocers, and butchers. People tended to live along the lines, leaving the areas between vacant. This gave the streetcar city something of a star-shaped pattern.

Concentric zone model

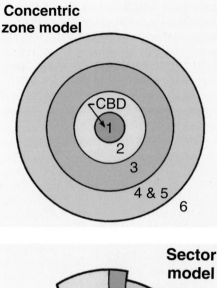

◀ **Figure 14D.3** With the success of the streetcar city, sociologists and geographers came up with the **concentric zone model** of cities. This model was most associated with Ernest Burgess.

(1) *Central business district*:

(2) *CBD fringe or frame*: occupied primarily by wholesale and warehouse functions, truck and railroad depots, and an industrial belt

(3) *Zone of transition*: area of deteriorating housing and where vice districts could be found: red light districts, skid rows, and cheap hotels

(4) *Zone of independent workingmen's homes*: composed primarily of workers who, while far from wealthy, usually owned their homes and were able to participate in some leisure; housing stock in this zone tended toward duplexes and three-deckers

(5) *Residential zone*: generally houses of the middle class; this zone was marked by the appearance of single-family houses and much lower densities

(6) *Commuters zone*: these are generally suburban towns and satellite cities, accessible by transit rails, composed of affluent residents living far from the city on large plots of land

Sector model

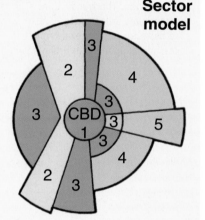

◀ **Figure 14D.4** Later, Homer Hoyt would develop a **sector model**, which took site factors explicitly into account.

• Outside the CBD, the *high-rent area (5)* would begin at the points farthest from the areas of industry. This could be a fashionable boulevard, lined with the more exclusive shops and white-collar services. This sector would be associated with certain amenities: closeness to a lake, higher elevations, or nice views of the city. There could also be site characteristics based on snob appeal.

• *Low-rent sectors (3)* would begin in areas where industry and more unsightly urban functions were invading. These would also be in areas not so attractive for residential development: low-lying land, fewer parks, and land near railroad tracks, industry, and noxious smells. Wealthier citizens moved out of these neighborhoods, leaving housing to be subdivided for the poor. This sector was synonymous with slums and disadvantaged ethnic groups.

• *Middle-income sectors (4)* would be found between high- and low-rent sectors. The middle class could not afford the best land in the city. So they took the next best land, leaving the worst land for the poor.

This is the distance that a person could comfortably walk from the edge to the center in about an hour. This horizontal compactness was further exacerbated by the fact that buildings could not go above a certain height. The only way in which a city could acquire more accessible land was through leveling hills, draining marshes, or filling in nearby waterways. Also, bridges and ferries were established to connect central cities with nearby communities, such as Boston to Cambridge and Manhattan to Brooklyn.

The combination of urban growth and an inability to expand spatially meant that density increased to the highest levels ever. New York had an overall density in 1850 of 136 people per acre (about 87,000 people per square mile). Philadelphia and Boston were about 83 people per acre (48,000 per mile). Land values in the center city also skyrocketed. A good example is Chicago, which with the opening up of railroads in the 1840s, really took off. All land within a 1-mile radius of the center was valued at $810,000 in 1842. By 1856, it was $50 million—growing 60 times in a dozen years!

The second stage is the omnibus/horsecar/streetcar stage. As industrialization took off after the Civil War, urban centers emerged as even more of a magnet. Immigration increased, and the migration of people from the country (including a stream of emancipated blacks from the South) meant that cities were bursting at the seams. The earliest transit systems were horse-drawn omnibuses that traveled a fixed route for a fixed fare. By the early 1850s, there were omnibuses operating in most northern cities and New Orleans. Later, horse-drawn streetcars were laid out over rails. These were easier to pull and so could be larger. Finally, toward the end of the nineteenth century, several varieties of electric streetcars were developed. We can therefore use the term **streetcar city** for this stage.

The third stage is that of the **recreational auto city**, as automobiles first came on the scene. Automobiles began as a bit of a novelty but had become affordable and popular among middle-class families. By 1930, there were 26 million cars, or one for every five people (a ratio not seen in Western Europe until the late 1950s).

◀ **Figure 14D.5** The car effectively expanded the radius of the city to about 30 or 40 miles in certain cases. In the very largest cities, such as New York, people began to move to places that transit systems could not go. In addition, the automobile allowed for the development of the areas *in between* the transit spurs. Because most people still worked in the CBD, and because parking was difficult there, many people would drive to the commuter train station, then take a train downtown. Auto traffic did not initially damage the integrity of the CBD. Most people still worked there, and the large number of people without cars still lived near there. It primarily led to the creation of more far-flung **bedroom communities**. The transit lines still defined the dominant urban patterns. Cars were used more for out-of-town trips than as a necessary component in urban commuting.

The fourth, and final, stage of transportation in cities occurred after World War II, when the automobile began to fundamentally alter city morphology. Much of this had to do with the influx of servicemen who needed places to live and a new breed of housing developers who built housing far from the city center (see Module 14E). Many of these new residences had less access to the existing transit systems, and burgeoning prosperity allowed Americans to buy more and more automobiles.

The new automobile dependency had some major effects on urban space by hastening decentralization. By 1960, a plurality of people lived in **suburbs**, as compared to either rural or central city locations. By 1990, about half of all people in the US lived in suburbs. By the early 1970s, the suburbs became places where most people shopped and worked. Cities were hemorrhaging manufacturing jobs as factories—which demanded large tracts of cheap land so that they could build on one floor—left the inner city for new greenfield locations in the outskirts. By the 1980s, two to three times as much office space—a traditional function of cities—had been created in the suburbs rather than in the city. Even corporate headquarters began to abandon their central city high-rises for new "corporate campuses."

Related to this, the new transportation era led to a decline in the central business district, in both relative and absolute terms. Downtowns had been highly valued because of their accessibility, but this depends on walking or taking mass transportation. In an automobile-dependent society, cars consume too much space to make it convenient to drive and park downtown. The new superhighways expedited movement around a city center. It became more convenient to locate near these beltways than downtown. Major regional shopping centers popped up near highway interchanges, offering the advantages of many different stores without the hassles of parking and inclement weather. In addition, with more people using airplanes and airports on the outskirts, central cities lost their importance as transit nodes. Certain intercity functions, such as courier services and hotels, found it more convenient to locate near the airports.

▲ **Figure 14D.6** The US road system was also improved. The **Interstate Highway System**, begun in the 1950s, created large, limited-access superhighways. While these connected cities, they also made it easier for people to live farther away from cities. Later, beltways would emerge to engirdle all major cities and connect the surrounding suburbs. The impact on the rural landscape outside of cities was immense as farm fields were rapidly converted into commercial strips and housing developments. These pictures show how Long Island, New York, developed after a freeway was put in place.

Figure 14D.7 ▶ The modern **auto-centered city** emerged, distinct from the earlier forms.

The old city center (CBD), still important for city hall and a few specialized functions, and the site of redevelopment efforts. In many cities, this downtown area has become a focus for tourism.

The inner streetcar suburbs built prior to WWII are now often regions of poverty. Still, many of the neighborhoods have shown some chic appeal, and some have been redeveloped and gentrified.

The third ring of emerging **edge cities** that have become office, employment, and shopping centers in their own right. Edge cities are a key new concept of the modern city. These combine all functions of a central business district but are located in the suburbs. There are many aspects of an edge city, but probably the most important one is that it provides many more jobs than homes.

A fourth ring (interspersed with the third) that functions as the suburbs of these urban villages.

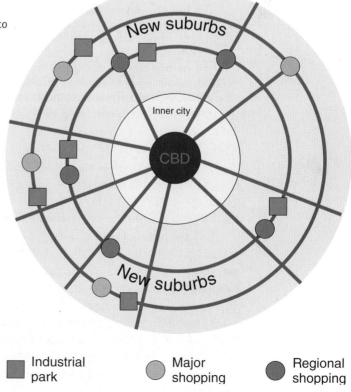

■ Industrial park   ● Major shopping   ● Regional shopping

14E Housing the City

The residential sector is by far the largest consumer of land in the city. A survey done in the late 1960s indicated that housing comprised one-third of all land in the city, with much of the rest devoted to streets and vacant property. The type of housing also determines the character of a city and its neighborhoods, whether it is multifamily or detached, rented or owned, newer or historic.

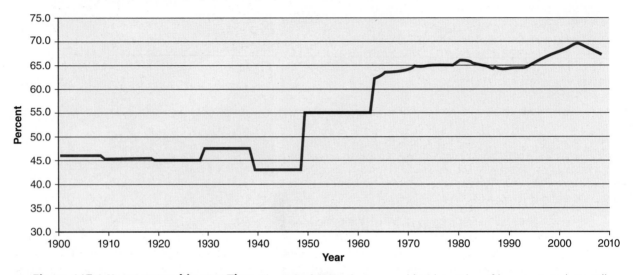

▲ **Figure 14E.1 Homeownership over Time** The United States is now considered a nation of homeowners, but until fairly recently, that was not true. Up until the 1940s, most people rented, but after that the percentage of homeownership increased a great deal and peaked at 68% to 69% in 2004. (Since the onset of the US housing crisis, the rate of homeownership has fallen to around 66%.) Several reasons account for this expansion of homeownership:

1. Because most houses require an initial capital outlay, homeownership became more of an option when a larger proportion of the population moved into the middle class and could afford to accumulate some wealth.
2. Before the 1930s, people paid most of the housing costs upfront, or they paid the costs after a short period. In the 1930s, the development of amortized mortgage spanning 15, 20, or 30 years allowed many middle- and working-class folks to buy a home.
3. The deduction for mortgage interest had been in the tax code since the income tax began in 1913. Now the US federal government subsidizes home mortgages to the tune of $76 billion a year, and this does not include the deductions for property taxes that also benefit homeowners.
4. Techniques in housing construction have probably made housing cheaper in real dollars. This is especially true when you consider that the quality, as measured by square footage and other amenities, has improved.
5. The psychology of homeownership means that people are more willing to buy a house because they consider it an American dream, a great investment, and a place where they can express their individuality. Rates of homeownership vary a great deal by age, family status, income level, and race.

◄ **Figure 14E.2** Abraham Levitt and his sons subdivided farms into hundreds of single-family houses. Levittown, New York, came first, located on Long Island potato fields. The Levitts took 4,000 acres, built each structure on concrete blocks at 60-foot intervals, and constructed the houses in an assembly line. The cost savings were enormous, and this system could provide housing for less per month than it would cost a returning soldier to rent an apartment. This is a picture of Levittown, New York, not long after it was first constructed.

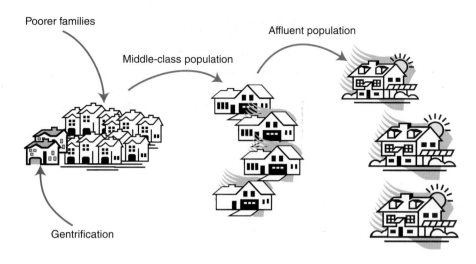

Figure 14E.3 ▶ Housing and neighborhoods carry many social connotations, based largely on the idea that status and prosperity have a lot to do with where you live. In a process known as **filtering**, more prosperous families move out of older housing and into newer housing. The movement of people out of this older housing creates a vacancy, which is filled by families that are a bit less prosperous. At the bottom are vacancies in less desirable locations, and these are often filled by immigrants. This filtering process creates a cycle whereby older neighborhoods can have more substandard, cheaper housing. Very often, the older housing is subdivided and not as well maintained. Owned housing may also be turned into rental housing. This process of neighborhood change helps explain the life cycles that various neighborhoods undergo. It also explains the process whereby metropolitan areas grow, as people continue to seek better housing, generally on the periphery of the city. There are exceptions, however. In some markets, some inner-city housing and older housing is prized. **Gentrification** occurs when the housing stock of a neighborhood is improved generally through the introduction of high-priced, more luxurious housing.

Every city contains several square miles of existing housing, dating to various time periods. One estimate is that 300 billion square feet of construction—mostly housing—now exists in US cities. Neighborhoods are best characterized by the prevailing age of housing. Except for the most blighted structures, all of this housing is in use. At the same time, new housing is constantly being built and households are continuously moving from one home to another.

According to the US Bureau of Labor Statistics, the construction industry, involved primarily in residential construction, accounts for between 4% and 5% of the economy, while real estate accounts for another 12%. The need to furnish and maintain these houses adds much more in terms of economic output.

Housing also remains among the most biddable of commodities. You decide to buy a house, and then you bid a price. The owner may choose to reject or accept. Likewise, in selling a house, you determine your sale price. This price has a lot to do with the quality of the house and the relative supply and demand for certain types of housing, but it also depends on price levels in the overall housing market and what people are willing to pay to locate in a particular neighborhood.

For most people, buying a house requires a mortgage loan, often for a long span of time. This is possible because of the nature of housing. You would not expect to pay for a car over 15 years, when the car would be junk at the end of the term. Housing is expected to appreciate in value—so by the end of the mortgage period, owners expect not only to pay off their loan but also to own something that is worth a lot more than it was initially. When housing does not appreciate, as happened most recently in many American cities, mortgage holders can get into trouble if they cannot make regular mortgage payments and they are unable to sell their house. In such a case, the house may go into **foreclosure**, a situation in which the mortgage holder loses all claims to his or her property.

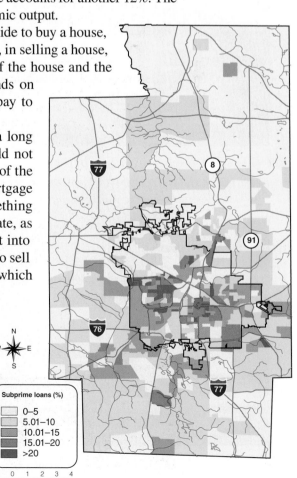

Figure 14E.4 ▶ **Subprime lending** describes mortgages made available to people who could not qualify for regular conventional, or prime, mortgages. Subprime mortgages always entail higher fees and/or rates to make up for a higher risk of default. This map of Akron, Ohio, and surrounding Summit County, shows subprime lending activity tends to be concentrated in specific neighborhoods, often marked by lower incomes and a higher African American proportion. **Predatory lending** occurs when these mortgages impose an undue financial burden on households by forcing debts that far exceed assets. In the worst case, the result may be foreclosure. In other cases, it means that households are paying more than they should on their mortgage.

Subprime loans (%)

- 0–5
- 5.01–10
- 10.01–15
- 15.01–20
- >20

1 0 1 2 3 4

14F Urban Development in Europe and Japan

While distinct from one another, European and Japanese cities are marked by several elements that place them apart from cities in the United States. These have to do with a rich historical legacy, a greater degree of planning, higher levels of compactness, and an eagerness to try out new urban forms. Cities in these countries are generally much older. Many European cities date back to the classical period of civilization and the Greek city-states. Japanese cities, while more recent, still have history that spans about 1,500 years. However, many cities in these regions can appear surprisingly new. This is partly due to the extensive rebuilding that had to go on after the devastation of World War II when cities such as Tokyo lost 70% of their buildings, but it also hearkens to a spirit of innovation and willingness to play around with new architectural and landscape forms.

Many European and Japanese societies have been eager to experiment with newer urban styles. In several European countries, architects have experimented with new forms of housing, including new towns built outside major cities. In the United Kingdom, there about 35 of these new towns, and they house about 4 million people. The Japanese have experimented with urban forms probably more than anyone else. Part of this is an attempt to accommodate residents comfortably within an extremely crowded society.

Cities in both Europe and Japan differ in that they must contend with much higher levels of centralized control compared to US cities. European governments employ a variety of growth control mechanisms that are intended to contain urban population within existing built-up areas and provide carefully limited outlets for growth beyond city lines. For example, many cities demarcate explicit boundaries beyond which city-type growth is not allowed to take place. The clear separation between urban and rural uses is especially apparent in densely populated countries, such as the Netherlands. Cities end abruptly and farm fields begin not too far from the central business districts. Great Britain provides **green belts** around its cities, where suburban land uses are restricted. Stockholm and Copenhagen have developed a series of land use plans based around extending the cities on transit lines.

(a)

(b)

◀ **Figure 14F.1** Many European cities provide an interesting juxtaposition of an old historic center, often oriented around a central plaza or square, with some startlingly innovative features that show off new architectural styles. The core is often the most attractive feature of the city, as far as tourists are concerned. (a) It usually offers amenities such as markets, cafés, interesting walks, and ancient buildings. For natives, residence in the core is highly valued, often in apartments that retain their historic exterior but with a renovated interior. To preserve the integrity of the historic core, many cities enforce lower building heights and require more modern skyscrapers to be located on the outskirts. (b) The outskirts of most European cities also contain the same mix of highways, shopping plazas, and parking lots found outside US cities, although these are usually less extensive and often located in more defined districts. Japanese cities, by contrast, do not have nearly the same level of public spaces and, while quite historical, have central business districts filled with high-rise buildings.

◀ **Figure 14F.2** One idea that combines the Japanese passion for miniaturization and some unique architectural innovations is the capsule hotels. These hotels provide "rooms" that are basically little sleeping boxes about 6½ feet long, with enough space for a small television and some lights. One other advantage of these hotels is that they are quite cheap in one of the most expensive places on earth, costing only about $30–40 a night.

(a)   (b)

▲ **Figure 14F.3** (a) In many European cities, bicycle use is far more prevalent as a major form of transportation. In Amsterdam, for example, close to half of the commuting population uses bicycles, and the urban infrastructure is set up for it. Bicycles look the part of an everyday workhorse. They are utilitarian, with only a few gears; they have fenders; and they are often dinged up from constant use. Most have multiple places to transport groceries, children, and even trailers. (b) Paris has also begun to greatly expand its bicycle infrastructure. In the past 10 years, Paris has expanded the network of bicycle paths and since 2007 has initiated a successful bicycle-sharing system.

The compactness of many European cities is experienced best on foot. These are truly walking cities, so it is possible to stroll from the city center to the countryside in less than two hours in a medium-sized city and less than one hour in a small city. Even in large cities, the walkability factor is very high. The high compactness is a legacy of several things. First, people enjoy living close to the city center. Second, many Europeans live in apartment buildings with a higher percentage of renters overall. Third, automobile use is discouraged in ways that begin with higher purchasing fees, gas prices triple to quadruple what they are in the United States, and much higher parking costs. The flip side of this is that most European cities have an excellent public transportation system. The network of trains and buses is more extensive and the pick-up times are more frequent. This level of compactness is also true of Japanese cities. Buildings are close together, most cities are intended for walking, and individual spaces are quite tight.

14G Cities in Less Developed Countries

It is difficult to do justice to the huge variety of cities in less developed countries, because they represent so many different cultural and social traditions. Some of these cities are found in the most historical civilizations in the world, while others are in places that were unurbanized until just a few decades ago. However, these cities have some aspects that show a major divergence from cities in the West.

Cities in less developed countries must contend with challenges based on massive growth combined with overall poverty. Most of these cities are growing at an alarming rate. With the exception of cities in Latin America, these cities are in the acceleration phase of the urbanization curve (see Module 13E). As a result, the urban population grows even more rapidly than the country's overall population, sometimes as much as 6% a year. No city could easily accommodate this increase, but overwhelming poverty makes matters worse. There is, of course, the poverty of individual residents—especially since most of the new migrants arrive because there is nothing left for them back home. But the cities are also poor, with limited budgetary resources to spend on infrastructure, safety services, and a professional civil service.

▲ **Figure 14G.1** Many of the largest cities in the less developed world emerged as centers of colonialism. These cities functioned as a conduit between the raw materials found in the colonial interior and the European power that controlled the colony and its resources. The colonial aspects of these cities developed, often with a district where the resident Europeans lived. In Calcutta (now Kolkata), which was established by the British as a Presidency town, the administrative section and western-style CBD acted as the center of the British community and was laid out in regular fashion. British colonialists lived splendidly in huge houses filled with servants. The Indian population, by contrast, was marked by extreme congestion and much poorer-quality housing. While most of the British have gone, these different sectors of the city still persist; many wealthier Indians now inhabit the older British enclaves.

◀ **Figure 14G.2** While migrants go to cities looking for jobs, the employment picture is often quite bleak. Opportunities in the **formal sector**—jobs in industry, established services, and government—are limited to a privileged few, so those who cannot find a job must find another way of making a living. This way is usually through the **informal sector**, which is labor-intensive, absorbs the remainder of the workforce, and is open to nearly everyone but which offers a very low standard of living. This informal sector is quite visible in third world cities. Activities include retail distribution (hawking newspapers), personal services, gambling services, and scavenging. Most people who work in the informal sector make a pittance, but it does provide work that is not restricted and does not require any additional credentials.

Figure 14G.3 ▶ Temporary structures built up by people with nowhere else to go are often described as **squatter settlements**, which suggests an illegal occupation. Although often this is the case, with settlements popping up in unutilized land owned by someone else, other times residents will provide some rental income to the landowner. The term *squatter settlement* has come to be associated with a number of other characteristics:

1. They are composed of some of the poorest people in the city, often new migrants with nowhere else to go.
2. They are unserviced, without water, sewage, toilets, electricity, or adequate roads. This creates a number of sanitation, safety, and health problems, and such settlements are often hotbeds of totally preventable diseases.
3. The housing is self-built out of whatever materials are available. Hundreds of people may take over a piece of land and construct dwellings of straw mats overnight. Over time, a process of autodevelopment takes place as the housing is improved. Straw is replaced by bricks and corrugated tin.

No matter how bad the conditions of the squatter settlements are, they offer great advantages over the places the squatters have left. Also, the settlements may improve with time. Unfortunately, governments and private owners may decide to reclaim the land or to simply clear the settlement without providing any alternative housing.

For many people moving to the city, one of the most pressing issues is a lack of proper housing. People can be too poor to afford private housing, and there is rarely enough government-financed housing to go around. Homelessness is a problem. As is true in wealthier cities in the United States, several cities in less developed countries are filled with people living on the sidewalks and in whatever public spaces are available. The difference between these cities and those in the United States is one of scope. Nearly half of all urban dwellers in poor cities suffer from a lack of decent housing. For many, the imperfect solution lies in developing self-built housing in the city's outskirts.

Figure 14G.4 ▶ The urban morphology of cities in less developed countries varies tremendously by region. A few basic items that they share relate to the fact that infrastructure and adequate housing simply cannot keep up with population growth. Most of these cities, like this model of a Latin American city, include a fairly modern central business district and a few well-serviced neighborhoods (zone of maturity) that include the more privileged members of society. There is also a sector, or spine, that goes from the central district to the more affluent outskirts, often including North American–style housing. The remainder of the city is composed of mixed areas of development (zone of in situ accretion) surrounded by areas of slums and squatter settlements on the outskirts.

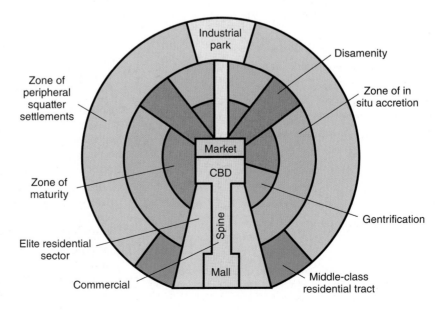

Key Terms

access (14C)
auto-centered city (14D)
bedroom communities (14D)
central business district
   (CBD) (14C)
concentric zone model (14D)
daytime density (14C)
density gradient (14C)
density peak (14C)
edge cities (14D)
filtering (14E)
foreclosure (14E)
formal sector (14G)
gentrification (14E)
green belts (14F)
grid (14A)
informal sector (14G)
Interstate Highway System (14D)
land value (14C)
morphology (14A)

nighttime density (14C)
nodal point (14C)
organic city (14A)
peak value intersection (PVI) (14C)
perimeter (14A)
planned cities (14A)
predatory lending (14E)
prime value intersection
   (PVI) (14C)
recreational auto city (14D)
sector model (14D)
squatter settlements (14G)
streetcar city (14D)
subprime lending (14E)
suburbs (14D)
transportation network (14A)
urban center (14A)
urban morphology (14A)
urban population (14A)
walking city (14D)

Basic Review Questions

1. What is meant by the term *urban morphology*?

2. How do the center, perimeter, and transportation network work to organize all cities?

3. When was a grid system first developed?

4. What were the key elements of the ancient city, and where were they located?

5. What were the key elements of the trading city, and where were they located?

6. What were the key elements of the industrial city, and where were they located?

7. How did an industrial city separate the workers from the factory owners?

8. What are some of the functions found in a city? What determines the distribution of the functions?

9. What is land value in various parts of a city based on?

10. How does the land value graph combine different types of urban functions?

11. What functions tend to have a greater stake in being close to the center of a city? What functions find access to the center less essential?

12. What are some of the features found in the central business district?

13. What is the density gradient?

14. What is the difference between nighttime density and daytime density?

15. What was the walking city composed of? How is it spatially constrained?

16. How did the streetcar stage of urban transportation affect the size and shape of the city?

17. Describe and diagram the concentric zone model of cities. Describe and diagram the sector model of cities. How do these two urban models compare and differ?

18. How does a recreational auto stage differ from the final auto-centered stage that occurred after World War II?

19. How do edge cities compare to the suburbs?

20. How has homeownership changed in the history of the United States, and why?

21. How does the process of filtering create a vacancy?

22. How has gentrification affected some inner-city neighborhoods?

23. What is the difference between subprime lending and prime lending?

24. How does predatory lending work, and why might predatory lending lead to housing foreclosure?

25. What are some of the ways in which the European city compares to American cities? What is the role of the central business district or historic center within European cities?

26. What are some of the major challenges faced by cities in less developed countries? How do these cities fit in the urbanization curve?

Advanced Review Questions (Essay Questions)

1. Describe the difference between an organic city and a planned city. What is the transportation network in a planned city more likely to resemble? How is the perimeter in the center of the cities more likely to be established? How was a center of a colonial Spanish city reflecting the power of particular people in the society?

2. In the ancient city, the trading city, and the industrial city, how did the political economic system determine their internal form? What were some of the principal features found in the ancient city, and how did they change as the ancient traditional city became larger and more complex? How do some of the major features of the trading city vary from that of the traditional city, and why? What elements of the trading city were abandoned or retained in the industrial city?

3. Draw the land value curve using all of the different functions that may be found within a city. What is the importance of access for each of these functions, and why? How might the land value of certain areas be affected by considerations of site? Describe how the central business district creates a set of features not found in other parts of the city.

4. What are the four stages of urban transportation? Did they influence the American city? How did the streetcar city solve some of the problems of the walking city in regard to spatial constraint? How did the streetcar city allow for greater functional separation, as well as greater social separation? How has the modern automobile-centered city altered the importance of the central business district?

5. Compare the concentric zone model to the sector model. How do these models differ in treating social class? How do they differ in addressing the central business district? How does the modern auto-centered city alter some of the major premises of these two earlier models? What is an edge city, and where would you find it?

6. What are the reasons behind the change in homeownership rates over the last 100 years? Has the process of filtering helped spark social change in different parts of the city? What is the role of gentrification in affecting some neighborhoods, and why might it be controversial?

7. Describe some of the major differences between European cities and cities in the United States. What are some of the key distinctions between how the core of the city is used? What are some key distinctions between how central government dictates land use? Why might

public transportation be much more popular in European cities than in American cities?

8. Diagram a model of a city in the less developed world. How does this model reflect the differences between the formal sector of the economy and the informal sector of the economy? What sorts of activities are found within the informal sector? How does this diagram also reflect the lack of housing for many people who move to these less developed cities?

- Housing foreclosure has become a key problem in many American cities. What have been some of the major factors responsible for the rise in foreclosures? Have these foreclosures concentrated in particular parts of the city, or are they more widely dispersed?

- What are some of the variations in housing prices between different parts of the United States? How have these prices changed over the last 20 years? What might be some of the factors leading to these variations in housing prices? Where would you expect housing prices to increase most rapidly, and where would you expect them to decline?

- Select a city in a European country and an American city with which you are familiar. Note some of the key differences between the European city and the American city. What are some of the major differences in terms of the compactness of the city? The use of public transportation? The degree to which social classes are arranged?

- Select a city from the less developed world. What are some of the factors leading to that city's growth? Where do the wealthy members of the city live? Where do most of the poor live? What are some of the main aspects of the informal sector in this city?

Further Study Topics

- One of the key consequences of an auto-centered city has been greater suburban sprawl. How would you define sprawl? How can a concern for sprawl be reconciled with the ability of people to live where and how they want to live? Does planning that tries to avoid sprawl impinge on personal freedom and private property rights?

- For a city you know, consider where the edge cities might be located. What do these edge cities comprise in terms of services, industries, retail, and offices? To what extent do the edge cities take over certain functions that are found within the central business district? Is the downtown area still an important segment of the city or not?

Summary Activities

The modern American city has become marked by suburbanization and edge city developments on the outskirts. Using this graphic or drawing something similar, for a city that you know, try to outline some of the major transportation corridors and some of the larger shopping and industrial zones that exist on the outskirts.

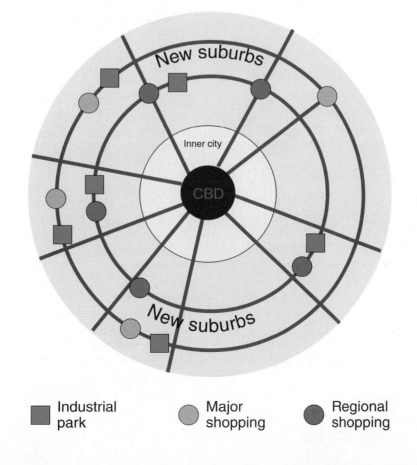

Industrial park   Major shopping   Regional shopping

CHAPTER 15

The Geography of Economic Activity and Agriculture

CHAPTER MODULES

An **economy** is defined as the extraction, production, consumption, and exchange of goods and services. Since this includes pretty much everything that people need to live—with the possible exception of air—**economic activity** is found in everything we do, from the management of a household to the regulation of global financial markets. No matter how primitive, all human societies need to sustain themselves through economic activity. But as human societies advanced, the nature of economic activity became increasingly sophisticated and the scope of activity expanded to where it encompassed the entire globe.

Economic geography examines economies and economic activities but gives special attention to location, distribution, and spatial interconnections. Economic geographers may analyze the attributes of a particular place: its physical characteristics, its material resources, the demand for different types of goods and services, and how all of this is regulated. Economic geographers try to fit these attributes together, within a place and across other places, to develop a sort of structure. They might look for "flows" or movements of various material and nonmaterial items between places, or perhaps they assess trends over time.

For most of human existence, the dominant economy was that of hunting and gathering—a refined version of what many animals did to procure food. When this economy changed to agriculture, humanity changed profoundly. Through agriculture, people were able to expand their numbers a hundred times over, generate surpluses, and put in motion the sequence of civilizations, armies, exchanges, cities, and inventions that define our history. This chapter examines both economic systems and the special significance of agriculture.

15A Small-Scale Economic Systems

All economic activity takes place within an economic system. An economic system is the way in which humans in a society organize themselves in regard to their economic activity. The economic system determines almost everything else in a society, including the political system and social relations. The economic system can be tied to levels of prosperity—perhaps some economic systems are better suited to creating wealth in a society—but it can also determine other issues such as how well people can access various goods and services. We take for granted that we live within one kind of system—a capitalist system—but there have been and still are many others. What is more, few economic systems are pure. Most societies combine two or more systems, although they are often dominated (and characterized) by one.

There are many possible varieties of economic systems, several of which have appeared historically. The earliest systems were marked by

1. reliance on subsistence food gathering or agriculture, which entailed the acquisition of food just for oneself, one's family, or possibly one's small group,
2. the vast majority of economic relations occurring within a small group, as part of either a clan or a village,
3. small-scale production, which was likely done within that small group, and
4. extensive use of a barter system, which involved the trading of goods and services.

▲ **Figure 15A.1** Today, we have very few examples of hunting and gathering economic systems. Most such systems are in remote locations threatened by the intrusions of modern life. For example, many such groups live in tropical forestlands and, so, will die out with deforestation. In fact, an organization called Survival International (www.survival-international.org) has made it its mission to protect the habitat, livelihood, and safety of these peoples.

Prehistoric life—most of the time that humans have been on earth—was a combination of **hunting and gathering**. As hunters, humans were quite successful at killing animals. They were able to work in teams, communicate effectively with each other, and construct weapons that made up for their lack of size, strength, claws, and powerful teeth. Gathering was the process of finding edible plant life; it, too, required a great deal of ingenuity.

As an economic system, hunting and gathering was fairly self-contained, based on small groups of people with little outside exchange. There were likely rules and traditions regarding the exchange and division of labor within the group and some possible specializations based on age and gender. We are not certain, but because there were so many groups involved, there were probably many variations of this economic system.

The Neolithic period (literally "New Stone Age") began the transition to **primitive agriculture**. The actual process will be discussed in Module 15D, but this was a very gradual transition, occurring in different parts of the world beginning about 9000 BC. While some early agricultural groups were nomadic and some involved shifting cultivation, most early agriculturalists settled in more permanent settlements, such as villages.

This primitive agriculture was almost entirely subsistence-based. Once the subsistence needs of the population were taken care of, the economic system could decide how to deal with the surplus—additional harvest beyond the subsistence needs of the farmer's family. But this early form of agriculture was unlikely to yield any large surpluses, and any surplus that did result was likely bartered within the village itself. Although we have some evidence of longer-distance trading in the far past, it does not appear to be the norm. Instead, based on some modern evidence of primitive agricultural communities, transactions within the community were highly ritualized. The village was headed by a big man, or chief, who had some control over the surplus. He stored some of it in buildings termed granaries.

Table 15A.1	Economic Systems						
	Scope of Exchange	Limits on Exchange	Medium of Exchange	Specialization?	Surplus Extraction	Power	Role of Government
Hunting and Gathering	Self-contained	Cultural reciprocal	None	No	Minimal	Within clan	None
Primitive Agriculture	Self-contained within village	Cultural reciprocal	None—barter; tithing	Little—some	Within village; to priestly class	Chief—later priests?	Minimal?
Feudalism	Self-contained within manor	Vertical allegiance	Forced labor; barter	Little	To lord; defense	Lord / bishop	Personal

Over time, the development of a surplus enabled more **occupational specialization**, as some individuals were provided food in return for their making things or providing special services. As the political community grew, perhaps to encompass several villages, the leaders controlled greater surpluses. As this was taking place, societies became less egalitarian and were marked by greater social stratification, headed by a defined elite group.

Feudalism is a small-scale economic system based on self-contained estates, controlled by a lord or master. Feudalism is defined by the following:

1. Farming is done by bounded peasants, termed serfs, on a manor.
2. Most of the surplus is ceded to the lord of the manor, which he uses to support himself, his household, and his retinue. Some lords controlled several manors. Most of the surplus was, in fact, needed to pay for the enormous demands of defense: knights, horses, armor. These all consumed a tremendous number of resources.
3. The feudal economic system was not based on cash or wages—surplus was simply passed over to the lords through the payment of rent in exchange for protection. This was the medium of exchange.
4. There was very little trade, as nearly all production, consumption, and exchange within the feudal system was contained within the manor.

The feudal system is based more on personal relationships than on an institutional structure, and it tends to emerge during periods of weak political control. The most famous period of feudalism occurred during Europe's Middle Ages, after the collapse of the Roman Empire (see Module 10B). Feudalism also occurred in other places and at other times. For instance, feudalism in sixteenth-century Japan differed in many ways from the medieval European system but shared similar economic characteristics.

◀ **Figure 15A.2** Diverting water from a wetland to farm fields has long been a preoccupation of agricultural societies. Early **irrigation** technologies required that a community work together, with someone or some people directing the labor of others, digging channels and constructing levees. In this picture, peasants are performing the arduous task of laying out and constructing dikes in order to control the water flow on the Yellow River.

15B Large-Scale Economic Systems

The development of kingdoms, empires, caliphates, and other larger political units in the world led to the development of **imperial economies.** These economic systems dominated the world up until 1300 or so. Famous empires—such as the Roman Empire, Byzantine Empire, Chinese Empires, and Islamic Empires—were agrarian societies with an economy based on agricultural surplus. Imperial economies were marked by the redistribution of surplus from peasants to large landholders, but with the imperial bureaucracy taking a substantial cut (see Module 10B). It was an extractive economic system, as wealth and resources flowed upward.

Imperial economies were far larger and much more complex than primitive agricultural or feudal economic systems. The sheer geographic size of an empire allowed for a great diversity of goods. Greater numbers of people enabled more occupational specializations. The ability to marshal surplus meant that many people did not have to farm and could congregate in large and small cities (see Module 13B).

Imperial economies also included some degree of **capitalism**. This entails the buying and selling of various goods in order to create **profit**, or the positive difference between how much revenue is made by selling a product and how much it costs to buy (or make) a product. The pursuit of profit is what drives the capitalist enterprise. In the beginning, capitalism depended on **merchants** who underwrote the costs of buying large quantities of a product, the shipping and storing of that product, and the trading itself. **Artisans**, or craftsmen who manufactured their own products, were also involved in profit-seeking, but their costs were more bound to the expense of materials and labor.

Imperial economies enjoyed a great deal of trading between regions and developed a distinct merchant class to guide and profit from this trade. But that trade was dominated by the demands of a political structure

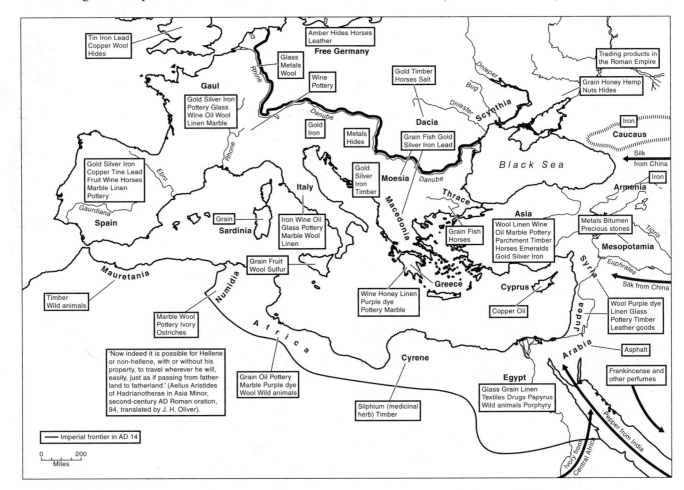

▲ **Figure 15B.1** The organization of large imperial economies allowed for some long-distance trade, but often these empires were large enough to promote specialization and trade within their borders. The Roman Empire included a wide variety of crops and resources and promoted a vigorous exchange between these far-flung regions. A system of established sea lanes and Roman roads facilitated the movement of goods and people within the empire.

that relied primarily on extraction. Merchants were given very little status or autonomy, and the economy and most of the political power were primarily in the hands of the great landowners.

The major transition in economic systems arrived about 1,000 years ago in Europe and involved the creation of a capitalist economic system. For most people who lived during that time, such a development would have gone unnoticed. This new system began in a few out-of-the-way pockets, far from the existing centers of civilization. Moreover, it developed at a time when the feudal economic system was still flourishing. The capitalist economic system developed independently of existing states. Ownership and control were mostly in private hands. Investment strategies, production decisions, and prices were determined privately and dictated by the demands of the marketplace. This is not to say that there was no government intrusion. There was, but trade was largely free and the merchant class developed an unprecedented degree of authority and wealth.

We can divide the capitalist economy into a capitalist commercial economy and a capitalist industrial economy. The **capitalist commercial economy** came first and was primarily concerned with the buying and selling of **commodities**. In this instance, a commodity is simply a product that can be exchanged for profit.

Between AD 900 and 1100, the capitalist economic system emerged in two places: the Mediterranean trade, anchored by a few northern Italian cities, and the Baltic and North Sea trade, based on a larger number of smaller trading towns. Since the collapse of the Roman Empire some 500 years prior, Europe had suffered through a period of drastic economic and population decline, propelled by privation, ignorance, and widespread violence, but the capitalist systems emerged when the continent as a whole was experiencing several positive changes. Much of the population had settled down and become more peaceful, more land had been cleared, and farming techniques had improved. By AD 1000, Europe was experiencing a sustained population increase and a greater demand for goods. From the nobility and churchmen came a demand for luxury goods, such as spices and silks. From the peasantry and lower classes came a demand for bulk goods, such as wool, flax, fish, and salt.

Of course, these changes did not *have* to lead to the creation of a capitalist economic system. In the past, demand was effectively met by merchant trading as well, but much of the surplus was channeled and controlled by larger and more intrusive governments. These new economies appeared, however, in areas without strong central governments, so there was no imperial bureaucracy to take the extra surplus and to keep merchants in their place. Then a new type of merchant class emerged to take advantage of this surplus through trade. Many of these early merchants were incredibly brave, traveling to areas hundreds of miles away for the chance to buy things not easily obtained at home. They also took huge financial risks by purchasing boats and hiring crews with no guarantee of a favorable outcome.

Over time, these separate economies expanded more lands and people. Rulers of manors found that it made more sense to specialize in certain goods that could be exchanged for other products, as opposed to producing everything on the manor. Pockets of capitalist activity grew in scope and profit. Eventually, all of the separate economies were folded into a single economy, and over time, the European capitalist economy grew to encompass other parts of the world as well, on terms favorable to European merchants. Protection of merchant privileges, markets, and supply routes became the business of the more powerful European states that later developed.

Table 15B.1	Economies						
	Scope of Exchange	Limits on Exchange	Medium of Exchange	Specialization?	Surplus Extraction	Power	Role of Government
Imperial Economy	Widespread throughout empire	Tradition, allegiances, obligations	Forced labor; money; influence	Yes, but mostly agrarian	Up through system to emperor	Emperor/ aristocracy; bureaucracy	Fairly intrusive
Capitalist Commercial Economy	Unlimited potential	Minimal; amount of capital	Money	Much	Via profits to merchants	Merchants	Little; regulatory
Capitalist Industrial Economy	Unlimited potential	Minimal; amount of capital	Money	Enormous	Via profits to industrialists	Industrialists	Little; regulatory
Planned Economy	Mainly within state; some exchange outside	State-imposed controls	Influence; money	Enormous	To state— redistribution	Bureaucracy	Controlling

The **capitalist industrial economic system** paved the way for a truly global capitalist economy, based on industrial activity. *Industrial activity* refers to the creation of finished products from raw materials. This was characteristic of artisan production based around small workshops, hand manufacturing, and tremendous skills. Later, the Industrial Revolution (see Module 16A) opened the way for mass production and the creation of massive profits.

The capitalist industrial economy followed the same principles as the capitalist commercial economy. The differences lay in degree rather than in kind. For one thing, the capitalist industrial economy changed the relations between regions. Production required a greater demand for resources, many of which came from far away. Places where goods were produced enjoyed vast profits, albeit very unevenly distributed, while the places that provided raw materials were often left at a disadvantage. The capitalist industrial economy also eventually altered the ways in which people worked. Factories required a great deal of labor, and many people streamed

▼ **Figure 15B.2** The capitalist economy began in two areas of Europe under two very different conditions. In the north, merchants located in several small towns began to trade primarily in bulk goods procured around the Baltic and North Seas. They obtained products such as salt from the North Sea coast, wool from England, flax from Belgium, herring from Norway, furs from Russia, and grains, wine, and beer from continental Europe. These merchants were somewhat independent of the feudal system, but they relied on it for many of their products. Later, the Hanseatic League was formed out of these towns, not based on a political affiliation but as an economic association that set prices and standards for different commodities and provided harbors that were safe and contained necessary services.

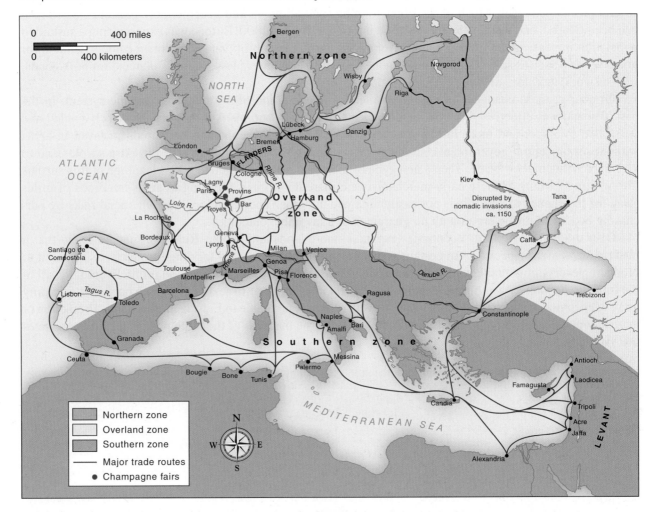

In the south, significant merchant activity first emerged in the (now) northern Italian cities of Venice, Genoa, Pisa, and Florence. The trade here spanned the Mediterranean. Because this included more sophisticated cultures—including some important empires—the trade was much more cross-cultural and sophisticated. The commodities tended toward luxury products, such as spices, silks, and porcelain. The trading relationships also relied on intermediary groups that enabled goods to be purchased from as far east as China and India. Source: From Dennis Sherman and Joyce Salisbury, *The West in the World, Third Edition*, © 2008 by The McGraw-Hill Companies, Inc., page 245. Used by permission.

to industrial towns from farming areas. As was the case with capitalist commercial economies, industrial economies transcended the sovereignty and authority of political states. Multinational companies, so common in this day and age, were introduced in the nineteenth century and some might say were descendants of some of the large, resource-extracting companies that were in place by the seventeenth century.

Capitalist economic systems are based on the idea of free enterprise and economic autonomy, and consumer demand (markets) determines what will be sold and produced. For example, the production of any commodity, such as minivans, is determined by the market demand for that item. If demand is high, more minivans are produced to satisfy demand. If it is low, fewer minivans are produced. Manufacturers can decide to increase or scale back production (which means hiring and firing personnel) or decide to change prices based on consumer demand. This makes life difficult for people who cannot afford the products, workers under threat of being laid off, and producers who fail.

▲ **Figure 15B.3** Capitalist industrial economies relied on the cultivation and extraction of resources throughout the world. In so doing, economies in far-flung regions were transformed. For example, the need for jute fibers in British textile production boosted the cultivation of this crop in Bengal.

An alternative is an economic system in which the economic decisions are made by "the people" whose voice is ostensibly channeled through a large government. In this system, factories, farms, services, and other economic activities are all publicly owned. **Planned economies** emerged as a response to unrestricted capitalist economies, and often to what were perceived as some of the inequities embedded in a capitalist system.

The twentieth century witnessed a large number of planned or command economies. In these systems, varying by their degree of strictness, all economic resources, production facilities, and land are owned by the government. Likewise, economic relations are determined by the government. All exchanges take place in a regulated manner, except for the often enormous black market. Most planned economies are relatively self-contained. Trade outside them relies more on barter—often through exchanges with other planned economies—rather than on currency transactions. What is interesting is that most such planned economies—China and the former Soviet Union, specifically—began in places where capitalism was just beginning.

There is plenty of space between unfettered capitalism and a completely planned economy. Many modern economies are **mixed economies** with government intervention and a capitalist orientation. Almost all countries provide for some form of free public education. With the exception of the United States, most wealthy societies also offer universal public health care. Even in the United States, there is a huge public sector at various levels of government; this accounts for one-third of the gross domestic product (see Module 15C). Government also has a hand in restricting certain practices, breaking up companies that appear too large and monopolistic, while attempting to regulate the rest. Likewise, China now contains a vigorous capitalist sector and has developed hundreds of thousands of large and small enterprises.

▲ **Figure 15B.4** Planned economies promise that material goods will be distributed equitably to everyone within the society—"to each according to his need." They also promise that people will not suffer from unemployment or a lack of education, health care, and other services deemed vital. In many instances, they deliver on these. Cuba is often held up as an example of a society that is able to provide all of its citizens with the necessities of life. At the same time, planned economies often suffer from a lack of dynamism, which stifles innovation and growth, and from the suppression of personal economic (and political) freedom that allows people to pursue their goals.

15C Economic Categories and Measures of the Economy

The health of the overall economy is always important news. People measure when the economy is growing and when the economy is stagnant. Occasionally, you will hear that the economy is in a recession. But what does this mean? Much of it has to do with some of the basic measures of the economy that are reported by governments and obsessed over by politicians, economic analysts, businesspeople, and ordinary workers. These measures also help us compare one economy with another.

One standard measure of the economy is the **gross domestic product (GDP)**. This is the total of all goods and services produced within a country. GDP is slightly different from **gross national product (GNP)**, which includes the total of goods and services produced by citizens of a country (whether the actual production takes place inside or outside a country's boundaries). **Gross national income (GNI)** is similar to GNP, except it does not include costs of indirect taxes, depreciation, and subsidies. All three of these measures are compared in a particular currency, often the US dollar and, so, are very susceptible to currency fluctuations. If the dollar is strong, it lowers the GDP, GNP, and GNI of other countries. Likewise, if the dollar is weak, then foreign economies appear to be stronger.

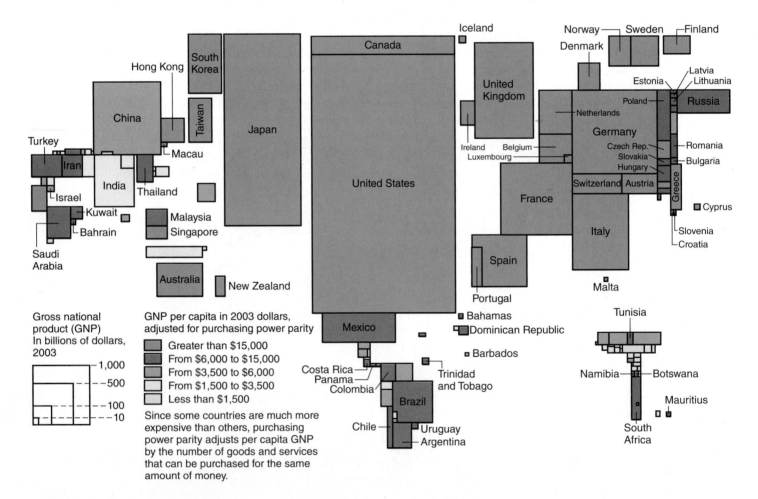

▲ **Figure 15C.1** This map of the world sizes each country not by its physical area but by the size of its economy. The map gives a good sense of the relative economic strength of different countries. Most European countries have a large economy well out of proportion to their land or population size. This is also true of Japan and some other fast-growing East Asian economies. Conversely, much of Africa contains small economies, as do many countries in southern Asia, the Middle East, and South America.

The relative sizes of individual national economies can change rapidly. Today, the United States is currently the world's largest economy, with a $14 trillion economy as of 2009. For the past several decades, Japan and Germany have been the second- and third-ranked economies. But as of 2010, China officially passed Japan to become the world's second largest economy (a development not yet reflected in this map). Some expect China to surpass the United States as early as 2030. How much do you think this map will change in 50 years?

A **recession** occurs when these measures of the economy decline, often for a sustained period of time, such as half a year. A **depression** indicates a much more severe downturn, for a longer period of time. Both recessions and depressions are marked by unemployment, unsold goods, and often many business closings.

An economy is categorized into different sectors. One distinction is made between the **private sector**, which includes all of the output produced by individuals working for themselves or privately owned businesses, and the **public sector**, which includes all of the output produced by government at all levels. The best-known private businesses are large corporations that control assets worth billions of dollars. *Fortune* and other magazines regularly put together rankings of these corporations based on a variety of criteria: market capitalization, or how much the company is worth in the stock market; the amount of revenues; and the amount of profits. Private sector output, however, can be quite small-scale and include goods and services produced by a single individual working for herself. This is also measured. Public sector output is fairly easy to measure. In the United States, this constitutes approximately 11% of the entire gross domestic product and includes output at the federal, state, and local government levels. State and local governments are responsible for many more functions, including most public education, and are about double the size of federal outlays. The public sector share of the economy varies considerably by country.

▼ **Figure 15C.2 Economic Sectors**

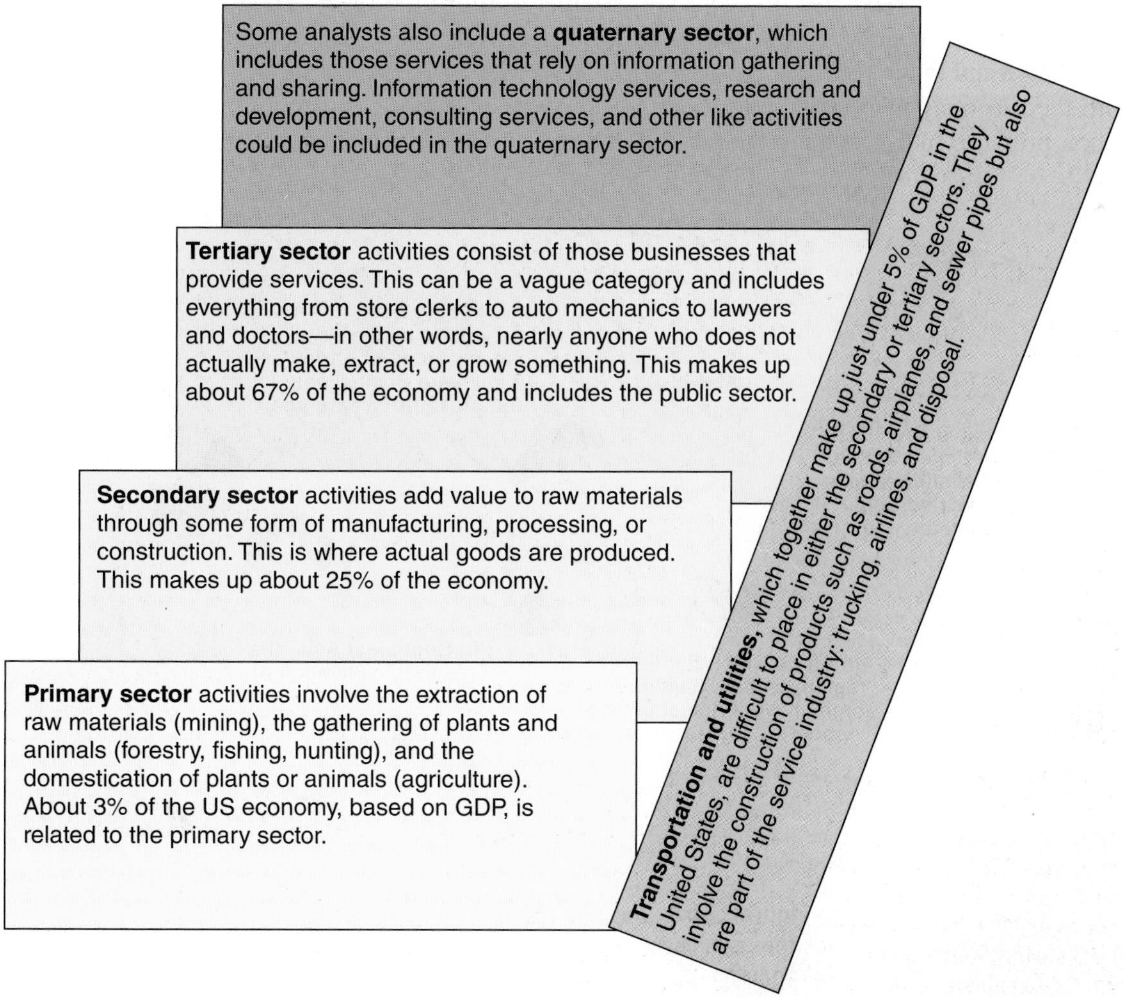

Some analysts also include a **quaternary sector**, which includes those services that rely on information gathering and sharing. Information technology services, research and development, consulting services, and other like activities could be included in the quaternary sector.

Tertiary sector activities consist of those businesses that provide services. This can be a vague category and includes everything from store clerks to auto mechanics to lawyers and doctors—in other words, nearly anyone who does not actually make, extract, or grow something. This makes up about 67% of the economy and includes the public sector.

Secondary sector activities add value to raw materials through some form of manufacturing, processing, or construction. This is where actual goods are produced. This makes up about 25% of the economy.

Primary sector activities involve the extraction of raw materials (mining), the gathering of plants and animals (forestry, fishing, hunting), and the domestication of plants or animals (agriculture). About 3% of the US economy, based on GDP, is related to the primary sector.

Transportation and utilities, which together make up just under 5% of GDP in the United States, are difficult to place in either the secondary or tertiary sectors. They involve the construction of products such as roads, airplanes, and sewer pipes but also are part of the service industry: trucking, airlines, and disposal.

15D Origins of Agriculture and the Process of Domestication

The development of agriculture was *the* watershed moment in human development, and it likely bridged the transition from prehistory to history. Prior to the development of agriculture, all human beings were involved in some form of a hunting and gathering economic system (described in Module 15A). This system required that people get their food from what was directly available, whether from animals that could be hunted, trapped, or fished or from plants that could be picked. In this regard, human beings fed themselves as highly intelligent animals that used their advantages of communication, tools, and food preparation.

Agriculture is the systematic cultivation of crops or the raising of livestock. With agriculture, people were able to grow or raise their own food, but this required a degree of planning that hunting and gathering systems did not. The adoption of agriculture also required some knowledge specific to the many different types of crops that were cultivated. The evidence is clear that knowledge of agriculture did not always lead directly to its adoption. Yet once the decision was made, people never looked back.

Because the origin of agriculture took place in prehistory, it is not possible to know exactly how and why some societies adopted it as a new way of life. Based on archeological evidence, we do know that agriculture emerged from multiple hearths scattered across the world. This means that it was adopted independently, in different places under different conditions.

We now take the development of agriculture as a given, but it did not have to turn out that way. Prehistoric societies probably did quite well for themselves and, in fact, rapidly rose to the top of the food chain. While lives were undoubtedly short, except for a lucky few, and the work may have been difficult, this was true for most early and late agricultural societies as well. In fact, the evidence we have from existing hunting and gathering societies is that there is a fair amount of leisure time available and that the diet can be quite varied. So what would make people adopt agriculture? Early in the twentieth century, two theories were introduced by noted scholars, trying to explain this all-important phenomenon. These theories are explained in Figure 15D.2 and Figure 15D.3.

Both theories may help explain agriculture in a particular place and time, but one theory that takes population pressure into account proves more generally valid. It may have worked something like this:

In northern China, off of the Huang Ho River, crops of millet were domesticated about 9,500 years ago; possibly related, along the Yangtze River, crops of rice were domesticated about the same time.

In the Middle East, in what is described as the Fertile Crescent, crops of barley and wheat were domesticated 10,000–12,000 years ago.

In what is now the eastern United States, crops of sunflower were domesticated about 4,500 years ago.

In Meso-America in what is now southern Mexico, crops of maize (corn) and squash were domesticated about 5,500 years ago.

In Africa within the Sahel region, crops of millet and sorghum were domesticated about 7,000 years ago.

In Southeast Asia, the planned cultivation of root crops (vegeculture) may have begun 10,000 years ago.

In the central Andes, crops of white potatoes were domesticated about 4,500 years ago.

▲ **Figure 15D.1** This map shows the primary hearths in agriculture, the crops domesticated, and the approximate time that domestication began. There may have been other hearths as well, with different crop complexes, but this is a good indicator of the variety of crop complexes and hearths available.

During the Pleistocene era, hunting and gathering humans were able to spread out and occupy virtually every corner of the world. But this also created ecological instability. For one thing, it probably caused widespread extinctions. Humans went first for big game, and many of these large mammals died off as a result.

These successes in hunting and gathering allowed the population to increase. This population increase was very slow by today's standards. People died young and most women would not be able to manage numerous children. Some estimates are that, on average, the population increased by about 0.002% a year, or 20 per million. This rate of increase is unnoticeable over a couple of generations, but over the course of tens of thousands of years it adds up.

Population pressures required that humans adjust their activities to focus on a particular place, possibly staying put for long stretches of time. This sort of complex foraging meant a need to gather a wide spectrum of food from a smaller number of places. People became more familiar with exactly where certain plants were located and when plants could be harvested for peak flavor. They may also have discovered better ways to get small game and fish.

It also meant less emphasis on big game and more emphasis on other foods. Evidence from ancient Mexico indicates a shift from a meat-based diet over the course of several thousand years. Archeological evidence suggests that humans used more plant food as opposed to animal food, more foods that require more preparation (poisons have to be leached out, for example), and more high-yield, low-prestige foods, such as shellfish. There is also evidence that these practices resulted in communities that settled down around a single place.

These new adaptations worked for a long time but still required a small number of people on the land.

▲ **Figure 15D.2** One theory, advocated by geographer Carl Sauer, saw agriculture as occurring in a favorable environment where plenty of food and water were available and where people led a reasonably carefree existence with a lot of leisure time. There was also a need for land that was wooded and easy to till, as well as communities amenable to experimentation. According to Sauer, the ideal locale would be near present-day Thailand. Here, the population began cultivating starchy, tropical crops, such as yams and bananas. These crops are grown by breaking off a part of the plant and burying it in the ground—a process known as vegeculture. This may have also had some religious significance, signifying destruction and regeneration. Tropical, well-watered environments were ideal for the domestication of crops such as taro root, one of the early staples for people in Southeast Asia and the Pacific islands. Every part of the taro plant is edible when cooked. The taro roots can be cooked and mashed somewhat as potatoes are.

Figure 15D.3 ▶ An opposed theory, advocated by the archeologist V. Gordon Childe, claimed that agriculture began during periods of environmental stress, perhaps as a result of global warming after the end of glaciation. This would have occurred in Southwest Asia, where drying conditions led to a scarcity of food. This caused a population implosion as people retreated to relatively moist areas near rivers and oases, as well as up to the higher elevations. The diminished environment led to a search for new sources of food and led to greater contact between people, plants, and animals. Necessity compelled the development of new food production techniques. It was likely through seed agriculture—in which seeds from plants such as wild barley (shown) are sown to later yield plants—that initial agriculture began in the region.

▲ **Figure 15D.4** Humans came to the American continents about 30,000 years ago and proceeded to occupy most of the lands here. These are a few of possibly 30 large animals in the New World that became extinct as a result of hunting. These included the ground sloth (at right), the mammoth (upper left), and the stag moose and saber tooth cat (lower left).

Even highly productive hunting and gathering societies could only sustain a population density of two people per square mile. At different places and different times throughout the globe, the **carrying capacity** of the land, or the number of people an area can support, given the technology, was exhausted.

At the same time, complex foraging resulted in greater knowledge of and intervention in the natural environment. Humans favored certain plants most beneficial to them. They tended to useful plants; removed useless plants (weeds) that competed for soil, sun and water; and perhaps dispersed seeds. They also favored plants that carried desirable traits, such as bigger fruit or more edible seeds. These traits would not have ordinarily mattered and may have been counterproductive for natural survival. But with human intervention, they could be sustained and propagated. In this way, *human selection* replaced *natural selection*. Geographer Jared Diamond provides the interesting example of almonds. Of course, we now know of almonds as flavorful and quite beneficial to health. But most almonds in the wild are bitter and poisonous, laced with cyanide. A mutation causes some almonds to lose this trait. This lack of bitterness is not advantageous in nature, because it causes the mutated almonds to be eaten by birds. But with human selection, these sweet-tasting, healthy almonds were nurtured and allowed to flourish.

This eventually leads to the stage in which actual planting takes place. Somehow, someone figured out that he or she could plant seeds (seed agriculture)—or in some cases (as for bananas), a part of the plant (vegeculture)—and a new plant would come up. Plants and animals become domesticated and dependent on humans for their survival.

Agriculture emerged as a new means of acquiring food, but not without cost. Agriculture probably required a great deal more work, and it may have been seen as a low-prestige way of producing food. But it allowed for an increase in the carrying capacity of the land by allowing more food production per unit area of land. When the extensive land requirements of hunting and gathering technologies were no longer feasible, human populations had the choice of either adopting agricultural methods or risking starvation.

Each area developed its unique style as different staples were grown. This resulted in distinct **crop complexes**, which became the basis of regional cuisines. The Middle East developed barley and wheat, northern

◀ **Figure 15D.5** Much of the complex foraging was focused on a place where there existed two or more separate environments, termed an **ecotone**. Ecotones were special places because they allowed for a greater variety of foodstuffs at different times of the year. It is in such places that agriculture most likely began.

China first domesticated millet, Southeast Asia was first with yams and the taro plant, and Meso-America made great use of maize.

From the early centers of domestication, agriculture diffused to eventually encompass the entire world. However, the process of acceptance could take a long time. It was not a question of knowledge. Some hunting and gathering populations, such as aboriginal groups in northeast Australia and prehistoric California, traded with farmers without adopting that technology for themselves. Other groups, such as peoples along the coast of northern Germany, waited over 1,300 years—over 65 generations!—before adopting this method of food production.

Most indications are that the introduction of agriculture in the Middle East, along the Fertile Crescent, eventually made its way to Europe. This is borne out by similarities in crop complexes, with Europeans adopting wheat and barley, both of which originated in the Middle East, and practicing a mixed agricultural economy that makes widespread use of animals. But there is also a significant time lag.

There is also a major difference between the climate along the coast of the Mediterranean Sea and the wetter and colder climates of northern and western Europe. This forced the domestication of new crops, such as rye and oats, which are more tolerant of moisture. It probably also led to the greater use of animals. Thus, while agriculture likely spread from the Middle East to Europe, it also lagged because European hunters and gatherers were hesitant to adopt farming techniques and had to come up with crops that were more locally useful.

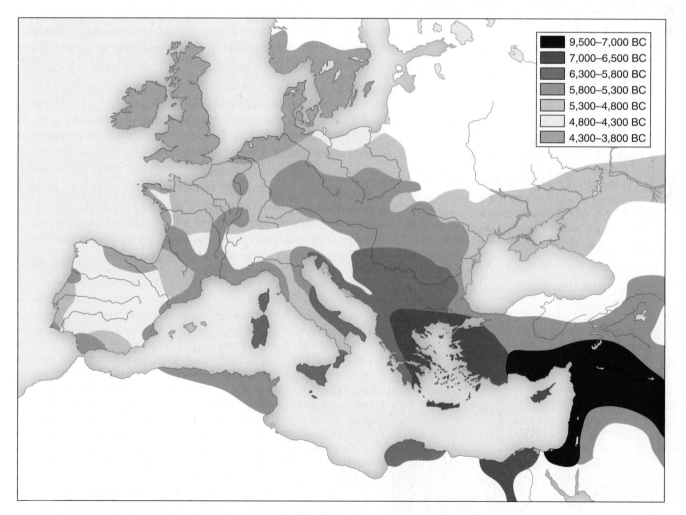

■	9,500–7,000 BC
■	7,000–6,500 BC
■	6,300–5,800 BC
■	5,800–5,300 BC
■	5,300–4,800 BC
□	4,800–4,300 BC
■	4,300–3,800 BC

▲ **Figure 15D.6 Expansion of Agriculture in Europe** Most early theories naturally assumed that agriculture developed in the Middle East, diffused first to Greece, then through the Mediterranean, up through the Balkan peninsula, and then north and west through the rest of Europe. There are indications of agriculture in the Balkans and the Danube basin as early as 6000 BC, in northern Italy as early as 5800 BC (certain types of pottery), in Germany by 5800 BC (also through analysis of pottery), in Switzerland near alpine lakes by 5000 BC, and as far to the north and west as the British Isles by about 4000 BC.

15E Different Types of Agriculture

▲ **Figure 15E.1** If you enjoy drinking a tall glass of milk with your cake and cookies, you are in the world's minority. Most people cannot adequately digest fluid milk—specifically, the lactose sugars found in milk. The result is an unpleasant, bloated feeling. This inability to digest milk, termed lactose intolerance, has an interesting geography because it is not spread evenly. There are only three regions where most people are not lactose intolerant: northern Europe among Germanic, Scandinavian, Finnish, and British populations; nomadic populations in Arabia, the Sahel, and Sudan; and the Tutsi population of Rwanda and Burundi. The northern European region is the largest and, through colonization, has spread this digestive enzyme to North America and Oceania. How did this ability come about? Probably it was introduced in early agriculture. The lactose in milk facilitates calcium absorption, most important in climates that are cool and cloudy. Over time, lactose tolerance proved a boon to survival, and a desirable genetic trait was passed on.

While it is difficult to designate uniform agricultural regions, today there are clear separations between places where humans practice one or more different types of agriculture.

The first distinction is between areas that are **arable**, or conducive to farming, and those that are not. Some parts of the world are simply too dry to sustain agriculture without a massive infusion of water. Agronomists call this the *aridity line*. Other parts of the world are too cold and are found behind the *thermal deficit line*. A few parts of the world are too mountainous, particularly near the Himalayas.

A second distinction can be found between regions where agriculture is primarily animal-centered, based on livestock, and regions where agriculture is primarily plant-centered, based on cultivating crops. People who raise livestock are considered herders or ranchers, and these regions tend to be where the climate and soil are less amenable to intensive cultivation of crops.

A third distinction lies between subsistence agriculture and commercial agriculture. In **subsistence agriculture**, nearly all of the crops and livestock are used to support the farmer, the farmer's family, and perhaps a larger group within a clan or village. In subsistence agriculture, people consume what they produce, whether for food, drink, fuel, or clothing. As a result, subsistence farmers cultivate a variety of crops, although they will likely focus on a few staples. In **commercial agriculture**, crops and livestock are farmed for cash and are considered commodities, intended to be exchanged for payment. Commercial farmers are more likely to focus on one or two items in order to gain a maximum return on their investment. The choice of what to farm depends on the comparative advantage of the land, market demands, and the quantity and skills of the farmers themselves.

◄ **Figure 15E.2** While many farming systems require lots of labor on smaller plots of land, other farming systems require a lot of land, resulting in lower densities and larger plots. Cultures found in the broad grasslands that extend from Manchuria through central Asia and into eastern Europe adopted a life of **pastoral nomadism**. *Pastoral* means "animals" and *nomadism* means "moving around and not settled." These cultures located in areas that were too harsh for crops and moved seasonally with their animals to locate the available water. This is still the life of the Lapps or Sami who live in northern Scandinavia. A more **mixed agricultural economy** prevailed in the Middle East and later in Europe. This involved a heavy reliance on both plants and animals. Cattle, goats, and sheep were important, but so were the grains to feed them and to feed the household. In such societies, animals were used for meat, for fertilizer, as a source of fabric, for traction in plowing, for mobility, and, of course, as a source of milk, butter, and cheese.

◀ **Figure 15E.3** The term *agribusiness* is often brought up in discussions of commercial agriculture. Commercial farming operations are businesses, but most are still family owned and operated. **Agribusiness** refers to a large company that owns the land and hires individuals to cultivate crops or raise livestock. It also refers to some of the other aspects of food production, from inputs (such as fertilizer, seeds, and equipment) to the delivery and storage of the farm products. Companies such as Tyson often contract out the raising of livestock to individual farmers but require certain practices. Such companies have been criticized for overuse of antibiotics and severe overcrowding among the livestock.

▼ **Figure 15E.4 Agricultural Regions of the World**

Commercial forestry and recreation: Heavily forested regions are often used primarily for forestry activities in order to provide wood and paper products. These same regions also serve as good places for recreational activities like hunting and fishing.

Dryland nomadic livestock herding, forestry, fishing, and hunting: Animals are herded from place to place, in search of forage vegetation. The animals—camels, goats, sheep—supply meat, milk, clothing, and building materials. This type of farming is found in marginal areas and is the one agricultural system that is not fixed in a single place. In addition, people in this category are also involved in some subsistence forestry, fishing, hunting, and gathering.

Tropical shifting subsistence cultivation: Farmers occupy an area of forest land, slash the vegetation, burn the remaining stumps to the ground, and then plant a variety of crops on the soil enriched by all of the organic matter. When the soil is exhausted after a few years, the farmers move along to another nearby plot. This type of agriculture is quite sustainable, but requires a great deal of land.

Commercial livestock ranching: A great deal of land is needed to raise cattle—several acres for one steer. In the United States, much of this land is government owned and leased to the ranchers. By and large, cattle ranchers are found in semi-arid regions of the world. Ranchers also focus on other animals, like sheep or alpacas.

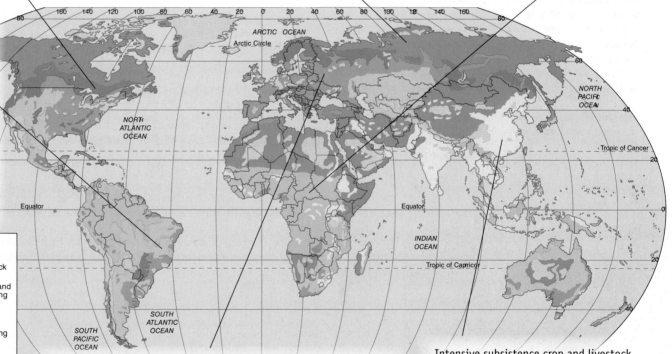

World Land Use
Predominant Activities by Region

- Commercial Crop and Livestock Agriculture
- Intensive Subsistence Crop and Livestock Agriculture, including Plantations
- Tropical Shifting Subsistence Agriculture
- Commercial Livestock Ranching
- Dryland Nomadic Livestock Herding, Forestry, Fishing, Hunting (Primarily Subsistence)
- Commercial Forestry and Recreation
- No Major Economic Activity

Commercial crop and livestock agriculture: This category includes many types of commercial agriculture. In some instances, grain crops, like wheat, are grown on large farms and utilize a great deal of technology. In other cases, farmers raise crops like corn and soybeans, as well as livestock such as pigs. Where conditions are appropriate, many fruits and vegetables are intensively cultivated. Sometimes, this has to do with the proximity of agricultural land to major market centers (see next module) or because some regions are particularly well suited, in terms of soil and climate, for the growing of fruits and vegetables. Some highly productive regions, like the Central Valley of California, rely on substantial irrigation.

Intensive subsistence crop and livestock agriculture, including plantations: Farmers cultivate small plots of land and grow staple crops, like rice and some other grains, in an intensive manner. Almost all of the work is done by hand with occasional animal labor (which also offers fertilizer). There is virtually no mechanization in this system. This map also includes plantation agriculture, which is the large-scale commercial cultivation of tropical crops, such as pineapples, sugar, coffee, and cocoa.

15F Theory of Rural Land Use

Commercial agriculture uses the principle of **comparative advantage**, which dictates that a specific region does a better job of producing something—in this case, a specific agricultural commodity—compared to another region, due to a more advantageous physical environment, the particular habits and skills of local farmers, and the proximity to markets. (The idea of comparative advantage can be extended to other economic activities as well; see Module 17B). Different crops are grown according to these factors and the choice of how to use the land—whether for urban uses, a particular crop, a range, a forest, or fallow land—is dictated by how profitable a particular land use might be. This profitability, or **land rent**, is governed by soil quality, climate, terrain, and cultural factors. All of these affect the costs and market price of the crops grown or developed on the land. Land rent is also dictated by the distance from the central market, where the crop would be sold.

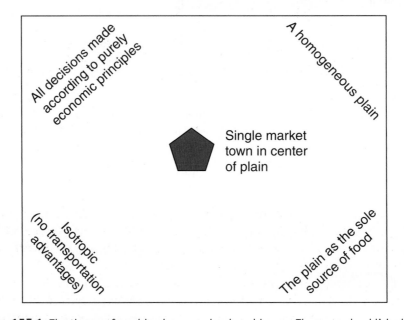

▲ **Figure 15F.1** The theory of rural land use, as developed by von Thunen and published in 1826, makes the assumptions as found on the graphic. The choice of what to cultivate depends on the following equation:

Land rent = (output × (price – production costs)) – (output × transport costs × distance from market)

The first part of the equation is the land rent received regardless of distance. The second part refers to the impact of distance. What types of commodities are especially sensitive to distance? Fluid milk is one, because it is highly perishable. When von Thunen developed this idea, distances and perishability were far more significant, but even today, they can play an important role. Another item that would be more affected by distance is something bulky and heavy to transport. One good example is firewood to heat a home. In von Thunen's day, timber for fuel was cultivated closer to city centers.

Figure 15F.2 ▶ Looking at different land uses, you can get a sense of which crops are likely to be found at which distances. What is important is the land rent of one crop relative to other crops. The land use generating the greatest land rent prevails. This graph can also be converted to a map of a plain surrounding a market center, with the likely agricultural land uses radiating out from the market center.

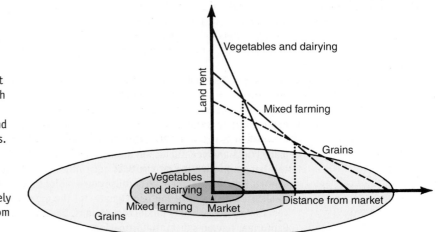

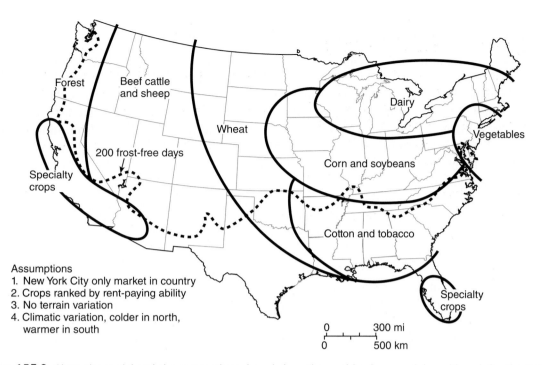

▲ **Figure 15F.3** Given the model and the assumptions, here is how the rural land use model would work for the United States. This is not too far from the reality of the actual land uses.

These ideas are particularly important to geographers because they help determine where certain crops would be grown. This was especially true in the past, when transportation was more difficult and the costs associated with transport could undercut the potential profit. The land rent concept is the basis for the **theory of rural land use**, associated with Johann von Thunen.

This model excels at showing the location of land uses in the past and how the distribution of certain crops shifted with changing transport costs. But does this model still apply to modern economies? Today, distances are shorter, so many items can be shipped in refrigerated trucks. But a number of perishable products—milk, fresh fruits, and vegetables—are still grown close by cities. This may become more important as people seek out locally grown food.

Figure 15F.4 ▶ The model in 15F.2 can be modified by relaxing many of the assumptions.

1. Assumption of a homogeneous plain. What happens if there is a section that is especially fertile? This alters the amount of yield for each crop and would push the line outward.
2. Assumption of isotropic plain. What happens if there is a river or some other transportation source near the farm? This lowers the transport costs for every crop that might be grown and stretches out the area where that crop might be grown.
3. Assumption of single market town. What happens if there is a second, smaller market town? This creates its own set of land use lines in its own hinterland, with an indifference line at some point between the two hinterlands.
4. Assumption of decisions according to economically optimizing behavior. What happens when farmers make a decision that is not always in their absolute economic best interest? It will blur boundaries because some farmers may not produce the more valuable crop, but simply a crop that yields some profit.

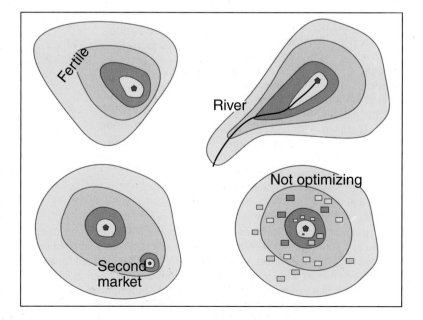

15G Agricultural Globalization, Then and Now

According to the Oxford English Dictionary, *globalization* is a fairly recent term, but the process it describes has been with us for a long time. This is nowhere more true than in agriculture, where the global exchange of crops and livestock forever transformed the world after 1492 and where the development of global corporations, distributions, and a world market have brought the products of the world into the local supermarket.

The global exchange of crops that occurred after 1492 is termed **The Great Columbian Exchange**. Fittingly, it was Christopher Columbus himself who took European crops, such as wheat, melons, grapes, and many others, to the island of Hispaniola. This began the largest exchange of agricultural products in the history of humankind.

The globalization of agriculture in the modern world takes many forms. While it is rare to see the introduction of new crops as took place during the Great Columbian Exchange, we now see the global infiltration of huge agricultural corporations and worldwide investment in farming, industrial farming practices, and a truly international marketplace. All of this creates a global food chain that stretches from ranches, plantations, fields, and groves across the world to your dinner table.

The nature of modern farming has changed quite a bit over the last several decades. Modern farmers in developed countries and in commercially owned acreages in the tropical regions have adopted industrial farming practices. This means that farmers use every device at their disposal to maximize yield, and this is accomplished through the choice of inputs, ways of farming, and the sale of food. The following are a few examples.

- Traditional fertilizer came from livestock (or even sometimes humans), but it is now based around synthetic nitrogen.
- Farmers purchase special hybrid seeds that can quadruple the amount of yield on an acre of land; the newest seeds are genetically modified.

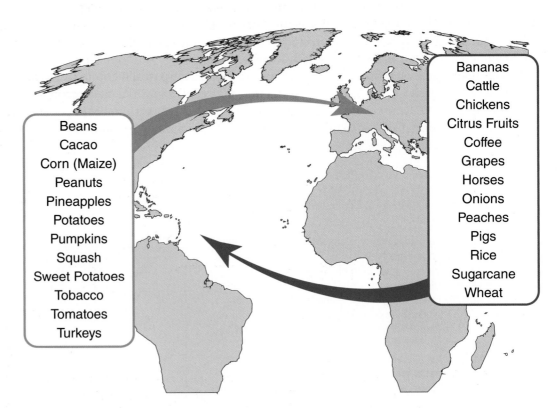

Figure 15G.1 ▶ In the wake of the European encounter with the Americas, hundreds of food crops and domesticated animals were exchanged. Nearly every crop from the Eastern Hemisphere was brought to the New World. The Spanish were especially intent on raising wheat for bread, grapes for wine, olives for oil, pigs and cattle for meat, and horses for transportation. Many of these items thrived in the tropical climate, pigs and cattle multiplied again and again in the wild, and others did better in more temperate regions. Sugarcane became a lucrative source of income for farmers throughout the Caribbean and South America. Orange groves prospered even without much tending. The result was that the number of food crops in the Americas tripled, with many doing better there than they had on the other side of the Atlantic.

The impact of American crops on the diets of Europe, Africa, and Asia was even more profound. There are foods that we now consider to be iconic of particular countries or cuisines—for example, the Irish potato, tomatoes in Italian cuisine, peanuts in Southeast Asian cooking, Indian chutney, cassava as a staple in tropical Africa. These are all crops that originated in the Americas. Maize, or corn, has become perhaps the most important crop in the world, either as a direct source of food for humans or as feed for animals. White potatoes and sweet potatoes are incredibly efficient, producing lots of food on small plots of land. Many American legumes, such as kidney beans, lima beans, and peanuts, help reinvigorate the fertility of the soil. Cassava grows in a variety of tropical climates and can be ground into a white flour that is the most important African staple. Other crops that are not staples, such as cacao, tobacco, and chili peppers, have been important as luxuries, or to enliven cuisines.

- Farmers require vast inputs of herbicides and pesticides to ensure that these expensive seeds are able to grow to maturity.
- Planting on the types of enormous acreages that constitute a modern commercial farm requires expensive farm equipment—combines and harvesters—each of which costs well over $100,000.

To increase efficiency, many farmers choose to focus on a single crop, or perhaps combine two. The result has been a huge bump in productivity. In his book *The Omnivore's Dilemma*, Michael Pollan estimates that the yield on an acre of corn has gone from 20 bushels per acre in the 1920s to 180 bushels per acre today.

In less developed countries, agricultural developments beginning in the 1950s and 1960s created a so-called **Green Revolution**. This was an attempt to import Western agricultural practices to subsistence farms in Asia, Latin America and Africa. New agricultural methods were diffused, including specialization, better seed selection, heavy use of fertilizers, better irrigation systems, more mechanization, and larger plots of land. New strains of wheat, rice, and corn were introduced that were much more responsive to fertilizer and to improved irrigation systems and, so, were much more productive. Fertilizer consumption increased markedly, as much as eight times in South Asia. Massive irrigation projects, financed by the World Bank, were built that provided water to agricultural regions and hydroelectric power to urban areas. To some extent, all of these innovations and inputs achieved the desired result of increasing food production. But problems also resulted because the Green Revolution did not necessarily jibe with local cultural methods. The modern techniques could be quite expensive for farmers to pursue—which often hurt the smaller, poorer farmers—and were not as environmentally friendly as some of the more traditional methods.

The distribution of food has also become far more globalized, as a few companies step into making sure that food from distant farms and plantations makes its way to the local grocery store. They are also responsible for processing food before it is sold to the consumer. Sometimes this reaches absurd lengths, such as cod caught off the coast of Norway, turned into filets in China, and then resold to Norwegian consumers. Lemons from Argentina are sold in Spain, even while local lemons are left to rot. Why is this? Much has to do with labor costs. Processing cod in China costs less than one-sixth as much as it would in Europe. Of course, this means that consumers can get a large variety of foods—kiwis, grapes, and shrimp—year round at reasonable prices. A country such as the United Kingdom, with a short growing season, now imports 95% of its fruit. The United States imports about $50 billion worth of fruit every year, including apples from New Zealand. But this global food chain requires a tremendous number of resources. All of these inputs require enormous amounts of energy, and the distribution of food to processing plants and then back to the consumer can be energy intensive as well, depending on the fuel needed for transport.

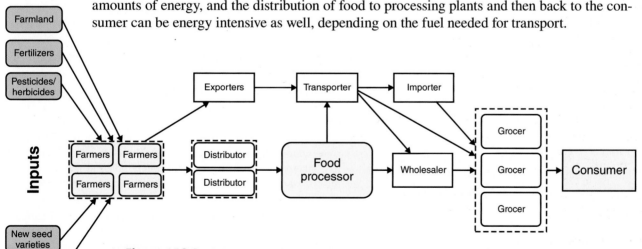

▲ **Figure 15G.2** Globalization of agriculture means that multinational agribusiness corporations hold tremendous sway in food production, even if they do not always own the land. Fertilizer is dominated by a few giant companies. Special hybrid seeds, which allow vastly more production on a given acre of land, are now sold to farmers by companies such as Monsanto. Likewise, the reliance of modern farming on herbicides and pesticides means a strong market for these products. A few manufacturers, such as John Deere and Caterpillar, are responsible for the sale of expensive farm equipment. The ownership and production are still primarily accomplished through family farmers, but more investment is finding its way into the purchase of land. Private investment firms are buying farmland in diverse places such as Argentina, Brazil, and England. Africa has begun to hold special appeal because the land is quite inexpensive by global standards; the plan is to consolidate holdings and introduce modern, industrial farming practices.

Key Terms

agribusiness (15E)
arable (15E)
artisans (15B)
capitalism (15B)
capitalist commercial
    economy (15B)
capitalist industrial economic
    system (15B)
carrying capacity (15D)
commercial agriculture (15E)
commodities (15B)
comparative advantage (15F)
crop complexes (15D)
depression (15C)
economic activity (15A)
economy (15A)
ecotone (15D)
feudalism (15A)
Green Revolution (15G)
gross domestic product
    (GDP) (15C)
gross national income (GNI) (15C)
gross national product (GNP) (15C)

hunting and gathering (15A)
imperial economies (15B)
irrigation (15A)
land rent (15F)
merchants (15B)
mixed agricultural economy (15E)
mixed economies (15B)
occupational specialization (15A)
pastoral nomadism (15E)
planned economies (15B)
primary sector (15C)
primitive agriculture (15A)
private sector (15C)
profit (15B)
public sector (15C)
quaternary sector (15C)
recession (15C)
secondary sector (15C)
subsistence agriculture (15E)
tertiary sector (15C)
The Great Columbian Exchange
    (15G)
theory of rural land use (15F)

Basic Review Questions

1. How would you define an economy and economic system?

2. What are some of the hallmarks of small-scale economic systems?

3. What were the features of the hunting and gathering economy?

4. How did the development of a surplus in primitive agricultural society allow for occupational specialization and possible social stratification?

5. How did a primitive agricultural society lead to a more settled and scheduled lifestyle?

6. What are some of the large-scale economic systems, and how do they differ from the small-scale systems?

7. What was the imperial economy composed of?

8. What are some of the aspects of capitalist economic systems?

9. What was the difference between trading within an imperial economy and trading within a capitalist economic system?

10. What are some of the key principles of the capitalist industrial economy?

11. What is a planned economy, and how does it deal with the exchange of goods and how these goods are distributed?

12. How do gross domestic product, gross national product, and gross national income measure the economy?

13. What is the difference between a recession and a depression?

14. What is the distinction between private sector output and public sector output in an economy? How does the public sector share of output vary between countries?

15. What is the distinction between primary sector activities, secondary sector activities, tertiary sector activities, and transportation utilities? About what percentage of the American economy does each of the sectors comprise?

16. What are some of the primary hearths where agriculture began?

17. What is the definition of agriculture?

18. What is the Carl Sauer theory of how agriculture may have begun?

19. What is the theory advocated by V. Gordon Childe?

20. What is the theory of agriculture that resulted from population pressure?

21. How does the idea of carrying capacity explain possible changes in the way in which people procured their food?

22. How have different regions of the world developed different crop complexes?

23. How did agriculture diffuse? Why did it take some time to spread from the Middle East to Europe?

24. What is pastoral nomadism?

25. What is the distinction between subsistence agriculture and commercial agriculture?

26. Describe each of the different agricultural regions.

27. Describe Von Thunen's theory of rural land use.

28. What was the importance of The Great Columbian Exchange?

29. How has the distribution of food become more globalized?

Advanced Review Questions (Essay Questions)

1. Describe the small-scale economic systems of hunting and gathering, primitive agriculture, and feudalism. How did these systems differ in regard to the use of barter, the level of specialization, and the role of government?

2. What was the difference in the nature of trade and the role of the merchant class in imperial economies and in capitalist economies? How did merchants within the capitalist economy deal with government? How did the Hanseatic League and Northern Italian economy grow to eventually encompass most of Europe?

3. What are some of the ways in which the economy can be measured? Where are the largest economies in the world?

4. Compare the three theories of how agriculture may have developed. What was the role of the environment in each of these theories? Overall, how many different hearths existed for early agriculture?

5. Why would it have been difficult for agriculture to diffuse? What are some reasons that the diffusion of agriculture from the Middle East to northern Europe likely took well over a thousand years? How did the diffusion of pastoral nomadism possibly lead to greater tolerance of milk?

6. How does subsistence agriculture compare to commercial agriculture? What are some of the locational demands of both subsistence and commercial agriculture? How does comparative advantage work to determine where things are grown?

7. Outline the theory of rural land use. What are some of its assumptions? How might the model of rural land use be modified based on differences in fertility, the presence of a river, or more than one market town?

8. Describe the importance of The Great Columbian Exchange. How did this alter the types of food used in the Old World and in the New World?

Further Study Topics

- Although hunting and gathering and primitive agricultural systems are fairly rare in the world today, they still exist. Research some modern-day hunting and gathering populations or some primitive agricultural economies—such as swidden, slash and burn, or pastoral nomadic. Examine the scope of the economy, the exchange system they have, the types of specializations, and the nature of organization.

- Almost every society is truly a mixed economy, with both private and public sector activity. But there are major variations in the size of the public sector. Examine two or three societies, including that of the United States. Note what the mix of private and public sector activity is in each of these societies. What are some activities taken over by the public sector in some societies that are found in the private sector in other societies?

- Examine the mix of agricultural regions and explore why these regions have developed the way they have. Is there any reason that some regions are involved in some forms of agriculture but not oth-

ers? How about for specific crops, such as wine grapes? List the factors determining the location of wine regions and explain some of the differences between them.

- A number of recent books and movies have highlighted the extent to which the food we eat is the product of far-flung, often unsustainable agricultural practices. In response to this, some communities have embraced locally grown products. Examine some of the local farming practices in your region. How do they operate? What are some of the challenges involved with these types of practices? Do you think that the food is healthier and better?

- Try to find a list of the top 25 corporations in the world, based on capitalization, revenues, profit, employees, or some other measure of size. Consider where these corporations are based and what kinds of products or services they provide. Try to find a similar list from 50 years ago. How would that list have changed? Would there be a difference in the countries represented? Would there be a different mix of products and services? Explain why.

Summary Activities

The theory of rural land use has become somewhat outdated with improvements in transportation and the rise of refrigeration. However, most cities still are surrounded by distinct agricultural zones. For example, most cities have a "milkshed" from where residents are able to get fresh milk.

For this exercise, take a city that you know (it should be a fairly large city) and try to locate the agricultural zones that surround it. You should consider dairying, fruits and vegetables, and other uses. Is there any logic to the location of these various agricultural land uses?

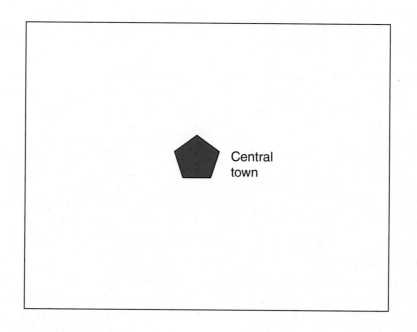

Central town

Geographies of Production and Consumption

Up until two centuries ago, most manufactured items were costly and rare. Energy came from people and animals, with some wind and water power thrown in as needed. Tools were often beautifully crafted and quite intricate, but they could only make things one at a time. As a result, only the rich could afford to purchase a lot of items. The masses of people made do with only a few, well-worn possessions.

After about 1800, a new mode of production based around factories and fossil fuel power began to change the quantity of things that could be produced, increasing manufacturing productivity 100 times over by expanding the productivity of every worker. This system made goods cheaper, provided a huge number of jobs in the new factories, and completely reoriented the way people lived. It also bestowed enormous advantages on those societies that were able to get there first. By 1839, Britain's position as an industrial powerhouse enabled it to defeat the Chinese Empire, with a population 20 times its size!

In more recent years, production and consumption have changed at a furious pace, and so have their geographies. The movement toward ever greater globalization, the development of high-technology industries, the creation of a predominantly service economy, and an increasing emphasis on consumer choice have transformed the world we live in.

16A Growth of Mass Production and an Industrial World

Production creates an object that is more valuable than the sum of the raw materials going into it. This is called **value added**: the difference between the price of the final product and the cost of raw materials, labor, and other inputs. For example, the actual value of many of the chief ingredients that go into a box of cereal—corn, rice, wheat, plus some sugar and other additives—may cost about 5 to 10 cents. Yet the value of the final product might be between 2 and 5 dollars! In this instance, there is a tremendous amount of value added in the production of cereal and allows such companies as Kellogg's, General Mills, and Post to employ many people and to make profits.

For most of human history, production occurred in small workshops. Artisans learned their craft over a period of many years, working as apprentices to a master craftsman before being allowed to strike out on their own. In Europe, most artisanal production was organized through guilds, associations of workshops that generally focused on a single industry, such as woolen textiles.

Mass production was the key outcome of **industrialization**, a process by which a greater proportion of a national economy is involved with manufacturing and that allowed more goods to be produced in greater quantity and at a lower price. While sometimes the term *Industrial Revolution* is used, industrialization was a long-term process that spanned a number of years, was associated with some major factors, and has taken decades to diffuse.

Industrialization opened the doors to the **mass production** of goods and helped spark demand for more goods as quantities rose and prices dropped. Industrial technologies required an enormous amount of financial capital, or money. Buying a steam engine, machinery, and a factory was more expensive and required deep pockets. Small artisans could not take advantage of the new technologies, so it was left to a new breed of entrepreneur, someone with a lot of extra money, to buy steam engines and put them to use. These needs also tended to favor particular places that had both the necessary capital and the human and raw material resources. Labor costs were also expensive, and many early industrialists did their utmost to squeeze every ounce of work out of their employees while paying as little as they could get away with.

▼ **Figure 16A.1** Industrialization was associated with three major changes.

Fɪɢ. 26.—Watt's Engine, 1774.

(a) The steam engine had been around for many centuries but had not been useful as a source of power until improvements were made in the 1760s by James Watt and others. Basically, coal was burned to boil water on a controlled basis. The steam that was generated forced the movement of pistons, which could then power all kinds of machinery, 24 hours a day, in any kind of environment. The steam engine also shifted the main power sources away from wind, water, and firewood to coal. This began industry's reliance on fossil fuels.

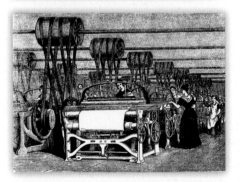

(b) New machinery was developed that could enhance the productivity of the human operator many times over. Some of these machines initially used water power from fast-moving streams, but they later adapted well to the more reliable steam engine. A mechanized or power loom enabled the age-old craft of weaving fibers into fabrics to be accelerated. It is because of power looms that textiles were the first craft to become industrialized.

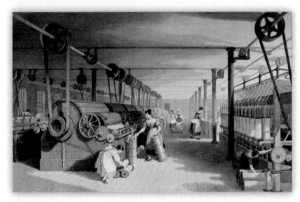

(c) Early steam engines were bulky and expensive, and they required a lot of coal. It cost a great deal of money to purchase some of the power machinery as well. The tools of industrialization were incompatible with the old workshop system. The **factory system** emerged, in which several people worked under one roof, bringing together all the necessary machinery to be powered from belts by one steam engine. This also changed the nature of artisan labor, generally requiring much less skill and allowing newcomers (often fresh from the countryside) to pick up the needed proficiency in a day or so. The factory system brought about a **division of labor**, in which each worker specialized in a single, repeated task, after which production was turned over to another laborer, who specialized in another task. Because no single task took too long to learn, this helped make labor cheaper and interchangeable.

Figure 16A.2 ▶ By 1800, Great Britain had about 11 million people, but it was poised to dominate the world economy in a manner that no other country had since the Roman Empire. Great Britain was able to capitalize on the following:

1. Efficiency: The demands of industrialization—ready resources and ready markets—required efficient economic systems. Great Britain was by far the most efficient economy around 1800. It had a compact area, no internal barriers, good turnpikes, and an excellent canal system. This allowed it to develop a domestic market and to reduce economic redundancies between regions. This also gave Britain and British merchants a huge amount of surplus financial capital, which could be invested in new modes of production.

2. Wealth: By 1800, Great Britain was also the richest and most global country. The American colonies played an important role as a source of raw materials for England and as a large market for British products. The British were successful in setting up the Britain—> Africa—> North America triangle with trade in slaves, sugar, and cotton. Merchants participating in this trading triangle, and other trading links, grew enormously wealthy.

3. Raw materials: Great Britain had started off as an outpost for wool. While it did not possess newer fibers, such as cotton, it did enjoy a big advantage in coal reserves, most of which were reasonably close to major population centers. As it was, most of the major industrial activity focused on areas near or on the coalfields. Cotton—the most essential fiber of the industrial era—was imported from places such as the American South. Later, Britain could also capitalize on an abundance of iron ore for making iron and later steel.

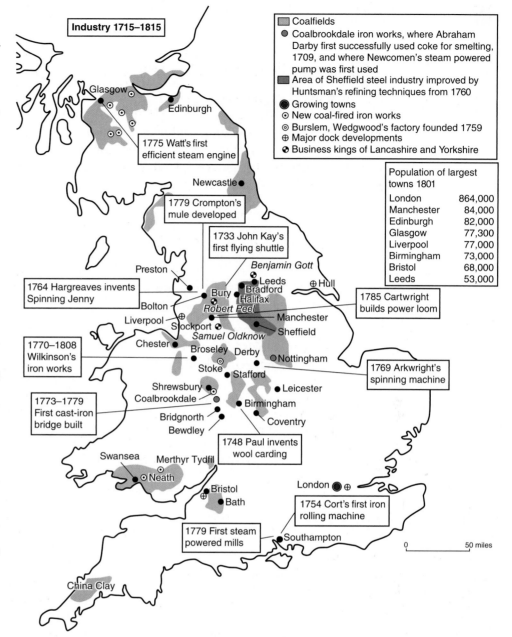

Industry 1715–1815

Coalfields
● Coalbrookdale iron works, where Abraham Darby first successfully used coke for smelting, 1709, and where Newcomen's steam powered pump was first used
■ Area of Sheffield steel industry improved by Huntsman's refining techniques from 1760
⬤ Growing towns
⊙ New coal-fired iron works
⊗ Burslem, Wedgwood's factory founded 1759
⊕ Major dock developments
❂ Business kings of Lancashire and Yorkshire

Population of largest towns 1801	
London	864,000
Manchester	84,000
Edinburgh	82,000
Glasgow	77,300
Liverpool	77,000
Birmingham	73,000
Bristol	68,000
Leeds	53,000

1775 Watt's first efficient steam engine

1779 Crompton's mule developed

1733 John Kay's first flying shuttle

1764 Hargreaves invents Spinning Jenny

1785 Cartwright builds power loom

1770–1808 Wilkinson's iron works

1769 Arkwright's spinning machine

1773–1779 First cast-iron bridge built

1748 Paul invents wool carding

1754 Cort's first iron rolling machine

1779 First steam powered mills

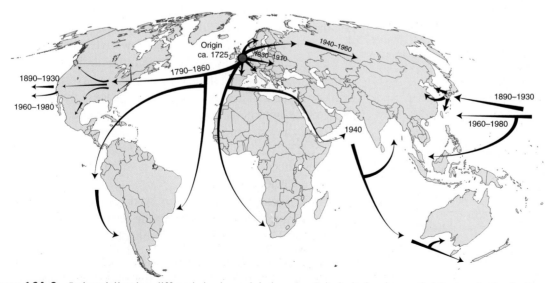

▲ **Figure 16A.3** Industrialization diffused slowly, mainly because Britain jealously guarded its new technologies. Other European countries, such as Belgium, France, and Germany, industrialized later (post-1850), followed by northern Italy and central Europe in 1880. The United States and Canada also industrialized in part during the middle nineteenth century. Around the turn of the twentieth century, Japan began to industrialize, followed by Russia and Eastern Europe. Industrialization in Latin America, China, India, and finally Africa occurred more in the mid to late twentieth century.

16B Factors of Production and Changing Geographies of Industrial Location

Manufacturing is a **production chain** that transforms raw materials into a finished product, then distributes that product for consumption by households, government, or other industries. While this process is fairly straightforward, it incorporates a number of direct and indirect **factors of production** considered in any industry (see also Module 17C on factors related to trading). Direct factors include the following:

- raw materials: the materials needed to make the product
- labor: the workers needed for the production process
- financial capital: the money needed to finance the production process
- markets: the households, firms, or government that will purchase the final product

Indirect factors, while important to any production process, are external to the actual production chain and include the following:

- technology: the nature of machinery in the production process
- infrastructure: logistic support in the form of communications, transportation, electricity, and water
- financial system: the availability of financing
- government role: government regulations, stability, tax policy, incentives, trade policies
- education/training: proximity to schools to create a trained labor force
- entrepreneurial climate: a number of intangible factors that foster entrepreneurship

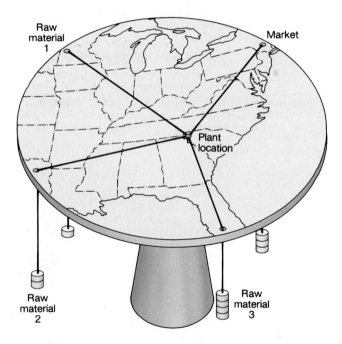

▲ **Figure 16B.1** In this example are three sources of raw materials and a single market. One raw material (Raw material 1) could be a power source, such as coal. Other raw materials (Raw material 2 and Raw material 3) might be important ingredients, such as iron and nickel. The market (Market) is located at some distance from all three. Where to locate the factory? It all depends on the cost of shipping each of the raw materials and the finished product. If the shipping costs are approximately equal for all three factors, then the factory will likely locate in the center of the triangle. However, if shipping costs are greater for one of the raw material sources, perhaps because the raw material was far heavier than the finished product, then the optimum location would be pulled toward the location of that material.

Each of these factors has a particular geography that must be considered, especially the factors of distance and transportation costs. Economist Alfred Weber developed a model of industrial location in 1909. He stated that the **optimum location** of a manufacturing plant is a balance between the locations of the various raw materials, the labor force, and the markets where the final products would be sold. Weber also distinguished between some raw materials, such as water, which are considered *ubiquitous* (available everywhere) and most raw materials, such as cotton or petroleum (as a source of power), which are *localized*. We need to consider how processing affects raw materials when discussing localized materials. Some raw materials, such as metallic ores, lose a great deal of weight in their processing. It does not make sense to transport these raw materials any great distance; rather, it is better to try to reduce the weight close to the source. Other raw materials gain a great deal of weight in processing, often through the addition of a ubiquitous material, such as water. This is true of many beverages, such as soft drinks and beer. Then, it is cheaper to process the raw material as close to the market as possible. Markets are generally localized as well, and they depend on who are the primary customers for the product. The labor force may or may not be localized, although in some instances labor, like capital, is more easily moved to where the factory is located.

These factors of production were undoubtedly important in determining industrial location in the past. But are they as significant today? There have been some big changes:

1. Transportation costs have steadily declined. This means that the costs of transporting raw materials and finished products are lower.
2. The costs and specialization of labor have increased. Most industries require a particular set of skills and they cannot rely

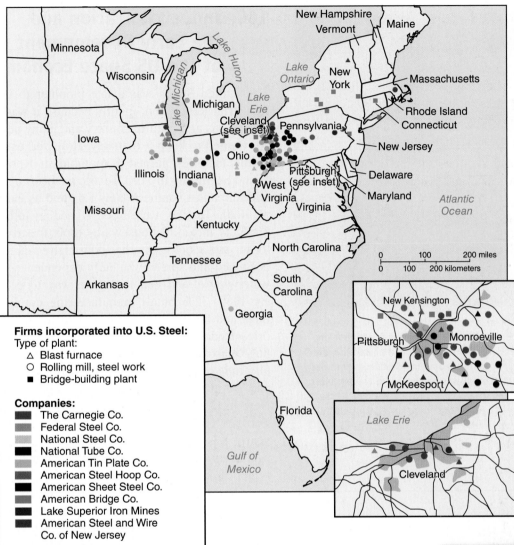

Firms incorporated into U.S. Steel:
Type of plant:
△ Blast furnace
○ Rolling mill, steel work
■ Bridge-building plant

Companies:
■ The Carnegie Co.
■ Federal Steel Co.
■ National Steel Co.
■ National Tube Co.
■ American Tin Plate Co.
■ American Steel Hoop Co.
■ American Sheet Steel Co.
■ American Bridge Co.
■ Lake Superior Iron Mines
■ American Steel and Wire
   Co. of New Jersey

◀ **Figure 16B.2** At the turn of twentieth century, the US steel industry was focused on a narrow belt that extended from just west of Cleveland to Johnstown, Pennsylvania (with important outposts in Chicago and Indianapolis). This location was no accident. The steel industry relied on iron ore as its primary ingredient and required huge blast furnaces fueled by bituminous coal. Great Lakes shipping made it fairly cheap to obtain iron ore from northern Minnesota, and bituminous coal was available along the northern Appalachians, just to the east of this steel-producing region. Transporting these raw and finished goods often required several modes of transportation: cargo ships, canal boats, and trains. The transfer of cargo from one transportation source to another, which also entails breaking the cargo into smaller units, occurs at the **break-in-bulk point**. These points developed into important cities ringing the Great Lakes. The markets for steel were many, from the major cities on the East Coast and Great Lakes to various forward-linkage industries (see Module 16C) that required steel for their own production chain. Many of these industries are also located in this steel-producing region.

Figure 16B.3 ▶ The garment industry is split between those segments that design clothes and those that produce the clothes. The design and some initial preparation, such as cutting, require much more specialized and higher-cost labor. These may be performed in high-income countries where particular labels are headquartered. The actual production of garments—which requires far more labor—is then outsourced to low-wage countries. The stratification of clothing among high-fashion houses, specialty stores, mass retailers, and discount stores is also reflected in various outsourcing arrangements. The significance of government policy, particularly the North American Free Trade Agreement (NAFTA), is also apparent in the rise of Mexico as a key production center, which became the world's sixth leading exporter in 2004. Many factories locate right near the border, in the **maquiladora** zone. But increasingly, factory owners have sought even lower wages in central and southern Mexico.

on the nearby labor force to possess those skills. As brainpower has replaced brawn power, there is an emphasis on educational facilities to train workers and the types of amenities that might keep workers at the site.

3. Most production is conducted transnationally, far beyond what existed before. If the primary cost factor for production is the cost of labor, then industries will locate factories in countries where labor is cheap.

4. Government also plays a bigger role as countries, states, and municipalities lure attractive industries with incentives and trade policies help channel outsourcing arrangements.

5. Production processes have changed to become more nimble, specialized, and flexible.

▲ **Figure 16C.1** Mills were built in New England towns such as Waltham, Lowell, Lawrence, Taunton, Fall River, and Providence. Many of the early mills relied first on water power, where streams and canals moved large water wheels and powered hydraulic turbines. New England capitalized on its early advantages as a mercantile region. Early industrialists, such as Francis Lowell (for whom Lowell was named) were the products of a prosperous Boston- and Newburyport-based merchant class that possessed the wealth needed to start new factories and were open to new innovations. Lowell himself helped establish the Boston Manufacturing Company in Waltham, which was responsible for a fifth of cotton textile production by 1850.

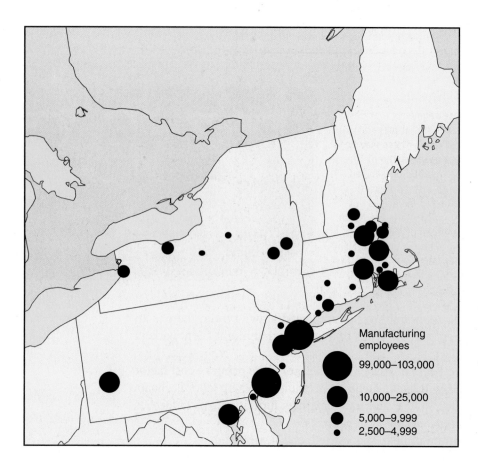

Manufacturing employees

● 99,000–103,000

● 10,000–25,000

● 5,000–9,999

● 2,500–4,999

16C Industrialization and the Early Development of the US Space Economy

The United States was a late bloomer to the Industrial Revolution, mainly because it was a prosperous agricultural country and many people wanted to keep it that way. However, early textile factories gained a foothold in Rhode Island beginning in 1790. Textile factories were widespread in southern New England as early as 1830. Textiles were soon joined by other products, including housewares, tools, firearms, locks, and clocks. As the industrial economy deepened and spread, the early dependence on water power and charcoal gave way to coal. By 1860, 72% of all manufacturing employment and 68% of all the manufacturing profits originated in the Northeast. In Pennsylvania, huge blast furnaces were developed to produce all kinds of ironworks, and Philadelphia alone had 7% of all US manufacturing employment. New York City produced engineering works, iron products, and machinery—accounting for nearly 8% of manufacturing employment—as well as serving as the financial and commercial center of the country.

These manufacturing centers relied on raw materials from a number of places. Iron was procured from Minnesota, beef and wheat from the Great Plains, cotton from the American South, minerals such as copper from the far West. These outside regions were economically integrated into the American economy, but in a way that strengthened the economic position of the Anglo-American Manufacturing Belt. In this way, they might be considered economic peripheries (see Module 18C) in that they provided raw materials to the core region but had

◀ **Figure 16C.2** These early advantages persisted as northeastern cities became home to the vast majority of all US manufacturing. Beginning with textiles, the industrial base soon diversified through forward and backward linkages. The **forward linkages**—those types of items that might be produced with cotton textiles—lay in the production of garments such as shirts, pants, and other cotton goods. The **backward linkages**—what textile production required as inputs—stemmed from the demand for textile machinery, machine tools, metal working, and iron casting.

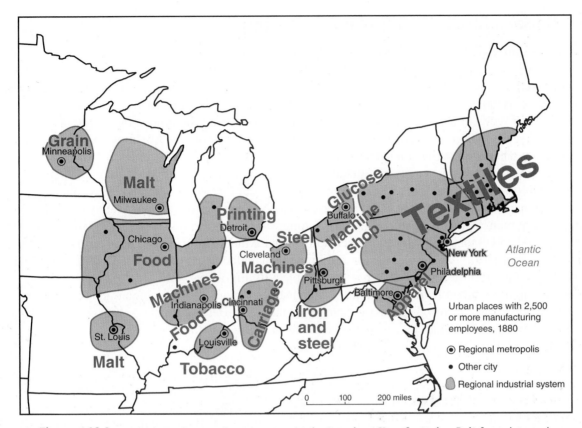

▲ **Figure 16C.3** By the late nineteenth century, an **Anglo-American Manufacturing Belt** formed a rough parallelogram, which extended to include important centers in Ohio, Indiana, Michigan, Illinois, and Wisconsin. These centers specialized in different industries. Textiles were still important to Philadelphia; clothing in Boston, New York, and Cincinnati; meatpacking in Chicago; and brewing in Milwaukee. Cleveland and Pittsburgh emphasized iron and steel production based on their factors of production (see Module 16D). By the turn of the twentieth century, several capital-intensive steel companies—Carnegie and U.S. Steel—had emerged as the largest in the world. Smaller cities, such as Johnstown, Pennsylvania; Youngstown, Ohio; and Gary, Indiana, also benefited. The development of petroleum refining, based on oil discoveries in Pennsylvania, Ohio, and Indiana, further consolidated the industrial prowess of Cleveland, Chicago, Philadelphia, and New York.

very little independent economic power. The South, for instance, was by far the poorest region of the United States, with average incomes only a third that of the Northeast.

In general, this core region was able to rely on several important aspects of comparative advantage (see Modules 15G and 17B) and a favorable relative location (see Module 1B):

- Railroads tied the area together, making it easy to go from one place to the other without too much difficulty. Distances between places in the core were short, and this helped facilitate commerce.
- The proximity between places also enhanced communication, which was vital to conducting business within and between cities. The idea of traveling for weeks to meet with a prospective business partner was just not feasible, so industries tended to locate close to other industries.
- Since money was such an important ingredient of commerce, being near the main banks was a benefit to industry.
- Natural advantages prevailed in this region. The eastern seaboard and the Great Lakes had several good ports, whereas the interior—with the exception of New England—contained plenty of prime farmland. Abundant coal in the area made it appealing to locate industries in this belt.
- The economic dynamism of the region attracted skilled and unskilled labor. Because of better schools and the presence of industry, skilled labor migrated here. Most of the immigrants also settled in the core cities, especially with the closing of the frontier in 1890.

16D Modern Shifts in US Manufacturing

By 1900, the United States was producing one-third of the world's industrial output, and nearly all of that capacity came out of the Anglo-American Manufacturing Belt. This region continued to enjoy economic dominance well into the middle of the twentieth century. But then things changed. Due to shifting factors of production (see Modules 16B and 17C), manufacturing moved from the northeastern and midwestern states to the South and West. At a smaller scale, manufacturing moved from the inner cities to the outer suburbs.

These changes profoundly affected the status of US regional economies. Any movement of manufacturing plants from one region to the other represented a movement of what had become fairly high-paying jobs. In 1950, manufacturing was a heavily unionized sector, and unions had been successful in raising wages and benefits to a fairly comfortable level. The dream of a house, a car (or two), vacations, and a college education for the children became attainable on a single income. The National Association of Manufacturers estimates that the average manufacturing compensation (including wages and benefits) was $69,000 in 2006, or about $12,000 more than US jobs as a whole. Furthermore, because manufacturing is a **base employment** sector, it supports a lot of jobs in the service sector and in other manufacturing industries. With the movement of all of these job opportunities, it makes sense that people will migrate as well.

What led to these broad regional changes? Much had to do with shifting comparative advantages. The comparative advantages of the Anglo-American Manufacturing Belt diminished and the region began to experience a number of distinct disadvantages relative to the rest of the country. We look at some of the principal factors behind this shift on the following pages.

▼ **Figure 16D.1**

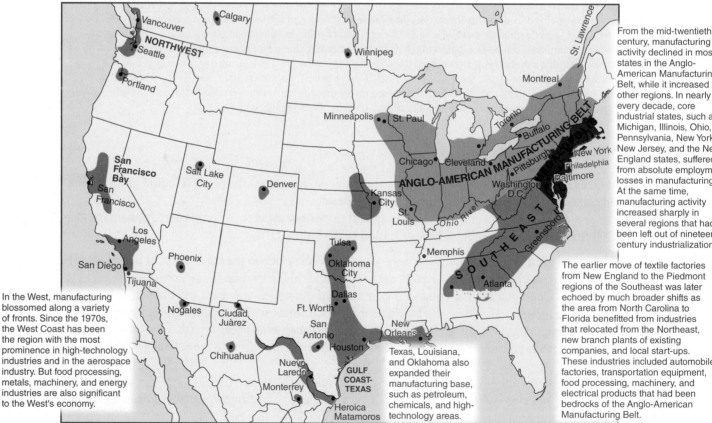

From the mid-twentieth century, manufacturing activity declined in most states in the Anglo-American Manufacturing Belt, while it increased in other regions. In nearly every decade, core industrial states, such as Michigan, Illinois, Ohio, Pennsylvania, New York, New Jersey, and the New England states, suffered from absolute employment losses in manufacturing. At the same time, manufacturing activity increased sharply in several regions that had been left out of nineteenth-century industrialization.

The earlier move of textile factories from New England to the Piedmont regions of the Southeast was later echoed by much broader shifts as the area from North Carolina to Florida benefitted from industries that relocated from the Northeast, new branch plants of existing companies, and local start-ups. These industries included automobile factories, transportation equipment, food processing, machinery, and electrical products that had been bedrocks of the Anglo-American Manufacturing Belt.

In the West, manufacturing blossomed along a variety of fronts. Since the 1970s, the West Coast has been the region with the most prominence in high-technology industries and in the aerospace industry. But food processing, metals, machinery, and energy industries are also significant to the West's economy.

Texas, Louisiana, and Oklahoma also expanded their manufacturing base, such as petroleum, chemicals, and high-technology areas.

Figure 16D.2 ▶ Most communities love to have industrial jobs, far more so than jobs in retail and other services. The reason for this is that most manufacturing is considered economic "base" employment. Manufacturing businesses are those that sell to companies, governments, and households outside the community. For example, steel produced in a factory is sold to customers outside the city in which the factory is located. Money then flows into the community. In contrast, non-base jobs produce goods and (mostly) services that are consumed locally. The money coming into a community by virtue of industrial employment can be used to purchase these non-base items. In this way, each base job can be multiplied to account for the additional non-base jobs created by the presence of one base job. If a job in a particular industry has a multiplier of 2.0, that means that this one job actually results in two jobs in the economy: the original industrial job as well as an additional non-base job. This is termed the **multiplier effect**.

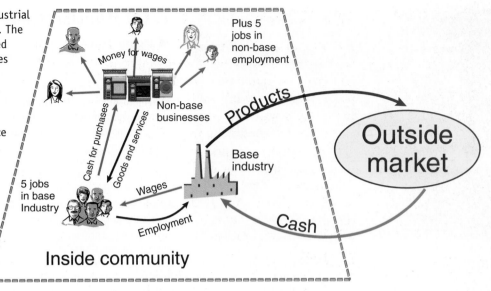

1. Shifting Labor Costs

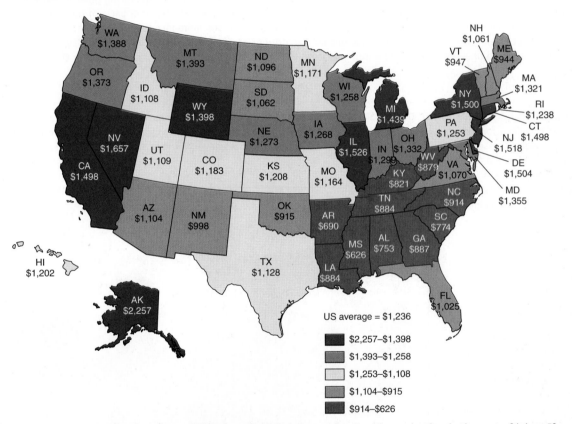

US average = $1,236

- $2,257–$1,398
- $1,393–$1,258
- $1,253–$1,108
- $1,104–$915
- $914–$626

▲ **Figure 16D.3 Per Capita Earnings, 1950** One of the key factors involved in production is the cost of labor. If everything else—including the necessary skills, transportation costs, and availability of infrastructure—is equal, factories will relocate to where they can achieve lower labor costs. This map shows that, by 1950, there was a huge earnings disparity between states—approaching 2:1 in many cases. Most low-income states were located in the Southeast and most high-income states were in the Anglo-American Manufacturing Belt. Industries that were less reliant on highly skilled labor, such as textiles, were the first to make the move to low-wage states. Later, other industries followed. More industries brought in better earnings and many of the poor states in 1950 have dramatically improved their economic position. In addition, many of these states offered other advantages to business. They tended to assess lower state and local taxes. They imposed fewer regulations. They were generally far less unionized. Despite the many negative impacts, this added up to what industry perceived as a favorable business climate.

2. Car Ownership and Highways

◀ **Figure 16D.4** In 1920, 1 out of 13 Americans owned an auto. By 1930, that ratio had shifted to 1 in 5, and by 1980, it was 1 in 3. Today, we have more motor vehicles on the road than there are licensed drivers. This movement toward the car, truck, SUV, and motorcycle came at the expense of railroad, streetcar, and bus travel and undercut the Anglo-American Manufacturing Belt's advantages of proximity to a well-integrated railroad web. Once a good road system was established (discussed more fully in Module 17E), the nature of travel changed, for both people and goods. The trucking industry burgeoned as an easier method of transportation, since it offered more flexibility. The development of highways and auto travel began to spread more advantages to places outside the old industrial core.

Initially, the development of the automobile industry was a boon to Michigan and Ohio. In the early twentieth century, southern Michigan focused on automobiles and auto parts. Other places benefited as a result of the vast backward linkages: steel, plastic, lead, copper, chrome, glass, rubber, textiles, machine tools, and ball bearings. Places such as Akron, Ohio, were built on tires, becoming the fastest growing city in the 1920s. Detroit's early dominance was linked to the dominance of the Big Three auto makers: General Motors, Ford, and Chrysler. In 1949, the United States made three-quarters of all the automobiles in the world, and the Big Three accounted for 95% of all US production. Detroit accounted for 42% of total auto production jobs in the country. After the 1950s, Detroit lost much of its comparative advantage vis-à-vis other parts of the country, and the United States lost its automobile advantage compared to other parts of the world. Even in a fairly recent period, there has been a movement of production from the Midwest to southern states such as Alabama, South Carolina, and Mississippi. This is a photo from the BMW manufacturing plant in Spartanburg, South Carolina. The more profound change has been the shift in automobile production to other parts of the world. In the 1970s, Japanese makers introduced smaller, high-quality, fuel-efficient cars, and more recently, another gas price shock has left American auto producers stranded with a huge unsold inventory of gas-guzzling pickups and SUVs. Today, the United States makes about one-sixth of all vehicles in the world, surpassed by Japan. About 20% of these are produced in the Detroit region.

3. Petroleum

Figure 16D.5 ◢ **Producing Oil and Gas Wells in the United States, Including Offshore** The shift to motor vehicles as the primary mode of transportation also affected the demand for certain resources, particularly petroleum. Before, the main energy source was coal. Petroleum was used initially for kerosene lighting, but with the rise of automobiles, the demand for oil skyrocketed. Moreover, oil (and natural gas) became more favored for home heating than coal, since it burned a lot cleaner.

The petroleum industry is capital intensive and very profitable. Oil rapidly became vital to the global economy because of its use in so many things. The United States was soon producing a lot of petroleum and consuming even more. The first sources were found in the same basic regions where coal was found: western Pennsylvania, eastern Ohio, and parts of West Virginia. However, the focus of the petroleum industry would shift to Texas, Oklahoma, and Louisiana, which took off with the discovery of oil wells. Gushers made millionaires out of wildcatters and boom towns out of hamlets. This oil was so important that the government built a pipeline system to connect with the resource to the industrial core. Huge corporations were spawned. The increasing importance of oil also gave these regions certain advantages that enabled them to spin off other industries, particularly petrochemicals.

The geographic shifts in the petroleum industry have had a big effect on the economic fortunes of places. Today, Texas is the headquarters for more of the top 500 corporations than any other state, surpassing California and New York. Because the petroleum industry is fairly volatile, those places that rely on oil have experienced economic difficulty when the price goes down, as it did in the 1980s. When the price of oil is high, as it has been in the last several years, these economies prosper.

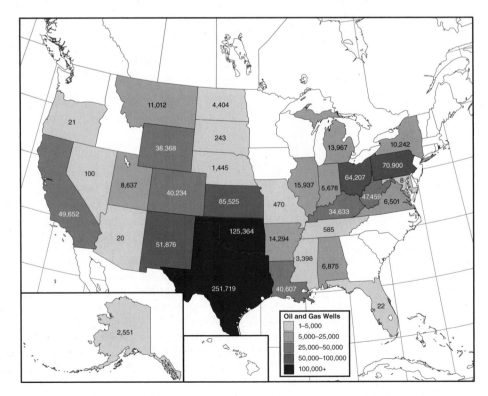

Oil and Gas Wells
- 1–5,000
- 5,000–25,000
- 25,000–50,000
- 50,000–100,000
- 100,000+

5. Role of Government

▲ **Figure 16D.7** The federal government played a much more active role in regional development during the twentieth century. Much of this had to do with its expanding size and reach, especially with the New Deal of the 1930s and after World War II. Federal redistribution of funds only occasionally had a specifically regional aim. The most significant redistributions of wealth from the Anglo-American Manufacturing Belt to the rest of the country took the form of big and small projects, including the following:

4. High Technology

◄ **Figure 16D.6** The development of new technologies has also changed the geography of the US economy. High-technology industry is key in this development and is discussed in more detail in Module 16E. *High technology* is a loose term for a variety of sectors, including computers, semiconductors, biotechnology, pharmaceuticals, and scientific, photographic, and telecommunications equipment. High technology became a major star of US manufacturing, accounting for 70% of new manufacturing jobs from 1960 to 1990. Between 1990 and 2005, high technology continued to increase as a percentage of US manufacturing, from 14% to 24%.

High-technology industries are considered clean, high-paying, and immune from business cycles. The products are characterized by high value and low weight and, so, are less sensitive to transport costs and more reliant on research and development. While these industries began largely in the Northeast, they began to move west. Unlike other industries, high technology did not necessarily shift as a result of lower labor costs. In fact, many firms located in places where costs were high. Instead, there was a tendency for new high-technology enterprises to locate near universities and where there were a variety of amenities.

Table 16D.1	States That Receive the Most and States That Give the Most		
Very few federal government policies have attempted to develop the economy of one region (the creation of the Appalachian Commission is one exception). But over the years, the flow of federal dollars has greatly favored states outside the manufacturing core. Taken as a whole, there has been a substantial outflow from the Northeast and Great Lakes states to states in the South and West. This table, based on 2005 data, shows the top states that have gained a great deal from federal tax revenues and the states that have provided far more tax revenue than they have received in federal funds.			

Top Federal Recipients	Federal Benefits as Percent of Tax Revenues	Top Federal Providers	Federal Benefits as Percent of Tax Revenues
Mississippi	202%	New Jersy	65%
New Mexico	200%	Nevada	67%
Louisiana	185%	Minnesota	73%
Alaska	183%	Connecticut	73%
West Virginia	175%	New Hampshire	75%
North Dakota	165%	Illinois	78%
Alabama	163%	Delaware	80%
Kentucky	151%	California	80%
Virginia	151%	New York	82%
South Dakota	148%	Colorado	83%

Source: Data from www.nemw.org/images/taxburdrank.pdf.

- Agricultural production in the Plains and the West was bolstered by the enactment of *farm price supports* in the 1930s. These were guarantees to purchase crops at a fixed price, and farmers were paid not to grow on their land. While the intent of support was to help poor family farmers, it enabled many of them to become quite well off. Many agribusinesses also took advantage of these supports to diversify into the food business.
- *Water policies,* such as the Tennessee Valley Authority (pictured above), provided irrigation and hydroelectric power to people in the South and West. This resulted in cheaper energy costs. After the oil embargo of 1973, for example, northeasterners paid 85% more for electricity and 50% more for natural gas than customers in western states.
- As the United States beefed up defense and overall military spending after World War II, *military bases* proliferated. Military bases are still an important economic engine because they bring federal dollars to an area. Bases are located disproportionately in the South, partly because of climate, perhaps partly because of a more military culture in the South, but also because most of the congressional leaders interested in defense hailed from the South and were able to use their longevity and clout to secure bases for their districts. In addition, government defense policy encouraged the dispersal of defense-related production from the core areas to "uncongested" areas, nearly all of these in the South and West.

16E The Geography of High Technology

The growth of **high-technology industries** has a special effect on the economic structure and geography of many societies. High-technology companies such as Microsoft, eBay, Apple, and Google did not exist 30 years or even 15 years ago, yet now they represent the leading edge of the US economy. In other countries, high technology has transformed cities such as Bengaluru (Bangalore), India.

High technology can be defined in several ways. One definition considers it as a set of particular industries. One international group lists aerospace, computers and office communication equipment, semiconductors, electrical machinery, pharmaceuticals, and science instruments as high-technology products. Software and Internet companies are often included as well. Another definition might consider the processes involved in high technology production. In this view, high technology industries incorporate a lot of research and development, technically sophisticated labor, and high value added in manufacturing.

Generally speaking, the factors of production related to the location of high-technology firms differ from those that determine the location of the steel and garment industries. For many high-technology firms, important factors include the proximity to some major universities, an entrepreneurial climate that includes a number of **venture capitalists** (financiers who are willing to risk their money on a risky, initial idea in hopes of great gains), environmental amenities that can attract the needed highly skilled labor, and excellent transportation and communications.

High technology benefits from *agglomeration economies* (see Module 13G). This occurs when the presence of a few similar industries creates economic conditions that attract other related industries. This lowers the cost of doing business while it increases the likelihood for success. Some aspects of agglomeration economies include a specially trained labor pool, access to needed suppliers (backward linkages), access to nearby companies that wish to buy a firm's products (forward linkages), necessary infrastructure, and other items.

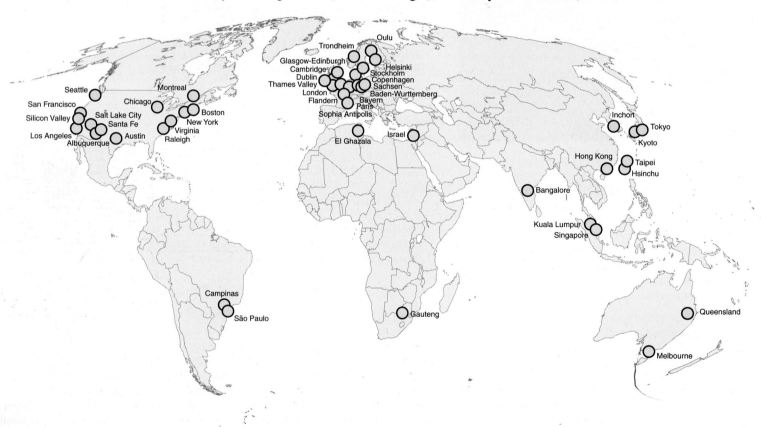

▲ **Figure 16E.1** This world map shows the location of global high-technology centers around 2000. Most of these centers still exist. While they share a common designator, they vary considerably in what they produce and in their labor requirements. Some centers correspond with the capital-intensive, highly skilled production most commonly associated with high technology. At the same time, other producers of high technology—for example, producers of semiconductors—continue to rely on cheap labor. Still other producers have managed to use the global assembly line (see Module 16F) to obtain highly skilled workers, but at lower prices.

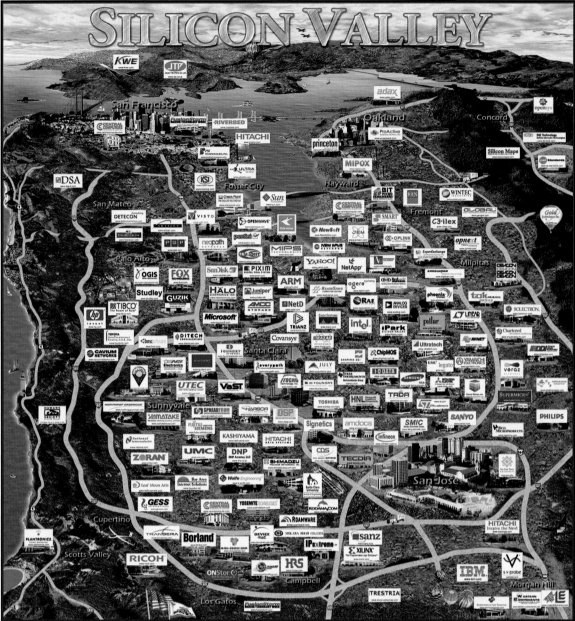

SILICON VALLEY

◀ **Figure 16E.2** If you were to list some places where the cost of living is out of sight, the region between San Francisco and San Jose, California, would probably be at the top. Yet it is also there that we find probably the oldest, largest, and richest concentration of high-technology firms in the world. Since its early development, Silicon Valley has continued to foster new companies, such as Google, which benefit from agglomeration economies and the presence of a high-technology cluster. This means that firms in Silicon Valley benefit from their proximity to other firms, access to a highly skilled labor pool, access to needed suppliers and markets, and the necessary sort of infrastructure.

A similar concept is that of clusters, and **high-technology clusters** share the following attributes:

- specialized labor: expertise in computer design, software programming, networks, and other skills essential to the high-technology world
- specialized inputs: a large number of nearby firms that possess specialized equipment, research tools, or specific technologies
- knowledge spillovers: highly technical information exchanged through formal and informal channels, and especially with the presence of universities
- market/user accessibility: accessibility is important because it lowers the friction of distance, but more importantly, it makes it easier for firms to respond to changes in market demand

Figure 16E.3 ▶ Many less developed countries have been able to reap certain advantages from specializing in various high-technology industries. Malaysia, for example, has become a major center for the production of silicon chips. The economy in India provides many of the attributes that high-technology firms are looking for. While it is still a poor country with a population that is predominantly agrarian and rural, India also contains a large population of well-educated workers who are fluent in English. Within India, high-technology activity has focused on southern cities, such as Hyderabad and especially Bangalore, pictured here. In fact, Bangalore (recently renamed Bengaluru) accounts for one-fourth of India's information technology industry and has evolved from a source of cheap labor for high-technology transnational corporations to an incubator for Indian-owned and Indian-operated software firms. It is estimated that, every week, several branch plants or joint ventures are established in Bangalore. Bangalore benefits from several factors that have helped it emerge as the high-technology center of India. It is located in a pleasant climate, it includes a cosmopolitan English-speaking population, it is the home of the Indian Institute of Science, and it contains many public sector agencies specializing in high-technology industries.

16F Globalized Manufacturing and the Rise of Transnational Corporations

We cannot discuss modern economic activity without invoking the term **globalization**. This pertains to all aspects of economic activity, especially to the production of goods. The term *globalization* is of relatively recent use, but the process it describes has been around for a long time. Definitions can differ, but broadly speaking, globalization is the elimination of national boundaries through ever greater integration of people, companies, and governments across the world. It includes some of the following aspects:

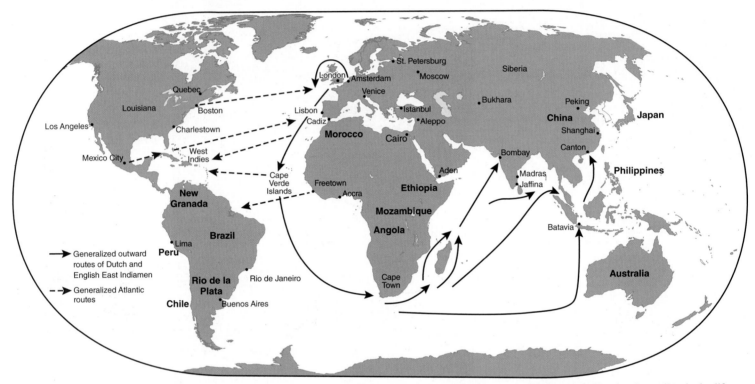

▲ **Figure 16F.1 Global Colonial and Trade Activity, 1500–1800** There is some question as to whether globalization is qualitatively different from simple internationalism, since trade, labor movements, and other forms of economic interaction that have been with us for quite some time. Whether we consider it to be simply a continuation of past trends or a truly distinct phenomenon, globalization is expressed in myriad ways in our economic world.

Table 16F.1 Stages of Globalization

While the term *globalization* is new, the process it describes has been with us for some time, but at far different levels of intensity. The beginning stage occurred when Europeans discovered the Americas and began to exploit it for their own purposes. Multinational trading companies, such as the Hudson's Bay Company, procured minerals, furs, spices, and agricultural commodities that could be sold to European markets.

I	Early transcontinental trading era as Europeans discover Americas and increased contact with Africa and Asia	Sixteenth through eighteenth centuries	The extraction of raw materials, the transfer of agricultural products, and the establishment of transcontinental trading networks were key aspects of this era. This was the first time that the entire world was part of a single economic system.
II	Industrialization and need for global resources	Nineteenth century	Industrialization sparks a need for globally obtained resources. Trade in raw materials, such as cotton, iron, nickel, rubber, copper, and even opium, intensifies and provokes wars for economic advantage. Still, most production is kept within a single country.
III	Global integration with protectionism	1900–1945	Huge new transnational corporations seek the development of global markets and a global labor force. Protectionism is a popular economic strategy.
IV	Free trade and Postcolonialism	1945–?	American corporations—joined by European and Japanese firms—successfully sell products abroad, establishing foreign branch plants that manufacture many of these products, and spark an era of worldwide communication. As decolonization severs the political bonds between countries in the late twentieth century, free trading blocs, most exemplified by the European Union but evident in other regions as well, cut down the barriers between the international flows of goods, services, labor, and markets.
V	New Era of Globalization	1990–?	More flexible forms of global production emerge as companies outsource much of their production requirements to subcontractors around the world. Internet explosion allows individuals, many outside traditional economic centers, to spearhead new economies.

- **deterritorialization**, which allows for social (and economic) activities to occur regardless of where people are physically located
- social and economic interconnectedness across political and geographical boundaries, facilitated especially through the use of the Internet
- the increasing speed of communications and transactions that allow goods to be bought, services to be rendered, and decisions to be carried out across the globe in a very short time
- a multipronged process that includes political, social, cultural, and economic movements

The transnational corporation is a prime example of how globalization has intensified with time. A **multidivisional corporation** is a corporation with many divisions based on product lines (such as snack products and cereal; scooters and motorcycles) or stages in the production chain (such as production of components and assembly into a final product). This becomes a **transnational corporation (TNC)** when these divisions cross international boundaries.

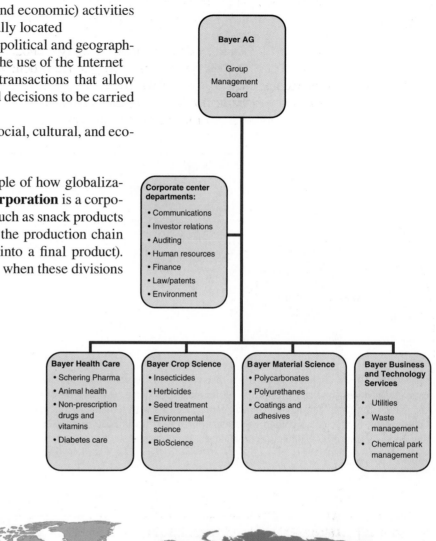

▲ **Figure 16F.2** One of the main hallmarks of a transnational corporation is a branch plant located outside of the country where the corporation is headquartered. Almost all of the largest corporations in the world are transnational. Even state-owned energy companies, such as PEMEX (headquartered in Mexico), develop international subsidiaries for the production or marketing of their products. Huge corporations, such as Ford Motor Company, IBM, or Intel, intentionally label foreign subsidiaries with their names: for instance, Ford Europe, IBM Japan (pictured), or Intel Malaysia. Other corporations may end up acquiring corporations that are located in another country. This is what happened when Daimler Benz acquired the Chrysler Corporation in 1998 to form Daimler-Chrysler (the corporation split apart in 2007).

▲ **Figure 16F.3** When you hear the name Bayer Corporation, you almost certainly think about aspirin. Yet Bayer, headquartered in Germany, is a diversified international corporation with a broad mix of product types. The organizational chart shows some of Bayer's key divisions and product groups. The map shows the location of Bayer's branch plants. Within each country, these plants are generally operated under chartered subsidiaries of the parent corporation. Many of the crop science production facilities, for example, are located in Brazil; the South African division includes animal health production facilities. Like all transnational corporations, Bayer figures out whether it makes economic sense to hold all of these different divisions. Some analysts have suggested that Bayer has suffered from diversifying beyond its core pharmaceutical operations into agricultural chemicals and plastics.

▲ **Figure 16F.4** Japanese automakers take great pains to point out that their cars are "made in America," often in factories closest to home. Toyota, now one of the world's top three automobile companies (closely tied with General Motors and Volkswagen), produced 1.5 million vehicles in North America in 2010, spent $23 billion annually in the US economy, and employed 35,000 workers.

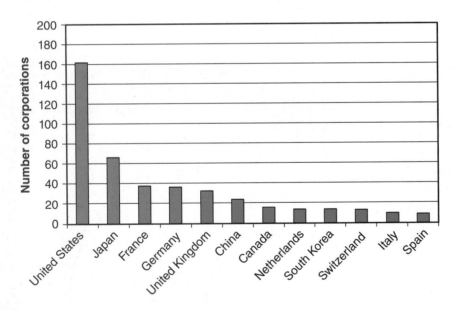

▲ **Figure 16F.5** While the world economy is shifting toward non-Western regions, the dominance of the West is still apparent here. Of the Global 500 (as compiled by *Fortune* magazine, 2007) the United States is headquarters for about one-third of all the top global corporations. When considered by region, North America and Western European countries are the headquarters for 358 of the top 500 corporations. Of the remainder, approximately half are headquartered in Japan. The newly emerging economies of China, India, Russia, and Brazil together contain 39 Fortune 500 corporations.

Geographers Philip Porter and Eric Sheppard demonstrate how the advantages of transnational corporations result in geographical expansion and geographical specialization. In regard to geographical expansion, TNCs might establish a subsidiary to ease their entry into a country's market. Much of this has to do with the desire of corporations to increase their revenues (and their stock price) by increasing the size of their market. At a certain point, because of competing firms and simply the number of potential consumers in the country, the home market becomes saturated or more and more difficult to sell to. Corporations seek new customers in other countries, thereby expanding their potential market and even getting a jump on the competition. However, many countries put up tariffs or other forms of trade barriers to limit the number of imports into a country (see Module 17C). But if a corporation decides to produce goods from a foreign-owned subsidiary, those products are not exposed to tariffs. In addition, potential customers may be more broadly receptive to items produced domestically.

In regard to geographical specialization, TNCs can end up reducing overall costs by producing goods in certain countries. For example, Xerox Corporation produces high-end photocopy machines near its Rochester, New York, headquarters, whereas simpler machines are manufactured in plants in Southeast Asia or South America. In this way, corporations are utilizing **locational advantages** that may be found in one of the factors of production. Very often, these locational advantages have to do with cheaper labor costs. According to the Bureau of Labor Statistics, the hourly compensation costs for a production worker in 2006 was about $24 an hour in the United States and $34 an hour in Germany. Yet in Brazil (a middle-income country), hourly wages plus benefits could be had for less than $5 an hour. In the Philippines, labor costs were about $1 an hour. Other locational advantages result from the benefits of diversification in general. Having an array of similar companies under one transnational corporate roof can enhance economies of scale by reducing costs related to duplicating technical support, marketing, administration, and so on. In the case of TNCs, a presence in many countries makes a corporation less dependent on government regulations or on labor unrest. This also allows a company to effectively move products, labor, and capital among its various international operations.

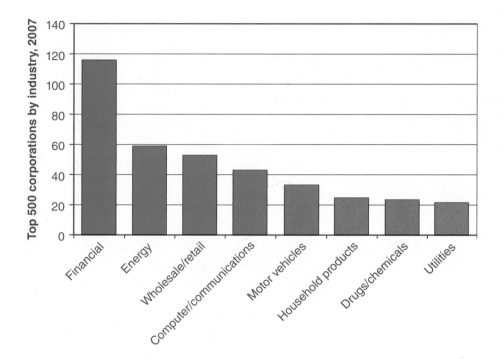

◀ **Figure 16F.6** This chart shows the types of products in which most corporations are involved. Both corporations involved in production and those involved in services are represented here. In fact, the largest category represents those corporations involved in some form of financial services: banks, securities, or insurance. This is followed by energy companies that provide petroleum, natural gas, and power generation.

The largest corporations in the world are all transnational corporations. Their gross revenues exceed the GDP for most countries. The top three corporations exceed the GDP for all but 26 countries, with a bigger economy than Denmark, South Africa, Iran, Ireland, and Finland. The top 25 companies would all rank in the top quarter of national economies if they were considered alongside countries.

Production chains are no longer completed all in one place. One way this occurs is through the production and transportation of various components in sites around the world, with the assembly in final factory. This has been termed a **global assembly line**. The manufacture of an automobile is a great example, since cars require tires, electrical, belts, mufflers, brakes . . . the list goes on and on. Many of these components are purchased from suppliers—all motor vehicle companies get their tires from tire companies—but some components are also made by corporate divisions. AC Delco is a division of General Motors, and it provides components ranging from batteries to brakes.

While discussion of a global assembly line often points to production in poorer countries, many times these components are produced in richer locales. Most automobile makers still prefer developed countries for their components, although that may be changing. A second method of worldwide production lies in a **global production line**, another way to characterize a **new international division of labor** that transcends international boundaries. In this case, the product is moved from one place to another in order to take advantage of favorable costs (often labor costs) or specific expertise. Further refinements in the division of labor, as production is broken down into more minute and easier-to-learn tasks, can make this process more reasonable.

Figure 16F.7 ▶ This graphic demonstrates how the global production line may work for some clothing. The clothing is designed in New York, where fashion designers utilize knowledge of current trends. The cloth is then transferred to northeastern Italy, where small firms weave and print the cloth. The cloth is then sent to China, where low-wage workers cut and sew the fabric into garments. The final apparel is then shipped back to a retailer in New York for sale.

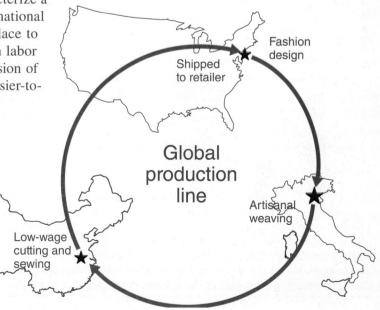

Table 16G.1 Medieval Consumption

Consumption levels differed markedly from society to society, even in the pre-industrial era. But some of these figures give an idea of how expenses may have operated in Medieval England in the fourteenth century. Of course, data were far less complete at this period but these estimates provide an idea of preindustrial consumption patterns. A percentage of the population—probably the two percent or less that belonged to the nobility or the successful merchant class—had amassed enough wealth to indulge in luxuries such as special foods, nice garments, spacious residences, and amusements. For the other 98 percent, necessities took up a huge portion of the budget. A year's worth of bread alone would make a significant dent. But there were opportunities to consume items such as alcohol, special clothing, or toys that went beyond the bare necessities. Alcohol, meat, perhaps a sword, and a nice tunic would have been an occasional expense.

Incomes	In Ducats*
Wealthy baron	785,000
Very rich knight	150,000
Wealthy esquire	66,000
Modest esquire	30,000
Annual "benefice" paid to support a parish priest	3,000–4,000
Annual income of building trades (masons and carpenters)	2,000–3,000
Annual cash income of yeoman farmer	1,000–3,000
Minimum annual income to sustain life for an individual	500–600

Expenses	In Ducats
Adult pig	150–200
Milk cow	300–400
Farmer's cart (iron fittings)	200–300
Mould board plow	30–40
Annual rent to feudal lord for an acre of land (varied considerably)	20–40
Axe	12–20
Cheap sword	15–20
Expensive sword (no jewels or precious metals)	100–200
Loom and treadle (for making cloth at home)	100–200
Shovel	10
Spinning wheel	30–40
Knife	5–10
Brass pot	50–100
Better-quality wool tunic, dyed various colors	250–350
Fur-lined wool tunic	300–400
Cheap cloth for peasant clothing (per yard)	20–60
Mattress cover (to be stuffed with hay)	5–10
Pair of leather shoes	15–40
Woman's chemise (linen undergarment)	20–25
Sheet for bed	10–20
Silk quilt	500–600
Chair	20–25
Bed covering (heavy blanket)	10–20
Stool	10–15
Table cloth	50–100
Hundred gallons of ale	75–125
Two-pound loaf of bread	1
Luxury townhouse with courtyard	20,000–60,000
Three-room peasant's house (600–900 square feet)	1,200–2,000
Two-story row house in a town	3,000–4,000
Two-story shop and living apartments in a town	6,000–10,000

*Each English pound is worth 600 ducats.

Source: Data from James Dunnigan and Albert Nofi, *Medieval Life and Hundred Years War.*
http://www.hyw.com/Books/History/1_help_c.htm

16G Geographies of Consumption

When discussing production, we must also consider **consumption**, since the two are so interlinked. Consumption is a necessary aspect of human existence, but it has evolved over the years. Consider what is meant by a **luxury**: something that provides enjoyment beyond the necessities of life. For most of human history (and prehistory), consumption was limited. Most individuals could only consume what they needed for their existence, living hand to mouth. This led to a very low level of overall consumption, since people "need" very little.

It was only during the eighteenth century and the advent of industrialization that consumption of large quantities by a substantial proportion of the population became the norm. Mass production required **mass consumption** and, of course, this meant that more and more people would be consuming "luxuries." In fact, many Europeans had by then become enamored of such items as ceramics, coffee, chocolate, tea, and tobacco. As the twentieth century progressed, consumption became even more pronounced and a couple of things happened. First, wants became needs, as what were previously considered luxuries became necessities. Today, even poor people in developed countries require items that would almost certainly fit under luxuries: televisions, automobiles, CDs. Yet they have become engrained in our lives such that a "luxury" is now considered to be an item or a service of great cost—for instance, an automobile such as a Rolls-Royce or a Bentley.

The second thing that happened is that consumption became an end in itself. The sociologist Thorstein Veblen remarked on this 110 years ago with his idea of **conspicuous consumption**, in which people feel a need to display their status by ostentatiously consuming goods and services. More recently, terms such as *materialism* and *affluenza* have been used to describe an insatiable need to purchase. This drive to consume has been abetted by the demands of a modern economy. Businesses live and die by growth, which can only occur if more people consume more stuff. So it becomes important to entice people to buy more things, even if they did not know they wanted them. The Index of Consumer Confidence, used as a barometer of economic health in the United States, is based on a sample of household views of current conditions and future expectations of the economy. This general overview is used by businesses to gauge their own expectations for economic growth.

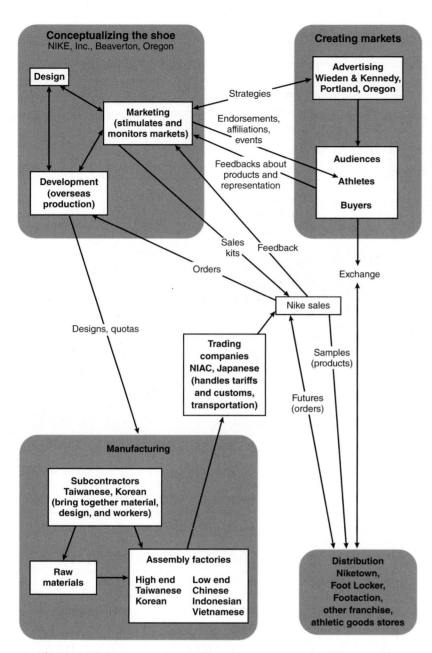

▲ Figure 16G.2 The consumption of a product often creates an idealized world. Nike ads routinely conjure up a variety of places emphasized by the "Just do it" catchphrase. Individuals are shown engaging in strenuous activity on the track, basketball court, and trails. Other products may grab an idealized aspect of their heritage in order to paint a picture. The image of Juan Valdez and Colombian coffee comes to mind.

▲ Figure 16G.3 Beyond a question of simple retail (discussed in Chapter 17), modern society has created a mind-boggling number of places and spaces to consume. These are a lot more than just stores. Niketowns—found all over the world—are a great example of how consumption spaces are created and, in effect, become destinations beyond what they sell. As with modern malls, the intent is to sell goods, but also to make people feel as if they are engaging in an experience that transcends simple consumption.

▲ Figure 16G.1 Consumption exhibits geography at many different scales. As consumers, we are now far removed from seeing the origins of the items we routinely purchase. Yet every product is the end result of a **commodity chain** that is all but invisible to the consumer. Nike shoes offers a good example.

- *Design*: The design of a Nike shoe starts at the Nike Research Lab, where researchers take into account the specific market, biomechanics, and aesthetics of the prototyped shoe.
- *Production*: Nike subcontracts production to factories located especially in China, Indonesia, and Vietnam. The raw materials of rubber, leather, and plastic are obtained and sent to the factories, which have become notorious for offering low wages and harsh conditions.
- *Marketing*: Nike makes extensive use of sports stars such as Michael Jordan and Tiger Woods. The swoosh and the phrase "Just do it" are parts of American culture. In other countries, Nike makes sure to use stars in locally popular sports, such as soccer.
- *Retail*: Nike operates its own stores and a few larger Niketowns and, of course, has been successful in gaining a prominent place in all footwear stores.

16H Consuming Places: Geographies of Tourism

One of the most important features of modern consumption has been the ability to vacation by getting in a car or an airplane and traveling to another destination. The **tourism** industry has grown to cater to that desire. It is a huge and varied industry made up of travel agents (and travel websites), hotels, restaurants, attraction developers, cruise lines, tour guides, guidebooks, and local and regional officials who seek to market their own place. Tourism is something that many places rely on as the main engine of their economy. While tourism is a service, it is also a basic industry that brings money in from the outside. It also takes advantage of whatever attributes a place has that make it desirable for people to visit, whether it is natural beauty or historical significance. Places without a lot of intrinsic allure can help create their own attributes by developing a theme park, a casino, or a major shopping opportunity.

▲ **Figure 16H.1** Back in 1930, Las Vegas, Nevada, would seem to have almost no desirable attributes. Most historically interesting places were farther north in Nevada, there were few inspiring natural features, and the climate was that of a hot, dry desert. But today, Las Vegas is one of the biggest travel destinations in the world, as well as a major center for US travelers and timeshare owners. The development of Las Vegas is legendary—thought up by dreamers, helped along by gangsters, and initially propelled by Nevada's permissive gambling laws. But the city has shed much of its seedy image by putting up spectacular hotels and providing entertainment that goes beyond just gambling. With its architecture, landscaping, and place-naming, Las Vegas pays tribute to other places, such as "New York, New York," and Bellagio, Italy. Of course, this dependence on imagery and tourism can be risky, as Las Vegas suffered from some serious downturns during the last recession. This has affected nearly every aspect of the city's economy.

Of all industries, tourism is probably the most geographically oriented. Even if a place is presented generically or is completely artificial, it is still the object of consumption. People travel to places because they seek something they cannot get at home. Tourism also operates at various scales. International tourism involves the most planning and expense, where people will often take two or more weeks to travel to another country or group of countries in a region. Domestic tourism can be especially important for many communities and for people who seek a particular attribute: a big cosmopolitan city, a historical landmark, a beach, or a mountain ski resort. Local tourism is also important. "One-tank trips" just a car ride away can lead people to nearby attractions where they will likely spend some money, buy souvenirs, and eat at a local restaurant. Downtowns in many less well-known cities have begun to market their tourist potential for the more local consumer. Cleveland, Ohio—not exactly a top draw nationally—has developed a series of downtown attractions, including a large Science Center and the Rock and Roll Hall of Fame, as a way to draw in more people.

What factors determine the tourist appeal of a place? Much of it has to do with what people seek to get out of travel. Some of the important motivators include a desire to escape a mundane environment, the pursuit of relaxation or recreational opportunities, the strengthening of family bonds, prestige, an opportunity for social interaction, educational opportunities, wish fulfillment, and shopping. Places need to be able to offer at least one of these amenities to be viable, and they must provide a measure of safety, accessibility, reliability, and reasonable value.

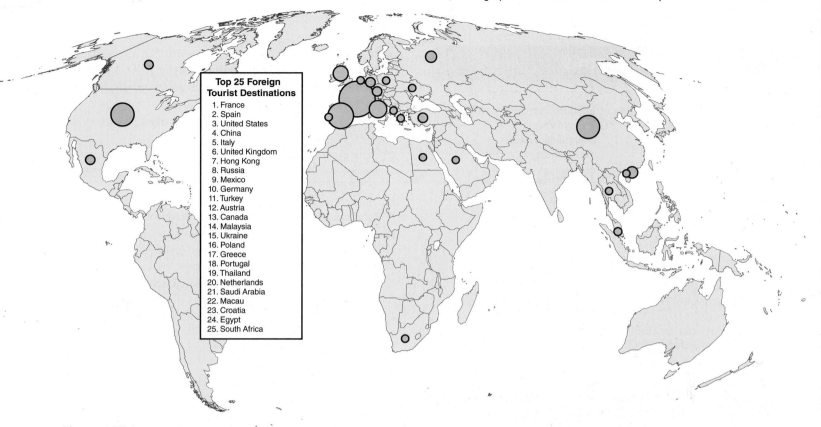

▲ **Figure 16H.2** With a few exceptions, such as North Korea, just about every country has a tourist industry. Many even have tourist ministries to promote and guide tourism. However, there is a great deal of unevenness in world tourist traffic. The countries of Western Europe enjoy very high tourist dollars per capita, despite the fact that these are expensive destinations. Many of the Caribbean islands are dependent on tourism for their economy and draw from North America and Europe. The United States, Canada, and Australia also have a great deal of international tourist traffic—and very robust domestic tourism. Most other countries have fairly low relative levels of tourism when measured on a per capita basis, although the absolute number of tourists to China, Russia, and Mexico is fairly high.

Top 25 Foreign Tourist Destinations

1. France
2. Spain
3. United States
4. China
5. Italy
6. United Kingdom
7. Hong Kong
8. Russia
9. Mexico
10. Germany
11. Turkey
12. Austria
13. Canada
14. Malaysia
15. Ukraine
16. Poland
17. Greece
18. Portugal
19. Thailand
20. Netherlands
21. Saudi Arabia
22. Macau
23. Croatia
24. Egypt
25. South Africa

▲ **Figure 16H.3 Straw Market in Coco Cay, Bahamas** Cruise ships have emerged as a big growth segment in the tourist industry. They provide a safe, stable environment for travelers and are usually all-inclusive in price. During a typical cruise of 4–10 days, ships "call" on a series of ports. Cruise passengers who disembark enter a land of kitsch, where "place" is reduced to stereotypes and shopping opportunities abound. Finding the authentic place can be quite a challenge, and many travelers are not able or willing to take the time.

Key Terms

Anglo-American Manufacturing
   Belt (16C)
backward linkages (16C)
base employment (16D)
break-in-bulk point (16B)
commodity chain (16G)
conspicuous consumption (16G)
consumption (16G)
deterritorialization (16F)
division of labor (16A)
factors of production (16B)
factory system (16A)
forward linkages (16C)
global assembly line (16F)
global production line (16F)
globalization (16F)
high-technology clusters (16E)
high-technology industries (16E)

industrialization (16A)
locational advantages (16F)
luxury (16G)
maquiladora (16B)
mass consumption (16G)
mass production (16A)
multidivisional corporation (16F)
multiplier effect (16D)
new international division
   of labor (16F)
optimum location (16B)
production (16A)
production chain (16B)
tourism (16H)
transnational corporation
   (TNC) (16F)
value added (16A)
venture capitalists (16E)

Basic Review Questions

1. How does production create value added?

2. Describes the changes associated with industrialization.

3. Discuss the changes associated with the steam engine, new machinery, and the factory system. How did the factory system bring about a new division of labor?

4. Why was Great Britain the first country to become industrialized?

5. Why did industrialization diffuse slowly after it was adopted in Great Britain?

6. Where was industrialization first found in the United States? Why?

7. How might you consider forward linkages and backward linkages as explanations for why a region that initially industrialized continued to enjoy further industrialization?

8. Where was the Anglo-American Manufacturing Belt located, and what sorts of items did it produce? What were some of the comparative advantages of the Anglo-American Manufacturing Belt?

9. How did the US space economy change in the twentieth century?

10. What is the importance of base employment? How does this fit into a multiplier effect?

11. What were some of the comparative advantages that other parts of the United States could use to attract industry? What sorts of industries did they attract?

12. What is the role of government in promoting regional development in the twentieth century—specifically, the role of water policies and military bases?

13. Discuss some of the factors of production important in any industry. What are the direct factors and what are the indirect factors of production?

14. Explain the industrial location model produced by Alfred Weber. What is the difference between ubiquitous materials and localized materials, and how does this affect the model?

15. What changing factors of production help us understand the location of garment factories in Mexico?

16. What is meant by *high-technology industry*? What is the importance of venture capitalism and high technology?

17. What are some of the common attributes possessed by high-technology clusters?

18. How has high technology shifted to other parts of the world, such as Bangalore/Bengaluru?

19. What are some of the aspects of globalization in relation to industrial production? What is the difference between a multidivisional corporation and a transnational corporation?

20. How are transnational corporations able to take advantage of certain locational advantages in the factors of production?

21. What is the global assembly line, and how does this relate to the global production line? How might the development of clothing be a good example of a new global production line?

22. How have consumption and luxuries changed over the course of human history?

23. How does the growth in consumption, and even conspicuous consumption, affect production levels?

24. What is a commodity chain, and how does it fit into the development of a particular product?

25. How does the development of tourism fit into a new style of consumption?

26. How might tourism be considered a way of geographically consuming different places?

Advanced Review Questions (Essay Questions)

1. What are the major changes associated with the beginning of industrialization? Why do these changes represent a major break from past practices? Where did the Industrial Revolution first begin, and why there?

2. Precisely where is the United States' industrial core region? How did the industrial core lose much of its dominance in the second half of the twentieth century in terms of (a) the loss of specific advantages relative to the periphery and (b) new advantages gained by the periphery?

3. What major industries were able to establish a beachhead in different parts of the United States? Specifically, why were automobiles centered in Michigan and Ohio? Why was petroleum production centered in Texas, Louisiana, and Oklahoma? How do these locations relate to different factors of production?

4. Describe how the industrial location model works. How does this help explain the development of the steel industry around 1900? Why are some of the aspects of this model less relevant today? What factors help explain the growth of maquiladora factories?

5. How do you define high technology? Why is it valued compared to other types of technology? How does high technology benefit from agglomeration economies? Why have aspects of high-technology production moved from original clusters in the United States and other developed countries to a number of less developed countries?

6. What are some of the ways in which globalization has altered industrial production? How does a transnational corporation take advantage of the global assembly line to reduce its costs?

7. Describe how consumption has changed over human history. How do the luxuries of one era become the necessities for another? How does the commodity chain fit into the development of different products? Specifically, how would it affect the production of shoes?

8. How does tourism fit into the geography of consumption? What are some of the things that allow a place to market itself for tourist purposes?

Further Study Topics

• Traditional factors of production don't necessarily pertain to modern industrial processes. Select a modern industry and discuss some of the factors of production that are significant to the success of that industry.

• Some experts argue that government's role in the development of the American space economy has not been balanced but instead has tended to favor certain regions. Looking at certain levels of government investment—for example, military investment or transportation projects—discuss the patterns of government investment and whether certain regions are favored at the expense of other regions.

• Why are some regions of the country more prone to high-technology investment and other related types of economic activity than other regions? Identify a few areas that seem to have a high proportion of high-technology investment and see whether you can determine what factors they share. What would be some of the suggested attributes in a region seeking to be a center for high-technology investment?

• Looking at the impact of globalization on the world, particularly in terms of industrial processes, identify what you think are some of the major advantages of transnational corporations, as well as some of the major disadvantages. Do you think that transnational corporations are more likely to exploit peoples in less developed countries, or are such corporations ultimately beneficial?

• In the chapter, we used the example of shoes as a product in a commodity chain. Examine another type of product in terms of how design, production, marketing, and retail are all based around the production and marketing of the product.

• Looking at the geography of tourism, consider the way in which the consumption of beautiful places can harm these very places. Is it possible for something like ecotourism to both generate the financial benefits of tourism and still preserve many of the values, both human and natural, of these places?

Summary Activities

Base jobs are an important source of economic activity for every community. Using the information provided by your local county business patterns (www.census.gov/econ/cbp/), consider your county or metropolitan area. Determine how many of these jobs would be considered as "base" (mostly jobs in manufacturing) and non-base (mostly jobs in services). Do you see any patterns?

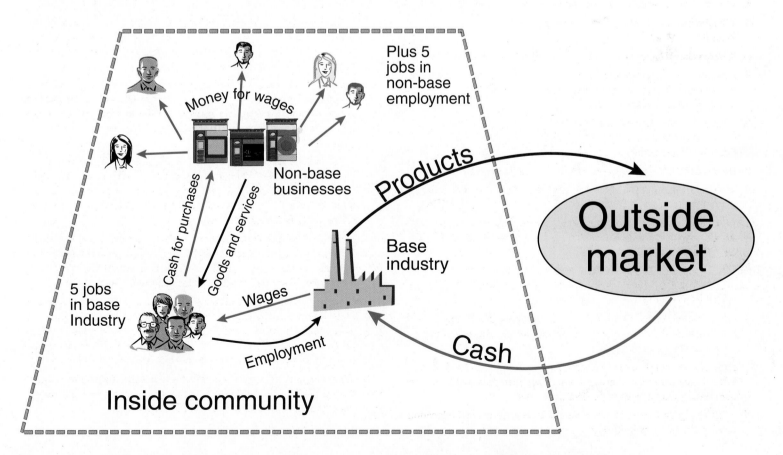

Distribution and Transportation

When you consider some of the most important advances in the past two centuries, surely the ability to "shrink" the world would rank among the most significant. For eons, people rarely ventured outside of their village and lived mostly within a space of just a few miles. Most of the things they needed were either made at home or acquired from people and places close by. But progress changed that. People found it easier and faster to travel great distances; to obtain resources, goods, and services across an ever wider field; and to enjoy greater access to information.

These all reflect the geographic concept of flows: the movement of people, things, or information from one place to another. Flows are a key aspect of spatial interaction, as discussed in Modules 1C and 1F, and are fundamental to the geography of human activity. Flows are often bound up in moving goods and services. But flows are also essential to human activity that is not purely economic. The development of transportation networks, for example, expedited the exchange of goods, but also the capacity for people to connect with others for cultural, social, and political purposes. The phenomenal growth of an information network that instantly ties together researchers from around the world has had a disproportionate impact on scientific exchange and advancement.

17A Growth of Trade

Trade involves any exchange of a tangible good or a service. Much prehistoric trade was likely in the form of **barter**, where a good or service is traded for another good or service as agreed upon by the people doing the trading. A man with extra wood, for example, might exchange it for some help plowing a field or hunting a deer. These barter economies have persisted into the present day and are often a survival strategy for people who eke out a living. As more people get involved and the economy becomes more elaborate, barter becomes rather unwieldy, so **cash exchanges** become more prevalent. Cash is just a way to place an abstract value on a product or service that allows for relatively easy exchanges.

While trade occurs at all spatial scales, when we speak of trade in the modern era most often we are referring to **international trade**, or the exchange of goods and services across country boundaries. What we would recognize as international trade also has a long history (see Module 15B). There is evidence of maritime trade in the Mediterranean region 9,000 years ago, with some trade regulations in place 4,000 years ago. Some societies, such as the Phoenicians, gained much of their livelihood through engagement in trade. And trade within and between large empires was extraordinarily important in moving goods, animals, and humans around. As the capitalist economic system emerged in Europe between AD 900 and 1100, the new economy was based on the ability to trade between regions and across political boundaries. In these earlier trading economies, trade was bimodal—divided between short-distance, local trade in basic goods and long-distance trade in luxuries. Such long-distance trade included intermediaries who helped bridge widely separate cultural and economic systems.

▲ **Figure 17A.1** Cities such as Venice, Bruges, and Amsterdam (shown above) grew rich by placing themselves at the center of trading networks. The development of territorial states in the sixteenth and seventeenth centuries (see Modules 10A and 10B) was an important milestone in trade, although countries promoted trade within their boundaries while working to stifle international trade. Still, international trade continued to expand throughout the eighteenth, nineteenth, and twentieth centuries as the world became more economically integrated, as markets grew richer and more demanding, and as production required a greater variety of raw materials.

Asian countries have increased their share of both exports and imports, fueled largely by China and Japan. North America has maintained its share of imports but lost ground in relation to exports, due mostly to a growing trade deficit on the part of the United States. Europe as a whole has increased its share of exports; although the United Kingdom's share has declined markedly, that of Germany, Italy and France has increased. The ever tighter economic integration of Europe has played a huge role in this development. The share of exports and imports from South America has dropped considerably as well, possibly related to protectionist policies.

So what accounts for the overall increase in trade and the differences between regions? While individual economies vary, a number of factors have influenced the overall growth of trade.

The first factor is a general increase in global prosperity. As a whole—and with some conspicuous exceptions—the world is richer now than it was 60 years ago. Initially, North America, Western Europe, and Japan enjoyed fabulous growth, and more recently East Asia, India, and some Latin American and Middle Eastern countries have expanded their economies. Greater prosperity leads to more goods produced that can be traded and a more affluent market that demands imported goods. The second factor can be pegged to the general decline in transportation costs, which will be discussed more fully in Module 17D. One of the chief barriers to trade is distance, and lowering transportation costs effectively reduces the costs of transporting goods across distances. Despite some ups and downs related to fluctuations in the cost of oil, transportation has become markedly cheaper and has brought places closer together. The third factor has been the most dramatic: expansion in communications technology, which has allowed suppliers and customers to communicate instantaneously across the world. Communications has been especially important in letting manufacturers develop more flexible production processes that depend on the current needs of customers. Suppliers coordinate the work of several factories, often located in different countries. With the World Wide Web, it is also possible for small entrepreneurs to import and export needed goods and services, something that would have been difficult before the technology was available. The fourth factor has to do with the increasing tendency of governments to adopt neoliberal policies (see Module 11C) that promote free trade.

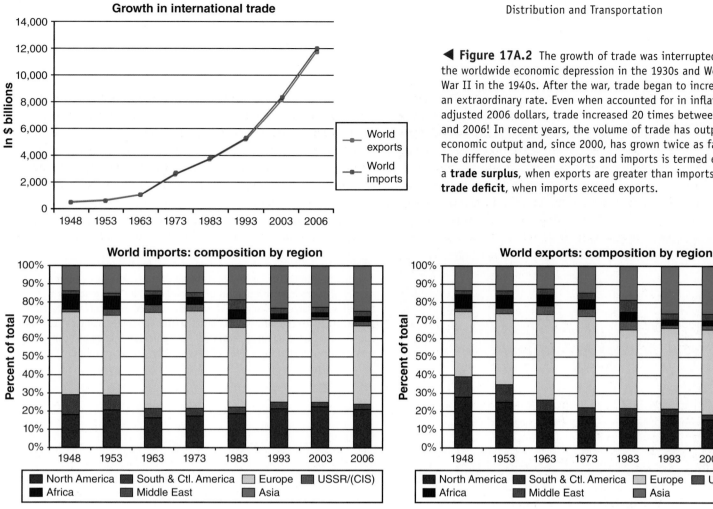

Growth in international trade

In $ billions (y-axis): 14,000, 12,000, 10,000, 8,000, 6,000, 4,000, 2,000, 0

x-axis: 1948, 1953, 1963, 1973, 1983, 1993, 2003, 2006

Legend: World exports, World imports

◀ **Figure 17A.2** The growth of trade was interrupted by the worldwide economic depression in the 1930s and World War II in the 1940s. After the war, trade began to increase at an extraordinary rate. Even when accounted for in inflation-adjusted 2006 dollars, trade increased 20 times between 1946 and 2006! In recent years, the volume of trade has outpaced economic output and, since 2000, has grown twice as fast. The difference between exports and imports is termed either a **trade surplus**, when exports are greater than imports, or a **trade deficit**, when imports exceed exports.

World imports: composition by region

Percent of total (y-axis): 100%, 90%, 80%, 70%, 60%, 50%, 40%, 30%, 20%, 10%, 0%

x-axis: 1948, 1953, 1963, 1973, 1983, 1993, 2003, 2006

Legend: North America, South & Ctl. America, Europe, USSR/(CIS), Africa, Middle East, Asia

World exports: composition by region

Percent of total (y-axis): 100%, 90%, 80%, 70%, 60%, 50%, 40%, 30%, 20%, 10%, 0%

x-axis: 1948, 1953, 1963, 1973, 1983, 1993, 2003, 2006

Legend: North America, South & Ctl. America, Europe, USSR/(CIS), Africa, Middle East, Asia

▼ **Figure 17A.3 Regional Trade Blocs, 2004** In the last several decades, a number of countries have joined together as free trade zones with minimal barriers to trade. These are common markets that allow for the free movement of labor, capital, and resources. The European Union has gone one step further by creating a consortium of countries that are politically independent but share a common currency and a common fiscal policy. In addition, the **World Trade Organization (WTO)** represents most of the world's economies and enforces the rules of free trade. WTO rules are negotiated and signed by most of the world's trading nations in order to smooth the flow of trade between countries. Critics charge that the WTO bolsters a trading system that is fundamentally unfair to poorer countries.

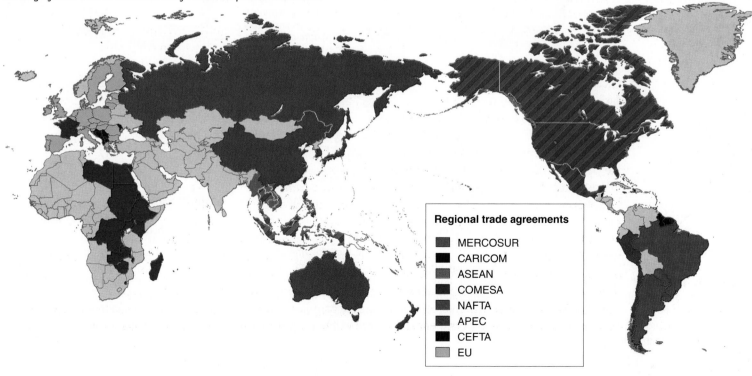

Regional trade agreements

- MERCOSUR
- CARICOM
- ASEAN
- COMESA
- NAFTA
- APEC
- CEFTA
- EU

17B Reasons for International Trade

What happens when countries do not trade? Self-sufficiency is fairly common among more primitive groups, who construct their own shelters, hunt, gather or grow their own food, and make their own clothing and tools out of nearby materials. A country is self-sufficient when its residents produce everything they need for their own consumption, with no need to trade beyond national borders. A self-sufficient country can also be described as an *autarky*. When a country seeks to limit trade through various mechanisms, this is termed **protectionism**.

◀ **Figure 17B.1** In 1973, a group of petroleum-exporting countries decided to punish the United States and other countries by limiting the supply of petroleum through an oil embargo. While this embargo went on, oil was scarce and expensive, and the US economy suffered a major shock. In 1979, the new fundamentalist Iranian government cut off the supply of oil once again. One of the most common scenes of both eras was high prices and long lines of cars waiting to get gasoline.

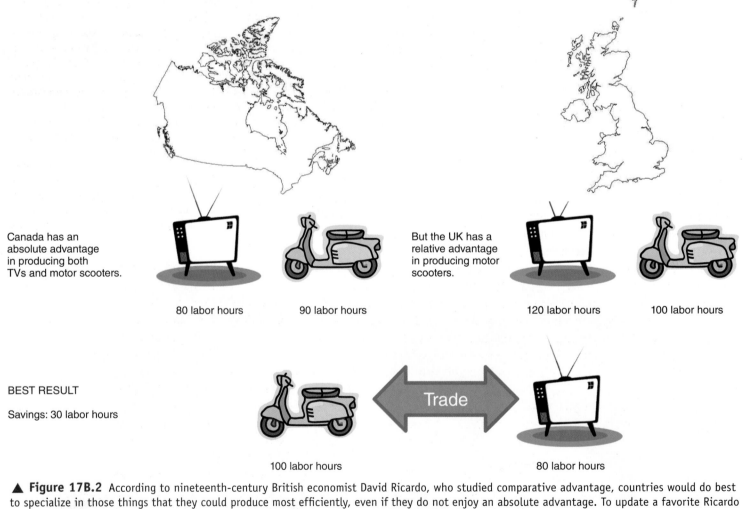

Canada has an absolute advantage in producing both TVs and motor scooters.

80 labor hours   90 labor hours

But the UK has a relative advantage in producing motor scooters.

120 labor hours   100 labor hours

BEST RESULT

Savings: 30 labor hours

Trade

100 labor hours   80 labor hours

▲ **Figure 17B.2** According to nineteenth-century British economist David Ricardo, who studied comparative advantage, countries would do best to specialize in those things that they could produce most efficiently, even if they do not enjoy an absolute advantage. To update a favorite Ricardo example, let's say it takes Canada an average of 80 labor hours to produce flat-screen televisions and 90 labor hours to produce motor scooters. British producers require 120 hours for televisions and 100 hours for motor scooters. While Canada has an absolute advantage in producing both of these items, it would make the most sense for Canada to focus on televisions and England to focus on motor scooters (where it has an advantage relative to its production of televisions). By having both countries specialize in items they make best, and by having them trade with each other, they can realize a savings of 30 labor hours.

One of the advantages of an autarky is that it does not rely on an external source, which might choke off supplies of a critical resource—what is termed an **embargo**. Another advantage of an autarky, or a protectionist economic system, is that it can help shield its own industries from foreign competition. This strategy has been employed by several countries, even those considered paragons of free trade. In the seventeenth century, England limited the import of cotton textiles from India (which it controlled) as a way to protect its own developing cotton textile industry. More recently, other countries have targeted particular sectors of the economy; Brazil, for example, protected many of its consumer industries, so that it could grow large enough to serve its market. Brazil banned automobile imports between 1974 and 1990 and relied on cars produced by Brazilian subsidiaries of General Motors, Fiat, and a Ford-Volkswagen consortium called Autolatina. The cars were limited in variety and considered substandard. But Brazilian consumers had no other choice.

The advantages of trade stem from the fact that natural and human resources are distributed unevenly throughout the world. Some places have certain resources that others do not, or they may have a pool of workers particularly adept at producing goods, or they may have lower labor costs. Because of this, the principle of *comparative advantage* (see Module 15F for an introduction) is that one country will likely have a cost advantage over another country in growing, extracting, or producing a product or in providing a service. International trade allows each country to specialize in an activity or activities for which it can extract, grow, produce, or provide more inexpensively (or at higher quality). If each country does this, more surplus and wealth are created in general.

▲ **Figure 17B.3** The proponents of free trade are likely to examine trade's benefits at an aggregate level. But critics of trade point out a number of flaws. First, trade terms are rarely "free" and can disadvantage some places at the expense of others. A country might decide to limit some imports—for example, in a distressed industry—and so follow aspects of protectionism. This may be because of political pressure or simply because there appear to be good strategic reasons to protect some portion of its economy. The Japanese, for example, fiercely protect their rice industry (Japanese rice paddies pictured above), even though land is scarce and rice can be cultivated more cheaply elsewhere. Second, a country's comparative advantage and what it chooses to specialize in can be forced on it, often by a colonial power. In the example in 17B.2 comparing Canada and Great Britain, let us say that Great Britain as the colonial power had compelled Canada to focus on lumber rather than on flat-screen televisions. While Canada may have some comparative advantage in lumber production, it is not as lucrative an industry as televisions and would have kept Canada mired in an economy that was resource-dependent rather than industrialized. Many colonies were forced into just such a specialization, concentrating on lower-value resources rather than on industries that required more skill and produced higher value. Third, free trade can cause a number of dislocations. It benefits companies with high levels of mobility and consumers who seek lower prices, but it can harm small, local producers and labor that is much more fixed in place. For example, since the North American Free Trade Agreement came into effect, a number of manufacturing jobs have been lost in the United States, while corn farmers in Mexico have suffered in competing against subsidized US corn.

While comparative advantage was initially viewed with regard to resources, many other factors come into play, such as labor productivity, the presence of capital, necessary infrastructure, and a climate of entrepreneurship. **Competitive advantage**—promoted by economist Michael Porter and others—takes into account the mix of infrastructure, skilled labor, government, domestic demand, levels of domestic competition, agglomeration economies, and other items. While the presence of raw materials can provide valuable short-term income to a country, several of the most successful economies have been able to promote industrial development without significant raw materials. Likewise, lower labor costs may not necessarily boost an economy, particularly if that labor is not especially productive. Japan is often cited as an economy that has enjoyed tremendous success without benefiting from a great number of resources or cheap labor. In this case, government policies (including an activist trade policy), steady increases in productivity, highly skilled labor, and necessary financing allowed Japan to become one of the world's largest economies by the latter half of the twentieth century. This also brings up another advantage of trade: **competition**. Producers who need to compete with other producers from other countries are forced to upgrade the quality of their goods or risk being undercut. Industries that have had to endure a great deal of internal domestic competition have been primed to compete successfully at the international level.

17C What Determines the Flow of Trade?
Elements of supply

Economies benefit from the resources found within their *land*. Many countries are endowed with abundant raw materials and other materials that may be relatively scarce. Oil is the classic example, since the countries with an abundance of this commodity are able to stake their entire economies on its export. This is also true on a regional level. Northern Minnesota, for instance, is based largely around an iron ore or taconite economy. The quality of agricultural land has a big effect as well and explains why some countries are able to export grain while others cannot. Individual crops, such as wine, rely on a particular mix of soil and climate.

Labor is considered in terms of its overall supply and its productivity. A large supply of labor creates a surplus. This means wages can be kept very low. Countries that are seeking to industrialize may exploit low wages to entice industry, since many products benefit from low-skilled, low-wage labor. Countries such as Taiwan, Hong Kong, Korea, Thailand, Mexico, and now China have used this tactic to promote lower-cost manufactured goods, which can then be exported abroad. The problem is that, as countries develop, their labor costs increase. Industries and a burgeoning service economy find a way to consume all the labor. Cost then becomes less of a competitive advantage. In this case, **productivity**, which is measured as the relative output per unit of labor, becomes important. This helps countries with a better-educated labor force. Each worker produces more "goods" of better quality and receives higher wages.

Capital comes in many forms. **Finance capital** covers the money that is available to finance industries. Generally speaking, countries that are endowed with investors, banks, and financial instruments have a much easier time producing things. Getting a loan is comparatively easy and huge conglomerates have access to pools of money. Poor countries do not have this access, and this is partly the reason the World Bank and the International Monetary Fund were established: to provide loans to developing countries. **Human capital** refers to the population's level of education and skills. **Fixed capital** is invested in existing facilities: buildings, machines, transportation, and other structural items needed to produce goods in the first place. This varies considerably by country. Compare the machinery owned by the average American farmer and by the typical farmer in Kenya.

Entrepreneurship concerns the ability of managers to develop new industries, seek out markets, and maintain a competitive edge. If you look at the hundreds of business books out there, entrepreneurship accounts for the vast majority of them. Entrepreneurship can be the "it" factor that helps create something like an iPod after digital music had been shared for years.

▲ **Figure 17C.1** Supply is based on a combination of four factors: land, labor, capital, and entrepreneurship. These factors of production are discussed elsewhere (see Modules 16B and 16D) but are vital in determining the types of goods that are traded and the particular flows of trade.

Barriers

Various impediments can slow down or sometimes stop the flow of trade between countries. *Distance* is clearly important because it relates to the cost of shipping goods. Most of the distance costs are affected by the web of highways, railroads, and airline and shipping routes that tie places together.

For instance, Canada is the United States' largest trading partner, with 20% of the total trade volume. This has a great deal to do with the fact that Canada shares a 4,000-mile border with the United States and that 90% of its population live within 100 miles of the border. Yet Canada is also well linked to the United States via many air, land, and sea *transportation networks*.

Trade between other countries that are close together can be hurt by poor transport ties. This harms trade between many African countries, which have a shortage of paved roads and operating railroad networks. Even air travel is hampered. Many airlines do not travel from country to country, but must go through European nodes instead!

In addition to the natural barriers posed by distance and other physical and transportation obstacles, governments routinely use policy to alter their trading relationships. This might protect domestic partners, reward certain countries, and punish others. Historically, some of the earliest territorial states, such as England and France, employed a policy of **mercantilism** that sought to reduce barriers to trade within their lands while creating a large number of external barriers. This policy was successful in limiting the ability of merchants and artisans from other countries to trade freely.

Today, countries continue to employ these tactics. Among these are **tariffs**: a tax on items leaving or entering the country. Most often, these are used to raise the price of imported goods. Tariffs also earn revenue for the government.

A recent example is a tariff that the United States imposed on imported steel in 2002 that increased prices by nearly 30%. (This was later dropped in 2003 under pressure from the WTO). A **quota** is a limit on the quantity of imports or exports. Sometimes this is imposed unilaterally but can also be a part of a bilateral negotiation. In the European Union, milk quotas have been used to regulate the production and supply of milk. Quotas were routinely used to restrict imports of textiles.

Currency manipulation is sometimes employed as well. If a country's currency can be kept artificially low, this makes the cost of imported goods high and decreases the costs of exported goods. The United States has long suspected that the Chinese government keeps its currency (the yuan) low in order to bolster Chinese exports.

Demand conditions

The other side of the trading equation involves **demand conditions**. What products are countries likely to import? This partly is related to wealth. Rich countries will be more open to a wider variety of goods than poor countries. Poor countries actually import a great deal, but much of what they import are necessities. Increased wealth has a disproportionate impact on disposable, or **discretionary, income**: the amount of money available to satisfy various whims. Because discretionary income goes to wants rather than needs, greater income increases the demand for certain products while having little effect on the demand for other products. For instance, greater income will go into sleeker sports cars and bigger homes but will have little effect on the amount spent on food. *Preferences* are also important. Sometimes a country can exhibit a marked preference for one product while spurning another. Koreans love American pop music, for example, but they shun American beef.

The main factors determining the flow of trade are

- *Supply* of certain products in one country
- *Demand* for certain products in another country
- *Barriers* involved in moving a product from one country to another

If country A produces something that country B wants (and does not produce), and if country A produces more than it needs for its own consumption and country B produces less than it needs, then country A will sell its surplus to country B.

17D Concepts in Transportation

The ability to move between places and the accessibility of different places depend on the level of transportation technology and how well transportation infrastructure is developed. As transportation technology has improved, accessibility has been enhanced and the scale at which humans interact has expanded tremendously.

Transportation is required for many activities, among them:

- military: the need to move a lot of people and material from one spot to another,
- freight: the need to move cargo, and
- personal mobility: the need to move oneself from one place to another, both long and short distances.

Each of these needs carries different demands. For military purposes, the demand is for speed, to move from point A to point B as quickly and safely as possible. People are willing to spend a lot of money for these efforts, but they are considered one-time and urgent. For freight purposes, the demand is more often one of cost. The ability to move stuff cheaply makes it easier to access raw materials for production and to get final goods off to the market. For daily personal transportation, time is of the essence. People like to get where they are going quickly and are not willing to travel for more than one hour a day in order to meet their daily travel needs.

Transportation **conveyances** are different from **transportation facilities**. Conveyances involve modes of travel, including various boats, horses,

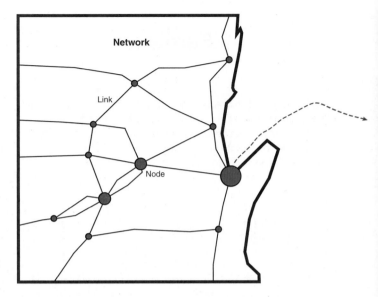

▲ **Figure 17D.1** There are a few basic elements to a transportation system. To begin with, every transportation system is composed of **nodes** and **links**. Nodes are either places in their own right or intersections. Links are the routes that connect nodes. In transportation, these can be roads, railroads, rivers, canals, footpaths, or sea or air routes. Some links have directionality; some do not. A **network** comprises the entire pattern of nodes and links. People often speak of **network connectivity**: the degree to which direct movements are possible over the network. More-connected networks tend to have more than one path or route between places. Less-connected networks have only one possible path between places. Disconnected networks have no path between places. Network connectivity affects mobility, or the ability to move between certain places. If you have ever tried to get an airplane flight between two cities, you can see how this works. Well-connected cities have a number of direct flights between them, whereas it might be impossible to fly between disconnected cities, even with intermediate connections.

Figure 17D.2 ▶ Many less developed countries are hampered by an inadequate **transportation infrastructure**. Case in point: Democratic Republic of the Congo, a country the size of Western Europe, is served by few passable roads and the only viable means of transportation lies in the railways. Unfortunately, most of these are quite old and unsafe, with usable portions extending for only about 2,300 miles total. Moreover, the railroad network is disconnected, made up of bits and pieces in different segments of the country.

Figure 17D.3 ▶ The cost of moving goods depends on the mode of transportation. Different conveyances have a big impact on the cost, but so do the available transportation facilities. In the years before the development of steam-powered transportation, water travel was significantly cheaper than land travel. This was especially true if water travel could take place downstream, using river power to move the cargo along. Three innovations dramatically cut freight costs. First, *canals*—artificial water channels cut to allow water travel across land where it had not been possible—were widely built. Second, *steam-powered ships* enabled the costs of traveling upstream and across any waterway to match downstream costs. Finally, *steam-powered railroads* made it relatively inexpensive to transport cargo across land. Later innovations, such as trucking, would further reduce costs, but these three innovations were key to nineteenth-century transportation.

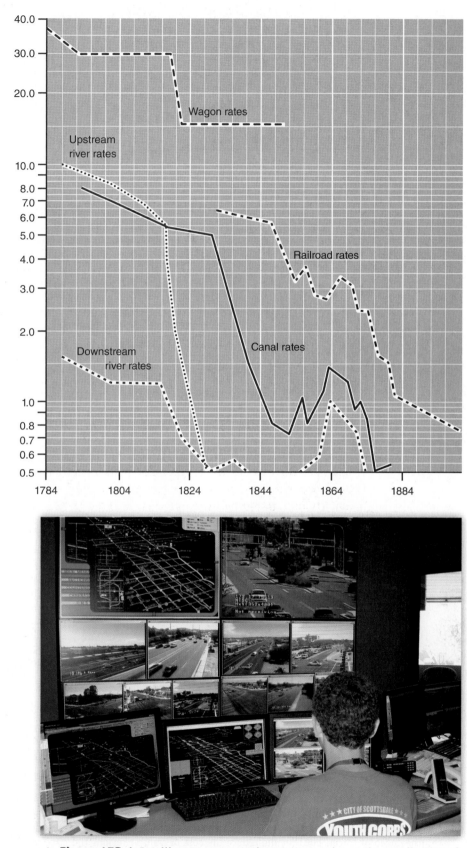

trains, motor vehicles, streetcars, and aircraft. Over history, we have progressed from relying on horses and sailing ships to automobiles and jet airplanes. These developments have had profound effects, but they could not be fully realized without complementary improvements in transportation facilities. These improvements include the development of airports, expansion of harbors and sea lanes, expansion of a uniform railroad network, and steady extension and upgrading of roadways.

First and foremost, transportation allows us to bridge distances and to increase our accessibility to different places. Distance represents both time and cost. Time is fairly intuitive: how long it takes to go from point A to point B. But sometimes the full time involved is not always considered. For instance, it may take a half hour to drive to a place, but another half hour to park. Cost is even more complicated. Sure, costs increase with distance, but they are also affected by the volume of what is being transported. Higher volumes often result in a smaller cost per unit weight. For example, transporting 1,000 pounds may be only twice the cost of moving 100 pounds.

▲ **Figure 17D.4 Intelligent transportation systems** enhance the coordination of traffic signal lights with the overall patterns and flows of traffic. These systems then can determine the placement and timing of specific lights at various intersections, helping minimize traffic congestions and implementing various emergency plans in case of collisions, stalled vehicles, fires, and major events.

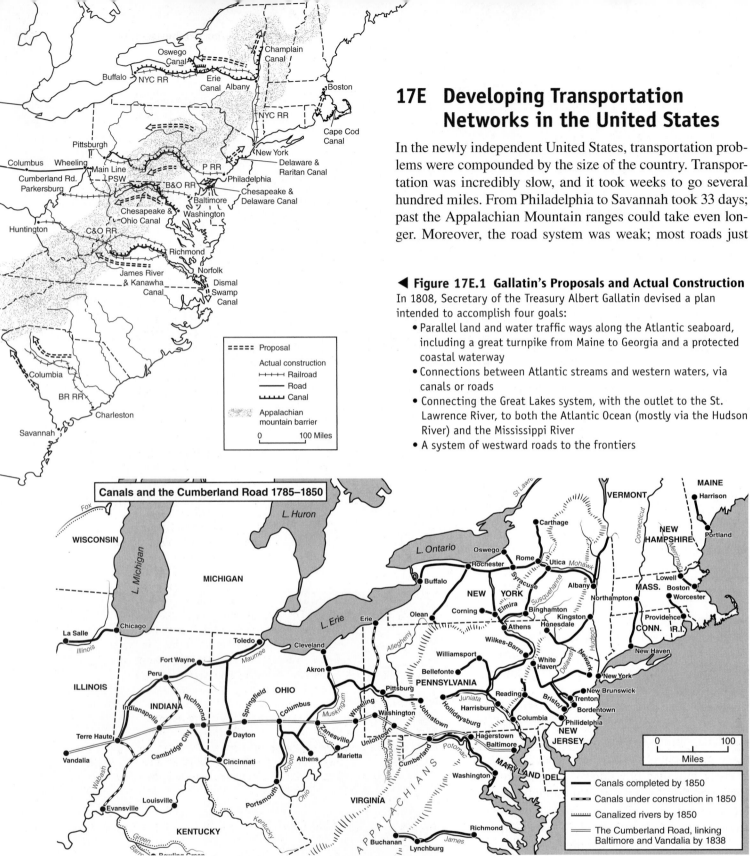

17E Developing Transportation Networks in the United States

In the newly independent United States, transportation problems were compounded by the size of the country. Transportation was incredibly slow, and it took weeks to go several hundred miles. From Philadelphia to Savannah took 33 days; past the Appalachian Mountain ranges could take even longer. Moreover, the road system was weak; most roads just

◄ **Figure 17E.1 Gallatin's Proposals and Actual Construction**
In 1808, Secretary of the Treasury Albert Gallatin devised a plan intended to accomplish four goals:
- Parallel land and water traffic ways along the Atlantic seaboard, including a great turnpike from Maine to Georgia and a protected coastal waterway
- Connections between Atlantic streams and western waters, via canals or roads
- Connecting the Great Lakes system, with the outlet to the St. Lawrence River, to both the Atlantic Ocean (mostly via the Hudson River) and the Mississippi River
- A system of westward roads to the frontiers

▲ **Figure 17E.2** The cost of transporting something by water is less than the cost of transporting over land using carts and animals. With the development of the steamboat in the 1810s, waterways became even more useful since boats could now travel upriver. Canals were developed as a means to link water systems so that freight and passengers could move about the country. Generally, canals did not enhance the speed of travel, but they did reduce the cost of transportation. The Erie Canal across New York opened in 1825 and linked the Great Lakes to the Hudson River. By 1825, Cleveland became the northern terminus of the Ohio Canal, which linked to Akron. The canal network created a situation where the northern third of the country could put cargo onto a canal and move it either directly or via the Great Lakes to the Atlantic. The southern and middle United States also used canals, but these generally led eventually to New Orleans. Certain cities, like Cincinnati, became relatively large because of their reliance on water transport via the Ohio and Mississippi rivers. For a farmer in southern Pennsylvania, it cost less to ship his goods the 1700 miles to New Orleans than the 300 miles overland to Philadelphia.

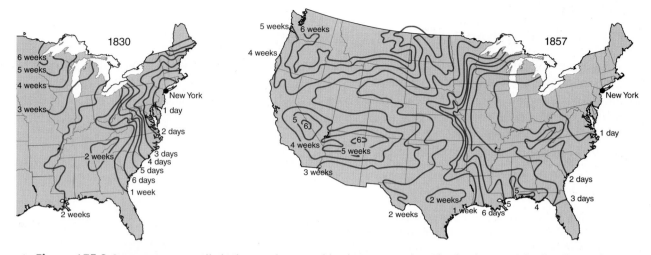

▲ **Figure 17E.3** Steam power propelled advances in sea and land transportation. The development of railroads—trains harnessed to a steam locomotive running on railroad tracks—moved goods and people faster than any other form of existing transportation. By the 1840s, a railroad network stretched out to the Great Lakes and penetrated into the Midwest. Chicago emerged as a new hub for railway expansion. Most farmers in these places lived within 20 miles of either a navigable waterway or a railroad. As these maps show, the development of railroads had a huge impact on travel times. What had once taken a week now took only a day. The first transcontinental railroad was completed by 1869, and there were four of these by 1883. By the end of the nineteenth century, the United States had by far the largest network in the world: more than 312,000 km of railroad network, bigger than all of Europe.

◀ **Figure 17E.4** The automobile would transform the American landscape in an unprecedented manner. But automobile use spread slowly after it was introduced to the public. Some of this had to do with the nature of automobiles themselves: They were too expensive, hard to operate, and considered a plaything of the rich. The mass production of Henry Ford's Model T in 1909 changed that. But a network of better roads was needed, too.

Most early roads were little better than farm roads. They were so bad that cars routinely got stuck in mud or lost a tire, and a small trip could be bone jarring—that is, if roads existed at all. In fact, the mileage of all surfaced roads—sand, gravel, and macadam—was less than that of railroad tracks in 1915. The financing of roads was still left up to the states, and poor states, especially in the South and West, suffered. Going cross-country was still an adventure. By the 1920s, a **national highway system** had been established, leading to the development of the US routes we see today as in the map above. North–south roads had odd numbers, from US 1 on the East Coast to US 101 on the West Coast. East–west routes had even numbers. The construction of these roads was financed through a gas tax. In the 1950s, the **Interstate Highway System**, composed of large, limited-access superhighways, revolutionized automobile travel, with the costs for this 41,000 mile network picked up primarily by the federal government.

made some connections to coastal harbors. Many roads began as an Indian path, then a trail, then a pack trail, then a wagon road that could actually sustain a wagon.

Another problem was that—unlike England or France—the federal government did not want to pay for roads. It had to be done by the states, so financing was a big headache, especially for poor states. Shortly after Ohio was admitted to the Union, federal intervention was needed to improve transportation networks.

While the **Gallatin Plan** was not adopted in every respect, it did point the way to a number of transportation changes. We can categorize transportation network development and its most important impacts into three eras:

- Canals: 1700s to early 1800s
- Railroads: mid-1800s to early 1900s
- Cars and roads: early 1900s until now

17F Modern Urban Daily Transportation

When it comes to moving people, the bulk of transportation takes place at a smaller, local scale. This type of transportation provides much of the rhythm of our daily lives as we move from home to work, run all of our errands, and add some social and recreational activities as well. As shown in Module 14D, changes in daily transportation have been the major factor in the changing form of the city. But how does urban transportation operate today? Several issues are significant: trip purpose, modal split, average length of trip, and the impacts of commuting and other urban travel.

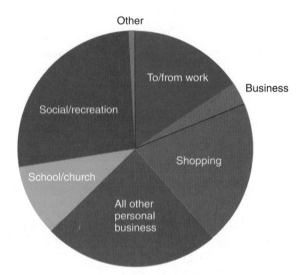

Figure 17F.1 ▶ What do people travel for? Many would suspect that the main purpose is getting to and from work. **Commuting** behavior, which describes this form of travel, is an important engine of urban traffic but accounts for only about one-quarter of the time spent on all household trips. Travel for social purposes, for shopping, and for other personal reasons also accounts for much of the time. These add considerably to how much time people spend traveling. The reason we often focus on travel time to work is because this is more likely to be captured in the US Census. The Census shows that commuting behavior varies a lot. More than half of Americans travel under a half hour, but nearly 1 out of 10 commute over an hour. In general, men tend to have longer commutes than women, but women are also more likely to pick up the brunt of the other forms of travel. In fact, men spend only 40% of their travel on family, shopping, and personal business, while women spend half. While it seems that commuting times are getting longer, in his book *Traffic*, Tom Vanderbilt suggests that the amount of time spent commuting has remained roughly the same over time. What has changed has been the mode of transportation.

Table 17F.1 Mode of Transportation in Commuting			
	1985 (%)	1993 (%)	2001 (%)
Automobile	86.5	88.0	87.8
Single-Occupancy	72.4	76.6	78.2
Carpool	14.1	11.4	9.7
Public Transportation	5.1	4.6	4.7
Taxicab	0.1	0.1	0.1
Bicycle or Motorcycle	1.0	0.7	0.7
Walks	4.0	3.1	2.8
Other Means	0.3	0.5	0.9
Works at Home	3.0	3.0	2.8

Source: Data from U.S. Census Bureau.

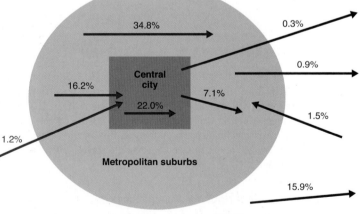

▲ **Figure 17F.2 Commuting Patterns in the US, 2000** In the United States, daily travel has increasingly been associated with **single-occupancy motor vehicle travel (SOV)**: cars, minivans, pickup trucks, and motorcycles. In fact, nearly 80% of Americans get to work this way. Carpooling is a distant second, followed by public transportation and walking or biking. As gasoline prices have increased, there has been a small but discernible decrease in SOV commuting, but most places we live in today are difficult to navigate without a car. As the schematic shows, most commuting is actually between suburbs, and it is impossible to walk, often dangerous to bike, and very time consuming to take public transportation systems, which often have limited network connectivity. Only in the New York City metro area, well serviced by commuter trains, subways, and an elaborate bus system, do more than a quarter of commuters take transit.

The impacts of urban, daily transportation are many and varied. Traffic congestion has been a historic bane. Even the ancient Romans experienced it, leading to some of the world's first traffic regulations. Congestion occurs when the demand for transportation facilities outstrips the capacity to handle the additional traffic. In the United States, congestion is felt most keenly on roads as the number of miles traveled in vehicles (the demand) has increased three times as fast as the additional lanes constructed (the capacity). More vehicles are using each lane, and this increases the likelihood of traffic jams. Trying to "fix" congestion has preoccupied many civil engineers and transportation planners.

The environmental impacts of urban, daily transportation have also become more prominent. Motor vehicles are the main source of air pollution, and they have led to some major problems in cities throughout the world. Traditionally, Los Angeles—with its massive freeway system, auto-dependent culture, bright sunshine, and physical configuration of sea breezes and mountains—was a poster child for smog. But lately it has been cities in the developing world, where automobile traffic has increased sharply and many drive older, less clean cars that suffer the most unhealthy air (see Module 12E).

Table 17F.2 Travel Modal Split for Urban Trips, Selected Countries, 1995

Modal split refers to the percentage of travel undertaken by each transport mode. These figures from 1995 show that the United States is unique in its overwhelming reliance on personal motor vehicles. In other economically developed countries, over half of commuting is accomplished by public transportation, walking, and bicycling. Even Canada, which is closest to the American urban model, has a far greater proportion of people who do not depend on driving. (Countries in the less developed world show even lower rates of driving, since motor vehicles are simply unaffordable to the mass of population.) What accounts for this difference? For one thing, gasoline costs substantially less in the United States, largely because it is taxed at a lower rate. The overall cost of owning and driving a vehicle—through registration rates, parking costs, and extra tariffs—is generally higher in other countries. Cities and suburbs in other countries have been developed in a more compact way. While sprawl is found everywhere, there is simply less of it. Finally, other countries have made more investments in public transportation and in facilitating bicycle travel. US federal support for public transit—very low to begin with—declined by two-thirds just between 1981 and 1990. It has recovered a bit since, but many politicians and transportation officials still question the need to add more public transportation facilities. As for bicycling, this is often seen as more of a recreational than a commuting option. Bike paths have been developed on old rail beds (rails to trails), but not many cities facilitate bicycle commuting.

Country	Automobile	Transit	Bicycle	Walk/Other	Automobile Trips per Transit Trip
United States	89	2	1	7	44.5
Canada	76	10	2	12	7.6
Denmark	42	14	20	24	3.0
Great Britain	65	14	4	17	4.6
France	56	13	5	25	4.5
Germany	49	16	12	23	3.1
Netherlands	45	7	28	20	6.4
Sweden	46	11	10	33	4.2
Switzerland	46	20	9	26	2.3

Source: Data from Jon Pucher in "Transportation Trends, Problems, and Policies: An International Perspective," *Transportation Research*, Vol. 33-A, Nos. 7/8, September 1999, pp. 493–503.

◀ **Figure 17F.3** Most recently, transportation has been implicated in personal health of another sort. Research has found that people who live in more pedestrian-friendly communities are clearly more likely to walk. This leads to significantly lower rates of obesity. In fact, the most walkable communities tend to be the trimmest, whereas sprawling communities contain a higher proportion of overweight people. This can be seen outside the United States as well, as many people living in places where walking is more common are much less likely to be heavy. The problem is that many communities are not friendly to pedestrians. In fact, they are often built without any amenities, such as sidewalks, that make walking possible. If a community is not perceived as a pleasant place for foot travel, or even a place where walking is downright perilous, like in this photo of Buford highway in Atlanta, people will be unwilling to walk.

17G Geographic Aspects of US Retailing

Today, the largest corporation in the world is a store, or, rather, a vast network of over 7,000 stores. Walmart Stores, Inc.'s ascendancy to the top of the business hierarchy demonstrates both the increasing significance of shopping to the economy and the consolidation of stores. Retailing has changed considerably in the last several decades, and so has the geography used to describe it. These changes make a dramatic impression on the landscape. Much of what is iconic about American places, from old-fashioned Main Streets to today's endless chain of big-box stores, derives from changes in retail geography.

Christaller's model of central place has been tested, modified, and tweaked since it was first introduced. To some extent, the principles behind it—stores clustering in central places and the hierarchical distribution of towns or shopping centers based on a market hinterland—have been borne out in rural areas, where it was first applied, and even in metropolitan areas, where one can see different orders of shopping areas, traditionally leading up to the downtown, or central business district (see Module 14C). However, retail operations have changed and models of retail that applied 70 years ago may not be as relevant today without considerable revisions.

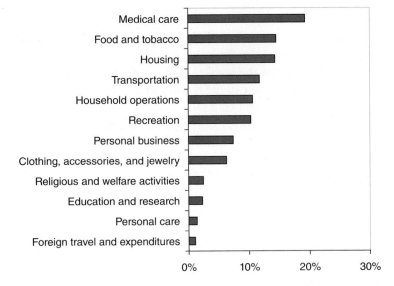

Consumption category

▲ **Figure 17G.1** As an aspect of economic activity, retailing can be viewed as the next-to-the-last stop on the supply chain from producer to consumer. Of course, not everything produced is sold to households. But consumer purchases do account for the majority (70%) of all spending—the rest divided between business investment and government. As this chart shows, much of this consumption takes place in stores: food, clothing, household goods, recreation, and many aspects of medical care, such as drugs. In that context, stores are the critical link in the distribution of goods to consumers. Retail is also important as an economic segment in its own right. It accounts for about 5% of economic output (wholesaling accounts for another 5%), 13% of all jobs (wholesaling another 5%), and 14% of all businesses in the United States (wholesalers another 5%).

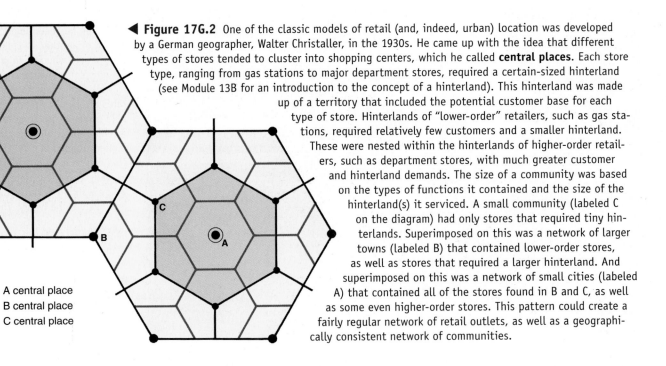

◀ **Figure 17G.2** One of the classic models of retail (and, indeed, urban) location was developed by a German geographer, Walter Christaller, in the 1930s. He came up with the idea that different types of stores tended to cluster into shopping centers, which he called **central places**. Each store type, ranging from gas stations to major department stores, required a certain-sized hinterland (see Module 13B for an introduction to the concept of a hinterland). This hinterland was made up of a territory that included the potential customer base for each type of store. Hinterlands of "lower-order" retailers, such as gas stations, required relatively few customers and a smaller hinterland. These were nested within the hinterlands of higher-order retailers, such as department stores, with much greater customer and hinterland demands. The size of a community was based on the types of functions it contained and the size of the hinterland(s) it serviced. A small community (labeled C on the diagram) had only stores that required tiny hinterlands. Superimposed on this was a network of larger towns (labeled B) that contained lower-order stores, as well as stores that required a larger hinterland. And superimposed on this was a network of small cities (labeled A) that contained all of the stores found in B and C, as well as some even higher-order stores. This pattern could create a fairly regular network of retail outlets, as well as a geographically consistent network of communities.

◉ A central place
● B central place
● C central place

▲ **Figure 17G.3** As retailing has changed, the classic models have had to undergo changes as well. As discussed in Module 14D, the downtown has gone from being the highest-order center in a metropolitan area—the place where everybody went to shop several times a year—to a place that sometimes has less retail than that found in the suburbs. The proliferation of suburban plazas in the 1950s and 1960s, indoor malls in the 1970s and 1980s, and big-box superstores in the 1990s and 2000s has drastically shifted the balance of marketing power. Edge cities, as discussed in Module 14D, have emerged on the city's outskirts as wholly new central places, often containing the functions and store types once found only in the downtown.

◄ **Figure 17G.4** In rural areas, the small town was there primarily to serve the needs of farmers and the operations that served family farms. Now, large-scale farms and a dwindling farming population can no longer support these small-town economies. Moreover, improved transportation systems make driving long distances to get to a larger center more feasible. These developments have dried up the customer base and expanded the necessary market threshold for the smaller towns. As a result, these small places just are not necessary anymore, as many of the stores once found in small towns can now survive only in larger towns.

The nature of retailing has been changing for a long time, and never more quickly than today. There are several major factors implicated in this change, most of which clearly apply to the United States but are present in other countries as well.

First, most retail outlets have simply gotten bigger, both in terms of the size of individual stores and in the overall quantity of retail space.

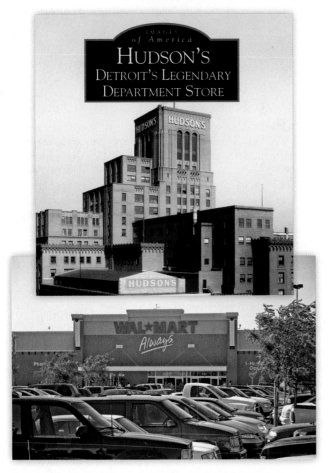

▲ **Figure 17G.5** In the mid-nineteenth century, a new type of store was built that contained multiple departments. These department stores were under single ownership and went on to be among the most imposing structures in the city, anchoring the growing downtowns and creating a landmark destination for customers from miles around. These and the other forms of retail that grew up in the expanding cities were particularly well suited for a city based on streetcar travel, and they continued to prosper well into the automotive era. Hudson's Department Store, shown here, was 25 stories high, with 12,000 employees and 100,000 daily shoppers. Despite the gargantuan size of these flagship stores, most other retail stores remained small. By the 1920s, however, average store sizes had grown and the old ways of retailing, with the proprietor fetching goods from behind a counter, gave way to the self-service environment we see today. The development of shopping malls encouraged a collection of many stores under one roof, with all but the anchor department stores ranging from 3,000 to 6,000 square feet. More recently, other types of stores expanded: Grocery stores, which used to be a couple of thousand square feet in size, now encompass more than an acre; the typical discount store often takes up 2 or 3 acres of shopping area; and a Walmart Supercenter or a SuperTarget averages about 4 acres in total.

The second factor is the change in retail locations—in particular, the move to the suburbs. Traditionally, retail was concentrated in the city. Many people lived in suburbs but shopped in the city. But by the 1960s, more retail was located in the suburbs than in the city. This process has continued so that suburban locations now include the vast majority of retail activity. Certainly, the movement of people out to the suburbs required a change in location. As more people drove, the zone of greatest accessibility was no longer found downtown. In fact, stores located downtown, with its congestion and expensive parking, would be hard pressed to compete with what (at first) were clearer streets and ample free parking. The growing size of retail also necessitated a change, since suburban locations offered lower costs per square foot and an ability for retail developers to control their environment. Finally, retailers began to see the development of stores as something more than just the direct purveying of goods. At a time when "shopping" has become perhaps the major form of recreation, stores need to create a more satisfying experience overall.

A third factor was the growth of **retail chains**. In the past, retailing was dominated by small, independent stores owned and operated by a family. In fact, each town and city contained local hardware and furniture stores, groceries, bookstores, even department stores. Some of these were quite grand and successful, but they were nearly always rooted in the community. According to the US Census Bureau, in 1948, 70% of total retail sales occurred in independent stores, with another 12% accounted for by retail chains with 10 or fewer stores. Today, the 20 largest US retail companies account for nearly a quarter of all retail sales, while stand-alone establishments account for less than 40%. But there are some major differences between store types. Some US stores have been given to tremendous consolidation. Department stores are at the very apex of consolidation, where 20 firms account for 98.5% of sales. Bookstores, shoe stores, electronics, and drug stores are likewise concentrated. At the other end of the spectrum, some categories—florists, car dealers, liquor stores, and furniture stores—are much less susceptible to consolidation. New car dealers with just one dealership, for example, account for the vast majority of sales.

This consolidation means that stores are increasingly isolated from the localities they serve. The retail landscape of cities and towns, even within the downtown areas, looks strikingly similar. The range of products is nearly identical—although each retail outlet stocks a bewildering array of goods, many times this excludes specialty products. Finally, the new retail economy effectively reconfigures the relationship between the retailer and the supplier. In the past, manufacturers pretty much made what they wanted to and sold their goods to a wide range of retailers. Now, retailers increasingly make decisions on how much products should cost and what sorts of products the manufacturer should supply. The risk of being cut out of the retail market altogether compels manufacturers to comply.

Figure 17G.6

◄ *Pedestrian-oriented commercial strips*, such as a Main Street, is the type of retail development that predominated from the late nineteenth until the mid-twentieth century. Stores were arrayed along a commercial street. Some of these streetscapes continue to thrive or have been revived. Since the 1970s, many communities have experimented with making these into pedestrian-only corridors, with mixed results.

▲ *Enclosed malls* can include up to 200 stores anchored by two or more big department stores. Patrons park and then walk into the mall. These originated in the mid-1950s and peaked in the 1980s. Few malls are built now and many have seen steep declines or complete shutdown. In the 1970s, a number of cities sought to replace their downtown stores with a mall. In the 1980s and 1990s, a few *megamalls* were built, notably the West Edmonton Mall in Alberta and the Mall of America near Minneapolis. These included a huge variety of stores as well as entertainment centers.

▲ *Neighborhood/community centers and strips* emerged after World War II as open strips or plazas around a supermarket or discount store, with several other stores. They were always surrounded by parking lots. In more densely packed urban areas, sometimes the parking is placed underground to maximize the amount of land given to retail spaces.

◄ *Specialty shopping centers* come in assorted types and include festival marketplaces such as Boston's Faneuil Hall and Baltimore's Harbor Place, outlet malls of various manufacturers, and fashion malls. These shopping areas are intended to attract people from a fairly long distance and become an aspect of tourism. These began being developed in the 1980s.

▲ *Power centers* emerged in the early 1990s and are suburban centers arrayed along a busy commercial stretch. These are made up primarily of large "category killer" stores that focus on one type of product, such as electronics or hardware, each of which is vast in its own right.

▲ *Open-air "lifestyle" centers* contain many of the features of a mall but are outside, do not contain anchor stores, and include many attractive outdoor fixtures. These generally cater to an upscale clientele and have become more popular since the late 1990s.

17H Changing Geographies of Retailing in the Internet Age

One of the more intriguing developments in retail distribution has been the impact of information technologies, particularly the Internet. While new, this also continues a long tradition of **nonstore retailing**. In the past, itinerant peddlers roamed the countryside, taking goods to their customers. Door-to-door salesmen, often with fixed routes, also sold to people at home. Montgomery Ward and Sears Roebuck popularized mail-order retailing, which relied on postal and other delivery services to bring goods to people. In 1895, Sears-Roebuck offered a 532-page catalog of goods, growing to be the dominant retail company in the United States well before it opened an actual store. Sears even sold kits to build houses by mail order; 75,000 of these were sold in the first half of the twentieth century. Within the last three decades, mail-order retailing has continued its popularity, especially with **niche marketers**, such as Lands' End. And certain television channels specialize in selling products, such as jewelry and electronics, to viewers. The growth of **e-tailing**, first popularized in the mid-1990s with such online-only vendors as Amazon.com, has continued into the 2000s. This has spawned a number of new terms. "Brick and mortar" now describes traditional stores that exist in a physical space. "Cyber Monday" marks the first Monday after Thanksgiving, when online purchases for Christmas peak.

Traditionally, retail commerce requires that retailers demonstrate an attachment to the places where they do business. Online retailing is not immune from this demand, either. It relies on customer familiarity and, so, must develop interfaces that correspond with the culture. For this reason, it is rare to find web portals that stretch across national boundaries. Moreover, the implementation of e-commerce needs to adhere to best practices that originate in the community. While the web presence itself appears aspatial, behind the screen are networks of suppliers, distributers, and employees rooted in various localities.

With the exception of the few purely online retailers, most e-commerce has adopted a hybrid approach that combines online retailing ("clicks") with the storefront retailing ("bricks") that has the advantages of having developed and nurtured some of these local networks. Such e-commerce has been shown to actually enhance customer relations in markets where the retailer does business. It helps retain old customers and bring in new ones. The website becomes an extension of the store's physical structure. Some retail websites, such as Lowes.com or Bestbuy.com, provide information on whether a product is in stock at a customer's closest store. Many retailers allow returns of merchandise purchased online at a physical store or provide free shipping to a store for customer pickup.

Online percentage of total retail spending, 2006

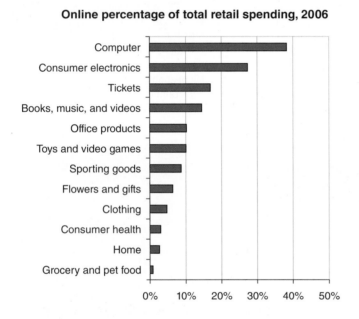

▲ **Figure 17H.1** While e-tailing has undoubtedly expanded, fortunes vary among product categories. Many of the largest online retailers took years to make a profit. Over 200 online start-ups from the 1990s collapsed in 2000 because they could not afford to wait or they specialized in product categories more resistant to online marketing. Online sites that marketed pet supplies, for instance, were especially hard hit. Successful online retailers have focused on books, computers, and electronics, some of these for different reasons. Books and music sites, such as Amazon.com, are not restricted to a limited stock but can offer nearly any item a customer would want. In this, they appeal to the "long tail," which means that they are able to sell small quantities of items to lots of people. Computer websites, such as Dell.com, offer a great way for consumers to customize their computer before it is actually assembled. Online electronics sites have benefited from their ability to sell the most current models from a wide range of vendors, the ability of potential buyers to comparison shop, and generally lower prices. This chart does not include the market penetration of eBay, which brings independent sellers together with potential buyers under the auspices of an auction site.

◀ **Figure 17H.2** What are some of the geographic implications of e-tailing? E-tailing should have an effect if it commands a significant market share of particular product lines. Taken to its logical end, some principles of central place theory (see Module 17G) are overturned as market hinterlands effectively span the globe. Online purchasing collapses the friction of distance and makes local retail outlets less relevant. One case in point: software stores, such as Egghead Software, were fixtures in malls throughout the late 1980s and 1990s. Yet these have largely been supplanted by online purchases of software and folding of software lines into other retail outlets. The much larger category of bookstores has also seen a major drop in so-called brick and mortar establishments. Bookstores are among the types of retail establishments most threatened by e-tailing. The rise of electronic readers, such as the Kindle and the iPad, could make these scenes rarer and rarer.

▲ **Figure 17H.3** The second major geographic implication of e-tailing is the need to develop massive spaces for distribution centers as well as for Internet servers. The promise of e-tailing lies in its speedy delivery, and this demands that much of the product line be in stock. So the whole operation relies on an extensive storage and distribution network. Since most e-tailers are still selling physical goods, distances must be accounted for. Amazon.com, for example, has over 30 "fulfillment centers," often located next to airports for speedy deliveries. The largest of these spans 13 football fields and employs hundreds of people.

Key Terms

barter (17A)
cash exchanges (17A)
central places (17G)
commuting (17F)
competition (17B)
competitive advantage (17B)
conveyances (17D)
currency manipulation (17C)
demand conditions (17C)
discretionary income (17C)
embargo (17B)
entrepreneurship (17C)
e-tailing (17H)
finance capital (17C)
fixed capital (17C)
Gallatin Plan (17E)
human capital (17C)
intelligent transportation systems (17D)
international trade (17A)
Interstate Highway System (17E)
links (17D)

mercantilism (17C)
modal split (17F)
national highway system (17E)
network (17D)
network connectivity (17D)
niche marketers (17H)
nodes (17D)
nonstore retailing (17H)
productivity (17C)
protectionism (17B)
quota (17C)
retail chains (17G)
single-occupancy motor vehicle travel (SOV) (17F)
tariffs (17C)
trade deficit (17A)
trade surplus (17A)
transportation facilities (17D)
transportation infrastructure (17D)
World Trade Organization (WTO) (17A)

Basic Review Questions

1. How does the barter system compare to a cash system?

2. How has international trade been important in world history?

3. What is the difference between a trade deficit and a trade surplus?

4. What accounts for the overall increase in trade?

5. What are some of the advantages of an autarky system?

6. What are some of the comparative advantages that are realized when countries trade with each other?

7. How might certain countries have a competitive advantage and be able to use this to promote more trade?

8. What are some of the criticisms of a complete free trading system?

9. What determines the flow of trade?

10. What are the four elements of supply in regard to certain products that a country might be able to trade?

11. What are the main conditions that allow for greater trade?

12. What are some of the barriers that might inhibit trade from occurring?

13. What are some of the reasons that transportation is required?

14. What are the differences between transportation conveyances and transportation facilities?

15. What are some of the elements of nodes, links, and networks in transportation systems?

16. How do the costs of different transportation systems compare to each other historically?

17. What was the Gallatin Plan, and what were some of the issues it was intended to resolve? What were some of its goals?

18. What spurred the canal building boom of the early nineteenth century?

19. How did the railroad have an impact on travel time in the United States?

20. What is the impact of the national highway system and Interstate Highway System on the transportation network?

21. In urban transportation, what are the main reasons people travel?

22. How does commuting behavior vary?

23. What are some of the modes of urban transportation?

24. How does the modal split vary by country?

25. Why does traffic congestion occur?

26. How is transportation related to physical health?

27. Why has retailing become more important than ever in a modern American economy?

28. Outline Christaller's central place theory.

29. How has the retail hierarchy and the location of markets changed over the years? What are three major developments in the nature of retailing within the last several decades?

30. What are six types of retail outlets?

31. How can you compare bricks and mortar retailing with the growth of e-tailing?

32. What are some geographical implications of e-tailing?

33. How have some stores developed a hybrid approach to retailing?

34. How has e-tailing allowed for more marketing at the long tail?

Advanced Review Questions (Essay Questions)

1. Discuss the factors that led to an increase in overall trade. How does international trade lead to a situation in which some countries develop a trade surplus but others develop a trade deficit? Which countries have enjoyed a large trade surplus in recent years, and why?

2. Discuss the differences between an economy based on autarky and an economy based on trade. What are some of the advantages of a system based on autarky? How does comparative advantage create a situation in which two partners in trade may both benefit?

3. Describe the factors that determine the flow of trade. What are some of the ways in which a country can seek to limit the amount of trade, particularly imports, that come into the country?

4. What is the significance of network connectivity in transportation, and how is it related to accessibility? How did the canal system promote accessibility, fit within the Gallatin Plan, and foster specific urban development? How did each of the phases of the railroad system increase connectivity, but more in some places than in others.

5. What hampered the early adoption of the automobile? How did the development of the national highway system and later the Interstate Highway System alter the transportation network in the United States in the twentieth century?

6. What have been some of the trends in driving over the last few decades (since about 1970)? What role does commuting play in overall driving? How would you characterize commuting in terms of modal choice and time and distance traveled? How does the United States compare with European countries in this regard?

7. How does Christaller's central place theory help us understand the location of different types of retail establishments and different locations of markets? How have changes in regard to (a) edge cities and (b) a dwindling farm population altered the basis of this theory?

8. Describe how retailing has changed in the last several decades. What have been some of the changes in terms of new types of stores, where stores are located, and the development of chains. What have been some of the major differences in regard to the consolidation of certain categories of retail as opposed to other categories, and what might explain these differences?

9. What is e-tailing? How does this compare to other forms of nonstore retailing? What are two major geographical implications of e-tailing?

Further Study Topics

- Up until the early 1960s, the United States had a trade surplus, but this soon changed. Explore some of the reasons the United States has experienced a massive trade deficit for several decades. Is this necessarily a bad thing? What are some of the ways in which the trade deficit could be reduced?

- International trade relies on the willingness of different countries to reduce barriers. The North American Free Trade Agreement, which includes the United States, Canada and Mexico, is very controversial because of the sense that it may cause jobs to leave the United States for cheaper opportunities in Mexico. Assess what some of the impacts of the North American Free Trade Agreement has been. Has it benefited or hurt the United States?

- Transportation is a big consumer of oil and a large contributor to pollution. Several proposals have called for the development of a carbon tax to alleviate pollution. How would the imposition of a carbon tax be likely to change transportation patterns and choices in the United States? Who would be the beneficiaries of these transportation changes, and whom might these changes harm?

- What are some of the differences between US cities in regard to share of bicycling and pedestrians in the overall modal split? What accounts for some of these differences, and how can a city try to increase the number of people who use public transportation or take some nonautomotive transportation?

- Chart some of the difference in the proportion of goods sold online. Why has e-tailing had a larger impact on some sectors of the retail world than on others? How has this altered the retail landscape? How can e-tailing exist without destroying the attachment that many stores have to place?

Summary Activities

This graphic shows the relations between nodes and links in a transportation network. Of course, a great deal depends on the type of transportation. For automobile traffic, nodes, links, and connectivity correspond to streets and highways. For bus users, these elements refer to bus routes.

For this activity, choose a transportation type in a town or city you know well. Then sketch out the main nodes and links. It might be interesting to determine the nodes and links involved with bicycling, for example, as compared to driving. Do you feel that there is adequate connectivity for your transportation mode?

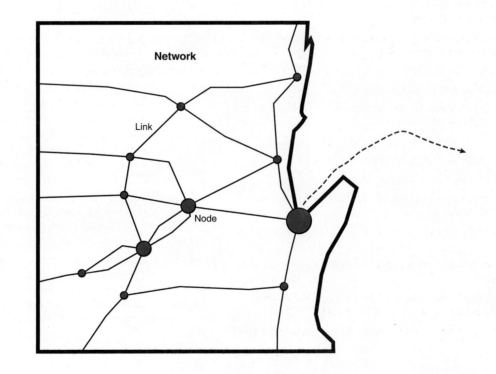

Development and Geography

Most of us reading this book are lucky to live in a society marked by relatively high degrees of prosperity. Periodic news reports—mass famines in the Sudan, catastrophic flooding in Bangladesh, a cholera crisis in Haiti, pavement dwellers in Indian cities, and a grinding poverty that affects so much of the world's people—underline just how bad it can be in so much of the world. Away from the tourist enclaves, visits to poor countries show us unfathomable hardships. An average American's standard of living is considered unattainable by all but a tiny few in most countries. In some societies, malnutrition, high mortality, and lack of decent shelter are considered normal conditions. Where you are born is probably the single most significant factor determining your life's prospects. To be born in a village in war-torn Afghanistan consigns you to the likely prospect of a miserable life and an early death. To be born in a wealthy country, such as Sweden, may not guarantee a prosperous and healthy life, but it makes it much more likely.

In their *Scientific American* article "The Geography of Poverty and Wealth," Jeffrey Sachs, Andrew Mellinger, and John Gallup ask, "Why are some countries stupendously rich and others horrendously poor?" Their answer relies to a great extent on geography. Development is not distributed randomly but instead shows clear differences between broad regions of the world. The wealthiest countries in North America, Europe, Japan/South Korea, and Australia/New Zealand are found in the temperate zones of the Northern and Southern Hemispheres. Most of the poorest countries are located in the tropics—only Singapore, Taiwan, and Hong Kong contradict this general trend. Geographical variations in climate, proximity to the sea, plant types, and diffusion possibilities have also been cited as possible factors responsible for development differences, although more comprehensive approaches have seen geography at work in many complex ways. The disparities we witness today are actually pretty recent, meaning that the current patterns have been determined by several historical events and processes.

This chapter aims to examine development issues from a geographic perspective, keeping in mind some of the material we have covered in previous chapters.

18A Meanings of Development and Development Disparities Today

A discussion of **world development** usually means raising the **living standards** of the world's poorest countries and, so, reducing disparities between countries in the world. A variety of terms are used to designate poor countries: **Third World**, **less developed countries**, sometimes *the developing world*—always with the implication that these countries aspire to a level of development that the rich countries—labeled **First World**, **developed countries**, or **more developed countries**—have already attained. However, development occurs everywhere, in countries rich and poor. It is a process with several related aspects—political, social, human, and economic.

The term **economic development** probably began with Karl Marx, who outlined stages of economic development that various societies go through. Others viewed development as part of the colonial enterprise of clearing forests, extracting resources, and otherwise harnessing nature's bounty for human goals. It was only during the twentieth century that development came to be associated with increasing the welfare of poorer countries. After World War II, economic development was considered primarily in regard to rising per capita incomes, with the aim of raising them in poor countries as rapidly as possible. Government agen-

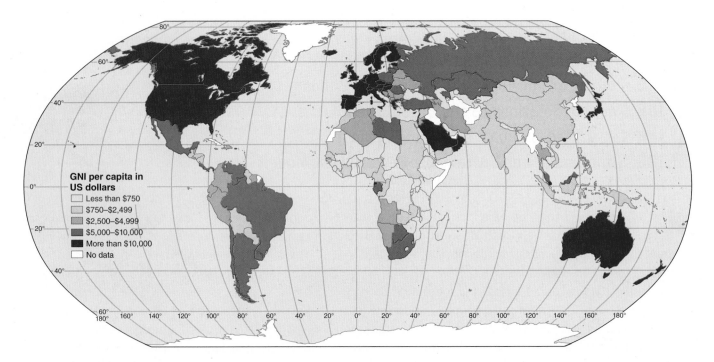

▲ **Figure 18A.1** In Module 15C, we discussed the different measures of economic activity and displayed some of the variations between countries in the world. This map takes gross national income (GNI)—a commonly used measurement of economic activity, which includes the total of all the goods and services produced within a country plus the net income from assets abroad—and divides it by total population. This per capita measurement exhibits enormous variations. Luxembourg, for example, has a GNI per capita of about $75,000. This is nearly two-thirds higher than the US figure. By contrast, about 45 countries show GNI per capita rates that are under $1,000 and about 15 countries where the per capita GNI is less than $1 a day! There are a number of cautions when examining a map like this. First of all, it is difficult to accurately gauge GNI, and agencies disagree on the exact dollar amounts. More significantly, the measurement does not take into the account what money will buy in different societies. In Luxembourg, the euro equivalent of $10 buys much less food than it does in a poor country, such as Ghana. For this reason, researchers have adapted these GNI per capita figures to include cost of living.

cies, nongovernmental organizations, and researchers all saw economic development as "a sustained, secular improvement in material well-being . . . reflected in an increasing flow of goods and services," to quote economists Bernard Okun and Richard Richardson. In other words, increasing economic development was the same thing as increasing the gross national product.

Most examples of economic development incorporate some measure of national production, often a combination of all goods and services produced in a country (see Module 15C). In this view, highly developed countries have substantial production relative to the size of their population. A country like Ireland has an economy similar in size to Nigeria. However, Ireland has about 4.5 million people, whereas Nigeria has 160 million. That is 25 times as many people to share the same size economy. In this case, Ireland would be considered more highly developed than Nigeria. Other refined measures also consider the economy's structure. An economy that is reliant on the export of raw materials may yield substantial income, however, it is considered less developed than an economy that produces more products and services requiring a highly educated labor force. Many Persian Gulf countries gain their wealth from the sale of petroleum, but have a way to go in regard to establishing the basis for an advanced economy.

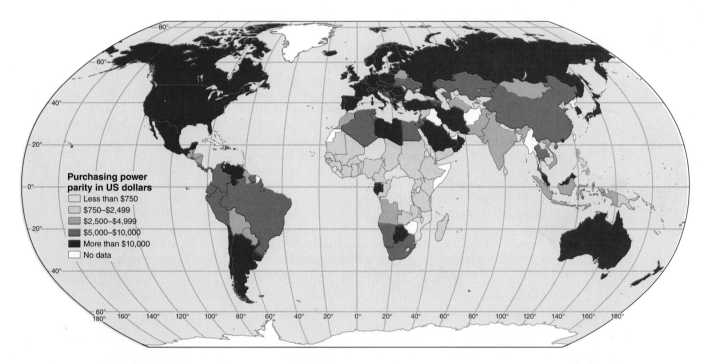

▲ **Figure 18A.2** This map shows just how the world's countries are arrayed along the spectrum of per capita income. **Purchasing power parity**, or **PPP**, ends up diminishing a little of the gross variation between countries, but development disparities are quite notable. When standardized to the US PPP, Luxembourg drops to about $65,000 per capita, but there are still about 15 countries that are under $1,000. Using these and other data, organizations such as the World Bank often classify countries by income. In the higher-income "club" are all countries with incomes higher than $10,000, primarily North American countries, European countries, Australia/New Zealand, and Japan. There are a few newcomers to this grouping: Singapore vaulted ahead to become the third-richest country, while South Korea and several Persian Gulf countries are also quite affluent. Israel and some Eastern European countries are in this category as well, although they are not quite as rich. Lower-income countries are those with incomes under $2,500 or so and are dominated by countries in sub-Saharan Africa, with some Southeast Asian and Central Asian countries listed. The broad middle-income category includes most of Latin America and many Asian and Eastern European countries.

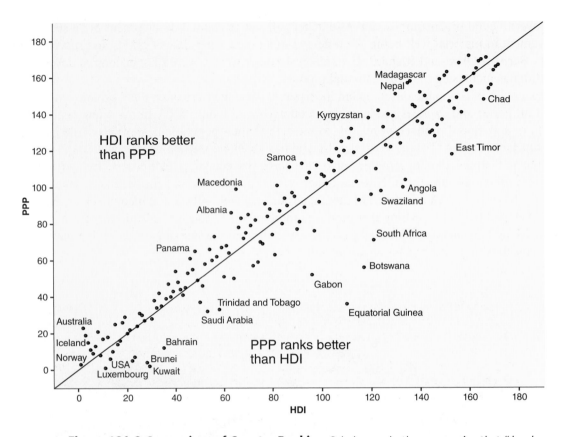

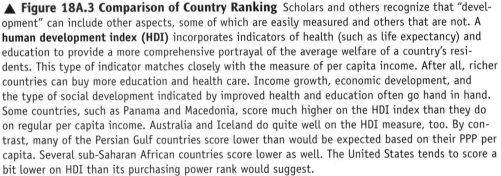

▲ **Figure 18A.3 Comparison of Country Ranking** Scholars and others recognize that "development" can include other aspects, some of which are easily measured and others that are not. A **human development index (HDI)** incorporates indicators of health (such as life expectancy) and education to provide a more comprehensive portrayal of the average welfare of a country's residents. This type of indicator matches closely with the measure of per capita income. After all, richer countries can buy more education and health care. Income growth, economic development, and the type of social development indicated by improved health and education often go hand in hand. Some countries, such as Panama and Macedonia, score much higher on the HDI index than they do on regular per capita income. Australia and Iceland do quite well on the HDI measure, too. By contrast, many of the Persian Gulf countries score lower than would be expected based on their PPP per capita. Several sub-Saharan African countries score lower as well. The United States tends to score a bit lower on HDI than its purchasing power rank would suggest.

Some social scientists have argued that these economic based measures of economic development miss significant dimensions of real human progress. The creation of a Human Development Index adds health, education, and welfare data to create a more balanced measure. Other indices, like the World Happiness Index, seek to incorporate subjective information that show just how content or "happy" people are in different countries.

Another approach is to consider a country's natural resources, especially its environmental richness, as a part of its wealth. Under conventional development measures, a country can cut down its forests, pollute its lakes and streams, decimate its wildlife, and poison its air, without reducing its national product. Yet these actions clearly harm its natural wealth. Unfortunately, the desire to boost short term economic production can create more pressures on a country's natural endowment. The establishment and acceptance of nonmonetary measures of development may be a good step in providing a helpful idea of what economic development can actually achieve.

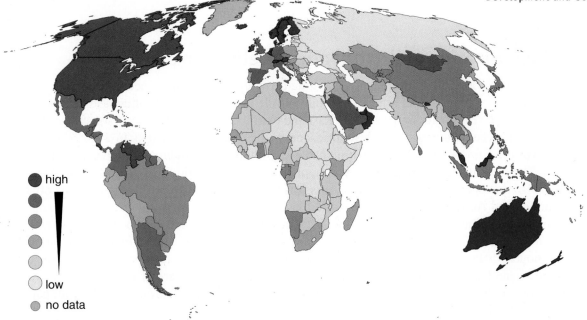

▲ **Figure 18A.4** The king of the South Asian country of Bhutan has famously promoted "gross national happiness," and other analyses have followed suit. This world map shows the variations in what the authors describe as "subjective measures of well-being" (SWB = subjective well-being). As with the human development index, this map correlates with conventional measures of development: The rich countries in North America and Australia tend to have high levels of well-being, while the poor countries in Africa are much less "happy." There are many discrepancies, however. People in Eastern Europe and Russia are far less content than people in China and Mongolia, even though they are far wealthier. Western Europeans seem less content than would be expected, although Scandinavia appears to be a very happy place, indeed.

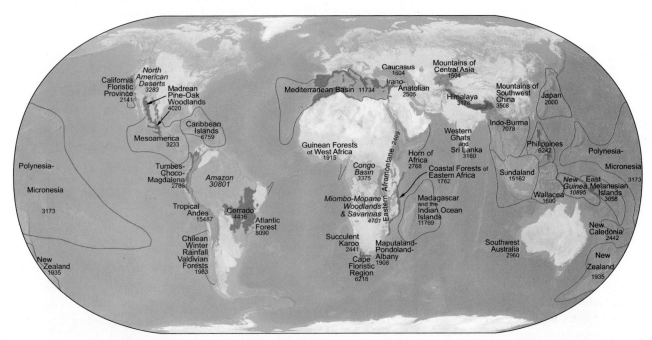

▲ **Figure 18A.5** The importance of environmental protection and sustainability has sometimes been looked upon as a luxury by developing countries. This map shows the number of biodiversity hot spots based primarily on a large number of unique species (the estimated number of unique species is given below the names of the regions). The main thing to notice is that these regions are concentrated in many less developed countries. Sustainable development (see Module 18G) attempts to reconcile economic advancement with the management of local natural resources, such as forests and soil, to keep them viable for long periods of time. It also seeks to limit pollution into water sources, the air, and the land. These goals, while laudable, are difficult enough to achieve in wealthy industrialized countries. For poor countries it is made more difficult by existing economic urgency and by relatively weak regulations.

18B Modernization and Economic Development

In the world of AD 1000, there were some economic differences between societies. However, this played to the disadvantage of most people living in Europe. While no society was wealthy (see Module 16G), the empires in China, the caliphates in the Middle East and North Africa, and the successor state of Byzantium were likely much richer than any duchy, bishopric, county, or kingdom in Europe. In 1400, a comparison of China and western Europe revealed that China had a slightly higher standard of living, as well as a larger population. The same comparison probably also applied to India, the Middle East, and North Africa.

The change that occurred in the next 600 years was truly dramatic. Western Europe and its offshoots in North America and Australia/New Zealand vaulted over every other society in terms of economic growth and development. By the twentieth century, the difference between western Europe and China was not just slight, but humongous. The European living standard was more than 10 times greater than that of China. The more modest differentiations that had marked the world in the past were supplanted by a yawning gulf between haves and have-nots. The reasons behind this evolving disparity are of more than academic inter-est. They may hold the answers to how poorer societies today can begin to develop and how all parts of the world may finally achieve prosperity.

While many academics and politicians have weighed in on the reasons behind **development disparities** in the world today, two basic approaches stand out. The first approach, stemming from the can-do mentality of the 1950s and 1960s but echoed today among some development economists, views underdevelopment as a function of progress. The second approach views underdevelopment as intrinsic to a global economic structure that began with colonialism and persists today with a pattern of **neocolonialism**. Neocolonialism is a term that reflects the sort of economic relationships that persist between the mother country and the former colony, even after independence. The former colony provides raw materials and cheap labor, for instance, at the risk of stunting its own development prospects and maintaining its dependency. Some critics

▲ **Figure 18B.1** The famed Italian explorer Marco Polo came from Venice—probably the most advanced society in Europe during the thirteenth century—and is best known for his long visit to China, at that time controlled by Mongol warrior Kublai Khan. The wealth Marco Polo witnessed in China surpassed anything he knew from Europe. He remained in China for many years and, on returning to Europe, wrote a book that documented the vast wealth and innovations he had discovered, includ-ing a complete postal system, the use of coal, paper, eyeglasses, and paper money.

Level of development (vertical axis label)

V. Age of mass consumption. This stage is marked by steady increases in the size of the economy. Overall economic growth is often lower than during the two earlier stages, but it initiates from a much greater base. Overall, the economy relies a great deal on middle-class consumption, so consumer spending and consumer confidence are key. This marks the experience of most affluent countries today.

IV. Drive to maturity. In this stage, the economy enjoys self-sustaining growth as it broadens to include several different sectors. More products are manufactured at home and more consumer goods are made available to a rising middle class, which becomes an engine of future economic growth through increased consumption. Great Britain entered this stage between 1820 and 1900.

III. Takeoff to sustained growth. In this stage, growth dominates society but there is a special concentration in lead sectors of the economy (such as cotton textiles in Britain). The rate of new investment rises continuously as productivity improves. This stage is also associated with major technological advances. Great Britain entered this stage during its Industrial Revolution between 1780 and 1820.

II. Preconditions for takeoff. In this stage, there is a rise in rates of investment, an increase in infrastructure, and the development of a more centralized state that is growth oriented. The first country to enter this stage was Great Britain between 1700 and 1800.

I. Traditional society. This is a pre-industrial economy that marked all societies prior to 1750 or so and is characterized by primitive technology and a hierarchical social structure with kings and emperors.

Time

▲ **Figure 18B.2** One of the most influential proponents of modernization theory, W. W. Rostow, described this process in his book *The Stages of Economic Growth*. According to Rostow, societies advance through a set of discrete stages. For a variety of reasons, wealthier societies have been able to advance more rapidly and are now at a higher stage. He used Great Britain, the first country to industrialize and the main economic power of the eighteenth and nineteenth centuries, as a model.

argue that world organizations such as the World Bank, the International Monetary Fund, and the World Trade Organization perpetuate neocolonialism.

Modernization theory is very much rooted in the experience of western Europe and North America and views these as models for the rest of the world to follow. This theory gained great popularity right after World War II, when the disparities between countries appeared overwhelming but also soluble. There was also a political motivation involved, since many of the wealthier countries in the so-called free world were poised against the threat of communism advanced by the Soviet Union and its allies.

The underlying idea behind these stages and modernization theory as a whole is that, in order to advance, each society needs to adopt elements of Western society. Specifically, to enjoy increased wealth requires industrialization, technological progress, and a reasonably unfettered capitalism. The government roles in the economy are limited to regulation and the provision of infrastructure. This capitalist transformation requires the right set of cultural conditions as well. **Western values**, including rationalism, science (as opposed to religion), and a strong work ethic, must be adopted. This also corresponds with particular social changes, including urbanization, greater separation of social roles, and the completion of the demographic transition. Politically, modernization was thought to go hand-in-hand with Western-style democracy. The establishment of a mass middle class would make democratic, stable governments more likely and act to deter tyranny. A society of homeowners, stockholders, and shopkeepers is much less likely to tolerate radicalism of any form.

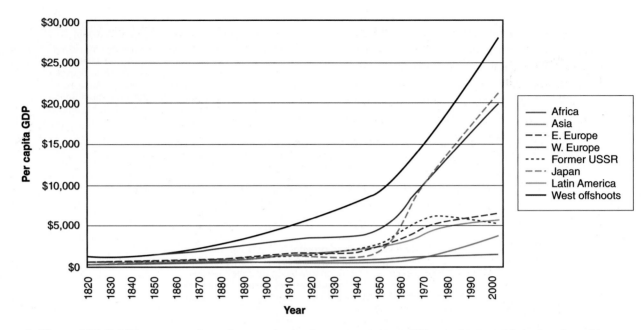

▲ **Figure 18B.3** Different countries underwent the development process at different times, and it is clear from this graphic that a few regions of the world prospered handily in the last two centuries. Western Europe—notably, Britain, Germany, France, and the Low Countries—expanded steadily during the nineteenth century. The Western offshoots of the United States, Canada, and Australia prospered even more. By the 1950s, Japan had begun to catch up with, and even surpass, Western Europe. Other regions have not been as successful, though this chart shows that, except for Africa, most regions have been able to improve their economic standing markedly in the last 60 years.

The political economic principle behind this idea has been termed neoliberalism (see Module 11C). In its purest form, neoliberalism involves the drive to enhance free markets, the development of capitalist transactions, and the elimination of barriers to trade. Modernization theory promotes this line of thinking.

A more contemporary take on the modernization approach is well articulated by economist Jeffrey Sachs, who is probably the academic most associated with development reform. Sachs views development as overcoming a series of **development traps** that can cause economies to stagnate.

Turning a society around requires the alleviation of many of these barriers. Most of all, it requires an infusion of capital in all forms. Sachs and other development researchers have called for governments in the developed world to increase their foreign aid and to make it more effective as a way to jump-start development. They have called for targeted investments needed to increase the amount of capital in a country to finance small businesses or to bolster the ability of farmers to increase yields. Public investments

Table 18B.1	Development Traps
Poverty	People in a society are unable to save and accumulate capital. In fact, countries that are desperately poor end up depleting their natural capital by exhausting soils and fisheries and by cutting down their forests.
Demography	The poorest countries have high total fertility rates and a high population growth rate (see Module 3E). The consequence is that a family cannot invest in the human capital of their children. In such societies, children, and especially girls, are left undernourished and undereducated.
Lack of Innovation	Invention in poor countries is stifled by a lack of capital, and especially a meager market.
Cultural Barriers	Conditions antagonistic to economic development are created by denying women their rights and/or by marginalizing particular ethnic groups.
Physical Geographic Issues	Economies are affected by their location, resources, climate, topography, and other aspects. Landlocked countries, for example, have to contend with the much higher cost of transportation. Tropical countries are prey to tropical diseases, such as malaria, which can exert a devastating toll.
Government Failure	Governments in much of the developing world are corrupt at best and unimaginably brutal at worst. The world's poorest countries tend to have the world's worst regimes. Money that could be paying for infrastructure projects is instead stolen or diverted to the military. Even well-meaning government initiatives may drive out foreign economic development.
Fiscal Traps	A huge problem for many governments in the developing world is the crushing burden of debt that they owe to banks, institutions, and governments in the developed world. This debt cycle makes it almost impossible to invest in development.

can be used to enhance infrastructures, finance schools, and improve public health. Providing every household with a mosquito net, for example, could dramatically reduce the incidence of malaria. The cancellation of debt would help many poor countries get on their feet, whereas now their debt service is greater than spending on health and education.

There have been global attempts to provide this assistance. Two of the best-known agencies in the effort to promote development are the **World Bank** and the **International Monetary Fund (IMF)**. Both agencies share similar goals. They both represent a consortium of most of the world's countries. However, the World Bank exists as primarily a lending institution, making loans available to poorer countries and often provides advice about the "correct" course of development. This has made it somewhat controversial. The International Monetary Fund acts more as a credit union that provides monetary resources that can be used by all countries in its network. A country experiencing a serious balance of payments problem, where the money going out greatly exceeds the money coming in, may apply to the IMF for advice and financial assistance.

▲ **Figure 18B.4** Individuals in the developing world often benefit from very small amounts of money, maybe a couple hundred dollars, which would escape the notice of most banks. They can use this money to invest in small enterprises that can improve their household finances considerably. Professor Muhammad Yunus was awarded the 2006 Nobel Peace Prize for his advocacy of such microloans through his **Grameen Bank**. His bank tends to provide loans to women, who are much more likely to use the money for productive uses. These women have almost no credit history, but they have proven over and over to have the capacity to use the funds wisely and to repay the bank. The additional benefit of such loans is that it raises the power and expectations of women and lowers poverty and birthrates.

Percent of population using the Internet
- 75%+
- 50%–74.99%
- 25%–49.99%
- 10%–24.99%
- 0%–9.99%
- no data

▲ **Figure 18B.5** The growth of Internet technologies has exposed yet another global inequity between those countries with good and growing access to the web and the many countries where Internet use is quite low. This **digital divide** has emerged as a major impediment to development, and it limits the opportunities for individuals to purchase supplies, gain information, and communicate. Fortunately, Internet penetration is growing fastest in many of those countries with lower levels of accessibility.

18C World Systems Perspective on Development

While modernization theory has been widely subscribed to, a number of problems are associated with it. First, because it uses the Western experience as a model, it assumes similar conditions among countries, when, in fact, the culture and historical experience vary greatly. Second, it examines the economic development of one country as an isolated phenomenon. It does not consider the links between the economic development of one country (or region) and the economic development of another country.

The **world systems perspective** views the economic system as a whole. Because the economy is global, events in one place have an effect on other places. Nowhere is this more apparent than in the experience of colonialism.

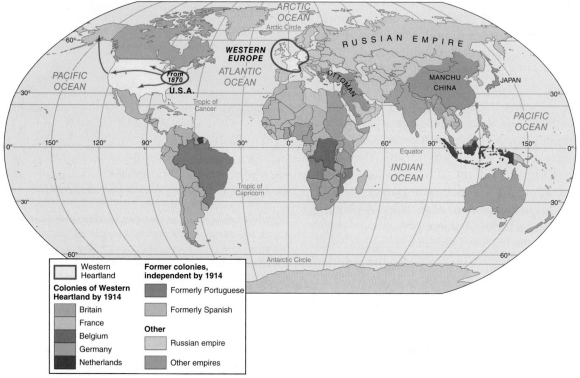

▲ **Figure 18C.1** This map shows all of the overseas colonies controlled by European countries at some point within the last 500 years. The purpose of colonialism was to provide resources for the colonizing country. Many of the earliest colonies were established as a means of acquiring precious metals and other valuable resources. Many colonies were used as a source of valuable agricultural and woodland products. Some colonies were primarily administered by the European power, whereas others invited settlement. Many of these colonies became part of a large **neo-European realm**, which consisted of those places colonized and settled largely by Europeans. This includes North and South America, Australia/New Zealand, and parts of South Africa.

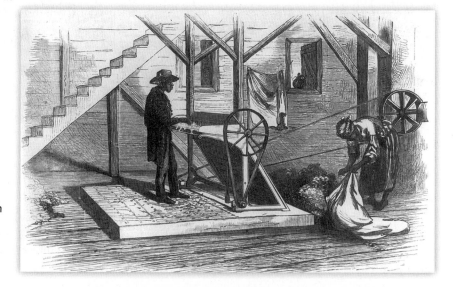

Figure 18C.2 ▶ **Cotton Gin** The demand for raw materials transformed many economies. Products from North and South America and Asia found their way into British factories. The American South was a major supplier of cotton in the mid-nineteenth century. In fact, much of the South's reluctance to give up slavery had to do with its dependence on the cotton economy. In India, British industrialism combined with parliamentary acts shut down Indian production of handmade textiles and clothing. By the late 1700s, British manufacturers had persuaded the government to outlaw the import of textiles from India. Indian workshops were forced out of business, and India became mainly a supplier of raw materials.

◀ **Figure 18C.3** Although China was never formally colonized, in the 1840s British warships forced a Chinese defeat, and a series of "unequal treaties" made China a virtual colony. China was divided into separate "spheres of influence," which gave British and other powers unfettered access to China's resources and forced the continued importation of opium into China.

The growth of Spanish, Portuguese, British, French, and Dutch empires in the Americas led to the rapid incorporation of the entire hemisphere in the 1500s and 1600s. While the Spanish and Portuguese, in particular, were primarily interested in the extraction of resources, they brought vast tracts of land and peoples into the European cultural sphere.

By the late 1700s and early 1800s, European power had been consolidated in South and Southeast Asia. These territories were brought in primarily to extend the mercantile interests of their mother countries. Several important colonies in the Americas gained their independence at that time, but these were supplanted later by new colonies acquired in Africa and Asia. Great Britain led the scramble for new colonies during this later stage but was joined by France, Belgium, Germany, Italy, and even the United States.

In the world systems perspective, the plight of various economies is seen in light of the overall expansion of the world economy, as well as the process of colonialism. As described in Module 15B, the expansion of the global economy led to the integration of the entire world, but this was a slow process. The establishment of colonies and the establishment of vast overseas empires were intended to create a large captive market and a vast resource base. Each European country vied with another to establish a bigger sphere. The transition from commercial to industrial capitalism changed the scope and character of colonialism. Raw materials were needed to manufacture industrial goods and these were often found in specific parts of the world.

Colonization and neocolonialism created inequalities in the development of regions. The regions under the domination of the European countries were devel-

▲ **Figure 18C.4** In the late nineteenth century, bananas became the primary crop grown in Central America. The US-owned United Fruit Company (which later became Chiquita Brands International) was established, with plantations in several Central American countries. Labor was recruited locally and brought in from Caribbean islands.

oped, but in a manner benefiting their mother countries. The demands of mass production combined with the ability to cover vast distances transformed societies far away from Europe. All development was in service to the mother country. These countries were mostly interested in acquiring raw materials, minerals, and agricultural goods from the colonies. At the same time, many colonizers actively discouraged any sort of domestic economic development. What is important to note is that the end of formal colonial control did not end the economic relationships that had otherwise been established. Postcolonialism led the way to a neocolonial relationship in which the same economic patterns applied.

One of the main theorists of the world systems approach, Immanuel Wallerstein, has categorized the world in terms of core, periphery, and semi-periphery. It is important to keep in mind that these are somewhat fluid categories and that there is some ambiguity as to which countries belong in each category.

Third, in the modern world economy, many countries have tried to shift away from the export of raw materials alone as a mainstay. In addition, several of these countries have turned toward the advantages of cheap labor in manufacturing production. In Module 16F, we discussed the global production line, in which production of a good takes place over several countries. Poor countries furnish many of the raw materials, but they may also furnish the inexpensive labor. Higher-end processes are conducted within the core countries.

Fourth, this model of a world system is intended to be dynamic. Over history, countries have shifted their positions as core, periphery, and semi-periphery. The significance of the **semi-periphery** is that these countries contain aspects of both core and periphery. They also demonstrate a transitional stage. Wallerstein points out that many of the important cities of Mediterranean Europe moved into semi-peripheral status as England and Holland took over the world economy in the seventeenth century. In the nineteenth century, the United States was clearly a part of the semi-periphery but moved into the core in the twentieth century. Now several Southeast and East Asian countries, once part of the periphery, have entered the semi-periphery. The fast-growing economies of China and India, while still quite poor by per capita income standards, have become more involved in manufacturing finished products, which are then exported to the core. China, in particular, has become the major manufacturer of clothing, toys, and many other items. India, in addition to manufacturing, now provides many services that are available more cheaply there than in wealthier countries. Countries such as South Korea and Singapore have arguably moved into the ranks of the core, as they now possess enough industrial and economic power to be able to finance their own futures.

Core

Core refers to those areas of the world that control the economic capital essential to economic exploitation. These countries are almost all colonizers, with the important exceptions of the settlement colonies of the United States, Canada, Australia, and New Zealand. The core is characterized by

- concentration of economic power
- diversified economic base
- high income relative to the periphery
- relative price stability
- greater social and political stability

Periphery

Periphery refers to areas that are economically dependent on the core. Almost all of these areas could be considered a part of the developing world, and most were former colonies. They share characteristics of

- lack of economic power
- an economic base that produces just a few commodities—these are commodity export economies
- very low income with a great deal of uneven distribution (very wealthy minority and impoverished majority)
- enormous price fluctuations as small changes in the core can produce vast changes in the periphery
- social and political instability

Semi-periphery refers to a transition stage from a status either as a core country or as a peripheral country. These economies are not fully dependent on the core but are not fully industrialized, either. Broadly, they are categorized as

- possessing some indigenous economic capital
- moderately developed, with the beginnings of an industrial base and often a focus on some important manufactured products
- medium income with a somewhat developed middle class
- they may choose protectionist policies to protect their native industries or choose to become quite export oriented, using exports of key manufactured products to increase their economic vibrancy

Semi-periphery

▲ **Figure 18C.5** We can observe several interesting aspects of the world systems model. First, the positions of countries are considered relative to each other. Peripheral countries could not exist unless there also existed a set of core countries. Therefore, the economies of **core** and **periphery** are interdependent. Second, as the global economy has changed, the types of items that are produced and exchanged between economies has shifted as well. Most economies in the periphery were at one point primarily involved in the export of a few raw materials. Bananas, cotton, coffee, jute, nickel—these were the types of commodities exported to core countries, which then used them in manufacturing. This relationship continues to exist in some cases.

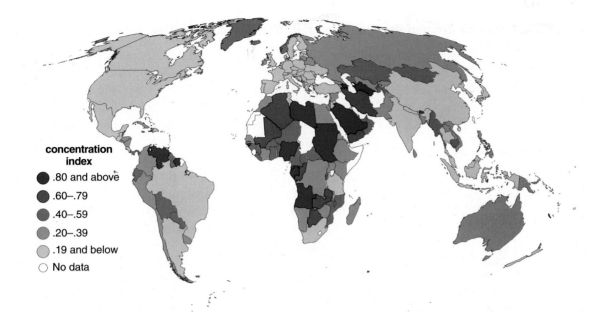

▲ **Figure 18C.6** Many countries concentrate on export of just a few agricultural or mining commodities. This map shows some of these **commodity export economies** and the products in which they specialize. An export concentration index of 1 means that a country is totally specialized in one commodity. An export concentration index closer to 0 signifies a completely diversified economy. There are several disadvantages to extreme specialization. A country's fortunes rely entirely on the success of particular crops. A bad harvest can send the economy into a tailspin. Beyond this, the actual price of the commodity can fluctuate tremendously, depending on the nature of demand and supply within the global market. Poor countries are rarely able to buffer against these price gyrations. Most fundamentally, reliance on a few primary sector products results in little additional value, since most of the profit lies in the production process. Economies that depend on raw materials are generally quite poor. One exception is petroleum, which has enriched a few economies but is subject to price fluctuations and has retarded the development of countries that rely on it.

▲ **Figure 18C.7** Malaysia has long cultivated many rubber trees and continues as the largest supplier of natural rubber. But rather than export the natural rubber to be processed elsewhere, Malaysia has been moving aggressively into the production of rubber products, especially medical gloves, catheters, and latex thread. These products are sold directly to hospitals and have come to command the lion's share of the world market. It also allows Malaysia to capture the entire production cycle from raw resource to finished product, transforming it from a commodity export peripheral economy to a clear member of the semi-peripheral economies.

18D Profiles of Development: The Bottom Billion

By economic and social welfare standards, many countries that seemed in desperate straits a generation ago have improved dramatically. They have seen incomes increase, manufacturing grow, steady improvements in health and education, and a decline in the most extreme forms of poverty. Bangladesh, for example, was considered the poorest country in 1970, prompting international outcries, concerts, and concern. Today, Bangladesh is still quite poor, but many of the economic indicators have begun to move in the right direction. More dramatic progress can be seen in southern India, eastern China, and many South American countries.

However, this improvement has not occurred everywhere in the world. According to economist Paul Collier, there now exists a three-way stratification of the world's population. There is a fortunate 1 billion people who live in affluent societies, where they enjoy tremendous material luxuries. There is a much larger group of 4 billion people living in societies that are truly developing. Many of these people are quite poor, to be sure, and work in sometimes horrific conditions but generally see their lives improving. It could be long hours in a sweatshop operated by a foreign apparel manufacturer, but it still represents some hope. Finally, there is a group of countries that have averaged periods of very small growth and periods of negative growth, as well as periods of stagnation. There is no improvement from one generation to the next. There is almost no foreign investment. The population in these economies belongs to the bottom billion.

The burden of disease is profound but, according to Collier, 73% of people living in countries of the bottom billion also suffer or have suffered through civil war. Civil war is much more likely to occur in very poor countries where the economy is stagnating. Rebel movements arise, often based on ethnic, regional, or

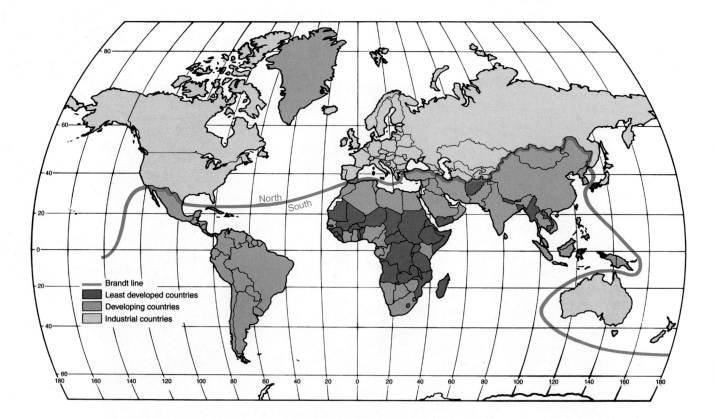

▲ **Figure 18D.1** The countries in the bottom billion are most accurately expressed as being a part of the **undeveloped world.** They are marked by extraordinarily low per capita national incomes, which place most of their people under conditions of extreme poverty. What is more, these are countries that have experienced virtually no economic growth in the past 30 years. Beyond the purely economic factors, people in the bottom billion suffer from low life expectancies, are more prone to diseases that are otherwise controllable, have generally abysmal education standards, and tend to bear the brunt of civil wars. The majority of these countries are in sub-Saharan Africa.

class grievances, and may receive support from overseas sympathizers. These conflicts tend to last a very long time—about seven years—and often perpetuate themselves as one group's atrocities spark reactions from an opposing group. Civil war leaves a legacy of killing and causes the economy to contract about 15%.

Collier notes that the countries in the bottom billion have been sucked into several interrelated traps, which keep them from advancing. These traps have been discussed by others as well and are listed in Module 18B. How to get over these traps is in the focus of the next module.

◀ **Figure 18D.2** Malawi is an example of a country in the bottom billion. It is a beautiful place, bordered on the east by Lake Malawi. It has been described as the "Switzerland of Africa." Yet Malawi is nothing like Switzerland when it comes to the welfare of its population. The human development index ranking is a miserable 164th among 177 countries and has not improved in recent years. Per capita gross domestic product averages less than US$2 a day, even when adjusted for purchasing power. Adult literacy is at 64% and is even lower for women. Malawi has benefited from less repressive politics than many sub-Saharan African countries but shares with them the ravages of disease. Fully 45% of the population does not survive past the age of 40. The lion's share of mortality is caused by infectious diseases and accidents: malaria, tuberculosis, diarrhea, and maternal mortality. But the biggest disease burden of all is AIDS. AIDS is so prevalent in Malawi that it has progressively stripped the countryside of able-bodied men and women. Under these conditions, children are raised by grandparents, and many of the villages have nobody to plow the fields or repair irrigation systems.

Figure 18D.3 ▶ Since independence in 1960, Somalia has been spiraling further and further backwards. In 1992, then-President George H. W. Bush decided to send in military troops to stop the violence in Mogadishu, the capital. US troops withdrew in 1993, and since then, the country has become essentially anarchic, under the sway of a variety of regional warlords. The central government controls only a small portion of the country. Beyond the ill effects on the people and the economy, one consequence of this political failure has been the growth of piracy along the coast. Pirates primarily attack freight ships but have become a major threat because Somalia has no way to stop them. Pirates make trade with Somalia impossible and choke off its economy.

18E Possible Solutions to the Development Crisis

While a good argument can be made that the global distribution of income is more uneven today than it was just a few years ago, many societies have managed to make significant gains since people began to think seriously about development in the 1950s and 1960s.

The problems of underdevelopment have spawned several ideas about the types of solutions that may work. As the preceding modules have shown, it can be immensely difficult to find a solution that works in any given case, much less in every case. Every society has its own set of problems, and the development of societies and economies is intertwined. Moreover, since development involves so many different dimensions—including population, politics, urbanization, and industrialization—the challenge grows even greater.

Possible solutions involve efforts to accelerate economic growth, mainly by way of industrialization, but proposals have become increasingly focused on promoting human capital and environmental sustainability. As indicated in Module 16A, industrialization involves a process in which a greater proportion of the national economy is devoted to manufacturing. It can also be expanded to include an ongoing process in which the manufacturing of lower-value-added products, such as textiles, is gradually replaced with the manufacturing of higher-value-added products, such as computer equipment. This would create conditions for a higher gross domestic product and higher incomes for a country's residents. The development of a robust service sector will come later as an economy moves to the "postindustrial" phase, but the primary goal is to move an economy away from a reliance on primary products toward one based on industry. At the same time, many societies have realized that raw economic growth is only one aspect of this equation. It is important to also promote the well-being of the entire population and to limit environmental degradation.

Raw materials
Some countries are blessed with an abundance of natural resources, but they may still be lacking some critical ingredients necessary for the production process.

Capital
Often indigenous private capital is scarce, yet this is probably the single greatest determinant of whether a country can kick-start its growth. Various strategies—including foreign direct investment, bank loans, foreign aid, and remittances from emigrants—can help increase the amount of money available for growth.

Infrastructure
An adequate supply of power and water is crucial for developing economies, as are functioning transportation and communication systems. These items can be unevenly distributed and completely lacking in certain regions of a country.

Industrialization

Markets
Many poor countries have a large population, but little purchasing power. The market for manufactured items is confined to a small middle class. Selling products to a global market requires that the items have the price and quality to compete successfully.

Skilled labor
This requires an adequate education system and incentives that keep children in school. Many countries lose their best-educated residents to more prosperous situations abroad. Less developed countries can also take advantage of low labor costs, which keep down the price of the final product.

▲ **Figure 18E.1** In order to industrialize, the various factors of production, as mentioned in Module 16B, need to be in place. Some of these are relatively easy to come up with, but some are more difficult.

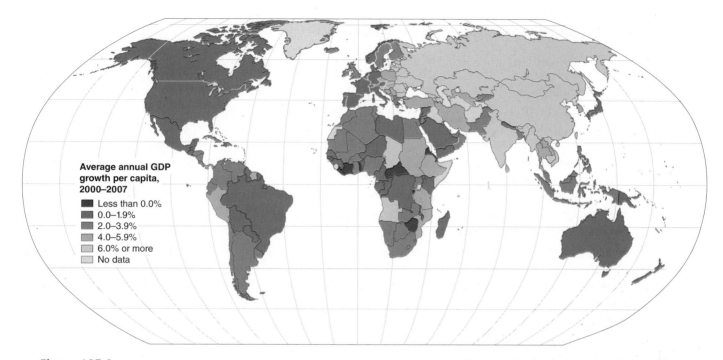

▲ **Figure 18E.2** This map shows how countries vary in terms of overall economic growth per capita. Several—most notably, China and India, but also countries such as Angola—have experienced tremendous growth, sometimes over 6% yearly, while others have stagnated. What is the role of various factors? Which can be altered? What can foreign aid do to help? These are the questions that development experts have sought to answer.

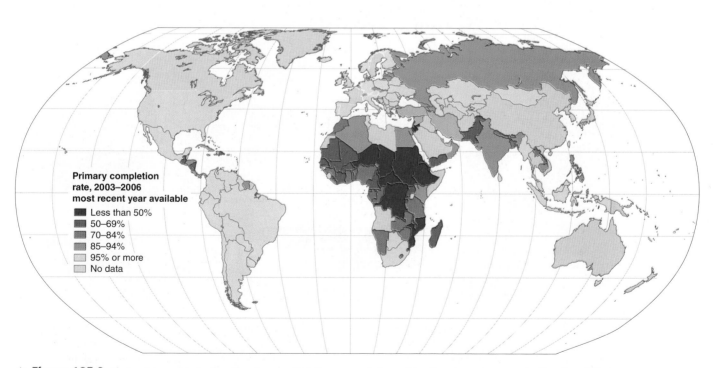

▲ **Figure 18E.3** Elementary school education is essential for any society seeking to advance economically, since this is where the basic skills of literacy and numeracy are learned. This map shows that primary completion rates in the developed world and in much of the less developed world—particularly Latin America—are high. Yet these rates continue to be quite low in many sub-Saharan countries, as well as in some countries in Asia.

18F Export-Led Approaches to Development

The export market school of development views production, perhaps aided by government, as the key to economic development. This approach could be implemented in several ways. The most extreme would be to get government, and all of its regulations, out of the way. However, most economies that attempted this approach were more likely to use government to cherry-pick and favor industries viewed as particularly important for success.

East Asia has shown the most success in following the export-led approach. Decades ago, Japan industrialized quickly and effectively by a concentration on its factory production, by government integration with industry, and by a reliance on exports. The newest success stories have followed much the same path. What marks these new **tiger economies** has been a strong reliance on exports, sometimes accounting for over half of gross domestic product. For many of the established "tigers," their small land areas and relatively small populations mean that exports are vital for companies to have sufficient market share.

China is a special case, of course. It has the largest internal market in the world and was long guided by a communist ideology that promoted self-sufficiency. Yet in the last couple of decades, China has emphasized exports. According to official sources, China's exports account for about 40% of its overall economy, and it runs an overall positive trade balance. But recently this export emphasis has been joined by more attention to its internal market. When that internal market fully awakens, nearly every analyst expects China to become the world's number one economy.

▲ **Figure 18F.1** The **export-led approach** identifies products that can be exported to the outside world, taking advantage of a country's specific advantages. The idea is that focusing on a couple of key resources and industries can bring in money to finance development of other things, such as schools, roads, or electric power. Then additional industries can be developed. Often the resource that is exploited is natural, such as oil. Or it can be a cheap labor force. In order to obtain capital, many countries rely on foreign investment. Many foreign companies set up a branch plant, taking advantage of a poor country's cheaper labor and land costs. South Korea's spectacular growth has been fueled by companies such as Samsung, which have catapulted the economy into the world's top tier.

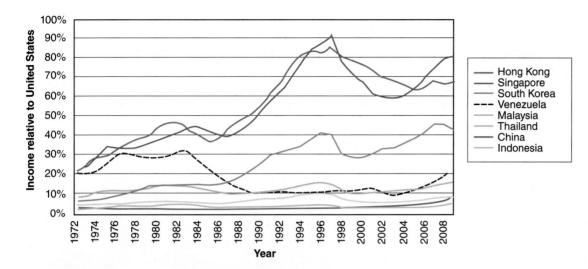

◀ **Figure 18F.2** Of all the success stories in less developed countries, the Asian tiger economies stand out. Generally considered to consist of Taiwan, South Korea, Hong Kong, and Singapore, these countries have clearly made the leap from less developed to more developed status, with a social profile, an economic prosperity, and a stability that rival those of First World countries. The chart, based on World Bank data, shows how these initial "tigers" have fared very well and have come close to US income levels. Taiwan indicators (not available here) would demonstrate the same thing, with an income now about equal to South Korea's. Other countries considered to share some of these attributes include Thailand, Malaysia, Indonesia and, biggest of all, China. These countries have made tremendous strides in growth, although they are still much poorer than Western industrialized countries. Venezuela, which long adopted more protectionist policies, saw its position slip considerably in the 1980s and 1990s.

▲ **Figure 18F.3** Singapore is a good example of a "tiger." It was founded on an island on the tip of the Malay Peninsula. While it provided major benefits to the trading position of the United Kingdom, its colonial overlord, Singapore achieved independence under a cloud of political strife and poverty. Today, Singapore has a per capita GDP that is higher than all but a handful of countries' and is among the sleekest and best-run countries in the world. In the 1960s and 1970s, Singapore placed its bets on textiles, apparels, and electronics, making use of its (then) cheap labor. By the 1980s and 1990s, Singapore had become both a financial center and regional headquarters for transnational companies. The Singapore model has relied heavily on exports and the promotion of its human capital resources. It has also followed an authoritarian path. Lee Kuan Yew, the principal leader of Singapore, embraces "Asian values," which combine economic freedom with political control. Singapore allows for restrained debate, but with so many restrictions that opponents say they effectively squelch any meaningful dialog. Rules that Westerners, and especially Americans, would find intolerable are regularly enforced there. The government mandates retirement savings, cleanliness and hygienic regulations (including fines for not flushing toilets), fertility restrictions, and automobile use. The government also has a great deal of control over a number of important media, utility, and transportation companies. Still, most people view the government as both effective and honest, which has helped attract a lot of business to the island. Moreover, the government has done a good job of providing a decent standard of living for the vast majority of its multiethnic population.

18G Structuralist and Sustainable Development Models

The alternative development models do not fall neatly into one type, but represent some reasonable alternatives to the export-led model and have been tried with varied degrees of success. Many of these approaches fit under the **structuralist school of development**, which views the intervention of government as key to economic development. Government intervention can be an important way to more directly control the production and consumption process. It can also be used to focus on expanding human capital.

▲ **Figure 18G.1** The emphasis in import substitution is on producing items not for export but for domestic consumption. The items that ordinarily would be imported are substituted with items made at home. Countries practicing import substitution encourage local industry and keep foreign goods out. The government wields various tools, including quotas on foreign goods and high tariffs on imports. This was seen as a way to even the playing field. Many of the former communist countries manufactured some legendarily horrible products, such as the East German Trabant (shown here). This approach may hinder higher economic growth because the lack of competition can lead to substandard products. It holds a general appeal, though, because it offers less foreign intrusion and promises an easier path to diversification.

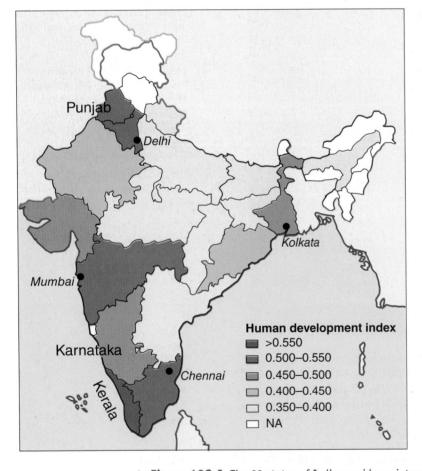

Human development index
- >0.550
- 0.500–0.550
- 0.450–0.500
- 0.400–0.450
- 0.350–0.400
- NA

▲ **Figure 18G.2** The 28 states of India provide an interesting laboratory in development because they have often followed quite different trajectories. Some states, such as Karnataka, have invested heavily in high technology. Others, such as Punjab, were heavily invested in the agricultural innovations of the Green Revolution (see Module 15G). The Indian state of Kerala has been an exemplar of most aspects of sustainable development. A small state on the southwestern coast of India, with an extremely high population density, Kerala has nonetheless racked up some very impressive numbers: It has a life expectancy of over 70 years, closer to that of the United States than to the rest of India. Fertility rates are low, even lower than the US rate. Its infant mortality rate is a low 14 per 1,000. Kerala's literacy rates for both men and women reach almost 90%—far better than most developing countries—and children in Kerala complete about twice as many years of schooling than in India as a whole. These achievements cut across region, caste, and gender, resulting in the highest human development index of any Indian state.

▲ **Figure 18G.3** Kerala has promoted environmental awareness through grassroots actions that oppose deep soil mining and sand mining and that promote ecotourism. Kerala's success, however, has come at an economic price. Much of its social and environmental progress has come about under a heavy emphasis on agriculture and a political policy that stresses redistribution, subsidies, and labor control. Rather than the type of Green Revolution policy that ended up promoting agricultural growth but at the expense of all but the wealthiest farmers, Kerala adopted ambitious land reform that transferred property from landlords to tenants, as well as sustainable farming practices such as in the rubber tapping pictured on the right. The upshot is that, while successful socially and environmentally, Kerala has not shown much success in promoting industrial growth. In fact, it belongs among the bottom third of all Indian states in economic growth performance. Its unemployment rate is high, and it depends a great deal on remittances from overseas workers. At the same time, Kerala does suggest a middle path of economic development, where it is possible to have a good standard of living even without a high income.

This approach is implemented in several ways. Under communist regimes, this can mean total government control of most of the means of production, labor transactions, and consumption. In noncommunist countries, this might involve more of a mix of these policies. For instance, the government can use trade policy to favor some industries over others but does so by focusing on the consumption of goods. For example, **import substitution** might be used to shelter young domestic industries from foreign competition by providing them with a secure market. Anytime a government decides that it will protect a particular industry with higher tariffs or quotas, for instance, it is employing a watered-down version of this approach.

One other development model that has been practiced has not led to tremendous gains in income but has shown itself effective in improving the well-being of the population. This sort of development, sometimes dubbed **sustainable development**, is primarily interested in evening out the distribution of wealth and providing decent health care, adequate shelter, and a solid education for citizens. It also focuses on environmental protection by maintaining and improving regional resources. This can be a tricky balance, since the needs of rapid development and environmental protection are sometimes opposed. As populations get wealthier, they often choose a lifestyle that requires more resources and can lead to greater levels of pollution.

Key Terms

commodity export economies (18C)

core (18C)

developed countries (18A)

development disparities (18B)

development traps (18B)

digital divide (18B)

economic development (18A)

export-led approach (18F)

First World (18A)

Grameen Bank (18B)

human development index (HDI) (18A)

import substitution (18G)

International Monetary Fund (IMF) (18B)

less developed countries (18A)

living standards (18A)

modernization theory (18B)

more developed countries (18A)

neocolonialism (18B)

neo-European realm (18C)

periphery (18C)

purchasing power parity (PPP) (18A)

semi-periphery (18C)

structuralist school of development (18G)

sustainable development (18G)

Third World (18A)

tiger economies (18F)

undeveloped world (18D)

Western values (18B)

World Bank (18B)

world development (18A)

world systems perspective (18C)

Basic Review Questions

1. What is development, and how can it be measured?

2. What are some of the variations in levels of development between countries?

3. How does the human development index incorporate different variables?

4. How might gross national happiness be considered part of development?

5. Historically, what sort of development disparities existed between places in the world?

6. What is modernization theory, and how is it portrayed in the stages of economic growth?

7. What are some of the development traps that can cause an economy to stagnate?

8. What is the value of micro-capital in improving the economy in poor countries?

9. What is the so-called digital divide?

10. Describe the world systems perspective on development. How is this rooted in colonization?

11. How did the European powers exploit their colonies economically?

12. What is a neocolonial relationship?

13. Define the terms *core*, *periphery*, and *semi-periphery*, and describe the different aspects of each of these categories.

14. How are peripheral countries forced to rely on primary sector commodities, and so become commodity export economies?

15. What does it mean to be part of the bottom billion? What are some of the factors that have caused countries to remain in that category?

16. What are some of the ways in which countries have been able to improve their overall situation and accelerate economic growth?

17. What are some of the factors that would allow less developed countries to industrialize?

18. How has industrialization sometimes led to greater environmental degradation?

19. What is the export market school of development, and how would this allow some countries to improve their economy?

20. How have export markets created a number of tiger economies? Where are these "tigers" located?

21. What are some of the approaches to economic development that fit within the structuralist school of development?

22. What are some of the means by which governments might intervene to try to improve their economies?

23. How does import substitution fit into models of economic development?

24. How has sustainable development fit into models of economic development?

Advanced Review Questions (Essay Questions)

1. Describes the major differences between countries related to their levels of development. What sorts of variables can be considered in relation to development? How might these variables be correlated, and what may be some exceptions, particularly in a measure such as the human development index or gross national happiness?

2. Describe some of the development disparities in the past. Why have disparities between countries widened over the last several centuries? To what extent do the stages of economic growth help explain this? Utilizing the different stages, show what some societies went through on their road to development.

3. Today, a number of countries are considered to be less developed. What are some of the major development traps that cause these economies to stagnate? What are some of the ways in which a poor country can try to turn itself around?

4. What is the world systems perspective on development? Specifically, how does it consider how core, periphery, and semi-periphery relate to each other? Is it possible for a country that is in the periphery to one day find itself in the core? How would this be the case?

5. How is the world systems perspective on development rooted in colonialism? Relate some of the reasons that a colonial economic relationship would have been developed. How has neocolonialism created a series of commodity export economies?

6. What are some of the characteristics of the countries that are among the least developed in the world? Where are many of these countries, and why? How does this lack of development create problems, including poverty, disease, and civil strife?

7. What are some possible solutions to the crisis of development? Specifically, how have some countries been able to use exports in order to improve their economies? What countries have been most successful in pursuing this strategy to foster economic development?

8. What is the structuralist school of development? Describe how it can be successful in a number of countries but can also create certain hindrances. How does import substitution help shelter an industry? How does sustainable development promote certain aspects of development?

Further Study Topics

- Look over some of the ways in which development has been defined—including the gross domestic product per capita, purchasing power parity, and the human development index—and identify some of the strengths and weaknesses of these definitions of development. Do they promote a certain way of looking at development and how it should be achieved?

- Jeffrey Sachs has shown that there are a number of development traps, which would prevent an economy from realizing its full potential. Taking a look at one or two countries that are considered to be underdeveloped, research their development traps. How difficult, or viable, would it be for these traps to be alleviated? Could it be done by the world community through additional foreign aid?

- Many countries in the periphery are involved in industrial activity. There has been some controversy as to whether the establishment of industrial plants that exploit a great deal of cheap labor is ultimately a positive thing for some of these developing economies. Examine the case of an economy that relies heavily on its cheap labor, and assess whether it improves economic prospects for its people and for the economy as a whole.

- Choose two economies, one that has been more involved in the export-led approach and one that has been more involved in the import substitution approach to economic development. What are some of the specific measures taken that would have facilitated these two approaches? How successful have they been?

Summary Activities

The human development index (HDI) has been used to gauge the true level of a country's development beyond gross national income per capita. As such, it has been adopted by the United Nations. The HDI is often closely associated with income levels, but there are several areas of divergence.

For this activity, choose 10 countries that interest you. Then go to the website http://hdr.undp.org/en/data/build/, which includes data for every country and allows you to build your own index. By just selecting the Income indicator, you can determine the rank of your countries in terms of purchasing power parity and then in the conventional human development index as calculated (HDI Rank). However, you can also select other indicators that you are interested in by exploring this interactive worksheet. You can select different indicators, determine their weights if you like, and build an index that you think is more accurate. In each instance, you need to scroll down to find the ranks of your selected countries. How do the ranks of your countries change when you use different criteria?

Country	Purchasing Power Parity Rank	HDI Rank (using conventional method)	HDI Rank A (using another method)	HDI Rank B (using another method)

GLOSSARY

The key terms are highlighted in bold within each module. The definition given here is referring to the module number of each term's first occurrence.

A

absolute distance (1F) A method of distance measurement using the straight line mileage between two places.

absolute location (1B) Dictates where each place exists on a reference system.

accent (7B) A way a language sounds or is pronounced in a particular location.

access (14C) The ability to travel between locations, such as workplaces, stores, and factories; is defined by an individual's situation.

accessibility (1F) Indicates ease of movement between places.

acculturation (9B) The process of learning how to operate within a new culture.

acid rain (12E) Precipitation that has elevated levels of sulfuric or nitric acid.

activity space (1G) A functional region in which individual activities occur.

African Traditional Religion (8I) Various, mostly animistic religions practiced in Africa.

Afro-Asiatic (7C) A large language family found primarily in North Africa and Southwest Asia.

agency (2G) Within social theory, the human capacity to make free, independent choices; often contrasted with **structure**.

agent (4C) An organism that causes a disease, such as bacteria, viruses, protozoa, or flukes.

agglomeration economies (13G) Different economic activities tend to locate next to each other and act as a powerful magnet, attracting other activities.

aggregate characteristics (1D) The dominant characteristics found within a place.

agribusiness (15E) A large company that owns the land and hires individuals to cultivate crops or raise livestock.

air pollution (12E) The introduction of chemicals, biological matter, or particulates into the atmosphere.

al-Idrisi (2B) A Muslim geographer and cartographer (1100–1165) educated in Spain who improved geographic knowledge by merging ancient knowledge with firsthand accounts by Muslim and European traders of his time.

American Manufacturing Belt (16C) In the late nineteenth century, the region that included Ohio, Indiana, Michigan, Illinois, and Wisconsin and represented different major industries located in these areas.

American Sign Language (7A) A language using hand gestures, primarily used by the deaf in the United States and Canada.

animism (8A) The belief that deities or souls inhabit everyday objects.

antecedent boundary (10H) A boundary created before an area is known or populated, often drawn with no recognition of the populations living there.

aquifer (12D) An underground area of permeable rock that can contain water or allow water to pass through.

arable (15E) Conducive to farming.

arithmetic density (3B) A statistic of population density calculated by dividing a country's population by its total land area. In other words, it is the number of people per square kilometer or square mile.

artifact (6C) Any physical object that a culture produces.

artisans (15B) Craftspeople who manufactured their own products and were involved in profit-seeking, but their costs were more bound to the expense of materials and labor.

assimilation (9B) The adoption of a new culture by a migrant and the abandonment of most aspects of an original culture.

asylum seeker (5D) A migrant hoping to be declared a refugee in a foreign country.

authoritarian states (11C) Also known as autocratic states; they concentrate political power in a single individual or clique.

auto-centered city (14D) With the rapid growth of vehicle use, cities developed automobile access. Effects include shopping centers near highways, decline in the central business district, and fewer downtown areas.

autocratic states (11C) Also known as authoritarian states, they concentrate political power in a single individual or clique.

autonomous regions (11G) Areas of some countries that feel they ought to have a special status partly because of their cultural distinctiveness and are given more autonomy by their government.

B

backward linkages (16C) The inputs required for production, such as machinery, machine tools, metal working, and iron casting.

Baha'i (8I) A universalizing religion founded in the nineteenth century and practiced in nearly every country today.

barriers to diffusion (6D) Things that slow or stop the spread of an idea, innovation, people, or other things.

barter (17A) The form of trade in which a good or service is traded for another good or service, as agreed upon by the people doing the trading.

base employment (16D) Employment that supports jobs in the service sector and other manufacturing industries.

basic demographic equation (3E) A simple equation that holds that a country's population in a future time period will equal births minus deaths plus immigration minus emigration.

bedroom communities (14D) Commuter towns inhabited by people who drive or take public transport to another city for work.

behavior (4B) In the triangle of human ecology, the effects of cultural norms or societal organizations on human health.

behavioral assimilation (9B) The situation in which a migrant or new ethnic group maintains a strong self-identity and much of the original culture but has adopted enough of the cultural traits of a host society to be a functioning member of it; also known as **cultural assimilation**.

behavioral geography (2F) A branch of human geography that focuses on the psychological processes that underlie human geographic decisions.

binary rank-size distributions (13H) The population of the top cities overwhelm the rest in terms of population.

border (10H) The region where a boundary exists, unlike a boundary, which is simply a line.

borderland (10H) A region centered around the boundary between places, often containing a lot of cultural diversity.

Boserup, Ester (3I) The Danish economist (1910–1999) who argued that rising populations will stimulate human societies to produce more food through innovation and technology.

boundary (1G) A line that distinguishes the area within the region from the area outside the region.

break-in-bulk point (16B) The point at which cargo is broken into smaller units to be transported.

Buddhism (8D) A religion founded in the sixth century BC and practiced today by over 400 million people. It emphasizes that life is suffering, but by living a proper life a human can achieve enlightenment and break free from the cycle of births and deaths.

built environment (13A) Human-made environmental elements, including buildings, monuments, and streets.

C

Cajuns (9A) An ethnic group possessing unique linguistic, religious, and other cultural traits, located in Louisiana and surrounding areas with historical roots in Canada.

cancer cluster (12G) A statistically unusual concentration of cancer in a particular area.

capital city (11F) Political center and necessary component of every state. It may or may not be in the core, and there may be more than one in a country.

capital region (11F) The area around the capital city in a country.

capitalism (15B) The buying or selling of various goods in order to create profit, driven by the pursuit of profit.

capitalist commercial economy (15B) An economic system primarily concerned with the buying and selling of commodities, or a product that can be exchanged for profit.

capitalist economy (11B) An economy in which a wide variety of private concerns are dominant and the state is far less involved in the production of goods and services.

capitalist industrial economic system (15B) The creation of finished products from raw materials, first by artisans and later by mass production, that paved the way for a truly global capitalist economy.

carrying capacity (15D) The number of people an area can support, given the technology.

cash exchanges (17A) A form of trade in which cash, a way to place an abstract value on a product or service that allows for relatively easy exchanges, is exchanged for a good or service.

caste system (8C) In Hindu areas, a complex division of society based on hereditary classes that are distinguished by their degree of ritual purity.

centers of absorption (5E) Places that attract migrants, according to Ravenstein.

central business district (CBD) (14C) In a city, the point with the greatest access to offices, banks, stores, and other activities. It is the most distinguishing feature and functions as a central marketplace, a major transportation node, and an administrative center, and it offers high-level services and contains heavy pedestrian traffic.

central places (17G) The idea by Walter Christaller in the 1930s that different types of stores tend to cluster into shopping centers.

centrifugal forces (10G) Factors, often negative, that tend to pull apart and disperse a population.

centripetal forces (10G) Factors, often positive, that tend to unify and bring together a population.

chemical insults (4B) Factors, such as drugs, dangerous gases, and harmful liquids, that negatively affect human health.

chiefdoms (10B) Tribal groups that inhabited particular places but at the same time were less likely to demarcate rigid boundaries.

child soldiers (5C) Youth that are either forced or impelled to serve as fighters or members of a militia.

choropleth map (1E) A type of map showing quantity or type of phenomena by area. It uses shades or colors to show class intervals and is often used for maps displaying density.

Christianity (8F) The world's largest religion, grounded in Judaic beliefs and based on the life and teachings of Jesus Christ, who Christians believe is the son of God.

citizenship (11D) Embodies the responsibilities and rights that some residents of a state possess.

city-state (10B) A system of small, city-centered states where political organization revolved around the city itself. People not engaged with agriculture lived in the city, while farmers resided in the surrounding hinterlands.

civic nations (10E) Nations based on shared principles, in contrast to ethnic nations, which are based more on cultural commonalities.

class intervals (1E) On a map, groupings of data assigned different shades or colors.

cluster migration (9C) The settlement of a whole town or area en masse by a particular ethnic group.

clustered (1E) A distribution in which data show distinct pockets of concentration.

coastal pollution (12I) Destruction or contamination of ecosystems along lakes, rivers, or oceans.

cognate (1A) A discipline that is in some way affiliated with a branch of human geography; for example, political science is a cognate of political geography.

cognitive distance (1F) A measure of distance based on perceived distance, rather than physical distance.

cognitive factors (12B) The ways in which a person's personality or attitudes toward nature, risk, or other factors might affect his or her reaction to a hazard.

colonial period (5F) In US history, the period from about 1600 until the American Revolution.

colonies (10B) Parts of an empire that are subordinate and have very little right to self-determination.

Columbian Exchange (2C) The interaction between the Eastern and Western Hemispheres after the arrival of Europeans in the Americas, including the sharing of cultural ideas as well as plants and animals.

Columbus, Christopher (2C) An Italian-born explorer (1451–1506) known for exploring the Caribbean and for erroneously believing that Asia was closer to Europe than it was.

commercial agriculture (15E) Crops and livestock that are farmed for cash and are considered commodities, intended to be exchanged for payment; more likely to focus on one or two items in order to gain a maximum return on investment.

commodities (15B) Products that can be exchanged for profit.

commodity chain (16G) The series of events that leads to the sale of a commodity to a consumer; design, production, marketing, and retail.

commodity export economies (18C) The export of just a few agricultural or mining commodities.

communist economy (11B) State that assume nearly all economic and social functions and try to impose comprehensive control over economic activities.

commuting (17F) Travel for the purpose of getting to and from work.

comparative advantage (15F) Dictates that a specific region does a better job of producing something than another region does.

competition (17B) When producers compete with other producers and are forced to upgrade the quality of their goods or risk being undercut.

competitive advantage (17B) The concept, promoted by economist Michael Porter, that takes into account the mix of infrastructure, skilled labor, government, domestic demand, levels of domestic competition, agglomeration economies, and other items.

compromise capital (11F) A capital of a country that is selected as a compromise between sectional interests within the country.

concentration of labor (13D) A large population of workers in close proximity to factories, which allows the factory system to function.

concentric zone model (14D) A visual representation of a city that categorizes parts of the city into CBD fringe or frame, zone of transition, zone of independent workingmen's homes, residential zone, and commuters zone.

confederation (11E) A system in which sovereign states agree to abridge some of their independent powers in order to work together as a group, but each state retains a great deal of sovereignty.

Confucianism (8I) A Chinese folk religion or philosophy that began about 2,500 years ago and that emphasizes proper social relationships and individual morality.

conspicuous consumption (16G) An idea by Thorstein Veblen that people feel the need to display their status by ostentatiously consuming goods and services.

Constructivism (10G) The view that nations are artificial creations that result from modernization, elite aspirations, or a series of events that makes nation-building a much more viable approach than anything else.

consumption (16G) A necessary aspect of human existence. Having evolved over time, it used to be what humans needed to survive but today includes luxury items that people desire.

contagious diffusion (6D) The transmission of a phenomenon through close contact with nearby places, such as with many diseases.

containment (10I) The policy that sought to limit Soviet advance to any countries not allied with the United States or the Soviet Union, thereby containing Communist expansionism.

contextual effect (11H) The geographical theory in which the characteristics of people in a local area help determine their political preferences; questions the overall importance of place in shaping people's attitudes or behaviors.

continuous data (1E) Data that occur everywhere, beyond observations.

conveyances (17D) Modes of travel, including boats, horses, trains, motor vehicles, streetcars, and aircraft.

Coptic Christians (8G) An early sect of Christianity primarily practiced in Egypt and Ethiopia.

core (18C) Countries that receive raw materials from peripheral countries to process into manufactured goods.

core region (11F) A place that can represent where the state and the dominant nationality emerged.

covariation (1E) The relationship between the spatial distributions of two or more phenomena that tend to vary in the same way.

creole (7B) A pidgin language that has been adopted by a group of speakers as its primary tongue.

criteria (1G) An established set of conditions that helps categorize and compare information.

critical geopolitics (10I) Used to dissect the ways state boundaries are perceived, relationships between states, and the ways the world is portrayed.

crop complexes (15D) Distinct crops grown in certain areas, which became the basis of regional cuisines.

crude birth rate (CBR) (3E) A simple measure of fertility that represents the number of children born per 1,000 people in a population in a given year.

crude death rate (CDR) (3F) A measure of mortality that represents the number of deaths per 1,000 people in a population in a given year.

cultural assimilation (9B) A situation in which a migrant or new ethnic group maintains a strong self-identity and much of the original culture but has adopted enough of the cultural traits of a host society to be a functioning member of it.

cultural convergence (6C) The process by which two cultures become similar.

cultural diffusion (6D) The movement of culture traits from one place to another.

cultural ecology (12A) The study of how human societies adapt to local habitats and how traditional societies engage in farming or other primary activities.

cultural landscape (6F) The cultural impacts on an area, including buildings, agricultural patterns, roads, signs, and nearly everything else that humans have created.

culture (6A) Shared patterns of learned behavior, attitudes, and knowledge.

culture complex (6B) A group of interrelated culture traits.

culture hearth (6E) An area from which important culture traits, including ideas, technology, and social structures, originated. Ancient Mesopotamia is an example.

culture region (6A) An area defined by a large number of common culture traits.

culture trait (6A) A single component of a culture; can be a thing, an idea, or a social convention.

cuneiform (7A) An ancient Mesopotamian form of writing made by pressing a reed into a tablet of wet clay.

currency manipulation (17C) A method by which a country keeps its currency artificially low in order to make the costs of imported goods high and decrease the costs of its exports.

cyclical movements (5A) A pattern of migration in which migrants move back and forth between two or a small number of places, such as their home and a distant worksite.

cyclone (12C) A hurricane in the Indian Ocean.

D

daytime density (14C) The time when people are at work, which results in a high concentration of people in and around the CBD.

de facto area (10H) According to the notion of effective national territory, the territory a state effectively controls and is not included in the legal area, or de jure area.

de jure area (10H) According to the notion of effective national territory, the legal area of the state that effectively controls the territory, or de facto area.

decolonization (10C) A trend in which colonies became independent from the states that colonized them after the United States declared its independence.

deforestation (12I) The process of clearing a forest.

demand conditions (17C) The products a country is likely to import based on its level of discretionary income, its preferences, and the availability of similar products at home.

democracy (10A) A government that is considered to rule with the consent of its people and, so, is internally legitimate but is not necessarily a government that is legitimate to other governments.

demographic consequences (5F) Changes in a society's population caused by a large influx or outflow of migrants.

demographic transition model (DTM) (3G) A model of demographic change based on Europe's population in the eighteenth through twentieth centuries. It argues that, as a country modernizes, its fertility and mortality rates drop, but not at the same time. Because death rates drop before birth rates, population increase will occur.

density (1E) The number of some phenomenon divided by some sort of control group.

density gradient (14C) A change in density of people over distance.

density peak (14C) The highest density an area in a city has ever experienced, which can be compared with current density to determine increase or decline.

depression (15C) A severe economic downturn for a longer period of time than a recession. It is marked by unemployment, unsold goods, and often many business closings.

description (2A) The recording of knowledge about the peoples and environments of the earth. In ancient times, many geographers simply described what they saw in the world without attempting to explain it.

deterministic (1A) Always resulting in a particular pattern.

deterritorialization (16F) Allows for social and economic activities to occur regardless of where people are physically located.

developed countries (18A) Rich countries that have established economic and political systems and are a model and aspiration to developing countries.

development disparities (18B) The inequity between developed and developing countries, which can be viewed as a function of progress or intrinsic to a global economic structure that began with colonialism and persists today.

development traps (18B) According to Jeffrey Sachs, a series of obstacles that cause economies to stagnate. Examples include poverty, lack of innovation, cultural barriers, and physical geography issues.

devolution (11E) A process that enables a central government to grant powers to lower administrative units.

dharma (8C) A key concept in Hinduism, one's proper duty in life.

dialect (7B) Variations of sounds and vocabulary in a language among different places.

diarrhea (4E) A symptom of various viral, bacterial, and parasitic infections, killing more than 2 million people each year.

diaspora (10F) A group that identifies with a particular homeland or territory but whose members are now dispersed.

diffusion (6D) The movement of a phenomenon from one location to another.

digital divide (18B) The inequity between those countries with good and growing access to the World Wide Web and the many countries where Internet use is quite low.

diplomatic relations (10A) Marks of state legitimacy, which include sending out a state ambassador, establishing an embassy, and signing treaties.

discretionary income (17C) Within a country's population, the amount of money available to be used to satisfy various wants.

dispersed (1E) A type of distribution in which there does not seem to be any type of agglomeration and incidences are well separated from one another.

distance (1F) A factor that heavily influences spatial interactions and can be measured in several ways.

distance decay (1F) The idea that, all else being equal, as the distance between two places increases, the volume of interaction between these places decreases. See also **Zipf's Law**.

distribution (1E) The spatial arrangement of a phenomenon.

division of labor (13A) Workers are given specific chores to do, with some prestige or value placed on certain tasks as opposed to others; can be used in a factory system in which each worker specializes in a single, repeated task.

domino theory (10I) The theory that looks at every political change in a country's government as a domino that causes other dominoes to fall in a chain reaction.

doubling time (3F) A statistic that shows how many years it will take for a population to double.

dual citizenship (11D) The case in which a person can be a citizen of two countries.

E

earthquake (12C) A violent shaking of the earth caused by tectonic or volcanic activity.

ecology (4B) The relationship between plants or animals and the environment.

economic activity (15A) Interaction in which a good or service is extracted, produced, consumed, or exchanged and can be found in nearly everything that people use to live.

economic consequences (5F) The positive or negative financial effects of immigration.

economic development (18A) The expansion of and improvement to a country's economy, which can mean harvesting natural resources, increasing the welfare of poorer countries, or raising per capita incomes.

economy (15A) The extraction, production, consumption, and exchange of goods and services.

ecotone (15D) A place where there existed two or more separate environments, which allowed for greater variety of foodstuffs at different times of the year and was most likely where agriculture began.

edge cities (14D) A key new concept of a modern city, they combine all functions of a central business district but are located in the suburbs and provide more jobs than homes.

effective national territory (10H) The notion that the legal area, or de jure area, of a state is not coincident with the territory that it effectively controls, the de facto area.

Eightfold Path (8D) In Buddhism, the proper way to eliminate desire and achieve enlightenment.

electoral geography (11H) Examines how people's political preferences are manifested in representation.

elite theories of state (11C) The view that governments, no matter what their political ideology or their constitution, are likely to support an elite class of people.

embargo (17B) An external source that has the ability to choke off supplies of a critical resource.

emergent ethnicity (9B) The process in which a new ethnic group or identity appears.

empires (10B) Large political entities made up of several culturally distinct regions held together by force, under the control of a single, dominant region.

enclave (11G) Part of or an entire country surrounded by another country.

endemic (4C) A disease, such as chicken pox, that is always present at some level in a population.

entrepreneurship (17C) The ability of managers to develop new industries, seek out new markets, and maintain a competitive edge.

environment (12A) Most commonly, the physical or natural conditions of an area.

environmental determinism (2D) The controversial idea, popular in the early twentieth century and largely discredited today, that climate or other physical qualities of an area dictate the culture of the people who live there.

environmental justice (12J) The concept that environmental laws and regulations should apply to all areas, regardless of the racial or ethnic composition of a location.

environmental perception (12B) How people perceive, feel about, and interact with the environment.

environmental racism (12J) The deliberate placement of polluting industries or activities in minority areas because those communities are less able or likely to fight the polluters.

epidemic (4C) An outbreak of a disease.

Eratosthenes (2A) The geographer and thinker (~276–195 BC) who is best known for his remarkably accurate calculation of the circumference of the earth.

e-tailing (17H) Online vending of goods, such as on Amazon.com.

ethnic islands (9C) Moderately sized areas of ethnic concentration in rural, or non-urban, areas, such as Amish or Hutterite communities.

ethnic nations (10E) Nations based on cultural commonality as opposed to civic nations, which are based on shared principles.

ethnic neighborhoods (9C) In cities, areas that have concentrated populations of a particular ethnic group, such as a Chinatown.

ethnic provinces (9E) Large areas associated with a particular ethnic group, such as French-speaking Quebec.

ethnic religions (8A) Religions that are primarily associated with one ethnicity, such as Shinto in Japan or Hinduism.

ethnicity (9A) A group's self-identification based on cultural, historical, physical, or other characteristics.

ethnoburb (9C) A suburb with a concentration of a particular ethnic group.

ethnocentrism (9A) An attitude of ethnic or cultural superiority.

ethnoregionalism (10G) Occurs where a minority national group is concentrated in a particular region of a country and may create small- or large-scale difficulties, including demands for autonomy.

Euclidean distance (1F) A method of distance measurement using the straight line mileage between two places.

Euclidean space (1C) A measure of space in which space operates as an area in which activities take place; also known as absolute space.

exclave (11G) When a part of a state's territory is geographically separated by another country.

exclusivity (10E) The expectation that a person is loyal to only one nation.

explosionists (3I) Population theorists who believe that the world will continue to see rapid population growth for decades to come.

export-led approach (18F) Identifies products that can be exported to the outside world, taking advantage of a country's specific advantages.

extraction economy (11B) A political economy that sought chiefly to enrich the ruler and the aristocracy and to maintain its armies; common in early modern states.

F

factor mobility model (5E) An economic model that argues that differences in wage rates cause people to migrate from low-wage areas to high-wage areas.

factors of production (16B) The elements necessary for production, including raw materials, labor, financial capital, and markets.

factory system (16A) The system in which several people worked under one roof, bringing together all the necessary machinery to be powered from belts by one steam engine, requiring very little skill.

federal states (11E) States in which each of the subunits is granted an independent constitutional authority, which defines its level of power, with the central state retaining greater sovereignty.

feminism (2H) In the social sciences, theories and philosophies that focus on the status, contributions, and rights of women.

feminist geography (9F) An approach to human geography that focuses on gender relationships as being central to our understanding of how space is created and arranged.

fertility (3E) How many people are born in a given time period.

feudal system (10B) A system based on the principles of personal allegiance and vassalage that results in a political organization not necessarily tied to complete territorial control.

feudalism (15A) A small-scale economic system based on self-contained estates, controlled by a lord or master.

filtering (14E) The process in which more prosperous families move out of older housing and into new housing, creating a vacancy, which is filled by families that are less wealthy.

finance capital (17C) The amount of money available to finance industries; includes available money as well as the capacity to obtain loans.

financial factors (4G) Whether or not someone can afford health or medical care.

first wave of European immigration (5F) The period from 1800 until 1880, when large numbers of Europeans, particularly from northern and western Europe, moved to North America.

First World (18A) Rich countries that have established economic and political systems and are a model and aspiration to developing countries.

Five Pillars (8H) Basic acts that Muslims are supposed to carry out, including a confession of faith, prayer, charity, observance of Ramadan, and participation in a pilgrimage to Mecca.

fixed capital (17C) The buildings, machines, transportation, and other structural items needed to produce goods.

flow map (1F) A type of map that is often used to depict the interaction between places.

folk culture (6G) Culture traits that are traditional, no longer widely practiced by a large number of people, and generally isolated in small, often rural areas.

foodways (6G) How a culture prepares and consumes food.

forced migration (5B) The situation in which migrants have no choice but to move or else face death or other severe penalty.

foreclosure (14E) A situation in which a mortgage holder loses all claims to his or her property due to nonpayment.

formal regions (1G) Places that have one or more characteristics in common.

formal sector (14G) Jobs in industry, established services, and government that are limited to a privileged few.

forward capitals (11E) Capitals that are intended to help move a population toward less populous areas.

forward linkages (16C) Items that can be produced from the output of an industry. For example, garments such as shirts, pants, and other cotton goods can be produced from cotton textiles.

fossil fuels (12H) Fuels that are formed when organic matter deposited on the earth's surface is changed by pressure and time over thousands of years to form coal, oil, or natural gas.

Four Noble Truths (8D) In Buddhism, principles that the Buddha taught concerning the nature of existence.

free migration (5B) The decision to relocate permanently to another location without coercion, support, or compulsion by any group.

friction of distance (1F) The amount of time it takes to get from one place to another.

frontier (10H) An area at the edge of any type of effective political control or at the edge of settlement with edges that shift frequently with settlement advances or increasing military control.

functional assimilation (9B) The nearly complete fusion of a minority ethnic group with its larger host society.

functional factors (4G) In regard to access to health care, the presence or absence of health care resources.

functional linkages (13C) Meaningful ties between cities that were historically political and administrative.

functional regions (1G) Regions constructed out of places that interact.

G

Gallatin Plan (17E) A plan, devised by Secretary of the Treasury Albert Gallatin in 1808, that attempted to parallel land and water trafficways along the Atlantic seaboard, establish connections between Atlantic streams and western waters, connect the Great Lakes system, and create a system of westward roads to the frontiers.

gender (9F) The societal norms and behaviors that are expected of males or females.

genocide (3H) The mass destruction of a population.

gentrification (14E) Occurs when the housing stock of a neighborhood is improved generally through the introduction of high-priced, more luxurious housing.

geographic information systems (2H) Computer systems that can capture, store, analyze, and output geographic data; commonly referred to as a GIS.

geographical coordinate system (1B) A type of reference system in which each place is given a unique value based on its latitude and longitude.

geographical factors (4G) In regard to access to health care, how close or accessible facilities are to users.

geographical grid (1D) A geographical spreadsheet in which places are represented in rows and have a specific geographical location.

geographical location (1D) Where a place is located. See also **absolute location** and **relative location**.

geometric boundaries (10H) Lines drawn on a map without much interest in whatever natural or cultural features are present.

geopolitical regions (10I) Regions that are formed by spatial contiguity and by political, military, cultural, and economic interactions between them.

geopolitics (10I) The study of how geographical space—including the types of interrelationships between states, the different functions of states, and the different patterns of states—affects global politics.

gerrymandering (11F) Manipulation that concentrates the support of one party or one group of people in one district and dilutes their support throughout a number of other districts.

ghettos (9C) Originally, an Italian term for areas of cities where Jews were forced to live; more broadly, poor urban neighborhoods where minorities are concentrated.

global assembly line (16F) The modern reality that production chains are no longer completed all in one place. Various components are produced in and transported to sites all around the world.

global production line (16F) A method of worldwide production in which the product is moved from one place to another in order to take advantage of favorable costs or specific expertise.

globalization (1D) The elimination of national boundaries through ever greater integration of people, companies, and governments across the world.

Grameen Bank (18B) The bank, established by Professor Muhammad Yunus, that provides microloans to primarily women in developing countries, who are more likely to use the money for productive uses, despite no credit history.

gravity model (5E) A model that defines the interaction between two cities in terms of each city's population and the distance between the two locations.

Great Schism (8G) The breakup, in 1054, of the major sect of Christianity into the Catholic Church and the Eastern Orthodox Church.

green belts (14F) Areas around cities where suburban land uses are restricted.

Green Revolution (15G) An attempt to import Western agricultural practices to subsistence farms in Asia, Latin America, and Africa between the 1950s and 1960s.

grid (14A) A street pattern with the greatest impact, first developed by the ancient Greek Hippodamus. Its advantages are that it is regular, simple, and repeatable for as far as the city expands.

Grimm's law (7C) A theory attributed to Jakob Grimm that modern German and English experienced consonant shifts since ancient times.

gross domestic product (GDP) (15C) The total of all goods and services produced within a country.

gross migration (5B) The total number of people who leave and enter a country in a given time period.

gross national income (GNI) (15C) Similar to GNP, except it does not include costs of indirect taxes, depreciation, and subsidies.

gross national product (GNP) (15C) The total of goods and services produced by the citizens of a country, whether the actual production takes place inside or outside a country's boundaries.

guest workers (5A) Laborers allowed to enter a country for a specific job and for a specified period of time.

guinea worm (4E) Also known as *Dracunculiasis*, this disease causes an infection by a roundworm that gets into humans when they drink water containing water fleas carrying the worm's larvae.

Gullah (7D) A creole language spoken on islands off the coast of South Carolina and Georgia.

H

habitat (4B) The natural characteristics and cultural aspects of an environment.

Hajj (8H) The annual pilgrimage to Mecca that all capable Muslims are expected to undertake at least once in their lifetime.

Hanification (9E) The Chinese government practice of moving Han Chinese citizens into minority ethnic areas to dilute the importance of the minority culture.

Harrison, John (2C) The British clockmaker (1693–1776) who invented a chronometer that worked while at sea, thus allowing accurate measurements of longitude to be determined.

hazardous waste (12G) Refuse that poses a risk either to the environment or to humans.

hearth (6D) The place where something begins.

Hecataeus (2A) The Greek historian (~550–476 BC) credited with writing the book *Ges Periodus*, a descriptive account of the ancient world.

Herodotus (2A) The historian (~484–425 C) who included geographic descriptions in his writings.

hierarchical diffusion (6D) A pattern whereby things move from one place to other places that have some similarities or are otherwise going to be more receptive, such as from a large city to smaller cities or from a boss to a subordinate.

high seas (10A) The parts of the ocean in which no government has sovereignty.

high-technology clusters (16E) Areas that have a high concentration of specialized labor, specialized inputs, knowledge spillovers, and market/user accessibility that benefits the high-technology industry.

high-technology industries (16E) Companies that support the growth and development of sophisticated technologies. It is a very new industry that has rapidly transformed many cities and countries.

Hijra (8H) The movement of Muhammad and his followers from Mecca to what is now Medina in 622 AD, an event regarded as the start of the Islamic calendar.

Hinduism (8C) The ancient and complex ethnic religion practiced primarily in India. It emphasizes reincarnation, the worship of any one of many gods, and the consequences of one's actions.

hinterland (13B) The area surrounding a city from which it obtains its food.

HIV/AIDS (4D) A worldwide disease caused by a virus that can cause a progressive breakdown of the human immune system.

homeland (10E) The distinct territory associated with a nation; however, unlike a state, the members of a particular nation may not be found in a territorially demarcated and contained place.

Homer (2A) The writer often considered the father of geography.

horizontal loyalty (10E) Powerful loyalty to a nation that is expressed toward all the people of that nation.

host (4C) A life form that has a disease.

human capital (17C) A population's level of education and skill.

human capital model (5E) A theory of migration that argues that people move not just for macroeconomic reasons but also for individual reasons.

human development index (HDI) (18A) A measure that incorporates indicators of health and education to provide a more comprehensive portrayal of the average welfare of a country's residents.

human ecology (4B) The interconnections between human populations and the physical world.

human trafficking (5C) The transportation of people against their will through the use of force, coercion, fraud, or other means.

humanistic geography (2F) A sub-branch of human geography that grew out of behavioral geography but put less emphasis on explaining the world and more focus on the meaning that humans place on the environment and their surroundings, as well as how people perceive the world around them.

hunting and gathering (15A) A feature of prehistoric human life, the combination of killing animals and finding edible plant life for food, which required teamwork, effective communication, and weapon construction.

hurricane (12C) A strong cyclonic storm system with low pressure, strong thunderstorms, high winds, and rain; also known as a **typhoon** or **cyclone**.

I

ibn-Battuta (2B) A Moroccan Muslim (1304–1368) who traveled over 75,000 miles and wrote an account of his journeys.

iconic landscapes (1H) A class of distinctive landscape types that bring to mind images and symbols essential to identity.

ideological subsystem (6C) The ideas, beliefs, values, and knowledge of a culture.

idiom (7B) Language that is peculiar to a certain group of people or a region; often used synonymously with **dialect**.

impelled migration (5B) Migration in which a person fears that failure to move will likely result in negative consequences or because of persecution.

imperial economies (15B) Systems marked by the redistribution of surplus from peasants to large landholders, but with the imperial bureaucracy taking a substantial cut.

implosionists (3I) Population theorists who believe that declining fertility rates indicate that the earth has turned the corner on population growth.

import substitution (18G) Used to shelter young domestic industries from foreign competition by providing them with a secure market.

index of dissimilarity (9C) A measure of segregation that indicates how isolated two groups are from each other in a particular area or city.

Indo-European (7C) A large language family of hundreds of languages, including English.

Industrial Revolution (3A) A series of agricultural and technological innovations that transferred European society beginning in the eighteenth century and eventually spread to much of the world.

industrialization (16A) The process by which a greater proportion of a national economy is involved in the manufacturing of goods. This allows more goods to be produced in greater quantity and at a lower price.

infant mortality rate (IMR) (3F) The number of babies who die before age one per 1,000 births.

infectious stimuli (4B) The effects on a person caused by viruses, bacteria, or other physical insults.

influenza (4E) Commonly known as the flu, a disease caused by a virus that affects humans, animals, and birds. Flu outbreaks can be regional or even global.

informal sector (14G) Employment that is labor-intensive, absorbs the remainder of the workforce, and is open to nearly everyone but offers a very low standard of living.

infrastructure (2G) In social theory, such as in structuralism, the hidden ideas and theories that help create the visible world around us. See also **superstructure**.

in-migration (5B) The total number of immigrants who arrive in a country in a given time period.

innovative diffusion (6D) See **diffusion**.

instrumentalism (10G) A view that nations emerge for a particular purpose, which meets the demands of a situation.

intelligent transportation systems (17D) A network that enhances the coordination of traffic signal lights with the overall patterns and flows of traffic.

interior landscapes (1H) Landscapes found inside a building, house, or other structure.

internal boundaries (10H) Boundaries within a country that separate substate units.

internal migration (5A) The movement of people within a country.

internally displaced persons (5D) People forced to leave their homes but who settle in another part of their own country.

international boundary (10H) A line that separates one state from another. Both sides usually have claims as to where the boundary should be located and it is rare to find an unattended boundary between two sovereign states.

International Date Line (1B) A line of longitude that is the other side of the prime meridian and is 180°.

international migration (5A) The movement of people between countries.

International Monetary Fund (IMF) (18B) An agency in the effort to promote development that represents a consortium of most of the world's countries. It acts as a credit union that provides monetary resources that can be used by all the countries in its network.

international trade (17A) The exchange of goods and services across country boundaries.

Interstate Highway System (14D) Begun in the 1950s and funded largely by the federal (US) government, it created large, limited-access superhighways, connected cities, and made it easier for people to live farther away from cities.

intervening obstacles (5E) Factors that a migrant must consider when weighing the pluses and minuses of a potential move, such as the cost or ease of crossing a border.

intervening opportunities (5E) Places along a migrant's route that might cause that person to stop and settle before reaching his or her final destination.

introduced capitals (11I) The introduction of a new city that can serve as a capital or to designate an existing smaller city as the new capital city, rather than use existing cities to form a capital region.

irredentist movements (10G) Ethnoregional movements that do not seek to create their own independent country but, rather, to separate from their existing state in order to join a neighboring state.

irrigation (15A) The process of directing water from nearby water sources to cropland. Early technologies required that a community work together through directing, digging, and constructing.

Islam (8H) A monotheistic religion with two major sects. It was founded in the seventh century by the prophet Muhammad and is now the second largest religion in the world. Its practitioners are known as Muslims.

isoline map (1E) A map that is used to display distributions. It consists of lines that connect points of equal value.

J

Jainism (8I) A small religion founded in the sixth century BC and practiced mostly in India or where Indians settle. It emphasizes the elimination of all activity that would accumulate bad karma.

Jesus (8F) A Jewish prophet, whose teachings form the basis for Christianity and whom Christians believe was the Messiah.

Judaism (8E) An old, monotheistic, and ethnic religion, which, despite its small size, has had a strong influence on human history and which formed a spiritual foundation for Christianity and Islam. Its practitioners are known as Jews.

jus sanguinis (11F) Citizenship based on parents' citizenship, regardless of place of birth; Latin for "right of blood."

jus soli (11D) Citizenship acquired through birth within a state's territory; Latin for "right of the soil."

K

karma (8C) In religions such as Hinduism and Buddhism, the notion that every action a person takes, whether good or bad, has a consequence in the future.

knot (2C) The unit of speed used by sailors; equal to 1 nautical mile per hour, which is equivalent to approximately 1.151 miles per hour, or 1.852 kilometers per hour.

kosher (8E) Prepared according to Jewish laws and traditions and most commonly used to refer to food.

L

land rent (15F) The profitability of a particular piece of land, dependent on soil quality, climate, terrain, and cultural factors.

land value (14C) The worth of a plot of land, affected by function (retail, industrial, residential, etc.), location, and ability to be developed.

landfills (12F) Places where waste material is buried and covered with soil.

landscape (1H) An area that is less defined than a region and is described in an abstract manner.

language (7A) A system of communication using sounds, gestures, marks, and signs.

language convergence (7E) The process of two languages merging together.

language divergence (7E) The process of a language splitting into two or more distinct languages.

language extinction (7E) The point at which a language no longer has any active speakers.

language family (7C) A collection of languages that have a common ancestor and is subdivided into smaller branches of related languages.

language isolate (7E) A language that belongs to no known language family.

latitude (1B) A measured distance north or south of the equator, with the North and South Poles as key reference points.

legitimacy (10A) The standing or right of the government of a unit to rule a state's people or territory.

less developed countries (18A) Impoverished countries that have frail or corrupt economic and political systems and that aspire to become developed countries.

life expectancies (3A) The average life spans of persons in a particular population.

lingua franca (7B) A language used in cross-cultural communication or trade.

links (17D) The routes that connect nodes. In transportation, these can be roads, railroads, rivers, canals, footpaths, or sea or air routes.

list system of proportional representation (11I) A system in which each party draws up a list of candidates in each electoral district, and people tend to vote for the parties rather than for the candidates themselves.

living standards (18A) Factors that affect the quality of life in a country, such as access to safe food and water, employment, and security.

loan words (7G) Terms used in one language that have an origin in another language.

locales (2G) Places where societal structures intersect with human decisions, according to structuralists.

locational advantages (16F) Reductions in production costs by locating in areas where wages are lower or some other factor makes it cheaper to produce in that area.

longitude (1B) A measured distance east and west of the prime meridian.

luxury (16G) Something that provides enjoyment beyond the necessities of life.

M

Mahayana Buddhism (8D) One of the two largest branches of Buddhism, practiced primarily in East and Southeast Asia. Generally, it has more mystical and spiritual elements than **Theravada Buddhism**.

majoritarian system (11I) A system in which elections are designed such that the winner must have a majority of the overall votes. For example, the top two candidates from the first round of voting compete directly against each other in the second round of voting.

malapportionment (11I) Manipulation in which some electoral districts vary in size even though they are equal in representation.

malaria (4E) A disease caused by a parasite and spread to humans by mosquitoes. About 40% of the world's population is at risk of contracting this disease.

Malayo-Polynesian (7C) A large language family of over 1,200 tongues spoken primarily in Southeast Asia and the South Pacific.

Malthus, Thomas (3I) The Englishman (1766–1834) who wrote *An Essay on the Principle of Population* and argued that population growth would lead to famine and disease.

maquiladora (16B) A factory located on the border, often to take advantage of low wage requirements in this area.

Marxist (2G) Related to the work of nineteenth-century thinkers Karl Marx and Frederich Engel.

Marxist theories of the state (11C) Views of the state as a vehicle promoting capitalism and the capitalist class; also those who control production.

mass consumption (16G) A large number of people purchasing large quantities of goods.

mass migration (5B) Population movements of a large number of people.

mass production (13D) A large output of goods, which both drops the price of the goods and sparks demand due to affordability.

measurement (2A) In geography, human understanding about the size and shape of the world as well as where things are located.

medical geography (4C) The sub-branch of geography that studies the pattern of and transmission of diseases as well as the spatial pattern of health care.

mental map (2F) A representation of the real world that humans have in their minds.

mentifacts (6C) Individual culture traits of the ideological subsystem, such as an idea.

mercantilism (17C) A policy that seeks to reduce barriers to trade within a country while creating a large number of external barriers, such as quotas and tariffs.

merchants (15B) Buyers of large quantities of products, who then ship, store, and/or trade the product; a necessary component of capitalism, especially in the early stages.

metropole (10B) The dominant part of an empire, distinguished from the subordinate colonies, which is normally the state that initiated colonization.

micro-states (10D) States that are very small but are still considered to possess a certain degree of sovereignty, legitimacy, and territory.

migration (5A) The permanent relocation of one's place of residence, usually implying a long-distance move.

militarized boundaries (10H) Heavily fortified boundaries that discourage the crossing of traffic, people, goods, and/or information.

Minamata disease (12J) A type of mercury poisoning that came to prominence in the 1960s after decades of industrial pollution in the city of Minamata, Japan.

minority national group (10G) A group that considers itself a nation but does not have control of the state.

mixed agricultural economy (15E) A system that involves a heavy reliance on both plants and animals for food, materials, and goods.

mixed economies (11B) Economies in which the government controls certain economic activities it considers key or appropriate to the public trust while leaving others in the hands of the private sector.

mixed system (11I) A system that combines both proportional voting (see **list system**) and a plurality system.

modal split (17F) The percentage of travel undertaken via each transport mode.

modern state system (10C) A system composed of territories that are more closely controlled and integrated than political territories had been and that eventually replaced many different types of political forms.

modernism (2H) Twentieth-century trends in art, architecture, and literature that represented a break from traditions of the past.

modernization theory (18B) A theory rooted in the experience of western Europe and North America. It views these as models for the rest of the world to follow.

moment magnitude scale (12C) A logarithmic scale used for measuring the strength of an earthquake.

monotheistic (8A) A type of religion that believes in one Supreme Being.

more developed countries (18A) Rich countries that have established economic and political systems and are a model and aspiration to developing countries.

morphology (14A) The form of a city, which varies but often includes an urban population, a center, a perimeter, and an internal transportation network.

mosque (8H) A house of worship in Islam and distinguished by a tower known as a minaret.

Muhammad (8H) The seventh-century prophet that Muslims believe is a messenger of God; the founder of the religion of Islam.

multidivisional corporation (16F) A corporation with many divisions based on production lines or stages in the production chain.

multinational state (10F) A country that contains more than one nation, which is true for many countries.

multiplier effect (16D) A job in a particular industry that has a multiplier of 2.0, meaning that this one job actually results in two jobs in the economy: the original industrial job as well as an additional non-base job.

multiscalar (1A) Taking place at different spatial scales.

multistate nation (10F) A nation that encompasses more than one state in which the nations may or may not have control of the state.

mystico-religious sites (8J) Places that are sacred to a religion because it is believed that a deity or other supernatural entity came into direct contact with humans at those locations.

N

nation (10E) A group of people who feel that they belong together as a polity for a number of reasons.

national highway system (17E) A highway system that had been established by the 1920s. It led to the development of the US routes seen today, consisting of odd-numbered north–south roads and even-numbered east–west routes.

national landscapes (10E) include Houses, churches, parks, monuments, and all manner of things that help determine the national flavor of a place.

nationalism (10E) The ideology that maintains that members of a nation should be allowed to form their own sovereign state.

nation-state (10F) A state that contains a single nation that is not disputed by anyone inside or outside.

nation-state ideal (10F) The ideal arrangement under nationalist ideology that every nation should have control over a state. Conversely, every political state should embody a specific nation.

natural boundaries (10H) Natural features that divide one country from another.

natural hazards (12B) Environmental events such as floods, hurricanes, earthquakes, tornados, tsunami, mudslides, volcanic eruptions, and droughts.

neighborhood effect (11H) See **contextual effect**.

neocolonialism (18B) The sort of economic relationships that persist between the mother country and the former colony, even after independence.

neo-European realm (18C) Former European colonies that were used for acquiring precious metals and other valuable resources and sometimes for settlement.

neoliberalism (11C) A set of policies that favor minimal government interference in markets and the promotion of free trade.

Neolithic Revolution (3A) The period in ancient times, approximately 12,000 years ago, when livestock and agriculture were domesticated, leading to the establishment of more permanent settlements and a rise in global population.

neo-Malthusians (3I) Modern population theorists that carry on Malthus's idea that population growth will lead to global chaos.

net migration (5B) The difference between the number of people who leave and the number of people who arrive in a country.

network (17D) The entire pattern of nodes and links.

network connectivity (17D) The degree to which direct movements are possible over a network.

new international division of labor (16F) A recent phenomenon in which the production process transcends international boundaries.

niche marketers (17H) Retailers that sell goods to fulfill a particular need, such as an outdoor equipment company.

Niger-Congo (7C) A large language family of 1,400 languages spoken primarily in Africa.

nighttime density (14C) The time when people are home from work, which results in a low concentration of people in and around the CBD.

NIMBY (12F) An acronym for "Not in My Back Yard"; refers to things that communities need and want, such as power plants and landfills, but that nobody wants in close proximity to his or her home.

nodal point (14C) A place at which things, such as transportation routes, converge.

nodes (17D) Components of every transportation system that are either places in their own right or intersections.

nonagricultural population (13A) The portion of the population not engaged in farming. They rely on farmers for food.

nonaligned countries (10I) After World War II, the countries that were not allied with either the Soviet Union or the United States.

nonstore retailing (17H) The buying and selling of goods that takes place outside of a store setting, such as by traveling salespeople or through mail-ordering.

nonstructural responses (12B) Actions taken by a society, a political body, or individuals to reduce the risk of a natural hazard.

O

occupational specialization (13A) Nonagricultural workers became involved in different types of trades and tasks, from metal workers to tanners to scribes; a hallmark of early cities as well as a characteristic of modern cities.

oligarchy (11C) A single individual or clique that holds concentrated power in an authoritarian or autocratic state.

One-Child Policy (3J) Begun by the Chinese government in 1979, a population control policy that restricts most couples to just one birth without special permission.

open boundaries (10H) Boundaries where crossing is unimpeded.

optimum location (16B) According to economist Alfred Weber, the ideal location for a manufacturing plant: where there is a balance between the locations of the various raw materials, the labor force, and the markets where the final products would be sold.

ordinary landscape (1H) A landscape that people encounter in their daily experiences.

organic city (14A) A city that is loosely planned, often featuring streets of varied width that might resemble labyrinths. Many medieval cities were organic, as are modern cities such as Boston.

out-migration (5B) The total number of immigrants who leave a country in a given time period.

P

Pali Canon (8D) The primary teachings of Buddhism; also known as the Tripitaka.

pandemic (4C) A worldwide outbreak of a disease.

pastoral nomadism (15E) A culture that locates in areas too harsh for crops and that moves seasonally with their animals to locate the available water.

patois (7B) Generally, rural or provincial speech or a nonstandard form of a language.

pattern (1A) The arrangement of various geographic phenomena at a given point in time.

peak value intersection (PVI) (14C) A single intersection with the greatest access, usually located at the intersection of two main streets.

perimeter (14A) An element that defines a city and is the manner by which a city is separated from the country.

period (1G) A way to slice up time. It is essential to historical understanding.

periodic movement (5A) Population movement, often over long distances, that occurs from time to time but is not permanent, such as going away to school or joining the armed forces.

peripheral (11G) In contrast to core areas, these regions are at the edge of political control, recently integrated into the state, culturally distinct, or exclaves.

periphery (18C) Countries that export raw materials to core countries to process into manufactured goods.

phenomenon (1A) Any attribute that can be considered geographically.

phonemes (7A) The sounds used in a spoken language.

physical insults (4B) Traumatic events, such as accidents, shock, or radiation poisoning, that negatively affect human health.

physiologic density (3B) A statistic of population density calculated by dividing a country's population by its area of arable land. In other words, it is the number of people per square mile or kilometer of farmable land.

pictographic writing (7A) A type of written speech in which small pictures are used for words.

pidgin (7B) A simplified language that is used by people who speak different languages for common communication; usually not the primary language of anyone using it.

place (1C) A basic unit and key concept in geography that indicates where something exists.

place interaction (1F) A wide variety of activities that occur between places.

place similarity (1F) One or more attributes that places have in common.

planned cities (14A) Cities laid out along more symbolic lines, often rich with symbolic elements, such as cosmological principles.

planned economies (15B) Economies that emerged as a response to unrestricted capitalist economies and often in response to what were perceived as some of the inequities embedded in a capitalist system.

pluralist theory of the state (11C) The view that the government is a neutral arbiter of all the different stakeholders.

point pattern (1E) The distribution of points on a map, which can be analyzed to determine patterns.

political economy (11B) The relationship among the state, the members of the state, and the economic activities contained within the state.

political subunits (11A) The division of territory into smaller, manageable pieces.

political unit (10A) Organizational entities at several different spatial scales that aid the study of political geography. The most important of these is the country, or state.

polygyny (4A) The cultural practice of a husband having multiple wives.

polytheistic (8A) A religion that believes in many deities.

popular culture (6G) The aspects of a culture that are widespread, fast-changing, and transmitted by the mass media.

population (4B) The number of people in an area as well as the age, gender, and genetic characteristics of a society.

population density (13A) The number of people per square mile.

population planning (3J) Government attempts to increase or decrease the birth rate in the country.

population profile (3H) A graphic that shows the number or percentage of men and women in a population per year group or range of years; sometimes called a population pyramid.

population size (13A) The number of people living in an area.

positivism (2E) A belief that all knowledge can be pursued by the scientific method. It puts a strong emphasis on observation and measurement.

possibilism (2D) The viewpoint that arose as a criticism of environmental determinism, holding that human populations develop their own cultures within constraints set by the environment.

postmodernism (2H) A complex set of ideas that arose as a criticism of modernism and that, in general, rejects that everything in the world is rational or neatly categorized.

poststructuralism (2H) A broad term that refers to social theories that questioned structuralism's search for deep structures and that focused on individuals and local differences. In geography, many poststructuralists focus on how marginalized groups view and use landscapes.

predatory lending (14E) A situation in which mortgages impose an undue financial burden on households by forcing debts that far exceed assets and can result in foreclosure.

primary loyalty (10E) The expectation that loyalty to a nation transcends that of other allegiances.

primary sector (15C) Activities involving the extraction of raw materials, the gathering of plants and animals, and the domestication of plants or animals.

primate city (13H) The largest city in a country that is much greater than the second largest, overwhelming the rest of the country in terms of population, as well as cultural and economic importance.

prime meridian (1B) The key reference line for longitude that is 0°; an arbitrary line that crosses through Greenwich, England, and connects the poles.

prime value intersection (PVI) (14C) A single intersection with the greatest access, usually located at the intersection of two main streets.

primitive agriculture (15A) The gradual transition to agriculture, occurring in different parts of the world beginning about 9000 BC. Some early agricultural groups were nomadic and some involved shifting cultivation; most early agriculturalists settled into more permanent settlements.

primitive migration (5B) Human movements that occur when a population runs out of food.

primordialism (10G) The view that nations are organically grown entities, that the world is divided into different national groups that have persisted for sometime, and that nationalist movements represent an awakening of already significant identities.

Prince Henry the Navigator (2C) A Portuguese royal (1394–1460) who contributed to European exploration and geographic discovery by employing cartographers, geographers, and other experts to further Portuguese maritime interests.

private sector (11B) In a capitalist society, all the factories, firms, and offices responsible for producing goods and providing services that are not run by the state; includes all of the output produced by individuals working for themselves and privately owned businesses.

probabilistic (1A) Tending to result in a pattern.

process (1A) An action that brings about a particular pattern.

production (16A) The process that creates an object that is more valuable than the sum of the raw materials going into it.

production chain (16B) The process that transforms raw materials into a finished product, then distributes that product for consumption by households, government, or industries.

productivity (17C) A measurement of the relative output per unit of labor.

profane landscape (8J) Places that are not holy or sacred; everyday places.

profit (15B) The positive difference between how much revenue is made by selling a product and how much it costs to buy or make a product.

protectionism (17B) When a country seeks to limit trade through various mechanisms.

Protestant Reformation (8G) An important religious movement, which began in Europe in the sixteenth century and was marked by a rejection of the power and rituals of the Catholic Church. It led to the rise of Protestant Christian sects.

proto-language (7C) The common ancestor of a family of modern languages.

psychosocial insults (4B) The effects of things such as crowding, anxiety, belonging, or love on a person's health.

Ptolemy (2A) A geographer, mathematician, and astronomer (90–168 AD), who wrote a long geography of the world. Versions of Ptolemy's maps were used for 1,500 years despite serious errors.

public sector (11B) In a capitalist society, state-run functions, including external relations, a system of adjudication or arbitration, and tax collection; includes all of the output produced by government at all levels.

purchasing power parity (PPP) (18A) A measure of per capita income that diminishes a little of the gross variation between countries and reveals development disparities.

pure democracy (11H) All citizens have a say in all the issues pertaining to their community.

pure characteristic (1D) A characteristic that can be applied to an entire place.

push-pull model (5E) A model of migration that argues that people are pushed from their homes by certain negative factors and pulled to other locations by positive qualities.

Q

Qur'an (8H) The holy book of Islam, believed by Muslims to be the actual words of God as revealed to Muhammad.

quantitative revolution (2E) In geography, the movement that grew in strength in the 1950s and 1960s and that focused on statistics, positivistic techniques, and the search for universal laws to explain geographic patterns and processes.

quaternary sector (15C) Services that rely on information gathering and sharing. These include information technology services, research and development, consulting services, and other similar activities.

quota (17C) A limit imposed on the quantity of a country's exports or imports, often used to restrict imported goods.

R

random distribution (1E) A phenomenon that is neither clustered nor dispersed.

rank-size relationship (13H) A relationship that typifies the overall urban hierarchy within a country. It is determined by dividing the population of the largest city in half to determine the size of the second largest city, the second by the third, and so on.

rate of natural increase (RNI) (3F) The difference in births and deaths in a population, usually expressed as a percentage; does not take into account migration into or out of an area.

rate of population growth (3F) A statistic, expressed as a percentage, that indicates the growth rate of a population in a given time period and that includes not only births and deaths but also migration.

Ravenstein's laws (5E) A set of theories about migration developed in the late nineteenth century by Ernst Georg Ravenstein.

Received Pronunciation (7D) Considered to be the standard form of English, spoken in and around London and often used on British radio and television.

recession (15C) The situation that occurs when measures of the economy decline, often for a sustained period of time, such as half a year.

recharge (12D) How quickly groundwater is replenished.

recreational auto city (14D) The time when automobiles were no longer a novelty and became more affordable and popular among middle-class families, raising ownership to one car for every five people in the United States.

refugee (5D) A person living outside of his or her own country who cannot return home because of fear of injury or persecution.

refugee warehousing (5D) The long-term housing of refugees in a specific location without allowing them to assimilate into the receiving country.

region (1G) A way of subdividing space into categorizable geographic units.

regional geography (2E) A type of geographic inquiry that focuses on the region as the main way to classify and understand the world. Regional geographies tend to focus on broad, holistic descriptions of regions.

reincarnation (8C) In religions such as Hinduism, the belief that souls are reborn after death in other life forms.

relative location (1B) The location of a place compared to other places.

relative significance (1D) The level of significance a characteristic has, depending on scale of analysis and the topic of interest.

religion (8A) A cultural system of beliefs, traditions, and practices, often centered around the worship of a deity or deities.

relocation diffusion (6D) The diffusion of a particular phenomenon over a far distance as a result of migration.

remittances (5A) Payments made by overseas migrants to their families back home.

repatriation (5D) The process of moving refugees back into their home country or region.

replacement level of fertility (3E) The total fertility rate necessary to keep a population at a constant size over time, assuming no migration; usually between 2.1 and 2.3.

representative democracy (11H) A complicated structure in which people elect representatives who are supposed to take the time to understand the issues and to represent their interests.

reservation (11G) A special region, most common in the Americas, established as a territory for indigenous peoples. It usually represents just a fraction of the land that these peoples had previously occupied.

restricted migration (5B) The fact that, in the modern world, there is very little "free" migration because of laws and border regulations. Thus, even when people make a free decision to move, they may not be able to migrate.

resurgent identity (9B) An ethnic group that reemerges after its importance faded or it was suppressed.

retail chains (17G) Stores that have several locations and are owned by the same company, as opposed to single, family-owned businesses.

reverse hierarchical diffusion (6D) Diffusion up a hierarchy, such as from a small town to large cities.

Ring of Fire (12C) Large areas of the Pacific Rim that are subject to volcanoes and earthquakes because of tectonic activity and their location along major crustal plate boundaries.

Ritter, Carl (2D) A German geographer (1779–1859), who emphasized observation of the landscape and who argued that geography must focus on understanding the interconnections among phenomena on the earth's surface and not just basic description.

Rosetta Stone (7A) A large stone discovered in 1799 with three languages inscribed on it. It eventually led to the deciphering of Egyptian hieroglyphics.

runic alphabet (7C) An early alphabet used by Germanic speakers before the adoption of the Latin alphabet.

rural-to-urban migration (5B) The movement of people from the countryside to the city.

S

sacred landscape (8J) A place that has religious or spiritual importance.

satellite state (10D) A state with less actual sovereignty, such as the freedom to exercise its own foreign policy or even to make internal changes.

scale (1D) This determines the frame of reference and shows which characteristics are especially important.

scale of analysis (1D) A scale that determines what is being studied based on the size of the area being examined.

schedule (13A) Cycles of the day, of seasons, and of rain and drought that determined the food supply.

Schengen Agreement (10H) In 1995, several European countries lifted all border controls between them, allowing for unimpeded access across international boundaries. It now includes most Western and Central European countries as well as many Eastern European countries.

schistosomiasis (4C) An endemic infectious disease caused by a fluke, which also lives in snails for part of its life cycle. The infection causes a massive immune response, affecting about 200 million people worldwide.

scientific exploration (2D) A movement that arose in the nineteenth century and focused on sending teams of scientists to explore certain parts of the world.

scurvy (2C) A vitamin C–deficiency disease common among sailors in premodern times.

second wave of European immigration (5G) The period in US history between 1880 and 1921, which saw millions of immigrants from Europe arrive in America.

secondary sector (15C) Activities that add value to raw materials through some form of manufacturing, processing, or construction.

sector model (14D) Developed by Homer Hoyt, a visual representation of a city that took site factors explicitly into account. These sites included the high-rent area, low-rent sectors, and middle-income sectors.

segregation (9C) The separation between or among different social or ethnic groups.

self-determination (10E) An idea whereby members of a nation are allowed to form their own sovereign state.

semi-periphery (18C) Countries that contain aspects of both core and periphery.

Semitic (7C) The branch of the Afro-Asiatic language family that includes Arabic.

sense of place (1C) A set of meanings attached to an area, particularly to the people who know that place well.

settlements (13A) Built out of more permanent materials, rather than being of temporary construction, they allowed for the development of agriculture.

Sharia (8H) Traditional Muslim law as set forth in the Qur'an and the example set by Muhammad in his lifetime.

shatterbelts (10I) Regions that are politically fragmented and are often areas of competition between two ideological or two religious realms.

Shinto (8I) The traditional animistic religion of Japan.

Siddhartha (8D) The Buddha; a noble born in the Himalayas approximately 2,500 years ago who rejected his life of privilege and sought a path to enlightenment. His teachings form the basis for Buddhism.

Sikhism (8I) Monotheistic religion founded in South Asia in the late 15th century by Guru Nanak as a reaction to perceived problems with the teachings of Islam and Hinduism.

single member plurality system (11I) A system in which an entire country or political subdivision is divided into electoral districts, each of which elects only one representative.

single-occupancy motor vehicle travel (SOV) (17F) The vehicles (such as cars, minivans, pickup trucks, and motorcycles) that are used by 80% of Americans to get to work.

Sino-Tibetan (7C) A large language family that includes various dialects of Chinese, including Mandarin.

site (1C) The immediate environment of a place.

situation (1C) The way in which a particular place relates to the space that surrounds it.

situation factors (12B) Realities such as where people are located, how old they are, their financial resources, and other truths that might affect a human's actual or perceived ability to deal with a possible hazard.

smog (12E) Air pollution produced by sunlight reacting with ozone released from cars, factories, and power plants.

social consequences (5F) The positive or negative effects of migration when two or more societies come together.

social construction of space (6F) The idea that society shapes the spatial nature of our world.

social factors (4G) Societal realities, such as racist or sexist policies, that might limit a person's access to health care.

sociofact (6C) A culture trait in the sociological subsystem.

sociological subsystem (6C) The part of a culture that guides how people are expected to interact with each other and how their social institutions are structured.

solid waste (12F) Essentially, garbage or trash, but it may include solid, semi-solid, or even liquid refuse.

sovereignty (10A) An indicator that a particular government has complete control and jurisdiction over a defined area.

space (1C) A two-dimensional area that contains a number of places and boundaries that may or may not be clearly defined.

spatial connectivity (1F) The network created by spatial interactions, which geographers attempt to understand.

spatial interaction (1F) The movement and interconnections between places.

special regions (11G) Political subunits that are granted different powers than those of regular subunits.

sprachbund (7C) A group of languages from different families or branches of a family that share grammatical or lexical similarities because of proximity.

squatter settlements (14G) Temporary structures built up by people with nowhere else to go, which usually suggest illegal occupation.

state (10A) A country; the most important spatial scale unit in political geography.

stateless nation (10F) A nation that has no state to call its own.

step migration (5E) When migrants move from a small town to a larger town, then stop and work for a while before moving on to an even larger town, and so on.

storm surges (12C) Walls of wind-driven water caused by a hurricane or tropical storm. They can be meters or tens of meters higher than sea level.

streetcar city (14D) That phase that took place after the Civil War in which city population ballooned, transit systems developed, and electric streetcars replaced horsecars and omnibuses.

structural responses (12B) The building of physical structures, such as levees, to reduce the impact of a potential natural hazard.

structuralism (2G) A set of social theories that generally look for deep structures or theories that guide human actions and societies.

structuralist school of development (18G) Views the intervention of government as key to economic development.

structuration (2G) A social theory that human action is partly constrained by social structures governed by laws and social norms and that societies can choose to either reproduce or change their behaviors.

structure (2G) In social theory, social, political, or economic systems that might limit or constrain the human capacity to make independent decisions; often contrasted with **agency**.

subjects (11D) In monarchical, feudal, or imperial settings, the residents of the state. They are given few rights, despite their many obligations for military service, labor, and taxation.

subprime lending (14E) Mortgages made available to people who could not qualify for regular conventional, or prime, mortgages. They always entail higher fees and/or rates to make up for a higher risk of default.

subsequent boundaries (10H) Boundaries created after recognized settlement. They are meant to separate existing cultural groups and may signify an attempt to align the boundaries that exist between nations.

subsistence agriculture (15E) Nearly all the crops and livestock are used to support the farmer, the farmer's family, and perhaps a larger group within a clan or village.

suburbs (14D) Inhabited areas around cities that grew rapidly due to decentralization of cities and automobile dependency.

Superfund Program (12G) A US government program that identifies and attempts to clean up the worst pollution sites in the country.

superstructure (2G) A social theory that argues that society has rules that humans can choose to act on or not.

surpluses (13A) Overabundances of food, often grain, resulting from organized agriculture and allowed for distributions, trade, and taxation.

sustainable development (18G) A development model that does not lead to tremendous gains in income but is effective in improving the well-being of the population.

synagogue (8E) A Jewish house of worship.

systematic geography (2E) An approach to studying geography that focuses on specializing in one subfield of the discipline and then applying that knowledge to a variety of regions or places.

T

Taoism (8I) An ancient Chinese philosophy or religion focused on individual morality, self-restraint, and humility.

tariffs (17C) Taxes on items leaving or entering a country, often used to raise the price of imported goods.

technological subsystem (6C) The material objects that a culture produces, as well as the procedures for using those objects.

territorial states (13B) Larger states that evolved from smaller city-states. They managed a number of cities and extended far beyond the hinterland of a single city.

territory (10A) An area in which a government has some measure of sovereignty. Outside the boundaries, a government does not have sovereignty.

tertiary sector (15C) Activities that provide services. This category includes everything from store clerks to auto mechanics to lawyers and doctors.

The Great Columbian Exchange (15G) The global exchange of crops that occurred after 1492, including the transport of European crops, such as wheat, melons, and grapes, by Christopher Columbus to the island of Hispaniola.

thematic maps (1E) Maps that show the distribution, flow, or connection of one or more characteristics and are used to show distribution.

theories of the state (11C) Theories used by geographers and other scholars to discuss how states operate, particularly those within democratic, capitalist systems.

theory of rural land use (15F) The theory, developed by von Thunen and published in 1826, that determines which crop to cultivate based on an equation that takes into account land rent, output, price, production costs, transportation costs, and distance from market.

Theravada Buddhism (8D) The oldest of the two major branches of Buddhism. Practiced mainly in Sri Lanka, Thailand, Burma, and Cambodia, its beliefs are relatively conservative, holding close to the original teachings of the Buddha.

Third World (18A) Impoverished countries that have frail or corrupt economic and political systems and that aspire to become developed countries.

tiger economies (18F) Quick and effective industrialization in East Asia by a concentration on factory production, government integration with industry, and a reliance on exports.

T-O map (2B) A type of medieval map that was based on Christian theology, showed the world as three continents (Asia, Africa, and Europe), and resembled a "T" inside an "O."

toponymy (7F) The study of place names.

topophilia (2F) A love of place.

topophobia (2F) A fear of place.

Torah (8E) In Judaism, the first five books of the Hebrew scriptures, believed to be the law of God.

tornados (12C) Violent rotating columns of air that are in touch with the surface of the earth.

total fertility rate (TFR) (3E) The number of children a woman can expect to have in her lifetime, given current fertility rates.

totalitarianism (11C) The type of autocracy that has been associated with ideologies of fascism, communism, and religious fundamentalism.

tourism (16H) A huge and varied industry made up of travel agents, hotels, restaurants, attraction developers, cruise, tour guides, guidebooks, and local and regional officials who seek to market their own place.

toxic waste (12G) Waste that poses a risk to human populations.

trade deficit (17A) When imports into a country exceed the number of exports going out of a country.

trade surplus (17A) When exports out of a country exceed the number of imports coming into a country.

traditional religions (8A) Faiths practiced by small, isolated groups of people who largely live in developing areas of the world.

transnational corporation (TNC) (16F) A corporation with many divisions based on production lines or stages in the production chain that cross international boundaries.

transportation facilities (17D) Improvements in the ease and volume of travel, such as airports, expansion of harbors and sea lanes, expansion of a uniform railroad network, and steady extension and upgrading of roadways.

transportation infrastructure (17D) The availability and quality of transportation networks in a country, such as roads and railways.

transportation network (14A) A framework that allows the movement of people and goods. In most cases, it has been composed of surface streets, but several cities have also adopted canals as a means of carrying heavy freight.

travel distance (1F) The distance traveled between places based on existing transportation routes.

travel time (1F) The time it takes to get from one place to another, accounting for different levels of connectivity.

trinary rank-size distributions (13H) The top three cities overwhelm the rest in terms of population.

Tripitaka (8D) The primary teachings of the Buddha; also known as the **Pali Canon**.

tsunami (12C) Large waves spawned by a massive displacement of water caused by volcanoes or earthquakes.

tuberculosis (TB) (4E) A potentially deadly lung disease, also known as TB. There are 9 million new cases each year.

typhoon (12C) A hurricane in the northwestern Pacific Ocean.

U

undeveloped world (18D) Countries in the "bottom billion"; countries that have averaged periods of very small growth and periods of negative growth, no improvement from one generation to the next, and almost no foreign investment.

unifying institutions (10G) Institutions that help promote nationalist ideology and bring members of a nation together.

unitary states (11E) States in which nearly all of the sovereignty and power reside with the central government.

universalizing religions (8A) Faiths that seek to convert nonbelievers to their ranks.

untouchables (8C) Within Hindu society, a group whose jobs are considered to be so spiritually and physically impure that they are below all other people in social status and historically have been widely discriminated against.

urban center (14A) Represents the organizing principle of the city and reflects the vital concerns of the population. In modern times, the main items that constitute the center is the "downtown," where land value is at its peak and where office, banking, and retail functions are located.

urban functions (13G) Specialized functions taken on by cities as a result of an interurban network.

urban hierarchy (13H) The idea that cities are rarely equal in size and importance to each other.

urban morphology (14A) A form of an urban area, which in developing countries tends to include inadequate housing, a fairly modern central business district, and a few well-serviced neighborhoods.

urban network (13C) Cities that are tied together in some meaningful way, which geographers and other urban researchers may describe as functional linkages.

urban population (14A) A population composed of individuals who are not themselves engaged in agriculture yet have to be housed and fed, which poses a challenge to the urban economy.

urbanization (13C) The increase in the percentage of people who live in cities, which eventually outstrips the number of people living in rural areas.

urbanization curve (13E) A way to describe the process by which a society becomes more urban. The curve is a general model of change based on time.

V

Vajrayana (8D) The branch of Buddhism practiced primarily in Tibet and Mongolia.

value added (16A) The difference between the price of the final product and the cost of raw materials, labor, and other inputs.

vassal (10B) Someone who must show fealty and pay some form of tribute to an overlord in return for being able to use the land.

vector (4C) The means by which a disease agent is transmitted to a host, such as a mosquito, tick, fly, or rodent.

Vedas (8C) The holy books of the Hindus.

venture capitalists (16E) Financers who are willing to risk their money on a risky, initial idea in hopes of great gains.

vernacular (7B) Local or isolated to a particular area. In the study of languages, words and phrases unique to a particular region.

vernacular region (1G) A region that people construct in their mind, making them difficult to dissect.

vertical loyalty (10E) A political structure in which the people were expected to owe allegiance to the ruler.

von Humboldt, Alexander (2D) A Prussian explorer and naturalist (1769–1859), who traveled widely, especially in the Americas, categorizing natural objects and writing about the importance of scientific inquiry.

W

walking city (14D) A city in which a majority of people walk to get from one spot to the other, which was the case for every city before 1850.

water diversion (12D) The human alteration of natural water patterns, such as irrigation channels, aqueducts, reservoirs, and similar structures.

water pollution (12D) Human contamination of water resources, such as lakes, rivers, and oceans.

Western values (18B) Important elements of Western culture, including rationalism, science as opposed to religion, and a strong work ethic.

Westphalian State System (10C) Dating from the Treaty of Westphalia in 1648, a system based on the idea of a world composed of autonomous, clearly bounded, sovereign territorial states.

White, Gilbert (12B) The geographer (1911–2006) who pioneered research on natural hazards and human response to flooding.

World Bank (18B) An agency in the effort to promote development that represents a consortium of most of the world's countries. It exists primarily as a lending institution, making loans available to poorer countries and providing advice about the "correct" course of development.

world cities (13I) Cities that are at the top of the global hierarchy; can be defined in terms of attributes or level of interaction and are usually highly populated.

world development (18A) Raising the living standards of the world's poorest countries and, so, reducing disparities between countries in the world.

world systems perspective (18C) The view that the economic system operates as a whole because the economy is global and events in one country have an effect on other countries.

World Trade Organization (WTO) (17A) Represents most of the world's economies and enforces the rules of free trade. The rules are negotiated and signed by most of the world's trading nations in order to smooth the flow of trade between countries.

Y

yellow fever (4E) A mosquito-transmitted viral disease that causes an acute hemorrhagic fever, affecting about 200,000 people worldwide each year.

Z

zero population growth (3E) See **replacement level of fertility**.

Zipf's law (5E) The idea that places or things that are farther apart will have less interaction between them. See also **distance decay**.

Chapter 1 Major Geographic Concepts

Adams, P. C., S. D. Hoelscher, and K. E. Till. *Textures of Place: Exploring Humanist Geographies.* Minneapolis: University of Minnesota Press, 2001.

Broek, J. O. M. *Geography, Its Scope and Spirit.* Columbus, OH: C. E. Merrill Books, 1965.

Carville, E. E., M. Kent, and M. Kenzer. *Concepts in Human Geography.* Lanham, MD: Rowman & Littlefield, 1995.

Clifford, N. J., S. L. Holloway, S. P. Rice, and G. Valentine, eds. *Key Concepts in Geography.* London: Sage, 2009.

Groth, P., and T. Bressi. *Understanding Ordinary Landscapes.* New Haven, CT: Yale University Press, 1997.

Hanson, S. *Ten Geographic Ideas That Changed the World.* New Brunswick, NJ: Rutgers University Press, 1997.

Harries, K. D. *Mapping Crime: Principle and Practice.* Washington, DC: US Department of Justice, Office of Justice Programs, National Institute of Justice, Crime Mapping Research Center, 1999.

Holt-Jensen, A. *Geography, History and Concepts: A Student's Guide.* London: Sage, 1999.

Kolars, J. F., and J. D. Nystuen. *Geography: The Study of Location, Culture, and Environment.* New York: McGraw-Hill, 1974.

Sack, R. *Human Territoriality: Its Theory and History.* Cambridge: Cambridge University Press, 1986.

Zelinsky, W. *The Cultural Geography of the United States.* Englewood Cliffs, NJ: Prentice-Hall, 1973.

Chapter 2 Geography through the Ages

Aitken, S. C., and G. Valentine, eds. *Approaches to Human Geography.* London: Sage, 2006.

Cloke, P., C. Philo, and D. Sadler. *Approaching Human Geography: An Introduction to Contemporary Theoretical Debates.* New York: Guilford Press, 1991.

Golledge, R., and R. J. Stimson. *Spatial Behavior: A Geographic Perspective.* New York: Guilford Press, 1997.

Gould, P., and R. White. *Mental Maps.* 2nd ed. London: Routledge, 1986.

Holt-Jensen, A. *Geography, History and Concepts: A Student's Guide.* London: Sage, 1999.

Ibn Battuta. *Travels in Asia and Africa.* Abingdon, Oxfordshire: Routledge Curzon, 2005.

Johnston, R., and J. Sidaway. *Geography and Geographers.* London: Hodder Education, 2010.

Johnston, R., et al., eds. *The Dictionary of Human Geography.* 5th ed. New York: Wiley-Blackwell, 2009.

Livingstone, D. N. *The Geographical Tradition: Episodes in the History of a Contested Enterprise.* Malden, MA: Blackwell, 1993.

Peet, R. *Modern Geographical Thought.* Malden, MA: Blackwell, 1998.

Sobel, D. *Longitude: The True Story of a Lone Genius Who Solved the Greatest Scientific Problem of His Time.* New York: Walker and Company, 1995.

Unwin, T. *The Place of Geography.* Harlow, Essex: Longman Scientific & Technical, 1993.

Chapter 3 Population

Boserup, E. *The Conditions of Agricultural Growth: The Economics of Agrarian Change under Population Pressure.* Piscataway, NJ: Aldine Transaction, 2005.

Greenhalgh, S., and E. A. Winckler. *Governing China's Population: From Leninist to Neoliberal Biopolitics.* Palo Alto, CA: Stanford University Press, 2005.

Newbold, K. B. *Population Geography: Tools and Issues.* Lanham, MD: Rowman & Littlefield, 2009.

Peters, G. L., and R. P. Larkin. *Population Geography: Problems, Concepts, and Prospects.* 9th ed. Dubuque, IA: Kendall Hunt, 2008.

Preston, S. H., P. Heuveline, and M. Guillot. *Demography: Measuring and Modeling Population Processes.* Malden, MA: Blackwell, 2000.

Veeck, G., et al. *China's Geography: Globalization and the Dynamics of Political, Economic, and Social Change.* Lanham, MD: Rowman & Littlefield, 2007.

Chapter 4 Geography of Health and Disease

Brown, T., S. McLafferty, and G. Moon. *A Companion to Medical Geography.* Malden, MA: Blackwell, 2010.

The Carter Center. "Guinea Worm Disease Eradication." Accessed March 15, 2011. www.cartercenter.org/health/guinea_worm/mini_site/index.html.

Centers for Disease Control and Prevention. "Malaria." Last modified December 3, 2010. www.cdc.gov/MALARIA/.

Centers for Disease Control and Prevention. "Tuberculosis (TB)." Last modified June 14, 2011. www.cdc.gov/tb/.

Centers for Disease Control and Prevention. "Yellow Fever." Last modified November 2, 2007. www.cdc.gov/ncidod/dvbid/yellowfever/index.html.

Crosby, A. W. *America's Forgotten Pandemic: The Influenza of 1918.* Cambridge: Cambridge University Press, 2003.

Joint United Nations Programme on HIV/AIDS (UNAIDS). *Global Report: UNAIDS Report on the Global AIDS Epidemic 2010.* Geneva, Switzerland: UNAIDS, 2010.

Meade, M., and M. Emch. *Medical Geography.* 3rd ed. New York: Guilford Press, 2010.

Oshinsky, D. M. *Polio: An American Story.* New York: Oxford University Press, 2005.

Snow, J. *On the Mode of Communication of Cholera.* London: John Churchill, 1855.

Chapter 5 Migration Flows

Brettell, C., and J. F. Hollifield, eds. *Migration Theory: Talking across Disciplines.* New York: Routledge, 2008.

Department of State. *Trafficking in Persons Report.* 10th ed. Washington, DC: US Department of State, 2010.

Honwana, A. *Child Soldiers in Africa.* Philadelphia: University of Pennsylvania Press, 2006.

Lee, E. S. "A Theory of Migration." *Demography* 3, no. 1 (1966): 47–57.

Manning, P. *Migration in World History.* New York: Routledge, 2005.

Shelley, L. *Human Trafficking: A Global Perspective.* Cambridge: Cambridge University Press, 2010.

Stouffer, S. A. "Intervening Opportunities: A Theory Relating Mobility and Distance." *American Sociological Review* 5, no. 6 (December 1940): 845–67.

United Nations Office on Drugs and Crime (UNODC). *Global Report on Trafficking in Persons.* Vienna, Italy: UNDOC, 2009.

Wessells, M. *Child Soldiers: From Violence to Protection.* Cambridge, MA: Harvard University Press, 2006.

Chapter 6   Culture and Cultural Landscapes

Bale, J. *Sports Geography*. 2nd ed. New York: Routledge, 2003.

Cloke, P. J., P. Crang, and M. Goodwin. *Introducing Human Geographies*. 2nd ed. London: Hodder Arnold, 2005.

Foote, K. E., ed. *Re-reading Cultural Geography*. Austin: University of Texas Press, 1994.

Foster, G. *American Houses: A Field Guide to the Architecture of the Home*. New York: Houghton Mifflin, 2004.

Gabaccia, D. R. *We Are What We Eat: Ethnic Food and the Making of Americans*. Cambridge, MA: Harvard University Press, 2000.

Gladwell, M. *The Tipping Point: How Little Things Can Make a Big Difference*. New York: Little, Brown, 2002.

Graff, T. O. Z., and D. Ashton. "Spatial Diffusion of Wal-Mart: Contagious and Reverse Hierarchical Elements." *Professional Geographer* 46, no. 1 (1994): 19–29.

Hagerstrand, T. *Innovation Diffusion as a Spatial Process*. Translated by Allan Pred. Chicago: University of Chicago Press, 1967.

McAlester, V., and A. L. McAlester. *A Field Guide to American Houses*. New York: Alfred A. Knopf, 1984.

Mitchell, D. *Cultural Geography: A Critical Introduction*. Malden, MA: Blackwell, 2000.

Norton, W. *Cultural Geography: Environments, Landscapes, Identities, Inequalities*. New York: Oxford University Press, 2006.

Pillsbury, R. "Carolina Thunder: A Geography of Southern Stock Car Racing." *Journal of Geography* 73, no. 1 (1974): 39–47.

Pillsbury, R. *No Foreign Food: The American Diet in Time and Place*. Boulder, CO: Westview Press, 1998.

Sauer, C. O. "The Morphology of Landscape." *University of California Publications in Geography* 2, no. 2 (1925): 19–53.

Tuan, Y. *Space and Place: The Perspective of Experience*. Minneapolis: University of Minnesota Press, 1977.

Tuan, Y. *Topophilia: A Study of Environmental Perception, Attitudes, and Values*. Englewood Cliffs, NJ: Prentice-Hall, 1974.

Wallach, B. *Understanding the Cultural Landscape*. New York: Guilford, 2005.

Zelinsky, W. *The Cultural Geography of the United States*. Rev. ed. Englewood Cliffs, NJ: Prentice Hall, 1992.

Chapter 7   The Geography of Language

Christin, A., ed. *History of Writing*. Paris: Flammarion, 2002.

Evans, N. *Dying Words: Endangered Languages and What They Have to Tell Us*. Malden, MA: Wiley-Blackwell, 2010.

Fennell, B. A. *A History of English: A Sociolinguistic Approach*. Malden, MA: Wiley-Blackwell, 2001.

Finegan, E. *Language: Its Structure and Use*. 5th ed. Boston: Thomson Higher Education, 2008.

Fischer, S. R. *A History of Language*. London: Reaktion Books, 1999.

Katzner, K. *The Languages of the World*. 3rd ed. New York: Routledge, 2002.

Lewis, M. P. *Ethnologue: Languages of the World*. Dallas, TX: SIL International, 2009.

Chapter 8   The Geography of Religion

Bass, D. B. *A People's History of Christianity: The Other Side of the Story*. New York: HarperCollins, 2009.

Brown, P. R. L. *The Rise of Western Christendom: Triumph and Diversity, A.D. 200–1000*. 2nd ed. Malden, MA: Blackwell, 2003.

De Lange, N. *An Introduction to Judaism*. Cambridge: Cambridge University Press, 2000.

Flood, G. *An Introduction to Hinduism*. Cambridge: Cambridge University Press, 1996.

Harvey, P. *Buddhism: Teachings, History, and Practices*. Cambridge: Cambridge University Press, 1990.

Keown, D. *Dictionary of Buddhism*. Oxford: Oxford University Press, 2003.

Klostermaier, K. K. *A Survey of Hinduism*. 3rd ed. Albany: State University of New York Press, 2007.

Murray, S. A., R. Huber, and E. Mechem. *Hammond Atlas of World Religions: A Visual History of Our Great Faiths*. Maplewood, NJ: Hammond World Atlas Corporation, 2008.

O'Callaghan, S. *The Compact Guide to World Religions*. Oxford: Lion UK, 2010.

Park, C. C. *Sacred Worlds: An Introduction to Geography and Religion*. London: Routledge, 1994.

Robinson, G. *Essential Judaism: A Complete Guide to Beliefs, Customs and Rituals*. New York: Pocket Books, 2000.

Skilton, A. *A Concise History of Buddhism*. Woodbridge Park, UK: Windhorse, 1997.

Smart, N., F. M. Denny, and F. W. Denny, eds. *Atlas of the World's Religions*. Oxford: Oxford University Press, 2007.

Sonn, T. *A Brief History of Islam*. Malden, MA: Blackwell, 2004.

Stump, R. *The Geography of Religion: Faith, Place, and Space*. Lanham, MD: Rowman & Littlefield, 2008.

Swatos, W. H., Jr., ed. *Encyclopedia of Religion and Society*. Walnut Creek, CA: AltaMira Press, 1998.

Waines, D. *An Introduction to Islam*. 2nd ed. Cambridge: Cambridge University Press, 2003.

Williams, A., ed. *Therapeutic Landscapes*. Farnham, UK: Ashgate, 2007.

Yao, X. *An Introduction to Confucianism*. Cambridge: Cambridge University Press, 2000.

Chapter 9   Race, Ethnicity, and Gender

Aitken, S. C., and G. Valentine, eds. *Approaches to Human Geography*. London: Sage, 2006.

Bayor, R. H., ed. *Race and Ethnicity in America: A Concise History*. New York: Columbia University Press, 2003.

Bernard, S. K. *The Cajuns: Americanization of a People*. Jackson: University of Mississippi Press, 2003.

Dinnerstein, L., and D. M. Reimers. *Ethnic Americans: A History of Immigration*. New York: Columbia University Press, 2009.

Frazier, J. W., and E. L. Tettey-Fio, eds. *Race, Ethnicity, and Place in a Changing America*. Binghamton, NY: Global Academic Publishing, 2006.

Gutman, I. *Resistance: The Warsaw Ghetto Uprising*. New York: Houghton Mifflin, 1994.

Houston, J. W., and J. D. Houston. *Farewell to Manzanar*. New York: Houghton Mifflin, 1973.

Inada, L. F., ed. *Only What We Could Carry: The Japanese American Internment Experience*. San Francisco: California Historical Society, 2000.

Li, W. *Ethnoburb: The New Ethnic Community in Urban America*. Honolulu: University of Hawai'i Press, 2009.

Massey, D., ed. *New Faces in New Places: The Changing Geography of American Immigration*. New York: Russell Sage Foundation, 2008.

Massey, D. *Space, Place, and Gender*. Minneapolis: University of Minnesota Press, 1994.

Miyares, I. M., and C. A. Airriess, eds. *Contemporary Ethnic Geographies in America*. Lanham, MD: Rowman & Littlefield, 2007.

Ng, W. *Japanese American Internment during World War II: A History and Reference Guide*. Westport, CT: Greenwood Press, 2002.

Rose, G. *Feminism and Geography: The Limits of Geographical Knowledge*. Minneapolis: University of Minnesota Press, 1993.

Chapter 10   A World of Nations and States

Agnew, J. A., K. Mitchell, and G. Ó. Tuathail. *A Companion to Political Geography*. Malden, MA: Blackwell, 2003.

Central Intelligence Agency (CIA). *World Factbook 2010*. Washington, DC: CIA, 2010.

Cohen, S. B. *Geopolitics of the World System*. Lanham, MD: Rowman & Littlefield, 2003.

Conversi, D. *Ethnonationalism in the Contemporary World: Walker Connor and the Study of Nationalism*. London: Psychology Press, 2002.

Dorel, G. *Atlas de l'empire américain*. Paris: Editions Autrement, 2006.

Jones, S. B. "A Unified Field Theory of Political Geography." *Annals of the Association of American Geographers* 44, no. 2 (1954): 111–23.

Kaplan, D. H., and J. Häkli. *Boundaries and Place: European Borderlands in Geographical Context*. Lanham, MD: Rowman & Littlefield, 2002.

Muir, R. *Political Geography: A New Introduction*. London: Macmillan, 1997.

Newman, D., and A. Paasi. "Fences and Neighbours in the Postmodern World: Boundary Narratives in Political Geography." *Progress in Human Geography* 22, no. 2 (1998): 186.

Tiryakian, E., and R. Rogowski. *New Nationalisms of the Developed West*. Boston: Allen & Unwin, 1985.

Chapter 11   Geography of Governance and Representation

Farrell, D. M. *Electoral Systems: A Comparative Introduction*. London: Palgrave, 2006.

Hartshorne, R. "The Functional Approach in Political Geography." *Annals of the Association of American Geographers* 40, no. 2 (1950): 95–130.

Lijphart, A., and D. Aitkin. *Electoral Systems and Party Systems*. Oxford: Oxford University Press, 1995.

Morrill, R. L. *Political Redistricting and Geographic Theory*. Washington, DC: Association of American Geographers, 1981.

Shelley, F. M. *Political Geography of the United States*. New York: Guilford Press, 1996.

Chapter 12   Environment and Conservation

Amery, H. A., and A. T. Wolf. *Water in the Middle East: A Geography of Peace*. Austin: University of Texas Press, 2000.

Bechtel, R. B. *Environment and Behavior: An Introduction*. Thousand Oaks, CA: Sage, 1997.

Bechtel, R. B., and A. Churchman. *Handbook of Environmental Psychology*. New York: Wiley and Sons, 2002.

Biello, D. "China Sacks Plastic Bags." Accessed September 24, 2010. www.scientificamerican.com/article.cfm?id=china-sacks-plastic-bags.

Bolt, B. A. *Earthquakes*. New York: W. H. Freeman and Company, 2006.

Castree, N., et al., eds. *Companion to Environmental Geography*. Malden, MA: Wiley-Blackwell, 2009.

Cole, L. W., and S. R. Foster. *From the Ground Up: Environmental Racism and the Rise of the Environmental Justice Movement*. New York: New York University Press, 2001.

Environmental Protection Agency. "Superfund." Last modified June 17, 2011. www.epa.gov/superfund/.

France, R. L., ed. *Handbook of Regenerative Landscape Design*. Boca Raton, FL: CRC Press, 2008.

Meadows, D., J. Randers, and D. Meadows. *The Limits to Growth: The 30-Year Update*. White River Junction, VT: Chelsea Green, 2004.

NOAA/National Weather Service. "The Deadliest Atlantic Tropical Cyclones, 1492–1996." Last modified February 7, 2005. www.nhc.noaa.gov/pastdeadlyapp1.shtml.

Sauer, C. O. "The Morphology of Landscape." *University of California Publications in Geography* 2, no. 2 (1925): 19–53.

Shrader-Frechette, K. *Environmental Justice: Creating Equality, Reclaiming Democracy*. Oxford: Oxford University Press, 2002.

Tchobanoglous, G., and F. Kreith. *Handbook of Solid Waste Management*. 2nd ed. New York: McGraw-Hill, 2002.

Thomas, D. S. G., and A. Goudie, eds. *The Dictionary of Physical Geography*. 3rd ed. Malden, MA: Blackwell, 2000.

Tiwary, A., and J. Colls. *Air Pollution*. 3rd ed. Abingdon, Oxfordshire: Routledge, 2010.

United States Geological Survey. "Earthquakes with 50,000 or More Deaths." Last modified April 14, 2011. http://earthquake.usgs.gov/earthquakes/world/most_destructive.php.

White, G. F. *Selected Writings of Gilbert F. White*. Edited by R. W. Kates and I. Burton. Chicago: University of Chicago Press, 1986.

Chapter 13   Urbanization and Urban Networks

Adams, R. M. *The Evolution of Urban Society: Early Mesopotamia and Prehispanic Mexico*. Chicago: Aldine, 1966.

Cotterell, A. *The Imperial Capitals of China: An Inside View of the Celestial Empire*. London: Pimlico, 2008.

Dublin, T., and P. Marion. "Lowell: The Story of an Industrial City: A Guide to Lowell National Historical Park and Lowell Heritage State Park." Lowell, MA: Official National Park Handbook, 1992.

Leick, G. *Mesopotamia: The Invention of the City*. London: Penguin, 2002.

Sjöberg, G. *The Preindustrial City, Past and Present*. New York: Free Press, 1965.

Smith, D., and M. Timberlake. "Conceptualizing and Mapping the Structure of the World System's City System." *Urban Studies* 32, no. 2 (1995): 287–302.

Chapter 14   The Changing Structure of the City

Berry, B. J. L., and J. D. Kasarda. *Contemporary Urban Ecology*. New York: Macmillan, 1977.

Burgess, E. W. "The Growth of the City: An Introduction to a Research Project." In *The City*, edited by R. Park, E. Burgess, and R. McKenzie, 47–62. Chicago: University of Chicago Press, 1925/1967.

Garreau, J. *Edge City: Life on the New Frontier*. New York: Doubleday, 1991.

Hoyt, H. *The Structure and Growth of Residential Neighborhoods in American Cities*. Washington, DC: Federal Housing Administration, 1939.

Kostof, S. *The City Shaped: Urban Patterns and Meanings through History*. London: Bulfinch, 1991.

Marcuse, P. "The Enclave, the Citadel, and the Ghetto: What Has Changed in the Post-Fordist U.S. City," *Urban Affairs Review* 33 (1997): 228–64.

Marcuse, P., and R. Van Kempen. *Globalizing Cities: A New Spatial Order?* Malden, MA: Wiley-Blackwell, 2000.

Morris, A. E. J. *History of Urban Form: Before the Industrial Revolution*. New York: Wiley, 1994.

Vance, J. *The Continuing City: Urban Morphology in Western Civilization*. Baltimore: Johns Hopkins University Press, 1990.

Chapter 15 The Geography of Economic Activity and Agriculture

Crosby, A. W. *The Columbian Exchange: Biological and Cultural Consequences of 1492*. Westport, CT: Greenwood, 2003.

Diamond, J. *Guns, Germs, and Steel: A Short History of Everybody for the Last 13000 Years*. London: Vintage, 1998.

Fagan, B. M. *Men of the Earth: An Introduction to World Prehistory*. Boston: Little, Brown, 1974.

Kiple Denneth, F., and O. K. Coneè. *The Cambridge World History of Food*. Cambridge: Cambridge University Press, 2000.

Pollan, M. *The Omnivore's Dilemma: A Natural History of Four Meals*. New York: Penguin, 2006.

Chapter 16 Geographies of Production and Consumption

Bernat, G. A. "Convergence in State per Capita Personal Income, 1950–1999." *Survey of Current Business* 81, no. 6 (2001): 36–53.

Dicken, P. *Global Shift: Reshaping the Global Economic Map in the 21st Century*. London: Sage, 2003.

Dunnigan, J., and A. Nofi. "Medieval Life and the Hundred Years War." DENO Partnership, 1997. Last modified 1997. www.hyw.com/Books/History/1_help_c.htm.

Haggett, P. *Geography: A Global Synthesis*. New York: Pearson Education, 2001.

Johnston, R. J., and P. J. Taylor. *Geographies of Global Change: Remapping the World*. Malden, MA: Wiley-Blackwell, 2002.

Jones, G. *Transnational Corporations: A Historical Perspective*. London: Routledge, 1993.

Kellerman, A. "Conditions for the Development of High-Tech Industry: The Case of Israel." *Tijdschrift voor economische en sociale geografie* 93, no. 3 (2002): 270–86.

Maddison, A. *Contours of the World Economy, 1–2030 AD: Essays in Macro-Economic History*. New York: Oxford University Press, 2007.

Meinig, D. W. *The Shaping of America: A Geographical Perspective on 500 Years of History*. Vol. 1, *Atlantic America, 1492–1800*. New Haven, CT: Yale University Press, 1986.

Meinig, D. W. *The Shaping of America: A Geographical Perspective on 500 Years of History*. Vol. 2, *Continental America, 1800–1867*. New Haven, CT: Yale University Press, 1995.

Meyer, S. P. "A Spatial Analysis of Small- and Medium-Sized Information Technology Firms in Canada and the Importance of Local Connections to Institutions of Higher Education." *Canadian Geographer/Le Géographe canadien* 50, no. 1 (2006): 114–34.

Mitchell, R. D., and P. A. Groves. *North America: The Historical Geography of a Changing Continent*. Lanham, MD: Rowman & Littlefield, 1987.

Murray, W. E. *Geographies of Globalization*. London: Routledge, 2006.

Scott, A. J. "The Changing Global Geography of Low-Technology, Labor-Intensive Industry: Clothing, Footwear, and Furniture." *World Development* 34, no. 9 (2006): 1517–36.

Sheppard, E. S., and T. J. Barnes. *A Companion to Economic Geography*. Malden, MA: Wiley-Blackwell, 2002.

Wial, H., and A. Friedhoff. *Bearing the Brunt: Manufacturing Job Loss in the Great Lakes Region, 1995–2005*. The Brookings Institution Metropolitan Policy Program, July 2006. www.brookings.edu/reports/2006/07useconomics_wial.aspx.

Chapter 17 Distribution and Transportation

Garrison, W. L. *Historical Transportation Development*. Research report, Institute of Transportation Studies, University of California, Berkeley, July 2003.

Goss, J. "Geography of Consumption 1." *Progress in Human Geography* 28, no. 3 (2004): 369.

Lowry, J. R. "The Life Cycle of Shopping Centers." *Business Horizons* 40, no. 1 (1997): 77–86.

Marston, S. A., and A. Modarres. "Flexible Retailing: Gap Inc. and the Multiple Spaces of Shopping in the United States." *Tijdschrift voor economische en sociale geografie* 93, no. 1 (2002): 83–99.

Pucher, J. "Transportation Trends, Problems, and Policies: An International Perspective." *Transportation Research Part A: Policy and Practice* 33, no. 7 (1999): 493–504.

Taaffe, E. J., H. L. Gauthier, and M. E. O'Kelly. *Geography of Transportation*. 2nd ed. Upper Saddle River, NJ: Prentice Hall, 1996.

Vanderbilt, T. *Traffic: Why We Drive the Way We Do (and What It Says about Us)*. New York: Knopf, 2008.

Wrigley, N., and A. Currah. "Globalizing Retail and the New e-conomy: The Organizational Challenge of e-commerce for the Retail TNCs." *Geoforum* 37, no. 3 (2006): 340–51.

Wrigley, N., and M. S. Lowe. *Reading Retail: A Geographical Perspective on Retailing and Consumption Spaces*. London: Arnold, 2002.

Chapter 18 Development and Geography

Arndt, H. W. "Economic Development: A Semantic History." *Economic Development and Cultural Change* 29, no. 3 (1981): 457–66.

Chari, S., and S. Corbridge. *The Development Reader*. London: Routledge, 2007.

Collier, P. *The Bottom Billion*. Vol. 7. Oxford: Oxford University Press, 2007.

Contreras, R. "Competing Theories of Economic Development." *Transnational Law & Contemporary Problems* 9 (1999): 93–108.

Easterly, W. R., D. Comin, and E. Gong. *Was the Wealth of Nations Determined in 1000 BC?* Brookings Institution, Global Working Papers 9, 2007. www.brookings.edu/papers/2007/09globaleconomics_easterly.aspx.

Friedman, T. L. *The World Is Flat: A Brief History of the Twenty-First Century*. New York: Picador USA, 2007.

Hoogvelt, A. M. M. *Globalization and the Postcolonial World: The New Political Economy of Development*. Baltimore: Johns Hopkins University Press, 2001.

Kapur, A. "Foreign Affairs: Poor but Prosperous." *Atlantic Monthly* 282, no. 3 (1998): 40–45.

Marks, N., S. Abdallah, A. Simms, and S. Thompson. *The Happy Planet Index*. London: New Economics Foundation, 2006.

Perry, M., L. Kong, and B. S. A. Yeoh. *Singapore: A Developmental City State*. New York: Wiley, 1997.

Potter, R. B., T. Binns, D. W. Smith, and J. A. Elliott. *Geographies of Development: An Introduction to Development Studies*. Upper Saddle River, NJ: Pearson Education, 2008.

Véron, R. "The 'New' Kerala Model: Lessons for Sustainable Development." *World Development* 29, no. 4 (2001): 601–17.

White, A. "A Global Projection of Subjective Well-Being: A Challenge to Positive Psychology." *Psychtalk* 56 (2007): 17–20.

Williams, G., P. Meth, and K. Willis. *Geographies of Developing Areas: The Global South in a Changing World*. London: Taylor & Francis, 2009.

World Bank. *Atlas of Global Development*. Washington, DC: World Bank, 2009.

Preface

Jaschik, S. "Why Students Read Textbooks (or Don't)." *Inside Higher Ed*, August 20, 2007.

Chapter Opener Design Element

NASA

Photos

Chapter 1

Opener: © PhotoLink/Getty RF; p. 3: NASA; 1A.2a: © www.sitesatlas.com; 1A.2b: Map courtesy of Ohio Department of Transportation; 1C.1a: © Medioimages/Getty RF; 1C.1b: © Getty RF; 1C.3a: ©RB-DESKKART www.welt-atlas.de; 1C.4: © Jon Malinowski; 1D.3: © Al Crespo; 1D.4: © Comstock Images/Alamy RF; 1E.1: © Susan C. Smith; 1E.2: CDC/NCHS; 1E.3: © New York City Police Department (NYPD), 1997/Doug Williamson; 1F.2: © ICOS; 1G.9: © Stacy Visconti; 1H.1a–c: © Megan Petroski; 1H.2a: © Jon Malinowski; 1H.2b: © Donley's Wild West Town, Union, IL; 1H.2c: © Brand X Pictures/Jupiterimages RF; 1H.3a: © Corbis RF; 1H.3b: © Leslie Horn.

Chapter 2

Opener: © Photodisc RF; p. 25: NASA; 2A.1: *The Yorck Project: 10.000 Meisterwerke der Malerei*. DVD-ROM, 2002. ISBN 3936122202. Distributed by DIRECT MEDIA Publishing GmbH; 2A.2: Reto Stockli, NASA Earth Observatory; 2A.3: Photograph is from The National Library of Poland; 2C.1b: Cover image from Richard Henry Major, F.S.A., *The Discoveries of Prince Henry the Navigator, and Their Results; Being the Narrative of the Discovery by Sea, Within One Century, of More Than Half the World*, 1877, Library of the University of Michigan; 2C.2: Reto Stockli, NASA Earth Observatory; 2C.3a: Marine watch, in silver pair-case, lying on cushions in mahogany carrying case, by John Harrison and Son, 1770, London (see also 71016 & 71017)/Worshipful Company of Clockmakers' Collection, UK/The Bridgeman Art Library International; 2C.3b: Charles Deering McCormick Library of Special Collections, Northwestern University Library; 2C.4b: © Melba Photo Agency/PunchStock RF; 2D.1a: © bpk, Berlin/Nationalgalerie, Staatliche Museen, Berlin, Germany/Klaus Goeken/Art Resource, NY; 2D.2: From Professor Carl Ritter of Berlin, *Geographical Studies, Translated from the Original German by William Leonard Gage*, 1863, Library of the University of Michigan; 2E.1: © Digital Vision/PunchStock RF; 2F.2–2F.3: © Jon Malinowski; 2G.2a: © Time & Life Pictures/Getty Images; 2G.2b: Project Gutenberg; 2H.1 (left, right): © Jon Malinowski; 2H.2: US Army, 1961.

Chapter 3

Opener: © Getty RF; p. 45: NASA; 3B.3: © Jon Malinowski; 3E.3: Senior Airman Stacia Zachary, United States Air Force; 3F.2: CDC; 3F.4: © Jon Malinowski; 3H.2: © David A. Harvey/National Geographic/Getty Images; 3I.2a: © Getty RF; 3I.2b: © Corbis RF; 3I.2c: © Jon Malinowski; 3J.1 (left): © PunchStock RF; 3J.2 (right): © Jon Malinowski.

Chapter 4

Opener: James Gathany/CDC; p. 71: NASA; 4A.1: © Bettmann/Corbis; 4A.2–4A.3: Reto Stockli, NASA Earth Observatory; 4B.1 (top left): Charles Farmer/CDC; 4B.1 (top right, bottom left): CDC; 4B.1 (bottom middle): Charles Farmer/CDC; 4B.1 (bottom right): Mary Hilpertshauser/CDC; 4C.1 (left): Courtesy of the National Library of Medicine; 4C.1 (right): Courtesy Professor R.R. Frerichs, UCLA Department of Epidemiology, http://www.ph.ucla.edu/epi/snow .html; 4C.2 (left): C. S. Goldsmith and A. Balish/CDC; 4C.3 (top right): Dr. Shirley Maddison/CDC; 4E.4 (left): © 2007 The Carter Center; 4E.4 (right): © 2010 The Carter Center; 4E.5 (right): Library of Congress, Prints & Photographs Division, LC-USZ62-138117; 4F.1: *World Health Statistics 2010.* © WHO 2010. All rights reserved. http://www.who .int/whosis/whostat/EN_WHS10_Full.pdf (Fig. 12, p. 114).

Chapter 5

Opener: © Doug Pensinger/Getty Images; p. 91: NASA; 5A.1: © Ingram Publishing RF; 5A.2a: Courtesy of National Archives and Records Administration; 5A.2b: © Corbis RF; 5A.2c: © Clark Brennan/Alamy RF; 5A.2d: © Marco Di Lauro/Getty Images; 5B.1: © PhotoLink/Getty RF; 5B.2: Reto Stockli, NASA Earth Observatory; 5B.3 (top): Image Science and Analysis Laboratory, NASA-Johnson Space Center. "The Gateway to Astronaut Photography of Earth." http://eol.jsc.nasa .gov/scripts/sseop/photo.pl?mission=ISS019&roll=E& frame=7720; 5B.3 (bottom): © Jon Malinowski; 5B.4: © Ingram Publishing RF; 5C.1 (right): © Jon Malinowski; 5C.2: © Eddie Gerald/Alamy; 5C.3 (left): © Marco Di Lauro/Getty Images; 5D.3 (left): USAID; 5E.2 (right): SMSgt. David H. Kipp/Department of Defense; 5E.3 (top left): © PhotoAlto/PunchStock RF; 5E.3 (bottom left): © Ingram Publishing RF; 5E.3 (bottom right): © Getty RF; 5F.2: © Corbis RF; 5F.3: Library of Congress, Prints & Photographs Division, LC-DIG-nclc-05054; 5F.4: © Jon Malinowski; 5G.2: © Volkmar K. Wentzel/Getty Images; 5G.3: © Comstock/PunchStock RF.

Chapter 6

Opener: © Jon Malinowski; p. 111: NASA; 6A.1: © Getty RF; 6B.1: © Koichi Kamoshida/Getty Images; 6B.2 (top left): US Army Photo; 6B.2 (top right): © Getty RF; 6B.2 (left): © Jon Malinowski; 6B.2 (bottom): © Corbis RF; 6C.1: © Jon Malinowski; 6C.2a: *The House Furnishing Review*, January 1902, p. 65. I.B. Scott & Company, Philadelphia; 6C.2b: *The House Furnishing Review*, July 1893. I.B. Scott & Company, Philadelphia; 6C.2c: *The House Furnishing Review*, January 1902, p. 65. I.B. Scott & Company, Philadelphia; 6C.2d: *American Monthly Illustrated Review of Reviews*, December 1905, p. 107; 6C.2e: *The House Furnishing Review*, January 1902, p. 7. I.B. Scott & Company, Philadelphia; 6C.2f: *The House Furnishing Review*, July 1893. I.B. Scott & Company, Philadelphia; 6C.3: © PhotoLink/Getty RF; 6D.1: © Mustafa Ozer/AFP/Getty Images; 6D.3: Engraving No. NWDNS-208-FS-3200-5. "Paul Revere's Ride." [Electronic Records]. Office for Emergency Management. Office of War Information. Overseas Operations Branch. New York Office. News and Features Bureau. Picture Division; Record Group 208: Records of the Office of War Information, 1926–1951; National Archives at College Park–Archives II (College Park, MD). NAIL Control Number: NWDNS-208-FS-3200-5; 6D.4: © Mark Lennihan, file/AP Photo; 6D.5–6D.7 (right): © Jon Malinowski; 6D.9: Library of Congress, Prints & Photographs Division, LC-DIG-ppmsca-25438; 6F.1 (left): © Alamy RF; 6F.1 (bottom left): © Creatas/Jupiterimages RF; 6F.1 (right): © PunchStock RF; 6F.1 (bottom right): © Jon Malinowski; 6G.1: © Getty RF; 6G.2: © Corbis RF; 6G.3: © Digital Vision/Getty RF; 6G.4: © Getty RF; 6H.1a–b: © Jon Malinowski; 6H.2a: Library of Congress, Prints & Photographs Division, HABS IND,39-MAD,34-in5; 6H.2b: Library of Congress, Prints & Photographs Division, HABS IND,39-MAD,5-in5; 6H.3a: © Jon Malinowski; 6H.3b: Library of Congress, Prints & Photographs Division, HABS DEL,1-DOV,10-de19; 6H.4a: Library of Congress, Prints & Photographs Division, HABS MO,26-JEFCI,4-mo13; 6H.4b: © Jon Malinowski; 6H.5a: Library of Congress, Prints & Photographs Division, HABS SC,30-LAUR,2-sc22; 6H.5b: Library of Congress, Prints & Photographs Division, HABS TENN,57-JASCO,2-tn18; 6H.6a: © Getty RF; 6H.6b: © Sears Brands, LLC. All rights reserved; 6H.7a–b: © Jon Malinowski; 6I.2b: © Greg Nicholas/iStockphoto; 6I.3: © Matt Hurdle; p. 133: US Geological Survey, Department of the Interior/USGS.

Chapter 7

Opener: © Jon Malinowski; p. 135: NASA; 7A.1: © Prehistoric/Getty Images; 7A.2: © Brand X Pictures/Jupiterimages RF; 7A.3: © Photodisc Collection/Getty RF; 7B.1: © PhotoLink/Getty RF; 7B.2: © Copyright 1997 IMS Communications Ltd./Capstone Design. All Rights Reserved RF; 7B.3: © Getty RF; 7C.1: © Jon Malinowski; 7C.2: © PhotoAlto RF; 7E.1: © Corbis RF; 7E.2: Reto Stockli, NASA Earth Observatory; 7F.1: © Comstock Images RF; 7G.1: © Comstock Images/Jupiterimages RF; 7G.2: © William Ryall 2010; 7G.3: © Robert Laberge/AFP/Getty Images.

Chapter 8

Opener: © Jon Malinowski; p. 155: NASA; 8A.1 (left, left middle): © Jon Malinowski; 8A.1 (right middle): © PhotoLink/Getty RF; 8A.1 (right): © Brand X Pictures/Getty RF; 8B.2: © Jon Malinowski; 8B.3: © Getty RF; 8B.4: © Corbis RF; 8B.5: © Jon Malinowski; 8B.6: © PhotoLink/Getty RF; 8B.7–8C.3a: © Jon Malinowski; 8C.3b: © Win Initiative/Getty Images; 8D.1: © Jon Malinowski; 8D.3: © Corbis RF; 8E.2: © 1998 Copyright IMS Communications Ltd./Capstone Design. All Rights Reserved RF; 8F.1: © Jon Malinowski; 8F.2: © Getty RF; 8F.3: © Image Source/PunchStock RF; 8G.2: © Reza/Getty Images; 8G.3: © PhotoLink/Getty RF; 8G.4: © Melba Photo Agency/PunchStock RF; 8G.5: © AGE Fotostock RF; 8H.1: © Nabeel Turner/Getty Images; 8H.2–8H.4a: © Corbis RF; 8H.4b: © Jon Malinowski; 8H.5: © Alamy RF; 8I.1: © Dr. Parvinder Sethi; 8I.2: © Bruno Barbier/Getty Images; 8I.3: © Jon Malinowski; 8I.4: © PhotoLink/Getty RF; 8I.5: © Mike Gadd. http://www.flickr.com/photos/mikegadd; 8I.6: © Jon Malinowski; 8J.1: © J. Stephen Conn; 8J.2: © Matthew J. Aho; 8J.3: © Jon Malinowski; 8J.4: © Mike Camille; 8J.5: © Corbis RF.

Chapter 9

Opener: © 2006 Glowimages, Inc. All Rights Reserved RF; p. 183: NASA; 9A.2b: © Louisiana Department of Culture, Recreation and Tourism; 9A.3a: Library of Congress, Prints & Photographs Division, LC-USZC2-1109; 9A.3b: Library of Congress Prints & Photographs Division, LC-USZ62-115416; 9B.1: Library of Congress, Prints & Photographs Division, LC-DIG-pprrs-00363; 9B.2: © Jon Malinowski; 9B.3: © Andreas Steinbichler/AP Photo; 9B.4: © Blend Images/Getty RF; 9C.1 (top, bottom): © Jon Malinowski; 9C.2: Library of Congress, Prints & Photographs Division, National Child Labor Committee Collection, LC-USZ62-29125; 9C.3: © PhotoLink/Getty RF; 9C.5: © WireImage for Omega Watches/Getty Images; 9C.6–9C.7: © Jon Malinowski; 9D.1: US Census Bureau, Census 2000 special tabulation. American Factfinder at factfinder.census.gov provides census data and mapping tools; 9E.1: Adapted by author from NASA/JPL/NGA; 9E.3: © Andrew Wong/Getty Images; 9F.1 (left): © Corbis RF; 9F.1 (right): © Patrick Baz/AFP/Getty Images; 9F.1 (bottom): © Corbis RF; 9F.2 (left): © Jon Malinowski; 9F.2 (right): © Corbis RF.

Chapter 10

Opener: © Alexander Zemlianichenko/AP Photo; p. 203: NASA; 10A.2: © Kyodo/AP Photo; 10B.1: Courtesy of the University of Texas Libraries, The University of Texas at Austin; 10C.1: From 1491: *New Revelations of the Americas Before Columbus* by Charles C. Mann, copyright © 2005 by Charles C. Mann. Used by permission of Alfred A. Knopf, a division of Random House, Inc.; 10C.3: © Chris Hellier/Corbis; 10D.1: © Bill Ray/Time Life Pictures/Getty Images; 10D.2: Courtesy of the University of Texas Libraries, The University of Texas at Austin; 10D.3: Reprinted from *Political Geography*, 16(6), N. Kliot, Y.

Line Art and Text

3J.1 (right): Data from US Census Bureau, "Focus on Adolescent Fertility in the Developing World," 1996; 3J.2 (left): Data from *World Population Prospects, 2008 Revision*, United Nations, Department of Economic and Social Affairs (DESA), Population Division, New York.

Chapter 4

4A.3: Data from Yale Center for the Study of Globalization; 4B.2: Redrawn after Meade and Earickson, *Medical Geography*, New York: Guilford Press; 4C.2 (right), 4C.3 (left), summary activity: Data from Centers for Disease Control; 4C.3 (bottom): Data from Centers for Disease Control, http://wwwnc.cdc.gov/travel/yellowbook/2010/chapter-5/schistosomiasis.aspx#1411; 4D.1, 4D.2: Data from the 2010 UNAIDS Report on the Global AIDS Epidemic at http://www.unaids.org/GlobalReport/Global_report.htm; 4E.1: Data from Center for Disease Control, http://www.cdc.gov/malaria/map/; 4E.2: Data from World Health Organization; 4E.3: Data from Centers for Disease Control, http://wwwnc.cdc.gov/travel/yellowbook/2010/chapter-2/yellow-fever.aspx; 4E.5 (left): Data from Office of the Public Health Service Historian, US Department of Health & Human Services; 4F.2: Data from UNEP/GRID-Arendal, *Access to safe drinking water, UNEP/GRID-Arendal Maps and Graphics Library*, http://maps.grida.no/go/graphic/access-to-safe-drinking-water; 4F.3: Data from UNICEF, http://www.unicef.org/wash/files/JMP_report_2010.pdf; 4F.4: Data from United Nations FAO, http://www.fao.org/fileadmin/templates/ess/documents/publications_studies/statistical_yearbook/yearbook2009/pdf/map14.pdf; 4G.1: Data from General Electric, http://www.ge.com/innovation/healthymagination/images/feature-health-cost.png; 4G.2: Data from Centers for Disease Control, http://www.cdc.gov/nchs/data/hus/hus09.pdf.

Chapter 5

5C.1 (left): Data from United Nations ODC, http://www.unodc.org/documents/data-and-analysis/tocta/3.Smuggling_of_migrants.pdf; p. 96: Tanya's quotation from US Department of State Publication 11150, *Trafficking in Persons Report*, June 2004; 5C.3 (right): Data from Coalition to Stop the Use of Child Soldiers, http://www.childsoldiersglobalreport.org/files/2008_child_soldiers_map.pdf; 5D.1, 5D.2: Data from UN High Commissioner for Refugees; 5D.3 (right): Data from USAID, http://www.usaid.gov/locations/sub-saharan_africa/countries/sudan/images/satellite/index.html; 5E.2 (top): Redrawn after E. Lee, "A Theory of Migration," *Demography* 1966, 3:47–57; 5F.1, 5G.1, 5G.4: Data from US Census Bureau.

Chapter 6

6A.2: From Arthur Getis and Judith Getis, eds., *The United States and Canada: The Land and the People, Second Edition*. Copyright © 2001 The McGraw-Hill Companies, Dubuque, Iowa. Reprinted by permission. All Rights Reserved; 6D.8: Data from Texas Education Agency, http://ritter.tea.state.tx.us/student.assessment/resources/online/2009/taks_g11_ss/11socialstudies.htm.

Chapter 7

7D.2: Redrawn after Raven I. McDavid, Jr. "The Dialects of American English," in W. Nelson Francis, *The Structure of American English* (New York: Ronald Press, 1958); "Regional Dialects in the United States," *Webster's New World Dictionary*, 2nd College Edition (New York: Simon and Schuster, 1980); and Gordon R. Wood, *Vocabulary Change* (Carbondale: Southern Illinois University Press, 1971), Map 83, p. 358; 7F.2: Redrawn after Zelinsky, W. (1967). "Classical Town Names in the United States: The Historical Geography of an American Idea," *Geographical Review*, 57: 463–495; summary activity: © Nova Development.

Chapter 8

summary activity: © Nova Development.

Chapter 9

9A.2 (left): Data from US Census Bureau; 9C.4: Data from US Census Bureau, "Racial and Ethnic Residential Segregation in the United States: 1980–2000"; 9E.2: Data from CIA; 9G.1, 9G.2: Data from United Nations Statistical Division.

Chapter 10

10D.2: Data from http://www.lib.utexas.edu/maps/africa/south_african_homelands.gif; 10D.4: Data from Dr. Steven Oluic; 10F.1: Basemap © Map Resources; 10F.2: Data from The Atlas of Canada, 2006; 10F.4: Data from http://www.lib.utexas.edu/maps/middle_east_and_asia/kurdish_86.jpg; 10F.5: Data from deBlij & Muller, 2003; 10G.2: Data from CIA; 10I.1: Data from Mackinder, Halford J., *Democratic Ideals and Reality: A Study in the Politics of Reconstruction*, New York: Henry Holt & Co., 1919; and Mackinder, Halford J., "The Geographical Pivot of History," *Geographical Journal*, Vol. 23, No. 4 (April 1904), pp. 421–437.

Chapter 11

11A.1: Data from Toyota Global Website, 2010; 11A.2: Data from http://www.catholicbishops.ie/dioceses/; 11C.4: Clay Bennett Editorial Cartoon used with the permission of Clay Bennett, The Washington Post Writers Group and the Cartoonist Group. All rights reserved; 11E.4: Redrawn after Geographic Guide Pictures of Europe, http://www.pictures-europe.com/map/france-map.jpg; 11E.6, 11G.4: © Map Resources; 11E.8: Data from GraphicMaps.com; 11E.9: Data from http://news.bbc.co.uk/2/hi/europe/country_profiles/1002141.stm; 11F.5, 11F.6, 11F.7, 11F.8, 11F.9, 11F.10, 11G.1: Data from CIA Factbook; 11G.2: Data from http://agonist.org/20100203/kremlin_shocked_as_kaliningrad_stages_huge_anti_government_protest; 11G.3: Data from http://media.photobucket.com/image/berlin%20map/artsglass/you%20rock/berlinmap_01.jpg?o=21; 11I.2: Data from http://atlas.nrcan.gc.ca/site/english/aboutus/100anniversary/carto_exhibit/elections.html/.

Chapter 12

12A.1: After Sauer, "The Morphology of Landscape," University of California Publications in Geography, 2(2), 1925; 12G.1: Data from Environmental Protection Agency; 12H.1, 12H.3: Data from CIA; 12H.2, 12H.4: Data from US Energy Information Administration; summary activity: © Map Resources.

Chapter 13

13B.3: Data from http://www.sacrificeworldwide.com/2011_History_ChangAnXian.asp; 13B.4: Redrawn after Burstein, Stanley M. and Richard Sheck, *World History: Ancient Civilizations*, Holt, Rinehart, & Winston; 13D.2: Redrawn after A. E. Morris, *History of Urban Form, Third Edition*, © 1994 Longman, Figure 8.55, p. 291; 13D.3: Data from http://christopherjoye.blogspot.com/2010/07/great-treasury-paper-on-china.html; 13F.1: Data from Population Reference Bureau; 13H.1: Data from Paul Knox and Linda McCarthy, *Urbanization, Second Edition*, © 2005, Pearson, Figure 3.15, p. 66; 13H.2: Redrawn after Gilles Pecout, *Atlas de l'histoire de France XIX–XXI siècle*, © 2007, Autrement; 13H.3 (left): Data from CIA Factbook; 13I.1, summary activity: Adapted from P. J. Taylor, D. R. F. Walker, and J. V. Beverstock, "Firms and Their Global Service Networks." In S. Sassen, ed. (2002), *Global Networks, Linked Cities*, New York: Routledge, pp. 93–115.

Chapter 14

14D.3, 14D.4: Redrawn from "The Nature of Cities" by C. D. Harris and E. L. Ullman in volume no. 242 of *The Annals of the American Academy of Political and Social Science*. Copyright © 1945 The American Academy of Political and Social Science, Philadelphia, PA; 14G.4: Redrawn from Larry Ford, "A New and Improved Model of Latin American City Structure," in *Geographical Review* 86 (1996), The American Geographical Society.

Chapter 15

15C.1: Redrawn and translated from Gerard Dorel, *Atlas de l'empire americain*, © 2006, Autrement, p. 22; 15F.3: Data from Kolars and Nystuen, *Geography: The Study of Location, Culture, and Environment*, © 1974 The McGraw-Hill Companies, p. 258.

Chapter 16

16A.2: Redrawn from http://www.tc.umn.edu/~tmisa/102/images/map_industry-7.gif; 16C.2: Redrawn after Paul Groves, *The Northeast and Regional Integration, 1800–1860 in North America: Historical Geography of a Changing Continent, Second Edition*, © 2001 Rowman & Littlefield, Figure 9.3, p. 200; 16C.3: Redrawn after *National Integration of Regional Economies in North America: Historical Geography of a Changing Continent, Second Edition*, © 2001 Rowman & Littlefield, Figure 14.4, p. 339; 16D.5: Data from National Resources Defense Council 2009 http://img36.imageshack.us/img36/9106/oilgasmaplg.jpg; 16E.1: Data from *Wired*, July 2000; 16F.1: Data from Williams et al., *Geographies of Developing Areas*, © 2009 Routledge; 16F.3: Data from Bayer Corporation http://www.bayer.com/; 16F.4: Data from Toyota Motor North America, Inc.; 16F.5, 16F.6: Data from *Fortune*, 2007; 16G.1: Redrawn after Peter Jackson, "Consumption in a Globalizing World," in *Geographies of Global Change*, by Johnnston, Taylor, & Watts, eds., © 2002 Blackwell Publishers, Figure 18.1; 16H.2: Data from World Development Indicators via NationMaster.

Chapter 17

17A.2: Data from World Trade Organization; 17A.3: Redrawn after Warwick Murray, *Geographies of Globalization*, © 2006, Routledge, Map 4.5; 17D.3: Data from McIlwraith and Muller, *North America: The Historical Geography of a Changing Continent*, © 2001 Rowman & Littlefield, Figure 8.1; 17E.3: Redrawn after William Cronon, *Nature's Metropolis: Chicago and the Great West*, © 1991 Norton, p. 77; 17F.1: Data from National Personal Transportation Survey; 17F.2: Data from US Census Bureau; 17G.1: Data from US Bureau of Economic Analysis, Survey of Current Business, April 2007, http://www.bea.gov/national/nipaweb/SelectTable.asp?Selected=N; 17G.2: Redrawn from Arthur Getis and Judith Getis, "Christaller's Central Place Theory," *Journal of Geography*, 1966; 17H.1: Unpublished data from Jupiter Research, Inc., New York, NY.

Chapter 18

18A.1, 18A.2: Data from the World Bank, 2008; 18A.4: Data from Adrian White, "A Global Projection of Subjective Well-Being: A Challenge to Positive Psychology?" University of Leicester School of Psychology, 2006; 18A.5: Data from Conservation International, 2008; 18B.3: Data from Angus Maddison, "Contours of the World Economy, 1–2030 AD: Essays in Macro-Economic History," © 2007, New York: Oxford University Press, p. 282; 18B.5: Data from International Telecommunications Union; 18C.6: Data from United Nations Conference on Trade & Development (UNCTAD) Handbook of Statistics http://www.nationsencyclopedia.com/WorldStats/UNCTAD-export-import-concentration-index.html; 18D.1: Data from UNCTAD and United Nations Development Program; 18E.2: Data from the World Bank and *Atlas of Global Development*, 2009, pp. 14–15; 18E.3: Data from the World Bank and *Atlas of Global Development*, 2009, pp. 32–22; 18F.2: Data from the World Bank; 18G.2: Data from http://commons.wikimedia.org/wiki/File:Human_Development_Index_for_Indian_states_in_2001.png.

INDEX

M

Macedonia, Republic of, conflict
    over naming, 150
Mackinder, Halford, 222
macrosale environment, 75
Mahan, Alfred, 222
Mahayana form of Buddhism, 162, 163
maize
    domestication of, 335
    gains from Green Revolution, 65
majoritarian electoral system, 250
malapportionment, 250–51
malaria
    effects of environment on, 72, 80
    global distribution of, 80
    overview, 80
Malawi
    HIV in, 79
    human development ranking, 405
Malawi, Lake (Malawi, Mozambique,
    Tanzania), 405
Malayo-Polynesian language family, 143
Malaysia
    Filipino refugees in camps in, 99
    high-technology industry in, 357
    rubber products, production of, 403
    as tiger economy, 409
Maldives, as micro-state, 210
males. See also gender
    treatment by parents, 197
Mali
    Guinea worm disease in, 82
    as part of culture hearth, 122
Malthus, Thomas (Essay on the
    Principle of Population, An), 64
manufacturing. See industry
Manzanar, 186
Mao Zedong (chief-of-state, China), 233
maps
    ancient, 26–27
    crime, 12
    demonstrating pattern with, 5
    during Renaissance period, 30
    spatial distributions, mapping, 12–13
maquiladora zone, 221, 349
Marchlewski, Julian, 149
Mardi Gras, 184
market capitalization, 331
marketing in commodity chain, 363
marketplace, 305
Marx, Karl, 39, 392
Marxism
    philosophies, 38, 39
    theories of the state, 232–33
Massachusetts
    functional specializations within
        Boston, 292
    location of 19th-century industry
        in, 14
    mental map of housing project in
        Boston, 36
    radius of Boston in 1850, 310
    rank-size shift of Boston, 294
mass consumption, 362–63
mass migration, 94
mass production, 287, 346–47
materialism, 362, 363
Mayans, as part of culture hearth, 122
Mayflower, 144
McCain, John, 4
Meadows, Donella (Limits to Growth,
    The), 272
measurement, as element of geographic
    knowledge, 26–27

Médecins Sans Frontières (Doctors
    without Borders), 99
Medicaid, 86
medical geography, 71
Medicare, 86
Mediterranean Sea
    ancient conceptions of, 26–27
    Venice (Italy) along the, 8
Mellinger, Andrew ("Geography of
    Poverty and Wealth, The"), 391
Mennonite people, 191
mental maps, 9, 36
mentifacts, 117
Mercalli scale, 260
mercantilism, 375
merchants, as part of capitalism, 326,
    327, 328
mercury poisoning, 274
Meso-America
    cities, emergence of, 282
    domestication of crops, 335
Mesopotamia
    as culture hearth, 122
    origins of modern writing found
        in, 136
mesoscale environment, 75
methyl mercury, 274
metropole, 207
Mexico
    city-size, disparities in, 295
    density of Mexico City, 308
    domestication of crops, 332
    as key production center, rise of, 349
    maquiladora on border with US, 221
    Mexico City as capital city and
        capital region, 242
    as tourist destination, 365
Mexico, Gulf of, damage from oil
    spills, 273
Michigan
    changes to culture from immigration
        in Dearborn, 93
    Dearborn as ethnoburb, 190
Michigan, Lake (Canada, US), 7
microscale environment, 75
Microsoft, 356
micro-states, 210
Middle Ages, decline of geography
    during, 28–29
Middle America
    as culture hearth, 122
    external voting rights, 235
    population densities, 48–49
    urbanization pattern, 290
Middle East
    conflict over names of places, 150
    domestication of crops, 332, 335
    urbanization pattern, 291
middle-income sectors, 311
migration
    consequences of, 104–5
    defined, 92
    flows, 91–107
    human trafficking, 96–97
    mapping human, 15
    measures of, 95
    versus movement, 92–93
    overview, 91
    reasons for, 100–3
    refugees, 98–99
    repatriation, 99
    types of, 94–95
    in United States, history of, 91, 106–7
militarized boundaries, 220
milk, problems with digesting, 336

millet, domestication of, 123, 335
Minamata Disease, 274
minaret, 176
Minoan civilization, as culture
    hearth, 123
minority national group, 216–17
Mississippi River (US), human
    adjustment to flooding along,
    258, 259
Missouri Compromise, 16
mixed agricultural economy, 336
mixed economies, 231, 329
mixed electoral system, 250
modal splits, 381
modernism, 40
modernization theory, 397, 398
modern state system, 208, 209
moment magnitude scale, 260
Monaco
    crude birth rate in, 54
    as micro-state, 210
    population density, 49
monks, in Buddhist society, 163
monotheistic religions, 157, 166
Montgomery Ward, 386
more developed countries
    development in, 392–95
    industrial farming practices in, 340
    life expectancies, 47
    migration, 91
    mortality rates, 56
    population growth, 45
    population transition model,
        problems with, 60
    total fertility rates, 55
    urbanism, early spread of,
        279, 281–83
    urbanization pattern, 289, 290–91
Morocco, housing stock of, 302
morphology of cities, early, 302–3
mortality
    measures of, 56
    and population change (see
        population change)
mosques, 171
mosquitos
    Anopheles, 80
    diseases spread by, 72, 80
Motherland Is Calling poster, 216
motor vehicles. See automobiles
movements between places, 92, 93
movement versus migration, 92–93
mudslides as environmental
    hazard, 258
muessin, 176
Mugabe, Robert (president,
    Zimbabwe), 233
Mughal Empire (India), 208
Muhammad, 170–71, 173, 179
multidivisional corporations, 359
multinational state, 214–15
multiplier effect, 353
multiscalar, patterns as, 5
multistate nation, 215
multivariate, patterns as, 5
Murdoch, Rupert, 232
music regions, 17, 121
Muslim law, 172
mystico-religious sites, 179

N

Nanak, Guru, 174
Napoleon, 207
Napoleonic Code, 241

NASCAR
    expansion of interest, 130
    home locations of drivers, 114
    patterns in, 130
nation
    boundaries and borderlands,
        218–21
    civic nations, 212
    defined, 212
    ethnic nations, 212
    markers of, 212–13
    nationalism as ideology and force,
        216–17
    sovereignty, legitimacy, and
        territoriality, 204–5
    and states, relationship between,
        214–15
National Association of
    Manufacturers, 352
National Geographic Society, 33
National Health Service (United
    Kingdom), 86
national highway system, 379
nationalism as ideology and force,
    216–17
nationalism as marker for nation, 213
national landscapes, 213
national powers in US, 238
nation-state, 214
nation-state ideal, 214
Native Americans
    forced migrations of, 94, 95
    place names derived from, 148, 149
    religions as traditional, 157
    reservations, 247
    sacred spaces, 179
natural boundaries, 218
natural disasters. See natural hazards
natural environment, 256–57
natural gas
    geography of, 270, 271
    production, 354
natural hazards, 258–61
    cognitive factors, 259
    defined, 258
    earthquakes (see earthquakes)
    hurricanes (see hurricanes)
    nonstructural responses to, 258–59
    perceptions of, 258
    situation factors, 259
    structural responses to, 258–59
    tornados (see tornados)
naturalization ceremonies, 94
natural landscape, 124, 256–57
natural population change, 56–59
natural selection, 334
nature as gendered, 197
Nauru, as micro-state, 210
Navajo, 179
neighborhood/community centers and
    strips, 384, 385
neighborhood effect, 249
neocolonialism, 396–97
neo-European realm, 400
neoliberalism, 232, 398
Neolithic Period, 324
Neolithic Revolution, 46–47
neo-Malthusians, 64–65
Nepal, Sarda River as natural boundary
    with India, 219
Netherlands
    development process in, 398
    as empire, 207
    growth through trading in
        Amsterdam, 370

population
  basic demographic equation, 54
  demographic transition model, 60–61
  in development of cities, 282
  doubling time, 59
  and environmental change,
    relationship between, 272–73
  fertility, 54–55
  health issues affected by, 75
  life expectancies, 47
  world (*see* world population)
Population Bomb, The (Ehrlich), 64
population change
  in the future, 64–65
  measures of, 56
  mortality and, 56–59
  natural, 56–59
population density, 49
population geography, as field of
  study, 35
population growth
  historical overview, 46–47
  rate of growth, 45–47
  in US, 104–5, 106–7
population planning, 66–67
population profiles, 62–63
Population Reference Bureau, 54
populist movement, 121
Porter, Michael, 373
Porter, Philip, 360
ports, development and maintenance
  of, 231
Portugal
  creation of Tordesillas boundary, 219
  as empire, 207
  geographers during Age of
    Exploration, 30
  loss of colonies, 209
Posidonius, 27
positivism, 35
possibilism, 33
postcolonialism, 401
postmodernism, 40
poststructuralism, 41
poverty in less developed
  countries, 318
power centers, 384, 385
Prairie-style homes, 129
predatory lending, 315
Presbyterian church, 169
primary loyalty, as marker of
  nation, 212
primary sector of economy, 331
primate city, 295
prime meridian, 6, 31
prime value intersection, 306, 307
primitive agriculture, 324–25
primitive migration, 94
primordialism, 216
Prince Henry the Navigator, 30
private sectors of economies,
  230–31, 331
probabilistic, patterns as, 5
process, 4–5
production
  in commodity chain, 363
  defined, 346
  factors of, 348–49
  global assembly line, 361
  global production line, 361
  hourly compensation for production
    workers, data on, 360
  mass production, 287, 346–47
  new international division of
    labor, 361

overview, 345
  value added, 346
production chain, 348
productivity, 374
profane landscapes, 178
profit, as part of capitalism, 326
Prohibition, 220
prostate cancer, 75
protectionism, 372, 373
Protestantism
  adherents, 167
  buildings, 176
  as major world religion, 158
  spread of, 169
Protestant Reformation, 169
proto-language, 140
psychosocial insults to health, 75
Ptolemy, Claudius, 27, 30
public sectors of economies, 230–31, 331
Pueblo Indians, 179
Puerto Rico, as special region, 246–47
purchasing power parity, 393
pure characteristics, 10–11
pure democracy, 248
push-pull model of migration, 101

Q

Qatar, crude death rate in, 56
Quakers, 166
qualitative methods, as field of study, 35
quantitative revolution, 35
quaternary sector of economy, 331
Quba Mosque (Medina, Saudi
  Arabia), 170
quota, trade, 375
Qur'an, 28, 142, 171, 173

R

racism
  environmental, 274, 275
  role in segregation, 190
random distribution, 12
rate of natural increase (RNI), 56–59
rate of population growth, 57–58
Ratzel, Frederich, 33, 222
Ravenstein, Ernst Georg, 100–1
Ravenstein's laws, 100
raw materials, in locating factories,
  348–49
Received Pronunciation version of
  language (RP), 144
recession, 331
recharge of aquifers, rate of, 263
recreation, commercial, 337
recreational auto city, 311–12
recycling
  increase of, in US, 273
  solid waste, 266, 267
red states/blue states division in US,
  248, 249
refugees, 93, 98–99
refugee warehousing, 98–99
regional geography, in birth of modern
  geography, 32, 34–35
regional trade blocs, 371
regions
  composition of, 16–19
  defined, 16
  formal, 16–17
  functional, 18–19
  vernacular, 19
Reilly, William J., 35

reincarnation, 160–61, 162–63
relative location, 6–7, 11
relative significance, 11
religion, 155–79. *See also specific
  religions*
  allocation of space for, 156
  artifact production by, 117
  buildings, design of, 176–79
  cities, design of, 177
  classifying, 156–59
  in culture complexes, 114
  defined, 156
  landscapes of, 176–79
  overview, 155
  sacred landscapes, 178
relocation diffusion, 120
remittances, 92
repatriation, 99
replacement level of fertility, 55
representative democracy, 248
reservation, 247
reserves, oil and coal, 271
reservoirs, changes to landscape
  from, 262
residential zone in concentric zone
  model of cities, 311
restricted migration, 94
resurgent identity, 186–87
retail chains, 384–85
retailing
  changes, 383, 384
  in commodity chain, 363
  enclosed malls, 384, 385
  geographical aspects of US, 382–85
  Hudson's Department Store, 384
  in Internet Age, changing
    geographies of, 386–87
  models of, 382, 383
  neighborhood/community centers
    and strips, 384, 385
  open-air lifestyle centers, 384, 385
  pedestrian-oriented commercial
    strips, 384, 385
  power centers, 384, 385
  specialty shopping centers,
    384, 385
  in supply chain, 382
Revere, Paul, 119
reverse hierarchical diffusion, 121
Ricardo, David, 372
rice
  domestication of, 123
  gains from Green Revolution, 65
Richardson, Richard, 393
Ring of Fire, 260
Rip Van Winkle (Irving), 148
Ritter, Carl, 32, 33
Roger II (king, Sicily), 28–29
Roman Catholic church
  adherents, 167
  buildings, 176
  control of territory by, 209
  creation of Tordesillas boundary
    by, 219
  dioceses, 177
  during fall of Roman Empire,
    284–85
  Latin, 146
  as major world religion, 158
  Protestant Reformation, 169
  Rome as headquarters for, 244
  territorial development of, 229
  views of world during Middle
    Ages, 28
  worship, 166

Roman Empire
  Christianity in Roman Empire,
    168, 169
  citizenship, beginning of use in, 234
  city-states, organized as, 207
  establishment of cities in, 282, 283
  execution of Jesus by Romans, 166
  fall of, 284
  Greco-Roman culture hearth, 123
  prosperity of Venice, 207
  Rome as capital of, 244
  territory of, 207
  towns in US named for Roman
    places, 149
Rosetta stone, 137
Rostow, W.W. (*Stages of Economic
  Growth, The*), 397
Rotokos, 136
"Route 66," 114
Royal Geographic Society, 33
runic alphabet, 141, 142
rural areas to urban, migration, 91, 95
Russia
  in beginning of capitalist economic
    system, 328
  industrialization of, 347
  Kalingrad as exclave, 246
  language as lingua franca, 138
  life expectancies, decline in, 47
  migrants to US, 107
  system of governing, 240
  as tourist destination, 365
Russian Empire, 209
Rwanda, refugee genocide in, 98
rye, domestication of, 335

S

Sachs, Jeffrey
  on development traps, 398
  "Geography of Poverty and Wealth,
    The," 391
sacred landscapes, 178
sacred spaces, 9, 179
Said, Edward (*Orientalism*), 223
Saint Helens volcano, Mount
  (Washington, 1980), 258
Salk, Jonas, 74
Salton Sea, 262
Sami people (Laplanders), 247, 336
samsara, 160–61
Samsung, 408
sanitation, worldwide access to
  proper, 85
San Marino
  as micro-state, 210
  overview, 211
San peoples, language spoken by, 136
Sarda River (India, Nepal), as natural
  boundary between India and
  Nepal, 219
Sardinia (Italy), 247
Sargon of Akkad (king, Sumeria), 282
satellite states, 210
Saudi Arabia
  gender differences in
    geographies, 41
  migrants as changing structure
    of, 104
Sauer, Carl
  agriculture, theory on occurrence
    of, 333
  cultural landscape, emphasis on,
    124–25, 176
  definition of landscape, 20